IBM AND THE HOLOCAUST

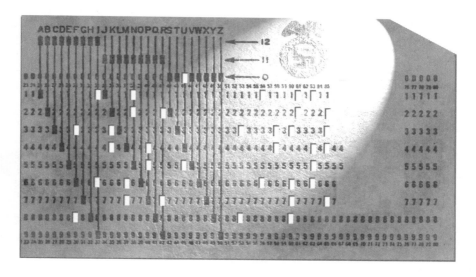

THE STRATEGIC ALLIANCE BETWEEN

NAZI GERMANY AND AMERICA'S

MOST POWERFUL CORPORATION

CROWN PUBLISHERS   NEW YORK

IBM AND

THE HOLOCAUST

EDWIN BLACK

Published by Crown Publishers, New York, New York.
Member of the Crown Publishing Group.

Random House, Inc.   New York, Toronto, London, Sydney, Auckland
www.randomhouse.com

CROWN is a trademark and the Crown colophon is a registered trademark
of Random House, Inc.

Printed in the United States of America

DESIGN BY BARBARA STURMAN

Library of Congress Cataloging-in-Publication Data is available upon request.

ISBN 0-609-60799-5

10 9 8 7 6 5 4 3 2 1

First Edition

CONTENTS

A Dehomag (IBM's German subsidiary) poster, circa 1934. Approximate
English translation is, "See everything with Hollerith punchcards."
(Courtesy of the author)

TO MY DAUGHTER, RACHEL,
who will read this book,

AND TO SIX MILLION
who will not.

ACKNOWLEDGMENTS

RARELY DOES A BOOK OF HISTORY INVOLVE SO MANY DOZENS OF PEOPLE who were so important. But this one does.

Because this investigation involved documents in so many countries and in so many languages, I relied on a network of researchers and translators, many of them volunteers. The team consisted of Holocaust survivors, children of survivors, retirees, and students with no connection to the Holocaust—as well as professional researchers, distinguished archivists and historians, and even former Nuremberg Trial investigators.

Ultimately, more than 100 people in seven countries participated, some for months at a time, many for a few weeks between jobs or during school breaks, and some for just a few hours when we needed specific documents translated. For most, their mission was simply to scour record groups or newspaper microfilm looking for certain key words or topics, knowing little about the implications of what they were finding. Once documents were located, they were copied and sent to me for review and analysis. When we discovered a lead, we would ask for follow-up research on a targeted theme or name.

Researchers and translators were recruited through Internet sites, university bulletin boards, Holocaust survivor organizations, archivists, historians, translator-researcher associations, and friends of friends of friends. Invariably, researchers were sorry to leave the project because of other commitments, and so they generally replaced themselves with trusted friends who could carry on their work.

Obviously, space does not permit me to list all those who helped in so many ways. But I would like to highlight a few. Gaylon Hecker and Mary Jo Osgood in Austin, Texas, organized a team of volunteers to screen the *New York Times* from 1933 to 1945. They worked lunch periods, evenings, and weekends in front of microfilm readers to create a unique newspaper history of the evolving business and persecution aspects of the Holocaust-era. The Texas group was joined by about a dozen researchers in several other cities. More than 1,500 hours of reviewing was required. Terra York in Washington, D.C., monitored the team's progress, and like a traffic manager broadcast the continuously changing microfilm reading assignments.

I personally labored in the archives of England, Israel, Germany, and America. But I was indispensably assisted in Britain by Jane Booth, Andy Farenden, Matt Martinson, and others. My efforts in Israel were advanced by several people, including Ariel Szczupak and Yitzhak Kerem; Kerem also worked in the archives in Paris, Washington, and New York. In Germany, I was at first helped by Barbara Haas, Katrin Reiser, and others, but then for many months by Thomas Kremer.

In America, I was assisted by the accomplished Holocaust author Gerald Schwab, former Nuremberg Trial investigator Fred Thieberger, former Allied occupation intelligence officer Werner Michel, business ethics professor Robert Urekew, and researchers Vanessa van der Linde and Kathleen Dyer-Williams, among many others.

In Holland, research depended upon two doggedly determined university students, Willemijn Ruberg and Martijn Kraaij. In Poland, we were helped enormously by the devoted assistance of Zbig Kanski and others. In France, Diane Goertz and several others undertook research.

Many translators were kind enough to help, and of course always on a rush basis. In German, two of the most important were Susan Steiner and Inge Wolfe, both of whom leapt into complex technical papers. Aldona Szostek-Pontchek tackled Polish. Especially diligent was the French translation team, including Jackie Holland, Virginia Rinaldi, and the French team leader, Terra York; when these fine people weren't translating, they were doing double duty with English language documentation. On the Labor Day weekend before publication, four French translators in four cities worked day and night to help unmask the facts in France.

A team of extraordinary researchers worked closely with me, often from 8 A.M. to midnight, as we searched through stacks of documents seeking clues and connecting dots. There was no rest for these hard-working, profoundly idealistic people, who often scrutinized hundreds of documents each day as we checked and triple-checked every granule of the story. These include Erica Ashton, Sally Murek, and Derek Kulnis during the day. Volunteer David Keleti, a genetic engineer, helped bolster the nightshift and weekend efforts. Keleti in particular helped us assemble the murky facts about IBM in Sweden and Switzerland. Susan Cooke Anastasi, our tireless copy editor, often worked the overnight shift; whatever errors we made at night, she would fix by morning.

Although many labored hard, without two heroic individuals this book simply could not have been completed. The first is Niels Cordes, formerly of the National Archives microfilm room. Cordes is one of the most methodical, intuitive, and knowledgeable historians and archivists I have ever met. We worked together in archives in New York, Washington, and London, and later he did research with a team in Berlin. Cordes translated many pages of German documents. He never failed to display the sharpest insights into the smallest details.

The second heroic figure is Kai Gloystein. Gloystein first worked on the project in archives and libraries in Bonn, Cologne, and Berlin, and then flew to America to help finalize the project working fifteen-hour days with every line of the manuscript and thousands of footnotes. He also translated voluminous documents, contemporary newspapers, and technical journals. Gloystein's indefatigable commitment to excellence, precision eye for detail and sharp intellect cast a profound benefit across every page of the manuscript. He was a warrior for perfection.

A number of leading historians and archivists bestowed great contributions to my effort through their advice, searches of their records, assistance in recruiting others, and special accommodations. These men and women are the stalwarts of history. In some cases, they selflessly offered their support, talent, and insights for more than a year. In Israel, this includes Gilad Livne at Israel State Archives who gave me full access to the Eichmann papers, and Rochelle Rubinstein at Central Zionist Archives, who also helped during my visit there. In Britain, John Klier from the University of London and the entire team at the Public Record Office rendered continuing assistance. In France, Agnes d'Angio and Herve Vernon of the French Economic Ministry Archive were always responsive. In Holland, Erik Somers of the Institute for War Documentation assisted for many months, recruiting interns and facilitating research.

In Germany, warm friendship and assistance was extended by Ulrich Soenius at Rheinisch-Westfälisches Wirtschaftsarchiv in Cologne, Peter Grupp of Politisches Archiv in Bonn, Gerhardt Hirschfeld of Stuttgart's Library of Contemporary History, Johannes Tuchel of the Memorial for German Resistance in Berlin, as well as Karola Wagner, Anette Meiburg, Siegfried Büttner, and the entire staff at Bundesarchiv in Lichterfelde. In Poland, Jan Jagielski at Warsaw's Jewish Historical Institute and Franciszek Piper at the Auschwitz Museum both found time in their overworked schedule to locate materials.

In the United States, Marek Web helped me at YIVO archives. Michael Nash at Hagley Museum extended scholar-in-residence privileges that were most helpful. Henry Mayer and Aaron Kornblum at the United States Holocaust Museum made a big difference to our demanding research. At the National Archives, I was blessed to encounter a group of irreplaceable archivists and other staffers, including John Taylor (OSS), Milt Gustafson (State Department), Fred Romanski (Justice), Greg Bradsher (Holocaust-Era Assets), Louis Holland (captured Nazi microfilms), Marie Carpenti, and many others in the reading room; these men and women worked with me for a year. They are the precious vanguard of America's effort to preserve its history.

All who read this book will see the influence of my pre-publication reader reviewers, each with their own broad or niche expertise. Each read the entire manuscript and most proffered extensive marginal notes. The reviewers included Robert Wolfe (Nazi documentation), Abraham Peck (Holocaust history), Henry Mayer (Holocaust documentation), Greg Bradsher (trading with the enemy), Werner Michel (Allied intelligence and Nazi technology), Fred Thieberger (Nuremberg war crimes investigation), Gerhard Hirschfeld (Holocaust in Holland), Erik Somers (Holocaust in Holland), Bob Moore (Holocaust in Holland), Esther Finder (survivor issues), Robert Urekew (business ethics), Bradley Kliewer (technology), Shlomo Aronson (Reich security and Nazi methodology), John Klier (Holocaust studies and Russian history), Byron Sherwin (ethics during the Holocaust), and many others in the fields of history, financial crimes, accountancy and business practices, who gave me the gift of their time and counsel.

All readers and reviewers helped me achieve greater precision. But a special mention must go to four of the finest minds on the period: Robert Paxton (Vichy France), William Seltzer (Holocaust census and statistics technology), Niels Cordes (German history and Nazi documentation), and Erik Somers (Holland). They influenced the manuscript in profound ways, immeasurably sharpening its precision.

I received telephonic assistance from Radu Ioanid (Holocaust in Romania), Henry Friedlander (sterilization and euthanasia), and many others.

Although dozens worked hard to advance my work, two eminent scholars made a towering contribution. The first is Sybil Milton, who helped initialize my research. Milton, former historian with the United States Holocaust Museum, had crusaded for years to discover the connections between IBM, its Holleriths, and the Holocaust. She warned me the road would not be easy. Her original guiding efforts launched me along the correct path. Unfortunately, Sybil passed away before the project was completed. This book is a testament to the pillar of Holocaust expertise she has represented for decades.

The other is Robert Wolfe, rightly at the very pinnacle of the world's respected experts in Holocaust and captured Nazi documents. Wolfe granted me his time and unparalleled expertise for over a year, constantly guiding me, prodding me, and assisting me in pursuit of the most complete and precisely documented story possible. Wolfe is a tireless warrior for truth in Holocaust documentation and accountability. His legendary reputation among the world's archivists and historians is richly deserved. His stamp on this book and my efforts is unmistakable.

History also recognizes that without a small group committed to uncovering the truth, this book would have never been written. These people made the difference: Aron Hirt-Manheimer, Arthur Herzberg, and Lawrence Schiffman, as well as Wolfe and Milton. Without their courage and stamina, it simply could not have been done.

Assembling the facts was ironically only half the struggle. Publishing those facts took a historic bravery and literary fearlessness that many lacked. At the head of the line is Philip Turner, formerly of Times Books, who acquired *IBM and the Holocaust* for Random House. Then, for almost eight months, I was closely supported—hour to hour—by Crown vice president and senior editor Douglas Pepper, who bonded with the text and the mission to boldly tell this unknown story to the world. During the past thirty years of investigative reporting and publishing, I have learned to quickly identify the genuine pros. Pepper and the entire team at Crown, all under the baton of Crown editorial director Steve Ross, never shirked. Others, such as William Adams, Whitney Cookman, and Tina Constable worked for precision and excellence. From the first moment, they mobilized the commitment and courage to place the full weight of Crown behind the project.

Crown's commitment was equaled overseas by some of the most distinguished editors and publishers of Europe and Latin America. All of them embarked upon the year-long process of chapter-by-chapter translation. They extended their support to me as an author and collectively joined to see this book become a worldwide phenomenon. Many became friends. These include Margit Ketterle and Christian Seeger of Germany's Propyläen Verlag (Econ/Ullstein/List); Abel Gerschenfeld of France's Editions Robert

Laffont; Paolo Zaninoni of Italy's RCS Libri/Rizzoli; Liesbeth de Vries of Holland's Kosmos Z&K; Zbig Kanski of Poland's Graal Agency and Ewelina Osinska of Muza; Claudio Rothmuller and Paul Christoph of Brazil's Editora Campus for the Portuguese-speaking countries, and Jorge Naveiro of Argentina's Atlantida for the Spanish-speaking countries. British publisher Little, Brown & Company UK, and its distinguished editorial director, Alan Samson, completed the book's global reach.

My book received the attention of the world's great publishers only because of the untiring efforts of one person, my agent, Lynne Rabinoff. Lynne's confidence in me and the project was the dominant force behind the book assuming a global scope. She fought valiantly—hour to hour—to preserve the quality and integrity of the final product. She was tireless in her efforts to bring this story to light in the most powerful fashion, and to ensure that it would reach not only the halls of academia, but readers in some fifty countries the book will appear in. These few words cannot express my respect for her as the best agent any author could ever have. As a result of energies and faith, this book became a reality.

Although I was always surrounded by researchers and translators, crafting the product required the continuous and highly amplified creative assistance of Hans Zimmer, Jerry Goldsmith, John Barry, BT, Moby, Tangerine Dream, David Arnold, Christopher Franke, Trevor Rabin, Trevor Jones, and many others.

Working virtually fifteen hours per day for a year, often never leaving my basement for days at a time, eating at my computer screen, imposed a profound hardship on my loving family—Elizabeth, Rachel, and my parents. They sustained, encouraged me, and mostly allowed me to detach from daily family life into the obsessive quest for this story.

I have seen many acknowledgment sections in many Holocaust histories. But one group always seems to be overlooked. Yet during my labors, they were never out of sight or out of mind. I acknowledge the six million Jews, including my grandparents, and millions of other Europeans who perished. Their memory and the image of their punch cards are with me always.

INTRODUCTION

THIS BOOK WILL BE PROFOUNDLY UNCOMFORTABLE TO READ. IT WAS
profoundly uncomfortable to write. It tells the story of IBM's conscious
involvement—directly and through its subsidiaries—in the Holocaust, as
well as its involvement in the Nazi war machine that murdered millions of
others throughout Europe.

Mankind barely noticed when the concept of *massively organized information* quietly emerged to become a means of social control, a weapon of
war, and a roadmap for group destruction. The unique igniting event was the
most fateful day of the last century, January 30, 1933, the day Adolf Hitler
came to power. Hitler and his hatred of the Jews was the ironic driving force
behind this intellectual turning point. But his quest was greatly enhanced
and energized by the ingenuity and craving for profit of a single American
company and its legendary, autocratic chairman. That company was International Business Machines, and its chairman was Thomas J. Watson.

Der Führer's obsession with Jewish destruction was hardly original. There
had been czars and tyrants before him. But for the first time in history, an anti-
Semite had automation on his side. Hitler didn't do it alone. He had help.

In the upside-down world of the Holocaust, dignified professionals
were Hitler's advance troops. Police officials disregarded their duty in favor
of protecting villains and persecuting victims. Lawyers perverted concepts of
justice to create anti-Jewish laws. Doctors defiled the art of medicine to per-
petrate ghastly experiments and even choose who was healthy enough to be
worked to death—and who could be cost-effectively sent to the gas chamber.
Scientists and engineers debased their higher calling to devise the instruments

7

and rationales of destruction. And statisticians used their little known but powerful discipline to identify the victims, project and rationalize the benefits of their destruction, organize their persecution, and even audit the efficiency of genocide. Enter IBM and its overseas subsidiaries.

Solipsistic and dazzled by its own swirling universe of technical possibilities, IBM was self-gripped by a special amoral corporate mantra: if it *can* be done, it *should* be done. To the blind technocrat, the *means* were more important than the *ends*. The destruction of the Jewish people became even less important because the invigorating nature of IBM's technical achievement was only heightened by the fantastical profits to be made at a time when bread lines stretched across the world.

So how did it work?

When Hitler came to power, a central Nazi goal was to identify and destroy Germany's 600,000-member Jewish community. To Nazis, Jews were not just those who practiced Judaism, but those of Jewish blood, regardless of their assimilation, intermarriage, religious activity, or even conversion to Christianity. Only after Jews were identified could they be targeted for asset confiscation, ghettoization, deportation, and ultimately extermination. To search generations of communal, church, and governmental records all across Germany—and later throughout Europe—was a cross-indexing task so monumental, it called for a computer. But in 1933, no computer existed.

When the Reich needed to mount a systematic campaign of Jewish economic disenfranchisement and later began the massive movement of European Jews out of their homes and into ghettos, once again, the task was so prodigious it called for a computer. But in 1933, no computer existed.

When the Final Solution sought to efficiently transport Jews out of European ghettos along railroad lines and into death camps, with timing so precise the victims were able to walk right out of the boxcar and into a waiting gas chamber, the coordination was so complex a task, this too called for a computer. But in 1933, no computer existed.

However, another invention did exist: the IBM punch card and card sorting system—a precursor to the computer. IBM, primarily through its German subsidiary, made Hitler's program of Jewish destruction a technologic mission the company pursued with chilling success. IBM Germany, using its own staff and equipment, designed, executed, and supplied the indispensable technologic assistance Hitler's Third Reich needed to accomplish what had never been done before—the automation of human destruction. More than 2,000 such multi-machine sets were dispatched throughout Germany, and thousands more throughout German-dominated Europe. Card

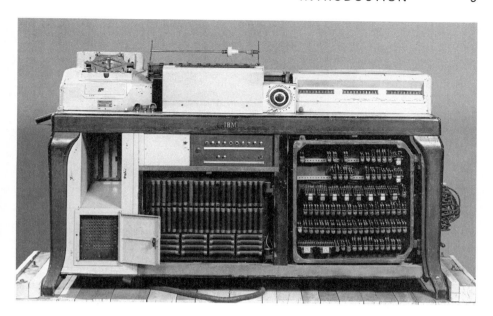

A Dehomag Hollerith machine. (Photograph courtesy United States Holocaust Memorial Museum, Washington, D.C.)

sorting operations were established in every major concentration camp. People were moved from place to place, systematically worked to death, and their remains cataloged with icy automation.

IBM Germany, known in those days as Deutsche Hollerith Maschinen Gesellschaft, or Dehomag, did not simply sell the Reich machines and then walk away. IBM's subsidiary, with the knowledge of its New York headquarters, enthusiastically custom-designed the complex devices and specialized applications as an official corporate undertaking. Dehomag's top management was comprised of openly rabid Nazis who were arrested after the war for their Party affiliation. IBM NY always understood—from the outset in 1933—that it was courting and doing business with the upper echelon of the Nazi Party. The company leveraged its Nazi Party connections to continuously enhance its business relationship with Hitler's Reich, in Germany and throughout Nazi-dominated Europe.

Dehomag and other IBM subsidiaries custom-designed the applications. Its technicians sent mock-ups of punch cards back and forth to Reich offices until the data columns were acceptable, much as any software designer would today. Punch cards could only be designed, printed, and purchased from one source: IBM. The machines were not sold, they were leased, and regularly maintained and upgraded by only one source: IBM. IBM subsidiaries trained the Nazi officers and their surrogates throughout Europe, set up branch offices and local dealerships throughout Nazi Europe staffed by a revolving door of IBM employees, and scoured paper mills to produce as many as 1.5 billion punch cards a year in Germany alone. Moreover, the fragile machines were serviced on site about once per month, even when that site was in or near a concentration camp. IBM Germany's headquarters in Berlin maintained duplicates of many code books, much as any IBM service bureau today would maintain data backups for computers.

I was haunted by a question whose answer has long eluded historians. The Germans always had the lists of Jewish names. Suddenly, a squadron of grim-faced SS would burst into a city square and post a notice demanding those listed assemble the next day at the train station for deportation to the East. But how did the Nazis get the lists? For decades, no one has known. Few have asked.

The answer: IBM Germany's census operations and similar advanced people counting and registration technologies. IBM was founded in 1896 by German inventor Herman Hollerith as a census tabulating company. Census was its business. But when IBM Germany formed its philosophical and technologic alliance with Nazi Germany, census and registration took on a new mission. IBM Germany invented the racial census—listing not just religious affiliation, but bloodline going back generations. This was the Nazi data lust. Not just to count the Jews—but to *identify* them.

People and asset registration was only one of the many uses Nazi Germany found for high-speed data sorters. Food allocation was organized around databases, allowing Germany to starve the Jews. Slave labor was identified, tracked, and managed largely through punch cards. Punch cards even made the trains run on time and cataloged their human cargo. German Railway, the *Reichsbahn*, Dehomag's biggest customer, dealt directly with senior management in Berlin. Dehomag maintained punch card installations at train depots across Germany, and eventually across all Europe.

How much did IBM know? Some of it IBM knew on a daily basis throughout the twelve-year Reich. The worst of it IBM preferred not to know—"don't ask, don't tell" was the order of the day. Yet IBM NY officials, and frequently Watson's personal representatives, Harrison Chauncey and Werner Lier, were almost constantly in Berlin or Geneva, monitoring activities, ensuring that the parent company in New York was not cut out of any of the profits or business opportunities Nazism presented. When U.S. law made such direct contact illegal, IBM's Swiss office became the nexus, providing the New York office continuous information and credible deniability.

Certainly, the dynamics and context of IBM's alliance with Nazi Germany changed throughout the twelve-year Reich. I want the full story understood in context. Skipping around in the book will only lead to flawed and erroneous conclusions. So if you intend to skim, or rely on selected sections, please do not read the book at all. If you believe that somehow the Holocaust would not have occurred without IBM, you are more than wrong. The Holocaust would have proceeded—and often did proceed—with simple bullets, death marches, and massacres based on pen and paper persecution. But there is reason to examine the fantastical numbers Hitler achieved in murdering so many millions so swiftly, and identify the crucial role of automation and technology. Accountability is needed.

What made me demand answers to the unasked questions about IBM and the Holocaust? I confronted the reality of IBM's involvement one day in 1993 in Washington at the United States Holocaust Museum. There, in the very first exhibit, an IBM Hollerith D-11 card sorting machine—riddled with circuits, slots, and wires—was prominently displayed. Clearly affixed to the machine's front panel glistened an IBM nameplate. It has since been replaced with a smaller IBM machine because so many people congregated around it, creating a bottleneck. The exhibit explained little more than that IBM was responsible for organizing the census of 1933 that first identified the Jews. IBM had been tight-lipped about its involvement with Nazi Germany. So although 15 million people, including most major Holocaust experts, have seen the display, and in spite of the best efforts of leading Museum historians, little more was understood about this provocative display other than the brief curator's description at the exhibit and a few pages of supportive research.

I still remember staring at the machine for an hour, and the moment when I turned to my mother and father who accompanied me to the museum that day and promised them I would discover more.

My parents are Holocaust survivors, uprooted from their homes in Poland. My mother escaped from a boxcar en route to Treblinka, was shot, and then buried in a shallow mass grave. My father had already run away from a guarded line of Jews and discovered her leg protruding from the snow. By moonlight and by courage, these two escapees survived against the cold, the hunger, and the Reich. Standing next to me five decades later, their image within the reflection of the exhibit glass, shrapnel and bullet fragments permanently embedded in their bodies, my parents could only express confusion.

But I had other questions. The Nazis had my parents' names. How?

What was the connection of this gleaming black, beige, and silver machine, squatting silently in this dimly lit museum, to the millions of Jews and other Europeans who were murdered—and murdered not just in a chaotic split-second as a casualty of war, but in a grotesque and protracted twelve-year campaign of highly organized humiliation, dehumanization, and then ultimately extermination.

For years after that chance discovery, I was shadowed by the realization that IBM was somehow involved in the Holocaust in technologic ways that had not yet been pieced together. Dots were everywhere. The dots needed to be connected.

Knowing that International Business Machines has always billed itself as a "solutions" company, I understood that IBM does not merely wait for governmental customers to call. IBM has amassed its fortune and reputation precisely because it generally anticipates governmental and corporate needs even before they develop, and then offers, designs, and delivers customized solutions—even if it must execute those technologic solutions with its own staff and equipment. IBM has done so for countless government agencies, corporate giants, and industrial associations.

For years I promised myself I would one day answer the question: How many solutions did IBM provide to Nazi Germany? I knew about the initial solution: the census. Just how far did the solutions go?

In 1998, I began an obsessive quest for answers. Proceeding without any foundation funds, organizational grants, or publisher dollars behind me, I began recruiting a team of researchers, interns, translators, and assistants, all on my own dime.

Soon a network developed throughout the United States, as well as in Germany, Israel, England, Holland, Poland, and France. This network contin-ued to grow as time went on. Holocaust survivors, children of survivors, retirees, and students with no connection to the Holocaust—as well as pro-fessional researchers, distinguished archivists and historians, and even for-mer Nuremberg Trial investigators—all began a search for documentation. Ultimately, more than 100 people participated, some for months at a time, some for just a few hours searching obscure Polish documents for key phrases. Not knowing the story, they searched for key words: census, statis-tics, lists, registrations, railroads, punch cards, and a roster of other topics. When they found them, the material was copied and sent. For many weeks, documents were flowing in at the rate of 100 per day.

Most of my team was volunteers. All of them were sworn to secrecy. Each was shocked and saddened by the implications of the project and intensely motivated. A few said they could not sleep well for days after learning of the connection. I was often sustained by their words of encouragement.

Ultimately, I assembled more than 20,000 pages of documentation from fifty archives, library manuscript collections, museum files, and other repositories. In the process, I accessed thousands of formerly classified State Department, OSS, or other previously restricted government papers. Other obscure documents from European holdings had never been translated or connected to such an inquiry. All these were organized in my own central archive mirroring the original archival source files. We also scanned and translated more than fifty general books and memoirs, as well as contemporary technical and scientific journals covering punch cards and statistics, Nazi publications, and newspapers of the era. All of this material—primary documents, journal articles, newsclips, and book extracts—were cross-indexed by month. We created one manila folder for every month from 1933 to 1950. If a document referred to numerous dates, it was cross-filed in the numerous monthly folders. Then all contents of monthly folders were further cross-indexed into narrow topic threads, such as Warsaw Ghetto, German Census, Bulgarian Railroads, Watson in Germany, Auschwitz, and so on.

Stacks of documents organized into topics were arrayed across my basement floor. As many as six people at a time busily shuttled copies of documents from one topic stack to another from morning until midnight. One document might be copied into five or six topic stacks. A high-speed copier with a twenty-bin sorter was installed. Just moving from place to place in the basement involved hopscotching around document piles.

None of the 20,000 documents were flash cards. It was much more complex. Examined singly, none revealed their story. Indeed, most of them were profoundly misleading as stand-alone papers. They only assumed their true meaning when juxtaposed with numerous other related documents, often from totally unrelated sources. In other words, the documents were all puzzle pieces—the picture could not be constructed until all the fragments were put together. For example, one IBM report fleetingly referred to a "Mr. Hendricks" as fetching an IBM machine from Dachau. Not until I juxtaposed that document with an obscure military statistics report discovered at the Public Record Office in London did I learn who Sgt. Hendricks really was.

Complicating the task, many of the IBM papers and notes were unsigned or undated carbons, employing deliberate vagueness, code words, catchphrases, or transient corporate shorthand. I had to learn the contemporaneous lexicon of the company to decipher their content. I would study and stare at some individual documents for months until their meaning finally became clear through some other discovered document. For example, I encountered an IBM reference to accumulating "points." Eventually, I discovered that "points" referred to making sales quotas for inclusion in IBM's Hundred Percent Club. IBM maintained sales quotas for all its subsidiaries during the Hitler era.

Sometimes a key revelation did not occur until we tracked a source back three and four stages. For example, I reviewed the English version of the well-known volume *Destruction of the Dutch Jews* by Jacob Presser. I found nothing on my subject. I then asked my researchers in Holland to check the Dutch edition. They found a single unfootnoted reference to a punch card system. Only by checking Presser's original typescript did we discover a marginal notation that referenced a Dutch archival document that led to a cascade of information on the Netherlands. In reviewing the Romanian census, I commissioned the translation of a German statistician's twenty-page memoir to discover a single sentence confirming that punch cards were used in Romania. That information was juxtaposed against an IBM letter confirming the company was moving machinery from war-torn Poland into Romania to aid Romanian census operations.

In the truest sense, the story of IBM and the Holocaust has been shattered into thousands of shards. Only by piecing them all together did I erect a towering picture window permitting me to view what really occurred. That verified account is retold in this book.

In my pursuit, I received extraordinary cooperation from every private, public, and governmental source in every country. Sadly, the only refusal came from IBM itself, which rebuffed my requests for access to documents and interviews. I was not alone. Since WWII, the company has steadfastly refused to cooperate with outside authors. Virtually every recent book on IBM, whether written by esteemed business historians or ex-IBM employees, includes a reference to the company's refusal to cooperate with the author in any way. Ultimately, I was able to arrange proper access. Hundreds of IBM documents were placed at my disposal. I read them all.

Behind every text footnote is a file folder with all the hardcopy documentation needed to document every sentence in this book at a moment's notice. Moreover, I assembled a team of hair-splitting, nitpicking, adversarial researchers and archivists to review each and every sentence, collectively ensuring that each fact and fragment of a fact was backed up with the necessary black and white documents.

In reconstructing the facts, I was guided on every page by two principles: context and consequences. For instance, although I enjoyed access to volumes of diplomatic and intelligence information, I was careful to concentrate on what was known publicly in the media about atrocities and anti-Jewish conditions in Europe. For this reason, readers will notice an extraordinary reliance on articles in the *New York Times*. I quote the *New York Times* not because it was the newspaper of record in America, but because IBM executives, including Thomas Watson, were headquartered in New York. Had they lived in Chicago, I would have quoted the *Chicago Tribune*. Had they lived in Cleveland, I would have quoted the *Cleveland Plain Dealer*.

Readers will also notice that I frequently relied upon reproducing the exact words the principals themselves used in telegrams, letters, or telephone transcripts. Readers can judge for themselves exactly what was said in what context.

With few exceptions (see Bibliographical Note), the Holocaust literature is virtually devoid of mention of the Hollerith machines—in spite of its high profile display at the United States Holocaust Memorial Museum. Historians should not be defensive about the absence of even a mention. The public documents were all there, but there are literally millions of frames and pages of Holocaust documents in the leading archives of the world. Many of these materials had simply never been accessed, many have not been available, and some are based on false chronologies or appear to be corporate minutia. Others were well known, such as Heydrich's 1939 instruction on concentrating Jewish communities near railroad tracks, but the repeated references to census operations were simply overlooked.

More than the obscurity of the documents, such an investigation would require expertise in the history of the Holocaust before and after the war began, the history of post–Industrial Revolution mechanization, the history of technology, and more specifically the archaic punch card system, as well as an understanding of Reich economics, multi-national corporations, and a grasp of financial collusion. In addition, one would need to juxtapose the information for numerous countries before assembling the complete picture. Just as important is the fact that until I examined the IBM documents, that half of the screen was totally obscured. Again, the documents do not speak by themselves, only in ensemble. I was fortunate to have an understanding of Reich economics and multi-national commerce from my earlier book, *The Transfer Agreement*, as well as a background in the computer industry, and years of experience as an investigative journalist specializing in corporate misconduct. I approached this project as a typical if not grandiose investigation of corporate conduct with one dramatic difference: the conduct impacted on the lives and deaths of millions.

Gathering my pre-publication expert reviewers was a process in itself. I sought not only the leading historians of the Holocaust, but niche experts on such topics as Vichy France, Romania, and census and persecution. But I also consulted business historians, technical specialists, accountants, legal sources on reparations and corporate war crimes, an investigator from the original Nuremberg prosecution team, a wartime military intelligence technology expert, and even an ex-FBI special agent with expertise in financial crimes. I wanted the prismatic view of all.

Changing perspective was perhaps the dominant reason why the relationship between IBM and the Holocaust has never been explored. When I first wrote *The Transfer Agreement* in 1984, no one wanted to focus on assets. Now everyone talks about the assets. The formative years for most Holocaust scholarship was before the computer age, and well before the Age of Information. Everyone now possesses an understanding of how technology can be utilized in the affairs of war and peace. We can now go back and look at the same documentation in a new light.

Many of us have become enraptured in the Age of Computerization and the Age of Information. I know I have. But now I am consumed with a new awareness that, for me, as the son of Holocaust survivors, brings me to a whole new consciousness. I call it the Age of Realization, as we look back and examine technology's wake. Unless we understand how the Nazis acquired the names, more lists will be compiled against more people.

The story of IBM and the Holocaust is just a beginning. I could have written twenty books with the documents I uncovered, one for every country in Europe. I estimate there are 100,000 more documents scattered in basements and corporate archives around the United States and Europe. Corporate archivists should take note: these documents are related to a crime and must not be moved, tampered with, or destroyed. They must be transferred to those appropriate archival institutions that can assure immediate and undelayed access to scholars and war crimes prosecutors so the accountability process can continue (see Major Sources).

Only through exposing and examining what really occurred can the world of technology finally adopt the well-worn motto: *Never Again.*

EDWIN BLACK
Washington, D.C.

PART **ONE**

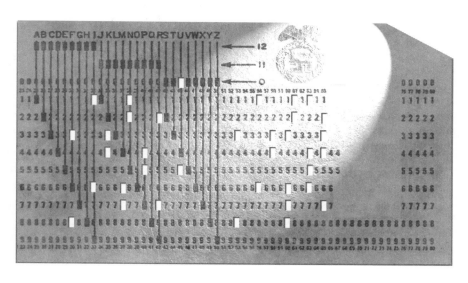

I
II
III
IV
V
VI
VII
VIII
IX
X
XI
XII
XIII
XIV
XV

NUMBERED PEOPLE

VEILS OF SMOKE HUNG ABOVE BERGEN-BELSEN CONCENTRATION camp. Many of the exhausted prisoners, insensate from torture and starvation, slumped lifelessly, waiting to fade into death. But most of the 60,000 human beings squeezed into this unimaginable clearing amongst the evergreens were still running from place to place, performing assigned chores quickly, proving their strength and viability for yet another day of existence. Surviving the moment was their quest.[1] This nightmare was Bergen-Belsen concentration camp, a special Hell on Earth created by Nazi Germany.

At the rear of the camp, just meters from its back fence, stood a solitary guard tower. Its cross-barred wooden frame rose some 25 feet in the air. Looking down from this commanding perch, one saw three orderly rows of wooden barracks down to the right. Along the left lay kitchens, workshops, storage areas, and latrines haphazardly arrayed between curved, muddy lanes. This length of incarceration all terminated several hundred meters away at the gate leading to the camp commandant's office and the SS encampment. A barbed-wire perimeter gave the camp definition even as a series of internal fences straddling patrol aisles segmented the cruel confines into six sub-camps.[2]

Just below the rear watchtower, a round-topped furnace squatted atop the mud. Black and elongated, the furnace resembled a locomotive engine, but with two weighty kiln doors at the front.

Its single, tall, sooty smokestack rose several meters into the air. A hand-made metal stretcher of sorts, used to slide emaciated corpses into the flames, was always nearby. Here was the crematorium. Not hidden out of sight, nor obscured by structures or berms, the crematorium was close enough to burn the eyes of any SS guard stationed in the watchtower. The ominous structure and its message were visible to all as the final way station should fate falter—or deliver.[3]

Situated between two rivers and the towns Bergen and Belsen, the site was originally established in spring 1943 as a prisoner transit camp for 10,000 Jews who might be ransomed or traded. But in the last months of 1944 and early 1945, as Nazi death camps, including Auschwitz, were liberated by the Allies, Belsen became a nightmare of human consolidation, receiving transports from other sites. By spring 1945, more than 40,000 were imprisoned under indescribable conditions. Starved, worked to death, and randomly tortured, the death toll rose to nearly 20,000 just for the month of March 1945. After liberation, horrified British medical teams were unable to save some 14,000 dying souls. Eventually bulldozers were deployed to gruesomely shovel bodies into trenches of twisted rigor mortis.[4]

Just meters from the Belsen crematorium, off to the left, near the kitchens and the cisterns, down a muddy path, stood the block leader's house. Inmates sometimes called this place "the lion's den." Within "the lion's den" was a room for the *Arbeitsdienstführer*, the Labor Service Leader. That is where the Hollerith punch cards were processed. At first glance, they seemed like simple rectangular cards, five and a quarter inches long, three and a quarter inches tall, divided into numbered columns with holes punched in various rows.[5] But they were much more than simple cards.

Beginning in December 1944, a Dutch Jew, Rudolf Cheim, was assigned to work in the Labor Service Office. Hungry and desperate to stay warm, Cheim tried every cold morning to locate a bit of extra food and some matches to make a fire. Kindling was stacked in the office. But no matches. For those, Cheim needed to venture into the other room where the SS officers slouched on chairs. Invariably, they viciously punched him in the face as the price for walking near to obtain a match. But it was worth it for Cheim. He could survive.[6]

Working in the *Arbeitsdienst* was good. The Labor Service Office held the power of life or death over prisoners, including him. If an inmate could work, he could live. Cheim was happy for an office assignment working with the Hollerith punch cards and their coded numbers. But as he did, he silently observed through the corner of his eye the SS men administering the card sorting procedure. For five weeks he took mental notes.[7]

Quickly, Cheim learned the method. Every day, transports of slave laborers were received. Prisoners were identified by descriptive Hollerith cards, each with columns and punched holes detailing nationality, date of birth, marital status, number of children, reason for incarceration, physical characteristics, and work skills. Sixteen coded categories of prisoners were listed in columns 3 and 4, depending upon the hole position: hole 3 signified homosexual, hole 9 for anti-social, hole 12 for Gypsy. Hole 8 designated a Jew. Printouts based on the cards listed the prisoners by personal code number as well.[8]

Column 34 was labeled "Reason for Departure." Code 2 simply meant transferred to another camp for continuing labor. Natural death was coded 3. Execution was coded 4. Suicide coded 5. The ominous code 6 designated "special handling," the term commonly understood as extermination, either in a gas chamber, by hanging, or by gunshot.[9]

As the trains and trucks rolled in from Belgium, France, and Holland, thousands of punch cards were examined, processed, and the information fed back to the Department of Statistics at the SS Economics Office in Oranienburg. The numbered men and women were compared to a list of work needs at Bergen-Belsen and other camps. "Never a name," Cheim remembers, "only the assigned numbers." How many died was just a statistic to note, a detail for the machines to digest. That December 1944, some 20,000 prisoners were registered; 50 deaths per day, on average, were recorded on punch cards.[10]

Cheim learned that to discover the occupational make-up of a prisoner group, each inmate's individual punch card was fed into the mechanical sorter. Then the dials were adjusted to isolate certain professions, labor skills, age groups, or language abilities needed for work battalions. If prisoners were selected for work, their names appeared on a Hollerith printout for transport to nearby sub-camps, factories, and even local farms.[11]

Labor requirements were reported and then matched by Office D II of the SS Economics Office, which administered all the camps under Gen. Oswald Pohl. Pohl, creator of the "Extermination by Labor" program, ardently argued that expeditiously gassing Jews deprived the Reich of an important resource. His idea, "Extermination by Labor," quite simply meant working Jews to death. Only after outliving their usefulness would they be deported to death camps for gassing. Office D II embraced SS Chief Heinrich Himmler's declaration: "If 10,000 Russian females collapse from exhaustion while digging a tank ditch interests me only so far as the tank ditch is completed for Germany."[12]

Cheim took special notice one day when five women escaped from Bergen-Belsen. Angry SS guards vowed to recapture them. They resented reporting the prisoner departures in column 34 of the punch card forms as code 7—escaped.[13]

He became fascinated with a young Dutch seamstress. Who was she? Her journey began in the Westerbork camp. Went to Auschwitz. She was born May 10, 1924. No name. Just a number. 53752. But who was 53752, Cheim wondered? Did she not have a name, only a number?[14]

Cheim soon began to understand the truth. Hundreds of thousands of human beings were being identified, sorted, assigned, and transported by means of the Hollerith system. Numbers and punch cards had dehumanized them all, he thought. Numbers and punch cards would probably kill them all. But Cheim never understood where the Hollerith system came from.[15]

One December morning, even as the numbered man Cheim, in his tattered uniform, stepped quickly toward the Bergen-Belsen Hollerith office to stay warm and to stay alive, another man, this one dressed elegantly in a fine suit and warm overcoat, stepped out of a new chauffeured car at 590 Madison Avenue in New York. He was Thomas J. Watson. His company, IBM—one of the biggest in the world—custom-designed and leased the Hollerith card sorting system to the Third Reich for use at Bergen-Belsen and most of the other concentration camps. International Business Machines also serviced its machines almost monthly, and trained Nazi personnel to use the intricate systems. Duplicate copies of code books were kept in IBM's offices in case field books were lost. What's more, his company was the exclusive source for up to 1.5 billion punch cards the Reich required each year to run its machines.[16]

Indeed, the systems were not only used in the concentration camps, but hundreds of them had been installed for years throughout the entire commercial, industrial, war-making, and anti-Jewish infrastructure of Nazi Germany and Nazi-dominated Europe.

On this cold December day, Watson was unyielding. His German subsidiary, Dehomag, was out of control. More lawyers would be called, more telegrams would be sent, more clever maneuvering with the State Department would be undertaken—not to stop Dehomag from its genocidal partnership with the Third Reich, but to ensure that all the proceeds and profits remained with IBM NY. No matter who won, IBM would prosper. Business was its middle name.

I
II
III
IV
V
VI
VII
VIII
IX
X
XI
XII
XIII
XIV
XV

THE IBM-HITLER INTERSECTION

ON JANUARY 30, 1933, THE WORLD AWOKE TO A FRIGHTENING
new reality: Adolf Hitler had suddenly become leader of Germany.
Hitlerites dressed in a spectrum of uniforms from gauche
to ominous, paraded, motored, and bicycled through Berlin in
defiant celebration. Hanging from trucks and stomping through the
squares, arms outstretched and often swaggering in song, the Nazis
were jubilant. Their historic moment—fraught with emotional expectations of revenge and victory against all adversaries—their long
awaited decisive moment had arrived. From this instant, the world
would never be the same.

Quickly, Hitler's Nazis moved to take over the entire government and virtually all aspects of German commerce, society, and
culture. *Der Führer* wanted an Aryan Germany to dominate all of
Europe with a master race subjugating all non-Aryans. For Jews,
Hitler had a special plan: total destruction. There were no secrets in
Hitler's vision. He broadcast them loudly to the world. They exploded as front-page headlines in every major city, on every radio
network, and in weekly cinema newsreels. Ironically, Hitler's fascism resonated with certain men of great vision, such as Henry
Ford. Another who found Hitlerism compelling was Thomas J. Wat-
son, president of one of America's most prestigious companies:
International Business Machines.[1]

The roads traveled by Hitler and Watson began in different parts of the world in completely different circumstances with completely different intentions. How did these two men—one an extreme capitalist, the other an extreme fascist—form a technologic and commercial alliance that would ultimately facilitate the murder of six million Jews and an equal number of other Europeans? These men and their philosophies could not have been more dissimilar. Yet as history proved, they could have hardly been more compatible.

It all began decades before in New York during the last gasp of the nineteenth century, at a time when America's rapid industrial growth spurred inventions to automate virtually every manual task. Swells of immigrants came to American shores to labor long days. But some dreamed of a better way to be industrious—or at least a faster and cheaper way. Contraptions, mechanizations, and patented gadgets were everywhere turning wheels, cranking cogs, and saving steps in workshops and factories. The so-called Second Industrial Revolution, powered by electricity, was in full swing. Turn-of-the-century America—a confluence of massive commerce and clickety-clack industrial ingenuity—was a perfect moment for the birthplace of the most powerful corporation the world has ever seen: IBM.[2]

IBM was born German. Its technology was originally created for only one reason: to count people as they had never been counted before, with a magical ability to identify and quantify. Before long, IBM technology demonstrated it could do more than just count people or things. It could compute, that is, the technology could record data, process it, retrieve it, analyze it, and automatically answer pointed questions. Moments of mechanized bustle could now accomplish what would be an impossibility of paper and pencil calculation for any mortal man.

Herman Hollerith invented IBM. Born in 1860, Hollerith was the son of intellectual German parents who brought their proud and austere German heritage with them when they settled in Buffalo, New York. Herman was only seven when his father, a language teacher, died in an accident while riding a horse. His mother was left to raise five children alone. Proud and independent, she declined to ask her financially comfortable parents for assistance, choosing instead a life of tough, principled self-reliance.[3]

Young Hollerith moved to New York City when, at age fifteen, he enrolled in the College of the City of New York. Except for spelling difficulties, he immediately showed a creative aptitude, and at age nineteen graduated from the Columbia School of Mines with a degree in engineering, boasting perfect 10.0 grades. In 1879, Hollerith accepted the invitation of his Columbia professor to become an assistant in the U.S. Census Bureau. In those days, the decennial census was little more than a basic head-count, devoid of information about an individual's occupation, education, or other traits because the computational challenge of counting millions of Americans was simply too prodigious. As it was, the manual counting and cross-tabulation process required several years before final results could be tallied. Because the post–Civil War populace had grown so swiftly, perhaps doubling since the last census, experts predicted spending more than a decade to count the 1890 census; in other words, the next census in 1900 would be underway before the previous one was complete.[4]

Just nineteen years old, Hollerith moved to Washington, D.C., to join the Census Bureau. Over dinner one night at the posh Potomac Boat Club, Director of Vital Statistics, John Billings, quipped to Hollerith, "There ought to be a machine for doing the purely mechanical work of tabulating population and similar statistics." Inventive Hollerith began to think about a solution. French looms, simple music boxes, and player pianos used punched holes on rolls or cards to automate rote activity. About a year later, Hollerith was struck with his idea. He saw a train conductor punch tickets in a special pattern to record physical characteristics such as height, hair color, size of nose, and clothing—a sort of "punched photograph." Other conductors could read the code and then catch anyone re-using the ticket of the original passenger.[5]

Hollerith's idea was a card with standardized holes, each representing a different trait: gender, nationality, occupation, and so forth. The card would then be fed into a "reader." By virtue of easily adjustable spring mechanisms and brief electrical brush contacts sensing for the holes, the cards could be "read" as they raced through a mechanical feeder. The processed cards could then be sorted into stacks based on a specified series of punched holes.[6]

Millions of cards could be sorted and resorted. Any desired trait could be isolated—general or specific—by simply sorting and resorting for data-specific holes. The machines could render the portrait of an entire population—or could pick out any group within that population. Indeed, one man could be identified from among millions if enough holes could be punched into a card and sorted enough times. Every punch card would become an informational storehouse limited only by the number of holes. It was nothing less than a nineteenth-century bar code for human beings.[7]

By 1884, a prototype was constructed. After borrowing a few thousand dollars from a German friend, Hollerith patented and built a production machine. Ironically, the initial test was not a count of the living, but of the dead for local health departments in Maryland, New York, and New Jersey.[8]

Soon, Hollerith found his system could do more than count people. It could rapidly perform the most tedious accounting functions for any enterprise: from freight bills for the New York Central Railroad to actuarial and financial records for Prudential Insurance. Most importantly, the Hollerith system not only counted, it produced analysis. The clanging contraption could calculate in a few weeks the results that a man previously spent years correlating. Buoyed by success, Hollerith organized a trip overseas to show his electromechanical tabulator to European governments, including Germany and Italy. Everywhere Hollerith was met with acclaim from bureaucrats, engineers, and statisticians.[9] His card sorter was more than just a clever gadget. It was a steel, spindle, and rubber-wheeled key to the Pandora's Box of unlimited information.

When the U.S. Census Bureau sponsored a contest seeking the best automated counting device for its 1890 census, it was no surprise when Hollerith's design won. The judges had been studying it for years. Hollerith quickly manufactured his first machines.[10]

After the 1890 census, Hollerith became an overnight tabulating hero. His statistical feat caught the attention of the general scientific world and even the popular newspapers. His systems saved the Census Bureau some $5 million, or about a third of its budget. Computations were completed with unprecedented speed and added a dramatic new dimension to the entire nature of census taking. Whereas in 1870 only five census topics were asked, amounting to little more than a head-count, many more personal questions were added. Indeed, now an army of census takers could posit 235 questions, including queries about the languages spoken in the household, the number of children living at home and elsewhere, the level of each family member's schooling, country of origin, religious affiliation, and scores of other traits. Suddenly, the government could profile its own population.[11]

Since the Census Bureau only needed most of the tabulators once every decade, and because the defensive inventor always suspected some electrician or mechanic would steal his design, Hollerith decided that the systems would be leased by the government, not purchased. This important decision to lease machines, not sell them, would dominate all major IBM business transactions for the next century. Washington paid Hollerith about $750,000 to rent his machines for the project. Now the inventor's challenge was to find customers for the machines in between the decennial federal censuses.

Quickly, that became no challenge at all. Governments and industry were queuing up for the devices. Census and statistical departments in Russia, Italy, England, France, Austria, and Germany all submitted orders. Hollerith's new technology was virtually unrivaled. His machines made advanced census taking possible everywhere in the world. He and he alone would control the technology because the punchers, sorters, and tabulators were all designed to be compatible with each other—and with no other machine that might ever be produced.[12]

Moreover, millions of punch cards would be needed to capture the data. Each disposable punch card could essentially be used only one time. Hollerith had the underpinnings of a monopoly and he had not even started the company. Most important, the whole enterprise quickly elevated Hollerith and his system to supranational status.[13] Governments were just customers, customers to be kept in check. In many ways, Hollerith felt that he and his technology were indeed bigger than governments. In many ways, he was right.

With the world waiting, it was time for the engineer to launch a corporation. Ironically, Hollerith was too busy garnering new business to create an actual company. Moreover, still in his twenties but already set in his ways, the handlebar mustachioed and often surly Hollerith was not well suited for the task. Hollerith could dress in top hat and elegant walking cane when the occasion required. But he lacked patience and finesse, abhorred the commercialization such a company required, and continually suspected his customers of planning to steal his designs. Maintaining a paternal connection to his invention, Hollerith took everything personally. Hence, no client or contact was too important to antagonize. Grudges were savored long. Feuds relished. Not infrequently, his attitude toward customers was take-it-or-leave-it. Outspoken and abrasive, he was ready to do combat with government officials whom he suspected of undermining his patent, here or abroad. The little annoyances of life riled him just as much, such as the car that suddenly broke down, prompting an angry letter-writing campaign to the manufacturer.[14]

Other than his inventions, Hollerith was said to cherish three things: his German heritage, his privacy, and his cat Bismarck. His link to everything German was obvious to all around him. Hollerith went out of his way to sail to Europe on German vessels. He once justified his friendship with a colleague's wife, explaining, "[She] is a German so I got along very well with her." And when colleagues thought he needed a rest, they suggested he take a long vacation in the one place he could relax, his beloved ancestral homeland.[15]

For privacy, Hollerith built a tall fence around his home to keep out neighbors and their pets. When too many cats scaled the top to jump into the yard, the ever-inventive Hollerith strung electrical wire along the fence, connected it to a battery, and then perched at his window puffing on a cigar. When a neighbor cat would appear threatening Bismarck's privacy, Hollerith would depress a switch, sending an electrical jolt into the animal.[16]

Hollerith's first major overseas census was organized for the brutal regime of Czar Nicholas II to launch the first-ever census of an estimated 120 million Russians. Nicholas was anxious to import Hollerith technology. So the inventor traveled to St. Petersburg to seal the enormous contract.[17]

Shortly after his return from Russia in late 1896, Hollerith finally incorporated. He located the company office in his austere two-story workshop-warehouse in the Georgetown section of Washington, D.C., just a few minutes drive from both the White House and Census Bureau. He named his new firm with predictable plainness: the Tabulating Machine Company, a name that would be quickly forgotten.[18] But that same entity would eventually become IBM, one of the most recognizable commercial names of all time.

SHORTLY AFTER the 1900 census, it became apparent to the federal government that it had helped Hollerith's Tabulating Machine Company achieve a global monopoly, one based on an invention the Census Bureau had—in a way—"commissioned" from an employee on the Bureau's own payroll, Herman Hollerith. Moreover, the new reform-minded Director of the Census Bureau, Simeon North, uncovered numerous irregularities in the Bureau's contracts for punch card machines. Hollerith was gouging the federal government. Excessive royalties, phantom machines, inconsistent pricing for machines and punch cards, restrictive use arrangements—the gamut of vendor abuses was discovered.[19]

Worse, instead of the Bureau being Hollerith's best-treated customer, Tabulating Machine Company was charging other governments and commercial clients less. North suspected that even the Russian Czar was paying far less than Uncle Sam. American taxpayers, it seemed, were subsidizing the newly ascended Hollerith empire.[20]

When he investigated, North was astonished to learn that his predecessor, William Merriam, had negotiated lucrative and sometimes inexplicable contracts with Hollerith's firm. Then, little more than a year after Merriam left the Census Bureau, Hollerith hired him as president of Tabulating Machine Company. A rankled North inaugurated a bureaucratic crusade against his own agency's absolute dependence on Hollerith technology, and the questionable costs. He demanded answers. "All that I desire to be satisfied of," North asked of Hollerith, "is that the [U.S.] government is given as fair and as liberal terms as those embodied in the company's contracts for commercial work and . . . for other governments."[21]

Hollerith didn't like being challenged. Rather than assuage his single most important customer, Hollerith launched a tempestuous feud with North, castigating him before Congress, and even to the man who appointed him, President Theodore Roosevelt. Tabulating Machine Company's technology was indispensable, thought Hollerith. He felt he could pressure and attack the U.S. government without restraint. But then North fought back. Realizing that Hollerith's patents would expire in 1906, and determined to break the inventor's chokehold on the Census Bureau, North experimented with another machine, and, finally, in July 1905, he booted the Holleriths out of the Census Bureau altogether. Tabulating Machine Company had lost its best client.[22]

A rival tabulator, developed by another Census Bureau technician named James Powers, would be utilized. Powers' machines were much faster than Hollerith devices. They enjoyed several automated advances over Hollerith, and the units were vastly less expensive. Most of all, Powers' machines would allow the Census Bureau to break the grip of the Tabulating Machine Company.[23]

Despondent and unapproachable for months during the self-inflicted Census Bureau debacle, Hollerith refused to deal with an onslaught of additional bad business news. Strategic investments porously lost money. Several key railroad clients defected. Tabulating Machine Company did, however, rebound with new designs, improved technology, more commercial clients, and more foreign census contracts. But then, in 1910, in an unbelievably arrogant maneuver, Hollerith actually tried to stop the United States from exercising its constitutionally mandated duty to conduct the census. Claiming the Census Bureau was about to deploy new machinery that in some way infringed his patents, Hollerith filed suit and somehow convinced a federal judge in Washington, D.C., to issue a restraining order against the Thirteenth Census. But the courts eventually ruled against Tabulating Machine Company. Hollerith had lost big.[24]

Continuing in denial, the wealthy Hollerith tinkered with new contraptions and delved into unrelated diversions while his company floundered. His doctors insisted it was time to leave the business. Frustrated stockholders and management of Tabulating Machine Company welcomed that advice and encouraged Hollerith to retire. Ambivalently, Hollerith began parceling out his interests.[25]

He began with Germany. In 1910, the inventor licensed all his patents to a German adding machine salesman named Willy Heidinger. Heidinger created the firm Deutsche Hollerith Maschinen Gesellschaft—the German Hollerith Machine Corporation, or Dehomag for short. This firm was owned and controlled by Heidinger; only a few of his relatives owned token shares. As a licensee of Tabulating Machine Company, Dehomag simply leased Hollerith technology in Germany. Tabulating Machine Company received a share of Dehomag's business, plus patent royalties. Heidinger was a traditional German, fiercely proud of his heritage, and dedicated to his family. Like Hollerith, Heidinger was temperamental, prone to volcanic outbursts, and always ready for corporate combat.[26]

The next year, a disillusioned, embittered Hollerith simply sold out completely. Enter Charles Flint, a rugged individualist who at the edge of the nineteenth century epitomized the affluent adventurer capitalist. One of the first Americans to own an automobile and fly an aeroplane, an avid hunter and fisherman, Flint made his millions trading in international commodities. Weapons were one of those commodities and Flint didn't care whom he sold them to.[27]

Flint's war profiteering knew no limits. He organized a private armada to help Brazilian officials brutally suppress a revolt by that nation's navy, thus restoring the government's authority. He licensed the manufacture of the newly invented Wright Brothers aeroplane to Kaiser Wilhelm to help launch German military aviation and its Great War aces. Indeed, Flint would happily sell guns and naval vessels to both sides of a brutal war. He sold to Peru just after leaving the employ of Chile when a border skirmish between them erupted, and to enemies Japan and Russia during their various conflicts.[28]

Of Flint it was once written, "Had anyone called him a merchant of death, Flint would have wondered what the fellow had in mind. Such was the nature of the Western World prior to the Great War."[29]

Flint had also perfected an infamous business modality, the so-called *trust*. Trusts were the anti-competitive industrial combinations that often secretly devoured competition and ultimately led to a government crackdown. The famous Sherman Anti-Trust Act was created just to combat such abuses. Newspapers of the day dubbed Flint, the "father of trusts." The title made him at once a glamorous legend and a villain in his era.[30]

In 1911, the famous industrial combine maestro, who had so deftly created cartel-like entities in the rubber and chemical fields, now tried something different. He approached key stockholders and management of four completely unrelated manufacturing firms to create one minor diversified conglomerate. The centerpiece would be Hollerith's enterprise.[31]

The four lackluster firms Flint selected defied any apparent rationale for merger. International Time Recording Company manufactured time clocks to record worker hours. Computing Scale Company sold simple retail scales with pricing charts attached as well as a line of meat and cheese slicers. Bundy Manufacturing produced small key-actuated time clocks, but, more importantly, it owned prime real estate in Endicott, New York. Of the four, Hollerith's Tabulating Machine Company was simply the largest and most dominant member of the group.[32]

Hollerith agreed to the sale, offering his stock for about $1.21 million, plus a 10-year consulting contract at $20,000 per year—an enormous sum for its day. The resulting company was given a prosaic name arising from its strange combination: Computing-Tabulating-Recording Company, or CTR. The new entity was partially explained by some as a synergistic combine that would bring ready cash and an international sales force to four seemingly viable companies stunted by limited growth potential or troubled economics. Rather than bigness, Flint wanted product mix that would make each of the flagging partners stronger.[33]

After the sale was finalized, a seemingly detached Hollerith strolled over to his Georgetown workshop, jammed with stacked machine parts in every corner, and declared to the workers matter-of-factly: "Well, I sold the business." Approaching the men individually, Hollerith offered one curt comment or another. He was gracious to Bill Barnes, who had lost an arm while assembling a belt mechanism. For Joe, a young shop worker, Hollerith ostentatiously handed him a $50 bill, making quite an impression on someone who had never seen so large a bill.[34]

Hollerith withdrew as an active manager.[35] The commercial extension of his ingenuity and turbulent persona was now in the hands of a more skilled supranational manipulator, Charles Flint. Hollerith was willing to make millions, but only on his terms. Flint wanted millions—on any terms. Moreover, Flint wanted CTR's helm to be captained by a businessman, not a technocrat. For that, he chose one of America's up and coming business scoundrels, Thomas J. Watson.

CARVED AMONG the densely wooded hills, winding, dusty back roads connected even the remotest farm to the small villages and towns that comprised the Finger Lakes region of New York State in the 1890s. Gray and rutted, crackling from burnt orange maple leaves in the fall and yielding short clouds of dust in the summer beneath the hoof and wheel of Thomas J. Watson's bright yellow horse-drawn organ wagon, these lonely yet intriguing byways seemed almost magical. Pastoral vistas of folding green hills veined with streams lay beyond every bend and dip. But even more alluring was the sheer adventure of selling that awaited Watson. Back then, it was just pianos and sewing machines.[36] But it took all-day tenacity and unending self-confidence to travel these dirt roads just for the opportunity—not the certainty, only the opportunity—to make a sale.

Yet "making the sale," that calculating one-on-one wizardry that ends as an exhilarating confirmation of one's mind over another's motivation, this was the finesse—the power—that came naturally to Watson. Tall, lanky, handsome, and intelligent, he understood people. He knew when to listen and when to speak. He had mastered the art of persuasion and possessed an uncanny ability to overcome intense opposition and "close the deal."

All born salesmen know that the addicting excitement of a sales victory is short-lived. No matter how great the sale, it is never enough. Selling, for such people, becomes not an occupation, but a lifestyle.

Any salesman can sell anything. Every salesman alive knows these words are true. But they also know that not all salesmen can go further. Few of them can *conquer*.

Watson was a conqueror. From simple merchandise inauspiciously sold to farmers and townsfolk in rural west-central New York, Watson would go on to command a global company consumed not with mere customers, but with territories, nations, and entire populations. He would identify corporate enemies to overcome and strategies to deploy. Like any conqueror, he would vanquish all in his way, and then demand the spoils. Salesmanship under Watson would elevate from one man's personal elixir to a veritable cult of commercial conquest. By virtue of his extraordinary skills, Watson would be delivered from his humble beginnings as a late-nineteenth-century horse-and-buggy back road peddler, to corporate scoundrel, to legendary tycoon, to international statesman, and finally to regal American icon—all in less than four decades.

Although born into a clan of tough Scottish Watsons, the future captain of industry was actually born Thomas J. "Wasson." His Protestant father, a brawling, scowling lumberman of little religious tolerance, was so opposed to having Catholic in-laws in the family, he changed his name to Wasson, just to disassociate. Eventually, the family let the protest drop and re-adopted the Watson name. Thus, young Tom could be a genuine Watson.[37]

Growing up in the Finger Lakes town of Painted Post offered few choices to the ambitious, young Watson. To escape a life of working the family farm and running horse teams pulling river barges, Watson declared early he would become a teacher. He even obtained his teaching certificate. But after just one day on the job, the impatient Watson confessed, "That settles my teaching career. I can't go into a schoolroom with a bunch of children at nine o'clock in the morning and stay until four."[38]

Watson wanted to dive into commerce. He began by peddling sewing machines and pianos on the road for a store in town. He had to provide his own horse. When his more experienced road partner drifted away, Watson took over—and did better. Even when economic times hardened, Watson learned to find lodging with befriended farmers, barter goods, and push on despite rain-flooded roads and every other adversity. Despite his admirable results, Watson's salary was generally $10 per week. Before long, he quit and looked elsewhere.[39]

Quickly, Watson learned that some sales positions offered something called a *commission*, that is, a cut. He joined a building and loan association in Buffalo where he sold shares up and down the populated roads south of the city. Watson's deal was straight commission. His manager was a slick and dapper operator who taught Watson how to smoothly sell stock in saloons, and how to always dress the role of a successful Gay Nineties businessman. Nothing drives glibness like a commission-only job. Watson excelled—and the feeling was invigorating. He loved to sell.[40]

In 1895, at age twenty-one, Watson bumped into John J. Range, the manager of the Buffalo office of one of the most rapacious companies of the day, the National Cash Register Company. Nicknamed "The Cash," NCR was the personal empire of the ruthless and belligerent tycoon, John Patterson. Patterson had created a sales manual designed to rigidly standardize all pitches and practices, and even mold the thought processes of selling. No deviation was allowed. Patterson's way was the only way. Range was one of Patterson's most successful sales supervisors, brutalizing and humiliating his underlings until they achieved their quotas. Range became a mentor to Watson. In no time, *The Cash* converted Watson into a youthful commercial mercenary.[41]

Within months, Watson was the territory's leading salesman, outearning Range himself, eventually becoming among the best *Cash* salesmen along the East Coast. His commissions reached as high as $100 per week. Patterson took notice, transferring Watson and his impressive skills to the undesirable Rochester office, one of the worst performing of *The Cash's* 160 branch offices. Watson worked his magic immediately. On his very first day, while tying his horse to the hitching post in front of the National Cash Register office, Watson encountered the angry saloonkeeper next door. The irate neighbor complained that *The Cash* enjoyed a dismal reputation and the prior sales agent was often too drunk to perform his job. Within minutes, Watson had somehow convinced the disenchanted man to buy a new cash register. Watson sold a second cash register while riding out to another complaining prospect.[42]

Patterson realized that Watson was good enough to go beyond simple sales. He was good enough to destroy the main competition in Rochester, the Hallwood Company, which also marketed a cash register. Adopting the brutal, anything-goes techniques of Patterson and Range, and adding a few devious tricks of his own, Watson began the systematic annihilation of Hallwood, its sales, and its customer base. Tactics included lurking near the Hallwood office to spy on its salesmen and customers. Watson would report the prospective clients so "intimidation squads" could pounce. The squads would threaten the prospect with tall tales of patent infringement suits by NCR against Hallwood, falsely claiming such suits would eventually include anyone who purchased Hallwood machines. The frightened customer would then be offered an NCR machine at a discount.[43]

Watson never missed an opening. A Hallwood salesman whom Watson had befriended one day mentioned that he was calling on a prospect the next day. In the morning, the Hallwood salesman arrived at the merchant's location just as Watson's horse and buggy was riding off, the sale in hand. Watson had risen at dawn and driven twenty miles to steal the account. Watson enjoyed the triumph so thoroughly, he bragged about the incident for years to come. Within a few years, Watson had virtually driven Hallwood out of Rochester. Later, Watson bragged that he had made Rochester "one of the best organized and cleanest territories."[44]

Patterson liked Watson's style. The unscrupulous NCR president had learned to use frivolous libel and patent suits to drive his competition into submission. Watson could add a whole new dimension to the war against anyone other than Patterson who dared buy or sell cash registers—even second-hand NCR cash registers. John Patterson believed that cash registers were his God-granted domain and no one else's. Watson would be the instrument of his hegemony.[45]

In 1903, Watson was called to Patterson's office and instructed to destroy second-hand dealers across the country. Although he had become a star in the Rochester office, Watson was still relatively unknown elsewhere. Patterson planted him in New York City, handed him a million-dollar budget, and asked him to create a fake business called Watson's Cash Register and Second Hand Exchange. His mission was to join the community of second-hand dealers, learn their business, set up shop nearby, dramatically undersell, quietly steal their accounts, intimidate their customers, and otherwise disrupt their viability. Watson's fake company never needed to make a profit—only spend money to decimate unsuspecting dealers of used registers. Eventually, they would either be driven out of business or sell out to Watson with a draconian non-compete clause. Funneled money from NCR was used for operations since Watson had no capital of his own.[46]

The mission was so secretive even the NCR sales force in Manhattan believed that Watson had simply defected from the Rochester office to set up his own shop. He reported directly to Patterson and his staff. It took years, but the enemy—second-hand dealers—was ruthlessly conquered.[47]

The victim list was long. Fred Brainin's second-hand business was on 14th Street in Manhattan—Watson bought him out with a proviso that Brainin would stay out of cash registers. Silas Lacey of Philadelphia merged into Watson's new front. The East Coast was easy. So Watson moved on to a real challenge: Chicago.[48]

One of the biggest Chicago dealers was Amos Thomas, located on Randolph Street in the Loop, just a few steps from the Elevated. Watson's fake company moved in across the street. Thomas remembered, "Watson . . . tried to get me to put a price on my business. He wanted to control the second-hand business. I told him I would not sell." But Watson and his cohorts, which now included his old supervisor John Range, would come by three or four times each day to press the man.[49]

Still, Thomas would not sell. So Watson opened a second competing store near Thomas. NCR had secretly acquired control of American Cash Register Company, the successor to Hallwood. Watson's second front, called American Second Hand Cash Register Company, only squeezed Thomas further. Weakened, Thomas finally offered a buy-out price of $20,000. But that was just too high for Watson.[50]

By now, it was clear to Thomas that Watson was fronting for Patterson's NCR. *The Cash* didn't care if Thomas knew or not. To prove it, they invited

Thomas to NCR headquarters in Dayton, Ohio, where he was first treated to a splendid dinner and then "handled" by a Patterson executive. Unless Thomas sold out for a "reasonable price," Thomas was told, NCR would rent yet another store near his and continue to undersell until his trade was entirely wrecked. Buckling under, Thomas at last agreed to sell for $15,875 plus $500 in cash. A battered and broken Thomas pleaded with Watson, as the new owner of his company, to be kind to a long-time devoted employee. Amos Thomas had been conquered.[51]

Patterson's school for scoundrels was unparalleled in American business history. A Watson aide once testified that Patterson would scream for merciless destruction of all competitors. "Kill them! . . . crush them," Patterson would yell at sales conferences. The vanquished included Cuckoo, Globe, Hallwood, Metropolitan, Simplex, Toledo, Union, and scores of other struggling cash register companies.[52]

NCR salesmen wore dark suits, the corporation innovated a One Hundred Point Club for agents who met their quota, and *The Cash* stressed "clean living" as a virtue for commercial success. One day during a pep rally to the troops, Watson scrawled the word THINK on a piece of paper. Patterson saw the note and ordered THINK signs distributed throughout the company. Watson embraced many of Patterson's regimenting techniques as indispensable doctrine for good sales. What he learned at NCR would stay with him forever.[53]

NCR's war tactics were limitless. Bribes, knock-off machines at predatory prices, threats of litigation, and even smashed store windows were alleged. The federal government finally stepped in. On February 22, 1912, Patterson, Watson, and several dozen other *Cash* executives were indicted for criminal conspiracy to restrain trade and construct a monopoly. Prosecutors called the conduct the most uncivilized business behavior ever seen and likened Watson and company to "Mexican bandits."[54]

A year later, in 1913, all defendants were found guilty by an Ohio jury. Damning evidence, supplied by Watson colleagues and even Watson's own signed letters of instructions, were irrefutable. Most of the men, including Watson, received a one-year jail sentence. Many of the convicted wept and asked for leniency. But not Watson. He declared that he was proud of what he had accomplished.[55]

Then came the floods. The late winter and early spring in Dayton, Ohio, had been brutal. Excessive rainfall swamped the city. The Mad and Miami rivers began overflowing. In late March 1913, a tornado tore through the area, turning Dayton into a disaster scene, with much of the area under water. Some 90,000 people suddenly became homeless. Communications were cut. But Watson and others at NCR controlled one of the few telegraph lines still on high ground.[56]

The Cash pounced. NCR organized an immense emergency relief effort. The company's assembly line was retrofitted to produce a flotilla of rudimentary rowboats—one every seven minutes. Bottled water and paper cups were distributed to flood victims along with hay cots for sleeping. NCR facilities were converted into an infirmary. Five babies were born there in one day. From New York, Watson organized a relief train of medical supplies, food, and more water. Where roadbed and rail switches were washed away, Watson ordered them instantly repaired. When NCR relief trains encountered irreparable tracks, just a few miles from Dayton, Watson recruited men to carry supplies in on their backs until the goods reached Dayton—all to cheering crowds.[57]

Patterson, Watson, and the other NCR men became national heroes overnight. A press room was established on NCR premises. Petitions were sent to President Woodrow Wilson asking for a pardon. Considering public sentiment, prosecutors offered consent decrees in lieu of jail time. Most of the defendants eagerly signed. Watson, however, refused, maintaining he saw nothing wrong in his conduct. Eventually, Watson's attorneys successfully overturned the conviction on a technicality. The government declined to re-prosecute.[58]

But then the unpredictable and maniacal Patterson rewarded Watson's years as a loyal sales warrior by suddenly subjecting him to public humiliation in front of a company assembly. Just as Watson was speaking to a festive gathering of *Cash* executives, Patterson histrionically interrupted him to praise another salesman. Everyone recognized the signs. Shortly thereafter, Watson was summarily fired.[59]

For seventeen years, NCR had been Watson's life—the fast cars and even faster commissions, the command and control of industrial subterfuge, the sense of belonging. It was now over. Shocked, Watson simply turned his back on his exciting lifestyle at *The Cash*. "Nearly everything I know about building a business comes from Mr. Patterson," Watson would admit. Now he added this vow: "I am going out to build a business bigger than John Patterson has."[60]

What was bigger than National Cash Register, one of America's largest corporations? Why stop at the American shoreline? Watson contacted the one man who could take him global, Charles Flint of CTR.

WHEN THOMAS WATSON walked into Charles Flint's Fifth Avenue suite, their respective reputations surrounded them like force fields. Watson's was national. Flint's was international. Watson had manipulated mere men. Flint had catered to the destiny of nations. Yet, the two did not instantly bond.

Flint was shorter and much older than Watson, although filled with just as much energy. After all, Flint had soared amongst the clouds in a Wright Brothers plane and driven automobiles, sailed the fastest boat on many a river or lake, and seen the world—all while Watson was still traversing back roads on horseback. Yet, during their first meeting, Watson was almost disappointed in the legendary financier's presence. But it was Flint's ideas that spoke louder than his physical stature.[61]

As a nineteenth-century international economic adventurer, Flint believed that the accretion of money was its own nurturing reward, and that the business world functioned much as the animal kingdom: survival of the fittest. Watson found nothing unacceptable in Flint's philosophy. Heading up CTR could be the chance Watson knew he deserved to be his own boss and make all the decisions. CTR's diverse line was better than cash registers because the dominant product was Hollerith's tabulator and card sorter. The two men could work together to make CTR great—that is, if Watson's management deal was structured right.[62]

But from Flint's point of view, he was hardly ready to stroll across the street to CTR's headquarters and install Watson. The supersalesman before him still walked under the shadow of a criminal conviction, which at that point had not yet been overturned. Although under appeal, it could cast the company in a bad light. During one of several board meetings to consider hiring Watson, at least one CTR director bellowed at Flint, "What are you trying to do? Ruin this business? Who is going to run this business while he serves his term in jail?"[63]

It was a process, one that Watson was determined to win, and so he spoke frankly to the reluctant directors. First, he sold himself—like any adroit salesman—and then worked around their collective worries about his conspiracy conviction. Visions of products and profits proliferating worldwide, million-dollar growth projections, ever-increasing dividends—these were the rewards the directors embraced as most important. CTR bought in. Watson was offered "a gentleman's salary" of $25,000 per year, plus more than 1,200 shares of the firm. But Watson wanted better. He wanted a slice of the profits. His commissionable days at NCR had whetted his craving for more of the same. Much more.[64]

"In other words," said Flint, "you want part of the ice you cut." Indeed.

Watson negotiated a commission of 5 percent of all CTR after-tax, after-dividend profits. However, in light of Watson's conviction, he would not join the firm as president, but rather as general manager. It didn't matter. Watson would call the shots. May 1, 1914, was his first day at CTR. Hollerith's company, now Flint's company, would never be the same. It would soon become Watson's company.[65]

Copying many of NCR's sales development and promotion techniques, Watson built an organization that even Patterson would have marveled at. Just as Patterson had organized the One Hundred Point Club for salesmen hitting their quota, Watson began a festive Hundred Percent Club. Patterson had demanded starched white shirts and dark suits at NCR. Watson insisted CTR employees dress in an identical uniform. And Watson borrowed his own NCR innovation, the term THINK, which at CTR was impressed onto as many surfaces as could be found, from the wall above Watson's desk to the bottom of company stationery. These Patterson *cum* Watson touches were easy to implement since several key Watson aides were old cronies from the NCR scandal days.[66]

But Watson understood much more about human motivation than Patterson had ever allowed to creep into NCR. Watson wanted to inspire men to greater results, not brutalize them toward mere quotas. His way would imbue a sense of belonging, not a climate of fear. As a general understood his troops, Watson well understood the value of the workingmen below to the executive men above. Moreover, any limitation in his general manager title was soon overcome. In 1915, his conviction was overturned and within forty-eight hours the board approved his ascent to the presidency of CTR.[67]

For the first years, Watson worked quietly out of his sparse office at CTR, cementing the firm's financial, labor, and technical position. He did his best to outmaneuver and neutralize the competitor tabulating machines. Patent wars were fought, engineering campaigns commenced, research undertaken, and major clients either conquered or re-conquered. When needed, Watson arranged bank loans to see the company through lean times and help it grow.[68]

Hollerith, although no longer in control, remained as an active consultant with the company, but found Watson's style completely alien. Years before, while still at NCR, Watson had ordered a Hollerith machine, but Hollerith declined to send one, fearing Watson would copy it for Patterson. Now that they were in the same firm, the two frequently butted heads on a range of issues, from commercialization to technical research. Unlike Hollerith, who was willing to do battle with customers over some barely discernible personal principle, Watson wanted to win customers over for the money. Money was his principle. Flint's chairman, George Fairchild, was also a towering force at CTR to be reckoned with. Watson navigated around both Hollerith and Fairchild. Without Flint's continuous backing, Watson could not have managed. Nonetheless, without his unique winning style, Watson could not have persevered.[69]

Watson became more than a good manager, more than just an impressive executive, more than merely a concerned employer, he became central to the company itself. His ubiquitous lectures and pep talks were delivered with such uplifting passion, they soon transcended to liturgical inspiration. Watson embodied more than the boss. He was the Leader. He even had a song.

Clad in their uniforms of dark blue suits and glistening white shirts, the inspirited sales warriors of CTR would sing:

> *Mister Watson is the man we're working for,*
> *He's the Leader of the C-T-R,*
> *He's the fairest, squarest man we know;*
> *Sincere and true.*
> *He has shown us how to play the game.*
> *And how to make the dough.*[70]

Watson was elevating to a higher plane. Newspaper articles began to focus on him personally as much as the company. His pervasive presence and dazzling capitalistic imperatives became a virtual religion to CTR employees. Paternalistic and authoritarian, Watson demanded absolute loyalty and ceaseless devotion from everyone. In exchange, he allowed CTR to become an extended family to all who obeyed.[71]

In 1922, Patterson died. Many have said his death was an emotional turning point for Watson, who felt his every move was no longer being compared to the cruel and ruthless cash register magnate. Some two years later, CTR Chairman Fairchild also died. By this time, Hollerith had resigned in ennui from the CTR board of directors and completely faded away in poor health. Watson became the company's chief executive and uncontested reigning authority.[72]

Now CTR would be completely transformed in Watson's image. A new name was needed. In Watson's mind, "CTR" said nothing about the company. The minor products, such as cheese slicers and key-activated time clocks, had long been abandoned or marginalized. The company was producing vital business machines for a world market. Someone had suggested a name for a new company newsletter: International Business Machines.[73]

International Business Machines—Watson realized that the name de-scribed more than a newsletter. It was the personification of what Watson and his enterprise were all about. He renamed the company. His intensely deter-mined credo was best verbalized by his promise to all: "IBM is more than a business—it is a great worldwide institution that is going on forever."[74]

More than ever, Watson fused himself into every facet of IBM's opera-tions, injecting his style into every decision, and mesmerizing into the psyche of every employee. "IBM Spirit"—this was the term Watson ascribed to the all-encompassing, almost tribal devotion to company that he demanded. "We always refer to our people as the IBM Family," Watson emphasized to his employees, "and we mean the wives and children as well as the men." He continually spoke in terms of "oneness" with IBM.[75]

Employees were well treated, generously compensated, entitled to ex-cellent working conditions with the most liberal benefits and vacation times, enrolled in the IBM Country Club at Endicott, New York, and invited to end-less picnics, rallies, and dances. Plus they were inducted into the IBM Club. "The company just won't let you get lonesome," assured one Club member. Children began their indoctrination early, becoming eligible at age three for the kiddy rolls of the IBM Club, graduating to junior ranks at age eight.[76]

"Look upon me as the head of the family," Watson would preach. "I want you to come to me as often as you feel that I can do anything for you. Feel free to come and open your hearts and make your requests, just the same as one would in going to the head of a family." So penetrating was the Watson father image that employees routinely did ask his permission for ordinary personal decisions. John G. Phillips, for example, a man so powerful within the IBM organization that he ultimately became its vice-chairman, did not own an automobile until 1926; in that year, he finally approached the Leader. "Mr. Watson," declared Phillips, "I have enough money to buy a car, but I would like your permission to do it."[77]

Watson's own son, Tom, who inherited his father's throne at IBM, admitted, "The more I worked at IBM, the more I resented Dad for the cult-like atmosphere that surrounded him."[78]

Large pictures of Watson in the weekly company publication, *Business Machines,* regularly sported headlines proclaiming even his ordinary accom-plishments, such as "Thomas J. Watson Opens New Orleans Office." The ever-present equating of his name with the word THINK was more than an Orwellian exercise, it was a true-life indoctrination. The Watson mystique was never confined to the four walls of IBM. His aura was only magnified by his autocratic style, barking out orders, demanding everywhere the pinnacle of service and action at a moment's notice, employing a secretary to ostentatiously follow him around scribbling notes and instructions on a steno pad.[79]

Newspapers constantly reported his movements and exploits. It was written during this era that, "probably no businessman in the country gets his name and picture in the newspapers more often than he does. Watson makes hundreds of public appearances every year at banquets, university commencements, the opening of art exhibits and similar occasions." *Fortune* referred to Watson as "the Leader," with a capital "L." So completely conscious was Watson of his mythic quality that he eyed even the porters on trains and waiters in restaurants as potential legend busters. He tossed them big tips, often as much as $10, which was largesse for the day. As he once explained, "there is a whole class of people in the world who are in a position to poor-mouth you unless you are sensitive to them. They are headwaiters, Pullman car conductors, porters and chauffeurs. They see you in an intimate fashion and can really knock off your reputation."[80]

By giving liberally to charities and universities, by towering as a patron of the arts, by arranging scores of organizational memberships, honorary degrees and awards, he further cultivated the man-myth for himself and IBM.[81]

Slogans were endlessly drilled into the extended IBM Family. *We Forgive Thoughtful Mistakes. There Is No Such Thing As Standing Still. Pack Up Your Troubles, Mr. Watson Is Here.*[82]

And the songs. They began the very first day a man entered the IBM culture. They never ended during one's entire tenure. More than 100 songs were sung at various company functions. There were several for Watson, including the "IBM Anthem":

> *There's a thrill in store for all,*
> *For we're about to toast*
> *The corporation that we represent.*
> *We're here to cheer each pioneer*
> *And also proudly boast*
> *Of that "man of men," our sterling president.*
> *The name of T.J. Watson means a courage none can stem:*
> *And we feel honored to be here to toast the IBM.*[83]

Revival-style meetings enthralled the men of IBM. Swaying as they chanted harmonies of adulation for the Leader, their palms brought together in fervent applause in hero worship, fully accepting that their families and destinies were intertwined with the family and destiny of the corporation, legions of company men incessantly re-dedicated themselves to the "Ever

Onward" glory of IBM. All of it swirled around the irresistible magnetism, the intoxicating command, the charismatic cultic control of one man, Thomas J. Watson, *the Leader*.[84]

WATSON'S CONNECTIONS to Germany set the stage for a technologic and economic alliance with the Third Reich. It began soon after America's entry into the Great War, when CTR's pre-Dehomag property in Germany, albeit marginal, was seized by the German government for being owned by an enemy national. As it happened, Watson was delighted with how CTR's assets were protected during receivership. His feelings were best expressed in a 1937 recollection he penned to Nazi Economics Minister Hjalmar Schacht.[85]

"From the day I returned to Germany after the [Great] War," Watson wrote Schacht, "to find my Company's affairs in the best safekeeping by your Alien Property Custodian, well-administered and conscientiously managed, from the highly satisfactory experience gained in my association with German industry after the War while building up my Company in Germany, all through the time of Germany's post-War suffering, recovery and setbacks, I have felt a deep personal concern over Germany's fate and a growing attachment to the many Germans with whom I gained contact at home and abroad. This attitude has caused me to give public utterance to my impressions and convictions in favor of Germany at a time when public opinion in my country and elsewhere was predominantly unfavorable."[86]

He added, the world must extend "a sympathetic understanding to the German people and their aims under the leadership of Adolf Hitler."[87]

More than fundamental sympathy, Watson in 1933 possessed an extraordinary investment in Germany. It began in the early twenties during the height of Germany's tornadic post-War inflation. It was a time when valueless German currency was transported from place to place in wheelbarrows and worth more as kindling than as legal tender. In 1922, Willy Heidinger's Dehomag was a mere licensee of Hollerith equipment. But the monetary crisis in Germany made it impossible for Dehomag to pay royalties and other monies it owed to Watson's CTR, which now controlled all of Hollerith's patents. Dehomag's debt was $104,000, or the astronomical sum of 450 billion marks. There was no way Dehomag could pay it.[88]

Watson traveled to Germany and ruthlessly offered Heidinger two options: bankruptcy, or handing substantial ownership of Dehomag over to Watson. It began by Watson asking for only 51 percent of the stock. But as Dehomag's financial position weakened, Watson abruptly upped his demand to 90 percent. Heidinger felt "cornered" with no choice: he ceded the German company to Watson, and Dehomag became a CTR subsidiary. When CTR was renamed IBM in 1924, Dehomag of course continued as an IBM subsidiary. Heidinger was allowed to retain approximately 10 percent of the stock. Dehomag could then still claim some token German ownership for appearance's sake.[89]

Ironically, Heidinger's shares were a virtual ruse because he could only own them as long as he worked for Dehomag. Even then, he could not control the stock. Once Heidinger left the company, he would have to sell the shares back to IBM and only IBM. Moreover, Heidinger's shares were used as collateral against large deferred company loans and a bonus system. For all intents and purposes, IBM now controlled the German company.[90]

For a decade after IBM acquired Dehomag, Watson tightly managed the German subsidiary's operation, setting its sales quotas, and at the same time benefiting from technical improvements to Hollerith systems devised by German engineers. Eventually, IBM began extending its influence overseas, creating subsidiaries or agencies in dozens of countries, each with its own name. With Watson's persona bigger than IBM's name, several of the companies were namesakes. Watson Belge was the Belgian subsidiary. Watson Italiana was the Italian subsidiary. In Sweden, it was Svenska Watson. In many places, the business names Watson and IBM were synonymous and inseparable.[91]

But the German subsidiary's revenues outshone them all. Many European countries were slow to adopt Hollerith technology. Germany, however, was more willing to accept the punch card systems. Indeed, of some seventy subsidiaries and foreign branches worldwide, more than half of IBM's overseas income came from Dehomag alone. By 1933, Dehomag had turned in a spectacular financial performance, 237 percent of its quota, and Willy Heidinger was due to be one of the stars at the forthcoming Hundred Percent Club convention in New York.[92]

WHEN HITLER came to power, in January 1933, he made an open promise to create a Master Race, dominate Europe, and decimate European Jewry. Numberless racial laws—local and national—appeared throughout the country. Jews could no longer advertise in the phone book or rent stalls in the markets. Thousands were terminated en masse from their employment. Even Jewish-owned companies were forced to fire their Jewish employees.[93]

Hitler's paper pogrom was the dull edge of the knife. The sharp edge was violence. Unrestrained acts of depraved Nazi brutality against Jews and other undesirables began at once, often in full view of newspapermen and photographers. Windows were broken. Jews dragged from their homes and shops were paraded through the streets with humiliating signs hung around their necks. Some were forced to wash the streets with toothbrushes. Not a few were kidnapped and tortured by Nazi gangs. Police looked the other way. On March 20, 1933, a concentration camp for political enemies was established at the pastoral town of Dachau, ten kilometers north of Munich. Many others soon followed. Scores of Jewish merchants in Essen and Muenster were delivered wholesale to the infamous camps. In Frankfurt, thousands of frenzied Storm Troopers paraded through the streets chanting, "Kill the Jews." A London newspaper actually published a Berlin street map locating a dozen Nazi torture houses.[94]

By April, some 60,000 Jews had been imprisoned and 10,000 more had fled the country, appearing as refugees throughout Europe and America. Professional associations were expelling their Jewish members. Signs were hoisted in front of hotels, restaurants, beaches, and sometimes even at the edge of town: "Jews Not Wanted Here." Jews were being swiftly driven into economic and social exclusion as a first step.[95]

Newspapers and radio broadcasts throughout the western countries declared Hitler a menace to world peace and indeed world civilization. The world reacted with boycott and protest movements springing up everywhere. Led by the Jews of New York and London, but supported by men and women of conscience from all faiths and all nations, boycotters and protesters noisily made sure that no one was unaware of the atrocities in Germany.[96]

On March 27, some 20,000 protesters gathered at a monster Madison Square Garden demonstration in New York that was broadcast around the world. Within days, similar rallies and sympathetic movements appeared in Paris, Istanbul, Toronto, Bombay, Warsaw, and London. In Salonika, 70,000 Greek Jews assembled to launch their anti-Hitler movement.[97]

Whether in Bucharest, Antwerp, Chicago, or Belgrade, a growing world movement would not stand by passively as Jews were being targeted. Anti-German boycott and protest actions erupted across the globe. The anti-Nazi boycott systematically identified merchants who imported German goods and forced them to stop by public pressure tactics. Whether it was small shops selling German china and camera film, or tourists sailing across the Atlantic on German vessels, outraged boycotters demanded they switch—or face a retaliatory boycott.[98]

Nor was energetic support for the whole idea of anti-German boycott the province of mere agitators. A Depression-wracked world was eager to replace the Third Reich's economic niche. Commercial interests and labor unions everywhere saw the anti-Nazi movement as one they could eagerly join for both moral and business reasons.[99]

On May 10, 1933, more than 100,000 marchers, businessmen and unionists alike, Jews and Christians, jammed midtown Manhattan. Newsreel cameras mounted on platforms filmed evocative scenes of anti-German placards in the air amid a backdrop of furling American flags and crowds loudly demanded that "in the name of humanity" all businesses stop doing business with Adolf Hitler.[100]

The question confronting all businessmen in 1933 was whether trading with Germany was worth either the economic risk or moral descent. This question faced Watson at IBM as well. But IBM was in a unique commercial position. While Watson and IBM were famous on the American business scene, the company's overseas operations were fundamentally below the public radar screen. IBM did not import German merchandise, it merely exported American technology. The IBM name did not even appear on any of thousands of index cards in the address files of leading New York boycott organizations. Moreover, the power of punch cards as an automation tool had not yet been commonly identified. So the risk that highly visible trading might provoke economic retaliation seemed low, especially since Dehomag did not even possess a name suggestive of IBM or Watson.[101]

On the other hand, the anticipated reward in Germany was great. Watson had learned early on that a government in reorganization, and indeed a government tightly monitoring its society, was good news for IBM. During the Depression years, when the Franklin D. Roosevelt Administration created a massive bureaucracy to assist the public and control business, IBM doubled its size. The National Recovery Act of 1933, for example, meant "businesses all of a sudden had to supply the federal government with information in huge and unprecedented amounts," recalled an IBM official. Extra forms, export reports, more registrations, more statistics—IBM thrived on red tape.[102]

Nazi Germany offered Watson the opportunity to cater to government control, supervision, surveillance, and regimentation on a plane never before known in human history. The fact that Hitler planned to extend his Reich to other nations only magnified the prospective profits. In business terms, that was account growth. The technology was almost exclusively IBM's to purvey because the firm controlled about 90 percent of the world market in punch cards and sorters.[103]

As for the moral dilemma, it simply did not exist for IBM. Supplying the Nazis with the technology they needed was not even debated. The company whose first overseas census was undertaken for Czar Nicholas II, the company Hollerith invented in his German image, the company war-profiteering Flint took global, the company built on Thomas J. Watson's corrugated scruples, this company saw Adolf Hitler as a valuable trading ally.

Indeed, the Third Reich would open startling statistical venues for Hollerith machines never before instituted—perhaps never before even imagined. In Hitler's Germany, the statistical and census community, overrun with doctrinaire Nazis, publicly boasted about the new demographic breakthroughs their equipment would achieve. Everything about the statistical tasks IBM would be undertaking for Germany was bound up in racial politics, Aryan domination, and Jewish identification and persecution.

WHEN HITLER rose to power, German intellect descended into madness. The Nazi movement was not merely a throng of hooligans pelting windows and screaming slogans. Guiding the Brown Shirts and exhorting the masses was an elite coterie of pseudo-scientists, corrupted professionals, and profit-blinded industrialists. Nazi jurists, medical doctors, and a clique of scientists—each with their prestigious academic credentials—found ways to pervert their science and higher calling to advance the cause of Aryan domination and racial persecution.

At the vanguard of Hitler's intellectual shock troops were the statisticians. Naturally, statistical offices and census departments were Dehomag's number one clients. In their journals, Nazi statistical experts boasted of what they expected their evolving science to deliver. All of their high expectations depended on the continuing innovation of IBM punch cards and tabulator technology. Only Dehomag could design and execute systems to identify, sort, and quantify the population to separate Jews from Aryans.

Friedrich Zahn, president of the Bavarian Statistical Office, phrased it best in recalling the role of Nazi statisticians. "The government of our *Führer* and Reichschancellor Adolf Hitler is statistics-friendly," wrote Zahn in *Allgemeines Statistisches Archiv (ASA)*, the official journal of the German Statistical Society. Zahn emphasized that Hitler's "government not only demands physical fitness and people strong in character and discipline, but useful knowledge as well. It demands not only political and economic soldiers, but also scientific soldiers."[104]

Zahn was a giant of statistics. Chairman of the German Statistical Society and president from 1931 to 1936 of the International Statistical Institute,

Zahn was by virtue of his prestigious international standing also an honorary member of the American Statistical Association. He was also a contributing member to the SS since the first days of the Hitler regime. Zahn was among those chiefly responsible for the immediate ouster of Jews from the German Statistical Society.[105]

The *ASA,* and technical journals like it, were closely followed at Dehomag since the publication was a virtual roadmap to the desires of Nazi statistical hierarchy. Anyone active in the statistics world read it. No IBM office, even in the United States, could afford to overlook a subscription. Within the pages of the *ASA* and similar statistical technical journals, Dehomag management and engineers could review proven statistical methodology that sought to step-by-step identify the Jews as undesirables. In many cases, *ASA* articles were written in conjunction with Dehomag experts, describing the tedious technical workings of specific IBM equipment, but more importantly how they were applied or could be applied to Reich policy and programs.[106]

From the very onset, the scientific soldiers of Hitler's statistical shock troops openly published their mission statement. "Above all," wrote Prof. Dr. Johannes Müller, in a 1934 edition of *ASA,* "remember that several very important problems are being tackled currently, problems of an ideological nature. One of those problems is race politics, and this problem must be viewed in a statistical light." Müller, president of the Thuringen Statistical Office, made his comments in a revealing 1934 *ASA* article entitled "The Position of Statistics in the New Reich."[107]

About the same time, Dr. Karl Keller, writing in an article, "The Question of Race Statistics," made clear that Jewish blood was to be traced as far back as possible. "If we differentiate in statistics between *Aryans* and *Non-Aryans,* we in essence talk about Jews and non-Jews. In any case, we will not look at religious affiliation alone but also ancestry." Like other Nazis, Keller was looking ahead to the domination of all Europe. Keller added, "beyond agreeing on the definition of race, we must move toward agreement on the number of races, at least as far as Europe is concerned . . . in reality, the Jews are not a race, but a mix of several races."[108]

Drawing on the emerging pseudo-academic notions of the exploding race science field in Germany, Keller urged doctors to examine the population for racial characteristics and faithfully record the information. "However, not every physician can carry out these examinations," Keller cautioned. "The physician must also undergo special anthropological training.[109]

"The only way to eliminate any mistakes," Keller insisted, "is the registration of the *entire* population. How is this to be done?" Keller demanded "the establishment of mandatory personal genetic-biographical forms. . . . Nothing would hinder us," he assured, "from using these forms to enter any important information which can be used by race scientists."[110]

Zahn, in his writings, was explicit in the need to annihilate inferior ethnic groups. In his 1937 *ASA* article entitled "Development of German Population Statistics through Genetic-Biological Stock-Taking," Zahn specified, "population politics, based on the principles of racial hygiene, must promote valuable genetic stock. It must prevent the fertility of inferior life and genetic degeneration. In other words, this means the targeted selection and promotion of superior life and an eradication of those portions of the population which are undesirable."[111]

In other articles, and in keynote speeches for statistical conventions, Zahn stressed, "There is almost no area of life in Germany which has not been creatively pollinated by the National Socialist ideology. . . . This is also true for the field of statistics. Statistics has become invaluable for the Reich, and the Reich has given statistics new tasks in peace and in war."[112]

Zahn declared, "Small wonder. In its very essence, statistics is very close to the National Socialist movement." He added, "German statistics has not only become the registering witness . . . but also the creative co-conspirator of the great events of time."[113]

Indeed, as co-conspirators, Nazi statisticians worked hand-in-hand with the battalions of Hitler's policy enablers and enforcers, from the Reich Race and Settlement Office and all its many allied agencies to the SS itself. Identifying the Jews was only the first step along the road to Jewish destruction in Germany.[114]

None of the publicly voiced statements of Hitler's scientific soldiers ever dissuaded Dehomag or IBM NY from withdrawing from their collaboration with the Reich. By necessity, that collaboration was intense, indispensable, and continuous. Indeed, the IBM method was to first anticipate the needs of government agencies and only then design proprietary data solutions, train official staff, and even implement the programs as a sub-contractor when called upon.

IBM machines were useless in crates. Tabulators and punch cards were not delivered ready to use like typewriters, adding machines, or even machine guns. Each Hollerith system had to be custom-designed by Dehomag engineers. Systems to inventory spare aircraft parts for the *Luftwaffe*, track railroad schedules for *Reichsbahn,* and register the Jews within the population for the Reich Statistical Office were each designed by Dehomag engineers to be completely different from each other.[115]

Of course the holes could not be punched just anywhere. Each card had to be custom-designed with data fields and columns precisely designated for the card readers. Reich employees had to be trained to use the cards. Dehomag needed to understand the most intimate details of the intended use, design the cards, and then create the codes.[116]

Because of the almost limitless need for tabulators in Hitler's race and geopolitical wars, IBM NY reacted enthusiastically to the prospects of Nazism. While other fearful or reviled American businessmen were curtailing or canceling their dealings in Germany, Watson embarked upon an historic expansion of Dehomag. Just weeks after Hitler came to power, IBM NY invested more than 7 million Reichsmarks—in excess of a million dollars—to dramatically expand the German subsidiary's ability to manufacture machines.[117]

To be sure, Dehomag managers were as fervently devoted to the Nazi movement as any of Hitler's scientific soldiers. IBM NY understood this from the outset. Heidinger, a rabid Nazi, saw Dehomag's unique ability to imbue the Reich with population information as a virtual calling from God. His enraptured passion for Dehomag's sudden new role was typically expressed while opening a new IBM facility in Berlin. "I feel it almost a sacred action," declared Heidinger emotionally, "I pray the blessing of heaven may rest upon this place."[118]

That day, while standing next to the personal representative of Watson and IBM, with numerous Nazi Party officials in attendance, Heidinger publicly announced how in tune he and Dehomag were with the Nazi race scientists who saw population statistics as the key to eradicating the unhealthy, inferior segments of society.

"The physician examines the human body and determines whether . . . all organs are working to the benefit of the entire organism," asserted Heidinger to a crowd of Nazi officials. "We [Dehomag] are very much like the physician, in that we dissect, cell by cell, the German cultural body. We report every individual characteristic . . . on a little card. These are not dead cards, quite to the contrary, they prove later on that they come to life when the cards are sorted at a rate of 25,000 per hour according to certain characteristics. These characteristics are grouped like the organs of our cultural body, and they will be calculated and determined with the help of our tabulating machine.[119]

"We are proud that we may assist in such task, a task that provides our nation's Physician [Adolf Hitler] with the material he needs for his examinations. Our Physician can then determine whether the calculated values are in harmony with the health of our people. It also means that if such is not the case, our Physician can take corrective procedures to correct the sick circumstances. . . . Our characteristics are deeply rooted in our race. Therefore, we must cherish them like a holy shrine which we will—and must—keep pure. We have the deepest trust in our Physician and will follow his instructions in blind faith, because we know that he will lead our people to a great future. Hail to our German people and *der Führer*!"[120]

Heidinger's speech, along with a list of the invited Nazi Party officials, was rushed to Manhattan and immediately translated for Watson. The IBM Leader cabled Heidinger a prompt note of congratulations for a job well done and sentiments well expressed.[121]

It was right about this time that Watson decided to engrave the five steps leading up to the door of the IBM School in Endicott, New York, with five of his favorite words. This school was the place where Watson would train his valued disciples in the art of sales, engineering, and technical support. Those five uppermost steps, steps that each man ascended before entering the front door, were engraved with the following words:

READ

LISTEN

DISCUSS

OBSERVE

The fifth and uppermost step was chiseled with the heralded theme of the company. It said THINK.[122]

The word THINK was everywhere.

III

THEY WERE SINGING TO THEIR LEADER.
Arms locked, swaying in song, male voices rising in adulation and expectation, they crooned their praises with worshipful enthusiasm. Clicking beer steins in self-congratulation, reassured by their vision of things to come, Storm Troopers everywhere sang the *"Horst Wessel Song"* as a Nazi testament and a prophecy both.

> *This is the final*
> *Bugle call to arms.*
> *Already we are set*
> *Prepared to fight.*
> *Soon Hitler's flags will wave*
> *Over every single street*
> *Enslavement ends*
> *When soon we set things right!*

Whether in beer halls, sports fields, or just swaggering down the streets, Brown Shirts throughout the Third Reich joyously chanted their most popular anthem. With good reason. For the *Sturm Abteilung (SA)*, or Storm Troopers, the ascent of Adolf Hitler was deliverance from the destitution and disconsolation of lives long disenfranchised by personal circumstance or character. But they needed a scapegoat. They blamed the Jews—for everything.

Jews had conspired to create the Depression, to enslave the German race, to control society, and to pollute Aryan blood. And now the followers of Hitler would exact their bizarre brand of justice and revenge.

More precisely, the Nazis planned to uproot the alien Jews from their prized positions within German commerce and culture. The angry young men of the SA, many of them dregs within German society, believed they would soon step into all the economic and professional positions held by their Jewish neighbors. Through unending racial statutes ousting Jews from professional and commercial life, relentless purges and persecution, unyielding programs of asset confiscation, systematic imprisonment and outright expulsion, the SA would usurp the Jewish niche. Nazis would assume Jewish jobs, expropriate Jewish companies, seize Jewish property, and in all other ways banish Jews from every visible facet of society. Once the Nazis finished with the Jews of Germany, they would extend their race war first to the Greater Reich in Europe they envisioned, and ultimately to the entire Continent.[1]

But Jewish life could only be extinguished if the Nazis could identify the Jews. Just which of Germany's 60 million citizens were Jewish? And just what was the definition of "Jewish"? Germans Jews were among the most assimilated of any in Europe.

Nazi mythology accused Jews of being an alien factor in German society. But in truth, Jews had lived in Germany since the fourth century. As elsewhere in Europe during the Middle Ages, what German Jews could do and say, even their physical dress, was oppressively regulated. Waves of persecution were frequent. Worse, anti-Jewish mobs often organized hangings and immolation at the stake. Even when left alone, German Jews could exist only in segregated ghettos subject to a long list of prohibitions.[2]

The pressure to escape Germany's medieval persecution created a very special kind of European Jew, one who subordinated his Jewish identity to the larger Christian society around him. *Assimilation* became a desirable antidote, especially among Jewish intellectuals during the Age of Enlightenment. When Napoleon conquered part of Germany in the early nineteenth century, he granted Jews emancipation. But after Napoleon was defeated, the harsh German status quo ante was restored. The taste of freedom, however, led affluent and intellectual Jewish classes to assimilate en masse. Philosophically, assimilationists no longer considered themselves Jews living in Germany. Instead, they saw themselves as Germans who, by accident of birth, were of Jewish ancestry.[3]

Many succumbed to the German pressure to convert to Christianity. German Jewry lost to apostasy many of its best commercial, political, and intellectual leaders. A far greater number were convinced that Jewish ethnic identity should be denied, but nonetheless saw quintessential value in the tenets of Moses. These German Jews developed a religious movement that was the forerunner of Reform Judaism. Yet, even many of this group ultimately converted to Christianity.[4]

Between 1869 and 1871, Germany granted Jews emancipation from many, but not all, civic, commercial, and political restrictions. Germany's Jews seized the chance to become equals. They changed their surnames, adopted greater religious laxity through Reform Judaism, and frequently married non-Jews, raising their children as Christians. Outright conversion became common. Many of Jewish ancestry did not even know it—or care.[5]

In fact, of approximately 550,000 Jews in Germany who were emancipated in 1871, roughly 60,000 were by 1930 either apostates, children raised without Jewish identity by a mixed marriage, or Jews who had simply drifted away. Even those consciously remaining within organized Jewish "communities" neglected their remnant Jewish identity. The Jews of twentieth-century Germany, like their Christian neighbors, embraced national identity far more than religious identity. In the minds of German Jews, they were "101 percent" German, first and foremost.[6]

But the Reich believed otherwise. The Jewish nemesis was not one of religious practice, but of bloodline. Nazis were determined to somehow identify those of Jewish descent, and destroy them.

IDENTIFYING THE Jews in Germany would be an uphill technologic challenge that would take years of increasingly honed counting programs and registration campaigns. From the moment Hitler was appointed Chancellor, fear gripped the entire Jewish community. No Jew wanted to step forward and identify himself as Jewish, and therefore become targeted for persecution. Many doubted they even possessed enough Jewish parentage to be included in the despised group. Indeed, not a few frightened Jews tried to join the denunciations of the Jewish community to emphasize their loyal German national character.[7] But that did not help them.

The identification process began in the first weeks of the Third Reich on April 12, 1933, when the Hitler regime announced a census of all Germans. Friedrich Burgdörfer, director of the Reich Statistical Office, expressed the agency's official gratitude that the "government of our national uprising had ordered the census." Burgdörfer, a virulent Nazi, also headed up the Nazi Party's Race Political Office and became a leading figure in the German

Society for Racial Hygiene. He was jubilant because he understood that Germany could not be cleansed of Jews until it identified them—however long that would take.[8]

The Nazis wanted fast answers about their society and who among them was Jewish. Censuses in Germany had long asked typical and innocent questions of religious affiliation. But since the Great War, European population shifts and dislocations had brought many more Jews to Germany, especially from Poland. No one knew how many, where they lived, or what jobs they held. Most of all, no one knew their names. The Nazis knew prior censuses were plagued by three to five years of hand sorting, rendering the results virtually useless for enacting swift social policies. If only the Nazis could at least obtain information on the 41 million Germans living in Prussia, Germany's largest state, comprising three-fifths of the German populace. How fast? Nazi planners wanted all 41 million Prussians processed and preliminary results produced within a record four months. The Prussian government itself was completely incapable of launching such a massive undertaking.[9]

But IBM's Dehomag was. The company offered a solution: it would handle almost the entire project as a contract. Dehomag would design a census package counting and classifying every citizen. Moreover, it would recruit, train, and even feed the hundreds of temporary workers needed to process the census and perform the work on Dehomag's own premises. If the government would gather the information, Dehomag would handle everything else. To secure the deal, Dehomag turned to its special consultant for governmental contracts, attorney Karl Koch.[10]

Koch enjoyed good Nazi Party as well as government connections. With Watson's help, Koch had recently traveled to IBM offices in New York to learn more about the company's technical capabilities and pick up tips on negotiating tough government contracts. By late May 1933, Koch was able to joyously report to Watson that he had secured a RM 1.35 million contract to conduct the Prussian census. This was a test case for Dehomag's relationship with the Nazi Reich. "We now have a chance to demonstrate what we are capable to do," Koch wrote to Watson.[11]

Koch was careful to credit his recent training in the United States. "Equipped with increased knowledge," Koch wrote Watson, "and strengthened by the experience collected during my highly inspiring trip to the States, I was able to conduct the lengthy negotiations and to accomplish the difficult work."[12]

Watson wrote back a letter of appreciation to Koch and hoped he would "have the pleasure of visiting your country next year."[13]

Organizing the census was a prodigious task. Dehomag hired some 900 temporary staffers, mainly supplied by the Berlin employment office, which had become dominated by the venomous German Labor Front. Dehomag enjoyed good relations with the German Labor Front, which ranked at the vanguard of radical Nazism. Coordinating with the Berlin employment office christened the enterprise as a patriotic duty, since relieving joblessness was a major buzzword objective of Hitler's promise to Germany. Dehomag's two-week immersion data processing courses instructed seventy to seventy-five people at a time in daily four-hour sessions.[14]

Statistical battalions were emerging. The Berlin employment office allocated large, well-lit halls for their training. Looking from the rear of the training hall, one saw a sea of backs, each a matronly dressed woman sporting a no-nonsense bun hairdo, tilted over census forms and punching machines. Packed along rows of wooden study benches, even behind view-blocking pillars, trainees diligently took notes on small pads and scrutinized their oversized census forms. Methodically, they learned to extract and record the vital personal details. Large "Smoking Prohibited" signs pasted above the front wall reinforced the regimented nature of the setting. At the front, next to a blackboard, an instructor wearing a white lab coat explained the complicated tasks of accurately punching in data from handwritten census questionnaires, operating the sorting, tabulating, and verifying machines, and other data processing chores.[15]

On June 16, 1933, one-half million census takers, recruited from the ranks of the "nationalistically minded," went door-to-door gathering information. Cadres of Storm Troopers and SS officers were added to create a virtual census army. In some localities, when recruitment flagged, individuals were coerced into service. The interviews included pointed questions about the head of the household's religion and whether the person was in a mixed marriage.[16]

In essence, the amount of data that could be stored on a card was a function of the number of holes and columns. A spectrum of data could be extracted by simply recording different combinations of hole punches. For that reason, Dehomag abandoned its standard 45-column cards and moved to a 60-column format. Sixty columns, each with ten horizontal positions, created 600 punch hole possibilities per card. Each column, depending upon how it was punched, represented a biographical characteristic. These 600 punch holes, arrayed in their endless combinations, yielded thousands of demographic permutations. Even still, Dehomag officials wondered whether all the data the Reich needed could be accommodated on the 60-column cards they were using. Dehomag declared in a company newsletter that it was willing to move to an 80-column format for the census, if required "for political reasons."[17] Soon the Reich could begin the identification process—who was Aryan and who was a Jew.

Population statistics had crossed the fiery border from a science of anonymous masses to the investigation of individuals.

———————

IN MID-SEPTEMBER, 1933, 6,000 brown cardboard boxes began unceremoniously arriving at the cavernous Alexanderplatz census complex in Berlin. Each box was stuffed with questionnaires manually filled out by pen and pencil, but soon to be processed by an unprecedented automated praxis. As supervisors emptied their precious cargo at the Prussian Statistical Office, each questionnaire—one per household—was initialed by an intake clerk, stacked, and then transferred downstairs. "Downstairs" led to Dehomag's massive 22,000-square-foot hall, just one floor below, specifically rented for the project.[18]

Messengers shuttling stacks of questionnaires from the Statistical Office to Dehomag bounded down the right-hand side of an enclosed stairwell. As they descended the short flight, the sound of clicking became louder and louder. At the landing, they turned left and pushed through the doors. As the doors swung open, they encountered an immense high-ceilinged, hangar-like facility reverberating with the metallic music of Hollerith technology. Some 450 data punchers deployed in narrow rows of punching stations labored behind tall upright secretarial displays perfectly matched to the oversized census questionnaires.[19]

Turning left again, and then another right brought the messengers to a long windowed wall lined with narrow tables. The forms were piled there. From these first tables, the forms were methodically distributed to centralized desks scattered throughout the work areas. The census forms were then loaded onto small trolleys and shuttled again, this time to individual work stations, each equipped with a device that resembled a disjointed typewriter —actually an input engine.[20]

A continuous "Speed Punching" operation ran two shifts, and three when needed. Each shift spanned 7.5 hours with 60 minutes allotted for "fresh air breaks" and a company-provided meal. Day and night, Dehomag staffers entered the details on 41 million Prussians at a rate of 150 cards per hour. Allowing for holidays and a statistical prediction of absenteeism, yet ever obsessed with its four-month deadline, Dehomag decreed a quota of

450,000 cards per day for its workforce. Free coffee was provided to keep people awake. A gymnast was brought in to demonstrate graceful aerobics and other techniques to relieve fatigue. Company officials bragged that the 41 million processed cards, if stacked, would tower two and a half times higher than the Zugspitze, Germany's 10,000-foot mountain peak. Dehomag intended to reach the summit on time.[21]

As company officials looked down upon a floor plan of the layout, the linear rows and intersecting columns of work stations must have surely resembled a grandiose punch card itself animated into a three-dimensional bricks and mortar reality. Indeed, a company poster produced for the project showed throngs of miniscule people scrambling over a punch card sketch.[22] The surreal artwork was more than symbolic.

Once punched, the columns were imbued with personal information about the individual: county, community, gender, age, religion, mother tongue, number of children, current occupation, and second job, if any.[23]

"Be Aware!" reminded huge block-lettered signs facing each cluster of data entry clerks. Instructions were made clear and simple. Column 22 RELIGION was to be punched at hole 1 for Protestant, hole 2 for Catholic, or hole 3 for Jew. Columns 23 and 24 NATIONALITY were to be coded in row 10 for Polish speakers.[24]

After punching, the cards were shuttled to a separate section of the hall, where they passed through long, squat Hollerith counters at the rate of 24,000 per hour. The system kept track of its own progress. Hence, Dehomag was always aware whether it was on schedule. Once counted, the cards moved to the proofing section. No errors would be tolerated and speed was essential. Proofing machines tabulated and verified proper punching for more than 15,000 cards per hour.[25]

When Jews were discovered within the population, a special "Jewish counting card" recorded the place of birth. These Jewish counting cards were processed separately.[26]

Then came the awesome sorting and resorting process for twenty-five categories of information cross-indexed and filtered through as many as thirty-five separate operations—by profession, by residence, by national origin, and a myriad of other traits. It was all to be correlated with information from land registers, community lists, and church authorities to create a fantastic new database. What emerged was a profession-by-profession, city-by-city, and indeed a block-by-block revelation of the Jewish presence.[27]

A Reich Statistical Office summary reported: "The largest concentration of Jews [in Berlin] will be found in the Wilmersdorf district. Approximately

26,000 Observant Jews account for 13.54 percent of the population within that district." Further: a total of 1,200 "Fur-Jews" accounted for 5.28 percent of the furrier trade, and nearly three-fourths of those are foreign-born. Further: based on existing emigration trends triggered by anti-Jewish persecution "only 415,000 to 425,000 Faith-Jews would remain in the German Reich by the middle of 1936."[28]

Dehomag's precious information would now help propel a burgeoning new binary of pseudo-science and official race hatred. Racial hygiene, race politics, and a constellation of related anti-Semitic disciplines were just so much talk in the absence of genuine statistics. Now a lightning storm of anti-Jewish legislation and decrees restricting Jews from all phases of academic, professional, governmental, and commercial life would be empowered by the ability to target the Jews by individual name. Moreover, by cross-sorting the Jews revealed in Column 22 row 3 with Polish speakers identified in Columns 26 and 27 row 10, the Reich was able to identify who among the Jews would be its first targets for confiscation, arrest, imprisonment, and ultimately expulsion. The so-called *OstJuden*, or Eastern Jews, primarily from Poland, would be the first to go.[29]

Friedrich Zahn, publisher of *Allgemeines Statistisches Archiv*, summed up the glee when he wrote, "In using statistics, the government now has the road map to switch from knowledge to deeds."[30]

DEHOMAG'S CENSUS undertaking was an unparalleled accomplishment for IBM. Watson was impressed from the moment Karl Koch secured the contract. Clearly, there was a lucrative future for IBM in Nazi Germany. At a time when other foreign companies were fleeing the Reich's violence, repression, anti-Semitism, and the inability to retrieve income from German operations, Watson moved swiftly to dramatically enlarge IBM's presence.

First, he ordered the merger of several small IBM subsidiaries in Germany. Optima, Degemag, Holgemag, as well as the existing Dehomag, were folded into a new corporation also to be named "Dehomag." Through a cunning twirl of losses and profits among the four German companies, and then manipulating balances owed by those subsidiaries to IBM NY for so-called "loans," Reich profit taxes would be avoided, despite record earnings in Germany. IBM NY would simply apply the incomes to the contrived loans it had extended to its own subsidiaries. IBM's Maryland division was used as a conduit for the loan transactions. A report from IBM's accountants to the corporate treasurer was explicit: "the motive for the merger was to effect an annual savings in taxes by reducing Dehomag's net profits by the amount of the net losses of Optima and [old] Dehomag . . . about $30,000 annually."[31]

Heidinger confirmed in a special report to Watson, "As the merger of Degemag, [old] Dehomag, and Optima is effected . . . corporation profits tax is out of the question . . . on account of the relief from [loan] claims of IBM, as thereby no profit, but merely a reduction of losses, is obtained."[32]

Second, IBM increased its investment in Dehomag from a mere RM 400,000 to more than RM 7 million—about a million Depression-era American dollars. This would include a million Reichsmarks to purchase new land in Berlin and build IBM's first German factory. IBM was tooling up for what it correctly saw as a massive economic relationship with the Hitler regime. In the midst of America's Depression, this expansion of manufacturing base would not relieve unemployment in the United States, but actually transfer American jobs to Nazi Germany where the Hollerith machines would be manufactured.[33]

Understandably, Watson decided to visit Germany to observe conditions first hand, which he did on October 13, 1933. Despite a highly publicized boycott against German ocean liners, he ignored picket lines and sailed on the German ship *Bremen*.[34]

Watson was impressed with what he saw in Berlin. The Watsons and the Heidingers managed many happy social moments together. Mrs. Watson even asked Heidinger for a copy of his portrait as a memento of their joyous time. Heidinger sent two.[35]

Watson also visited the massive census operation at Alexanderplatz. There among the rows of data clicking clerks arrayed before their large block- letter instructions to enter Jews in Column 22 row 3, amid the clatter of shiny, black sorters flickering punch cards into a blur, Watson was moved to donate money to buy meals for everyone at IBM expense. As an added gesture, he authorized Dresden pastries for each and every member of the Statistical Office's Census Department. Heidinger later wrote to Watson that the total bill for his "bountiful gift" of 6,060 meals disbursed to 900 staffers came in at just under 4,000 Reichsmarks.[36]

More than just hot meals and baked goods, Watson wanted to make sure Dehomag was successful and effective. He personally dispatched Eugene Hartley, a top IBM census expert and manager of the firm's statistical department, to advise Dehomag. Hartley would oversee costs in Berlin and become acquainted with all details of Dehomag's census operation and its methods. These details were to be recorded in a special handbook. No copies would exist. Senior management at Dehomag sent Watson an RCA Radiogram declaring, "We especially appreciate your foresight in sending Mister Hartley who as a census expert is especially helpful to us at a time when we are undertaking greatest service job ever done by any IBM agency."[37]

Most gratifying to the Germans was the secret pact between Watson and Heidinger, entered into that October 1933, while Watson was touring Dehomag. At a time when the Hitler government was declaring its war intentions in Europe, Watson's secret deal granted Heidinger and Dehomag special commercial powers outside of Germany. Although there were IBM agencies and subsidiaries throughout Europe, Dehomag would be permitted to circumvent and supplant each one, soliciting and delivering punch card solution technology directly to IBM customers in those territories. That gave Dehomag entrée to the major foreign corporations, foreign national railroads, and foreign government offices across the Continent. IBM subsidiaries, such as those in Brussels, Paris, and Warsaw would still exist. But now Nazified Dehomag could usurp their clients and even their manufacturing base.[38]

The extraordinary arrangement virtually reinvented Dehomag as a de facto "IBM Europe." Subject to IBM NY oversight, the German subsidiary was granted free rein to cultivate its special brand of statistical services to other nearby countries, especially Austria, Czechoslovakia, Poland, Belgium, France, and Holland. Where census, registration, and other statistical operations did not exist, or where they could be updated along the lines of Germany's anti-Semitic model, Dehomag could now move in. In essence, before the Third Reich advanced across any border, its scientific soldiers would already have a vital outpost.

With its new potency to create a German sphere of statistical influence across the continent, no wonder senior management in November 1933 sent Watson a jointly signed cable proclaiming, "Your visit to Germany has brought encouragement not only to Dehomag, but to the German people."[39]

CONSIDERING THE far-reaching importance of the Watson-Heidinger agreement for commercial hegemony, and the certainty of upsetting other IBM subsidiaries, Watson committed nothing to paper about his secret territorial agreement with Heidinger. Deniability seemed to be the order of the day.

Clearly, Watson possessed an understanding of the value of deniability. When he was prosecuted for criminal conspiracy in the National Cash Register case, he was confronted by exhibit after exhibit of his own incriminating writings, such as instructions to destroy competitors and create fake companies. That error would not happen again. Moreover, IBM was at that very moment being prosecuted by the U.S. Justice Department's anti-trust division for additional secretive acts of monopoly and unfair competition involving punch card technology.[40]

Watson developed an extraordinary ability to write reserved and cleverly cautious letters. More commonly, he remained silent and let subordinates and managers do the writing for him. But they too respected an IBM code—unwritten, of course—to observe as much discretion as possible in memos and correspondence. This was especially so in the case of corresponding with or about Nazi Germany, the most controversial business partner of the day.

For example, a few weeks after Watson left Germany, one of IBM's European managers in Paris, M. G. Connally, was assigned to monitor details of the merger of IBM's four subsidiaries. On November 18, 1933, Connally wrote a letter to Heidinger concluding with the sentiment: "I only wish we had someone here to do things the way you people do in Germany." Shortly thereafter, Connally circulated a copy of that letter to Watson and other executives at IBM NY. Connally sheepishly scribbled under the last sentence, "I think now I shouldn't have said this."[41]

Whether or not Watson wanted to keep the Dehomag expansion deal a secret, Heidinger was clearly irked by the absence of any proof that he could literally invade any other subsidiary's territory. Census offices and other IBM customers in other countries would be surprised if abruptly contacted by a Dehomag agent. And any IBM subsidiary manager would surely challenge a Dehomag attempt to steal its business.

After many months of waiting, Heidinger suddenly demanded some written proof.

On August 27, 1934, he pointedly cabled Watson, "We need urgently by cable and following letter confirmation for our right granted by you personally to deliver our German manufactured machines for entire European market. . . . This right does not include any obligation of your European companies to give any orders."[42]

Watson gave in. The next day, August 28, he dispatched a radiogram to Berlin: "Confirming agreement reached between us last conference in Berlin. We extend German company rights to manufacture machines under our patents for all European countries. Formal contract following by mail. Thomas Watson."[43]

But the contract that followed by mail was not acceptable to the Germans. Heidinger detested negotiating with Watson and bitterly remembered how he had lost his company during the post-War inflation. Now, during the new Hitler era, Watson wanted Dehomag to proliferate punch card technology throughout the continent, generating huge contracts. But sales would be funneled through the local IBM subsidiaries rather than through Dehomag's blocked bank accounts. Heidinger reluctantly agreed, but didn't trust Watson and insisted that he be vindicated not just with a new agreement, but written confirmation that this expansion pact was originally sealed almost a year before.[44]

So on September 11, Watson again cabled Heidinger: "Confirming agreement reached between us in Berlin October 1933. We extend by that agreement your company rights to manufacture and to sell our machines to all European Hollerith companies." Watson followed it up with a signed letter confirming that he had indeed sent the cable, and quoting the exact text. The cable and letter were sent to Nazi Germany. In America, however, the carbons were carefully placed in the file of IBM Financial Vice President and close Watson confidant, Otto E. Braitmayer. A hand-scrawled note confirmed exactly where the carbons were being kept: "Carbons of Letter of September 11, 1934 to Willy Heidinger in which Mr. Watson confirmed cable of Sept 11 regarding agreement that German Co has rights to mfg and sell IBM machines to all Europe in Braitmayer files."[45]

Deniability in the face of the undeniable required a special mindset. At every twist and turn of IBM's growing relationship with Adolf Hitler, Watson and the other executives of IBM NY were confronted with four undeniable realities.

First, barbaric anti-Semitic violence and general repression were everywhere in Germany and clearly part of a methodical program to destroy the Jews. Second, popular and diplomatic protest against the Hitler regime in America, and indeed throughout the world, was highly visible and threatening to any business that traded with Germany. Third, any corporation willing to ignore the moral distaste and public outcry accepted the stark realities of doing business in the Third Reich: unpredictable local and national Nazi personalities and regulations, confiscatory taxes, revenues trapped in blocked German bank accounts that could only be used within Germany, and the absolute certainty that the company and its employees would be integrated into the fabric of the Nazi game plan. Fourth, he who helped Germany helped Hitler prepare for war.

Anti-Semitic violence and general repression in Germany was an undeniable fact for all in America, but especially for anyone who could read the front page or the first few pages of the *New York Times,* listen to a radio broadcast, or watch a newsreel. In the formative months of February, March, and April 1933, Watson and his colleagues at IBM were exposed to not just several articles in the *New York Times,* but scores of them each week detailing ghastly anti-Semitic brutality. On many days, the New York papers were filled with literally dozens of repression and atrocity reports.

March 18, *New York Times*: In an article detailing Nazi plans to destroy Jewish professional life, the paper reported that a quarter of all Jewish attorneys would be forced to retire each year until they were all gone. It wasn't just the legal profession. Within weeks all German Jews expected to be ousted from their professional positions and occupations, the paper wrote.[46]

March 20, *New York Times*: The page one center headline decried, "German Fugitives Tell of Atrocities at Hands of Nazis." Making clear that "iron-clad censorship" in Germany was preventing most of the truth from emerging, the paper nonetheless enumerated a series of heinous acts. For example, at Alexanderplatz in Berlin, just down the street from the Prussian Statistical Office complex, Brown Shirts invaded a restaurant popular with Jewish businessmen. Waving a list of names of the restaurant's Jewish customers, the Brown Shirts "formed a double line to the restaurant door." They called each Jew out by name and made him run a gauntlet. As a Jew passed, each Storm Trooper "smashed him in the face and kicked him with heavy boots, until finally the last in the line, knocked him into the street." The last Jew to run the gauntlet was beaten so severely, "his face resembled a beefsteak," the newspaper reported.[47]

March 21, *New York Times*: Under a page one banner headline declaring, "Reichstag Meeting Today is Prepared to Give Hitler Full Control As Dictator," was a special two-column dispatch from Munich. "Chief of Police Himmler of Munich today informed newspaper men here that the first of several concentration camps will be established near this city."[48]

By April 20, about the time Watson decided IBM should solicit the census project, *New York Times* headlines reported more than 10,000 refugees had fled Germany in the face of daily home invasions, tortures, and kidnappings; 30,000 more were already imprisoned in camps or prisons; and another 100,000 were facing economic ruination and even starvation. On May 10, about the time IBM was at the height of its negotiations for the census, the world was further shocked when Nazis staged their first and most publicized mass book burning. By the end of May, when Dehomag's contract with the Reich was finalized, the *New York Times* and the rest of America's media had continuously published detailed accounts of Jews being brutally ousted from one profession after another: judges ceremoniously marched out of their courtrooms, lawyers pushed from their offices, doctors expelled from their clinics, professors drummed out of their classrooms, retailers evicted from their own stores, and scientists barred from their own labs.[49]

On June 11, the day before the door-to-door census taking began, the *New York Times* reported that the government was searching through the backgrounds of more than 350,000 government workers to identify which among them might be of "Jewish extraction who are liable to dismissal." In that same edition, the *New York Times* rendered a page-specific summary of Adolf Hitler's book, *Mein Kampf,* explaining how completely public his program of Jewish annihilation was. Hitler declared on page 344, reported the *New York Times,* "If at the beginning of the [Great] War, 12,000 or 15,000 of these corrupters of the people [Jews] had been held under poison gas . . . then the sacrifice of millions at the front would not have been in vain . . . 12,000 scoundrels removed at the right time might perhaps have saved the lives of one million proper Germans."[50]

By the time Watson was organizing his plans to set sail on the *Bremen,* on August 29, 1933, the *New York Times,* in a page one article, reported the existence of sixty-five brutal concentration camps holding some 45,000 Jewish and non-Jewish inmates; an equal number were incarcerated at a variety of other locations, creating a total of some 90,000 held.[51]

Banner headlines, riveting radio broadcasts, and graphic newsreels depicting the systematic destruction of Jewry's place in Germany must have seemed endless. Blaring media reports made it impossible for anyone at IBM to deny knowledge of the situation in the Third Reich. But what made a technologic alliance with the Reich even more difficult—moment-to-moment—was an America that everywhere was loudly protesting the Hitler campaign of Jewish destruction. To ally with Germany at that time meant going against the will of an enraged nation—indeed an enflamed world.

Although anti-German protest marches, picket lines, boycotts, and noisy demands to stop the atrocities were in full swing on every continent of the world, nowhere would protest have appeared more omnipresent than to a businessman in New York City. In New York, the air burned with anti-Nazi agitation. All sectors of society—from labor unions to business leaders, from Catholic bishops to Protestant deacons to defiant rabbis—rallied behind the battle cry that humanity must starve Depression-battered Germany into abandoning her anti-Semitic course. "Germany Will Crack This Winter," read the placards and the leaflets.[52]

Typical of the vehemence was the giant demonstration at Madison Square

Garden on March 27, 1933. Culminating days of loud marches throughout the New York–New Jersey area and highly publicized denunciations, the Madison Square Garden event was calculated to shut down New York—and it did.

At noon on March 27, business stopped. Stores and schools closed across Greater New York as employees were released for the day. The rally didn't start until after 8:00 P.M., but by that afternoon, large crowds were already lined up outside the Garden. Once the doors were unlocked, the flow of protesters began. It continued for hours. Traffic snarled as thousands jammed the streets trying to wedge closer. Demonstrators heading for the rally were backed all the way down the subway stairs. Six hundred policemen formed a bluecoat chain along the crosswalks just to allow pedestrians to pass.[53]

When the doors shut, only 20,000 boycotters made it inside. So public loudspeakers were hastily erected for an estimated 35,000 keyed-up citizens crammed around the streets of the Garden. Police and protest marshals diverted several thousand to a second ad hoc rally at nearby Columbus Circle. It wasn't enough. More overflow rallies were frantically set up along the nearby intersections.[54]

Synchronized programs were at that moment waiting in Chicago, Washington, Houston, and about seventy other American cities. At each supportive gathering, thousands huddled around loudspeakers waiting for the Garden event to commence. That day, at least one million Jews participated nationwide. Perhaps another million Americans of non-Jewish heritage stood with them shoulder-to-shoulder. Hundreds of thousands more in Europe were preparing sympathetic demonstrations, fasts, and boycotts.[55]

New York and Thomas Watson had never seen anything like it. From the windows of IBM at 270 Broadway, the massive demonstration was an unmistakable message: Don't do business with Hitler. Moreover, boycott leaders promised vigilant retaliation for any American firm that did.[56]

Protests, larger and smaller than the one on March 27, were repeated throughout the year and indeed throughout the life of the Third Reich.

The stakes must have been high for Watson to disregard the gargantuan protest of a nation, and the world's battle cry to isolate Germany commercially. But IBM maintained its steadfast commitment to an alliance with Nazi Germany. It was just days later that Watson launched the effort to garner the Prussian census contract.

Germans understood Watson to be a friend of the Reich. Just after the Madison Square Garden event, senior management at Dehomag sent their company Leader a jointly signed appeal on firm letterhead. German managers implored Watson to help suppress the "cruelty stories depicting pretended abominable crimes against German jews . . . [which] are untrue." The word "Jews" was not capitalized. Heidinger could not bring himself to capitalize the letter "J" when typing the word "German" next to the word *Jew*. "We are applying to our esteemed foreign personal and business friends," Dehomag wrote, "with the most urgent request, not only to reciprocate our cooperation but—as champions of truth—not only not to believe similar unfounded rumors, but to set yourselves against them."[57]

Watson did not disappoint his colleagues in Berlin. Just after the worldwide rallies in late March, Dehomag board meetings in Berlin confirmed, "President Watson and vice president Braitmayer were fully agreed that we should manufacture all suitable items in Germany according to our best lights and by our own decision." Hence, plans to establish a factory were to proceed, even though certain highly technical parts would still be imported from the United States. Watson's office routinely received translated copies of the meeting minutes a few days later.[58]

Watson's commitment to growing German operations seemed indefatigable. He ignored the tide of America's anti-Nazi movement and the risk of being discovered as a commercial associate of the Third Reich. But doing so meant ignoring the inescapable financial risk any businessman could see in Nazi Germany. Simply put, doing business in Germany was dangerous.

Foreign business was fundamentally considered an enemy of the German State. Incomes earned by foreign corporations could not be transferred overseas. They were sequestered in blocked German bank accounts. The money was usable, but only in Germany. Hence, a dollar of profit made by Dehomag could only be spent in Germany, binding any foreign enterprise to continued economic development within Germany. Companies were frequently required to invest their profits in Reich bonds. Many considered this monetary move little more than Hitler's effort to take American business hostage. Others understood that as corporations fled Germany, the Reich was forced to decree that their money would have to remain behind.

IBM's Paris office began regularly receiving statements from the Deutsche Bank und Disconto-Gesellschaft, listing Dehomag's distributions as blocked funds in the name of International Business Machines Corporation. For example, one account balance of RM 188,896 was suddenly boosted by RM 90,000—almost none of which could be sent back to America.[59]

Rapid-fire regulations designed to subdue the independence of foreign business were being promulgated almost daily. Often regional rules were simply decreed by a local party potentate. Companies were obligated to fire

Jews, hire from the ranks of the NSDAP—the Nazi Party—pay special contributions, and sometimes even defer plans for mechanization on the theory that certain types of machinery displaced jobs. Conflicting rules from conflicting authorities were commonplace.

Most of all, Germany loudly warned all foreign business that they were subject to a concept known as *Gleichschaltung,* loosely translated as "total coordination" with the State. Within days of Hitler's rise to power, the process of *Gleichschaltung* began as every political, organizational, and social structure within German society was integrated into the Nazi movement and therefore made subordinate to NSDAP goals and instructions. *Gleichschaltung* applied to business as well. Foreign business quickly realized it. And they were reminded often.[60]

April 7, 1933, *New York Times*: A page one article bannered "Nazis Seize Power to Rule Business; Our Firms Alarmed," led with the assertion, "Adolf Hitler, having made himself political dictator of Germany, today became dictator of German big business as well." The *New York Times* explained that, "every phase of German business had already been thoroughly organized. By taking control of the business organizations, the Nazis have obtained control of the interests they represent."[61]

April 28, 1933, *New York Times*: In an article headlined "Germany Cautions Foreign Business," the newspaper prominently reported a promulgation by Reich Economics Undersecretary Paul Bang, "The German government . . . must demand that foreign business establishments unreservedly participate in the realization of Germany's economic program."[62]

To complete the circle of apprehension, everywhere the talk was of renewed war. Any economic transfusion to the Hitler regime was seen by many as a mere prelude to another horrific military conflict. Officials in Washington, diplomats in London and Paris, and business leaders throughout the world feared that the advent of Hitler would throw humanity back into a global war. Signs of German rearmament were reported continuously. Open declarations by Germany that it would reoccupy tracts of land seized by the victorious Allies were blared throughout the media. A key source of alarm was Hitler's so-called employment program.

Germany was disarmed as part of the Versailles Treaty. Now labor forces were becoming façades for military recruitment. Organized "labor units" were subject to conscription, wore uniforms, and underwent paramilitary training. Typical was a *New York Times* report on May 21 headlined "Reich Issues Orders for New Labor Units." The subhead read, "Military Tone Is Evident in the Conscription Regulations—Storm Troops Favored."[63]

Why would one of America's leading businessmen and his premier corporation risk all by participating in a Nazi economy sworn to destroy Jewry, subjugate Europe, and dominate all enterprises within its midst? For one, IBM's economic entanglements with Nazi Germany remained beneath public perception. Few understood the far-reaching ramifications of punch card technology and even fewer had a foreground understanding that the company Dehomag was in fact essentially a wholly-owned subsidiary of International Business Machines.

Boycott and protest movements were ardently trying to crush Hitlerism by stopping Germany's exports. Although a network of Jewish and non-sectarian anti-Nazi leagues and bodies struggled to organize comprehensive lists of companies doing business with Germany, from importers of German toys and shoes to sellers of German porcelain and pharmaceuticals, yet IBM and Watson were not identified. Neither the company nor its president even appeared in any of thousands of hectic phone book entries or handwritten index card files of the leading national and regional boycott bodies. Anti-Nazi agitators just didn't understand the dynamics of corporate multi-nationalism.[64]

Moreover, IBM was not importing German merchandise, it was exporting machinery. In fact, even exports dwindled as soon as the new plant in Berlin was erected, leaving less of a paper trail. So a measure of invisibility was assured in 1933.

But to a certain extent all the worries about granting Hitler the technologic tools he needed were all subordinated to one irrepressible, ideological imperative. Hitler's plans for a new Fascist order with a "Greater Germany" dominating all Europe were not unacceptable to Watson. In fact, Watson admired the whole concept of Fascism. He hoped he could participate as the American capitalistic counterpart of the great Fascist wave sweeping the Continent. Most of all, Fascism was good for business.

THOMAS WATSON and IBM had separately and jointly spent decades making money any way they could. Rules were broken. Conspiracies were hatched. Bloody wars became mere market opportunities. To a supranational, making money is equal parts commercial Darwinism, corporate ecclesiastics, dynastic chauvinism, and solipsistic greed.

Watson was no Fascist. He was a pure capitalist. But the horseshoe of political economics finds little distance between extremities. Accretion of wealth by and for the state under a strong autocratic leader fortified by jingoism and hero worship was appealing to Watson. After all, his followers wore uniforms, sang songs, and were expected to display unquestioned loyalty to the company he led.

Fascism, the dictatorial state-controlled political system, was invented by Italian Dictator Benito Mussolini. The term symbolically derived from the Roman *fasces*, that is, the bundle of rods surrounding a ceremonial axe used during Roman times. Indeed, Nazi symbols and ritual were in large part adopted from Mussolini, including the palm-lifting Roman salute. Ironically, Italian Fascism was non-racial and not anti-Semitic. National Socialism added those defining elements.

Mussolini fascinated Watson. Once, at a 1937 sales convention, Watson spoke out in *Il Duce*'s defense. "I want to pay tribute . . . [to the] great leader, Benito Mussolini," declared Watson. "I have followed the details of his work very carefully since he assumed leadership [in 1922]. Evidence of his leadership can be seen on all sides. . . . Mussolini is a pioneer . . . Italy is going to benefit greatly."[65]

Watson explained his personal attraction to the dictator's style and even observed similarities with his own corporate, capitalistic model. "One thing which has greatly impressed me in connection with his leadership," conceded Watson, "is the loyalty displayed by the people. To have the loyalty and cooperation of everyone means progress—and ultimate success for a nation or an individual business . . . we should pay tribute to Mussolini for establishing this spirit of loyal support and cooperation."[66]

For years, an autographed picture of Mussolini graced the grand piano in Watson's living room.[67]

In defense of Fascism, Watson made clear, "Different countries require different forms of government and we should be careful not to let people in other countries feel that we are trying to standardize principles of government throughout the world."[68]

Years after *der Führer* seized power, Watson drafted a private letter to Reich Economics Minister Hjalmar Schacht, in which he argued "the necessity of extending a sympathetic understanding to the German people and their aims under the leadership of Adolf Hitler." Watson described Hitler's threatening posture toward other nations as a "dynamic policy." In referring to the "heroic sacrifices of the German people and the greatest achievements of their present leadership," Watson declared, "It is the sincere and earnest desire entertained by me and countless other friends of Germany . . . that these sacrifices and achievements should be successful and that the New Germany should reap the fruits of its present great effort to the fullest extent." Watson concluded the draft with "an expression of my highest esteem for himself [Hitler], his country and his people."[69]

Watson was equally appreciated and admired by Fascists, especially in Germany. In its struggle with the democratic governments and popular movements that opposed Germany's anti-Semitic drive, Nazis greatly valued their unexpected and influential ally. To them, it was a subtle green light of quiet approval because Watson seemed, in the Nazi mentality, to speak for more than one American firm—he seemed to represent President Franklin D. Roosevelt and indeed America itself.

The man who began his career as a turn-of-the-century horse-and-buggy peddler had graduated to become America's number one private international statesman. Watson used charitable donations to telescope his own importance. The roll call of honorary appointments of power and prestige was long and enviable. He was the chairman of the Carnegie Endowment for Peace, trustee of New York University, and chairman of the American section of the International Chamber of Commerce—and the lengthy gilded list proceeded from there. In fact, in the very days before the Reich awarded Dehomag the census contract, American newspapers prominently reported that Watson had been both nominated unopposed as a director of the Federal Reserve Bank and appointed trustee of Columbia University.[70]

His access to Secretary of State Cordell Hull, and more importantly to President Franklin D. Roosevelt, was unparalleled. While the Hoover Justice Department was at the height of its anti-trust investigation of IBM in 1932, Watson donated large sums to the Roosevelt campaign. Roosevelt's election over Hoover was a landslide. Watson now had entrée to the White House itself.[71]

Watson carefully curried favor with Roosevelt by publicly supporting some of his more controversial policies. Soon, Watson was sending policy suggestions to the President. The two men began to correspond regularly. Watson was so proud of the letters, some of them mere presidential tokens, he would carry them around in a pocket, showing them off when the moment would permit.[72]

Soon, Roosevelt came to rely on Watson for advice. White House staffers would occasionally ask for Watson's schedule in case the President needed to contact him quickly. Watson visited Hyde Park for tea several times and even stayed overnight at the White House. Eventually, Roosevelt offered to appoint Watson Secretary of Commerce or Ambassador to England. But Watson declined to leave IBM.[73]

Instead, Watson's son remembers, "he served unofficially as Roosevelt's representative in New York." If a foreign dignitary arrived, the White House might ask Watson to stage an honorary luncheon. "All Father had to do was press a button," his son remembers. "He had a whole department that did nothing but set up company dinners and other functions . . . all at IBM expense." Indeed, Roosevelt once remarked, "I handle 'em in Washington and Tom handles 'em in New York."[74]

Watson leveraged his position with the Administration to develop extensive contacts with Secretary of State Cordell Hull, numerous ambassadors and consuls, and the State Department in general. Cloaked in officialdom, Watson never failed to undertake the often months-long process of formally soliciting official greetings to private functions from Roosevelt, Hull, or other Administration luminaries. These letters, often gratuitous, broadcast arcs of power to those observing overseas, especially in a Reich that believed in bigger-than-life personages.

No wonder Nazi Germany considered Watson a very powerful friend. Indeed, when in October 1933 Dehomag encountered unexpectedly high customs duties on IBM machinery it hoped to import as part of its new expanded portfolio, Heidinger wrote a thinly veiled threat to Reich Customs bureaucrats. "The president of our American co-associate, the International Business Machines . . . Mr. Watson, is one of the most prominent American personalities," asserted Heidinger. "Among other things, he is one of the well-known 25 intimate counselors of President Roosevelt, president of the New York Chamber of Commerce . . . he also holds many, many other positions of honor in the United States. In keeping with his friendliness for Germany, proven at all times, he has up to now done everything possible which appeared to be to the interest of Germany. I am quite sure that Mr. Watson would never understand . . . a country to raise supplementary customs . . . on his machines." Heidinger added, "I do not know what the attitude of the above-named would be if the customs increase were permitted. I am recommending," Heidinger concluded, "that the above facts be placed to the knowledge of the two gentlemen [customs officers] examining the situation."[75]

Watson did everything he could to reinforce in Germany his image of special American potency and friendship. The German consul in New York was a houseguest at Watson's home, and Watson insisted on arranging for him complimentary country club privileges at the IBM Country Club. His socializing with the German Ambassador was equally robust, making certain that special invitations for luncheons and dinners were regularly circulated to German diplomats, and punctual acceptance or gracious regrets were sent in response to theirs.[76]

So a happy medium was found between Watson's desire to maintain deniability in IBM's lucrative relations with Germany and his personal desire to hobnob with Third Reich VIPs. But, the demands of the growing business in Germany would not be free of Watson's famous micro-management. Too much was at stake.

Watson would travel to Germany regularly during the thirties for first-hand information about the situation in the Nazi Reich. These visits would be augmented by his personal New York representatives who would monitor Dehomag on-site for months at a time. Verbatim translations of Dehomag's voluminous memos, correspondence, even routine bureaucratic forms and applications, were continuously transmitted to IBM in New York for review and comment.

Watson had created the IBM Europe office, headquartering it in Paris and then Geneva, to function as the eyes and ears of the New York office in Europe. When Watson's personal representatives were not in Germany, continuous supervision of Dehomag was effected by executives in the Swiss branch of IBM, and often the Paris office. More than just routine oversight of the German operation, the Swiss office of IBM would become the all-important nexus for instructions, profit funneling, and continent-wide coordination in support of Dehomag's technologic activities throughout Europe. The combination of Watson's micro-management from afar and persistent Swiss examination gave IBM an ever-present hour-to-hour grasp of the smallest operational details at Dehomag, from miniscule bank discrepancies amounting to just a few dollars to the most vital issues facing the subsidiary's relations with the Nazi regime.

From the very first moments and continuing throughout the twelve-year existence of the Third Reich, IBM placed its technology at the disposal of Hitler's program of Jewish destruction and territorial domination. IBM did not invent Germany's anti-Semitism, but when it volunteered solutions, the company virtually braided with Nazism. Like any technologic evolution, each new solution powered a new level of sinister expectation and cruel capability.

When Germany wanted to identify the Jews by name, IBM showed them how. When Germany wanted to use that information to launch programs of social expulsion and expropriation, IBM provided the technologic wherewithal. When the trains needed to run on time, from city to city or between concentration camps, IBM offered that solution as well. Ultimately, there was no solution IBM would not devise for a Reich willing to pay for services rendered. One solution led to another. No solution was out of the question.

As the clock ticked, as the punch cards clicked, as Jews in Germany saw their existence vaporizing, others saw their corporate fortunes rise. Even as German Jewry hid in their homes and wept in despair, even as the world quietly trembled in fear, there was singing. Exhilarated, mesmerized, the faithful would sing, and sing loudly to their Leaders—on both sides of the Atlantic.

Some uniforms were brown. Some were blue.

I
II
III
IV
V
VI
VII
VIII
IX
X
XI
XII
XIII
XIV
XV

THE IBM-NAZI ALLIANCE

WILLY HEIDINGER HATED THOMAS WATSON. BITTER AND defiant, Heidinger saw Watson as the incarnation of the financial calamity that had befallen Germany after the Great War. Heidinger had possessed the vision in 1910 to introduce Hollerith's contraption into Germany. He founded a company, Dehomag, to bring data processing to his country. But for the monetary manipulations that arose after World War I, the Diktat of the Versailles Treaty, and the wild ensuing hyperinflation of the twenties, Heidinger would still own that company.[1]

Back in 1922, worthless German currency was devalued by the hour. Heidinger was unable to remit some $104,000 in royalties to CTR, the IBM predecessor company, because it amounted to trillions of inflated Reichsmarks that were impossible to obtain. Watson seized upon Germany's inflation crisis to take possession of Dehomag. During contentious negotiations, Watson first offered to demur on the royalty debt in exchange for 51 percent of the company. Heidinger felt it was better to own nearly half of a going concern than all of a bankrupt one. So he agreed to yield half of Dehomag. But then Watson abruptly upped the demand from 51 percent of Dehomag to 90 percent. Heidinger felt "cornered" by his own private *Diktat*. Under Watson's new terms, Heidinger would own 10 percent—or nothing. Watson had outmaneuvered Heidinger.[2]

It was more than a decade earlier. But Heidinger never forgot it. He spent the rest of his career biting back.

Watson, on the other hand, was a steel-nerved businessman. He saw the Dehomag takeover of 1922 as just another opportunity to swoop up a lucrative business for virtually nothing. What could be more natural? Hating a business contact was of no use to a man like Watson. Heidinger merely represented a factor to control in the pursuit of profits.

But Heidinger was woven from too much feisty fabric. His austere face pulled tight over high cheekbones beneath a worried brow framed the very picture of contentiousness. "I would be the last to submit to domination," Heidinger wrote to IBM's Nazi oversight panel in recalling his dislike for Watson. "I do not, as a matter of principle, let anyone tell me to do anything."[3]

Warlike in his business demeanor, Heidinger enjoyed corporate combat and tenacious lawsuits. He could litigate a narrow commercial issue for years and obstruct a crucial company program at the eleventh hour unless he received his due. Like Hollerith himself, Heidinger was willing to battle colleagues as well as adversaries. An IBM assessment of Heidinger termed him a "hardened survivor" whose "life . . . was not a serene one." The description added, "He throve on fights."[4]

More than just volatile and unpredictable, no one at IBM trusted Heidinger. Company executives constantly suspected him of chiseling IBM for small and large sums, and thwarting their routine audits to identify the amounts. "Mr. Heidinger is a very selfish man," wrote one IBM auditor who in spring 1934 tried to verify Dehomag's tax information. At about that time, another IBM auditor in Paris reported back to the New York office, "Just in order to avoid any misunderstanding, we wish to advise that we are not aware of what is taking place . . . insofar as the recording of the inventories and the closing of the books is concerned." The company's staid blue-suited accountants learned to be reluctant in approaching Heidinger less they incur his volcanic temper. In that vein, another auditor, also writing in spring 1934, complained, "it is practically impossible to do anything by correspondence, due to the fear of unduly exciting our German friends."[5]

Even before Hitler seized power, IBM had profited enormously from Dehomag. By 1927, profits had returned more than 400 percent of IBM's purchase price.[6] Now, as part of the Third Reich's industrial team, Dehomag's future was catapulting. Nazi demands for a universe of punch card applications promised horizonless profits. Merged IBM entities, a Europe-wide territory, and a new factory presaged a magnificent new Dehomag whose fortune would rise along with the fortune of the Third Reich. Yet who would prosper? Would it be the German people? the Aryan race? Heidinger personally? No. It would be Watson and IBM. Heidinger roiled at the prospect.

Normally, Watson would not tolerate even a spark of rebellious management, let alone continuous insolent defiance. It was indeed a measure of Dehomag's indispensable importance to IBM's long-range global goals that the micro-managing, egocentric Watson would endure clash after clash with his own executives in Germany. Likewise, Heidinger was resourceful and energetic enough to walk away from any distasteful foreign enterprise and pursue his own commercial dominion. In truth, the two men desperately needed each other.

Watson needed Heidinger's connections to the NSDAP to turn Nazi plans into IBM profits. And he needed Heidinger's cooperation if those profits were to discreetly detour around the Reich payment moratorium. One method was requiring its own German subsidiary to pay IBM "royalties." Revenues could then be deemed a "necessary expense" to Dehomag rather than a profit to the parent company. Dehomag monies could occasionally be transmitted to IBM in this form. As IBM's European manager reassured New York executives in a 1934 letter, Dehomag Manager Herman Rottke promised to "pull every wire and use every effort to continue [royalty] payments."[7]

For Heidinger's part, he needed Watson to arm the statistical soldiers of the Third Reich for the coming war against European Jewry and territorial conquest. For now, the machines would still be imported from the United States. But even after the new factory was rushed into operation, allowing Hollerith machines to be manufactured in Berlin, the precious punch cards themselves, painstakingly produced to an exacting specification, could still be ordered from only one source: IBM in the United States.

Both men would vault their tempers and stratagems across the Atlantic as Heidinger labored to expand Dehomag's commercial cooperation with the Third Reich, and Watson struggled to retain all the profits, often cutting Heidinger out.

To achieve his goals, each man had to cooperate in an international campaign of corporate schizophrenia designed to achieve maximum deniability for both Dehomag and IBM. The storyline depended upon the circumstance and the listener. Dehomag could be portrayed as the American-controlled, almost wholly-owned subsidiary of IBM with token German shareholders and on-site German managers. Or Dehomag could be a loyal German, staunchly Aryan company baptized in the blood of Nazi ideology wielding the power of its American investment for the greater glory of Hitler's Reich. Indeed,

Heidinger and Watson both were willing to wave either banner as needed. Both stories were true. Watson had seen to that.

Dehomag's Aryan façade was carefully constructed. In newly Nazified Germany, many good and decent businessmen looked the other way, dreading the day stern-faced men sporting swastika armbands knocked on the door demanding anti-Semitic loyalty oaths, subscriptions of financial support, and ultimately invasive Party control via *kommissars*. At the same time, some could not wait to join the movement. Dehomag was among those who could not wait. IBM was among those who did not mind.

Early on, Heidinger sought out the sponsorship of the Nazi Party hierarchy. He wanted Dehomag draped in the authority not only of the government but the Nazi Party itself. However, before the NSDAP would ally with Dehomag, the powerful Political and Economics Division demanded, in December 1933, that the company answer some pointed questions. The Party's probe was designed to detect just who controlled the corporation, whether the firm was German enough, Nazi enough, and strategic enough to receive the Party's seal of approval.[8]

Heidinger proffered incisive, if dubious, written replies. "My company is an entirely independent organization which has acquired patent rights from their American owners," he insisted, and is merely bound to pay "royalties." But, argued Heidinger, "any worries as to whether or not excessive amounts of German funds are being exported are thoroughly unjustified," especially since most of the royalties remained in blocked German bank accounts until released by the government.[9]

One Party question inquired why Dehomag could not sell any wholly German-built office equipment instead of American products. Heidinger explained that the Reich could not achieve its goals without Hollerith tabulators. "[A]side from ours, no other punched card machinery is manufactured in Germany," asserted Heidinger, adding, "Our machines cannot possibly displace other machines, because the work they are called upon to perform cannot be accomplished by the other machines."[10]

Heidinger concluded his written comments by reminding the Party examiners that Dehomag had been "entrusted . . . with the compilation of statistics for the Prussian census." He added knowingly, with that air of ominous lack of specificity so common in those days, "Moreover, negotiations are now pending in Berlin, their object being an agreement between my company and the SA [Storm Troopers] high command in that city for the compilation of certain necessary statistics."[11] Nothing more need be said. Dehomag was approved.

Verbatim translations of the NSDAP's questions and Heidinger's answers —along with the German originals—were delivered to the New York office within several business days for review by Watson and other IBM executives.[12]

New York agreed with a sub-rosa approach if it could garner the Nazi Party affiliation needed to secure more government contracts. IBM willingly diminished its own identity as part of the effort. New York executives were advised of a Dehomag request: "in the future, on all machines shipped to them [Dehomag], the following designations are to be omitted: 1) International Business Machines, 2) International." A 1934 memo from IBM's Paris managers didn't even want IBM billed for small German registration fees, explaining, "we all should be very careful in exploiting or advertising the name of IBM Corp. in Germany."[13] Watson himself would continue his high visibility, but would be portrayed during his frequent visits not as a foreign controller of Dehomag as much as a supporter of IBM technology in Nazi Germany.

Heidinger's assertions of allegiance to Nazi ethics and independence from foreign influence were certainly acceptable to IBM in New York—so long as everyone in the company understood the truth: Watson remained in charge. To ensure that Watson in fact retained full control of Dehomag's activities, IBM NY insisted on several provisions.

First, Dehomag by-laws would allow New York to supercede the German board of directors at any time. Dehomag's corporate by-laws five and six declared that the corporation would be comprised not only of shareholders and a board of directors, but of an unusual third component: "representatives and attorneys—in-fact . . . determined by the shareholders." These would be IBM accountants, managers, and lawyers who could project Watson's authority on a day-to-day basis. The fifth by-law added, "The shareholders shall be in a position to annul the board of directors." By-law seven ordered, "The representatives [Watson's attorneys and accountants] shall follow the instructions of the shareholders and the board of directors, if there is one."[14]

Second, Heidinger's token 10 percent share of the Dehomag were his to own, but only so long as he remained with the company. The stock could not be sold without the shareholders' permission, according to by-law four.[15]

Clearly, the power at Dehomag was wielded by the shareholders. Watson and IBM NY owned 90 percent of the stock. This gave Watson and his attorneys veto power over any Dehomag activity and indeed over Heidinger himself.

Watson also wanted his own people on the Dehomag board to counterbalance Heidinger. Representing IBM NY were trusted Watson representatives Walter Dickson Jones, who operated out of IBM's Paris office, and John E. Holt, who mainly operated out of IBM's Geneva office.[16] Heidinger acquiesced to the concept of foreign control, but he resented Watson's interference. The first test came quickly. It involved German Sales Manager Karl Hummel.

Watson had cultivated a personal alliance with Hummel. He had arranged for Hummel to attend IBM's sales training school at Endicott, New York, and entertained Hummel and his wife in his home. The Hummels and Watsons periodically exchanged gifts. Watson knew how to develop loyalty. He wanted Hummel on the German board. December 15, 1933, Watson made his move, sending a radiogram to Dehomag General Manager Hermann Rottke: "To give Dehomag fuller representation in Germany, I request that Karl Hummel be made second director *(Geschäftsführer)* and his name so listed. . . . Kindly notify me when this is done."[17] Watson had not asked Heidinger first.

Heidinger erupted, and just days before the new factory was to open in a grand ceremony, Rottke cabled back: "According to German law, not I but only shareholders meeting and board of directors have authority to promote Karl Hummel . . . sending your cable and a copy of this answer to Heidinger."[18]

Sarcastic and threatening, Heidinger on December 20 dashed off a warning to Watson. "I do not seriously fear . . . your positive will in the future to put me aside in questions of importance for the Dehomag. Nevertheless, I of course feel deeply depressed that you are not interested to hear my opinion [about] . . . such an important decision. . . . That feeling of depression . . . might be considered as not important. But what could be important is the following.[19]

"As you know," Heidinger continued, "we all considered it of greatest importance to proof [*sic*] that the Dehomag is a German-managed company . . . free from American influence . . . our authorities are very sensitive if they should believe to be fouled." He hinted that the Nazi Party might feel the need to install two of its own *kommissars* on the board. During a recent conference at the Nazi Party headquarters, Heidinger had reassured ranking officials that Dehomag would function free of American influence. Now the Hummel appointment was showing the opposite, he claimed, adding that Watson's move would "shock" Party stalwarts and create a "dangerous" situation for the company.[20]

Watson went into damage control mode. Upon receiving Heidinger's irksome missive, he cabled Rottke, who would soon sail to America for meetings at IBM: "Do nothing further about Hummel until I see you in New York."[21]

It was difficult, but Watson humbled himself. In a rambling, two-page letter filled with spelling errors, Watson apologized over and over again, regretted Heidinger's upset, professed his unqualified friendship to Germany, recalled his pleasant times in Berlin, enumerated his forthcoming dinner engagements with the German ambassador, and staunchly assured, "you have nothing to worry about in connection with the German government, so far as my connection with our German business is concerned." Watson blamed not his lack of respect for Heidinger, but a simple typo. In his original cablegram asking for Hummel's appointment, Watson averred, "one word was misquoted. The cablegram dictated was 'I suggest,' and I find in the copy it was written 'request' . . . it is always my policy . . . to make a suggestion, rather than a request."[22]

Suggest. Not request.

Unappeased, Heidinger shot back in a melodramatic flourish, "it was a real and great joy for me to receive your letter . . . [and] to see that the biggest part of the trouble arose from the mistake of using the word 'request' instead [of] 'suggest' which . . . formally settles the most dangerous point . . . I hardly can express how happy I am about the friendly manner in which you explained . . . the mistaken wording of your cable."[23]

Heidinger's message was cabled to Rottke, who at that moment was steaming across the Atlantic on the SS *President Roosevelt*. Rottke had the cable retyped on letterhead and handed it to Watson once he landed in New York. Hummel, it was decided, would be promoted to senior management, but not sit on the board. The conflict was over. Watson filed his original dictation copy of that December cablegram to Rottke. On line two the word "request" was originally typed. Watson edited the cable, scratched out "request" but then upon reflection wrote it back in by hand and signed it. "Suggest" was never in the document. It was always "request."[24]

JANUARY 8, 1934.

In a corner of Dehomag's vast punch card operation within the great Karstadthaus census complex at Berlin's Alexanderplatz, with morning light streaming in behind them through banks of tall parallel windows, several dozen officials of the Prussian Statistical Office were joined by leaders of the Nazi Party in full uniform and Dehomag officials in their finest suits to solemnly recognize the coming revolution of data processing and the newly forged alliance with International Business Machines.[25]

Hands reverently clasped either behind their backs or across their belt buckles, shoulders and arms touching in fellowship, the assemblage stood in awe of this day, the day Germany would unveil its own factory producing Hollerith machines. The President of the Prussian Statistical Office, Dr. Höpker, delivered brief remarks using the euphemisms and crystal clear ambiguities of the day. "[T]he irresistible force of the National Socialist government . . . demands the [census] results faster than ever before," he declared, adding, "German statistics understands this impatience." He then explained exactly how the punch card process worked, distilling the anonymous German masses into specific names organized by race and religion, as well as numerous other characteristics.[26]

Accompanied by a dense din in adjacent halls that clicked and whirred like locusts swarming a field, Heidinger stepped to the front to speak. With the passion of a die-hard ideologist simultaneously presenting an omnipotent gift to the nation and fulfilling a life-long personal dream, he spoke of the demographic surgery the German population required.

"The physician examines the human body and determines whether . . . all organs are working to the benefit of the entire organism," asserted Heidinger to a crowd of company employees and Nazi officials. "We [Dehomag] are very much like the physician, in that we dissect, cell by cell, the German cultural body. We report every individual characteristic . . . on a little card. These are not dead cards, quite to the contrary, they prove later on that they come to life when the cards are sorted at a rate of 25,000 per hour according to certain characteristics. These characteristics are grouped like the organs of our cultural body, and they will be calculated and determined with the help of our tabulating machine.[27]

"We are proud that we may assist in such a task, a task that provides our nation's Physician [Adolf Hitler] with the material he needs for his examinations. Our Physician can then determine whether the calculated values are in harmony with the health of our people. It also means that if such is not the case, our Physician can take corrective procedures to correct the sick circumstances. . . . Our characteristics are deeply rooted in our race. Therefore, we must cherish them like a holy shrine, which we will—and must—keep pure. We have the deepest trust in our Physician and will follow his instructions in blind faith, because we know that he will lead our people to a great future. Hail to our German people and *der Führer*!"[28]

The entire group then filed out of the massive building and motored to

IBM's new factory in the quiet Berlin section of Lichterfelde to attend the official opening. At 10:30, Dehomag employees stopped their work to gather for the great event. Tall trees along the perimeter were still nearly barren from the Berlin winter. The swastika-bedecked square in front of the four-story factory complex was already jammed with hundreds of neighborhood onlookers and well wishers.[29]

Just before noon, two columns of Storm Troopers took up positions along either side of the walkway leading to Dehomag's front door. A band from the SA's 9th Regiment played Nazi victory songs. Finally, the NSDAP hierarchy arrived.[30]

Dehomag had invited Nazi higher-ups representing the organizations most important to the future of IBM's partnership with the Third Reich. From the German Labor Front came Rudolf Schmeer, a last-minute stand-in for Dr. Robert Ley, leader of the organization. The German Labor Front was the militant coalition responsible for mobilizing unemployed Nazi millions into both newly created jobs and vacated Jewish positions. The Front also inducted Germans into regimented squads that functioned as veritable military units. So important was Dr. Ley and his German Labor Front that the entire Lichterfelde factory opening was delayed two days because he took ill. Only when it became clear he would not recover for days was the event suddenly rescheduled with Schmeer, accompanied by an entourage of potentates, standing in.[31]

At Schmeer's side was A. Görlitzer representing the SA, the rough and ready Storm Troopers, the violent edge of Hitler's forces. Görlitzer was a powerful Nazi. When Goebbels became Propaganda Minister, Görlitzer took his place in the Storm Trooper organization. Now, the presence of Görlitzer, in gleaming, black leather boots and fighting uniform, would testify to the importance of Dehomag in Hitler's future plans.[32]

As the invited Nazi officials paraded through echelons of honor guard, the Brown Shirts pumped their arms rigidly diagonal. Schmeer, Görlitzer, and the other leaders returned the disciplined Hitler salute with a casual, almost cocky bent-elbowed gesture, their open palms barely wafting over their shoulder.[33]

Bouquets decorated Dehomag's reception hall. One large swastika emblem dominated the front of the podium, and an even larger swastika flag hung across the wall. Music inside was provided by an NSDAP men's choir. To record the event, a tall, circular microphone stood nearby.[34]

The company's most important users were there as well. Heidinger's guest list included the directors of the *Reichsbank* and other financial institutions, the Police, Post Office, Ministry of Defense, Reich Statistical Office, and an executive contingent from the *Reichsbahn,* that is, German Railway.[35]

The future was in the cards—a future of names, of police files and concentration camps, of bank accounts and asset transfers, of war offices and weapons production, of endless statistical campaigns and registrations, and of trains. So many trains. The men and organizations assembled would help shape that future in ways people were only beginning to imagine.

Representing Watson at the event was his personal representative, Walter Jones. Jones was the Paris-based manager of all European operations and a man who would one day become chairman of IBM Canada.[36]

Framed by swastikas front and rear, a clearly impressed Jones was the first to speak. He proclaimed in German, "It is an outstanding honor and privilege for me to be with you and to represent Mr. Thomas J. Watson, president of International Business Machines, on the occasion of the formal opening of this magnificent factory . . . the new and permanent home of Dehomag."[37]

Repeatedly using Nazi buzzwords for economic recovery, Jones made clear that Mr. Watson agreed to the new construction "because he realized your organization had outgrown the facilities . . . [and] the time was propitious . . . as it would give employment to many idle workmen and thus help . . . the unemployed." Peppering Watson's name and imprimatur throughout his address, Jones praised, "the noble work undertaken by your government in its aim to give work to every German citizen."[38]

When Heidinger came to the front, nattily dressed with a small handkerchief peeking from his suit jacket pocket, the man was clearly emotional. "I feel it almost a sacred action, if in this hour I consecrate this place of our mother earth," he began. Reviewing Dehomag's turbulent history, he described how the tiny company had persevered despite a lack of financing, the Great War, and the suffocating post-War inflation.[39]

Although at that very time, Heidinger was battling Watson over the appointment of Hummel, in this moment of Nazi fulfillment, Heidinger was effusive. Recalling IBM's acquisition of Dehomag, he recast the story not as an acrimonious takeover but as a financial rescue by a benevolent friend of the German people. "I express our deepest appreciation and our thanks for the noblesse not to be surpassed, proved by our creditor . . . International Business Machines Corporation under the management of their president, Thomas J. Watson, in our condition of distress. . . . [IBM] could have been in a position to take over our entire firm by . . . enforcing their claim for bankruptcy . . . but [instead] purchased a share in our company."[40]

Continually invoking Nazi re-employment clichés, Heidinger promised that Dehomag would provide "bread and work" for German citizens. In that vein, he said that IBM had calculated the cost of a grand opening banquet and instead would contribute the 10,000 Reichsmarks to the Winter Subsidy, a Nazi program donating funds and food to those thrown into deeper joblessness by the international anti-Nazi boycott.[41]

He concluded by unveiling a building plaque commemorating the factory both to "the national awakening of the German people" and to its future. Heidinger concluded by asking that "the blessing of heaven may rest upon this place."[42]

Final remarks were offered by Schmeer on behalf of the powerful German Labor Front. "German men, German women," he proclaimed, "the fact that we are on the way up under Hitler's leadership despite the present conditions was doubted by many, not just by our enemies, but also by people who were willing to work honestly and diligently. The opening of this factory . . . shows that the road Hitler has prescribed and which he took last year was right, namely to bring trust into the German economy. People in the past were not lacking commitment to hard work but they lacked trust . . . the *Volks* community now present in this factory is here to stay, and stay for all eternity. . . . It will produce goods, which will help our people in their ascent."[43]

Snapping into respect, Schmeer pumped his arm forward exclaiming, "I now ask you to collect our joy and cry out: 'Our Führer, Adolf Hitler, *Sieg Heil!*'" The crowd reciprocated with fire: *Sieg Heil*! The choir burst into the national anthem, "Deutschland über Alles."[44]

Marching out enthusiastic and reassured, swept into the moment, the regaled Brown Shirts chanted the "Horst Wessel Song."[45]

> *Soon Hitler's flags will wave*
> *Over every single street*
> *Enslavement ends*
> *When soon we set things right!*

For IBM and Dehomag both, it was an extraordinary day of Nazi communion. Two days later, Jones sent off verbatim translations of the speeches to Watson with an enthusiastic cover letter declaring, "as your representative, I attended the formal opening . . . I have never witnessed a more interesting ceremony." Jones attached a list of all the Nazi figures that attended, and even made clear that the dignitaries included the SA's "Görlitzer, who succeeded Dr. Goebbels in the latter's former position." Jones' letter proudly mentioned "a full company of Nazi storm troups [*sic*] with band" and promised IBM's Leader that plenty of photos would follow.[46]

Watson sent a personal letter to Heidinger. "Mr. Jones sent me a copy of the speech you made at the opening of the new factory in Berlin . . . and I have read it with a great deal of interest . . . you are certainly to be congratulated upon the manner in which you conveyed your thoughts." The company was so proud of the event that Dehomag printed commemorative programs of the event with photographs and transcripts of the speeches made at both the census complex and the factory.[47]

There was no turning back now. IBM and the Nazi party had bonded. Swastikas and corporate slogans had found their common ground. Day and night, the Jewish names clattered through IBM systems, faster and faster, city by city, profession by profession. Dehomag was the Third Reich's informational deliverer. As such, they were afforded a special place in the mindset of Nazi planners. It was an awesome responsibility for Dehomag and IBM, but one they accepted with doctrinaire devotion.

The feeling was captured by one Nazi newspaper, *Der Deutsche,* which sent a reporter to cover the Lichterfelde ceremonies. The paper quoted Heidinger on the nature of the company. Heidinger explained it this way: "Children's character is determined by their parents. Firms' by their founders."[48]

GERMANY WAS quietly tabulating.

While Hitler's rhetoric was burning the parade grounds and airwaves, while Storm Troopers were marching Jews through the streets in ritual humiliations, while Reich legislative decrees and a miasma of regional and private policies were ousting Jews from their professions and residences, while noisy, outrageous acts of persecution were appalling the world, a quieter process was also underway. Germany was automating.

Hollerith systems could do more than count. They could schedule, analyze, and compute. They could manage.

Several dozen Hollerith systems were already in use by a small clique of German industrial firms and government offices.[49] But now Hitler's Reich discovered that in its quest for supremacy, it could mechanize, organize, and control virtually all aspects of private and commercial life, from the largest industrial cartel to the humblest local shopkeeper. Just as people would be categorized and regimented down to the least characteristic, so would all of German business be analyzed to the smallest detail—and then subject to

Nazi discipline. The economy could recover. People could go back to work. But it would all be done toward a single, totally coordinated Nazi goal.

A global movement was loudly organizing to shatter the German economy and topple the repressive Hitler regime by denying economic recovery, prolonging German joblessness, and boycotting German commerce. But IBM was mobilizing its financial and engineering might to do the opposite. General Manager Rottke echoed IBM's attitude at the Lichterfelde factory opening, declaring, "We are able to hereby assist our government in its battle against unemployment." *Work and bread* was the theme IBM and Dehomag used again and again to describe their venture—all in support of the National Socialist goal. As Heidinger told his audience, "Public interest prevails over private interest."[50]

Hollerith technology had become a German administrative way of life. Punch cards would enable the entire Reich to go on a war footing. For IBM, it was a bonanza.

Dehomag's client list sparkled. Electrical combines such as Siemens in Berlin and Lech-Elektrizitätswerke in Augsburg. Heavy industry such as Mannesmann in Düsseldorf and I.G. Farben in Frankfurt. Automakers such as Opel in Rüsselsheim and Daimler-Benz in Stuttgart. Retail stores such as Woolworth and Hertie in Berlin. Optical manufacturers such as Zeiss in Jena and Zeiss Ikon in Dresden. Chocolate factories such as Schokoladenfabrik in Tangermünde. Coffee producers such as Kaffee Handels A.G. in Bremen.[51]

Aircraft engines: 10 customers; coal mining: 7 customers; chemical plants: 18 customers; electrical products: 10 customers; motor vehicle industry: 11 customers; shipbuilders: 2 customers; railroads, buses, trams, and other transportation: 32 customers; insurance companies: 26 customers; banks: 6 customers; public utilities: 16 customers; iron and steel: 19 customers; turbines, engines, and tractors: 7 customers.[52]

Leather tanning, washing machine manufacture, liquor, paint and varnishes, cigarettes, perfumes, railway car assembly, ball bearings, rubber, petroleum, shoes, oleomargarine, asbestos, explosives.[53]

Reichspost, Reichsbahn, Pension Funds, the *Luftwaffe,* the Navy.[54]

Payroll, inventory control, material strength calculations, personnel, finance, scheduling, product usage, and manufacturing supervision.[55] There was virtually no business that could not benefit from punch card technology. Dehomag deftly controlled the data operations of the entire Reich.

Moreover, one Dehomag customer account could represent dozens of machines. Hollerith systems involved an ensemble of interconnected devices that could be manufactured in a variety of configurations. Punchers, proofers, verifiers, sorters, tabulators, alphabetizers, multipliers, printers. I.G. Farben installed arrays in Offenbach, Bitterfeld, Berlin, Hoechst, and other locations. Daimler-Benz utilized machines in Berlin, Stuttgart, Genshagen, and other sites. Junkers employed Hollerith devices in Magdeburg, Leopoldshall, Kothen, Dessau, and numerous other cities. Municipalities everywhere used the machines. Frankfurt am Main's Public Works Department alone maintained an extended suite of punchers, verifiers, tabulators, multipliers, and sorters. Statistical offices—federal, regional, and local—could not lease enough systems.[56]

Gleichschaltung, that is, total central coordination, demanded that endless accountings be submitted regularly to government bureaus, Nazified trade associations, and statistical agencies. *Kommissars* and government regulations required companies to install Hollerith machines to ensure prompt, uniform, up-to-the-minute reports that could be reprocessed and further tabulated. The Reich Statistical Office's Department I was officially charged with the responsibility of helping companies transition to the elaborate Hollerith methodology. Statistical bureaus hired thousands of new staffers just to keep up with the data flow.[57]

Hitler's Germany began achieving undreamed of efficiencies. The *Reichsbahn* was a vital customer for Dehomag, deploying full or partial systems in Essen, Cologne, Nuremberg, Mainz, Frankfurt, Hannover, and nearly every other major connection point. Some 140 million passengers annually were booked through Dehomag card sorting systems. Punch cards made the trains run on time and even evaluated engine efficiency when pulling certain types of freight. Records in some railway operations that previously required 300 people six months to organize could now be computed by a staff of fifteen working for just a week.[58]

Customers such as Krupp, Siemens, and the Deutsche Bank were able to reduce their operating costs and clerical staffs by as much as half, and plow those human and financial resources into sellable goods and services. Manpower could be shifted as needed from plant to plant by companies and deployed from city to city by the German Labor Front.[59]

To meet fast-expanding demand, Dehomag hired more than 1,000 new employees to staff the new factory at Lichterfelde. Everywhere throughout the plant, newly installed machine tools were fabricating Hollerith devices. Workshops buzzed, cranked, and whirred with Beling & Lübke precision lathes, Jung surface grinders, Boley milling machines, Hille high-speed drills, Auerbach & Scheibe 3-spindle drill presses, Thiel metal saws, Karger thread-cutting lathes, and Universal grinding machines.[60] Metal shavings, oil cans, iron rods, tin coils, ball bearings, alloy sheets, and rubber rollers combined with bent elbows, squinting eyes, wedging hands and brows wiped by the sleeves of work smocks to create a manufacturing miracle. IBM zeal and Nazi devotion coalesced to help the Reich recover and strengthen.

Lichterfelde was overwhelmed with orders. It established a "shock department" for the speedy manufacture of spare parts, retrofitted an old disused IBM plant from pre-merger days, and converted it to a workshop. Outside storage, some 1,200 square meters costing more than RM 12,000 annually, was rented. Workmen shuttled materials back and forth from the storage site to the overcrowded Lichterfelde site where even corridor space was at a premium. "Our own workshops (technical) grew to such an extent," complained Heidinger in a report to IBM NY, "that every square meter of space was overfilling with machines and persons, and the acute shortage of space became more and more critical."[61]

Dehomag's explosive growth arose not only from a dictatorial marshalling of all commerce, but also because of a completely new industry within Nazi Germany: race science. Identifying who was a Jew—either by certifying Aryan lineage or exposing Jewish ancestry became big business overnight. Hollerith alone possessed the technology to efficiently provide the answers Nazi raceologists craved.

RACE SCIENCE had long been a pseudo-scientific discipline within the Nazi culture. The field suddenly transformed from vague debates into a lucrative reality when two factors converged. It began when a multiplicity of anti-Jewish decrees and private provisos demanded Jewish ousters and pure Aryan descent. But these racist requirements clashed with the reality Dehomag had exposed when it compiled the 1933 census: not all the Jews could be identified by a mere census.

Census tabulations isolated nearly a half million Jews, less than 1 percent of the overall German population, and 65,000 less than the previous national census in 1925. Reich statisticians saw this drop as validation that "the new political order had induced a strong emigration trend." But in the Nazi mindset, the half million identified were merely the most obvious Jewish layer, the so-called "practicing Jews."[62]

Nazi ideology defined Jewishness not as a function of religious practice, but bloodline. How far back? Nazi theoreticians debated tracing parentage. Some looked at grandparents. Some suggested searching back four generations. Still others focused on the year 1800, before Jewish emancipation, that is, before assimilation into German society.[63]

Reich statisticians concluded from the occupational yields of the Dehomag census that "there are quite a number of Jews in these 'independent occupations' who have left the community of the Jewish faith. Those 'Jews' could not be recorded as Jews in the 1933 Census. That means that Jewish infiltration into our cultural life is probably much greater than the numbers for practicing Jews would otherwise indicate."[64]

Estimates of how many ancestral Jews, baptized or not, really dwelled within the Reich ranged far above the traditional 600,000. But no one knew just how many. Nazi raceologists devised a bizarre pseudo-mathematical formula that grouped ancestral Jews into a series of grades, such as *fully Jewish, half-Jewish,* and *quarter-Jewish,* depending upon how many Jewish parents and grandparents could be calculated from their past. All of it defied logic once one added other generation-to-generation dynamics such as remarriages and divorces.[65]

Logical or not, everywhere Germany was buzzing with the need to trace ancestry by cross-indexing births, deaths, baptisms, and other data going back generations. Since racial decrees mandated that only Aryans could participate in many walks of life, German individuals, companies, schools, associations of every size and caliber, and even churches, were gripped by the necessity to prove their Aryan purity and to exclude everyone else. Moreover, physical characteristics such as height, stature, and blond, blue-eyed features, were all thought to be coefficients of racial descent.

Linguistics played a dynamic role. Words such as *public health and medicine, nationality, foreigners, family* and *family genealogy, hereditary,* and even the word *German,* took on special anti-Semitic implications. Jews were foreigners, and in many cases thought to be disease carriers. Racial impurity was a public health issue. Only Aryans could be Germans. The word *German* became exclusionary.

A competitive, confusing, and often overlapping network of governmental, private, and pseudo-academic agencies with constantly evolving names, jurisdictions, and sponsors sprang up into existence. All of them were directly or indirectly dependent on Hollerith's high-speed technology to sort through the voluminous handwritten or manually typed genealogical records needed to construct definitive family trees. This complex of race science agencies ultimately took on a bureaucratic life of its own.

Powered by Hollerith technology, the *Führer*'s Office operated the Race Political Office. The SS created the Reich Race and Settlement Office. The

Justice Ministry empowered one of its lower court divisions to rule on matters of hereditary health. Josef Goebbels' Ministry of Propaganda vested its Department II with questions of Jewish policy, popular health, and population. Labor and unemployment offices under the aegis of the Labor Ministry maintained an index of "foreigners," meaning Jews and non-Aryans.[66]

Race science in the Interior Ministry was the provenance of the Reich Committee for the Protection of German Blood. Department I dealt with issues of race law and policies. Department IV studied population politics, genetic hygiene, and medical statistics. Department VI was concerned with foreign groups within Germany.[67]

The Reich Health Office, also part of the Interior Ministry, included two special units: Department L supervised genetic health and racial hygiene; Department M was authorized to oversee genetic research. In addition, the Reich Committee for Popular Health, which advised the Interior Ministry, maintained a sub-office for genetic and race hygiene.[68]

In the Reich Statistical Office, which was completely dependent upon IBM equipment and technical assistance, Department IV was responsible not only for traditional data such as census, household, and family data, but nationality and race statistics as well. The Ministry of Science and Education developed special offices for racial and genetic research and oversaw the work of the Kaiser Wilhelm Institute for Anthropology, Human Genetics and Eugenics.[69]

The Nazi Party itself also maintained a plethora of structured and informal special advisory bureaus on race and public health.[70]

Offices devoted to race science melded genuine documentation with rumors, poison pen letters, and vengeful tips. Challenges to one's Aryan background were commonplace. Whether driven by a sense of national duty or ordinary fear, everyone was forced to confront their racial make-up. At the apex of racial grading was a bureaucratic entity attached to the Interior Ministry. This section began its existence before 1933 as the Nazi Information Office. Ultimately, after numerous name changes, it became known as the *Reichssippenamt*, or Reich Family Office, endowed with the final authority to decide who was Jewish or Aryan.[71]

Lists were distributed, exchanged, and updated continuously, often in a haphazard fashion. To cope with the growing bureaucratic fascination with punch card records, senior Interior Ministry officials reviewed one fanciful proposal for a twenty-five-floor circular tower of data to centralize all personal information. The proposal was rejected because it would take years to build and stock. But the futuristic concept opened the eyes of Reich planners. Each of the twenty-five floors in the imagined tower would be comprised of 12 circular rooms representing one birth year. Every circular room would contain 31 cabinets, one for each day of the month. Each cabinet would in turn contain 7,000 names. Registrations and updates would feed in from census bureaus. All 60 million Germans could then be organized and cross-indexed in a single location regardless of changes in residence. Data could be retrieved by some 1,500 couriers running from room to room like so many magnetic impulses fetching files.[72]

Lists were indeed everywhere. Non-German Registries were maintained in police stations, employment bureaus, professional associations, church organizations, local Nazi departments, and the SS Security Office, the *Sicherheitsdienst,* known as the SD. The SD was under the control of Reinhard Heydrich, nicknamed the Hangman.

Buried within the bowels of Heydrich's Berlin office was the Department of Research, which developed registries on Freemasons. In 1934, one of the SD's nameless specialists on Freemasons demonstrating particular zeal was a corporal who had just transferred in from the Dachau concentration camp. He showed such promise working with registries that he was reassigned to *Referat* II 112, the Jewish Department, where he could work with more lists. The corporal's name was Adolf Eichmann.[73]

As the cross-indexing capabilities and sorting routines of Dehomag's machinery became more sophisticated, race researchers continuously discovered greater informational depth about Jews and those of Jewish bloodline. For Dehomag, such statistical feats were both its science and its competitive edge. Educating its customers was an everyday occurrence.

An August 1934 article in the Dehomag publication, *Hollerith Nachrichten,* extolled the benefits of advanced data processing. The article, entitled "An Improved Analysis of Statistical Interdependencies via Hollerith Punch Card Process," illustrated how difficult data calculations could be better interpreted and predict probabilities. As a prime example, the journal cited "the field of medicine, and the science of genetics and race." Complex tabulations could be rendered, the article suggested, regarding "the size of fathers and their children, number of children and parents. Diphtheria and age, and the different racial characteristics." The article explained, "Even though the gathering of statistical material in industrial and commercial businesses has steadily grown in size . . . in administrative archives and because of censuses and other surveys, the interpretation has not kept pace. Due to the lack of manpower . . . one is limited . . . to sorting out past developments. . . . This is not always enough. . . . The actual justification for the collection of data in great quantity is the ability to draw conclusions . . . and ensure a safe estimate of future and current occurrences."[74]

Racial purity was not just a catchphrase for Nazis, it was an obsession. Germany wanted more than a society of Aryans, it wanted a master race: tall, strong, blond, and blue-eyed, intellectually and physically dominant. Eugenics became an elite cult. Nazis sought to weed out the weaker elements of its population, regardless of parentage—even from among their own people. The mentally ill, diseased, handicapped, homosexual individuals, certain Jews, Gypsies, and a group of misfits termed "anti-social," were not to be part of Germany's future.

Beginning in summer 1934, the Third Reich took the next step. Armed with statistical data and other information collected from medical offices, doctors, and insurance companies across the nation, Germany began organized sterilization.

TWO DECREES were promulgated by mid-1934. One was *The Law for Simplification of the Health System*, enacted in July 1934, requiring doctors and other clinicians to fill out detailed forms about the health condition of their patients. These were filed with Health Offices and eventually processed by Hollerith systems at the Reich Statistical Offices in Berlin and its regional divisions. The information, combined with extensive information from health insurance questionnaires, created a eugenic profile.[75]

The second decree was *The Law for the Prevention of Genetically Sick Offspring*, made active in January 1934. Eugenic theorists in Germany had developed a maze of precepts mandating exactly which bloodlines should be terminated based on the statistical probability of endowing defective genes. Sterilization guidelines initially specified individuals deemed insane, retarded, epileptic, or manic-depressive, among others.[76]

But now eugenic pseudo-academicians and Nazi statisticians evolved an additional belief that a man's right to live was determined by his net worth to Nazi society. "The only value of man—and this is a direct object of statistics—is his economic value . . . his human labor productivity," wrote Friedrich Zahn in a 1934 edition of the German statistical journal, *Allgemeines Statistisches Archiv*. Zahn's article, "The Economic Value of Man As an Object of Statistics," reminded that, "statistics is identical in character with the National Socialist idea."[77]

Zahn called for a "registration of the various risks which threaten the value of productivity . . . [as a result of] . . . illnesses, disability, unem-

ployment and non-accomplishment of occupational goals." Population engineering, he emphasized, would rely upon extensive data analysis, including
statistics from a gamut of health bureaus, disability and liability insurers,
unemployment offices, and even academic testing data from schools.[78]

Nazi genetic experts worried about not only those individuals exhibiting undesired traits, but the parents and/or children who might carry those
traits and therefore contaminate the gene pool. One census theoretician pos-
tulated that the potential for contamination could be set at a 25 percent
chance per diseased parent. Hence, once an undesirable person was identified, the parents and offspring, including newborn children, required sterilization as well.[79]

Quickly, the notion of sterilizing the physically undesirable expanded
to include the *socially* undesirable. So-called *anti-socials,* that is, misfits who
seemed to be unsuited for labor, became special targets. A leading raceologist described anti-socials as "those who, based on their personality, are not
capable of meeting the minimum requirements of society, *i.e.,* personal,
social, and *völkisch* behavior." One official definition cited: "human beings
with a hereditary and irreversible mental attitude, who . . . have repeatedly
come into conflict with government agencies and the courts, and thus appear
. . . a threat to humanity." Included were traitors, race violators, sexual per-
verts, and "secret Jews." But, "the numerically largest group consists of 'the
work-shy and habitual parasites.'"[80]

Compulsory sterilization was aimed principally at those adjudged physically and mentally inferior regardless of their race or nationality. However,
the criteria applied not only to general groups exhibiting the proscribed
characteristics, but, in the new lexicon of anti-Semitism, to virtually all Jews
within Germany.

Dehomag systems compiled nearly all the medical, health, and welfare
statistics in Germany, either at the compilation site or through the Reich Statistical Office. *Hollerith Nachrichten* aggressively proliferated its population-
engineering technology to new customers. An article entitled "The Hollerith
Punch Card Process in Welfare and Social Security" boasted, "sorting procedures are done by Hollerith machines with such speed and reliability that
the directors of the welfare administration are unrestricted in their catalog of
questions." It added, "The solution is that every interesting feature of a statistical nature . . . can be summarized . . . by one basic factor. This basic factor is
the Hollerith punch card."[81]

Questionnaires, although to be filled out by hand, were jointly designed
by Dehomag engineers and Nazi disability or welfare experts for compatibil-

ity, since ultimately all information would be punched into Hollerith cards. Yet, as a Dehomag notice to users advised, the questionnaires would have to be adapted to the technical demands of the Hollerith system, not the other way around. A vertical notice printed along the bottom left of typical welfare forms often indicated the information was to be processed "by the punch card office," generally an in-house bureau.[82]

People seated in a doctor's office or a welfare line never comprehended the destiny of routine information about their personal traits and conditions. Question 11 required a handwritten checkmark if the individual was a *foreigner*. Later, this information was punched into the correlating punch card in columns 29–30 under *nationality*.[83]

For many clerks and doctors, coding was a new procedure. Various editions of *Hollerith Nachrichten* tutored readers on the proper method of filling out Hollerith-compatible forms. In one issue it reminded form processors to code Special Characteristics in the several columns field 12. Antisocial was to be coded 1 in one column. In a second column, diseases such as blindness were coded 1. Mental disease was 2. Cripples were 3. Deaf people were 5. Parents who had already been sterilized were to be noted with an "*s*"; children already sterilized "because of a parent's sickness" were noted "*as*."[84]

Uniform codes were established for occupations. Factory workers were coded 19, hotel and guesthouse workers were 23, theatre artisans were 26. Unemployed persons received the code number 28. These codes were handwritten into field 8 on the forms.[85]

Diseases were also coded: influenza was 3, lupus was 7, syphilis was 9, diabetes was 15; they were entered into field 9.[86]

Once coded and punched, all data was then sorted by machine.

If agencies lacked the manpower to undertake their registrations, or the money to buy the equipment, Dehomag would perform the work for them. Insurers, for example, could send quarterly data directly to the Lichterfelde office for processing. Volume was important. "Since the work is done by Dehomag," advertised a company solicitation, the approach was recommended for any insurance company carrying "more than 15,000 members."[87]

Graphs, organizational charts, and work flow diagrams published by Dehomag bolstered the modern technological feat of its data processing. One work flow diagram showed the complex method by which handwritten forms and questionnaires in any agency's master personnel file were marshaled through a dozen separate sorting, proofing, resorting, and tabulating stages until results were finalized.[88] An individual looking at a plain paper form filled out by pen or pencil might never comprehend the tortuous route that document would take through the Hollerith process.

One of the most aggressive locales implementing Hollerith technology for race science was the city of Hamburg. Doctors there submitted extensive forms on all their patients to a Central Health Passport Archive where the information could be retrieved when needed and exchanged with other registries. Archive officials asked for reciprocal exchanges with "health and welfare institutions of all kinds, economic welfare, youth and education welfare, court decisions, special foster care, sterilizations . . . and all other sentences where personality evaluations are considered."[89]

Raceology was enabled as never before. Statistician Zahn extolled the fact that "registered persons can be observed continually, [through] the cooperation of statistical central offices . . . [so] other statistical population matters can be settled and regulated." Zahn proposed "a single file for [the] entire population to make possible an ethnic biological diagnosis [to] turn today's theory into tomorrow's practice. Such a file would serve both practical considerations as well as science," he argued, adding, "Clarified pictures of the volume of genetic diseases within the population . . . now gives science a new impetus to conduct research . . . which should promote good instead of bad genetic stock."[90]

Genetic denunciations and routine evaluations were adjudicated by the Genetic Health Courts based on a combination of anecdotal evidence and Hollerith data. The accused included parents guilty of no more than the misfortune of a birth-defected child, innocent newborns of the statistically suspect, helpless individuals condemned as depressed or psychiatric within a world gone mad, and those who just didn't fit into the new Nazi milieu.[91]

In the sterilization program's first year, 1934, more than 84,600 cases brought to the Genetic Health Courts resulted in 62,400 forced sterilizations. In 1935, 88,100 genetic trials yielded 71,700 forced sterilizations.[92]

Eventually, sterilization was viewed as merely preliminary to more drastic measures for cleansing the Reich. Zahn warned in a statistical journal article: "population politics, according to the principles of racial hygiene, must promote valuable genetic stock, prevent the fertility of inferior life, and be aware of genetic degeneration. In other words, this means superior life selection on the one hand, and the eradication of genetically unwanted stock on the other hand. The ethnic biological diagnosis is indispensable to carry out this task."[93]

WHEN HERMAN HOLLERITH designed his first punch card, he made it the size of a dollar bill.[94]

For IBM, information was money. The more Germany calculated, tabulated, sorted, and analyzed, the greater the demand for machines. Equally important, once a machine was leased, it required vast quantities of punch cards. In many cases, a single tabulation required thousands of cards. Each card was designed to be used only once, and in a single operation. When Dehomag devised more in-depth data processing, the improvements only bolstered card demand. How many punch cards were needed? Millions—per week.[95]

Punch cards sped through the huffing machines of the Third Reich like tiny high-speed mechanized breaths rapidly inhaled and exhaled one time and one time only. But Hollerith systems were delicate, precision-engineering instruments that depended on a precision-engineered punch card manufactured to exacting specifications under ideal conditions. Because electrical current in the machines sensed the rectangular holes, even a microscopic imperfection would make the card inoperable and could foul up the entire works.

So IBM production specifications were rigorous. Coniferous chemical pulp was milled, treated, and cured to create paper stock containing no more than 5 percent ash, and devoid of ground wood, calk fibers, processing chemicals, slime carbon, or other impurities that might conduct electricity and "therefore cause incorrect machine sensing." Residues, even in trace amounts, would accumulate on gears and other mechanisms, eventually causing jams and system shutdowns. Electrical testing to isolate defective sheets was mandatory. Paper, when cut, had to lie flat without curl or wrinkle, and feature a hard, smooth finish on either side that yielded a "good snap or rattle."[96]

Tolerances necessitated laboratory-like mill conditions. Paper thickness: .0067 inches plus or minus only a microscopic .0005 inch. Width: 3.25 inches with a variance of plus .007 inches or minus .003 inches. Two basic lengths were produced: 5.265 inches and 7.375 inches, plus or minus only .005 inch in either case. Edges were to be cut at true right angles, corners at perfect 60 degree angles, with a quarter-inch along the top and three-eighths along the side, all free from blade creases with the paper grain running the length of the card. Relative humidity of 50 percent and a temperature of 70–75 degrees Fahrenheit was required at all times, including transport and storage.[97]

Printing of the customer's name and specific project name was to be legible but not excessively inked and in no circumstances sufficient to dent the card or nudge it out of its plane, which could microscopically alter thickness. Text or numbers had to be printed in precise positions to line up with punching devices and machine gauges. IBM instructions to mills declared, "These specifications are absolutely necessary" and any variation "could distort the result."[98]

Only IBM could make and sell the unique punch cards for its machines. Indeed, punch cards were the precious currency of data processing. Depending upon the market, IBM derived as much as a third of its profit from card sales. Overseas sales were even more of a profit center. Punch card profits were enough to justify years of federal anti-trust litigation designed to break the company's virtual monopoly on their sale and manufacture.[99]

When Herman Hollerith invented his technology at the close of the previous century, he understood the enduring commercial tactic of proliferating a single universal system of hardware and ensuring that he alone produced the sole compatible soft goods. Hollerith was right to size his card like the dollar. IBM's punch card monopoly was nothing less than a license to print money.

In the Third Reich's first years, Germany was completely dependent upon IBM NY for its punch cards. Even after the factory in Lichterfelde opened, German manufactured machines were useless without cards imported from the United States. Card presses would eventually be built in Germany, but until that time, Dehomag was constantly scrambling to import the millions of cards ordered each week by its customers. To guard against sudden shortages, Lichterfelde needed a six-month supply—enough to fill fifty-five railroad cars. Half the stock was stored off-site in leased warehouses, and the rest in the factory.[100]

So vital was the production of paper products that in May 1934 the Reich Ministry of Economic Affairs sought to regulate mills. An Economics Ministry decree placed an eighteen-month moratorium on establishing, closing, or expanding paper mills without the specific permission of the Reich. Dehomag hoped to have its card presses in operation before the moratorium expired.[101]

IBM was making so much profit in Germany, it was causing problems. About $1 million profit was suddenly earned by the end of 1933, this at a time when nearly all of German industry was being battered due to the international anti-Nazi boycott. Dehomag had sold an unprecedented 237 percent of its 1933 quota—outpacing all IBM foreign operations combined. Yet Nazi business precepts denounced large corporate profits, especially those earned by foreign corporations. No wonder a nervous IBM auditor in Europe conceded to IBM NY, "Dehomag is in an extremely dangerous position, not only with respect to taxation, but it may be cited as a sort of monopolistic profiteer and, where primarily owned by foreigners, it may be seriously damaged by unfriendly publicity."[102]

For Heidinger, IBM profits were good news. His personal bonus, expressed as a stock dividend, would total nearly a half million Reichsmarks. He wanted his share. But Watson was not so inclined. Reich currency regulations sequestered profits into frozen bank accounts disbursable only within Germany. Heidinger could be paid, but not Watson. Moreover, newly enacted decrees taxed profit dividends harshly. If Watson couldn't receive his money, he saw no reason why anyone else should either. As the chief stockholder, Watson voted that no dividends would be paid.[103]

Heidinger would not abide Watson first usurping Dehomag and now usurping his share of the profits. Dehomag's extraordinary growth was an accomplishment Heidinger had personally sculpted by virtue of his Nazi connections. He wanted the financial reward he felt he deserved. The war for control of IBM's money in Germany only escalated.

Conflict arose in 1933 as soon as IBM announced the merger of its existing German subsidiaries, the million-dollar expansion, and new factory construction. Since Heidinger owned a token share of one of the old minor companies being folded into the new larger Dehomag, he expected his stock to be purchased as part of the consolidation. Watson refused, even though the buyout amounted to only RM 2,000, or about $500.[104]

On September 25, 1933, IBM's European Manager, Walter Jones, placed the question squarely with Watson personally. Heidinger, reported Jones, "now thinks IBM should take this [RM 2,000] off his hands and asked that the matter be submitted to you." A New York auditor acknowledged on Watson's behalf that IBM did in fact need Heidinger's shares to effect the merger. But the auditor added, since "the stock at the moment is worthless . . . [because it has] lost its entire capital through its operations . . . we do not think it would be fair for IBM to pay him anything for it."[105]

Heidinger knew his stock had become worthless only by virtue of the losses engineered by Watson to avoid taxes.

Heidinger fought back. He went directly to the Reich tax authorities, briefed them on IBM's entire complex merger plans, and asked for a formal ruling on the company's tax avoidance strategy. If Heidinger couldn't get his $500, it would be costly for the parent company. Quickly, IBM learned it was very expensive to fight the feisty Heidinger.[106]

Tax officials proposed an assessment as high as a half million dollars.

Protracted negotiations ensued with the tax boards. Streams of letters and cables crisscrossed the Atlantic. Numbers, from the ferocious to the moderate, bandied between IBM offices. Heidinger had positioned himself to "save the day" by negotiating the taxes down to a quarter of their proposed assessment. New York began to comprehend the process. IBM auditor Connolly at one point understated the predicament: "I should not be surprised if he [Heidinger] set up scares [with government officials] and talked them off for the sound of it."[107]

Financial battling between Berlin and New York seemed endless. Heidinger continuously tried to extract bits of compensation and sometimes trivial sums of expense money. IBM would block him through its controllers, managers, and attorneys. Heidinger would then retaliate by aggressively "consulting" Reich bureaucrats, which invariably led to added costs. Connolly openly asked in one letter if Dehomag could just pursue its corporate business without Heidinger "running to the German government every time for approval."[108]

One conflict came to a head at the June 10, 1934, Dehomag board meeting. Heidinger wanted IBM NY to pay his dividend taxes resulting from the merger. He also resented the highly detailed financial reports required each month by IBM auditors. Watson refused to pay Heidinger's dividend taxes and his auditors would not relent on their micromanaging oversight. At the board meeting, Heidinger angrily threatened that if his view did not prevail, than Dehomag was no longer an independent German company, but a foreign-dominated firm. As such, he would notify authorities in Berlin. Dehomag would then be assessed an extra quarter-million in special taxes and "prohibited from using . . . the word *Deutsche*" in its name, since that term was reserved for Aryan businesses. Without the word *Deutsche* in Dehomag, he warned, government and commercial contracts would be lost. Minutes of the June 10 exchange were omitted from the meeting's written record. Details, however, were summarized in a separate letter to New York.[109]

Ironically, when it came time to making capital investments, Heidinger took a completely opposite approach. In a memo asking IBM NY to undertake an expensive expansion of facilities, Heidinger asserted, "The management can merely submit proposals; the decision as to whether something should be done about it, is the responsibility of the owners."[110]

Ultimately, IBM and Heidinger forged one battle-scarred compromise after another, howsoever transient. But no matter how insolent or disruptive Heidinger became, Watson refused to disengage from Dehomag's lucrative partnership with Nazi Germany. In fact, Watson was determined to deploy as many lawyers, accountants, and managers as necessary—and personally visit Berlin as often as required—to make sure IBM received all the profit—frozen or not. The fight with Dehomag would continue—not to reign in its technologic alliance with the Third Reich, but rather to ensure that the profits continued and remained unshared.

WATSON KNEW he needed to stay close to developments in Germany. In 1934, he visited twice. The first was a brief stay in late June to oversee the final merger of four IBM subsidiaries into the new larger Dehomag, a transaction long delayed by negotiations with the tax authorities. In addition, a new management and stock participation contract was needed for Heidinger. Watson wanted to be on hand if any last-minute disputes arose with Heidinger.[111]

When Watson visited Berlin that June, the Reich's forced sterilization program was just ramping up. Everywhere, Jewish misery was evident. Nazi Brown Shirts noisily blocked the doorways of Jewish-owned shops. Unemployed Jews were moving out of their homes. Signs declaring Jews "not wanted" were prominently posted outside stores and cafes. But Watson did not focus on the Nazi war against the Jews and other non-Aryans. He was concerned with IBM's market victories in Germany and his war against any potential competition. IBM's only possible rival was Powers.

Dehomag didn't own the entire German market for punch cards—only 95 percent of it. Since the first days of Herman Hollerith's census contracts at the start of the twentieth century, IBM and its predecessor companies had been dog-fighting the Powers Accounting Machine Company in the United States and indeed anywhere in the world Powers tried to do business.

James Powers was a Russian immigrant to America who had helped the U.S. Census Bureau break free of Hollerith's monopoly in 1905 by developing a similar card sorter. As such, Powers and the Hollerith companies constantly jousted and litigated on patent rights. In 1914, while Watson's criminal conviction for anti-trust was in appeal, a financially battered Powers, anxious to avoid further confrontations, simply asked Watson's CTR to license its punch card technology. Without that license, Powers declared it would go out of business. Under the specter of federal charges, Watson ostentatiously agreed to license his competitor, Powers, but at an exorbitant 25 percent royalty. This would ensure that Powers would survive as a miniscule player in the punch card field, thus obviating federal charges of total monopoly. But the 25 percent royalty also meant that Powers' machines were more expensive for customers and therefore profoundly less competitive. Besides, IBM would receive a good share of all of Powers' revenues.[112]

After the government dropped its anti-trust case against Watson, he was less inclined to let Powers survive. Recalling a tactic from his NCR days, Watson litigated against Powers extensively for various forms of patent infringement, raided its key managers in America and abroad, and systematically pressured clients to switch to Hollerith systems.[113]

In Germany, Powers did enjoy some minor installations dating back to the 1920s primarily because it sold rather than leased its machines and had developed some highly specialized models. What's more, some machines, even though old, were simply still functioning. *Some* was too many for Watson. Dehomag continued the IBM legacy of litigation by suing Powers in Germany. But this time, it was not for patent infringement. It was for not being sufficiently Aryan.

In the highly charged Nazi business environment, where certain words possessed special meaning, Powers was one of many firms that rushed to declare themselves "under German management." But in reality, charged Heidinger in the court complaint, two Americans were managing the Powers firm. Even after the Powers board of directors ousted its two American managers, Heidinger claimed that the foreigners were nonetheless secretly controlling the company. All this, he argued, was designed by Powers "to facilitate marketing for its products" within the Third Reich, thereby competing unfairly with Dehomag through false advertising. Dehomag, on the other hand, was pure German and free from foreign influence, the complaint attested.[114]

In late April 1934, the court agreed and permanently enjoined Powers from representing that it was "German." Punishment for infractions, the court ruled, would be an unlimited fine or imprisonment up to six months for each infraction.[115]

Watson had specifically authorized the Powers suit and been kept up to date on its developments. What's more, Watson wanted to identify Powers' clients and convert them to IBM equipment. Dehomag salesmen kept detailed intelligence on all Powers customers. Upon request of the New York office, Lichterfelde was able to produce a list of every Powers customer, in perfect columnar fashion, listing the year the client purchased Powers equipment, which units were rented or purchased, the machine's application, and which Dehomag sales office was nearby. That list was regurgitated alphabetically, chronologically, and geographically.[116]

The uses for a finely tuned Hollerith surveillance system were unlimited. Germany never lost sight of its most important objective: the war against the Jewish people and other undesirables. In that war, Germany would undertake a steep, years-long technologic climb as IBM systems improved, Nazi registration campaigns multiplied, and the net tightened. The Third Reich was just beginning to apply Dehomag solutions.

By the end of 1934, medical, welfare, and insurance offices were joined in their punch card registrations by nursing homes and sanitariums as well as an ever-increasing number of German healthcare practitioners. A Registry of anti-social persons was launched. Heinrich Himmler, head of the SS, inaugurated the *SS Statistical Yearbook*. And "continuing education" courses in racial hygiene conducted by noted statisticians became widely advertised.[117]

In addition, preparations were finalizing for a national *Work Book*. Employers were to fill out a booklet for each employee and then submit it to the appropriate Labor Office. Eventually, 354 such Labor Offices would be opened across Germany. While the *Work Book* was overtly a means of identifying and regimenting every worker in the Third Reich, a data field near the top right asked whether, under the current Nazified definitions, the worker was a "foreigner or stateless." *Work Books*, tabulated by punch card, would become the basis for ever-increasing population scrutiny. Jews, of course, were not permitted to work. When they were discovered, they were terminated. He who did not work would starve. Eventually, without a *Work Book*, Jews could not obtain ration cards to purchase food.[118]

Ultimately, card by card, sort by sort, those of any Jewish blood would be weeded out from every corner of German society no matter how they tried to hide.

In 1934, statistician Karl Keller expostulated the popular expectation that genealogical tracing technology would eventually discover all the Jews. Writing in *Allgemeines Statistisches Archiv,* Keller assured, "The determination of Jewish descent will not be difficult because membership in the Jewish faith and membership in the Jewish culture were nearly identical before the emancipation of the Jews. It is therefore sufficient to check the change of denominations in church registers and registry offices for the last 130 years."[119]

Statistical sweeps with the help of Hollerith technology were already canvassing baptism records, birth and death registries, and other church records, not only to certify Aryanism, but also to isolate Judaism. Dehomag's customers included such bodies as the Catholic Burial Society in Munich and the Church Council in Eisenach. Some church groups processed information on their own equipment, some merely reported their data to other monitoring agencies. Eventually, the Non-Germanic Family Baptismal Registry, compiled by evangelical bodies, would list a million names of Jews and others who had converted to Christianity during the previous century.[120]

Understanding it possessed the technology to scrutinize an entire nation, Dehomag proudly advertised its systems with a certain unmistakable flair. The company created two surrealistic promotional posters. One was a giant punch card hovering over a factory beaming its X-ray-like searchlights into every room of every floor. The caption read: "Hollerith illuminates your company, provides surveillance and helps organize." A second poster depicted a giant odious eye floating in the sky projecting a punch card over everything below. The caption read: "See everything with Hollerith punch cards."[121]

No one would escape. This was something new for mankind. Never before had so many people been identified so precisely, so silently, so quickly, and with such far-reaching consequences.

The dawn of the Information Age began at the sunset of human decency.

I
II
III
IV
V
VI
VII
VIII
IX
X
XI
XII
XIII
XIV
XV

A NAZI MEDAL FOR WATSON

THOUSANDS OF SWASTIKA FLAGS FLAPPED TEN-ABREAST across long marching columns of *Sturm Abteilung,* goose-stepping under a warm Nuremberg sun. Chevroned glockenspielers and drummers festively tapped martial rhythms beneath tasseled regimental standards that wagged astride 100,000 rippling shoulders of National Socialism. Dressed in paramilitary garb, a legion of stern-eyed conscripted laborers, each bearing a long shovel slung across their collarbone like a rifle, tramped along boulevards bannered with fifty-foot swastika bunting. A throng of 56,000 jack-booted disciples sprawled the length of a vast field until their image vanished into the distance. September 15, 1935, was Party Day, a momentous climax to a week of choreographed Nazi demonstrations. It was epic.[1]

Over cobble-stoned streets, paved market squares, tar-topped avenues, and embedded trolley tracks, the stage-managed multitudes flowed in testament to *Führer* worship. As rectangular human masses passed reviewing points, officials of the NSDAP and German government stood at attention and pumped their arms stiff, palms outstretched. Everywhere the rallying call trumpeted: *"Sieg."* Everywhere the crowd answered: *"Heil! Sieg . . . Heil! Sieg . . . Heil!"*[2]

Nuremberg was kinetic with cordons of artillery and air defense guns, light tanks, and horse cavalry brigades lumbering beside armies of uniformed men. Warplanes roared above in acrobatic fly-bys. Then they theatrically bombed and burned a sham village constructed on a field. Hundreds of miles away, German U-boats suddenly emerged from beneath the waves to conduct naval maneuvers coordinated with the other land-air shows of military might.[3]

The Third Reich was at war—even if the invasions had not yet begun. Those would come. For now, Germany wanted the world to know that it was ready for territorial defense and conquest. The world understood and recoiled. All of Germany's illicit rearmament was in flagrant violation of the Treaty of Versailles, which after the Great War guaranteed a demilitarized German republic. Front-page headlines and worried diplomatic dispatches openly wondered when a hot new conflict would erupt. International anti-Nazi agitation—boycotts and energetic protest gatherings—demanded civilized nations break Germany's economic back to deter her from aggression and Jewish persecution.

But even if Germany's territorial war had not yet begun, its battle against Jewish existence was raging. So despite the military marching and ostentatious weaponry, this day, September 15, 1935, would be dominated not by border threats, but by Nazism's anti-Semitic frenzy.

Since 1933, the Reich had legislated Jewish dislocation from virtually every facet of German professional, commercial, and social life. Many Jews were so thoroughly excluded by Aryan mandates, they were reduced to buying and selling mainly to each other just to survive. Pauperization of German Jewry was a real threat and malnutrition of Jewish children was already attracting the attention of international aid agencies. Yet many Jews still clung to their relative anonymity. In businesses owned or controlled by Jews, or where their participation was essential, Jews felt they could continue unidentified, unnoticed, unmolested.[4] If they could just stand in, they would not stand out.

Nazi theorists continued to bicker over what amount of Judaic parentage constituted an excludable Jew, and how far to trace bloodline. Determining Aryan pedigree was complicated by endless demographic and geographic variables that simply slipped through the punch cards. Cagey replies to questionnaires from individuals or companies nervous about their answers, as well as changing residential and business addresses, undermined the process. Moreover, suspect citizens rushed to baptismal fonts and church pews to assume new or more pronounced Christian personas. In consequence, tens of thousands of racial purity examinations had been convened since 1933.[5]

Laxity and ambiguity helped. About a third of Germany's nearly 450,000 remaining registered Jews dwelled in Germany's smaller cities and towns where in many instances they continued to exist unmolested. Many local and national government agencies often found it easier to continue trading with reliable Jewish firms than locate an untested alternative. *Hausfraus* managing a tight budget commonly sneaked away to Jewish retailers seeking discounts after their dogmatic husbands went off to work.[6]

Doctrinaire Nazis fought back. Night classes for housewives instructed women how and why to avoid Jewish shops. A court ruled that husbands were not legally bound to pay for purchases their wives made at Jewish stores. The mayor of Baden was fired when his dealings with Jews were discovered. Jew-baiters such as Julius Streicher published rabid, pornographic newspaper accounts of ritual murder and rampant sexual perversion by Jews, and then cajoled and humiliated all loyal Germans into boycotting Jewish enterprises. Brown Shirts blocked the doors of Jewish establishments and graffittied their exteriors. But too many Germans simply would not or could not comply with the complex confusing strictures to not buy from Jews. Most importantly, too many simply did not know where all the Jews were.[7]

In the absence of an explicit law defining exactly who in Germany was a Jew, Nazi persecution was far from hermetic. For years, such a definition would have been a cloudy exercise. Even if Nazis could agree on such an exegesis, no one could back up the definition with hard data. Since the advent of the Third Reich, thousands of Jews nervously assumed they could hide from the Aryan clause.

But Jews could not hide from millions of punch cards thudding through Hollerith machines, comparing names across generations, address changes across regions, family trees and personal data across unending registries. It did not matter that the required forms or questionnaires were filled in by leaking pens and barely sharpened pencils, only that they were later tabulated and sorted by IBM's precision technology.

Even as Hitler's fanatic followers thunder-marched through Nuremberg, Hollerith machines in Berlin were dispassionately clicking and rattling through stacks of punch cards slapping into hoppers to identify the enemy for the next drastic measures.

Throughout 1935, race specialists, bolstered by population computations and endless tabular printouts, proffered their favorite definitions of Jewishness. Some theorems were so sweeping as to include even the faintest Jewish ancestry. But most tried to create pseudo-scientific castes limited in scope. These latter efforts would encompass not only full Jews who professed the religion or possessed four Jewish grandparents, but also the so-called *three-quarter, half,* and *one-quarter* Jews of lesser Jewish lineage.[8]

Adolf Hitler was personally aware of preliminary Hollerith findings that while only about a half million Germans registered as Jews in the census, the veins of many more coursed with traces of Jewish blood. About a million more.[9] He wanted something done about the continuing Jewish presence. The Jews Hitler feared most were the ones not apparent. *Der Führer* had been working on the long-awaited racial definition for some weeks, but the enforceable formulae and calculations were still inconclusive.[10]

On September 10, 1935, he flew from Berlin to Nuremberg to open the Party Day celebrations. Church bells sounded and flowers were thrown adoringly as his automobile wended through the streets paced by newsreel cars. But belying the flourish was a Hitler impatient to intensify Jewish obliteration.[11]

Suddenly, on September 13, 1935, Hitler demanded that a decree be hammered out—now—within forty-eight hours, in time for his appearance before the *Reichstag* as the culmination of Party Day festivities. Top racial experts of the Interior Ministry flew in for the assignment. Working with drafts shuttled between Hitler's abode and police headquarters, twin decrees of disenfranchisement were finally patched together. *The Law for the Protection of German Blood* and a companion decree entitled the *Reich Citizenship Law* deprived Jews of their German citizenship and now used the term explicitly—*Jew*, not non-Aryan. Moreover, Jews were proscribed from marrying or having sexual relations with any Aryan. Jewish employers could not even hire an Aryan woman under the age of 45—a concession to Streicher's hysteria regarding sexual perversion. The laws would apply not only to full Jews, but also to half and quarter Jews as well, all according to complex racial mathematics.[12]

Despite the decree language, the precise arithmetic of Jewish ancestry had still not been finalized. How could one differentiate a quarter Jew from a so-called *Mischling*, or person of some mixed Aryan and Jewish blood? Indeed, it would be months of drafting and redrafting before those fractions were finally settled.[13]

Laborious and protracted paper searches of individual genealogical records were possible. But each case could take months of intensive research. That wasn't fast enough for the Nazis. Hitler wanted the Jews identified en masse. Once drafted, the Nuremberg regulations would be completely dependent upon Hollerith technology for the fast, wholesale tracing of Jewish family trees that the Reich demanded. Hollerith systems offered the Reich the speed and scope that only an automated system could to identify not only half and quarter Jews, but even eighth and sixteenth Jews.[14]

With the denouement of September 15 approaching, Germany's own sense of Jewish numbers was changing dynamically. As Security Police Chief Heydrich had concluded, "it has become apparent that a great number of Jews in Germany have become baptized in the Evangelical and Catholic faiths with the idea that once they changed their residence, they would no longer appear as Jews in the registries."[15]

Earlier in 1935, the Party's Race Political Office had estimated the total number of "race Jews." Thanks to Dehomag's people-counting methods, the Nazis believed that the 1933 census, which recorded a half million observant Jews, was now obsolete. Moreover, Nazis were convinced that the often-quoted total of some 600,000 Jews, which was closer to Germany's 1925 census, was a mere irrelevance. In mid-June 1935, Dr. Leonardo Conti, a key Interior Ministry raceologist, declared 600,000 represented just the "practicing Jews." The true number of racial Jews in the Reich, he insisted, exceeded 1.5 million. Conti, who would soon become the Ministry's State Secretary for Health overseeing most race questions, was a key assistant to the officials rushing to compose the Nuremberg Jewish laws for Hitler.[16]

Working in bureaucratic anterooms and elegant villas, the race scientists tore up version after version until their paper supply ran out. So they finished writing on menus. Finally, at 2:30 A.M. on September 15, armed with the most up-to-date statistical information, the decrees were cobbled into presentable form.[17] The scene was set for Hitler's announcement that evening.

At 9 P.M., September 15, a grandiose if improvised hall decorated with streamers and ceiling fabrics was convened as a *Reichstag* for 600 deputies. They gathered for the sole purpose of ratifying the laws their *Führer* would declare. Hitler outwardly appeared as his usual charismatic self, carefully attired in riding pants tucked into polished jack-boots, a red swastika armband around his left elbow, and a tie neatly buried under a fully buttoned soldier's jacket. His hair, austerely slicked to one side, bannered above his unmistakable narrow mustache to create Nazism's emblematic face. But to at least some observing him, *der Führer* seemed tired from the long debate over Jewish definition. From his seat on the stage, he ascended three steps to a podium overlooking a massive assembly of the devoted stretching dozens of rows back and more dozens left and right of a great center aisle that was empty except for the obligatory photographer and a newsreel cameraman. Behind, a full orchestra and organist sat stilled, their instruments set down. Facing him, thousands waited, rapt with anticipation.[18]

Hitler's speech, revised at the last minute, lasted only twelve minutes. Even though passionate, and at times fiery, his voice sounded weak. He rambled from point to point. Throughout, *der Führer* tore into a world community that was offending German honor and boycotting German goods. As usual, he blamed the Reich's one great enemy. "We must notice here," he accused, "mostly Jewish elements are at work." He ripped into "international Jewish agitation" and declared, "The time had come to confront Jewish interests with German national interest."[19]

Referring to the population statistics rendered by his raceologists but rounding off the numbers, *der Führer* cried out, "a nation of 65 million persons has a right to demand that she is not respected less than the arbitrariness of 2 million persons." For the first time, Hitler had left behind the well-worn totals of 400,000 to 600,000 German Jews and now pronounced the updated Hollerith tabulated numbers.[20]

New racial laws, he promised, would immediately strip German Jews of their citizenship, even more severely restrict their activities and outlaw their ability to hoist a German flag. More than once, Hitler remonstrated, "the law is only an attempt at legal regulation. However, should this not work . . . should Jewish agitation within and without Germany continue, we will then examine the situation again."[21]

Gesturing fanatically, he concluded with this warning: The new law "is an attempt at the legal regulation of a problem, which, if it fails, must be turned over to the Nazi Party for final solution."[22]

The pleasant Nuremberg night and reverberating *Sieg Heils* suddenly turned to rain. Hitler's well-photographed smile was now nowhere to be seen, not even as the crowd cheered him all the way from the *Reichstag* hall to his hotel.[23]

Everywhere, the new formulaic approach to Jewish persecution exploded into worrisome headlines. Under a page one banner story, the *New York Times* lead was typical: "National Socialist Germany definitely flung down the gauntlet before the feet of Western liberal opinion tonight . . . [and] decreed a series of laws that put Jews beyond the legal and social pale of the German nation." The paper went on to detail the legal import of the ancestral fractions.[24] The news was everywhere and inescapable.

The League of Nations' High Commissioner for Refugees Coming from Germany issued all member governments a long, detailed, and scathing report of the Reich's determination to persecute Jews on an unprecedented basis, all based on tabulating the percentages of their ancestry. The report's opening page sounded a special alarm: "Even more ominous was the declaration of the German Chancellor: '. . . should, however, the attempt at legal regulation fail, then the problem must be turned over to the National Socialist Party for final solution.'"25

Ironically, while all understood the evil anti-Jewish process underway, virtually none comprehended the technology that was making it possible. The mechanics were less than a mystery, they were transparent.

In 1935, while the world shook at a rearmed Germany speeding toward a war of European conquest and total Jewish destruction, one man saw not revulsion, but opportunity—not horror and devastation, but profit and dividends. Thomas Watson and IBM indeed accelerated their breakneck alliance with Nazism. Now Thomas Watson, through and because of IBM, would become the commercial syndic of Germany, committed as never before to global advocacy for the Third Reich, helping his utmost to counteract Hitler's enemies and further *der Führer*'s military, political, economic, and anti-Semitic goals. Even as he continued as a statesman of American capitalism and a bulwark of international commerce, Watson would become a hero in Nazi Germany—both to the common man and to Adolf Hitler himself.

NAZI GERMANY was IBM's second most important customer after the U.S. market.

Business was good. Hitler needed Holleriths. Rigid dictatorial control over all aspects of commerce and social life mandated endless reporting and oversight. What's more, Germany's commercial isolation and preparation for war compelled the National Socialist regime into a frenzied campaign of autarky that necessitated upward spirals of surveillance and bureaucratic meddling into the smallest industrial details. Nazi planners wanted every object in daily life—from trucks to paper clips—coded, inventoried, and regimented. But no matter how preoccupied with economic and armament drives, the Reich inculcated every program with its maniacal desire to eradicate the Jewish presence.

IBM was guided by one precept: know your customer, anticipate their needs. Watson stayed close to his customer with frequent visits to Germany and continuous daily micro-managed oversight of the business.

Everywhere one turned in America or Germany in 1935, it was clear that identification and exclusion of the Jews was only the beginning. The next step was confiscation and Aryanization. During the two previous years, most Aryanizations were disorganized. Jews were forced from their business or profession and then pressured to sell their enterprises to Aryans for a fraction of the value. Thousands of others fled the country as refugees with their portable possessions worriedly stuffed into bulging suitcases. Homes, vehicles, and chattels were left behind, often to be seized in satisfaction of trumped-up juridical penalties or simply taken over as abandoned property.[26]

Jewish presence in smaller towns now became the most precarious. Once identified, Jews were unable to earn a living, then unable to even purchase food or medical supplies. Local shopkeepers, kept in line by neighborhood anti-Jewish boycott vigilantes, prominently displayed signs forbidding Jews to shop within. Pointed threats and a late night visit from hooligans usually sealed the family's departure decision. During 1935, dozens of localities were able to post signs on their outskirts declaring that they were *Jew-free* and/or Jews were no longer permitted to purchase lands or even enter the town limits. As Jews were methodically driven to lodge with friends and family in larger cities, they left behind their real estate and often much of their goods. Now the body of unattended Jewish property was growing.[27]

When a town became Jew-free, it became a publicized event. In Germany, the town administration or local Nazi groups would eagerly advertise the accomplishment. Foreign newspaper and radio broadcasts chronicling Nazi oppression frequently reported the development as well. Typical was an article in the *New York Times,* May 28, 1935, headlined "All Jews Quit Hersbruck." The article reported, "A swastika flag has been hoisted over a house in Hersbruck, near Nuremberg, which has been the home of the last remaining Jewish resident in the district."[28]

But Watson didn't need to read about Aryanization in newspapers. He discovered it personally. In July 1935, Watson visited Berlin. That July, Nazi thugs ran wild in the streets of Berlin smashing the windows of fashionable Jewish stores. One of those department stores was owned by the Wertheims, family friends of the Watsons. The Watson family learned that to protect the store, Mr. Wertheim first transferred the property to his Aryan wife, but then ultimately decided to sell "for next to nothing" and escape to Sweden. On another visit to Berlin, the Watsons and other IBM executives were invited to an elegant reception at the Japanese embassy. While sipping tea in the garden, a German diplomat boasted that the exquisite home formerly belonged to a Jew who fled the country. Such new ownership of greatly discounted homes was now common in Berlin.[29]

By late 1935, however, the Nazis envisioned a more systematic and state-controlled process to expropriating Jewish property. Just after the enactment of the Nuremberg Laws, the Nazis began floating plans for a clearinghouse to gobble up all Jewish holdings for a pittance. This plan was no secret. It was widely promoted in Germany through the Party's Economic Information Agency. And the news traveled abroad. A *New York Times* article on September 24, 1935, was headlined "Nazis Plan to Buy Out All Jewish Firms; Stress Bargains Resulting from the Boycott." The article reported, "The plan calls for the purchase of Jewish firms by a central corporation, and their redistribution among ambitious Aryan businessmen. It is suggested that such businesses can be obtained cheaply. . . . The Nazi organ responsible for this 'solution of the Jewish problem' makes startling guesses as to what the prices would be. It says, 'some fairly large Jewish firms can be purchased for 40,000 marks.' Evidently . . . the Jews can be induced to feel a very pressing desire to sell." The newspaper noted that under such conditions, Jews might then be faced either with the prospect of "emigration or semi-starvation."[30]

As part of the drive to liquidate Jewish assets, Nazis began visiting Jewish homes and invalidating their passports. Now Jews could not even become refugees without paying a confiscatory flight tax of 25 percent of their holdings in Germany.[31] Identifying Jewish possessions was the next step.

Banks, financial institutions, and pension funds were among Dehomag's most important clients. Indeed, Dehomag maintained an entire department for the banking industry. IBM designed highly specialized tabulating equipment for banks, including the BK and BKZ models, which were capable of producing customer statements and recording specific transactions. On August 12, 1935, savings banks were suddenly required to provide the *Reichsbank* with detailed information about all their depositors. Some banks used the Hollerith process by coding accounts into one of ten professional categories Dehomag had established. *Hollerith Nachrichten* published a notice for those institutions that did not yet own sorting machines, advertising that Dehomag could do the sorting in-house for a fee. The company bragged that it possessed the ability to cross-reference account numbers on bank deposits with census data, including grouping by profession or industry.[32]

Dehomag's financial documentation capabilities soared when it unveiled a powerful new model dubbed the D-11, which could process numerous account developments, compute interest, and help create detailed customer records. Within months, the new D-11 would allow high-speed data management of bank accounts at dazzling levels.[33]

At the same time, the human identification process proliferated. Local and regional statistical offices registered new births on Hollerith cards, carefully noting the religion of both parents. Marriages were also registered on punch cards, again noting the religion of both partners. These cards were then forwarded to regional Dehomag service bureaus, such as the one in

Saarbrücken at Adolf Hitlerstrasse 80. More than half the local regional statistical offices operated card punchers, but could not purchase their own
sorters because of the backlog and expense of the machines. So Dehomag
conducted the sorts on its own premises, just as it did for so many tabulations. Once Dehomag completed its work, the data was sent on to the Reich
Statistical Office where it was combined with a confluence of other data
streams.[34]

Personal information about Jewish people in Germany was always
changing—precisely because of the innumerable dislocations Jews suffered.
For this reason, starting in 1935, the authorities required Jewish communal
leaders to report their members by age and gender no longer annually, but
quarterly.[35] Such data was just one more trickle comprising the river of cross-
indexed information Hitlerites processed to isolate the Jewish nemesis.

Eventually, the Hitler regime felt statistically ready to espouse regulations defining just what constituted a Jewish business.

A firm was labeled "Jewish" if the owner or a partner was Jewish, if
even a single Jew were in management or on the board of directors. If a
quarter of its shares or votes were held by Jews, or under Jewish influence
through nominees or agents, the company was classed Jewish; this regulation
made it increasingly difficult and dangerous to mask ownership. A company
could be owned and operated by undisputed Aryans, but if it maintained a
branch managed by a Jew, that branch would be declared Jewish.[36]

Naturally, it would be impossible to certify a company as being Jewish
unless denouncers knew the identities of all business principles and were
profoundly certain which of those individuals qualified as Jewish under the
Nuremberg Laws. But fewer Jews could hide from the dragnet IBM had
helped the Reich construct. This forced companies to quickly identify and
terminate, even if reluctantly, any of its Jewish management, and even its
own Jewish ownership.

Once a company was deemed to be Jewish, as defined under the special
regulations, its inventory and assets would ultimately be registered. Hollerith
systems that could inventory people could inventory merchandise as well.
Among Dehomag's most important customers were the Trade Statistics Office
in Hamburg, the *Reichspost,* and various national and local taxing offices.
Decrees of the Reich Economics Ministry's *Kommissar* for Price Control, beginning in 1936, required uniform reporting procedures by key industries. In
most cases, the installation of IBM machinery was mandatory in order to
comply. Government statisticians and Dehomag had developed coding systems for virtually all raw materials and finished goods. Eventually, the coding

system would make it possible for the Nazis to organize its seizures with stunning specificity.[37]

None of Germany's statistical programs came easy. All of them required on-going technical innovation. Every project required specific customized applications with Dehomag engineers carefully devising a column and corresponding hole to carry the intended information. Dummy cards were first carefully mocked-up in pen and pencil to make sure all categories and their placement were acceptable to both Dehomag and the reporting agency. No information could be input unless it conformed to Dehomag specifications. Therefore, the Reich tailored its data collection to match Hollerith requirements. Moreover, there was only one source to purchase the cards: Dehomag. The company sold them, generally in lots of 10,000, often preprinted with project names. Of course, once Dehomag approved the formats, it trained the reporting agency's personnel to execute the work.[38] Dehomag was Germany's data maestro.

During the frenetic rush to expand business with the Nazis and automate more and more Reich projects, never once was a word of restraint uttered by Watson about Dehomag's indispensable activities in support of Jewish persecution. No brakes. No cautions. Indeed, to protest Germany's crusade against Jewish existence would be nothing less than criticizing the company's number two customer. Despite the innumerable opportunities to disengage or decline to escalate in the war against the Jews, IBM never backed away. In fact, the opposite occurred.

Watson became intensely proud of the German subsidiary's accomplishments. In late November 1935, two months after the Nuremberg Laws were espoused, and just days after more headlines were made when the Reich issued highly detailed genealogical dicta defining just who was Jewish under the decree, Watson traveled to Berlin to celebrate Dehomag's twenty-fifth anniversary. A lavish company banquet was scheduled for November 27 at the exclusive Hotel Adlon. More than 150 invitations were distributed. IBM offices in New York, Switzerland, Italy, France, and Norway were represented by their top executives. Dignitaries such as U.S. Ambassador to Germany, William E. Dodd, Hitler's press attaché, Ernst Hanfstaengl, former German consul in New York, Otto Kiep, and Reich Economics Minister, Hjalmar Schacht were invited. Important industrial contacts were on the list. Even if some, such as Schacht, could not attend, most did.[39]

Sumptuous food was served in the Watson tradition of elaborate dinner events. The Heidingers, Rottkes, and Watsons toasted their success. But even as the precious crystal glinted and ornate silverware gleamed, the utilitarian machine rooms of Lichterfelde and countless other data processing offices throughout Germany continued their own demographic clatter. The machines never slept.

Not everyone could be as jubilant and splendid as the Watson revelers at the Hotel Adlon. Unseen and unheard were Jews, cowering in their homes, fearing visibility. Goebbels had already warned them. "We have spared the Jews," asserted Goebbels, "but if they imagine they can just stroll along the [fashionable] Kurfürstendamm as if nothing at all had happened, let them take my words as a last warning." In another warning, Goebbels demanded, "Jews must learn to break with their past behavior and leave public places in Germany to the Germans." These were not quiet comments murmured at obscure party meetings but public threats reprinted worldwide, including in the *New York Times* under headlines such as "Nazi Warns Jews to Stay at Home."[40]

Now Watson eagerly launched a program to expand Dehomag's capability. Ten more boxes of machinery had been shipped from New York to Hamburg in November 1935 on the SS *Hansa*. Millions of additional punch cards would be rushed across the ocean until Dehomag could produce them in Germany. Branch offices were opened throughout the Reich, the Lichterfelde factory was enlarged, and a second factory was established to manufacture spare parts.[41]

While in Berlin that November 1935, Watson attempted to gain technical information from Dr. Fels, a key Reich Statistical Office expert who had helped organize the 1933 census. Watson learned that despite Fels' expertise, he had been ousted from his position because he was Jewish. Dehomag delivered a note to Watson's hotel explaining that Fels was now living as an unemployed refugee with his family in New York, "in quite a bit of misery." The note added that IBM in America had declined to give him a job. But Watson wanted Fels' expertise. So immediately upon his return to America Watson arranged a meeting. On February 3, 1936, Fels briefed Watson in his Manhattan office and they spoke of such wide-ranging issues as the German census and the prospects for similar projects elsewhere. As for employment, Watson did assure he would ask around and see if any of the many organizations he was associated with might offer Fels a job.[42]

After the Fels briefing, joint exchanges on both sides of the Atlantic between IBM NY and Dehomag sales and technical staff became constant. These exchanges were highly selective, well thought out, and very costly investments in future work. Dozens of Dehomag salesmen, engineers, and managers came to America for training and exchange of expertise. IBM established a special sales training school in Endicott, New York, predominantly attended by German and other European IBMers. Sales training was necessary because despite all the proliferation in punch card systems, representatives encountered continual resistance from government officials on just how the elaborate new technology worked. At Endicott, salesmen learned how to fire the imagination of bureaucrats and convince them that IBM's technology could provide solutions for any governmental requirement—no matter how unprecedented.[43]

Four of IBM NY's brightest engineers and managers, all of Germanic descent, were eventually transferred from America to the Berlin operation: Walter Scharr in 1936, and Otto Haug, Erich Perschke, and Oskar Hoermann in the following years. One Austrian inventor, Gustav Tauschek, was so prized, he demanded—and was granted—an annual contract guaranteeing him six months with IBM in the United States and six months in his beloved Austria. Tauschek generated dozens of valuable patents. Indeed, anticipating Dehomag's expansion, IBM NY filed for patents in various European countries to protect the inventions of its German subsidiary.[44]

New devices never stopped appearing. Numbered gang punches type 501 for multiple punching. Electrical interpreters type 550 for analysis. Electrical accounting machine type 400 for zone punching. Summary punch type 516 for cumulative information. Dehomag developed its own motor-driven duplicating printing punch type 016 for high-speed processing, and calculating punches type 621 and type 623. Multiplying punches were able to tally the sum of two punched holes on a single card, shortening sort time. High-speed reproducers, alphabetic tabulators, numeric and alphabetic interpreters, horizontal sorters—a parade of metal magicians joined the repertoire.[45] Many of these devices were of course dual-purpose. They as routinely helped build Germany's general commercial, social, and military infrastructure as they helped a heightening tower of Nazi statistical offensives.

In Germany, some of the devices, such as the IBM Fingerprint Selecting Sorter, were only usable by Nazi security forces.[46]

Specialized printing presses for punch cards were finally installed in 1935, allowing Dehomag to print its own punch cards. In a typical eight-hour shift, allowing for pauses to change plates and re-ink, each press could produce 65,000 cards. Within two years, IBM would install fifty-nine such presses in Germany—fifty-two from the only European press source that could manufacture them, and seven from the United States, including several high-speed units five times faster than the European models.[47]

In 1936, Dehomag opened its first full-time school for customer training. Courses for beginning card punchers typically required two weeks of intensive study. Additional courses were needed to master the more delicate skills of operating the sorters and tabulators. Each new device required additional training. A Development Laboratory, staffed by ten engineers, was opened. Initial projects included high-speed punches and automatic paper feeders for the new D-11. Ironically, despite all its increased factory space, technical support from America, and extra investment, demand was so high that Dehomag was still two years behind in filling its mounting list of orders.[48] It was a never-ending battle to supply systems. And the Reich needed them so urgently.

IBM WAS MAKING a fortune. Since the day Hitler came to power, the company had been reaping millions from its German operation. How many millions might never be known because the company buried its profits in bizarre inter-company transactions. But the outward manifestations of IBM's growth and prosperity and the "admitted profits" it reported were amazing to a nation struggling to recover from the Depression.

"December 1933 was the largest December in the company's history," Watson boasted to stockholders during one early 1934 meeting. He added that January 1934 was also the largest January in the company's history and February 1934 saw conceded profits of $103,000 above the year before. Watson predicted the trend would continue throughout 1934. These profits were declared despite every attempt to weave revenues into complicated, untaxable inter-company shunts. Net income for 1933—to the extent it was identified given blocked accounts in Germany—was reported as $5.73 million, including income from foreign subsidiaries. Most telling, of $55.4 million in assets, $16.2 million was surplus cash.[49]

Net income for the first six months of 1934 was $3.4 million over the $2.9 million posted in 1933, even after adjusting for various inter-company charges. Income increased to $5 million for the first nine months of the year, or $7.18 per share over $6.22 per share the previous year. A dividend of 2 percent was declared in addition to the regular quarterly dividend.[50]

Equally impressive to the business press were the numbers for 1935. Watson began the year by predicting IBM's continued upsurge. "Our trade abroad is improving," reassured Watson, "as shown by the fact that for the first ten months of 1934 our exports increased about 35 percent over the corresponding period of 1933. One of the main factors contributing to industrial recovery may be found in the constantly increasing cooperation among political, industrial, and financial leaders." Million-dollar profits continued to rise in 1935. Shares for the year bloated to $9.38.[51]

However the funds were classed or categorized, Dehomag alone paid some $4.5 million in dividends to IBM during the early Hitler years.[52]

IBM announced it would erect a building at 32nd Street and Fifth Avenue in Manhattan. Then the company purchased $1,000 life insurance policies for all 6,900 of its employees on the job since January 1933 or earlier. While dedicating a new addition to the company's plant in Endicott just before Christmas 1934, Watson extravagantly announced a Yule gift—a 37 percent minimum wage increase for 7,000 workers. Shortly thereafter, newspapers revealed that Watson had become the highest paid executive in America. They dubbed him the "thousand dollar per day man." Watson received a bonus of 5 percent of all IBM profits worldwide. So his total salary amounted to $364,432 per year, or nearly as much as the combined salaries of the chairmen of Chrysler and General Motors. With characteristic aplomb, Watson defended his unprecedented compensation. Then IBM bought another Manhattan building site, this one at 57th and Madison.[53]

In mid-1935, Congress had passed a new law with an extraordinary impact on IBM: the Social Security Act. Congress had invented a bureaucracy no one was sure could even be implemented. Social Security would require a central file on nearly 30 million Americans.[54] Until this point, Hollerith systems had still not attained the technologic ability to create a single central registry. That is why so many repetitive sorts by statistical agencies were undertaken and updated so frequently.

When the Social Security law was passed, no budget appropriation and no infrastructure were in place because bureaucrats were convinced that "the machinery . . . to do the job . . . did not exist." Nor did the first Social Security officials believe that nearly 30 million Americans could be quickly punched into a first-time-ever system, and then sorted, assigned a number, and eventually alphabetized. Nor did anyone imagine that such voluminous records could be searchable and retrievable based on name and number.[55]

Hollerith machines, as they were understood to exist in America at the time, could do no more than add, subtract, tabulate, and tally punch cards. But Social Security required *collation*, "the ability to take two sets of records and do a [simultaneous] matching to see whether . . . they were related to one another," as government technicians described it.[56]

To the amazement of the bureaucrats, IBM was ready. The company was quickly able to unveil a so-called "collator" that could achieve precisely what the government had in mind: compare and cross-reference two sets of records in a single operation. Therefore, it was not necessary for the government to invent its own equipment. IBM would provide the solution.[57]

Washington awarded IBM an on-going contract so substantial it permanently boosted IBM into a corporate class of its own. Watson's people boasted that Social Security was "the biggest accounting operation of all-time." Actually, it was the second biggest. The dress rehearsal had already taken place in Germany in 1933. It will never be known whether the collator was invented in Germany or the United States, or as a collaborative effort of IBM's cross-Atlantic development programs. But shortly after it appeared in the United States, the collator also appeared in Dehomag's inventory. Dehomag was so impressed with the talented machine, the subsidiary deployed dozens of them, and planned to produce or import 50,000 more.[58]

From the moment Washington anointed IBM with the Social Security contract, the company's income catapulted six-fold within several years. Social Security and a diverse parade of lucrative contracts from the Department of Labor to the War Department created a veritable federal partnership with IBM.[59] The company became quasi-governmental. Large-scale research and development into punch card registration, identification, and storage and retrieval systems were now funded by the U.S. government as well as Nazi Germany. IBM's technology jumped. As a result of massive American taxpayer-funded research, more people-managing punch card capabilities than ever before would be available to the Hitler regime.

WATSON'S STRUGGLE to retain profit in Nazi Germany was all consuming. Reich regulations were constantly tightening the rules for business in cash-starved Germany. Austerity measures required ever-increasing domination of industry. Moreover, Heidinger never paused in his battle to reap his portion of the Dehomag money. Watson could handle Reich regulations. But Heidinger was something else.

Barely a day passed without numerous position papers, contract drafts, legal opinions, and explanatory memos wafting between IBM offices in Geneva, Paris, Berlin, and New York trying to maintain an edge in Watson's profit war with Heidinger. Every time one fire seemed doused, new flames erupted.

For example, IBM was faced with a Dehomag profit of RM 1.2 million at the end of 1934. Watson didn't want to pay the taxes in either Germany or the United States. To both take the profit, yet make it disappear, European auditors in late February 1935 concluded that "the new Dehomag will simply have to show a deficit as of December 31, 1934, after payment of the RM 1.2 million 1934 dividends. The deficit will be made up within the first few months of 1935." That dividend of course would be classed a "royalty," making it appear as an expense. However, at about the same time, even the royalty loophole dried up. IBM accountants reported to IBM that "royalty payment to New York is no longer possible." Confronted with a technical deficit for the first quarter of 1935 and unable to transfer profit, Dehomag petitioned the Berlin authorities for temporary tax relief, claiming "a hardship."[60]

The problem was that Heidinger earnestly wanted a profit shown so he could qualify for a bonus. Without a formal profit showing, Heidinger's 10 percent bonus would never materialize. Before the merger, Heidinger was accustomed to receiving a monthly bonus of RM 10,000. Under the new arrangement, IBM reaped huge earnings as royalties or other "fees," but his income suddenly disappeared. Until the profits could again be declared, Heidinger demanded a monthly "loan" of RM 5,000 just to make living expenses.[61]

Only Watson could authorize it. He did agree, but kept Heidinger on a short leash. The loans would extend only until August 1935, at which time "the whole position will be reviewed again."[62]

Upon learning of his temporary morsel, Heidinger, on March 3, 1935, shot off a saccharine thank you to IBM NY Vice President Otto Braitmayer. "It was indeed a great pleasure for me to receive . . . your kind letter of February 21 by which you allow me to receive from the Dehomag during the first eight months of this year a monthly advance of RM 5,000—instead of dividends which will be declared later on. . . . thank you very much for your kind thinking of me on occasion of my 60th birthday . . . which brings me nearly into your class of age."[63]

But then an additional Reich regulation hit, this one completely undercutting windfall profits. New rules prohibited distributed profits in the form of dividends above 8 percent of a company's original investment. Since Dehomag's soaring profits were now vastly in excess of IBM's original capitalization, the dividend cap applied. As it became increasingly difficult for IBM NY to extract monies from Germany, profits still remained undeclared. It seemed that no matter what was done, Dehomag's growing business made money but profit was never declared.[64]

An IBM comptroller's analysis conceded that by fiddling with losses, "It is obvious that Mr. Heidinger would draw about 40 percent of the total dividends which could be declared." At the same time, the analysis added, IBM would only be able to receive 60 percent of what it was expecting.[65]

Finally, Heidinger caught on that IBM losses were just as valuable as profits. If he couldn't get a bonus on profit—he demanded it on the losses. Ironically, IBM managers were unable to deny the logic. "Mr. Heidinger is justified to a certain extent," conceded one internal memorandum, "in asking that the losses in the other divisions be taken into consideration . . . because . . . the surplus is reduced."[66]

IBM agreed to give Heidinger a bonus on losses, but struggled to phrase the arrangement since German taxing authorities would never believe genuine losses could create a bonus. Finally, to assuage Heidinger, the company agreed to declare a phantom dividend first, pay Heidinger a 10 percent bonus on that amount, and then recast those same numbers as losses to avoid tax.[67]

But what should be done with the blocked funds? In July 1935, during a Dehomag board meeting Watson attended in Berlin, he directed that "the money should rather remain invested in the firm and be credited to the license account [royalties], as direct remittances are not possible." Heidinger was offered extra incentives, such as insurance and a generous pension.[68] The feisty German agreed, but that only postponed the next round of financial fisticuffs.

Meanwhile, to realize blocked profits, Watson channeled money into tangible assets. He expanded Dehomag's Lichterfelde factory, retrofitted an old underutilized pre-merger facility in Sindelfingen outside Stuttgart, and installed additional card printing presses. The race was on to build those presses and expand factories, because shortly, the Reich would decree that German companies could no longer pay for any imports from America. The new rules prohibited such imports, by either cash or credit. Hence intra-company accounts could no longer be manipulated to create losses. Dehomag could no longer mask as a legitimate expense its own machinery shipped from one IBM company address to another. The German subsidiary would have to become completely self-sufficient.[69]

Rottke bragged to the Dehomag board chairman in New York that he had beat the new regulations because "I have still imported as much merchandise as ever possible" from IBM NY before the new regulations took effect.[70] Stockpiling IBM supplies, machines, spare parts, fabricating equipment, and punch cards meant that Dehomag received a decisive manufacturing impetus without the need to remit any money to New York. That only strengthened Dehomag's balance sheet, and made it a more powerful component of IBM.

But now surplus cash escalated in Germany beyond even Dehomag's needs. Watson needed to invest in German assets that would retain their value. They could be sold later. Eventually, IBM commissioned its outside auditors—Price Waterhouse—to join IBM managers in making investment recommendations. An extensive written report was submitted. Stocks of other German companies were considered too volatile. Timberlands were debated, but deemed unlikely to be approved by the Reich as a precious natural resource. Buying an independent paper factory was rejected since paper was now highly regulated by the Reich.[71]

"Rental property might be acquired, preferably in Berlin," an IBM European manager suggested to Watson in a letter. The decision was Watson's. He chose apartment buildings. These could be turned over to local rental agents for leasing, thereby generating income as well.[72] Berlin was filled with some very discounted real estate at the time.

IBM began buying apartment buildings. The properties purchased were not prime locations, but reliable sources of rental income. One building was at Schützenstrasse 15/17. A second was at Markgrafenstrasse 25. Attorney Konrad Matzdorf, whose office was near one of the addresses, managed the sites, and according to one IBM assessment, "accumulated a substantial amount of money for the rentals."[73]

As IBM plowed its Reichsmarks into hard assets, it already anticipated a wider European presence. In 1935, Watson shifted the company's European headquarters from Paris to a city with a better banking environment, Geneva, Switzerland. A Price Waterhouse report later confirmed that while dividends and profits destined for the United States were indeed blocked in Germany, "the regulations quoted above do not apply to transfers to Denmark, Belgium, Holland, Switzerland and Italy, since these countries have made special arrangements with Germany in connection with the transfer of interest and dividend payments."[74] As it happened, IBM maintained operations in Denmark, Belgium, Holland, Italy, and now Switzerland.

Although the arrangement to pay Heidinger bonuses on losses originated in 1935, the small print of any agreement with the Dehomag founder consumed months of wrangling. During that time, IBM was astonished to learn that Heidinger had never quite filed all the many merger papers from 1934, thus preserving some or all of his original corporate compensation rights. More than that, the language in some of the merger documents Heidinger drew up was so convoluted, no IBM translator could understand it. At the end of 1935, an IBM manager confessed to New York, "the translation is still very confusing and actually it is hard to tell exactly what it means. Also you will be interested to know that both Mr. Rottke and Mr. Zimmerman of the German company are unable to determine the exact meaning of the German original."[75]

Pure and simple, Heidinger would not finalize the merger papers until his bonus was rectified. The matter had been dragging on since late 1933. IBM was operating companies that arguably did not quite legally exist for lack of the proper paperwork.

Once and for all, IBM wanted to straighten out its contractual messes with Heidinger. Both sides, in spring 1936, agreed to new bonus language. Heidinger visited New York in early 1936 to attend the Hundred Percent Club, the international IBM celebration of those executives meeting or exceeding their annual sales quota. Dehomag was always the number one foreign revenue producer. While Heidinger was in New York, there was plenty of face-to-face time for him and Watson to work out the smallest details of the final agreement governing the merger and bonus. A special letter was crafted by a Berlin attorney confirming that the contract was just a private undertaking between two stockholders with Dehomag, not with Watson in his capacity as chairman of IBM. This continued the fiction that Dehomag was not under foreign influence.[76]

So little trust remained that each side secured its own attorney. IBM Vice President Braitmayer sent a letter to a European manager in Geneva, and in a postscript asserted, "You will understand that I wish to avoid any unnecessary legal expenses, yet it is essential that IBM interests be fully protected and that you avoid any such complications as were involved in the 1934 contract drawn by Mr. Heidinger." Braitmayer added, "I am depending upon you to use some tact and judgment in handling this situation. And I hope you will understand that this letter is [only] for the perusal of yourself."[77]

Finally, on June 10, 1936, with numerous translations, multiple translated copies, attorneys in abundance, and signatures inked everywhere, an extensive array of eight document sets was executed, thus finalizing the Dehomag merger of 1933 and securing Heidinger's bonuses. To further bolster the image of German ownership, IBM ultimately arranged so-called "loans" for directors Hermann Rottke and Karl Hummel so they could purchase nominal shares of Dehomag. The loans were collateralized by the shares themselves and neither individual enjoyed "the right to sell or transfer to any third parties" any of their shares. No money changed hands. In consequence, it appeared to Reich authorities that three Germans owned Dehomag, even if in fact it was controlled 100 percent by IBM NY.[78]

As Watson reviewed a passel of final signed, notarized, sealed, and registered documents, America's most powerful businessman undoubtedly hoped that the war for profits in Germany was over. Heidinger might now be pacified. Watson was wrong.

GERMAN JEWRY did not understand how, but the Reich seemed to be all-knowing as it identified and encircled them, and then systematically wrung the dignity from their lives. Indeed, it was clear to the world that somehow the Reich always knew the names even if no one quite understood how it knew the names.

Confiscation and Aryanization escalated throughout 1936, as did physical brutality. On September 8, 1936, a *New York Times* report headlined "Reich Seizing 25% of Fortune of Jews" reported: "The order served on Jews by local tax authorities demands that they deposit within eight days 'security' equal to the Reich escape tax . . . one-fourth their total assets. Jews on whom the order was served were frank in stating that sudden withdrawal of 25 percent of their capital meant ruin to their business and nothing was left except to shut down."[79]

On September 17, 1936, a *New York Times* report headlined "Nazi Penalties Heavier" reported: "The *Stürmer*, Julius Streicher's anti-Semitic weekly, announces that the Reich Justice Ministry has instructed public prosecutors to demand more severe punishment for Jewish race defilers—Jews convicted of having had relations with German women. The *Stürmer*, which regularly prints a list of Jews sentenced during the week throughout Germany, has long complained that German courts are too lenient."[80]

The day before, the *New York Times* was one of many publications that printed Streicher's explicit remarks to newspapermen. The article, sub-headlined "The Way to Solve Problem Is to Exterminate Them," reported: "The Nuremberg high-priest of anti-Semitism . . . announced that in the last analysis, extermination is the only real solution to the Jewish problem. Mr. Streicher made it clear in his address that he was not discussing the question in regard to Germany alone . . . but of a world problem. He declared there were some who believed the Jewish question could be solved 'without blood,' but . . . they were seriously mistaken. . . . if a final solution was to be reached 'one must go to the bloody path.' Such measures would be justified, Mr. Streicher declared, 'because the Jews always attained their ends through wholesale murder and have been responsible for wars and massacres. To secure the safety of the whole world, they must be exterminated,' he said."[81]

The world could not help but know the dismal result of Nazism. What they did not read, they saw. Refugees were everywhere.

Trains screeched into Paris, Prague, Warsaw, Brussels, Geneva, and Madrid. Ships lowered their gangplanks at Boston, New York, Mexico City, London, and Johannesburg. On every arrival, refugees were an unmistakable sight. Emerging as a family group, wearing their finest, towing suitcases and footlockers filled with clothes and memories, they stepped with hard-summoned pride and irrepressible confusion into the dim of displacement. Many were professors toting books bundled with cord. Some were doctors and lawyers lugging well-worn briefcases. A number were merchants stowing precious leather ledger books. Not all of them were Jewish. Some didn't even believe they were Jewish. Many were intellectuals or dissidents of various religions. Children were told stories about sudden vacations. Parents wondered what the night would bring. Not all had papers. Some carried smuggled gold and jewels to re-establish themselves. But most had little to defray their existence. The machinery of confiscation had sent them out virtually penniless or with their dwindled assets trapped in a hostile Reich.

An amalgam of disorganized rescue and relief was underway. The League of Nations, Jewish organizations, Zionist bodies, church groups, governmental committees, labor unions, and ad-hoc municipal agencies struggled to find housing, jobs, and moment-to-moment succor for the refugees. But all of the several dozen helping drew upon money and resources that fundamentally did not exist at a time when all nations were suffering from the weight of their own domestic depression. The world's brittle ability to assist was cracking. By late 1935, more than 125,000 had escaped Germany. In Holland, more than 5,000 had arrived. Czechoslovakia also extended asylum to more than 5,000. Poland absorbed 30,000. France had received 30,000 refugees but transferred 20,000 to other countries. Nearly 37,000 had escaped to the United States, Palestine, and Latin America.[82]

So global was the crisis that the League of Nations appointed James G. McDonald a special High Commissioner for German Refugees. McDonald's compelling report on the mounting catastrophe, issued as he resigned in frustration, declared, "Perhaps at no time in history have conditions been less favorable to the settlement of such a difficult international problem." The gates were closing. Zionist leader Chaim Weizmann declared the world was divided between places where Jews could not stay, and places where Jews could not go.[83]

It was against a backdrop of human misery everywhere that Watson proved that he was a special friend of the Nazi Reich. More than just his investments in Germany, and his strategic socializing with German diplomats and industrialists, Germany felt Watson was an ally in the Nazi battle for economic recovery and conquest. Watson never spoke a word of criticism against his customer Nazi Germany. But more than that, he worked to breach the gorge of isolation surrounding the Reich. One of his main venues was the International Chamber of Commerce and its U.S. affiliate, the United States Chamber of Commerce.

The American Chamber of Commerce, comprised of the nation's most powerful magnates and corporate executives, was a powerful political influence in America. Its Foreign Department functioned as the American Section of the International Chamber of Commerce. The ICC was a nongovernmental organization created by the League of Nations to promote world trade and study the hard mechanics of treaties governing such international commerce as postal, shipping, currency, banking, and patent rules.

Watson was elected chairman of the Foreign Department, which also made him the chairman of the American Section of the ICC. This, in essence, made Watson America's official businessman to the world.[84]

In his new capacity, Watson seized the opportunity to rapidly organize the Eighth Biennial Congress of the International Chamber of Commerce to be held in Paris in June 1935. Quickly, he secured the U.S. Government's imprimatur for the event, thus elevating its status and glitter. To that end, numerous letters were exchanged with Secretary of State Cordell Hull and his subordinates. State Department officers were invited to sail on the same ship with Watson and his ICC co-delegates as a cohesive entourage. American ambassadors, consuls, and attachés from across Europe were beckoned to attend. Hull himself was importuned by Watson for a message of congratulations for the ICC's related Council meeting and referring to "world peace." Such a greeting from Hull, prominently printed in program notes and shown to key contacts, would reinforce the image of Watson as a political dynamo within the Roosevelt Administration.[85]

After a flurry of minute revisions, Hull strung together a sequence of inconsequential words that Watson could publish to show the American government's seeming approval of the Paris event and, more importantly, of Watson's leadership of it. "I take this means," cabled Hull, "of expressing my interest in the purpose of the meeting which you will attend to discuss ways in which business organizations can cooperate most effectively to secure a more adequate and practical economic approach to world peace. The meeting is timely and I shall be glad to learn its results on your return."[86]

In the bright glare of the international media, Watson assembled the world's leading corporate leaders, including those from the Third Reich, to discuss the most pressing economic problems of the day. The topics debated: avoidance of competitive currency depreciation; uniform treatment of foreign corporations; payment of international debts; and international protection of inventions, trademarks, patents, and models.[87] Grandiloquent speeches before the plenary, debates among working groups, elaborate communiqués to government leaders, and hastily organized press dispatches spotlighted the official agenda of the Congress.[88]

But one pressing economic topic was never raised during the eminent conclaves. The issue was not an abstruse fiscal machination that dwelled in the unnoticed realms of international economic theory. It was the one financial crisis that threatened to overwhelm civilized governments throughout the Western world by the sheer crush of its tragic sorrow and economic implication. Refugees were never mentioned.

Indeed, the whole issue of the Hitler menace was sidestepped as Watson encouraged all to assume a "business as usual" posture with Germany. Hitler's Reich craved respite from the torrent of international criticism battering its economy. Watson did what he could to help. Germany believed that if it could just export its products and be left alone to pursue its militancy, the Third Reich would prevail. In the Nazi mindset, whenever it could function routinely in world commerce, it won fleeting validation for its course.

During the Paris Congress, Watson was elected the next president of the entire ICC. He was now the undisputed paragon of world trade. He would be installed as president at the next ICC Congress scheduled for June 1937. As such, he was proud to announce his personal selection for the host site. The world may have been isolating Germany. All Western nations were suffering the financial burden of Nazi oppression. Refugees flowed to their cities. Tension arising from Hitler's threats of invasion and exported Fascism spurred an expensive arms race. But Watson staunchly urged all to join him in what he promised would be the biggest and most grandiose Congress yet.

"We are going . . . to Berlin," he told his Chamber colleagues. "We are free from those particular antagonisms which strong political feelings have caused so much to break nations apart."[89]

Watson would not criticize Hitler. On the contrary, in his countless interviews and public speeches, Watson somehow seemed to emphasize ideas the Reich found profoundly supportive. At any other time in history, Watson's words might have been received as visionary gems. But in the tenor of the times, they struck a chord of grateful resonance with the Reich.

Speaking at both IBM and ICC events, Watson regularly pleaded for "an equitable redistribution of natural resources," and expressed his support for a rearmed Germany. He voiced his oft-quoted opinions at a time when the Reich was daily violating the Versailles Treaty by rebuilding its war machine, and threatening to invade neighboring regions to acquire the very natural resources it felt it deserved.[90]

Watson was explicit at one key conference when he asked ICC colleagues to press their contacts in government for "some sound understanding in regard to limitation of armaments," and then admitted, "we are not talking about disarmaments." As usual, he added that progress was needed on one other point, "which is of the greatest of importance, a fairer distribution of raw materials." Addressing the crippling boycott facing Germany, Watson repeated his mantra, "We believe that as soon as we can have the proper flow of trade both ways across the border, there will not be any need for soldiers crossing those boundaries."[91]

Even when spoken to his face, Watson maintained aphasic disregard for any criticism of the Hitler regime. At an April 26, 1937, ICC banquet in Washington preparatory to the Berlin Congress, the guest speaker was John Foster Dulles, former American legal counsel to the Treaty at Versailles and one of the nation's foremost international law experts. His presentation was entitled "The Fundamental Causes of War." Watson was not happy about the topic. Before Dulles spoke, Watson even lobbied Dulles to change the title. Dulles openly quipped that Watson had complained: "Nobody wants to hear about war, let's hear about peace." To this, Dulles told the members, "I said, 'Alright, you [Watson] can write the title if I can write the speech. Before I get through, I think you may wish that . . . I had written the title and he had written the speech.'"[92]

Dulles tore into Germany, saying all the things Watson had considered impermissible. "Take the case of Germany," said Dulles, with Watson standing next to him. "Inability to get foreign exchange [due to the anti-Nazi boycott] has blockaded Germany almost as effectively as she was blockaded during the war by fleets and the armies of the Allies. There is a shortage of food, a shortage of raw material, and the same sense of being circled by hostile forces. . . . It may be that in fact a country has all the facilities, which it requires to develop within its borders . . . It may be possible to prove all that as a matter of logic. But logic has never cured a mental disease."[93]

Caustically declaring that the well-worn catchphrase of "peace" bandied by Germany and its intellectual allies was a fraud, Dulles forcefully insisted, "A state to remain peaceful, must afford its individual citizens an opportunity to work and to enjoy the fruits of their labor. There must be no undue repression of the individual . . . where such repression occurs on a large scale, peace is threatened. The outbreak, when it comes, may be civil war, but it may equally be international war."[94]

When Dulles finished his long speech, Watson declined to even acknowledge it had taken place. Departing from his usual toastmaster effusiveness, Watson simply introduced the next speaker, the American Secretary of Agriculture. Minutes later, Watson tried to counteract Dulles' comments by exhorting his fellow entrepreneurs to support the ICC gathering in Germany. "At our meeting in Berlin," urged Watson, "we hope to see as many of you people as possibly can get over because it is of great importance to your country that you be there and assist us in carrying on that meeting."[95]

Watson reviled any detraction of Germany. One typical comment to the Associated Press, reported in the *New York Times,* used some of the same formulations Hitler defenders themselves had so frequently invoked. "Mr. Watson scoffed at the possibility of another world war," said the *Times.* "'World peace,' he [Watson] declared, 'will result when the nations of the world concentrate on their own problems and set their individual houses in order.'"[96]

When challenged, Watson would insist, "I'm an optimist." Those among friends and family who knew him best later tried to excuse his behavior as "naïve."[97] But there was none shrewder than Watson. He calculated his words like a carpenter: measure twice, cut once.

Watson confessed his feelings shortly thereafter in a draft letter to none other than Reich Economics Minister Schacht. "I have felt a deep personal concern over Germany's fate," Watson wrote, "and a growing attachment to the many Germans with whom I gained contact at home and abroad. This attitude has caused me to give public utterance to my impressions and convictions in favor of Germany at a time when public opinion in my country and elsewhere was predominantly unfavorable."[98]

Moreover, Watson knew war was imminent. So did Heidinger. In October 1936, long before the intellectual showdown with Dulles, Heidinger sent a memo to IBM NY detailing plans to build bomb shelters for Dehomag in case war broke out. "The authorities have approached us," reported Heidinger, "with demands that sufficient care should be taken to protect our plant and operations against air attack. In view of the fact that we are located close to a railway station, such demands seem justified . . . in the interest of the safety of the lives of the workers and employees . . . we believe we should recommend immediately the setting up of air raid shelters. . . . Something must surely be done immediately."[99]

With metric specificity, Dehomag's memo called for two massive bomb shelters, each large enough for 950 people or a mass of machinery, as well as an underground tunnel linking factory buildings at the Lichterfelde complex. The bomb shelters were later approved by Watson.[100] Thus IBM assured that Hitler's punch card capability would be protected from Allied strikes, even if those included American bombers.

Thomas Watson was more than just a businessman selling boxes to the Third Reich. For his Promethean gift of punch card technology that enabled the Reich to achieve undreamed of efficiencies both in its rearmament program and its war against the Jews, for his refusal to join the chorus of strident anti-Nazi boycotters and isolators and instead open a commercial corridor the Reich could still navigate, for his willingness to bring the world's commercial summit to Berlin, for his value as a Roosevelt crony, for his glitter and legend, Hitler would bestow upon Thomas Watson a medal— the highest it could confer on any non-German.

The Merit Cross of the German Eagle with Star was created for Thomas Watson to "honor foreign nationals who made themselves deserving of the German Reich." It ranked second in prestige only to Hitler's German Grand Cross.[101]

Watson was honored. At the next ICC Congress, he would not only be installed as president of the ICC, he would be decorated by *der Führer*. Working with Goebbels as stage manager, Watson would make the 1937 ICC conference in Berlin a commercial homage to Germany. Hitler in turn would make that event a national homage to Thomas Watson.

———

THE GREAT 24,000-ton oceanliner *Manhattan* brought ninety-five American executives and their families to Hamburg on June 24, 1937, where they refreshed and boarded trains for Berlin to attend the ICC gathering. As usual, Watson made arrangements for the State Department, its ambassadors, consuls, and other envoys to sail with the group or otherwise become abundantly visible. In Berlin, the Americans would join more than 2,500 delegates and others from forty-two other countries marshaled by Watson to make a strong showing. The group included 900 from Germany. The suites of the Hotel Adlon, Bristol, and Continental were waiting. The Adlon doubled as Watson's nerve center for the Congress. Scenic tours were arranged for the after hours.[102]

Watson had already declared that after the Berlin gathering he would travel to Italy for a private meeting with Mussolini and that the next ICC conference scheduled for 1939 would be held in Tokyo, Germany's Pacific ally. IBM had been cultivating a thriving business in Japan, helping that nation develop its air force and aircraft carriers.[103]

Greetings to the Berlin Congress were not only conveyed by Hull, but this time President Roosevelt himself issued an official, if innocuous, felicitation. Again, such communications emphasized Watson's primacy as much as the event itself. "My hearty congratulations and warmest greetings on your election as President of the International Chamber of Commerce," Roosevelt cabled the Adlon. "For many years, I have followed with interest your efforts to advance the work of this organization. . . . Your Congress in Berlin is taking place at a time when many serious problems call for wise and mature counsel. . . . On this very important occasion, I extend to you and to the participating delegations my best wishes for a successful conclusion to the deliberations."[104]

On June 28, 1937, over a peaceful cup of tea served in dainty china cups atop elegant saucers, in a quiet corner of the Reich Chancellery, huddling over a small serving table and seated on cushy, floral armchairs, Watson and Hitler would finally talk. Sitting with them was a Hitler cohort and two other prominent Hitler supporters from the ICC convention. No one knows exactly what Hitler told Watson during their exchange. Watson paraphrased it later for the *New York Times* as, "There will be no war. No country wants war, no country can afford it."[105] But no one really ever knew the exact exchange between the men. Whatever Hitler did say, Watson was encouraged and entranced.

Later, the ICC thousands assembled at the German Opera House, which doubled as the *Reichstag*. Nazi flags fluttered monumentally from the balconies as a massive orchestra played Beethoven's Lenore Overture #3. The *New York Times* reported, "At times . . . it seemed to be a purely National Socialist rally."[106]

And then Adolf Hitler suddenly walked in. Dressed in his familiar brown party uniform, he made his way directly to the royal box festooned with a swastika flag. As he did, the familiar command crackled through the air: *"Sieg!"*[107]

The assemblage of distinctive businessmen, including dozens from the United States of America, in the year 1937, gripped by the moment, awed by the occasion, imbued with the spirit, under the leadership of Thomas J. Watson, jumped to their feet amid roars, cheers, and wild applause, reached for the sky in a loyal salute and chanted back *"Heil!"*[108] Watson lifted his right arm halfway up before he caught himself. Later, a colleague denied to a reporter for the *New York Herald* that Watson's gesture was a genuine salute.[109]

Hermann Goering was one of the first main speakers. He hammered at Nazi Germany's constant themes. The Third Reich's "mighty rearmament," Goering insisted, was merely to defend Germany's long borders and protect her honor. He demanded justice for Germany, and access to the raw materials she was entitled to. *Reichsbank* President Hjalmar Schacht in his address also stressed "honest raw material distribution."[110]

Many more Nazi speakers argued their case, hopeful for appeasement if possible, committed to conquest if necessary. Even Schacht, whose rhetoric was generally subdued, described racial prerogatives that arose from a "God-given division of nations according to race."[111]

When the plenary finally dismissed, a signal was given and the orchestra played the theme of the Storm Troopers, the "Horst Wessel Song" and then the German national anthem, "Deutschland über Alles." Caught up in the hypnotic invigoration of it all, delegates sang along with stalwart Brown Shirts.[112]

Then the merriment began in earnest. Berlin had not seen so monarchical a reception in recent memory. Watson was wined, dined, and honored everywhere in Berlin. Josef and Magda Goebbels entertained the Watsons at the Opera House. The Schachts invited the Watsons and delegates to a grand party for hundreds at the Berlin Palace. The Goerings hosted a majestic banquet for the Watsons and delegation presidents at the immense Charlottenburg Palace. Berlin's mayor organized a sumptuous dinner for the delegates.[113]

But all prior splendor was surpassed by the elaborate Venetian Nights staged by Goebbels on Peacock Island, an extravaganza thought by many to be the grandest party of the Nazi era. Located a short drive from Berlin in pastoral Wannsee, Friedrich Wilhelm III's romantic eighteenth-century castle on Peacock Island had been converted for the evening into an Arabesque fantasy at a cost of 4 million Reichsmarks. Watson and the other guests crossed to the isle atop a narrow pontoon bridge, which brought them to a long path lined with hundreds of charming Berlin schoolgirls daintily outfitted in white blouses over white silk breeches and white leather slippers. Each girl waved a white fairy's wand and angelically bowed as Watson and his fellow industrialists promenaded in.[114]

Three thousand—some said four thousand—guests were then invited to imbibe at a bar of seemingly endless length, manned by eighty bartenders pouring and mixing any cocktail, vintage cognac, fine wine, or robust beer.

Corks popped continuously as champagne flowed with abandon. A regal dinner remembered as gigantic was served to hundreds of tables, each seating as many as twelve. Thousands of chefs, waiters, and their kitchen helpers whisked dome after dome of gourmet specialties back and forth across the lawns in a spectacular demonstration of precision table service. Enchanting Prussian porcelain figurines were bestowed upon the wives. Ballerinas and singers from a nearby artist's colony performed an enchanted display of dance and song beneath a prodigious rotunda, which later became an immense dance floor.[115]

But no fanfare could compare with the crowning moment, the decoration of Watson. Hitler's medal was bestowed by Schacht as newsreel cameras whirred and government functionaries snapped to stiff attention. The eight-pointed gold-framed cross of white enamel embedded with German eagles and Nazi emblems dangled about the neck from a broad red, black, and white ribbon in tandem with a second six-pointed star worn over the left breast. To Watson, it was magnificent. When wearing it, he was draped by two swastikas, one to the right and one to the left.[116]

The majesty and fantasy of Berlin 1937 swept Watson and IBM into an ever more entangled alliance—now not only in Germany, but in every country of Europe. Soon, the metallic syncopation of Hollerith technology would echo across the continent. There were frightening new applications for punch cards in store, applications no civilized person could envision. France, Poland, Italy, Bulgaria, Czechoslovakia, Holland, Norway, Romania, Hungary, and the other nations would soon be set ablaze.

Through it all, the songs never stopped. Swaying with exuberance, all dressed in one color, lyrics shouted in almost hypnotic fervor, the songs never stopped. Endicott reverberated with the prospects as followers sang out.

> *That's the spirit that has brought us fame!*
> *We're big, but bigger we will be.*
> *We can't fail*
> *for all can see.*
> *. . .*
>
> *We fought our way through—and new*
> *Fields we're sure to conquer too.*
> *For the ever onward IBM.*[117]

PART **TWO**

I
II
III
IV
V
VI
VII
VIII
IX
X
XI
XII
XIII
XIV
XV

JULY 5, 1937
Your Excellency
Adolf Hitler
Berlin

Before leaving Berlin, I wish to express my pride in and deep gratitude for the high honor I received through the order with which you honored me. Valuing fully the spirit of friendship which underlay this honor, I assure you that in the future as in the past, I will endeavor to do all in my power to create more intimate bonds between our two great nations. My wife and my family join in best wishes for you.

Thomas J. Watson
International Business Machines[1]

JULY 4, 1938
Mr. Thomas J. Watson
International Business Machines
New York

Dear Sir:

I must offer you my apologies for taking the liberty to write you and to request your kind attention for the following matter. Like many [of] Jewish confession, I am facing a

137

very terrible moment in life and I am obliged to leave this country and to procure in another land my means of living. I am born on the 17th of June 1906 and was educated in the elementary and high school in the country. During eight years until 1933, I have worked as an operator of the Hollerith punching machine for the Reich Statistical Office in Berlin.

Now I have spoken with Mr. Drines, the manager of the Hollerith company in Berlin about my plans to find work abroad. Mr. Drines has advised me to write to you somehow with my plans and I hope that with your kind help I would be able to find work in a foreign country. No doubt you know the condition of living here and it would be useless to give any further reasons for my immigration.

I would be very grateful to you for your kind assistance and please accept in anticipation my thanks.

Hoping to be favored with your reply, I remain

Sincerely Yours,
Ilse Meyer
Berlin[2]

GERMANY WAS bitter for the Jews. By 1937, thousands had escaped as pauperized emigrants. But for those Jews remaining within the Reich, existence became a progressively fainter shadow of its former self. Driven from the small cities, Jews began to flood into Berlin where they attempted to continue a fraction of the civilized life they once knew. Small things became important: a cup of coffee in a cafe, a stroll in the park, cinema on the weekend, an afternoon concert, these were the precious relics of normalcy German Jewry clung to. But the Nazis would not permit a moment of peace. Jews were subjected to unending acts of personal degradation as they were marginalized. The national humiliation effort was more than a cruelty unnoticed except within the borders of Germany. The campaign was the source of never-ending American newspaper articles and radio reports, including those in the *New York Times*.

Nazis would enter cinemas and demand all Jews rise so they could be escorted out. Cafes catering to Jews were ordered closed and the patrons taken into custody. Local authorities disbanded virtually all Jewish athletic teams, musical societies, and social clubs. Indeed, any gathering of more than four Jews in a single place was forbidden. Placarded park benches warned that Jews could not sit down. Synagogues were shuttered and often razed; the grand principal synagogue of Munich was replaced with a parking lot.[3]

Hundreds of disenfranchised middle-class German Jews from the provinces tried to reestablish themselves in Berlin with small retail businesses. Former boot manufacturers reappeared in shoe shops. Liquidated apparel makers set up shop as haberdashers. Evicted professors opened bookstores. As soon as the Nazis discovered these shoestring enterprises, customers were frightened away and the assets targeted for confiscation. Jewish shops were defaced with painted epithets exclaiming "Jewish Swine" or "Out with the Jews." Not infrequently, armed Storm Troopers blockaded the doorways. One day, the world awoke to headlines reporting a massive racist display as several miles of Berlin's main shopping streets were obstructed with crude, three-foot-high signs identifying exactly which stores were owned by Jews.[4] Nazi agitators always seemed to know if owners were Jewish, no matter how new the stores.

Yet for the Hitler regime, the pace of Jewish destruction was still not swift enough nor sufficiently complete. Although Germany's professing Jews had been identified, thousands of so-called "racial Jews" with Jewish ancestors dating back to the prior century had yet to be marked. In 1937, the Reich ordered another nationwide census that would prepare the country for military mobilization, and for the Jews would be the final and decisive identification step. Dehomag eagerly agreed to organize the project.[5]

The racial portion of the census was designed to pinpoint ancestral Jews as defined by the Nuremberg Laws, ensuring no escape from the Reich's anti-Semitic campaign. In addition to the usual census questions, a special card asked whether any of the individual's grandparents was Jewish. When completely filled out, the card would be isolated in a separate envelope for processing by both the census authorities and security offices.[6]

The project, originally scheduled for May 1938, would be an enormous undertaking for IBM, requiring a huge expansion of manpower, machinery, and processing space. Seventy sorters, some sixty tabulators, seventy-six multipliers, and 90 million punch cards would be needed for the RM 3.5 million contract. IBM supervisors in Geneva, Stockholm, and New York understood how difficult the challenge would be. A memo from IBM's European Factory Manager J.G. Johnston to IBM NY supervisors in Sweden specified, "we also have to raise considerable funds for the financing of the RM 3.5 million census order" even though the Reich's payments would be distributed over a fifteen-month period. Other IBM executives seemed to sense that the forthcoming racial census would represent a project so far-reaching, it would be the last of its kind, and therefore IBM's investment would have to plan for a temporary surge. "You should take into consideration . . . the fact that the German census order is a peak load which may not reoccur."[7]

The Nazi establishment was ecstatic about the implications for German Jewry. "In May of next year," bragged the leading NSDAP newspaper, *Völkischer Beobachter,* "the largest and most comprehensive census will take place. It will be larger and more comprehensive than Germany, and even the rest of the world, has ever known. . . . it is the duty of every Volks-comrade to answer every single question completely and truthfully . . . [thus] giving the Führer and his colleagues the basis for the future legislation of the next five to ten years."[8]

One Nazi bureaucrat enthused, "The general census of 1938 is intended to also determine the blood-wise configuration of the German population. . . . the results could also be recorded on the police department's technical registration cards. The police would thus gain an insight into the racial composition of the persons living in their jurisdictions. And this would also accomplish the goals set by the Main Office of the Security Police."[9]

But the much-anticipated May 1938 census was delayed. On March 13, 1938, the Third Reich absorbed Austria, creating a Greater Germany of 73 million people. Hitler called it the *Anschluss,* or "Annexation." The anti-Semitic program that had evolved over the years in Germany now rapidly took hold in the Austrian provinces—virtually overnight. First came the violence. Jewish merchants were rounded up and publicly beaten, their stores looted. Viennese crowds cheered when Jewish men and women were forced to their knees to scrub streets as rifle butts flailed them.[10]

Page one headlines in the *New York Times* immediately decried an "Orgy of Jew-baiting." The article described sadistic cruelties calculated to coerce Jews into immediately emigrating penniless to anywhere. "In Vienna and Austria," the *New York Times* declared, "no vestige of decency or humanity has checked the will to destroy, and there has been an unbroken orgy of Jew-baiting such as Europe has not known since the darkest days of the Middle Ages."[11]

Then came the arrests. Thousands of Jews were extracted from their homes and offices, loaded onto wagons, and shipped to concentration camps, such as Dachau, where they suffered bestial tortures, starvation, and back-breaking labor. The camps, too, were designed to convince Austrian Jews to leave the country—should they ever be released from incarceration. And only those who promised to emigrate at once were even considered for release.[12]

When the pace of emigration was not quick enough, Jews in the Austrian provinces were simply expelled from their homes with no notice. More than 3,000 Jewish men, women, and children in the Burgenland region of Austria, many with roots dating back centuries, were loaded onto trucks, driven to the Jewish quarter of Vienna, and summarily dumped. The Vienna Jewish community housed them in synagogues and other buildings as best they could, but the weather was unusually cold and many of the children suffered extreme exposure and near starvation from the ordeal.[13]

On June 30, 1938, nearly 10,000 Jewish-owned businesses in Austria were ordered to immediately fire all Jewish employees—30,000 men and women—and replace them with Aryans. The mass media described "heart-breaking scenes" across Vienna as trusted Jewish employees—many of ten- and twenty-year tenure—were suddenly ousted without warning or severance.[14]

Expulsions, exclusions, and confiscations raged across Vienna, stripping Jewish citizens of their dignity, possessions, and legal status. No one was spared. Middle-class Jews from Sigmund Freud to nameless victims were forced to board any ship, train, or bus out of Austria with no possessions other than what they could carry.[15] Once Jews were identified, their lives in Austria were over.

Suicide became a frequent alternative. In the first 10 days of German annexation, ninety-six persons committed suicide. As more Jews found themselves dispossessed or facing the prospect of Dachau, they entered into suicide pacts and even suicide clubs.[16]

With stunning precision, the Nazis knew exactly who in Austria was Jewish. Indeed, the *New York Times,* in its initial coverage of the round-ups, could not help but comment, "Many of these patrols are engaged in rounding up the thousands on lists of those due for imprisonment and 'correction.' These lists were compiled quietly year after year in preparation for the day of Germany's seizure of power."[17]

IBM was in Austria. Before Hitler came to power, the company was represented only by an agency called Furth & Company, operated in part by Stephan Furth. But in 1933, after Hitler declared the Third Reich, Watson established a wholly-owned IBM subsidiary in Austria. Furth then went to the United States to undergo sales training with IBM in New York. Shortly thereafter, Furth returned to Vienna as co-manager of the new wholly-owned IBM subsidiary. That subsidiary had the benefit of one of IBM's most talented punch card engineers, Gustav Tauschek, and Manager Victor Furth. Another Dehomag-trained manager named Berthold later joined Furth. In 1934, IBM undertook the Austrian census, and two years later, Watson approved a card printing plant for the country.[18]

In early 1938, in the weeks leading up to the March *Anschluss,* Adolf Eichmann was dispatched to Vienna as a specialist on Jewish affairs to organize forced Jewish emigration. Once in Vienna, he found an enormous punch card operation working around the clock. The Hollerith program superseded every other aspect of German preparations.[19]

"For weeks in advance [of the *Anschluss*]," remembered Eichmann, "every able-bodied man they could find was put to work in three shifts: writing file cards for an enormous circular card file, several yards in diameter, which a man sitting on a piano stool could operate and find any card he wanted thanks to a system of punch holes. All information important for Austria was entered on these cards. The data was taken from annual reports, handbooks, the newspapers of all the political parties, membership files; in short, everything imaginable. . . . Each card carried name, address, party membership, whether Jew, Freemason or practicing Catholic or Protestant; whether politically active, whether this or whether that. During that period, our regular work was put on ice."[20]

The German racial census scheduled for May 1938 was postponed a year to allow Dehomag to draw up new plans to count the population of Austria as well. Dehomag opened several additional branches throughout the greater Reich to accommodate the extra load. More than twenty-five offices would tackle the task of profiling the expanded base of some 70 million Germans and Austrians.[21]

Hitler's reign of terror against the Jews continued throughout 1938 to the continuing astonishment of the world. The final stage of confiscation was launched on April 27 as the Reich ordered Jews to register virtually all possessions.[22] Hollerith machines were kept busy tabulating assets.

Conditions in Nazi Germany became ever more nightmarish. Beheading was adopted as the dreaded new punishment of the unappealable Peoples' Court, which adjudicated in secret but announced its executions to the world media as a warning to all those the Reich considered special enemies. Scores of ghastly concentration camps were opened throughout the Greater Reich, each spawning its own infamy of cruel torture and degradation depicted in the newsreels and magazines of the day. Mob violence during the day, a dreaded knock on the door in the middle of the night, humiliating public campaigns, and endless decrees forcing Jews further into starvation and impoverishment rained terror on Jewish existence in the Greater Reich.[23]

World revulsion against Germany was inspired not just by its anti-Semitic outrages, but by a continuous assault of highly publicized oppression against Catholics, Protestant church groups, intellectuals, and others the Nazis did not agree with.[24] Hitler's war menacing clearly identified Czechoslovakia for imminent takeover. Poland and France seemed next. Many thought it was just a matter of time before Europe re-ignited into a total war that America would be compelled to enter. It became increasingly hard for anyone to argue Germany's case, even euphemistically in code. Then came the turning point for Americans and indeed the world: *Kristallnacht*—The Night of the Broken Glass.

November 10, 1938, on the twentieth anniversary of Germany's surrender in the Great War, all Germany exploded into a national pogrom of depravity and violence against Jews heretofore not seen. The Reich's pretext was the assassination of a German consular official in Paris by a despondent Jewish refugee. Within hours of the news, disciplined cadres of shock troops driving in open cars, directed by uniformed SA leaders, with merciless synchrony, deployed in virtually every town and city of the Third Reich during the early hours. Almost on cue, Hitler's Germany erupted into a tempest of shattered glass. Store panes, display cases, fixtures, office doors, and ordinary windows—if it was glass, the Nazis smashed it. Synagogues, cafes, schools, offices, homes—wherever there was unexcised Jewish presence, the Brown Shirts struck.[25]

Then Jewish possessions were systematically ripped, splattered, and looted. Brown Shirts spread Torahs across the ground and danced upon the scrolls. Furniture was thrown into the street. Valuables were carted away as trophies. Pictures, books, and curtains were torn.[26]

Kerosene came next. Floors and drapes were methodically doused. An enthusiastic drenching was reserved for Torahs, prayer shawls, holy books, and devotional *bimahs* in synagogues. Tossed matches. Rolled incendiary bombs. Lobbed petrol bombs. Nearly everything Jewish was set aflame. Not just in Berlin. Not just in Vienna. In every town and city of the Third Reich.[27]

More than 15,000 Jews dragged from their homes were brutalized before the cheering onlookers, herded into trucks, dispatched to jails, and in many cases, directly to concentration camps. Firemen watched the flames with laughter, taking care that neighboring Aryan structures were unaffected. Policemen studiously directed traffic, allowing the marauders complete freedom of operation.[28]

Here among the ruins was the final overnight summary of Jewish existence in Germany and a prophecy for their bleak fate in Europe. Jewish life would ultimately be incinerated everywhere. The consequences of identification had been irrevocably unmasked. Whatever doubt the world had about the intentions of the Hitler regime, that doubt vaporized with the curls of smoke rising from hundreds of synagogues and Jewish offices in Germany.

Newspapers, newsreels, and radio broadcasts across the globe burned with headlines condemning Hitler's Reich as savage and barbarous. The *New York Times* printed a tall page one banner headline: "Nazis Smash, Loot and Burn Jewish Shops and Temples." The newspaper tellingly noted that the only Vienna synagogue not torched was one "that the authorities have protected . . . because it contains records of the Jewish community of Vienna that could not be replaced."[29]

Washington recalled its ambassador from Berlin. Western diplomats called for concerted action to stem the anti-Semitic outrages. President Franklin D. Roosevelt issued a sharply worded denunciation in which he personally penned the words, "I myself could scarcely believe that such things could occur in a twentieth century civilization." Gallup Polls asked whether Hitler could be believed when he said he had no more territorial ambitions in Europe beyond Czechoslovakia; 92 percent of American respondents and 93 percent of British respondents declared Hitler could not be believed. Hitler's followers in America had already been prosecuted in high-profile cases under various civil rights statutes. Now, the term "Nazi sympathizer" became widely used. And Nazi collaboration and propagandizing was deemed sufficiently subversive and "un-American" that eventually a special Congressional committee investigated.[30]

American reaction to the riots was almost wholly disregarded by Hitler. After *Kristallnacht,* Jews were forced to vacate their apartments, sometimes on just a few days' notice, as Hitler loyalists queued up to move in. In Munich, all Jewish families were given just forty-eight hours to permanently leave the city. The order was soon rescinded as impossible—although later the demand was re-imposed. Jews were collectively fined 1 billion marks for inciting the *Kristallnacht* riots. And the last phases of confiscation and asset registration were set in motion.[31]

The German government issued dire warning after dire warning that the situation could worsen. But a *New York Times* feature on November 14, 1938, ominously asked, "Inasmuch as everything has been done to the Jews in Germany that can be done to a people short of physical extermination, there are arising some obvious speculations as to what these continued warnings may imply." The question was answered just days later on November 30, when the newspaper published an article headlined "Jews in Germany Get

Extermination Threat," quoting the *Schwarze Korps,* the organ of Hitler's SS, as it advertised the potential for wholesale Jewish murder.[32]

Watson had visited Germany twice in 1938, once in late May, just after the *Anschluss* of Austria, and once in early October, during the tense build-up to *Kristallnacht.*[33]

Germany was threatening invasion daily. War preparations were no secret. Reich propagandists spread the word, ensuring headlines and debates. Commanders fortified borders. Mobilization plans were disseminated. Aircraft engineers received special awards for new bomber and fighter designs. Passenger trains were restricted so rail stock could be devoted to troop movements. Housewives were publicly asked to dramatically reduce consumption of fats to save money so the Reich could purchase raw materials urgently needed for its weapons production.[34] War was in the air.

Yet, throughout the year, Watson argued passionately for Germany's demands. He barely made an appearance at an international commercial meeting, university commencement ceremony, ribbon-cutting, or press conference without reiterating his well-worn Hitleresque appeal that the world "redistribute its raw materials" and lower so-called "trade barriers" as "the path to peace." This public lobbying was undertaken even as the mass media regularly published articles and broadcast explanations that Germany desperately only needed those raw materials to arm her war machine. Even though Watson's pronouncements sounded to many as mere code for the Nazi agenda, he held fast to his script. More than that, whenever Watson returned from a tour of the Continent, his dockside remarks always spoke glowingly of the optimism throughout Europe and the steadily increased standard of living for all—this at a time when the world was teetering on the brink of total war and witnessing the dispossession of the Jews.[35]

Prominent writers and personalities would rebut Watson's brand of thinking. One foreign correspondent in the *New York Times* reflected the common view when he wrote, "It must be remembered . . . the series of boycotts due to worldwide resentment against German domestic policies . . . play almost as large a part as do the trade barriers." In May 1938, just after the *Anschluss* and just before sailing to Germany, Watson answered such sentiments. "Unjust criticism of business is a trade barrier," he lectured his fellow industrialists at an ICC gathering, adding, "Unjust criticism of government is another trade barrier."[36]

For Watson, whatever Hitler was doing to the Jews and other perceived enemies of the Third Reich was no obstacle to realizing profit on Germany's plans. "You know, you can cooperate with a man without believing in everything he says and does," Watson sermonized to his followers after one trip to Germany, adding, "If you do not agree with everything he does, cooperate with him in the things you do believe in. Others will cooperate with him in the things they believe in." On another occasion, Watson illuminated his steeled indifference this way: "I am an American citizen. But in the IBM I am a world citizen, because we do business in 78 countries and they all look alike to me—every one of them."[37]

Yet when Watson's ocean liner anchored at New York just days after the November 10 *Kristallnacht* outrage, it was all different. IBM's Leader finally realized that American sentiment had become so extremely anti-Nazi, he now needed to distance himself from the very regime he had so publicly saluted.

> NOVEMBER 25, 1938
> Dr. Hjalmar Schacht
> President
> Reichsbank
> Berlin, Germany
>
> Dear Dr. Schacht:
>   I returned from Europe about ten days ago, and I feel I owe it to you and the German people to tell you of the tremendous loss of good will to Germany, which is increasing on account of the latest policies of Germany in regard to dealing with Jewish minorities in your country. I feel that I would be unfair to my long list of Jewish friends if I did not appeal to your Government to give fair consideration to the Jews as human beings, and to their property rights. As you know, for many years, I have put forth my best efforts to improve trade relations between Germany and the United States, and I want you to know that it is my honest judgment that if the Jewish situation today is not improved, it will have a very serious effect on Germany's trade with our country.
>
>   Yours very truly[38]

Watson reviewed the typed letter from his secretary. A diagonal line was drawn through the entire letter canceling its message and the words "Yours very truly" were vigorously crossed out. The letter would not be sent.[39] Second try, this one directly to Adolf Hitler.

November 25, 1938

Your Excellency:

In July 1937, as President of the International Chamber of Commerce, I received by your order the Merit Cross of the German Eagle, which was presented to me by Dr. Schacht on behalf of the German Government, in recognition of my efforts for world peace, and better economic relations between Germany and other nations.

In expressing my thanks to you, I stated that I would cooperate with you in the future as I had in the past in connection with these two important issues. This, I am still most anxious to do; but upon my recent return to my country after an absence of several months I find a change in public sentiment and a loss of good will to your country, and unless something can be done to bring about a more friendly understanding on the part of our people, I feel it is going to be difficult to accomplish mutually satisfactory results in connection with our trade relations.

The change in sentiment referred to has been brought about through the decisions of your Government in dealing with minorities, and I respectfully appeal to you to give consideration to applying the Golden Rule in dealing with these minorities.

I have read with the greatest interest the statement that your Government is prepared to make arrangements with a committee of leading Quakers to assist German Jews in the spirit of charity and the Golden Rule, I venture, therefore, to accept this act as a symbol of willingness on your part to grant more generous treatment to minorities.

If your Excellency would follow up this act of kindliness with policies inspired by its humanitarian effort, it would, in my opinion, be the one way by which those interested in the exchange of goods and services and high ideals might find the opportunity to help Germany regain the valuable trade and good-will which she has lost.

Very respectfully yours,
Thomas Watson[40]

Watson would be able to show his direct and unequivocal protest letter to anyone as evidence of vociferous objection to Hitler's anti-Semitism. Presumably the letter could be exhibited with the same flourish Watson employed in displaying other letters to and from world leaders, some of which he routinely carried in his inside suit pocket. Surely, the November 25, 1938, letter would put Watson on record as unalterably opposed to Hitler's campaign. But somehow, Watson's explicit letter to Hitler was . . . misaddressed. Watson could always say it had been mailed. But in truth the Post Office returned it—unopened. Watson's secretary tried again four months later.[41]

People of conscience throughout the world were outraged at the Hitler regime. Yet Germany was on the verge of expanding its use of Hollerith systems to an unprecedented level. Watson needed to cover himself in the Reich and at home. He would now pursue a strange public posture, essentially speaking from both sides of the punch card. Deftly, he would mix his messages of subtle advocacy for Reich territorial and economic hegemony with patriotic assertions supporting American defense measures, and almost pollyannaish aphorisms offered to Germany about its brutal anti-Semitism. Watson would always be able to point to out-of-context portions of his remarks to satisfy any audience—be it those listening in the Nazi Reich or the United States. At the same time, all mention of Germany as the linchpin of IBM's overseas operation was conspicuously dropped from IBM press statements.

For example, just after *Kristallnacht,* when Watson returned from Europe, his usual dockside remarks to the media listed the many countries he had visited, including Greece, Italy, Romania, Portugal, Turkey, and France. But Germany was not mentioned—the first time since the rise of Hitler that Watson had omitted the country name from his proudly detailed itineraries. A newspaper article about IBM's foreign employees studying at the company sales school in Endicott spoke of students from twenty-four countries. Yet Germany's name was the only one not listed—again, the first time the Reich's place in IBM's international commerce was omitted, even though, as usual, representatives from Germany were there.[42]

Platitudes were dispensed in abundance. "World Peace through World Trade" became Watson's official jingo to explain away IBM trading with Nazi Germany. Beckoning Hitler to please "observe the Golden Rule" paled as a schoolboy-like admonishment in the face of the ruthless torture and dispossession gripping German Jewry. But Watson was an expert at calculated public pronouncements on troublesome topics. When he first assumed the helm of the IBM organization—back in the CTR days—he scheduled a company assembly to demonstratively and publicly lecture his sales force, "You must not do anything that's in restraint of trade . . . or that could be construed by anybody as unfair competition." Ironically, these stern moralistic directives were conspicuously broadcast just at the height of the Justice Department's decision-making process on re-prosecuting Watson for his role in one of America's most aggravated cases of anti-competitive tactics.[43]

So, at the same time the IBM Leader was advocating "the Golden Rule," he wrote a letter to the world's governments urging them to "collaborate regardless of divergent ideals and opinions" to avoid war. In international economic forums, he asserted "the divine right of every people to choose its own government" and demanded "adjustments that would give all countries an opportunity to share in the resources of the world."[44] Watson's choice of words bore the unmistakable ring of Germany's party line, which likewise demanded that it be allowed to share in all of Europe's natural resources for the greater glory of the Reich.

None of Watson's public posturing stopped him from accelerating Dehomag's ability to do Hitler's bidding throughout Europe—so long as IBM could keep its distance and Watson could remain removed from the process. In late May 1938, shortly after Germany annexed Austria, Watson visited Berlin on Dehomag business. Watson requested Dehomag's management to prepare to extend its operations into Austria, thus replacing the existing subsidiary controlled by IBM NY. Dehomag was going to develop some unique tabulating equipment, based on its powerful new D-11, engineered for special applications that could generate significant revenues. However, these new efforts would have an impact on complicated issues of profit sharing, tax, bonus, and general compensation—all of which Watson wanted carefully negotiated.[45]

More and more, Watson tried to work through intermediaries. The negotiation itself was delayed until shortly after Watson left Germany. Then, on the morning of June 24, 1938, Dehomag convened a shareholder meeting attended by two Geneva-based IBM executives representing the New York office. Although Watson was not there, he controlled the decisions from afar through his 85 percent vote, cast through his European General Manager John E. Holt who held a power-of-attorney. Point six of the minutes called for negotiations "as soon as possible."[46]

It was left to a member of the IBM NY's board of directors, Oscar L. Gubelman, to work out the details of Dehomag's expansion into Austria, along with certain loan provisions and stock options as inducements for Dehomag Directors Rottke and Hummel. Gubelman agreed that the directors' loan provisions and stock options could be incorporated into a formal supplemental employment contract, but the Austrian expansion itself was to be kept as an oral arrangement recorded only by memo. On July 6, 1938, Rottke and Hummel jointly confirmed the oral arrangement in a letter to Gubelman, who was staying at Berlin's Hotel Adlon. Their letter listed three main points: "a) New Products, b) New Territories, c) reduction of [stock] repurchase price in case of premature leaving the Dehomag due to notice of resignation."[47]

The joint Dehomag letter acknowledged New York's primacy in no uncertain terms. "IBM," the letter emphasized, retains "unlimited power to dispose of such new products, and in view of its [IBM's] position within Dehomag, is absolutely in a position, even without our express declaration of assent, on its part to formulate the conditions for the inclusion of Dehomag in such new business."[48]

Only IBM NY could authorize Dehomag to develop new products or expand into Austria, but if it did so, the business would be maintained separately from the regular books and would appear instead as loan or bonus transactions. Dehomag's confirmation letter expressed the understanding in cautious, stilted language. For New Products: "It has been orally agreed," the letter recited, "and is confirmed herewith by us in writing, in case IBM entrusts Dehomag with the sale and/or manufacture of new products which lie outside the present scope of business of the Dehomag and also do not come under the license agreement between the Dehomag and the IBM, we agree that upon the request of the IBM, we can be totally or partly excluded from the results of the business transactions in these new products, as they have been agreed upon in the form of a bonus in the loan agreements and supplementary agreements concluded between the Dehomag and us."[49]

For New Territories: "In case the IBM should voluntarily transfer the working of territories outside of Germany to the Dehomag, we also agree that, upon the request of the IBM, we can be totally or partly excluded from the results of the business transactions in these new territories as they have been agreed upon in the form of a bonus in the loan agreements and supplementary agreements concluded between the Dehomag and us."[50]

The letter added, "After careful deliberation, you have considered it proper to let the points a) [New Products] and b) [New Territories] be dealt with merely in this letter in the sense of our discussion, while point c) will be included in the supplementary agreement." Rottke and Hummel's letter concluded with their gratitude for helping the Reich: "We confidently hope that the contents of this letter will convince Mr. Watson . . . that we see our life's task in our present work and sincerely wish to contribute to the development of the Dehomag for many years to come. We thank you very much for the great assistance you have given in this matter."[51]

Although the arrangement to expand Dehomag was handled through intermediaries, Watson micro-managed every detail. On August 2, 1938, Watson sent a letter to John Holt, IBM's European general manager, confirming approval of both the loan additions to the employment contracts and the special letter about the expansion. "Mr. Gubelman has handed me the final draft of the proposed amendment to the Rottke-Hummel contracts," wrote Watson, "and also the letter from Rottke-Hummel addressed to Mr. Gubelman as a Director, dated July 6, 1938. . . . You are authorized to sign for IBM."[52]

The scene was set for Dehomag to immediately expand into every new Nazi-conquered nation, so long as IBM approved in advance. Austria was only the beginning, and IBM understood it well. On August 4, 1938, J.C. Milner, a Geneva-based IBM supervisor of Dehomag, wrote to J. T. Wilson, the manager of IBM NY's so-called Foreign Division, explaining, "Rottke has made arrangements . . . which include equipment for seven or eight different countries to fill customers orders." The letter added that Dehomag could not fill all the orders from its inventory, so "five or six sets of Valtat equipment . . . we shall have shipped [from the U.S.] to the freeport at Geneva."[53]

A key mission for Dehomag machines was census in neighboring countries. "During 1940, the census will be taken in several countries," Milner's August 4 letter confirmed, "and we expect a number of orders." He added, "One of the problems which confronts us is that of providing special machines for census work. . . . Since Endicott has discontinued manufacturing the Printing Counting Sorter, we do not seem to have any machine particularly adapted to census work. As you know, Germany does construct a Census Tabulator, and we have always figured on being able to get the machines from them for forthcoming work." But production in Germany was backlogged and was becoming less economical because of Reich currency restrictions.[54]

So Milner wondered whether Endicott wanted to develop its own census tabulator capable of high-speed counting, continue to rely on the German version, or perhaps produce them in another European country and ship them on Dehomag's behalf. "If Endicott does not propose to undertake such work," he wrote in the August 4, 1938, letter, "it is quite possible that we shall have to look into the situation in France, and see whether they can economically construct a machine equivalent to the German Census Tabulator."[55] IBM NY now began viewing its various subsidiaries throughout Europe as coordinated to support Dehomag's operation.

Moreover, IBM NY wanted to maintain strict controls on each and every Dehomag lease. Special rebates and discounts for Reich operations could not be extended unless approved by New York. J. T. Wilson sent a memo to IBM's Europe headquarters on August 25, 1938, entitled "Shipment of German Machines Beyond Germany," demanding to know whether corporate controllers in Geneva were "setting prices for machines shipped beyond the borders of Germany." Wilson wanted to make sure the proper mark-up above cost was preserved. That same day he sent a second letter off to Harrison Chauncey, another IBM NY management troubleshooter in Europe, explaining, "Their costs are very much higher than our costs at Endicott. For instance, the cost of building a Sorter in Germany is $292, while the cost at Endicott is $220."[56]

Holt replied to Wilson, "We have a fixed charge . . . and do not take into consideration whether it comes from the United States, or Germany, or another factory." He added, however, that "in the case of special machines, such as [Dehomag's] D-11, we have always set prices which are, we believe, somewhat higher than the United States would charge. . . . Since the German company has a schedule of rebates to its customers of which you are well aware, in taking a special German machine and placing it in a foreign country, we have always tried to approach the net German price, using the official rate of exchange."[57]

Holt offered an example. "In other words," he wrote, "should a machine be supplied to Holland, we would . . . add 25%, and [then] add a further 10%." But Holt made unequivocally clear that IBM NY controlled pricing on all of Germany's machines. "[I]n all cases, we set the prices, and Germany does not."[58]

Complicating all IBM efforts to profit on Dehomag's Europe-wide sales in fall 1938 was yet another Reich monetary decree. Germany was nearing bankruptcy. The anti-Nazi boycott had virtually crippled a once-thriving export-dependent Reich economy. Despite desperate cashless barter efforts to boost foreign sales and unverifiable trade statistics to the contrary, Germany's currency-earning exports were down to the United States by as much as 95 percent for many commercial sectors. Schacht had confided as much to Watson at the 1937 ICC Congress.[59] Without foreign exchange, Hitler could not rearm. So it was hardly a surprise to IBM when the Third Reich prohibited exports by German companies unless they earned actual cash. In other words, Dehomag could no longer ship Hollerith machines across its borders and then forward the sales income to IBM NY as so-called debt repayment.

"As you are aware," IBM's Milner in Geneva wrote Wilson in New York, in an early August 1938 letter, "for a number of years we have been able to charge such goods against the debts owing to IBM in New York, but this permission has now been withdrawn by the Government." Milner added that the arrangement was a surprise even to IBM auditors. "Price Waterhouse people in Berlin . . . stated it was most unusual and they did not know of any other foreign concern who had the same privilege."[60]

Nonetheless, "I'm sorry to tell you," Milner lamented, "that we have just been advised by Mr. Rottke that from now on it will not be possible to ship tabulating equipment and other goods out of Germany to our various countries without the German company receiving payment for the goods."[61] Hence, profits would not only be trapped in German blocked mark accounts, other IBM subsidiaries in Europe acting as intermediaries for Dehomag would have to transfer foreign currency to Berlin to complete the transaction.

Moreover, Dehomag income in Europe, unless somehow shrouded, might now subject IBM profits to double taxation. Double taxation was a particular irritant to Watson, and he had worked for years to legislate a solution. IBM Geneva's M. G. Connally, a key Dehomag auditor, revealed the company's attitude to a U.S. State Department officer earlier in 1938. He let it slip that "some concerns have actually resorted to the fiction of royalties in order to avoid taxation," but quickly added, that in the case of IBM, "no such fiction existed and that royalties are the result of clearly worded contracts."[62]

More than just controlling which machines would be distributed throughout Europe, and at what price, IBM understood by fall 1938 that it was now an integral part of the Nazi war machine. Wilson circulated on August 25, 1938, a memo to senior management in the New York office, reviewing problems in exporting machines from Germany. "As you know," Wilson informed, "both brass and copper and alloys play a big part in the mechanism of all of our machines and these metals are very scarce in Germany, at least, I am told they require them for war materials."[63]

Indeed, by 1937, the Reich concluded that punch card technology was too important to its plan for Europe not to be strictly regulated. Henceforth, machines would be rationed only to those users approved by the military. In 1937, a secret unit was created within the Reich War Ministry's Office of Military Economy. The department became known under the innocuous name *Maschinelles Berichtwesen*, or Office of Automated Reporting, and was dedicated to one main function: punch card technology. This agency went through several bureaucratic metamorphoses, chiefly through the Reich Ministry for Armaments and War Production. The *Maschinelles Berichtwesen*, also known as the *MB*, wielded complete control over the ordering, sale, use, reporting, and coordination of all Hollerith systems in Greater Germany. It worked in complete tandem with all aspects of Hitler's campaigns in Europe, opening so-called "field offices" in conquered countries.[64]

From the Reich's point of view, punch card technology would be indispensable to its war-making capability. A February 1938 secret military report declared that "technologizing the Wehrmacht [armed forces]" was imperative. The report listed the continual regimentation, tracking, and redeployment of the general population, work force, and military personnel, as best accomplished by Hollerith systems. "A punch card system," the *MB* report concluded, "must be introduced for the statistical survey of workers and for shifting workers" to create "perfectly structured personnel planning."[65]

A later memo from the Office of Military Economy called for a universal punch code system. The document reviewed Dehomag's many prior efforts, such as the census, labor statistics, and the *Work Book,* but that these "all have the disadvantage of existing for singular purposes and being incompatible with each other." The report made clear, "it is impossible to reliably separate industrial demand for armament purposes from total industrial demand. The punch card is appropriate for the solution of this problem," adding, "The punch card does not replace all considerations, judgments and decisions, but it makes them easier."[66]

While it was obvious to all that Germany was preparing for imminent war, it was also apparent that the Reich was aggressively utilizing statistics and punch card technology to track Jews and implement its program of persecution. "Statistics issued today show that 12,094 Jews left Berlin last year for Palestine, Great Britain and the Americas," led a July 4, 1937, *New York Times* article datelined Berlin, adding, "The statistics are confined to 'Jews by faith,' the authorities declaring that Jews by race alone could be included in such records." Wire services regularly reported on the facts of Nazi demographic tracking: religion percentages based on census returns; quotas on goods Jews could purchase; an August 17, 1938, regulation compelling all identified Jews whose names did not "sound Jewish" to add the first name Israel or Sara.[67]

Newspapers, on May 15, 1938, listed a number of large cities outside Berlin and exactly how much their Jewish population had decreased through the end of 1937. Nuremberg had 7,502 Jews in 1933, but only 4,000 in 1937. Worms went from 1,016 Jews in 1933 to 549 in 1937. Hagen dropped from 508 to 299.[68]

Nazi raceology was becoming an all encompassing obsession evident on virtually every street and within every organization in Germany. A June 22, 1938, *New York Times* article reported, "twenty-six research organizations have been established throughout the Reich which go from family to family" to identify bloodline. Wire services informed that the curriculum for all German medical students had been altered to include mandatory courses on race science and population policy. Local prosecutors could order compulsory divorces of Jews and Aryans. At the same time, hundreds of thousands of marriages of urban Aryan women to what the Germans termed "virile, hereditary" farmers were required by Nazi demographers to achieve population health; the authorities began combing factories and offices for state-mandated brides.[69] Few in America outside of IBM understood that these highly publicized racial policies were facilitated by Dehomag's population, health office, and labor office tabulations.

Personal data that could not be tabulated by an organization for lack of an on-site Hollerith system were assembled on simple handwritten cards, forms, or copied onto registries that were forwarded to race offices and security services for punching and sorting. Churches were among the leading sources of such information. Their antique, ornately bound church books were often bulky and difficult to work with so supply companies developed a variety of index cards in various sizes designed to facilitate the tracing of ancestry. Often the process was awkward and anything but fast.[70]

One small church office in Braunlage in the Harz Mountains was typical when it complained in a letter to the *Reichssippenamt*, the Reich's leading raceology agency, that the cards were too small and the data too large. "We have received samples of cards for the carding of church books," wrote Pastor Stich. "Once we started to work with these cards, we noticed that these are rather small. . . . For [those of] us who are doing the work and bearing the costs, it is important we record not just some of the data, but all of the data, so that each card gives complete information about ancestry. . . . we are not served well if we have to open and move the pages of the heavy and irreplaceable church books." Pastor Stich asked for larger index cards, making clear, "We are glad to serve the cause . . . and ready to do the job right."[71]

The *Reichssippenamt* promptly replied, "The primary function of the carding of church books is that it makes the research easier and at the same time preserves the church book. . . . if you follow my guidelines for an alphabetical name index, then use of the church books itself should be reduced by a factor of fifty."[72]

Local NSDAP leadership in Düsseldorf debated whether cards should be filed phonetically or alphabetically. Either way, the office felt it wise to color code the cards. "Whenever full Jews or mixed Jews appear," a local official wrote, "the former are marked by a red line, the latter by a blue line.

However, both also receive a tab. Without the tab, the red and blue lines could otherwise not be easily identified after the sorting and filing has taken place."[73]

Detailed instructions were developed for recording baptisms to make sure Jews could not hide their identity through conversion. "For every Jewish baptism," the instructions read, "two double cards are to be filled out in addition to the normal card. (One for the *Reichssippenamt* and one for the file of Persons of Foreign Descent in the Berlin central office). With name changes (for example, the Jew Israel receives the family name Leberecht through baptism), the Christian or Jewish name is to be entered in parentheses in the field for family name." The name was then coded R, and the Jew's occupation and address were to be written on the reverse side.[74]

To help standardize methods, the Publishing House of Registry Office Matters published a guide entitled *How Do I Card Church Books?*[75]

So precise were the tabulations that, in some areas, the authorities had identified people considered "sixteenth Jews." The county of Bautzen, for example, summarized its extensive race tracking in a December 5, 1937 study, bragging that it had expanded the local Race Political Office from four employees to twenty-one during the previous two and a half years, with additional race experts deployed in local Party offices as well as women's associations. "For the entire county area," officials asserted, "there exists a file for Jews, Half-Jews, Quarter-Jews, Eighth-Jews, etc. with the following information: name, residence, occupation, date of birth, place of birth, citizenship, religion . . . spouse, children, ancestors." As a result, local officials had identified 92 [full] Jews, 40 half-Jews, 19 quarter-Jews, 5 eighth-Jews, and 4 sixteenth-Jews "whose connections are continuously observed."[76]

Race offices developed a mutual help network that constantly traded and updated their data. For example, Bautzen's information collection was helped by registries from the State Health Offices; those offices were tabulated by Hollerith systems. In June 1938, 339 local labor offices took a so-called "labor census" of 22,300,000 German workers employed in approximately 247 occupational groups and subsets; the labor agencies also exchanged information assembled by Dehomag. Eichmann's office *Referat* II 112, the Jewish Section of the Main Security Office, traded its synagogue and church sects lists with the *Reichssippenamt*; both offices used Hollerith systems.[77]

The exponential growth of demand for Dehomag services spurred Watson to push his entire organization to manufacture more German machines faster. He even pushed his German managers at Dehomag to break production records. In mid-June, Watson agreed to add equipment and work space if the German subsidiary could double its output. IBM managers in Paris monitored Dehomag's monthly progress, and asked for hard numbers. By the end of 1937, Rottke was able to report to IBM that monthly punch card production was at 74 million per month, production of horizontal sorters would double from 15 to 30 per month, tabulating machines would increase from 18 per month to 20 per month, multiplying punches would double from 5 to 10 per month, and counters would rise from 200 to 250 per month.[78]

To speed production, IBM approved the purchase of more machine tools for the assembly shops. Three inclinable presses, a jig bore, five 6-spindle drill presses, four vertical drill presses, five bench drills, and a variety of milling machines, saws, grinders, lathes, and screw presses.[79]

In early June 1938, IBM again pushed for greater productivity. Holt reminded IBM's Paris-based European Factory Manager J G. Johnston, "Mr. Watson states that you told him last year . . . it should be possible to produce twice the number of parts [at Sindelfingen] . . . Mr. Rottke informs us that only 60% of the parts are now being manufactured at Sindelfingen." Johnston traveled to Berlin immediately, and reported back in minute detail on proposed expansion plans, explaining on a veritable floor-by-floor basis which improvements had been approved by Watson, and which were still awaiting permission. Watson's consent was required for even the smallest change in factory layout. For example, wrote Johnston, "if we should obtain the authorization of Mr. Watson for the shaded part of the plan for the new building, we could expect an increase of 3 x 462 sq. meters or a total of 1,386 sq. meters space . . . which increase would be sufficient for our needs for some length of time."[80]

Johnston assured Holt, "The figure of 60 of the total output of parts now being manufactured in Sindelfingen will be greatly increased." He stressed that many of the new machine tools were just being delivered and would be brought on line soon.[81] More machines would be built—faster, better, cheaper.

Europe was hurtling toward all-out war. Dehomag would be ready.

CZECHOSLOVAKIA WAS NEXT.

Hitler, in 1938, demanded the largely Germanic Sudetenland region of Czechoslovakia be handed to the Reich. Not only were there 3 million German-speaking residents in the Sudetenland, but Czechoslovakia possessed the raw materials that Hitler coveted. German generals had already drawn up invasion plans. But hoping to avert war, Britain and France, in tandem with Italy, negotiated with Hitler for a compromise.[82]

After dramatic ups and downs, the last-minute Munich Pact of September 30, 1938, ceded the Sudetenland to Germany as of the next day. The deal was called appeasement and was foisted upon Czechoslovakia by the European powers without regard for the Czech nation.[83]

On October 1, 1938, German forces moved in according to a pre-arranged takeover schedule. Within hours of entering any town, it was transformed. Streets and buildings were bedecked with Nazi bunting and swastika flags. For months, highly organized Sudeten Nazis functioned as a vanguard for the oppression to come, burning Jewish homes and boycotting Jewish stores. Now they ensured that Jewish shops were smeared with white paint.[84] No one doubted what would come next.

By October 2, thousands of Jews flooded across the new border by car, train, and on foot into what remained of Czechoslovakia.[85]

Jews remaining behind found themselves identified, in spite of their highly assimilated Czech national character. Nazi contingents would systematically appear on their streets, drag families from their homes, herd them into trucks, and either deliver them to concentration camps or dump them penniless on the border with remnant Czechoslovakia. Many women and children, already beaten and bloody, were forced to cross the frontier crawling on their hands and knees, some on their bellies. Soon, their overwhelming numbers—as many as 40,000 had either fled or been expelled—were too much for the Czechs. Nor were the Czechs willing to provoke the Germans by seeming to create a refuge for deported Jews. The Czechs refused them entry.[86]

Ousted from the Sudetenland, and barred from the reduced Czechoslovakia, thousands of expelled Jews were now stranded in slender tracts of no-man's land between border crossings. Dispossessed of everything, hundreds dwelled in roadside ditches, completely exposed to the elements without food, water, sanitation, or an understanding of how they had been identified or why they were suffering this fate. South of Bruenn, 150 huddled beneath hedges. Near Kostitz: 52 people. Outside Reigern: 51 people. Food shipments sent by relief committees were blocked by Czech guards, German soldiers, or Party stalwarts. Then came rains to magnify their misery and muddy their nightmare.[87]

The agony of these ditch people became an on-going spectacle for the world's media. They survived from moment to moment only on the morsels of food thrown in pity by passersby transiting the borders and disregarding prohibitions on aid. When the trapped Jews were finally forced back to the German side, vicious mobs of jeering Nazis brutalized them.[88]

But the Sudetenland was not enough for Hitler. In early 1939, the Third Reich pressured Czechoslovakia to commence its own anti-Jewish ousters, including those Jews who had fled Germany, Austria, and the Sudetenland. Czechoslovakia complied, hoping to forestall an invasion. At 6 A.M. on March 15, 1939, the Reich invaded anyway. German troops pushed into all of Moravia and Bohemia. Hitler declared the whole of Czechoslovakia a Reich Protectorate under the iron-handed rule of appointed Governors. Now all of Czech Jewry would be disseminated. A staccato of anti-Semitic registrations, expulsions, and confiscations soon descended upon all of what was once known as Czechoslovakia.[89]

Within days, newspapers were reporting the same sorrowful fate for Czech Jewry as experienced elsewhere. Doctors and merchants were expelled from their posts and professional associations. Synagogues were burned. Signs forbidding Jews at cafes and other stores appeared.[90]

The suicides began. Thirty per day in Prague. In Chicago, a number of Czech refugees who had been admitted on temporary visas formed a "suicide colony." One member of the colony was Mrs. Karel Langer, who ended her family's life in the Congress Hotel. First she hurled her two young boys, six and four years of age, out of the window of the thirteenth floor. She leapt after them just seconds later. Police recovered all three bodies from the Michigan Avenue sidewalk.[91]

Registration of property and family members was extended not only to those who outwardly practiced Judaism, but those defined by the Nuremberg Laws as having three and in some cases, two, Jewish grandparents. An estimated 200,000 would be involved.[92]

IBM was already in Czechoslovakia. Shortly after Hitler came to power, IBM NY had established a service bureau in Prague. The first school for Czech salesmen was opened in 1935 about the time the Nuremberg Laws were passed. In November 1936, Watson approved a card printing plant in a small town near Prague, where sixteen printers and two cutting machines were installed. Some months later, as IBM ramped up operations, the company protested when Czech Customs changed the company's tariff classification from simplistic mechanical punches to statistical machines.[93]

In 1937, Georg Schneider was hired as an additional salesman for Prague. Within about a year, Schneider was transferred to Dehomag in Berlin "as a salesman and studying the German organization." He met Watson in Berlin, as well as the company's leading Swiss-based supervisors. By that time, Czechoslovakian State Railways was utilizing 52.2 million punch cards per year. In 1939, IBM Geneva and Dehomag agreed that Schneider should return to Prague, where about sixty employees worked, as the new co-manager working with Director Emil Kuzcek. At about that time, the Reich opened the Statistical Office for the Protectorate of Bohemia and Moravia, located in Prague. IBM did not list itself in Czech commercial registries as owning its own subsidiary. Instead, the subsidiary's 200,000 Korunas value was held 102,000 by IBM's attorney in Prague, Stefan Schmid, and 98,000 by IBM's European General Manager John Holt, both men acting as nominees for IBM NY.[94]

For IBM, the question was not how deeply Dehomag would control all Hollerith activity in Czechoslovakia, but once again, who would share in the profit. In the first days of 1939, after Germany's takeover of the Sudetenland, and at the height of the Reich's threats to take over the rest of Czechoslovakia, IBM worried about the bonus question with Heidinger, Rottke, and Hummel.

On January 11, 1939, Watson's personal emissary, Harrison Chauncey, drafted a letter for European Manager Holt in Geneva, reviewing how the oral arrangement with Dehomag for "new territories" might work once Czechoslovakia was included. So there was no mistake, Chauncey recited the language from the oral arrangement. "'In case the IBM should voluntarily transfer the working of territories outside of Germany to the Dehomag,'" Chauncey quoted, "'we also agree that, upon the request of the IBM, we can be totally or partly excluded from the results of the business transactions . . . as they have been agreed upon in the form of a bonus in the loan agreements.'"[95]

Then Chauncey posited the question: "In the case of Austria and Czechoslovakia, should determination be made whether or not at this time as to whether Rottke and Hummel should receive the benefits from any business within these two countries."[96]

In an effort to create deniability about the decision, Chauncey added, "under present circumstances it might be unwise for the IBM to make the determination." Written by hand, the sentence appended, "but Dehomag should when time is proper." Thus, IBM NY could claim that Czech activity was undertaken at Dehomag's sole decision—even though no such activity could take place without Watson's permission.[97]

Addressing the time constraints, Chauncey wrote, "You might consider whether Dehomag should have an understanding immediately, because, of course, there will also be involved a transfer of the assets in Austria and

Czechoslovakia."[98] Chauncey's letter did not refer to "the Sudetenland," which had already been swept into the Reich, but "*Czechoslovakia*"; although Czechoslovakia was being daily threatened with forcible annexation, Germany was still weeks away from its invasion.

A senior IBM executive, John G. Phillips, scribbled on the draft, "have Chauncey see me." On January 17, 1939, the heavily edited letter to Holt was formally typed on letterhead and again submitted to senior executives for review. Still maintaining deniability, the revised version suggested, "Under present circumstances, we wonder whether it would be unwise for IBM to make the determination relating to territory and products. We might consider whether it would be more proper to have Rottke and Hummel write Dehomag setting forth substantially the same thing as in the letter to Mr. Gubelman. . . . You might consider whether Dehomag should have an understanding immediately, because, of course, there will also be involved a transfer of the assets in Austria and Czechoslovakia."[99]

But Chauncey's letter still seemed too sensitive for senior IBM executives. Newspaper headlines and newsreels were blasting Germany daily for the Czech situation. After ten days, the letter was still not approved, and finally on January 27, Chauncey was instructed by Phillips, "suggest we hold on this for the present."[100]

Dehomag lost no time in proceeding in Czechoslovakia—with or without settling the question of bonuses for Czech activity. But even if Rottke and Hummel were willing to wait for a decision on bonuses, Heidinger was not. As Germany prepared to launch an invasion against Czechoslovakia, Heidinger unleashed his own battle plan to secure a share in the profit the IBM organization expected in newly conquered territories.

GERMANY WAS facing economic collapse and began clamping down on taxpayers and profiteers. Watson had refused to declare a profit since 1934, despite record multi-million mark earnings. Tax authorities reviewed RM 180,000 in IBM advances and loans to Heidinger in lieu of actual profit dividends. Heidinger's money was declared a bonus no matter how it was disguised—and he was ordered to pay RM 90,000 in taxes. On January 20, 1938, Heidinger wrote to IBM's Holt in Geneva complaining that no matter what IBM called it, "The German government considers it as a dividend and I have to pay the [income] taxes." The levy was in addition to his normal income taxes. "That is impossible for me," he conceded. "I would have to burden my properties with a mortgage or to change my standard of life."[101]

Heidinger offered IBM an ultimatum: either declare a bona fide profit and pay a dividend for prior years that would net him RM 250,000—or he would exercise an option requiring IBM to buy back his shares in the company. For now, he was offering just one of his ten shares. He would still retain 9 percent. "Find out which . . . Mr. Watson would prefer," Heidinger asked.[102]

Alarms went off in Geneva, Paris, and New York. IBM had no objection to a stock buy-back. But everyone understood that if Heidinger reduced his holdings below 10 percent that might cause Nazi authorities to re-examine the Aryan nature of Dehomag. The company could lose the ability to use *"Deutsche"* in its name, and might even be taken over by *kommissars*.[103] Moreover, in Germany's current state of war preparedness, punch card technology overseers in the Ministry of War could even decree a takeover.

Letters flew across the Atlantic as IBM tried to plan its next move. IBM's Geneva Controller J. C. Milner coolly informed Rottke that the company had no difficulty declaring a dividend, but German law limited such distributions to 6 or 8 percent—and that amount would not be much more than monies already advanced. As for Heidinger selling back his stock, Milner curtly wrote, "we can take no decision on this." Rottke wrote back, encouraging New York to pay Heidinger. Stalling for time, Milner replied, "it will not be possible to come to a final decision . . . until such time as I receive a reply from Head Office."[104]

Rottke's reply was explicit: "I would gather . . . the IBM does not wish to purchase this interest [Heidinger's stock] . . . inasmuch as a change of German interests into foreign hands would be a disadvantage at the present time. However, something will have to be done, because Heidinger needs money and can or will obtain it by other means; nobody will be able to legally prevent him from selling."[105]

Throughout spring 1938, more letters, conferences, and debates streamed between IBM offices on both sides of the ocean. Watson personally called for written recommendations and proposed agreements from special advisors, accountants, and attorneys both in and out of Germany. In some cases, one translation wasn't enough for Watson. The whole dispute was all coming at a difficult time in view of Dehomag's expansion plans. Austria had just been annexed, and Germany was openly planning the takeover of Czechoslovakia. Even as Watson was battling Heidinger's demand for bonuses, he was cautiously negotiating the nature and bonuses of Dehomag's expansion into "new territories," such as Austria and Czechoslovakia.[106]

Watson compromised—in a way. With his consent, Dehomag adopted a shareholder resolution for "an eventual dividend to be declared for the years 1935, 1936 and 1937." When it was, Heidinger would be paid his long awaited bonus, less all his advances, of course. In the meantime, Watson's many outside advisors would provide the written opinions about how much profit was legally permissible to declare under existing German law without incurring confiscatory taxes and mandatory loans to the Reich. To assuage a nervous Heidinger, Watson agreed to provide yet more advances, RM 7,000 monthly for the remainder of 1938.[107]

But Heidinger was impatient. While he had appealed the tax decision, he did not expect to prevail. Soon, Heidinger would have to pay a huge assessment. Dehomag's books reflected one multi-million mark record after another—1938 alone would yield RM 2.39 million in conceded profits even after IBM applied various intra-company devices.[108] Yet Watson still delayed any decision on declaring a profit.

Finally, in late November 1938, just days after *Kristallnacht,* a furious exchange of correspondence between New York and Berlin escalated into a stubborn standoff over dividing the money.

The squabbling culminated with Heidinger implying that Watson was involved in defrauding the Reich tax authorities. In a long, rambling and sarcastic five-page letter to one of Watson's Berlin attorneys, Heidinger openly conceded his stock was a sham. Referring to his so-called "preferred shares in Dehomag," Heidinger declared, "My company shares are no real preferred shares, if for instance the Tabulating Division would yield no net profit, while the remaining divisions would earn a net profit of say five percent, on my shares, I would not obtain anything and the remaining five percent are therefore not preferred in that case but disadvantaged."[109]

Heidinger's letter repeatedly insisted the bogus share arrangement might be viewed by the authorities as a scheme "flatly to evade paragraph 3 of the law." He invoked strong words, uncharacteristic of IBM's usual ambiguity. At one point, he referred to "a tax liability evaded by abnormal measures." The word "evade" was used repeatedly, as in "tax evasion." Heidinger even added an unsubtle hint of criminality, writing, "But by no means must we expose the Dehomag to the risk of a penal prosecution." As was his style, he flamboyantly concluded his pejorative missive "with renewed hearty thanks."[110]

Watson sought help from Price Waterhouse. But the prestigious accountancy firm could only conclude Dehomag's finances were in supremely profitable condition and that Heidinger deserved his bonus. In its lengthy thirteen-page single-spaced analysis, dated December 30, 1938, Price Waterhouse declared: the only question is when and how much to pay Heidinger. Moreover, warned Price Waterhouse, if Heidinger insisted on selling his shares, the value of that stock—real or not—was far greater than when the original merger took place in 1934. Using rigid principles of valuation, Price Waterhouse examined the pluses and minuses of the German political and tax environment, and the problem of blocked bank accounts. The firm concluded that each share of Dehomag was actually "worth more to a purchaser in Germany, than to a resident abroad." The report underlined the words "in Germany."[111] For Watson, this meant that his shares were now actually less valuable than Heidinger's.

Indeed, Price Waterhouse asserted, Dehomag by any measure had only become more valuable. The net worth of the company had essentially doubled from its RM 7.7 million total investment in 1934 to more than RM 14 million. Annual earnings were about RM 2.3 million, a 16 percent return on net assets.[112]

At the same time, more bad news came. Dehomag was supplying machinery and spare parts to IBM for resale throughout Europe. IBM in turn merely credited Dehomag's loan balance account. Frustrated and defiant, Dehomag managers in mid-December 1938 unilaterally began terming those shipments "exports." This triggered the Reich's rule requiring actual foreign currency payment, which Dehomag obtained by debiting IBM's precious few dollar accounts in Germany.[113]

On January 3, 1939, IBM's Geneva Controller J. C. Milner mailed Watson a long, detailed letter explicating the adverse Price Waterhouse report, searching for silver linings, parsing Heidinger's contract language, and ultimately trying to construct loopholes around the inevitability of either paying Heidinger dividends or buying part of his stock. Milner conceded that buying just one of Heidinger's shares would expose the subsidiary as American-controlled.[114]

Milner explored all the possibilities. "If he [Heidinger] died and the stock was offered to IBM, in accordance with his contract, the higher book value combined with the earnings of the company would probably force a high valuation of the stock," asserted Milner. Maybe the company could pay the elderly Heidinger in ten annual installments? Could Dehomag purchase Heidinger's stock with blocked marks as an internal obligation? Milner offered a range of options, none of them promising.[115]

It seemed to be a no-win dilemma for IBM. Purchase of Heidinger's stock was out of the question, asserted Milner, because no one could predict what the Reich economic and taxing authorities would do. On the other hand, once dividends on the 1935–1937 period were formally paid to Heidinger, he would next ask for dividends for 1938. It would continue annually even as the company's value escalated.[116]

Clearly, money was a pressure tactic IBM could use. Heidinger was receiving a monthly allowance of RM 7,000 for all of 1938. Milner had some weeks earlier reminded IBM attorneys in New York, "the last payment on this account will fall due in December. It will then be necessary for a decision to be made regarding the year 1939."[117]

Heidinger was being squeezed. Not only was he liable for a RM 90,000 tax, but because of the protracted reporting delay, German tax authorities had added a mandatory loan to the government, made retroactive for the three years 1934–1937, and that loan totaled RM 151,000. He could never afford that without help from the company. Watson understood that, and cut off Heidinger's RM 7,000 monthly advance.[118]

In a March 13 letter, Rottke implored Milner to advance Heidinger the money needed for the mandatory loan.[119] Heidinger was clearly desperate. Tax monies would be due within a matter of weeks. He had accommodated Watson all these years. Now he needed help.

Watson was unmoved. On March 15, the day the Nazis smashed into the remainder of Czechoslovakia, Milner calmly answered Rottke, expressing regret for a "very awkward condition." But in fact, insisted Milner, it was Heidinger who had insisted that dividends be paid. If now the taxing authority had imposed mandatory loans, that was Heidinger's problem. Indeed, IBM attorneys in Berlin had carefully studied current regulations and determined that IBM had actually advanced monies above the legal limit. "Therefore," asserted Milner, "it is Mr. Heidinger who has received too much money, and it is he who should make arrangements to invest the surplus with the Loan Stock Bank."[120]

In describing the mess to the IBM NY officers, Milner caustically noted, "We cannot be blamed if Mr. Heidinger's own government will not let him draw adequate cash dividends. On the other hand, this increases the hazard of his offering to sell us some of his stock."[121]

In the meantime, IBM was negotiating with the subsidiary's two other managers, Hummel and Rottke, over the profit sharing plan for Dehomag's activities outside of Germany. On March 21, six days after Czechoslovakia had been seized, even as Poland, Lithuania, and other countries were being actively threatened with German invasion, IBM European troubleshooter

Harrison Chauncey dashed a short note off to Phillips about the bonus terms for "new territories" to be handed to Dehomag. "I wonder," Chauncey asked, "if the further changes in the German political situation require any consideration of this subject at this time?" Phillips in New York scrawled a note back, "Considering present changes in the map of Europe don't you consider it best to wait?"[122]

It was no longer just Austria and Czechoslovakia. Clearly, other nations would soon come under Dehomag's sphere of influence. IBM was trying to plan ahead.

BRINKSMANSHIP WAS Watson's specialty. First he instructed Holt not to go to Berlin to participate in a scheduled shareholders meeting. Hence, no decision could be voted on Heidinger's request. As each day passed, Heidinger's financial situation worsened.[123]

Then, on March 31, 1939, Watson cabled Holt: "Loan Heidinger 150,000 marks to pay Loan Stock Account and also authorize you to vote for payment of 8% dividend, you to invest our dividend money in real estate." Under German law, 8 percent was the legal limit IBM could pay without incurring additional taxation. The 8 percent dividend was to be paid monthly just as the advance was. But 8 percent would total RM 3,500, just half of what Heidinger needed to pay his bills and half the 16 percent return identified by Price Waterhouse.[124] Heidinger needed RM 7,000 per month. He was fed up with IBM and Watson.

APRIL 26, 1939
Thomas J. Watson
President of the IBM
New York

Dear Mr. Watson!
   As you know, up to the end of last year, I received a monthly payment of RM 7000—as an advance on account of dividends. . . . these payments have been stopped since Jan. 39 . . . since that date, no shareholders meeting took place and therefore a corresponding resolution could not be formed.
   A meeting has been called for April 11 . . . Mr. Holt replied . . . "it is not convenient for him to come Berlin" and that he acts solely in the capacity of the chief stockholder, the IBM. . . .

April 14, Mr. Rottke wrote to Mr. Milner . . . saying among other words: "I seriously fear that Mr. Heidinger gets in economic difficulties . . . therefore I beg you kindly to discuss this item with Mr. Watson in Paris . . . Today, Mr. Rottke informed me that he received a letter of Mr. Milner . . . "to advance to Mr. Heidinger on account of dividends for 1939, a sum equal to eight percent of his capital share in Dehomag. (That means RM 3,500). This may be advanced monthly . . . and can be ratified at an eventual meeting of the partners." . . . That means that the IBM either does not like my partnership or at least that it does not attach great value to maintain my partnership in the Dehomag.

Unnecessary to say how sorry and how deeply depressed I feel about such an attitude, which in all probability ends my partnership . . . I herewith offer my shares . . . in the Dehomag to the IBM . . . negotiate with me about the purchase price . . . accept the transfer of the shares to IBM.

I would be very happy and highly appreciative if the personal relations which have been created during the past 29 years between me and the different gentlemen of the IBM . . . and between you and me will not be changed . . . Again expressing my deepest regret, I beg to accept my personal regards and remain

very sincerely yours,
Willy Heidinger[125]

Rottke openly conceded the contract between IBM and Heidinger had "been made under an unlucky star, [and] appears to be the source of all evil." But he nonetheless warned Watson again that if Heidinger's shares were transferred to a foreign source Dehomag would probably not be permitted "the use of the word *Deutsche* (German) as an enterprise recognized in Germany as German."[126] That disaster had to be avoided at all costs. To IBM's doctrinaire German managers, including Heidinger, Dehomag represented far more than just a profit-making enterprise. To them, Dehomag had the technologic ability to keep Germany's war machine automated, facilitate her highly efficient seizure of neighboring countries, and achieve the Reich's swiftly moving racial agenda. If IBM's subsidiary were deemed non-Aryan, the company would be barred from all the sensitive projects awaiting it. Hitler's Germany—in spite of itself—would be deprived of the Holleriths it so desperately required.

From Watson's point of view, Germany was on the brink of unleashing its total conquest of Europe. IBM subsidiaries could be coordinated by

Dehomag into one efficient continental enterprise, moving parts, cards, and machines as the Reich needed them. The new order that Hitler promised was made to order for IBM.

In July 1939, Watson arrived in Berlin to personally mediate with Heidinger. A compromise would be necessary. The stakes were too high for the Nazis. The stakes were too high for capitalism. But it was the Germans who gave in, deferring on Heidinger's demands for a few months under terms Watson dictated. Watson now controlled something the Third Reich needed to launch the next decisive step in the solution of the Jewish question, not just in Germany—but all of Europe. Until now, the fastest punchers, tabulators, and sorters could organize only by numbers. The results could then be sorted by sequentially numbered profession, geographic locale, or population category. But now Watson had something new and powerful.[127]

He had the alphabetizers.

ON MAY 17, 1939, GERMANY WAS SWEPT BY 750,000 CENSUS takers, mainly volunteers. They missed virtually no one in the Greater Reich's 22 million households, 3.5 million farmhouses, 5.5 million shops and factories. Teams of five to eight census takers fanned out through the big cities such as Berlin, Frankfurt, Hamburg, and Vienna. Towns and villages were divided into districts of thirty homes with one census taker assigned to each. Some 80 million citizens in the Greater Reich, including Germany, Austria, the Sudentenland, and the Saar, would be classed according to their ancestry.[1]

There was little question to the world that the May 1939 national census was racial in nature. *New York Times* coverage of the mammoth project made clear that this census would "provide detailed information on the ancestry, religious faith and material possessions of all residents. Special blanks will be provided on which each person must state whether he is of pure 'Aryan' blood. The status of each of his grandparents must be given and substantiated by evidence in case of inquiry."[2]

Certainly, by May 1939, virtually every "practicing Jew" had been registered, surveyed, numbered, and sorted numerous times in a series of overlapping, often disjointed, campaigns. The purpose of the 1939 census was to identify the so-called "racial Jews" in

Germany proper, add Jews of any definition in the new territories of the expanded Reich, and locate each individual before being ghettoized or subjected to other action. Indeed the ghettoization decrees had begun that very month. In addition, Germany was preparing for all-out war and without the census, it could not identify exactly where all its draftable men were, and which women would step into their economic shoes once mobilized.[3] As such, the census was vital to Hitler's two-front war—one against the Jews, and one against all of Europe.

Understandably, Dehomag's 1939 undertaking dwarfed anything it had attempted before, including the 1933 Prussian census. Months of intensive training, conducted in thousands of sessions, prepared legions of volunteers for the critical mission. Police and their auxiliaries were mandated to support the count "with all their powers" and "to function as census-takers in difficult and confusing residential areas," according to official regulations.[4]

The additional Hollerith machinery assembled was massive: 400 electrical key punches, 10 gang punches, 20 summary punches, 300 key punch verifiers, 70 sorters, 50 tabulators, 25 duplicators, and 50 D-11 VZ tabulators. The Reich had imposed seemingly impossible target delivery dates for November 1939. So to increase speed, Dehomag's engineers converted their versatile D-11 calculating tabulator into a pure counting machine dubbed the D-11 VZ. The improvised device could process 12,000 60-column punched cards per hour in sixteen counters and then precision-punch its own summaries onto 80-column cards. Eighty million cards were actually used.[5]

A special envelope containing a so-called Supplemental Card was created. This all-important card recorded the individual's bloodline data and functioned as the racial linchpin of the operation. Each head of household was to fill out his name and address and then document his family's ancestral lines. Jews understandably feared the newest identification. Census takers were cautioned to overcome any distrust by assuring families that the information would not be released to the financial authorities.[6]

But it was not German taxing agencies that were the most eager for the new data. It was the Nazi Party structure and Reich security forces seeking to locate additional Jews and other undesirables. Indeed, the final data was intended to help comprise a single national register for the entire Greater Reich. Each card carried a single column coded for descent, designed into the card prototype long before the census was launched. A letter from the Order Police to the Ministry of the Interior at the end of 1938 explained: "This column on the registration card is included to be filled out at the right time. That time should come in May of next year during the population, occupation, and company census. The regular questionnaire will be supplemented by an additional card. This card will include the question of whether the person had any fully Jewish grandparent. Survey results will then be evaluated using this registration card."[7]

The 25 million Supplemental Cards—one for each household—represented a virtual doubling of census files. To cope with the volume and still meet deadlines, the census tabulation was divided into two operations. First, each special envelope containing a Supplemental Card was labeled to correspond to the household's general questionnaire, along with the district and municipality of origin. Then local officials, generally the police, affixed the letter "J" to both the questionnaires and cards of all Jewish families.[8]

The words "Do Not Send Directly to the [Berlin] Statistical Bureau" were printed on every envelope. Instead, both the general questionnaire and its companion special envelope were sent to the regional statistical offices for the tedious quality control procedures. Did the envelopes match up to the questionnaires? Were Supplemental Cards containing racial data and the general questionnaires filled out completely? Just preparing the 25 million census forms and 25 million Supplemental Cards for processing required a behemoth manual operation. Once approved, the questionnaires and cards were transported to Berlin and separated. The Supplemental Cards were sorted into three groups: non-Aryans, "higher educated people," and all others. These were then tabulated to yield the racial data.[9]

Never before had so many been counted so thoroughly and quickly. The Reich Statistical Office hired an additional 2,000 staffers to process the forms and race cards, which were enough to fill more than seventy boxcars. As in 1933, Dehomag created cavernous counting rooms and management offices at the Statistical Office headquarters in Berlin to tabulate the information. Initially, Dehomag's army of operators punched 450,000 cards per day. With time, the volume reached one million daily. The company met its deadline. Preliminary analyzed results were ready by November 10, 1939, the one-year anniversary of *Kristallnacht,* and, more importantly for Hitler, the anniversary of Germany's surrender in the Great War.[10]

Intense demand to access the final information on racial Jews came from competing Nazi organizations as well as state and national government bureaus. But anxious local and state agencies would have to wait. For example, municipal officials throughout Saxony asked their regional statistical offices if they could examine the census data first to speed their ghettoization and confiscation campaigns. But the Reich Statistical Office in Berlin said no. Greater priority was granted to the SD and Adolf Eichmann's *Referat* II 112, which both received copies of all census registration lists.[11]

The census yielded exactly the data Nazi Germany needed, including data for the areas beyond Germany. Within months, for example, bureaucrats in the Austrian Statistical Office had compiled a complete profile of Jewish existence in the country. A report dispatched to Reich officials opened with the explanation: "In the census of May 17, 1939, the question was put for the first time whether one of the individual's grandparents was a full Jew by race." With stunning specificity, the extensive summary concluded, "According to the initial results of this year's census, there were 91,480 full Jews and 22,344 part Jews of Grades I and II in Vienna as of May 17, 1939. In the remaining Reich Districts of the Ostmark there were 3,073 full Jews and 4,241 part Jews." Tables displayed the Jewish totals divided into full Jews, as well as Grade I and Grade II Jews. Each of those designations was subdivided between male and female and then delineated district by district for all of Vienna. In Innere Stadt: 116 Grade II female Jews. In Aimmering: 27 Grade II males. In Wieden: 31 Grade I males. Precise numbers were tallied for key regions as well: Salzburg, Tirol, and others.[12]

Dehomag's final calculations yielded a grand total of 330,539 so-called "racial Jews" still dwelling within the expanded Reich—Germany, Austria, and the Sudetenland. This was far less than the wild projections of 1.5 million generated four years earlier when the Nuremberg Laws were drafted. The new count showed 138,819 males and 191,720 females—more females because about 35,000 Jewish wives had become widowed or detached from refugee men. Clearly, through persecution, emigration, death during incarceration, and outright execution, Greater Germany had lost about half its originally counted Jewish population of some 502,000, including Jews added when the Saar region was annexed in 1935. But, by adding Austria and the Sudetenland, the Third Reich discovered that by 1939 it had actually *gained* an additional 96,893 Jews.[13]

Moreover, there were hundreds of thousands more Jews in the old Czechoslovakia, now called the Protectorate of Bohemia and Moravia. Millions more existed in Poland and other countries in Europe that Germany planned to conquer or dominate. Indeed, the same German refugees would be encountered again and again as they fled from nation to nation.

Emigration and deportation would not work. Jewish refugees were being, or would be, reabsorbed as Germany annexed or invaded new territories in Europe. Dehomag's numbers told them exactly how many Jews could be found in the Greater Reich, and soon IBM subsidiaries throughout Europe would help compile the numbers for invaded territories as well. It seemed the more the Reich achieved its territorial goals, the more Jews it encountered.

A better solution would be needed.

BY 1939, Nazi race policy had evolved. No longer was Germany's anti-Semitic crusade content with just ridding the Greater Reich of Jews. Hitler had always wanted all Europe completely Jew-free. In pursuit of that goal, NSDAP forces had spent years subversively cultivating paramilitary Fascist surrogates worldwide—from Brazil's Integralite Party to Syria's Phalange militia. Europe, of course, was the Nazi success story. Romania's Iron Guard was highly organized and impatient. In Holland, it was the Dutch Nazi Party. Polish Brown Shirts terrorized Jews. In Hungary, the Arrow Cross Party agitated. In Croatia, blood-lusting Ustashi could not wait. Whether their shirts were black, brown, or silver, whether of German extraction or merely anti-Semites in other lands, these people could be relied upon to preach Hitler's ideology of Jew-hatred, racial castes, and Aryan superiority.[14]

Wherever those of German ancestry or ultra-nationalists existed, the Reich sought to use them as advance troops organized around strict Aryan principles. The *Auslandsorganisation* of the NSDAP, an association of German Nazis living abroad, was the backbone of this movement. Berlin expected members to help achieve its goals. Typical was a published exhortation in the German press demanding all Aryans to observe rigid racial purity. In that same vein, Goering had demanded quite publicly in his speeches that Germans living in other countries terminate all Jewish employees and "be the servants of this Homeland."[15]

But keeping track of potential German sympathizers globally was a prodigious task. As early as summer 1938, the German Foreign Institute at Stuttgart began compiling what it called a "German world migration register" to help identify its friends in other countries. Advocates insisted "[t]he World Migration Book must represent more than a card index but a German world . . . [where] eternal Germanism may live." The *Stuttgart Kurier* asserted that the Migration Book would remind Germans worldwide of their "never ending task to work with word and deed for the maintenance of the German race."[16]

Even as it rallied Nazi cohorts throughout Europe, Berlin pressured its neighbors to adopt anti-Semitic policies along Aryan lines to forestall German aggression. For example, just days before the Reich invaded Czechoslovakia, Berlin offered to respect Prague's borders only if it submitted to a three-prong ultimatum: delivery of one-third of its gold reserves, dismantling of its army, and an immediate "solution of the Jewish problem" according to Nuremberg racial definitions.[17]

Country after country adopted laws identical to German race policies, ousting Jews, confiscating their assets, and organizing their expulsion long before the Reich crossed their borders. By spring 1939, Hungary had already passed a series of anti-Jewish measures, including land expropriation, professional exclusion, and citizenship annulment. A *New York Times* headline on the question declared, "Aim to Head Off Nazis." Waves of pogroms and Nazi-style anti-Jewish boycotts and economic expulsions had long been sweeping Poland, especially in areas with many so-called *Volksdeutsche,* those of German parentage. By 1937, the Polish government declared the popular campaign had become official, to the delight of German-allied Polish Fascists. Similar persecution was regularly debated in Romania, Czechoslovakia, and Lithuania. Eventually the majority of Europe would soon legislate Jews out of existence. It was all part of Berlin's new continent-wide irresistible sphere of anti-Semitic influence.[18]

While Berlin was igniting anti-Jewish campaigns everywhere, NSDAP forces were quietly gathering population details on Jews throughout the Continent and preparing for the day when Nazi-inspired coups or outright invasion would permit the instant liquidation of one Jewish community after another. Nazi race and population scientists utilizing punch card systems were a crucial component of this effort.

Typical was a Nazi operative named Carl Fust, who was scouting church records for familial information in Lithuania as far back as 1936. On June 29, 1936, he reported his progress to the *Reichssippenamt* in Berlin. "I have now also registered all known books of the Tilsit Mennonite Community," wrote Fust. "It was quite a task to find the present location of the books . . . The entries . . . go partly back to the year 1769; however, individual data goes back as far as 1722."[19] The *Reichssippenamt* automated its files with Hollerith machines.

On July 2, 1936, several Nazis met in a Breslau inn to discuss the services of Fritz Arlt, a Leipzig statistician. Arlt had created a cross-referenced card file on every Leipzig Jewish resident, down to so-called quarter-Jews. What made Arlt's expertise desirable was that his cards also listed exactly which ancestral Polish towns their families originated from. At the Breslau meeting, Arlt was assigned to work with the security offices of the *Auslandsorganisation.* His groundbreaking Polish demography was deemed so pivotal, Arlt was asked to journey to Berlin to assist Eichmann's *Referat* II 112, with travel expenses to be paid by the SD.[20]

The Reich did everything in its power to extend its census, registration, and genealogical reach throughout Europe. Once it invaded or forced its political domination in a neighboring country, it could then immediately locate both racial and practicing Jews. Berlin proved it could be done in Austria and the Sudetenland. But such demographic feats Europe-wide would be impossible without detailed, automated information about Jewish citizens in other lands. That required more than the resources of the Reich Statistical Office, it required multi-national statistical cooperation.

IBM subsidiaries throughout Europe had long been working in unison to take advantage of political and military events in Europe. Salesmen constantly shuttled from various countries to either New York or Berlin for training, and were then transferred back to their original countries to oversee punch card operations. In late 1939, with Thomas Watson's consent, an international training school for IBM service engineers throughout Europe was opened in Berlin. IBM lectures and demonstrations for military leaders and government leaders were frequent—all under the watchful eye of IBM's Geneva office.[21]

In the first three months of 1939 alone, IBM Sweden sold 1.9 million punch cards to Denmark, 1.3 million to Finland, and 696,000 to Norway. IBM NY sold 1 million cards to Yugoslavia, and 700,000 to Spain. Dehomag sold 261,000 to Hungary.[22]

On February 16, 1939, Reich legal authorities announced that the term *Aryan* would be replaced in many instances by a new term: *European racial.* Under the new guidelines, other ethnic groups and races, such as Germany's Romanian and Hungarian allies, could be allowed to exist.[23] But a Jewish presence would be allowed nowhere on the Continent.

By late spring 1939, Europe was wracked by incremental Nazi land grabs and invasions in Austria, Czechoslovakia, and the Memel region of Lithuania. Massive German military buildups, including troop concentrations on its extended frontiers, threatened Denmark, Poland, Hungary, Luxembourg, Belgium, Holland, France, and England. European Jewry, including thousands of refugees, was threatened with extinction.

Regardless, Watson went full speed ahead with plans for the 1939 International Chamber of Commerce Congress. Originally scheduled for Tokyo, Watson had relocated the conference to Copenhagen after a troubled Japan withdrew. In Copenhagen, Watson planned to make his most strenuous appeal yet for raw materials to be handed over to Germany. As usual,

Watson sought political cover for his activities. He wrote to President Franklin D. Roosevelt on June 9, 1939, for the usual open letter of support. This time, Watson was more careful. "We should like very much to have a message from you to be read at our opening session on June 26 . . . [as] in our last Congress in Berlin in 1937, and if it's still consistent with your policy."[24]

The world had changed dramatically since 1937. Germany was a prominent participant of the Watson-dominated ICC Congress. Diplomatic relations with the Reich had been sorely strained since *Kristallnacht* and the various invasions. War was around the corner. Washington did not want to act as though it was business as usual for Nazi Germany in international parleys. Unsure White House staffers shunted the letter to Secretary of State Cordell Hull, asking him to prepare Roosevelt's comment "if you approve the sending of such a message."[25]

In Copenhagen, at the ICC Congress, Watson's pro-Axis proposal exceeded anything the State Department could have expected. He championed a resolution whereby private businessmen from the three Axis and three Allied nations would actually supercede their governments and negotiate a radical new international trade policy designed to satisfy Axis demands for raw materials coveted from other nations. The businessmen would then lobby their respective governments' official economic advisors to adopt their appeasement proposals for the sake of averting war. Ironically, the raw materials were needed by Axis powers solely for the sake of waging war.[26]

On June 28, under Watson's leadership, the ICC passed a resolution again calling for "a fair distribution of raw materials, food stuffs and other products . . . [to] render unnecessary the movements of armies across frontiers." To this end, the ICC asked "the governments of France, Germany, Italy, Japan, the United Kingdom and the United States . . . each collaborate with their own leading businessmen . . . with respect to national needs . . . [and therefore] give all countries of the world a fair opportunity to share in the resources of the world."[27]

Even as Watson angled for Germany to be ceded more raw materials, Germany was openly raping invaded territories. Just days before, on June 2, the *New York Times* carried a prominent story headlined "Terrors of Nazis Related by Benes," based on an international radio broadcast pleading for anti-Nazi resistance. In the article, purged Czechoslovakian President Eduard Benes detailed the Reich's methodical theft of Czech resources since the March 15, 1939, invasion. "Dr. Benes told of a nation of 10 million persons," the *New York Times* related, "until a few months ago proud and free, being systematically enslaved, degraded and robbed of its material and cultural possessions." The article indicated that Germany "has robbed and transported to Germany more than 35 billion crowns . . . [$1.22 billion] of Czecho-Slovak property."[28]

Benes declared, "You all must have heard how the German dictatorship is devastating the beauty that was Czecho-Slovakia, how splendid forests are being destroyed and the lumber carted away to Germany, how public build-ings . . . are being divested of their window frames, of their glass windows, of all materials . . . all supplies have been taken and transported to Germany. . . . Factories are being ruined and industry crippled as machinery is carried away for war purposes."[29]

He added, "Czech families spend nights in the woods, not daring to sleep in their own beds for fear of Nazi pogroms. And German peasants, excited by the Nazis who have come from Germany for that purpose, bran-dish scythes and cry, 'The bloody night is coming.'"[30]

No wonder the German delegate to the ICC enthusiastically lauded Watson's proposal, which only sought to legitimize by private consultation what the Third Reich was undertaking by force. In his final speech of the Congress, Watson himself summed up the misery and devastation in the world as a mere "difference of opinion." His solution of businessmen confer-ring to divvy up other nations' resources to avoid further aggression was offered with these words: "We regret that there are unsatisfactory economic and political conditions in the world today, with a great difference of opinion existing among many countries. But differences of opinion, freely discussed and fairly disposed of, result in mutual benefit and increased happiness to all concerned."[31]

But so enthusiastic was Watson that he quickly wrote to President Roosevelt, attaching transcripts from the conference and explaining that the concept of a private survey by businessmen to resolve and rewrite trade bar-riers was his invention. "You will note that this resolution does not suggest a political conference," Watson pointed out to the President, stressing the non-governmental procedure. But, he added, once the private recommendations were tendered, the six nations might then call for an international meeting to ratify the suggestions. Watson concluded his letter indicating that he had a "great deal of background" on the topic "which I prefer to present to you in person." He added a tantalizing triviality: "I also have a very interesting per-sonal message to deliver to you from [the Danish monarch] His Majesty, King Christian X."[32]

Watson's embarrassing correspondence asking to brief Roosevelt began bouncing around the State Department, Division of European Affairs, Advisor on Political Relations, Division of Trade Agreements, Department of Protocol, Division of International Conferences, Office of the Advisor on International Economic Affairs, and Cordell Hull personally. One protocol chief wrote, "it is not a matter for us . . . Mr. Watson being an American, we would have nothing to do with making an appointment for him to see the President." Another offered a hairsplitting technicality: Watson was the outgoing president of the ICC. His July 5 letter to Roosevelt was written a few days after being succeeded at the ICC. Therefore, "It does not appear that it is necessary to comment . . . inasmuch as Mr. Watson is no longer President of the International Chamber and the resolution does not come to us officially from that body."[33]

Finally, an innocuous three-sentence say-nothing reply was cobbled together for the President's review after being initialed by no fewer than ten Department officials. It read: "My Dear Mr. Watson: I have received and read with interest your letter of July 5, 1939, in regard to the meeting of the Tenth Congress of the International Chamber of Commerce. I note that you desire to discuss some of the background of this meeting with me in person and to deliver to me a personal message from His Majesty King Christian X. I shall look forward to seeing you after you return to this country."[34]

In explaining so unresponsive a reply to Watson's elaborate letter, a key State Department official, John Hickerson, caustically wrote, "It seems to me that the attached draft letter for the President to Mr. Watson says about as much as the President could appropriately say. I do not see how the President could well comment on the resolution discussed in this letter recommending that the Governments of France, Germany, Italy, Japan, the United Kingdom and the United States appoint economic representatives of their respective governments to work with businessmen in regard to 'their own needs and what they are able to contribute to the needs of other countries.'"[35]

Watson sent Hull a letter almost identical to the one he sent to Roosevelt. The same State Department group that formulated Roosevelt's response proffered a similar reply for the Secretary of State, amounting to little more than a simple and non-committal thanks to Watson for "your letter regarding the activities of the Congress."[36]

But Watson would not desist. He sent formal lithographed resolutions to the State Department hoping to rally its support for an international conference of business executives to parcel out the world's resources. One State Department assistant secretary could not help but comment on the similarity of Watson's suggestion to the Axis' own warlike demands. "This is, of course, a political question of major world importance," wrote the assistant secretary, "and one upon which we have been hearing much from Germany, Italy and Japan. It occurs to me that it is most unfortunate that Mr. Thomas J. Watson, as an American serving as the president of the International Chamber of Commerce, should have sponsored a resolution of this character. It may well be that this resolution will return to plague us at some future date." That comment was written on October 5, 1939.[37] By then it was unnecessary to reply further.

Poland had already been invaded. World War II had begun.

HOURS BEFORE dawn on September 1, 1939, SS Officer Alfred Naujocks was preparing to launch World War II. For days, Naujocks' detachment of German soldiers had been waiting. Sometime before 5:40 A.M., he received the code word from Berlin. Working methodically and according to plan, Naujocks' men donned Polish uniforms and staged a fake attack against a German radio station. Drugged concentration camp inmates were dragged into position and smeared with blood to become the "German casualties." This sham provided Hitler with the pretext to launch Operation Case White —the invasion of Poland.[38]

Germany's assault was the fiercest and fastest in history. Hundreds of airplanes mounted a sustained bombardment of Poland's railroads, storage facilities, troop encampments, and cities. Six divisions of coordinated troops, tanks, and artillery ravished Warsaw. Within days, three-fourths of the firebombed and shell-battered capital was reduced to smoking rubble. So unique was this attack, it was dubbed *Blitzkrieg,* or lightning war. Britain and France declared war just days later.[39]

Poland, essentially unarmored and in many cases deploying horse cavalry, held out for twenty-seven fierce days before its complete capitulation. News of barbarous massacres, rapes, inflicted starvation, systematic deportations, and the resulting unchecked epidemics made headlines around the world. In one incident in Nasielek, some 1,600 Jews were whipped all night in what was termed a "whipping orgy." Two Jewish sisters were dragged from their beds in the night and taken to a cemetery; one was raped and the other given five zlotys and told to wait until next time. Shortly after the war began, a *New York Times* article headlined "250,000 Jews listed As Dead in Poland."[40]

Polish Jewry numbered more than 3 million persons—10 percent of the Polish population. Atrocities, rapes, and massacres could not wipe them all away. Deportation to labor camps was underway. But something more drastic was needed. A German military review of specific actions in Poland declared, "It is a mistake to massacre some 10,000 Jews and Poles, as is being done at present . . . this will not eradicate the idea of a Polish state, nor will the Jews be exterminated."[41]

On September 13, the *New York Times* reported the Reich's dilemma with a headline declaring, "Nazis Hint Purge of Jews in Poland," with a sub-head, "3,000,000 Population Involved." The article quoted the German government as declaring it wanted "removal of the Polish Jewish population from the European domain." The *New York Times* then added, "How . . . the 'removal' of Jews from Poland [can be achieved] without their extermination . . . is not explained."[42]

SEPTEMBER 9, 1939
Mr. Thomas J. Watson, President
International Business Machines Corporation
590 Madison Ave.
New York NY USA

Dear Mr. Watson:

During your last visit in Berlin at the beginning of July, you made the kind offer to me that you might be willing to furnish the German company machines from Endicott in order to shorten our long delivery terms. I . . . asked you to leave with us for study purposes one alphabetic tabulating machine and a collator out of the American machines at present in Germany. You have complied with this request, for which I thank you very much, and have added that in cases of urgent need, I may make use of other American machines. . . .

You will understand that under today's conditions, a certain need has arisen for such machines, which we do not build as yet in Germany. Therefore, I should like to make use of your kind offer and ask you to leave with the German company for the time being the alphabetic tabulating machines which are at present still in the former Austria. . . .

Regarding the payment, I cannot make any concrete proposals at the moment, however, I should ask you to be convinced that I shall see to it that a fair reimbursement for the machines left with us will be made when there will be a possibility. . . .

. . . [A]t the time that the German production of these machines renders it possible, we shall place at your disposal . . . a German machine for each American machine left with us.

This offer, made orally by you, dear Mr. Watson . . . will undoubtedly be greatly appreciated in many and especially responsible circles. . . . We should thank you if you would ask your Geneva organization, at the same time, to furnish us the necessary repair parts for the maintenance of the machines. . . .

Yours very truly,
H. Rottke

cc: Mr. F. W. Nichol, New York
cc: IBM Geneva[43]

IBM's alphabetizer, principally its model 405, was introduced in 1934, but it did not become widely used until it was perfected in conjunction with the Social Security Administration. The elaborate alphabetizer was the pride of IBM. Sleek and more encased than earlier Holleriths, the complex 405 integrated several punch card mechanisms into a single, high-speed device. A summary punch cable connector at its bottom facilitated the summarizing of voluminous tabulated results onto a single summary card. A short card feed and adjacent stacker at the machine's top was attached to a typewriter-style printing unit equipped with an automatic carriage to print out the alphabetized results. Numerous switches, dials, reset keys, a control panel, and even an attached reading table, made the 405 a very expensive and versatile device. By 1939, the squat 405 was IBM's dominant machine in the United States. However, the complex statistical instrument was simply too expensive for the European market. Indeed, in 1935, the company was still exhibiting it at business shows.[44] Because the 405 required so many raw materials, including rationed metals that Dehomag could not obtain, IBM's alphabetizer was simply out of reach for the Nazi Reich.

But the 405 was of prime importance to Germany for its critical ability to create alphabetized lists and its speed for general tabulation. The 405 could calculate 1.2 million implicit multiplications in just 42 hours. By comparison, the slightly older model 601 would need 800 hours for the same task—fundamentally an impossible assignment.[45]

More than 1,000 405s were operating in American government bureaus and corporate offices, constituting one of the company's most profitable inventions. But few of the expensive devices were anywhere in Europe. Previously, Dehomag was only able to provide such machines to key governmental agencies directly from America or through its other European subsidiaries—a costly financial foreign exchange transaction, which also required the specific permission of Watson. Germany had taken over Poland and war had been declared in Europe. Such imports from America were no longer possible. But Dehomag wanted the precious alphabetizing equipment still in Austria: five variously configured alphabetical punches, two alphabetical interpreters, and six alphabetical printing tabulators, as well as one collator. However, these valuable assets were still owned and controlled by the prior IBM subsidiary.[46]

Watson would not transfer the assets or give the Austrian machines to Dehomag without something in return. The exchanges began by a return to the issue of Heidinger's demand to sell his stock if he could not receive the bonuses he was entitled to. Watson tried to defuse the confrontation by suddenly agreeing to advance Heidinger the monies he needed. Watson wrote Rottke, "When I was in Germany recently and talked to Mr. Heidinger, he gave me to understand that he was in need of some money to meet his living expenses. As a stockholder in your Company, I am writing this letter to advise you that it will be agreeable to us for you to lend Mr. Heidinger such amounts as you think he will require to take care of his living expenses."[47] Watson's letter, of course, expressed his incidental approval as a mere stockholder—not as the controlling force in the company—this to continue the fiction that Dehomag was not foreign-controlled.

At the very moment Watson was dictating his letter about Heidinger, Germany was involved in a savage occupation of Poland. WWII was underway. So Watson was careful. He did not date the letter to Rottke, or even send it directly to Germany. Instead, the correspondence was simply handed to his secretary. She then mailed the authorizing letter to an IBM auditor, J. C. Milner in Geneva, with a note advising, "I have been instructed by Mr. Watson to forward the enclosed letter for Mr. Hermann Rottke to your care. Would you kindly see that the letter reaches him." The undated copy filed in Watson's office, however, was date-stamped "September 13, 1939" for filing purposes.[48]

But Heidinger was not interested in further advances, as these only deepened his tax dilemma. He wanted the alphabetizers and made that known to J. W. Schotte, IBM's newly promoted European general manager in Geneva who acted as Watson's intermediary on the alphabetizer question. On September 27, 1939, the day a vanquished Poland formally capitulated, Schotte telephoned Rottke and a Dehomag management team in Berlin to regretfully explain that Watson refused to transfer the alphabetizers. Instead, Watson merely offered to arrange for Dehomag to take possession of thirty-four broken alphabetizers returned from Russia and lying dormant in a Hamburg warehouse. They could be repaired and rehabilitated back into service.[49]

An indignant Rottke refused "most energetically on the grounds that these are 'old junk' in which we are not the least interested." Schotte upped the offer, saying Watson wanted Dehomag to take over the entire Russian territory. Rottke thought the prospect in principle seemed rather attractive because Dehomag could then gain foreign exchange. But, thought Rottke, all the benefits of Russian sales would be negated if the German subsidiary was still compelled to pay IBM NY a 25 percent royalty. Preferring not to verbalize any of that, Rottke simply replied to Schotte that any ideas on servicing the Russian market should be expressed in writing.[50]

Returning to the alphabetizers, Rottke repeatedly insisted Schotte call Watson to recommend that he "let us have these few machines." Schotte would not budge, saying they had been "set aside for urgent needs." From Rottke's view, the machines were in Nazi-annexed Austria, a territory now granted to Dehomag, and Watson would not let the Germans deploy the existing machines? Incensed and threatening, Rottke told Schotte, "IBM is big enough to take care of its customers," adding, "depriving us of these few machines might later be regretted." Schotte saw that Rottke's limit was being reached. He promised to call Watson again and convey the sentiment in Berlin.[51]

Schotte called Rottke the next morning, September 28, in friendly spirits. It was all just a mistake on Watson's part, he was happy to say. Watson, claimed Schotte, thought the machines had never even been delivered to Austria. Watson had backed down again. Rottke was able to send a letter to Heidinger confirming that Dehomag is "keeping the machines I had asked for until further notice."[52]

Dehomag's paperwork was quickly finalized:

Alphabetical Summary Punch . . .
    serial #517-10674-D9   *Transferred to Dehomag
Alphabetical Summary Punch . . .
    serial #517-10072   *Transferred to Dehomag
Alphabetical Duplicating Printing Punch . . .
    serial #034-11722-M8   *Transferred to Dehomag
Alphabetical Duplicating Punch . . .
    serial #034-11252   *Transferred to Dehomag
Alphabetical Duplicating Punch . . .
    serial #034-11253   *Transferred to Dehomag
Alphabet-Interpreter . . .
    serial #552-10494-C9   *Transferred to Dehomag
Alphabet-Interpreter . . .
    serial #552-10495-C9   *Transferred to Dehomag

Alphabetical Printing Tabulating Machine . . .	
serial#405-13126-D9	*Transferred to Dehomag*
Alphabetical Printing Tabulating Machine . . .	
serial#405-13127-D9	*Transferred to Dehomag*
Alphabetical Printing Tabulating Machine . . .	
serial#405-13128-D9	*Transferred to Dehomag*
Alphabetical Printing Tabulating Machine . . .	
serial#405-11332	*Transferred to Dehomag*
Alphabetical Printing Tabulating Machine . . .	
serial#405-11000	*Transferred to Dehomag*
Alphabetical Printing Tabulating Machine . . .	
serial#405-10206	*Transferred to Dehomag*
Collator . . .	
serial#077-10577-D9	*Transferred to Dehomag* [53]

Just a week before, on September 21, 1939, Reinhard Heydrich, Chief of Himmler's Security Service, the SD, held a secret conference in Berlin. Summarizing the decisions taken that day, he circulated a top secret Express Letter to the chiefs of his *Einsatzgruppen* operating in the occupied territories. The ruthless *Einsatzgruppen* were special mobile task forces that fanned out through conquered lands sadistically murdering as many Jews as they could as fast as they could. Frequently, Jews were herded and locked into synagogues, which were then set ablaze as the people inside hopelessly tried to escape. More often, families were marched to trenches where the victims, many clutching their young ones, were lined up, mercilessly shot in assembly line fashion, and then dumped into the earth by the hundreds.[54] But these methods were too sporadic and too inefficient to quickly destroy millions of people.

Heydrich's September 21 memo was captioned: "The Jewish Question in the Occupied Territory." It began, "With reference to the conference which took place today in Berlin, I would like to point out once more that the total measures planned (i.e., the final aim) are to be kept strictly secret." Heydrich underlined the words "total measures planned" and "strictly secret." In parentheses, he used the German word *Endziel* for "final aim."[55]

His memo continued: "A distinction is to be made between 1) The final aim (which will take some time) and 2) sections of the carrying out of this goal (which can be carried out in a short space of time). The measures planned require the most thorough preparation both from the technical and the economic point of view. It goes without saying that the tasks in this connection cannot be laid down in detail."[56]

The very next step, the memo explained, was population control. First, Jews were to be relocated from their homes to so-called "concentration towns." Jewish communities of less than 500 persons were dissolved and consolidated into the larger sites. "Care must be taken," wrote Heydrich, "that only such towns be chosen as concentration points as are either railroad junctions or at least lie on a railway." Addressing the zone covered by *Einsatzgruppe I,* which extended from east of Krakow to the former Slovak-Polish border, Heydrich directed, "Within this territory, only a temporary census of Jews need be taken. The rest is to be done by the Jewish Council of Elders dealt with below."[57]

Under the plan, each Jewish ghetto or concentration town would be compelled to appoint its own Council of Elders, generally rabbis and other prominent personalities, who would be required to swiftly organize and manage the ghetto residents. Each council would become known as a *Judenrat,* or Jewish Council. "The Jewish Councils," Heydrich's memo instructed his units, "are to undertake a temporary census of the Jews, if possible, arranged according to sex [ages: (a) up to 16 years, (b) from 16 to 20 years, and (c) over], and according to the principal professions in their localities, and to report thereon within the shortest possible period."[58]

Once in the ghetto, the instruction declared, Jews would be "forbidden to leave the ghetto, forbidden to go out after a certain hour in the evening, etc."[59]

Heydrich demanded that "the chiefs of the *Einsatzgruppen* report to me continually regarding . . . the census of Jews in their districts. . . . The numbers are to be divided into Jews who will be migrating from the country, and those who are already in the towns."[60]

Some 3 million Polish Jews, during a sequence of sudden relocations, were to be catalogued for further action in a massive cascade of repetitive censuses, registrations, and inventories with up-to-date information being instantly available to various Nazi planning agencies and military occupation offices.[61] How much food would the Jews require? How much usable forced labor for armament factories and useful skills could they generate? How many thousands would die from month to month under the new starvation regimen? Under wartime conditions, it would be a marvel of population registration—a statistical feat. No time was to be lost.

The Reich was ready. During summer 1939, the Office for Military-Economic Planning, with jurisdiction over Hollerith usage, had conducted its own study of the ethnic minorities in Poland. By November 2, 1939, Arlt, the statistics wizard who had already surveyed Leipzig Jews and their city-by-city ancestral roots in Poland, had been appointed head of the Population and Welfare Administration of the "General Government," the new Reich name for occupied Poland. Arlt was devoted to population registrations, race science issues, and population politics. He edited his own statistical publication, *Volkspolitischer Informationsdienst der Regierungen des Generalgouvernments* (Political Information Service of the General Government), based in Krakow. It featured such detailed data as Jewish population per square meter with sliding projections of decrease resulting from such imposed conditions as forced labor and starvation. Arlt ruled out permanent emigration, since this would only keep Jews in existence. Instead, one article asserts, "We can count on the mortality of some subjugated groups. These include babies and those over the age of 65, as well as those who are basically weak and ill in all other age groups." Only eliminating 1.5 million Jews would reduce Jewish density to 110 persons per square kilometer.[62]

In October 1939, the next counts began.

UNLIKE GERMAN, Austrian, and Czech Jewry, most of Polish Jewry was not assimilated. Intensely religious and not infrequently cloistered into very separate communities, they were often discernible by certain physical features that Eastern Europeans associated with Jews. Characteristic dark beards and other facial attributes made their appearance very different from many Poles. Openly speaking Yiddish and Germanic dialects only set them further apart. In some neighborhoods, Jews wore traditional attire. Persecuted into the portable professions, Jews inhabited the merchant class and artisan crafts. Indeed, the Polish word for "commerce" was the German word *handel*, which Jews had Yiddishized. With well-developed schools and other institutions, as well as a unifying corporate communal body, a flourishing Jewish and Yiddish culture thrived in Poland. The Jews of Poland were often highly recognizable and frequently resembled the stereotypical notion anti-Semites harbored. In short, one didn't need a punch card–driven census to identify most of Polish Jewry.

But for special measures Hitler had in mind, the Jews of Poland did need to be counted and their possessions inventoried. Moreover, the Nazis did need to identify the thousands of Jews who did not fit the physical and social stereotypes, had drifted away from the communal group or its neighborhoods, had become baptized, or who had simply assimilated successfully into overall society.

Once Germany invaded Poland, the vibrant Jewish existence there was quickly obliterated. First, as instructed by Heydrich, Nazi forces created

Judenräte, that is, Jewish Councils, across the country. In Warsaw, where a third of the city's million-plus residents were Jewish, a balding engineer named Adam Czerniakow was abruptly appointed chairman of the local *Judenrat.* Undoubtedly, he was chosen for his methodical, engineering mind. Czerniakow and his council of twenty-four handpicked elders were charged with managing all civic affairs of the trapped Jewish population. It was the Council's responsibility to gain rigid compliance with the torrent of oppressive measures decreed by the Nazis as the Reich speedily dismantled the once-thriving community of some 375,000 Warsaw Jews. In their impossible task, the *Judenrat's* every move was closely regulated by the Gestapo, SS, *Einsatz-gruppen,* and other Nazi bodies. Nazi officers sometimes lurked just a few feet away at the window as Czerniakow worked in his office.[63]

Statistics, registrations, and census would be an all-consuming duty for Czerniakow and his council during the coming days.

On October 4, 1939, Czerniakow was called to the *Einsatzgruppe* offices on Szuch Avenue. As instructed, he immediately went to work on a statistical questionnaire. He continued to meet with Nazi officials daily. Each time he was summoned, he noted their escalating, almost non-negotiable demands and commands. October 7, the issue of statistics came up again. October 12, during a meeting with the SS, Czerniakow reviewed questions about the community's finances, forced labor contingents, and the forms to be used to record data. October 13, in meetings with the SS, Czerniakow again conferred on statistics wanted by the Germans and the forms to be used.[64]

To swiftly transfer the Jews out of their homes and businesses across Warsaw and compress them into a small prison-like neighborhood was a major population transfer that required detailed planning. The Nazis were already gathering house-by-house lists of residents from German-appointed "courtyard commandants," this ostensibly to qualify occupants for food in a city where nearly all water, electricity, and transportation had ceased. In addition, the *Judenrat* was required to compile lists of all Warsaw Jews between the ages of sixteen and sixty.[65]

None of it was fast enough or complete enough. On October 14, *Einsatzgruppen* officers ordered the *Judenrat* to conduct a full Jewish census broken down by city district. Somehow, the *Judenrat* would also have to identify the baptized Jews who were not part of the Jewish community.[66]

German statistical officials already possessed the published figures of the Jewish population from the 1931 general Polish census. That census routinely recorded citizens by religion and mother tongue. So the Nazis could easily estimate that about 350,000 Jews lived in Warsaw. But many had fled as the *Blitzkrieg* advanced into the Polish heartland and during the years of pre-war anti-Jewish agitation. Berlin needed precise numbers. They didn't care how. The Nazis demanded Czerniakow plan and execute the census taking.[67]

The next day, as Czerniakow prepared for his task, *Einsatzgruppe* officers and their Polish-born auxiliaries patrolling the Jewish quarters continued to sadistically terrorize Jews directly outside his office. Their favorite sport was pouncing on defenseless, pious Jews walking the streets and demonstratively cutting off their beards. Other times, they forced Jews down on all fours and then ordered neighbors to ride them like donkeys in a race. Brutality to Jews on holy days or just before the Sabbath was the most intense. Pork and butter were smeared across their lips to violate their kosher observance. Soldiers snapped endless photos of the merriment for keepsakes. As such outrages took place outside his window, Czerniakow struggled to outline the logistics of the census.[68]

On October 16, at 5 A.M., Czerniakow resumed working on census taking logistics and the questionnaire. On October 17, Czerniakow rose at dawn to begin a day of meetings to explain his duties, including a stop at the Polish Statistical Office to confer with its staff. On October 19, another meeting was held at the Polish Statistical Office.[69]

On October 20, an *Einsatzgruppen* officer came to the Jewish Community Center for a 3 P.M. meeting with Czerniakow, but the *Judenrat* chairman had already gone to the Security Police headquarters for the meeting. It was a mix-up. Czerniakow was threatened with retaliation unless he came back quickly. By 5 P.M., Czerniakow was summoned to yet another meeting, this one with the SS, again to review census plans. Of the several competing Nazi entities occupying Warsaw, the SS decided its group would issue the census proclamation.[70]

On October 21, Czerniakow met with officials from noon until 2 P.M. at the Polish Statistical Office. From 3 P.M. until 6 P.M. he was at the SS again, hammering out plans for the census. During the difficult conference, Czerniakow tried to explain that the operation should be postponed until early November 3—but the Nazis refused to wait that long. Czerniakow was sent to another official for a protracted, stressful conference and then ordered to conduct the census within one week, on October 28, and at Jewish expense. There was no time to deploy an army of census takers. Instead, Jews would be ordered to appear at local census sites to fill out their forms. Czerniakow was dispatched to the Currency Control Office where officials unblocked some frozen Jewish accounts to defray census costs, such as printing questionnaires. Czerniakow then rushed to meet a printer and together they hurried to the printing shop to discuss the final format of the questionnaires demanded by the Germans, as well as posters announcing the count. It was Czernaikow's responsibility to drive throughout the city that night hanging the announcement posters so they were visible in the morning. Very late that day, fatigued and disconsolate, trying to reconcile with his God, Czerniakow finally returned home. He vomited.[71]

In the morning, Czerniakow continued preparations for the census, including naming twenty-six commissioners to oversee its thoroughness and reliability. The SS had a habit of taking hostages when compliance was required.[72] These men would surely be held responsible if anything went amiss.

On October 23, SS officers came to the Jewish Community Center to monitor the *Judenrat*'s plans to execute the count. October 26, at 1 P.M., Czerniakow toured census stations all over the city. Czerniakow spent the next day making final preparations, conferring with the census commissioners and attending to last-minute details.[73]

Chaim Kaplan was one of Warsaw Jewry's many eloquent men of letters. A teacher, poet, and journalist, Kaplan had traveled to America and Palestine during the pre-War years. In his diary, on October 21, he wrote, "Some time ago, I stated that our future is beclouded. I was wrong. Our future is becoming increasingly clear." He added, "blessed be the righteous judge," the traditional invocation chanted at funerals and upon hearing of a death.[74]

On October 25, Kaplan recorded, "Another sign that bodes ill: Today, notices informed the Jewish population of Warsaw that next Saturday there will be a census of the Jewish inhabitants. . . . Our hearts tell us of evil— some catastrophe for the Jews of Warsaw lies in this census. Otherwise there would be no need for it."[75]

Kaplan had witnessed rabbis brutally beaten and their beards forcibly cut. He had seen elderly women yanked at the jaw with riding crops. Innocent people were compelled to dance atop tables for hours on end. On the day of the census, Kaplan wrote, "These people must be considered psychopaths and sadists, because normal people are incapable of such abominable acts. . . ." He also wrote: "The order for a census stated that it is being held to gather data for administrative purposes. That's a neat phrase, but it contains catastrophe. . . . We are certain that this census is being taken for the purpose of expelling 'nonproductive elements.' And there are a great many of us now. . . . We are all caught in a net, doomed to destruction."[76]

Kaplan was not alone in fearing the census. Czerniakow was besieged with questions about the purpose of this count.[77] The deeply Talmudic community, which had little left except its faith and teachings, understood well that censuses were ominous in Jewish history. The Bible itself taught that unless specifically ordered by God, the census is evil because through it the enemy will know your strength:

I Chronicles 21: Satan rose up against Israel and incited David to take a census of Israel. . . . This command was also evil in the sight of God . . . Then David said to God, "I have sinned greatly by doing this. Now I beg you to take away the guilt of your servant. I have done a very foolish thing."[78]

On October 28, 1939, for the Jewish people of Warsaw, everything stopped. That day they were counted.

Throughout the day, thousands of census forms were brought to the Jewish Community Center, generally by the house superintendents in Jewish buildings.[79]

The results came with almost magical speed. In a little more than forty-eight hours, all the forms had been counted. By October 31, Czerniakow had been informed there were some 360,000 Jews in Warsaw. The exact number was 359,827, revealing the community's precise dimensions: Jews infancy to age 15: . . . 46,172 men and 45,439 women; Jews aged 16–59 . . . 104,273 men and 131,784 women; Jews aged 60 and over . . . 13,325 men and 16,933 women; undetermined . . . only 537 men and 1,364 women. Employed . . . 155,825. Unemployed, including infants and invalids . . . 204,002. Artisans . . . 73,435. The Germans even knew that many Jewish artisans were practicing without a license by comparing the census results with the actual number of artisan licenses previously issued by the local authorities.[80]

The next day, Czerniakow was ordered to submit a complete report on the census within two weeks. On November 2, even as crews began burying masses of typhus and dysentery victims created by the squalid conditions, Czerniakow discovered he could not pay all of the collateral expenses of the census.[81]

By November 20, all census matters had been completed, although the Nazis were planning the ghetto to approximate the outlines of the already overcrowded Nalewki district. The signs at its boundary would read: *Achtung! Seuchengefahr. Eintritt verboten* (Attention: Epidemics—Entry Prohibited). The seizure of all Jewish funds was being readied. But the Nazis still wanted the baptized Jews. It was Czerniakow's problem. He solved it somehow by producing a list of Christian converts, which he handed over on December 6, 1939. By December 9, the authorities had revised their number of Jews in Warsaw to 366,000, the extra 6,000 apparently accounting for the so-called racial Jews.[82]

Now the Reich knew exactly how many Jews were under their jurisdiction, how much nutrition to allocate—as low as 184 calories per person per day. They could consolidate Jews from the mixed districts of Warsaw, and bring in Jews from other nearby villages. The transports began arriving. White armbands with Jewish stars were distributed. Everyone, young or old, was required to wear one on the arm. Not the forearm, but the arm—visible, above the elbow. The Warsaw-Malkinia railway line ran right through the proposed ghetto. It was all according to Heydrich's September 21 Express Letter. Soon the demarcated ghetto would be surrounded by barbed wire. Eventually, a wall went up, sealing the residents of the ghetto from the outside world. Soon thereafter, the railway station would become the most feared location in the ghetto.[83]

The Nazi quantification and regimentation of Jewish demographics in Warsaw and indeed all of Poland was nothing less than spectacular—an almost unbelievable feat. Savage conditions, secrecy, and lack of knowledge by the victims would forever obscure the details of exactly how the Nazis managed to tabulate the cross-referenced information on 360,000 souls within forty-eight hours.

But this much is known: The Third Reich possessed only one method of tabulating censuses: Dehomag's Hollerith system. Moreover, IBM was in Poland, headquartered in Warsaw. In fact, the punch card print shop was just yards from the Warsaw Ghetto at Rymarska Street 6. That's where they produced more than 20 million cards.

WATSON DID NOT really want Poland until 1934. Why? Because that's when Powers had encroached on IBM business in the Polish market. Watson would not tolerate that.

There were so few potential punch card customers in Poland, in the years before Hitler, that IBM didn't even maintain a subsidiary there. Watson's company was only represented by the independent Block-Brun agency. Since the struggling Powers Company sought its few customers wherever IBM didn't dominate, Powers felt free to operate in Poland. Then, in a 1934 sales coup, Powers convinced the Polish Ministry of Posts to replace its Hollerith equipment with rival Powers' machines.[84]

Just as Patterson believed all cash register business "belonged" to the NCR, Watson believed all punch card business innately "belonged" to IBM. When IBM lost the Polish postal service, Watson reacted at once. First, he replaced the Block-Brun agency with a full-fledged IBM subsidiary named

Polski Hollerith.[85] But who would run the new subsidiary? Watson wanted J. W. Schotte.

Jurriaan W. Schotte was born in Amsterdam in 1896, just about the time Herman Hollerith incorporated his original tabulating company. Schotte was eminently qualified for the international punch card business. His background included civil engineering and military service. He was fluent in Dutch, French, and German, and could speak some Romanian and Malay. He had traveled extensively throughout Europe, and enjoyed good commercial and governmental connections. After a stint at the Dutch Consulate in Münster, Germany, he was employed by Dutch import-export companies in New York, San Francisco, and the East Indies. He knew manufacturing, having managed a factory in Belgium. Schotte was perfect for another reason: He was Powers' European sales manager. Schotte was the one who had sold the Powers machines to the Polish Post Office.[86]

Schotte had worked his way up through the Powers organization. Starting as a factory inspector at its U.S. affiliate, he had risen to maintenance supervisor and instructor throughout Europe. A fierce sales competitor, he had deftly operated out of Powers' offices in Paris, Vienna, and Berlin. Most valuable, Schotte knew all of Powers' customers and prospects throughout the continent.[87]

By 1934, however, Dehomag had so thoroughly squeezed Powers in Germany, including its lawsuit for falsely claiming to be an Aryan concern, that Schotte admitted he had "nowhere to go but out." He traveled to New York to meet with J.T. Wilson, the head of IBM NY's Foreign Trade Department. Schotte hoped to salvage his career by becoming a European representative for IBM. Wilson was unsure. Schotte brought a great deal of insider knowledge, but he had been the bitter competition for some time. So Wilson only tentatively hired Schotte, and then cabled the various subsidiaries asking their opinion.[88]

The reports were not good. Heidinger curtly dismissed the suggestion, calling Schotte "an unscrupulous price-cutter." IBM's Geneva office was equally unenthusiastic. But Watson thought otherwise—Schotte was just what IBM needed in the new Europe. During a meeting in Watson's office, Watson dramatically painted a tantalizing picture of the future of Europe, one that excited Schotte because he could play a central role in IBM's plans. He could return to Europe as IBM's Manager for Southeast Europe with a handsome compensation package. Schotte was later described as "in awe" and "walking over clouds" as the meeting ended and he stepped to the door of Watson's office. But his euphoria was cut short when Watson abruptly declared, "Mr.

Schotte, your employment in IBM depends on your getting IBM machines back into the Polish Postal Service."[89]

Schotte sailed back to Europe and, as Watson had insisted, persuaded the Polish Postal Service to switch back to Hollerith machines.[90] Watson would have Poland again.

Hitler also wanted Poland. Nazi doctrine had long called for the conquest of Polish territory, the subjugation of its people as inferiors, and the destruction of its 1.3 million Jewish citizens that comprised the largest Jewish community in Europe. Moreover, the Reich was determined to confiscate Poland's significant natural resources and industry, including timber, coke, coal, and steel making in Upper Silesia. Upper Silesia was adjacent to the Sudeten region and many *Volksdeutsche* lived in its cities. Hitler considered the area German.

By 1935, the year of the Nuremberg racial laws, Polski Hollerith had opened a card punching service bureau in Warsaw. The next year, IBM opened a second Polish office, this one in the Upper Silesian city of Katowice, and then a card printing facility in Warsaw serving a customer base requiring 36 million cards per year. In 1937, Polski Hollerith signed the Polish Ministry of Railroads. That year, IBM changed its name to Watson Business Machines sp. z. o.o. and appointed an IBM salesman of Polish extraction, Janusz Zaporski, as temporary manager. Ironically, although IBM owned and controlled 100 percent of the company, as he had done so often before, Watson chose to register the stock not in the company's name, but in the name of his Geneva managers. In this case, it was IBM Europe General Manager John Holt and IBM's Geneva auditor J. C. Milner, as well as a token share—the equivalent of $200—in the name of a Polish national. By the time the company changed names to Watson Business Machines sp. z. o.o in 1937, IBM had garnered only twenty-five customers in Poland. But the list included some of the country's most vital industry giants, such as the Baildon steelworks. More importantly, by this time, the subsidiary had organized the nation's freight cars and locomotives, and through the Polish Postal Service could control access to every address in Poland.[91]

After Hitler invaded Poland in September 1939, IBM NY awarded the lucrative Upper Silesia industrial territory to Dehomag, negotiating the disposition of each of the pre-existing machines. Then Watson recast his Polish subsidiary as an Aryan entity by re-incorporating as a German company and affixing a German language name, Watson Büromaschinen GmbH, with the recognizable, German incorporation suffix. The office in war-torn Warsaw was moved to Kreuz 23, and the company appointed a German manager,

Alexander von Dehn. Von Dehn was only in charge of the remnant Polish territory, that is, the vanquished and subjugated remainder known in Hitler parlance as the "General Government." All but two of the previous Polish customers of the remnant subsidiary had disappeared, since the Polish government ceased to exist except as a vassal to the Germans.[92]

Yet, after adjusting for the effects of the invasion, the subsidiary thrived for years under the murderous Nazi regime. IBM's German or Polish subsidiaries, separately or in tandem, serviced the occupying Nazi needs through the German military's constantly changing punch card agency, which ultimately became known as *Maschinelles Berichtwesen* (*MB*), or the Office for Automated Reporting. The *MB* maintained Polish field offices in Posen, Krakow, Stettin, and Danzig. Each *MB* office was typically equipped with one alphabetical tabulator and duplicator, ten alphabetical punchers and proofers, eight magnetic punchers and proofers, one D-11 tabulator with summary capabilities, and two or three sorters. One or two Wehrmacht officers supervised a typical support staff of several dozen as well as one or two on-site so-called Hollerith experts. Dehomag itself was in charge of all *MB* office training, leasing, upkeep, and custom-printed punch cards and design of specialized applications. The projects were as diverse as a so-called "horse census" of all horses and mules in Poland, which would help move German elements through the harsh Polish winter, to the shipments of coal. IBM Geneva was so proud of the horse census, conducted in spring 1940, that they quickly included it in a special report to IBM's Washington office describing the lucrative war profiteering of the various European subsidiaries.[93]

During the years of Nazi-dominated Poland, deniability continued to be a precious imperative. IBM NY continued to operate through its intermediaries, nominees, and Geneva managers. It would always be able to say it was unaware of Watson Büromaschinen's activities and the paperwork would be nearly impossible to trace.

For example, the subsidiary's account at Handlowy Bank in Warsaw, referred to as "number 4B," was actually an IBM account, controlled from Geneva. An administrator later described the arrangement in these words: "In this manner, the IBM's account was at the same time the business capital of the Warsaw company, as Herr von Dehn was entitled to take sums from the account for the purposes of the Warsaw company." Despite the horrific conditions in Warsaw, IBM maintained close control of the account after the invasion. On February 10, 1940, IBM gave von Dehn written authority to receive customer payments, that is, physically "receive" them. The actual permission for von Dehn to deposit the payments in IBM's account, "after deduction of the sums necessary for the conduct of the management," was only oral.[94]

In summer 1940, long after Hitler had invaded numerous other countries in Europe, and after the Warsaw Ghetto was being sealed, Watson wanted his Polish operation to stay intact. On July 29, 1940, a key official of the IBM Geneva office, known as P. Taylor, had written to von Dehn conveying Watson's instruction that the families of all married men who had worked for the subsidiary prior to the invasion should be given special financial assistance. This subvention was to be paid from the company account. Initially, the gesture was prompted by confiscatory Nazi economic decrees and labor restrictions, which canceled the expected Christmas 1939 bonus. Two months pay was offered as a so-called "loan," and, as an administrator later explained, "in order to keep up the appearance of the loan, the recipients paid back minimal amounts each month." Von Dehn was included in the company welfare, which exemplified the IBM ethic of taking care of "the company's own." Such assistance encouraged loyalty from employees even during the war. The company also granted food loans. Soon, the loan policy was extended to unmarried employees as well. Eventually, the employee loan program, which was similar to programs Watson had declared in other countries, amounted to more than 135,000 zlotys or approximately $27,000. IBM Geneva also authorized small loans to its war-devastated suppliers totaling more than 8,000 zlotys.[95]

IBM machinery was placed throughout the General Government, including two alphabetizers and accessory machines, which had been brought in by the invading German army. Dehomag rented them to the Polish users, retaining 25 percent of the income. The remainder went to Watson Büromaschinen. Among the few remaining clients were Polish Railways and the Krakow Statistical Office.[96]

The subsidiary's machinery in occupied Poland was insured in the United States. In 1940, von Dehn asked IBM to increase the insurance in view of wartime conditions. But this would have involved paperwork. IBM declined to do so.[97]

As for Block-Brun, IBM's former agency, it was excluded from nearly all of IBM's expansion in Poland. Block-Brun switched to Powers, the only minor competitor left in punch card technology. But the residual Powers business was paltry. So Block-Brun was eager to retain a tertiary role as a local supplier of IBM control mechanisms. An administrator who later looked for a written contract with Block-Brun could never find one. This relationship also appeared to be oral. Under the cloudy arrangement, IBM sold the control mechanisms at Block-Brun's own risk, requiring the Polish agency to pay the import freight to Warsaw. These parts were not sold into Poland by Dehomag, but directly by IBM either in New York or Europe. Watson required Block-Brun to pay the import fees. All sales were final with Block-Brun immediately assuming ownership once the apparatuses were ordered. But IBM's terms often allowed the agency to pay into the Bank Handlowy account only after the merchandise was sold, generally six to fifteen months after receipt.[98] IBM was receiving the money for years after the invasion.

Block-Brun's sales on behalf of IBM were often wrongly listed as "consignments," which meant IBM would have owned the devices until sale, paid tax immediately, and assumed all risk for war damage. IBM refused to honor any appearance of consignment. For example, in 1939, a shipment worth $12,134 was severely damaged. Block-Brun negotiated with IBM for years before IBM finally agreed to take the machines back via Sweden. Due to war conditions, the machines never made it back.[99]

After the Nazis invaded Poland, IBM maintained its punch card printing operation at Rymarska Street 6. Three printing machines and one card cutter employed just two people, using paper brought in from Germany. Ultimately, during the occupation years, the shop at Rymarska produced as many as 10 million cards per year.[100]

In 1939, Rymarska Street 6 stood along a very short, tree-lined lane, opposite a plaza fountain, just yards from the Jewish district that in 1940 would become the walled-in Warsaw Ghetto. The street itself had long possessed a Jewish character. In 1928, before IBM inhabited it, Rymarska 6 housed the Salon for Jewish Art. The property had been owned, at one point, by the Hirszfeld brothers. In addition to a gallery, the street had become known for print shops. Rymarska 8 housed the Pospieszna printer and the "Union" printer was a few doors down. But after the Nazis arrived, Jews lost their property to Aryan or Polish concerns. When, in 1940, the Warsaw Ghetto was walled in, the often-adjusted perimeter cut right through Rymarska Street, oddly circumventing the print shops in an almost U-shaped deviation. Rymarska 1–5 and Rymarska 11–20 ended up within the Ghetto. Rymarska 6 and a few other shops remained outside the ghetto. Thus, most of the printing operations continued undisturbed.[101]

Statistical operations resembling the Warsaw census were established in ghettos all across Poland. Although the incessant counts and voluminous card files were implemented and maintained by the *Judenräte* under merciless Nazi coercion, the vital statistics were not certified as final until they were approved by the fully equipped city statistical offices outside the ghetto walls. Ultimately, the ghettos developed elaborate statistical bureaus. In some cases, they were required to publish their own statistical yearbooks. The Czestochowa Ghetto's three statistical bulletins in 1940 totaled some 400 pages of detailed demographic and subsistence analysis.[102]

Poland was not the only focal point for Reich statistical action. A Statistical Office for the Protectorate of Bohemia and Moravia was opened in Prague in 1939. Data services were also opened in Upper Silesia and the Warthe region where IBM had transferred the territory to Dehomag.[103]

After the 1939 invasion, Heydrich of the Security Service, the official who had sent out the all-defining September 21 Express Letter, sent a follow-up cable to his occupying forces in Poland, Upper Silesia, and Czechoslovakia. This cable outlined how a new census scheduled for December 17, 1939, would escalate the process from mere identification and cataloging to deportation and execution as people were rapidly moved into Polish ghettos to await the next step.[104]

Heydrich's memo, entitled "Evacuation of the New Eastern Provinces," decreed: "The evacuation of Poles and Jews in the new Eastern Provinces will be conducted by the Security Police . . . The census documents provide the basis for the evacuation. All persons in the new provinces possess a copy. The census form is the temporary identification card giving permission to stay. Therefore, all persons have to hand over the card before deportation . . . anyone caught without this card is subject to possible execution. . . . It is projected that the census will take place on December 17, 1939."[105]

More than a half-million people were to be deported from the Warthe region alone, based on "Statistical information (census lists, etc.) from German and Polish sources, investigative results of the Security Police and the Security Service, and surveys . . . [which would] constitute the foundation."[106]

How long would it take to quantify and organize the deportation of millions from various regions across Eastern Europe based upon a December 17 census? Relying upon the lightning speed of Hollerith machines, Heydrich was able to assert, "That means the large-scale evacuation can begin no sooner than around January 1, 1940."[107]

Ultimately, the late December census took place over several days, from December 17 to December 23, 1939. Each person over the age of twelve was required to fill out census and registration in duplicate, and was then fingerprinted. Part of the form was stamped and returned as the person's new identification form. Without it, they would be shot. With it, they would be deported.[108]

December was a busy month for IBM's German subsidiary—and

extremely profitable. Throughout Germany and the conquered territories, Dehomag frantically tried to keep up with the pace of unending censuses, registrations, and analyses of people, property, and military operations that required its equipment, repair services, and card processing. Millions of cards were printed each week just to meet the demand. Understandably, whereas Rottke had been incensed at Watson's initial refusal to transfer the alphabetizers as requested, all the hard feelings were now gone.

DECEMBER 6, 1939
Mr. Thomas J. Watson, President
International Business Machines Corporation
590 Madison Ave.
New York NY USA

Dear Mr. Watson:
    As Christmas is approaching I feel an urgent desire to express to you and your family my most sincere and best wishes for a joyful Yuletide. Mrs. Rottke and my two sons add their good wishes hereto. I take this opportunity to thank you again most heartily for the understanding by you in regard to my requests during the past year. I hope that the difficult times, which have come over the European nations once more, will not last too long. My family and I are enjoying good health, which I sincerely trust is also the case with yourself and your family.

With very kindest regards, I am
Very sincerely yours,
Herman Rottke[109]

    In early 1940, IBM Geneva sent Watson a statement of Dehomag's 1939 profits. The numbers were almost double the previous year, totaling RM 3,953,721 even after all the royalty income and other disguised revenue. The Dehomag profit statement to Watson also explained that somehow almost half the 1939 profit, RM 1,800,000, was suddenly recorded in December 1939.[110]

    The strategic alliance with Hitler continued to pay off in the cities and in the ghettos. But now IBM machines would demonstrate their special value along the railways and in the concentration camps of Europe. Soon the Jews would become Hollerith numbers.

I
II
III
IV
V
VI
VII
VIII
IX
X
XI
XII
XIII
XIV
XV

WITH BLITZKRIEG EFFICIENCY

HITLER'S ARMIES SWARMED OVER EUROPE THROUGHOUT the first months of 1940. The forces of the Reich slaughtered all opposition with a military machine unparalleled in human history. *Blitzkrieg*—lightning war—was more than a new word. Its very utterance signified coordinated death under the murderous onslaught of Hitler's massive air, sea, and 100,000-troop ground assaults. Nothing could stop Germany.

Nazi Europe—and Berlin's new world order—was becoming a reality. *Austria*: annexed in March 1938. *Sudetenland*: seized October 1938. *Czechoslovakia*: dismembered March 1939, and the Memel region ceded from Lithuania that same month. *Poland*: invaded September 1939. By January 1940, nearly 42 million people had come under brutal German subjugation. Disease, starvation, shattered lives, and fear became the desolate truth across the Continent.

The Jews were running out of refuges. One overrun sanctuary after another slid back into the familiar nightmare of registration, confiscation, and ghettoization. No sooner did the Swastika flag of occupation unfurl, than the anti-Semitic decrees rolled out. Eastern European countries not yet conquered emulated the pattern as German sympathizers and surrogates in Romania, Hungary, and Italy undertook Berlin's bidding to destroy local Jewish populations.

As the winter receded, the Reich prepared for further aggression. By spring 1940, Nazi Germany began dismembering Scandinavia and the Low Countries. April 9, the *Wehrmacht* invaded Denmark. May 2, Norway was stormed. Several days later, tiny Luxembourg was taken. May 15, Germany crushed Holland into complete submission. May 28, Belgium capitulated to German forces. During April and May, Germany's enslavement jurisdiction grew to 65 million Europeans.[1]

Cities across Europe smoldered in ruin. Warsaw was pulverized into a shambles. Rotterdam was mercilessly bombed even after its surrender on May 14 because, as Berlin propagandists explained, Dutch officials exceeded the ultimatum deadline by some twenty minutes. An elaborate Nazi newsreel, filmed by parachuting cameramen, showed Rotterdam almost completely aflame. Airports at Brussels and Antwerp were bombed and strafed by hundreds of *Luftwaffe* planes.[2]

Nazi-commandeered trains crisscrossed the continent hauling into Germany looted coal, scrap metal, foodstuffs, machinery, and the other essentials Berlin craved. When they weren't carrying raw materials, or transporting troops, the railroad cars freighted conscripted labor en route to work projects as well as expelled Jews destined for concentration camps.[3]

Mass executions, organized plunder, and ruthless invasion—these blared across the front pages of the newspapers, the frames of newsreels, and the broadcasts of radio news. Germany was portrayed in emotional headlines and feature articles as a savage, murderous nation bent on destroying and dominating all of Europe no matter how many people died. On April 2, Poland's exile government declared that in addition to a million prisoners and forced laborers transported to German work sites, an estimated 2.5 million had died as a result of military action, executions, starvation, or frigid homelessness. In the five days of Germany's invasion of the Netherlands commencing May 10, a quarter of the Dutch army was killed—more than 100,000, plus a casualty rate of 80 percent.[4]

Moreover, millions of Jews were now clearly earmarked for death by virtue of Hitler's oppressive measures. In November 1939, the *New York Times* published reports from Paris declaring that 1.5 million Jews trapped in Poland were in danger of starving to death. On January 21, 1940, World Jewish Congress Chairman Nahum Goldmann warned a Chicago crowd of 1,000, as well as wire service reporters, that if the war continued for another year 1 million Polish Jews would die of calculated starvation or outright murder. Such dire predictions only capped years of saturation media coverage about inhumane Jewish persecution and horrifying concentration camps.[5]

Indeed, whenever Jewish persecution was reported, the media invariably reported the incessant registrations and censuses as Nazidom's initial step. The methodology, technology, and the connection to IBM were still far below public awareness. But some specifics were beginning to appear. For example, a March 2, 1940, *New York Times* article, entitled "Jews in Cracow Move to Ghettos," described how 80,000 Jews had been herded into overcrowded flats in a squalid urban district devoid of resources. "A common sight," the report asserted, "is the white armband with the blue Star of David, which all Jews must wear by government decree . . . [signifying] their registration in the government card file."[6]

Only with great caution could Watson now publicly defend the Hitler agenda, even through euphemisms and code words. Most Americans would not tolerate anyone who even appeared to be a Nazi sympathizer or collaborator. So, as he had done since *Kristallnacht* in late 1938, Watson continued to insert corporate distance between himself and all involvement in the affairs of his subsidiaries in Nazi Europe—even as he micro-managed their day-to-day operations. More than ever, he now channeled his communications to Nazi Europe through trusted intermediaries in Geneva and elsewhere on the Continent. He controlled subsidiary operations through attorneys and employees acting as nominee owners, following the pattern set in Czechoslovakia and Poland.[7]

In May 1940, as American society prepared for an inevitable war with Hitler, Watson worked to secure the underpinnings of his public image. He intensified his advocacy for peace, and against all war.

"Universal peace is one of the most desirable, most worthwhile ideals in the world today," Watson insisted in a May 4 speech to reporters. "It cannot be sold by a few people working in widely scattered communities. The project requires a worldwide organization of enthusiastic, hard-working individuals selling the gospel of peace."[8] Watson advertised IBM as such an organization.

Four days later, on May 8, Watson told reporters that the company's latest course held in Endicott, New York, for IBM sales representatives from twenty-four countries was to "enable the students . . . to make greater contributions to the cause of world peace through world trade."[9]

Watson's advocacy for peace was limitless. May 13, 1940, was proclaimed IBM Day at the World's Fair being held that month in New York. IBM Day was nothing less than an extravaganza of orchestrated adulation for the company. A dozen chartered trains brought in 7,000 IBM employees and their wives from company facilities across the nation to visit the architectonic

IBM Pavilion. Each IBMer wore a red ribbon of solidarity with the company. Two thousand lucky ones were chosen to be feted at a massive Waldorf-Astoria dinner. Special congratulations to IBM, as usual, were issued by leading politicians from President Roosevelt to the Mayor of New York. To underscore the drama, Watson commissioned an original orchestral work, *The IBM Symphony*, a bombastic composition dedicated to the uplifting spirit of the firm.[10]

The climax of IBM Day, however, was Watson's speech on the subject of peace. He delivered his sermon to 30,000 specially invited guests gathered at the vast Court of Peace located in front of the sweeping USA Pavilion. Mutual Radio broadcast the highly publicized event countrywide.[11]

Peace was Watson's message. War was bad, he argued at every opportunity. It would prove nothing but military might, waste lives and precious resources. War was in fact the worst recourse for the world, and all right-thinking men should be opposed to any involvement with it, Watson pleaded. As head of the Carnegie Endowment for International Peace, Watson everywhere proclaimed his driving mantra: "World Peace through World Trade." Indeed, Watson must have seemed to the public like the very champion of peace and the arch adversary of all conflict. Ironically, at that very moment, Watson and IBM were in fact Europe's most successful organizers not of peace, but of the ravages of war.

Even as Watson was preaching the imperatives of peace, IBM was ecstatic about its accomplishments revolutionizing warfare not only for the Third Reich, but also for its Axis allies and even other European nations about to be vanquished by Hitler. In spring 1940, J. W. Schotte, IBM's general manager for Europe, dispatched a confidential report from his Geneva office to senior IBM executives in America. Schotte's dispatch addressed the activities not only of just Dehomag, but also of the two dozen European subsidiaries and agencies that worked as inter-connected branches of the New York company.[12]

Schotte's enthusiastic memo was entitled "Our Dealings with War Ministries in Europe." It began, "Up to about one and a half years ago [about the time of *Kristallnacht* in 1938], our negotiations with the war ministries of the twenty-four countries which are under the jurisdiction of IBM European headquarters in Geneva, had not been very successful. This was due to several reasons, but mainly to the fact that in military circles administration was considered a 'necessary evil' of little importance for the defense of the country."[13]

IBM had finally succeeded in gaining the necessary insider access to sensitive military projects, Schotte reported, so that company engineers could properly design punch card applications for war use. Schotte explained that in prior years "the military men in Europe have been reluctant to reveal their problems and programs to civilians. It has been overlooked in such instances that there is a distinct difference between knowing which problems exist and what system is applied, and the data and figures to which the system has to be applied."[14] As such, Schotte drew a fine theoretical distinction between IBM possessing specific knowledge of the facts about a military operation, such as the number of people to be counted or a list of German bombing raids, and the actions themselves.

The big change in military acceptance of Hollerith systems appeared at the end of 1938, confirmed Schotte, when "in Germany a campaign started for, what has been termed . . . 'organization of the second front.'" He elaborated, "In military literature and in newspapers, the importance and necessity of having in all phases of life, behind the front, an organization which would remain intact and would function with 'Blitzkrieg' efficiency . . . was brought out. What we had been preaching in vain for years all at once began to be realized."[15]

Schotte's memo made clear that only at IBM's initiative did the militarists comprehend what magic they could achieve with Hollerith automation. "Lectures on the punched card system were held by our representatives before officials of the general staff of various countries and, with our men, the study of possible applications was begun . . . progress was rather slow, and it was not until about eight or nine months ago [summer 1939] when conditions in Europe clearly indicated that a war was more or less unavoidable, that the matter became acute."[16]

Asserting that IBM sold to either side and had enjoyed an ever-escalating volume since the summer of 1939, Schotte's memo declared, "The War Ministries of Yugoslavia, Rumania, Hungary, Poland, Sweden, Holland and France (these are the ones that I remember very distinctly from memory) sent us orders for punched card equipment, some of which is already installed, others being installed when the war started, and further equipment not yet installed or still in transport."[17]

Revenues from IBM's dominant customer, the Third Reich, was growing so rapidly, Schotte said he did not yet possess the sales numbers. "We have no details of Germany," he reported, "but know that a large amount of punched card equipment is being used by the War Ministry." He added that so great was Germany's need in the months before and after the invasion of Poland that the Reich began requisitioning machines. Indeed, the agency ultimately known as the *Maschinelles Berichtwesen (MB)* had exercised full authority over all punch card technology since 1937. "In the second half of

1939," wrote Schotte, "most of our equipment was 'seized' and used to supplement the installations already in operation."[18]

Once war erupted, the haste to add machines for military use was not confined to Germany. Schotte's report noted that "rush orders were placed with us" by those countries not yet properly automated. Most IBM subsidiaries were two years behind in filling orders, so many war ministries hurried their orders just to get in queue. "To make up for lost time," Schotte continued, "Holland and France gave us blank orders for a large quantity of machines, although our studies were not completed for several of the uses, and the quantities of required machines not established. As late as February 1940, the French War Ministry ordered a very substantial quantity of machines."[19]

Schotte's report clarified that not all war applications were handled directly by war ministries. Numerous systems had been conveyed to private industry, "but are for their [war ministry] use and under their control." Therefore, even though a coal mine or insurance company might be listed as the account, utilization of the machines was dictated by military needs either on the original corporate premises or moved to a more secure location altogether. Indeed, by spring 1940, his memo confirmed, many such systems had already been relocated to more protected sites, the report acknowledged.[20]

Widespread expansion of punch card systems for war was ironically undermined in various countries by the draft itself, which infringed on the punch card workforce, asserted Schotte. However, eventually, military officials exempted "key men in our installations [who then] remained at their posts." Moreover, "supervisors and our indispensable servicemen were released for such work." Even still, he added, "A great inconvenience was caused due to the sudden extension of equipment in most countries, a shortage of trained supervisors and punch operators. Ads were placed in the papers and such operators lured away from one installation to another by offering higher salaries. We hurriedly started training schools for key punch operators and supervisors, and of course servicemen who would be exempted from military service due to age or physical condition."[21]

Europe's militarists had finally realized the indispensable advantages Hollerith instilled into modern warfare, boasted Schotte. Punch cards freed up manpower. Schotte cited a typical case: "For example, in Hungary with one set of machines and a few operators we replaced about sixty men." He added that the machines "work twenty-four hours without vacation. The place and location is immaterial, and machines have been installed in bomb-proof cellars. . . . There is no limit to the flexibility and adaptability of the machines, provided the mass of data to be handled is sufficiently large."[22]

Most importantly, stressed Schotte, Hollerith machines guaranteed "speed in handling mass records and data. Such speed would be absolutely impossible by manual methods," he stressed.[23]

Schotte's report included a list of IBM's remarkable accomplishments for the armies of war-ravaged Europe. Personal information about every officer and soldier resided on Hollerith systems. In France, for example, the actual "mobilization call to each officer was printed by our equipment by means of punch cards." Hollerith machines controlled all payrolls to both armies and civilian workers in munitions factories.[24]

So comprehensive was IBM Europe's data on both Germany and its enemies that Schotte's memo was able to assert that the punch cards maintained "records of each and every Communist and Nazi."[25]

Records were also kept "on skilled laborers by profession, industry, etc. Such records are kept to control the potential of war material manufacture," Schotte's memo specified.[26]

The labor data tersely alluded to in just a few words in Schotte's memo was profoundly vital to Hitler. These automated reports allowed the Reich to strategically deploy both the skilled laborers within Germany and the conscripted work brigades and slave gangs shipped in from occupied countries. It was a daunting organizational challenge. By the end of 1940, the number of such conscripted and other slave workers totaled nearly 2.5 million. Reporting formats continuously evolved as the Reich's needs changed and Hollerith technology improved to keep up. Eventually, reporting categories included what Germany considered its entire manpower pool, from company owners to skilled workers to unskilled laborers, divided into male and female columns. As time evolved, the various cross-indexed reports further classified the categories into "Reich residents, civilian foreigners, prisoners and Jews," as well as others. Germany's punch card control agency, *Maschinelles Berichtwesen*, coordinated the reports. The agency considered its labor data, "without a doubt, *MB*'s most important statistical survey on the deployment of individuals," as a key senior *MB* official later expressed it. "For all participating offices," the *MB* officer emphasized, "this was the major tool for the coordination and surveillance of work employment in the individual territories and in the entire Reich. Its results laid the foundation for the ongoing monthly negotiations on the assignment of workers for armaments production."[27]

Three years later, Schotte, while in his New York office, would describe to a government official exactly how the personnel tracking system worked in Nazi-occupied territories. "For example," wrote the official that Schotte briefed, "if a Gauleiter [the ranking regional Nazi Party official] in Poland needs a number of technicians who speak Polish but are not Poles, it is possible to secure the exact names and locations of the men in their present units by placing the punched cards in the sorting machine and setting the machine to provide the correct answer. When the required number has been determined, the machine stops."[28]

People weren't all that IBM counted and tracked. Schotte, in his spring 1940 memo to IBM, was also proud of the company's ability to count "animals: a record of each horse, mule, etc."[29]

Although mentioned by Schotte only in passing, animal censuses were complex logistical projects. The Nazis ordered the first such "horse census" in Poland in early 1940. Jews operated many of the stables and equine operations in Poland. As part of the confiscation of Jewish assets, horses were seized and then mobilized by the army to move materials, prisoners, and even corpse wagons through the frigid, often snowbound Polish countryside, as well as the cities. By seizing horses, the Reich also cut off an important means of escape for Jews fleeing Nazi invaders. Orders to German police units stationed throughout Poland reflected the gravity of the horse count. Those instructions proclaimed: "In order to secure the *Wehrmacht*'s census of horses, conducted to avoid a secret shifting around, I request that you, in conjunction with the county's farmers and all *Wehrmacht* offices dealing with the horse census, employ police forces, especially at night, to establish that horses are not secretly moved from their census districts into other sections. Captured horses which may have been moved are to be confiscated and their owners punished." British intelligence agents monitoring the horse census called the project "tremendous," and in a secret report could only marvel at the "thoroughness of preparations."[30]

The spring 1940 cow census in occupied Belgium, also monitored by British intelligence, reflected an equal feat of livestock counting. After the count, each animal was required to wear an identity card.[31]

Schotte's spring 1940 memo also listed the extraordinary programs of material control covering inventories as diverse as "arms, clothes, airplane spare parts" and all raw materials, such as "rubber, oil, steel, iron." Moreover, reported Schotte's report, "records [are] kept of each factory with the type and class of its machines" and whether they were currently being used for battle or classed as potential suppliers.[32]

In occupied lands, material censuses and registrations organized Nazi plunder of resources. For example, a butter census was scheduled for occupied Denmark to discover large stores of butter hoarded by Danes. As railroad cars loaded with the material and merchandise of a foreign country entered Germany, punch cards kept track of the inventory. This system was refined as the months progressed and as Germany's occupation broadened. Schotte later described the evolved system for a government official who summarized it this way: "The original inventory throughout a country is represented by cards," the official wrote. "For a period of ten days in Germany, cards are punched of incoming and outgoing movements and then at the end of ten days are sorted by commodity, together with the inventory card . . . [so] the inventory is never more than ten days behind time."[33]

Schotte's spring 1940 memo also cited the organization of all "automobile records: (military and in some cases also the private cars)." Private vehicles were routinely seized by invading Germans, first from Jews, and then from other citizens as well. Identifying cars and trucks was one of the first statistical efforts Germany generally mounted after invading any foreign territory.[34]

Hollerith machines were deeply involved in combat records as well, according to Schotte's spring 1940 memo. For example, *Luftwaffe* missions were all duly recorded to calculate the details of aviator combat, asserted the report. Schotte's memo bragged that punch cards maintained a "record of each flight of a military aviator, for his personal record and calculation of premiums." In addition, all German war injuries were analyzed by complex Hollerith programs that allowed Reich planners at the Central Archive for War Medicine in Berlin to conduct sophisticated medical research. In World War I, it was Hollerith analyses of head-wound injuries that helped the Austrian military design the most protective helmet possible.[35]

Schotte's spring 1940 report also listed "decoding" of enemy dispatches as a prime Hollerith application.[36]

As each month advanced, Hollerith machines became more involved in each and every move of the German forces. Eventually, every Nazi combat order, bullet, and troop movement was tracked on an IBM punch card system.[37]

In 1940, IBM NY knew the exact location of each of its machines in the Greater Reich on an updated basis. Without that tracking, it could not audit IBM Europe's charges and depreciate its equipment. One typical machine list in its Manhattan office was entitled "International Business Machines Corp. New York" and labeled in German words "Machines as of September 30, 1940." This particular thirteen-page inventory identified each machine by client, location, type, serial number, and value. Five alphabetizers in the 405 model series, for instance, were located at the German Army High Command. Those five machines bore serial numbers 10161, 10209, 11316, 13126, and 13128, with each one valued between RM 8,750 and RM 11,675.[38]

Other alphabetizers were placed at a myriad of offices, according to the list, including various military inspectorates, offices of the punch card control agency, the census bureau, the branches of Reich Statistical Office, and strategic arms manufacturers such as Krupp and Junkers Aircraft. Again, each installation reflected the type of machine, serial number, and value.[39]

Ironically, all the rush orders placed into the militaries of such countries as Holland and Poland worked to the Reich's advantage. When the Nazis invaded, all Hollerith machines were seized and converted to German use. IBM subsidiaries were then on hand to service the Reich's needs. Sales to Germany's enemies never bothered IBM's hypersensitive Reich sponsors. Indeed, some in the Nazi hierarchy may have even viewed such sales as a virtual "pre-positioning" of equipment in neighboring nations, nations that many throughout Europe and America expected to be invaded imminently. In the case of Poland, for example, IBM leased Hollerith equipment to the Polish military in 1939 just before the German invasion, and then immediately after the invasion created a new Berlin-based subsidiary for the occupied territory. Accounts in annexed regions were transferred to Dehomag. In the case of Holland, systems were leased to the military in early 1940; a completely new subsidiary was planned in March 1940, just weeks before the invasion, and rush-formalized just after the invasion.[40]

IBM had almost single-handedly brought modern warfare into the information age. Through its persistent, aggressive, unfaltering efforts, IBM virtually put the "blitz" in the *krieg* for Nazi Germany. Simply put, IBM organized the organizers of Hitler's war.

Keeping corporate distance in the face of the company's mounting involvement was now more imperative than ever. Although deniability was constructed with enough care to last for decades, the undeniable fact was that either IBM NY or its European headquarters in Geneva or its individual subsidiaries, depending upon the year and locale, maintained intimate knowledge of each and every application wielded by Nazis. This knowledge was inherently revealed by an omnipresent paper trail: the cards themselves. IBM—and only IBM—printed all the cards. Billions of them.

Since Herman Hollerith invented his tabulators at the close of the nineteenth century, the feisty inventor had fought continuous technologic and legal battles to ensure that no source but his company could print a card compatible with the sorter's complex mechanisms. Once a customer invested in a Hollerith machine, the customer was continuously tied to the company for punch cards. This exclusivity was nothing less than the anchor of the lucrative Hollerith monopoly.[41]

Watson vigilantly continued Hollerith's legacy. During the Hitler years, the Department of Justice litigated IBM's monopoly, focusing on the firm's secret pacts with other potential manufacturers, which forbid any competition in punch card supply. Unique presses, extraordinary paper, near clinical storage, exacting specifications, and special permission from Watson were required for any IBM subsidiary to even begin printing cards anywhere in the world. Should any non-IBM entity dare enter the field, Watson would shut them down with court orders. For example, when the German paper manufacturer Euler, associated with the Powers Company, tried to print IBM-compatible punch cards, Watson restrained them with an injunction. For good measure, IBM wrote special clauses into its German contracts prohibiting any client—whether an ordinary insurance company or the NSDAP itself—from utilizing any card other than one produced by IBM. In short, Hollerith cards could only be printed at IBM-owned and -operated printing facilities and nowhere else.[42]

Until 1935, IBM NY was the sole exporter of punch cards to Hitler's Germany. Eventually, Watson invested in high-speed presses for Germany so Dehomag could print and export its own throughout Europe. During the next few years, he authorized IBM printing presses in Austria, Poland, Holland, France, and greatly expanded capacity in Germany. Deep into the war, as late as 1942 additional IBM printing facilities were opened in Finland and Denmark. All these plants acted as a coordinated cross-border European supply line. For example, in the first three months of 1939 alone, IBM Sweden sold 1.9 million punch cards to Denmark, 1.3 million to Finland, and 696,000 to Norway. IBM NY sold 1 million cards to Yugoslavia and 700,000 to Fascist Spain. Dehomag sold 261,000 to Hungary. It was all done under the constant supervision of IBM Geneva, which in turn kept in continuous contact with IBM NY. European General Manager Schotte regularly flew back and forth from Switzerland to America conveying reports.[43]

IBM printed billions of its electrically sensitive cards each year for its European customers. But every order was different. Each set was meticulously designed not only for the singular client, but for the client's specific assignments. The design work was not a rote procedure, but an intense collaboration. It began with a protracted investigation of the precise data needs of the project, as well as the people, items, or services being tabulated. This required IBM subsidiary "field engineers" to undertake invasive studies of the subject being measured, often on-site. Was it people? Was it cattle? Was it airplane engines? Was it pension payments? Was it slave labor? Different data gathering and card layouts were required for each type of application.[44]

Once the problem was intimately understood, Hollerith technology was carefully wedded to the specific mission. This process required a constant back and forth between the IBM subsidiary's technical staff and client user as they jointly designed mock-up punch cards to be compatible with the registration forms, and then ensured that the plug and dial tabulators could be configured to extract the information. Only after careful approval by both IBM technicians and the client did the cards finally go to press.[45]

Once printed, each set of custom-designed punch cards bore its own distinctive look for its highly specialized purpose. Each set was printed with its own job-specific layout, with columns arrayed in custom-tailored configurations and then preprinted with unique column labels. Only IBM presses manufactured these cards, column by column, with the preprinted field topic: race, nationality, concentration camp, metal drums, combat wounds to leg, train departure vs. train arrival, type of horse, bank account, wages owed, property owed, physical racial features possessed—ad infinitum.[46]

Cards printed for one task could never be used for another. Factory payroll accounting cards, for example, could not be utilized by the SS in its on-going program of checking family backgrounds for racial features. Differences in the cards were obvious. Dehomag's 1942 accounting cards for the Böhlerwerk Company, for instance, featured the manufacturer's name centered. The card contained only 14 columns preprinted with such headings as *hours worked* above column 8, *pieces produced* above column 9, and *suggested processing time* above column 11. The right hand third of the punch card was empty.[47]

In contrast, SS Race Office punch cards, printed by Dehomag that same year, featured a bold *Rassenamt SS* logo. *Rassenamt* cards carried custom-labeled columns for *years of marriage* above column 7, *height* above column 47, *height while seated* above column 48, and *weight* above column 49. A separate grouping on the *Rassenamt* card listed "ethnic categories," including subdivisions such as *Nordic* printed above column 50, *Oriental* above column 57, *Mongolian* above column 59, and *Negroid* above column 60. SS Race Office cards were crowded from margin to margin with column designations.[48]

Dehomag's 1933 Prussian census cards featured a large Prussian Statistical Office label and used only 48 columns in total. The census card bore such preprinted demographic headings as *religion* over column 24 and *mother tongue* over column 28; columns 49–60 were left empty. Coal survey cards listed sources, grades, and carloads. *Luftwaffe* cards listed bombing runs by pilots. Ghettoization registration cards listed Jews block by block.

Railroad punch cards listed cities along a route, schedule information, and the freight being hauled—whatever that freight might be.[49]

Each card bore the distinctive ownership imprimatur of the IBM subsidiary as well as the year and month of issue, printed in tiny letters—generally red—along the short edge of the card. An IBM punch card could only be used once. After a period of months, the gargantuan stacks of processed cards were routinely destroyed. Billions more were needed each year by the Greater Reich and its Axis allies, requiring a sophisticated logistical network of IBM authorized pulp mills, paper suppliers, and stock transport. Sales revenue for the lucrative supply of cards was continuously funneled to IBM via various modalities, including its Geneva nexus.[50]

Slave labor cards were particularly complex on-going projects. The Reich was constantly changing map borders and Germanizing city and regional names. Its labor needs became more and more demanding. This type of punch card operation required numerous handwritten mock-ups and regular revisions. For example, *MB* Projects 3090 and 3091 tracking slave labor involved several mock-up cards, each clearly imprinted with Dehomag's name along the edge. Written in hand on a typical sample was the project assignment: *"work deployment of POWs and prisoners according to business branches."* Toward the left, a column was hand-labeled *"number of employed during the month"* next to another column hand-marked *"number of employed at month's end."* The center and right-hand column headings were each scribbled in: *French, Belgium, British, Yugoslavian, Polish.*[51]

Another card in the series was entitled *"registration of male and female workers and employees."* Hand-scribbled column headings itemized such conquered territory as *Bialystok* [Poland], *Netherlands, Protectorate* [Czechoslovakia], and *Croatia.* Noted in pen near the bottom were special instructions about the left-hand row: *"columns 56–59 members of Polish ethnicity go with hole 1"* and *"columns 56–59 members of Ukrainian ethnicity go with hole 2."*[52]

Yet another Dehomag mock-up card in *MB* Project 3090 was hand-titled *"registration of male and female foreign workers and employees."* The scrawled column headings included: *road worker, miners, textile workers, construction workers, chemists, technicians.*[53]

Cards were only the beginning. All decisions about precisely which column and which row could be punched in order to properly record, tabulate, and sort any portion of data were studiously determined in advance by Hollerith engineers. Making the cards readable by IBM sorters required special settings on the machines that only company engineers could adjust. This involved review of machine schematics to ascertain which adjustments were needed for each data run. Once an assignment was undertaken, the subsidiary or its authorized local dealers would then continuously train the Nazi or other personnel involved to use the equipment, whether puncher, sorter, or tabulator. The delicate machines, easily nudged out of whack by their constant syncopation, were serviced on-site, generally monthly, whether that site was in the registration center at Mauthausen concentration camp, the SS offices at Dachau, or the census bureau in any country.[54] Without this abundance of precision planning, assistance, and supply of systems, IBM's Holleriths just could not work—nor could their benefits be derived.

Naturally, IBM profits boomed. In February 1940, IBM Geneva sent IBM NY a month-by-month review of Dehomag's record profit increases in the last half of 1939. June profits increased RM 96,680 over May profits. July bettered June's amount by RM 123,015. August continued to set another record, beating July by RM 98,006, and so on for the rest of the year.[55]

In April, IBM executives in both Geneva and New York continued to marvel at Dehomag's unprecedented profit increases, including the unexpected nearly RM 1.8 million boost in December 1939. Auditors could not wait for details, reporting, "we telegraphed to Berlin for further information which we are now awaiting."[56]

It was never clear exactly how much true profit IBM earned worldwide because of the stealthy way its many subsidiaries classified and reclassified revenues to avoid taxation. Not all that was profitable was declared a profit. However, in mid-1940, even after applying its best accountancy transmogrifications, the New York office was compelled to announce yet another in a string of profit records, this one for the first half of the year. Just less than a $6 million gross profit for the six-month period was conceded, and that was without adding about a million-dollar foreign profit blocked in Germany and elsewhere. That $6 million half-year profit was about a half million higher than the same period a year before. Few in the financial community were surprised. IBM profits had been in a steep climb since the day Hitler came to power.[57] Clearly, the war was good to IBM coffers.

Indeed, in many ways the war seemed an ideal financial opportunity to Watson. Like many, he fully expected Germany to trample over all of Europe, creating a new economic order, one in which IBM would rule the data domain. Like many, Watson expected that America would stay out of the war, and when it was over, businessmen like him would pick up the post-war economic pieces.

In fact, Watson began planning for the post-war boom and a complete reorganization of the world's economic system almost as soon as the war began. By late April 1940, he had convened a stellar Committee for Economic Reconstruction jointly sponsored by the two organizations he dominated, the ICC and the Carnegie Endowment for Peace. This group planned to rewrite the rules of international trade and economic sovereignty, essentially parceling out the world's resources when the war concluded. Watson introduced the plan to his fellow industrialists attending an April 29, 1940, ICC dinner in Washington D.C. "Our program," asserted Watson, "is for national committees in the individual countries to study their own problems from the standpoint of what they need from other countries and what they have to furnish other countries." It was the same Hitleresque message Watson had been preaching for years. Some countries, both men believed, were simply entitled to the natural resources of another. War could be avoided by ceding these materials in advance.[58]

No time was wasted in making plans. "We are carrying on just as though there wasn't any war, if you can believe it, and probably you don't," declared Eliot Wadsworth, chairman of the ICC's American Committee, when he convened the April 29, 1940, meeting. Wadsworth, a Watson confidant, revealed that "already two meetings have been held among representatives of the sections of the International Chamber in spite of the fact that it is contradictory to the regulations of the belligerent countries. . . . England, France and Germany have allowed the representatives of their sections to meet in friendly discussion at The Hague to consider the . . . future program."[59]

Just days after the ICC's dinner, Hitler launched his savage *Blitzkrieg* invasions overrunning Norway, Luxembourg, Holland, and Belgium. An outraged public could turn nowhere without seeing German atrocities depicted on newsreel screens or the front pages of newspapers. Horror stories from refugees, governments–in–exile, diplomats, and journalists alike would not stop. Although the nation was divided on the wisdom of entering the war, many nonetheless felt certain America would soon join the battle against Germany. Anti-Nazi sentiment intensified. A Gallup poll taken shortly after the Reich's spring offensive began showed only 2 percent of Americans felt Hitler's invasion of Belgium or Holland could be justified.[60]

As the public mood swelled against all things Nazi, Watson was now confronted with one major public relations problem: his medal.

Despite all the persecutions, atrocities, plunder, and invasions, Watson remained the proud holder of *der Führer*'s Merit Cross of the German Eagle with Star bestowed in 1937 at the ICC Congress in Berlin. Hitler's medal was a very public link. Holding it in the face of daily aggression was inherently an acceptance of Hitler's actions.

At the same time, Watson had avoided virtually all criticism of the Hitler regime beyond offering boyish aphorisms to observe the Golden Rule, and calling the invasion of Poland "a difference of opinion." He could not afford to offend his second-biggest customer, a customer that would soon emerge as the new dictatorial ruler of Europe. On the other hand, Watson would never allow his legendary and patriotic position in the United States to be compromised.

Events were squeezing Watson.

On May 16, 1940, the day after Holland capitulated, Watson did as he always did: he reached out to his friends in the White House and State Department for political cover. That day, he dispatched a note to Secretary of State Cordell Hull asking if the United States government wanted him to return the medal. Watson could then attribute his return or refusal to return the decoration to Hull's specific counsel. Now, however, the American government was openly anti-Nazi.[61]

Hull would not even become involved. The Secretary immediately wrote back: "I feel that this is a matter upon which the decision will have to rest entirely with you, and is not one upon which this Government would be able to take a position." Hull penned a personal regret in the margin, "I would offer advice to no person sooner than you."[62]

Four days later, on May 24, Watson took his first overt step of identification with the victims of Nazi aggression. He agreed to chair an emergency committee to raise $3 million for the relief of Dutch refugees.[63]

But now, IBM itself was coming under scrutiny for its Nazi connections. The company had become a virtual way station for German nationals transiting in and out of New York for training, meetings, and conferences. Some of these men were now moving with the vanguard of the German destruction machine in Austria, Czechoslovakia, Poland, and Holland. Others had been transferred to South America. A number of German nationals were actually stationed at IBM offices in the United States. Some of them were openly anti-Semitic and pro-Nazi. To even express pro-Nazi opinions was now considered anti-American.[64] Beyond the vaunted publicity stunts and symphonies, IBM's Nazi alliance was quietly emerging from the haze.

At the end of May 1940, FBI Director J. Edgar Hoover became interested in IBM's Nazi connections. Suspecting the company of hosting a hotbed of Nazi agitation, the Federal Bureau of Investigation, in late May, launched wide-ranging investigations on at least four German nationals employed by IBM and suspected of espionage or other subversive conduct. Although no charges were ever brought, more probes would follow and they would continue for years. Assistant Secretary of State Adolf Berle became the State Department's point man for espionage concerns at IBM. Berle and Hoover began to regularly trade information on the suspected spies at IBM. In short order, federal agents and local police intelligence officers were dispatched to IBM offices in Manhattan, Endicott, Albany, Cincinnati, and Milwaukee asking probative questions.[65]

Eventually, the FBI interviewed senior company executives in their IBM offices, including the executive secretary, sales manager, education department director, and even Executive Vice President and General Manager Frederick Nichol. The field investigations soon came to the door of several IBM clients. Customers were asked about any pro-Nazi remarks overheard from at least one suspect IBM salesman in Milwaukee. The postmaster in Darien, Connecticut, was asked about rumors involving a leading IBM technical editor, a German national working in New York who was said to be part of an anti-Jewish society and expressing pro-Reich feelings.[66]

As soon as Watson learned of the FBI's interest, indeed even before the agency could organize its investigations, he went into action. Watson and Nichol visited Undersecretary of State Sumner Welles on June 6 to volunteer personal details about potentially suspect IBM employees in the U.S. and Latin America. Watson made it clear he would cooperate in any way, and take immediate steps to sever corporate relations with any individual the government thought questionable, including several specifically discussed in the Colombia and Mexico City offices. Welles referred the information Watson proffered to Berle, who in turn forwarded it on to J. Edgar Hoover. Ironically, when Watson and Nichol met with Welles at the State Department on June 6, the two IBM executives forgot to mention one particular salesman by the name of Karl Georg Ruthe.[67]

The FBI soon took an intense interest in German-born Ruthe for the many reports of his rabidly pro-Hitler statements while in IBM offices and even at customer sites. One widely distributed FBI file memo related the comments of an auditor at Blatz Brewery in Milwaukee, one of the IBM customers Ruthe had visited. A Blatz auditor passed on Ruthe's remarks reportedly expressing "strong sympathies for Germany and [the] thought that Hitler was justified in everything he did, inasmuch as Germany was given a very unfair deal in the last World War."[68]

Another FBI report quoted IBM's Milwaukee manager reporting that Ruthe "was quite boastful and would predict the outcome of the battles that are taking place in Europe, and that he kept the office force in a general turmoil with his constant talk about Hitler and what he [Hitler] was going to do to the European nations." Ruthe was also rumored in FBI files to be a member of the *Bund,* an association of German-American Nazis.[69]

Few could understand Ruthe's continuing position in the company since he was hired in 1936. He did not fit the IBM mold. Reported in FBI files as a "drunk" and "a poor salesman," Ruthe was said to have seriously under-performed at the Endicott sales training school. Indeed, when Ruthe was transferred from the New York office to IBM Milwaukee, his superiors were asked to keep tabs on him.[70]

Although Watson and Nichol forgot to mention Ruthe during their June 6 discussion, they did remember several days later, when Nichol sent a letter to Welles marked "Strictly Confidential." Nichol wrote, "In the discussion which Mr. Watson and I had with you on Thursday June 6, we overlooked mentioning the name of Mr. Karl Georg Ruthe. The facts concerning him are as follows." Nichol then listed in a column Ruthe's date and place of birth in Germany, graduating school in Germany, the four languages he spoke, home address, and citizen status—which was "American Citizen."[71]

Nichol added some other background: "Mr. Ruthe was first employed by us on December 1, 1936, in New York in a sales capacity. He spent three months at our school at Endicott, N.Y., from July to October 1937, when he was assigned to Milwaukee, still in a sales capacity. Prior to working for us, Mr. Ruthe was a tutor of modern languages in New York City; had his own school in Schenectady (the Schenectady School of Languages) and was an instructor of German at Union College in Schenectady. We understand him to be an American citizen, and believe that his parents reside in Germany. It so happens that we saw fit to ask for this man's resignation last week, based solely, however, on his inability to produce a record as a salesman in this business." Nichol included nothing more on Ruthe.[72]

Ironically, when the FBI inquired as to how a person such as Ruthe could remain at IBM so long, they discovered that Watson had omitted some pertinent details. The FBI file cited observations received from IBM Sales Manager Fred Farwell: "Subject's work was so poor," an FBI report recorded, "that he would have never been allowed to finish the IBM School and go out into the Field as a salesman had it not been for his close relationship to Mr. Watson, President of IBM; that as a matter of fact, Subject had been a constant source of trouble to all men in administrative positions who came in contact with Subject. And that Subject was only kept as an employee for the length of time, in view of his relationship to the President of the Company." Farwell added that Ruthe had married Watson's niece.[73]

The first week of June was a tense one for Watson. On June 3, 200 German planes dropped 1,060 explosive bombs and 61 incendiaries on Paris itself. More than 97 buildings were struck, including two hospitals and ten schools, killing 45. Ten children died at one demolished school alone. U.S. Ambassador to France William Bullitt himself narrowly missed death. While he was lunching with the French Air Minister, a bomb crashed through the roof and into the dining room, showering everyone with glass shards, but the device failed to explode.[74]

The public mood was reflected in a page one story in the *New York Times*, June 4, reporting a mere off-hand comment to an elevator boy by a German diplomat arriving in Buenos Aires, Argentina. The diplomat asked if the young man could speak German. When the youth replied that he could not, the diplomat shot back, "Well, you'd better learn it, you are going to need it."[75]

On June 6, newspapers across the country, including the *New York Times*, reliably reported that the Gestapo was scouring Amsterdam armed with special lists of the "enemies of Germany." Those rounded up were "liquidated. . . . Nearly all have faced firing squads," the syndicated articles reported. Rumors that the names and addresses of all Jews living in Holland had already been turned over to Nazi agents were also circulating in both German and American papers. That same day, some 2,000 German tanks began rolling toward Paris for what was being called the "Battle of France." Reich bombers hit the British coastline. All this was happening on the very day Watson was in Washington, D.C., assuring Undersecretary of State Welles that IBM would rid itself of Nazi sympathizers.[76]

The long delayed moment had come. That day, June 6, Watson wrote a reluctant letter to Adolf Hitler. This one would not be misaddressed or undelivered. This one would be sent by registered mail and released to the newspapers. Watson returned the medal Hitler had personally granted—and he chose to return it publicly via the media. The letter declared: "the present policies of your government are contrary to the causes for which I have been working and for which I received the decoration."[77]

In Germany, Watson's action would be considered the highest form of insult to *der Führer* at a moment of German glory. The public manner of Watson's rejection only heightened the affront. This would change everything.

In Berlin, at Dehomag, all hell broke loose.

I
II
III
IV
V
VI
VII
VIII
IX
X
XI
XII
XIII
XIV
XV

THE DEHOMAG REVOLT

JUNE 10, 1940
Memo to Willy Heidinger
Re: Mr. Watson

I am setting up a confidential file in this matter . . . [and]
sending you a copy of yesterday's edition of the *Völkischer
Beobachter*. It states that Mr. Watson has returned the medal,
which the Führer had bestowed upon him. . . . This stupid
step of Mr. Watson's opens up a number of possibilities. At
the moment, we have decided not to start anything ourselves
but will wait to see who might approach us, if anybody. It is
not improbable that such a step may harm the company, and
all of us, very seriously—sooner or later—since it must be
considered as an insult to the Führer and therefore the German people.

Mr. Hummel has been deliberating whether we can even
continue in the management of the Dehomag in light of this
deliberate insult. . . . I have assumed the position that our
first duty and obligation is to place all our strength at the
disposal of this enterprise which is so important for the conduct of the war. It is imperative that this company meet all
the tasks that the German economy has imposed on it, particularly in time of war. Moreover, there is no reason to cause

the Dehomag and its employees any harm merely because of the personal hatefulness and stupidity of one American.

It appears that Mr. Watson is surrounding himself with a group of Jews who fled from Europe. . . . It appears that the influence of these Jews, in addition to the anti-German Jewish and other lies in newspapers, are beginning to affect his mind and to impede his judgment. Even if he [Watson] should have pretended friendship for Germany and if his true opinion did not become apparent until now, it is evident that this act is terribly inane, looking at it from a purely commercial point of view. It seems Mr. Watson, with great vanity, wants to insult the *Führer* of the German people, but he does not realize that there can only be one result of this act, if there is any at all, namely, that Mr. Watson's personal economic interests can be affected.

Nevertheless this step is indicative of the great excitement in America; therefore the danger that America may enter the war is somewhat closer. If this should happen we would have to examine the possibility of separating ourselves from [IBM] America in view of the new conditions. Naturally the Economics Ministry will examine carefully whether Germany receives more royalties from America or vice versa. . . . we would welcome it if the royalty agreement between Dehomag and IBM could be dissolved entirely. One could assume the position that the mutual contributions should stop with an exchange of patents. . . . Therefore, if we renounce any further contributions [from IBM NY], no royalties should have to be paid in the future. The IBM interest in the Dehomag would then have to be transferred into German hands in some form or other. . . . Savings of royalties could be paid into a war fund and at a future time the rentals could be lowered to correspond to the present royalty.

In any case I have the feeling that Mr. Watson is sawing the branch on which he and his IBM are sitting.

From Hermann Rottke[1]

The war was on.

Nazism's favorite capitalist had fallen from the Reich's imagined cloud line. By returning the medal, Watson had turned on *der Führer*, insulted the German people, and proved that IBM was no longer a reliable ally of the Third Reich. Everywhere among the insider echelons of Nazidom and German media, Watson's name was reviled. Hitler's personal paper, *Völkischer*

Beobachter, declared that the "vultures of profit smell the fry," adding with regret, "it might have been expected that . . . Thomas Watson would have a broader outlook than the hate-blinded Jewish editors and journalists."[2]

Nazi castigation was not limited to the Greater Reich, but was broadcast by German radio and newspapers in the invaded countries as well. Quickly, IBM managers in occupied Czechoslovakia, Poland, Norway, and other Nazi-dominated lands learned of Watson's affront. They felt the impact immediately as their German customers, corporate and government, expressed displeasure. Fascists in other Axis countries were equally offended. Mussolini's people in Rome were furious with Watson Italiana, summoning the subsidiary's director to a formal reproach.[3]

All the suppressed but long festering resentment at Dehomag now coalesced into a unified list of grievances. Dehomag was a German company that Watson stole. IBM NY represented foreign domination and therefore the very antithesis of National Socialist doctrine. The American parent company was charging exorbitant royalties and reaping huge profits, thereby exploiting the German nation. Most of all, Heidinger hated Watson. It all became a single impetus for open corporate rebellion.

The backlash was immediate. In Dehomag's Lichterfelde office, Watson's picture was removed from the wall. Stuttgart employees did the same. In the Hamburg, Frankfurt, and Vienna branches—and ultimately in every one of the German subsidiary's offices—the pictures of Watson were quickly taken down.[4] That was only the beginning.

Spurred by equal parts personal greed and Nazi fervor, Heidinger and Rottke began scheming to completely eliminate IBM NY's influence from Dehomag's realm. Step-by-step, they would now pressure IBM either to sell the subsidiary to German nationals, or at least reduce the foreign ownership from a majority to a minority. Ousting his personal representatives from the Berlin subsidiary's board of directors would also end Watson's micromanagement of Dehomag operations. Plain and simple: Heidinger, Rottke, and Hummel now saw Thomas J. Watson and IBM NY as little more than a foreign nemesis—a nemesis they were determined to cast off.

To begin his *putsch*, Heidinger retreated into a precise reading of German corporate law. On July 1, 1940, he sent a registered letter to IBM Geneva convening a special board meeting to discuss the crisis caused by Watson's insult to Hitler and to expel IBM NY's representative, Geneva-based John Holt, from the three-seat board.[5]

Using charged language, the meeting agenda declared that Holt would be "eliminated" by a vote of the local board because he was an absentee director and thereby "prevented from fulfilling his obligations." IBM responded to the challenge with coolness. Geneva cabled a power of attorney to IBM's local representative, Albert Zimmermann, authorizing him to *discuss* the issue, of course, but then to vote IBM NY's majority *against* replacing Holt.[6]

Insufficient, declared Heidinger. Under a strict reading of German corporate law, a power of attorney required a certain sworn written form, and an authorizing cable alone was legally unacceptable. On July 15, Heidinger convened a brief sixty-minute board meeting, disallowing Zimmermann's dissenting proxy. Then the two resident board members, Heidinger and his brother-in-law, Dr. Gustav Vogt, voted Holt out. "All persons present agree that it is advisable to straighten matters," the rebellious German board resolved by "the elimination from the board of directors of Mr. Holt. . . . Considering the present situation . . . all persons present propose a personality [as a replacement] who is also esteemed by the German [authorities]." Technically, however, with Zimmermann's proxy disqualified, a voting quorum was not present. Therefore, while Holt could be voted out by the board alone, his replacement could not be properly voted in under German law except by the stockholders themselves. IBM was the largest, holding 85 percent.[7]

Knowing Watson's proclivity for hiring lawyers to defend hairsplitting legal positions, Dehomag adhered to the explicit letter of the law. Heidinger scheduled another immediate meeting, just two weeks later, on July 29, to elect the "replacement of the eliminated member, Mr. Holt," as the board minutes phrased it. Under German corporate law, the minutes noted, if IBM declined to provide a proper written proxy for the second meeting, then the token minority 15 percent ownership—that is, Heidinger, Rottke, and Hummel—could vote in whomever they wished to replace Holt.[8] Doing so would neutralize Watson.

Just after the July 15 meeting adjourned, a brusque Dehomag letter was dispatched to IBM Geneva. Citing German law and company statute down to the sub-paragraph, Dehomag's notice advised Geneva that its previous cabled proxy to Zimmermann was unacceptable in its form. With or without the approval of IBM NY, the letter bluntly warned, the re-scheduled July 29 meeting would address the Watson medal crisis "and its eventual consequences for our company," as well as the "replacement of the eliminated member, Mr. Holt."[9]

For years, cabled instructions from Geneva and New York projecting Watson's micro-management had been routine facts of corporate life for Dehomag. But all that was before Watson returned the decoration. Now Heidinger had the momentum to work his own will. He would force his issues with a combination of strict legal interpretation and rapid-fire corporate maneuvers.

Heidinger's July 15 correspondence to IBM Geneva warned the parent company that should it fail to provide the proper proxy form for the July 29 meeting, or fail to ratify Berlin's choice for a new board member, a stalemate would prove just as destructive. Then, "no decisions binding the company can be taken," Heidinger warned, adding, "To enlighten matters, we wish to state that according to . . . [German corporate] law, the board of directors has to be composed of three persons at least."[10] Holt's ouster left only two sitting board members: Heidinger and his brother-in-law Vogt. Without three on Dehomag's board, the firm would be illegitimate and incapable of functioning as a corporate entity.

To ensure that Watson could not litigate the board *putsch* as setting "unreasonable" deadlines in view of difficult wartime circumstances, Heidinger scheduled the July 29 meeting not in Dehomag's Berlin headquarters, but in the subsidiary's Munich branch. Munich was much closer to IBM's Geneva office, "thus diminishing your traveling time," Heidinger carefully wrote to IBM Geneva.[11]

This time, IBM rushed to comply. Watson's Geneva representatives did not feel comfortable entering Germany with officials agitated. But they did present their resident German agent, Zimmermann, with a proper power of attorney. The July 29 board meeting in Munich convened at 10 A.M. with a reading of the rules and relevant statutes. Quickly, they did away with the traditional balance sheets showing losses resulting in zero bonuses. Heidinger forced adoption of the true profits totals: nearly RM 2.4 million for 1938 and almost RM 4 million for 1939. Management bonuses of nearly RM 400,000 were approved for Rottke and Hummel. Heidinger reserved his own bonus for later.[12]

The medal crisis was then vigorously debated "in view of the great urgency of this question." Heidinger demanded that Holt's seat on the board be filled not by one German director, but two. He nominated Emil Ziegler on the suggestion of the Berlin Chamber of Commerce. The second nomination was a leading Nazi official, Ernst Schulte-Strathaus, a key advisor in Deputy Führer Rudolf Hess' office.[13]

Dehomag was to become completely Nazified. The hierarchy had plans for Hollerith machines that stretched to virtually all the Reich's most urgent needs, from the conflict in Europe to Hitler's war against European Jewry. Some of the plans were so sensitive they could not be discussed with outsiders. It was absolutely essential that Dehomag be controlled by the highest Nazi party and government circles. Heidinger had connections at those levels, which had benefited Dehomag through the Hitler years.

Heidinger had been a friend of Hess' since their soldiering days in World War I. The Schulte-Strathaus family had, in 1910, helped Heidinger launch the original Hollerith Company in Germany. Bonds remained tight during the post-War years. Ernst Schulte-Strathaus had emerged as one of the bizarre and mysterious personalities at the top of the Nazi leadership. A doctrinaire astrologer, Schulte-Strathaus read the stars for Hess.[14]

In the July 29 board meeting, Heidinger demanded that Schulte-Strathaus be ratified. In fact, Heidinger had already invited him to join the board and Schulte-Strathaus had already accepted.[15] So he expected a unanimous yes.

But Watson was not ready to allow Heidinger to dictate who could sit on the board—even if the proposed man was a personal advisor to Deputy Führer Hess. Zimmermann declared that he was instructed to vote against Schulte-Strathaus. Wielding IBM's majority, the measure was defeated. Watson preferred either Rottke or Hummel, both of whom owned token stock options, or Zimmermann himself. Heidinger staunchly refused to even allow Watson's suggestions to be voted, asserting that German corporate law made employees ineligible for seats on a board of directors. Heidinger insisted on Schulte-Strathaus as a representative of Hess.[16]

Heidinger adjourned the meeting in a stalemate. Next, he decided to either cash out of the company, or pressure IBM into essentially walking away from its subsidiary. The stakes were immense for Germany.

Hess' office was not the only one determined to ensure the complete cooperation of Dehomag. Other key Party advisors to *der Führer*'s office, soon to emerge, also had plans for IBM's equipment. But the strategic alliance with IBM was too entrenched to simply switch off. Since the birth of the Third Reich, Germany had automated virtually its entire economy, as well as most government operations and Nazi Party activities, using a single technology: Hollerith. Elaborate data operations were in full swing everywhere in Germany and its conquered lands. The country suddenly discovered its own vulnerable over-dependence on IBM machinery.

Millions of cards each week were needed to run the sorters. Indeed, the military alone employed some 30,000 people in their Hollerith services. Adding other governmental and commercial clients, at any given time, thousands of operators were working at Holleriths. Watson presses printed all the cards these people needed moment to moment. IBM's paper and pulp supply lines extended to mills throughout the world. IBM owned the patents for the unique paper stock the Holleriths required. At the same time, Germany's war industry suffered from a chronic paper and pulp shortage due to a lack of supply and the diversion of basic pulping ingredients to war propellants. Only four specialized paper plants in Germany could even produce Hollerith card stock—all were on contract to IBM. The few paper houses in France were running low on coal and cellulose supplies, hence their deliveries could never be assured for more than a month or two at a time. IBM was constantly pooling its global paper resources, including its abundant North American suppliers, to meet the ever-increasing demand. The Reich could not tap into the vital North American paper markets. Holleriths could not function without IBM's unique paper. Watson controlled the paper.[17]

Printing cards was a stop-start process that under optimal conditions yielded 65,000 cards per eight-hour shift. The Third Reich consumed cards at an almost fantastic rate. In 1938, more than 600 million per year were consumed from German sources alone. In 1939, that number almost doubled to 1.118 billion. Projected use by 1943 was 1.5 billion just within the Reich. Building a printing press was a six-month process at best, much longer when the metals were not available. Dehomag clients typically stockpiled a mere thirty-day supply of finished punch card paper. Holleriths could not function without cards. Watson controlled the cards.[18]

Precision maintenance was needed monthly on the sensitive gears, tumblers, and cogs on thousands of machines that syncopated millions of times each week throughout Nazi Europe. Building new factories might take six months to a year just for the first machine tools to arrive from specialized machine tool works. Long tool manufacturing lead times were always needed. In 1937, IBM ordered three inclinable power presses for planned factory expansion; delivery times for the power presses required ten or eleven months. Three six-spindle drill presses required eight to twelve months. A three-spindle drill required sixteen months. A radial arm drill required twelve months. Two plain milling machines and a vertical miller required twenty-four months. Even working at peak capacity in tandem with recently opened IBM factories in Germany, Austria, Italy, and France, Nazi requests for sorters, tabulators, and collators were back-ordered twenty-four months. Hollerith systems could not function without machines or spare parts. Watson controlled the machines and the spare parts.[19]

Watson's monopoly could be replaced—but it would take years. Even if the Reich confiscated every IBM printing plant in Nazi-dominated Europe, and seized every machine, within months the cards and spare parts would run out. The whole data system would quickly grind to a halt. As it stood in summer 1941, the IBM enterprise in Nazi Germany was hardly a stand-alone operation; it depended upon the global financial, technical, and material support of IBM NY and its seventy worldwide subsidiaries. Watson controlled all of it.

Without punch card technology, Nazi Germany would be completely incapable of even a fraction of the automation it had taken for granted. Returning to manual methods was unthinkable. The Race and Settlement Office of the SS was typical of those Nazi agencies frustrated over their long-back-ordered Holleriths. While it was waiting, Race and Settlement department heads complained in one typical statistical report that the office simply could not keep up with its prodigious raceology responsibilities without a punch card system. "At least 7,000 applicants," the report conceded, "who ful-filled the [racial] requirements for marriage have been waiting years for their Certificates of Approval from the *Reichsführer*-SS." What's more, 50,000 additional applicants were also waiting for further documentation reviews, the report continued, and more than 100,000 applicants had only been provi-sionally accepted into the SS until the office could properly "complete their family trees back to 1800."[20]

"I have determined," wrote the SS Race and Settlement Office's statisti-cal chief, "that the Hollerith punch card system, which is being used success-fully by the Reich Statistics Office, *Reichsbahn, Reichspost, Reichsbank*, etc, as well as various research facilities . . . is necessary and would serve our inter-ests best."[21]

The Race and Settlement statistical chief succinctly explained the Hollerith difference in these words: "The [manual] way in which the files are [currently] stored, makes any quick and efficient survey impossible. It would require months of work looking through individual files to answer even one [racial] question." He added, "For every single one of the additional future tasks, months of tedious clerical work would be necessary just to determine how many and which [racial] petitions are involved. The punch card system would be able to determine this easily, quickly to the desired date. . . . There-fore, card indexing is indispensable." The SS statistician concluded that the high cost of the IBM equipment was justified because this was the "exact instrument for complete surveillance both on a large scale and down to the smallest detail."[22]

The SS Race and Settlement Office was finally allocated its Hollerith, but only in 1943, two and a half years after inaugurating the collection of the marriage data it sought to automate.[23]

With punch card technology so vital to German operations, it was no wonder that after Watson ostentatiously returned Hitler's medal, Reich planners suddenly worried about their entire Hollerith infrastructure. Berlin launched the same struggle for autarky, that is, national self-sufficiency, already underway for armaments and raw materials, such as rubber. Outraged Nazi leaders became determined to replace IBM technology with a punch card system they could control. It was a matter of Nazi necessity. It was a matter of Nazi pride.

The quiet effort began in France, which had fallen to German domination in mid-June, just days after Watson returned the medal. Nazi engineer and Dehomag-trained punch card specialists from Berlin quickly began pilfering the machines of IBM's French subsidiary, bringing them back to Germany for urgent assignments. No longer bound to honor Watson as a business partner, Reich agents categorized the machines as "war booty" that could simply be seized.[24]

Next, Hermann Goering's circle purchased a majority control of the tiny Powers operation in France, hoping to merge it into a Germanized cartel. Nazi representatives even brought in for examination a rival machine produced by a small fledgling French company called Bull, which enjoyed about 25 percent of the fragmented French market. Plans were already underway to purchase a majority control of Bull, which had wielded no mass manufacturing operation but offered a replicable design. Watson had long tried to neutralize the tiny Bull operation with patent litigation, buy-out offers, employee raids, and even outright purchases of Bull's operations in Switzerland. But Bull, even though dwarfed by IBM, still had a number of machines in operation. And its machinery was considered as good as any Hollerith.[25]

But Berlin really didn't know what to do. They stole some IBM machines in France, purchased control of a Powers subsidiary, and brought in Bull machines, all envisioning a new cartel. None of it was coordinated, but something had to be done to counteract Germany's dependence on IBM.

From the Reich's point of view, Watson and IBM clearly possessed an insider's understanding of virtually everything Germany did and indeed all of its advance planning. That had to stop. Argue as they might, IBM NY officials were unable to convince Nazi officials otherwise, even when New York emphasized that only non-American IBM employees possessed access to the Reich's most sensitive secrets. Watson's Berlin attorney, Heinrich Albert, offered a written opinion summing up the problem. "The military authorities are greatly concerned with the whole matter," wrote Albert shortly after the Dehomag revolt began. "Not only are most military agencies and offices equipped with these special machines but the authorities are also afraid that via the majority of IBM in the Dehomag, the USA [itself] might get a far-reaching insight into the activities not only of Dehomag itself, but also of the big German rearmament plants and the German economic structure as a whole. This fear is based on the particular organization of the business of Dehomag and is not quite as unfounded as it might appear from the very beginning.[26]

"The Dehomag does not sell its machines," Albert continued, "but lets them out on lease. Before concluding a contract of lease, a thorough study of the [client] company, or business enterprise which wants to have the machines, is made from the point of view whether the use of the machines fits into the system of the prospect, whether the use of them is advantageous, and how the business must be organized to use the machines to the greatest possible advantage. There can be no doubt that this method . . . secures to the Dehomag a contact and insight into the big business of the nation superior to any other company."[27]

Albert added that IBM's counterarguments and rationales were simply not credible to the authorities. "It is no use to argue that this fear is absolutely theoretical and has no foundation [in fact] whatever in practice, as not only no American citizen is employed in this part of the business . . . [or that] these studies are kept most confidential and secret according to the strictest general rules and regulations. There the objection and the handicap is and must be taken into consideration."[28]

From IBM's point of view, the struggle to create an alliance with Nazi Germany had been too great and the potential for continuing profits too rewarding to simply walk away. Nor would Watson tolerate competitors— existing or newly created—invading IBM's hard won territory. Since the dusty horse-and-buggy days of National Cash Register, Watson had learned not to compete, but to eliminate all competition—no matter how marginal— by any pernicious tactics necessary.

IBM Geneva troubleshooter, P. Taylor, in an August 1940 letter to the New York headquarters, worried openly about the threat should the Third Reich develop Bull machines or an *ersatz* hybrid—even though it would take years to switch. "The danger of this is, of course, that the Bull machines do exactly the same as Dehomag's," wrote Taylor, "whilst also having alphabetic and printing units, and [if obtained] they can easily be exchanged to replace Dehomag machines."[29]

Heidinger had obtained a one-week travel permit and on August 15, 1940, he visited Taylor in IBM's Geneva office to lodge his threats and demands. He was not subtle.[30]

"Foreign partnerships in German companies are not very much liked," Heidinger told Taylor, "particularly where the foreign interest is a majority. The IBM majority in the Dehomag was not very helpful, but did not cause too much harm—up to now. The situation is entirely changed by the step of Mr. Watson giving back his German decoration and writing a letter to the *Führer* published in the American press. That step is considered as an insult of the highest degree not only to Hitler, but to each individual German. What could be the consequences? Each customer or prospect will try to avoid getting punched card machines from a company which proved or at least appears to be hostile to Germany. Therefore an already existing or a new-formed German company taking up the manufacture and sale of such machines will have excellent chances. Dehomag's business would no longer exist."[31]

Exaggerating how easy it would be for any new competitor to emerge, Heidinger asserted, "Patent difficulties do not exist [and] if necessary it would be easy to get a compulsory license for a modest royalty of say five percent instead of twenty five percent which [now] Dehomag pays [to IBM NY]. No difficulties would exist to get experts for such a system: workmen, engineers, salesmen, managers."[32]

Heidinger threatened to call for a vote of employees as loyal Germans, whether they would continue working with an IBM subsidiary or a newly formed German one. "The IBM should consider what result a vote within Dehomag would have," said Heidinger menacingly. "Who of the Dehomag people is willing to continue working for the Dehomag of which a majority is owned by a hostile IBM or who is willing to work for a new German company?"[33]

There were more complications. All the open undercurrents against Dehomag as an American business with German management were now confirmed. IBM's subsidiary had been unmasked as a non-Aryan business—something many always knew but begrudgingly overlooked. Now many in Berlin were preparing for the day when the U.S. would join England against the Third Reich. In such a case, explained Heidinger, Dehomag would be considered enemy property, a custodian would be appointed to run the business and make all decisions. "Such [a] trustee would be the only manager," continued Heidinger, "while the rights of the old managers and the board are suspended. The consequences would be disastrous. One of the several possibilities is . . . [that] the trustee would discover that our profit and therefore the prices are too high. He certainly could and probably would reduce at once the prices. There would practically be no possibility to raise the prices again in normal times. Supposing the Dehomag pulled through this crisis—the return to shareholders could then only be very modest.34

"With or without the entry of the U.S.A. into the war," stressed Heidinger, "the danger of the total ruin of the Dehomag is immediately present. No member of the board of directors or management could assume the responsibility of passively awaiting events."35

Heidinger offered IBM several ultimata. One: sell the entire subsidiary to the Germans at a negotiated price. Two: use the millions of surplus profits in Dehomag's blocked accounts to double investment in the subsidiary. Issue new shares, but all the new voting rights would be held by Germans, either Dehomag managers or an Aryan committee. IBM would still retain its majority ownership, but lose its control. Three: In a complicated scheme, IBM NY buys out some of the captive stock held by Heidinger, Rottke, and Hummel and transfers that stock to employees.36

Whatever Watson decided, insisted Heidinger, Dehomag must now be allowed to exercise further control. "The advice I give you now is of more value than any advice given in the past," Heidinger told Taylor. But he would not wait for the protracted decision-making process Watson was known for. He demanded that Taylor cable the threats and options to Watson. Heidinger would wait in Geneva for an immediate response.37

Taylor cabled Heidinger's remarks to New York with his observation that "a plan exists already for the formation of a new [rival] German company."38 Whatever Watson did now to enrich its local managers or relinquish control, eventually IBM would be dethroned. At the same time, IBM people understood it was far easier to talk about replacing IBM than to actually do so. Harrison K. Chauncey, Watson's top emissary in Berlin, reported after one key meeting with a ranking Nazi official, "We are threatened with possible elimination of Dehomag through competition which may be sponsored by the authorities." But he followed by countering, "The government at the present time needs our machines. The army is using them evidently for every conceivable purpose." He added, "During the war it would be very difficult for competition to get started, unless they used the French Bull manufacturing plant." W. C. Lier, another senior IBM auditor negotiating in Berlin, commented on the prospect of Germany not allocating raw materials for machines manufactured by IBM's subsidiary in occupied France. Lier wrote to Chauncey, "the whole point is—who will manufacture since the Dehomag is not in a position to deliver most of the units before one or even two years?" Lier underlined his rhetorical question, adding, "[who] will produce the machines which are indispensable to the German war economy?"[39]

Since 1933, Watson had refused all opportunities to restrain or disassociate from Dehomag, or even reduce IBM's breakneck expansion program for the Third Reich. Yet now, in August 1940, as never before, Watson was confronted with one genuine last chance—perhaps the most decisive chance—to walk away.

If Watson allowed the Reich—in a fit of rage over the return of the medal—to oust IBM technologic supremacy in Nazi Germany, and if he allowed Berlin to embark upon its own *ersatz* punch card industry, Hitler's data automation program might speed toward self-destruction. No one could predict how drastically every Reich undertaking would be affected. But clearly, the *blitz* IBM attached to the German *krieg* would eventually be subtracted if not severely lessened. All Watson had to do was give up Dehomag as the Nazis demanded. If IBM did not have a technologic stranglehold over Germany, the Nazis would not be negotiating, they would simply seize whatever they wanted. For Watson, it was a choice.

He instructed IBM General Manager F. W. Nichol to telephone Geneva manager P. Taylor on August 19 and enthusiastically approve the ratification of Hess' staff advisor Schulte-Strathaus and German businessman Emil Ziegler as new board members. Watson also agreed to offer former German counsel in New York, Otto Kiep, as a third addition. Watson had known and trusted Kiep as a family friend for years; Watson's daughter even served as godmother to Kiep's child. Kiep could at least try to mitigate further Dehomag efforts to exclude IBM NY from the business proceeds and help shore up ties to the government. At the August 31 Dehomag board meeting in Berlin, under direct instruction from the New York office, IBM's representative voted with Heidinger. The details were recorded in the minutes. "Mr. Holt is barred by unanimous vote. Messers. Kiep, Schulte-Strathaus and Ziegler are elected unanimously."[40]

But Watson would not detach Dehomag from the global IBM empire. He would not allow Bull and Powers or any other competitor to intrude upon his domain. IBM would not back down from what it considered its rightful commercial place in Nazi Germany's New World Order.

Over the coming months, Watson would fight hour to hour, deploying lawyers, special emissaries, and government intermediaries to protect his privileged and profitable position in Hitler's enterprise. Watson would not allow IBM to be replaced. As a result, millions of cards, millions of lives, and millions of dollars would now intersect at the whirring stations of Hitler's Holleriths.

EVEN THOUGH Watson had agreed to director's seats for three influential Nazis—Schulte-Strathaus, Ziegler, and Kiep—it just wasn't enough. The pressure on IBM's empire would not subside. On August 20, a special committee of some undetermined Nazi authority launched an investigation of Dehomag and its practices. There was no let-up on Heidinger's insistence that IBM relinquish control of Dehomag either by becoming a minority owner or selling outright. If that was not possible, he wanted his now valuable shares purchased by IBM for dollars.[41]

At first, the fact that Heidinger was insisting on both a buy-back of his shares and transfer of the subsidiary ownership appeared to be a contradiction. If Heidinger wanted as much of the stock as possible in German hands, why insist on IBM repurchasing his shares, which would return ownership to New York? But Watson soon understood: Heidinger was trying to cash out his position in dollars even while he helped German circles dismantle Dehomag or weave the firm's resources into a purely German cartel. This was becoming all too apparent to Watson's negotiators as they explored any avenue to quietly separate from Heidinger.[42]

In late August 1940, Taylor in Geneva suggested New York might want to simply pay off Heidinger with an enticing financial arrangement by either increasing his percentage of the company or undertaking a one-time buy-out of some or all of his shares on the condition that he cancel his special contract altogether. Knowing Watson's aversion to paying actual dollars, Taylor suggested IBM trade "one of our buildings in Berlin," and add in more accounting maneuvers. "If we have to pay in Reichsmarks," wrote Taylor, "get Mr. Heidinger to take the first building at our purchase price of 2,178,000 marks, plus the difference in a cash payment, such cash to be obtained from Dehomag as a payment on account of their indebtedness to us for royalties." To keep Heidinger out of any competitive company, Taylor suggested IBM "would continue to pay 40,000 marks a year to Heidinger for his advisory services, and in the event of his death, pay it to his widow as long as she lives."[43]

Pages and pages of financial and political analyses shot back and forth between IBM offices in Berlin, Geneva, and New York. It was a constant state of corporate crisis as the vicissitudes of one option after another were floated and sunk, revived, and then shunted.[44] Through it all, Heidinger remained adamant.

IBM's Berlin attorney, Heinrich Albert, was one of Germany's leading experts on foreign corporations operating in the Third Reich. Of course, IBM was not alone in its lucrative dealings with the Third Reich. Many American companies in the armament, financial, and service arena refused to walk away from the extraordinary profits obtainable from trading with a pariah state such as Nazi Germany. Indeed, Watson led them in his capacity as chairman of the American section of the International Chamber of Commerce. Albert counseled many of these American companies about protecting their subsidiaries. Based on his experience, Albert sent Watson dozens of pages of dense legal opinions, settlement theories, and cautiously parsed recommendations. But much of it built on one of his earliest observations: "It cannot be denied that the situation is serious," wrote Albert. "What it practically amounts to is the question whether the IBM prefers to hold a secure and safe minority interest in a sound and safe company, [or] . . . the holding of a controlling, but endangered majority in an endangered company."[45]

The prevailing view among many was that Nazi aggression in Europe was unstoppable and the economy that would soon be imposed over an entire subjugated Continent would flow only to those companies Berlin favored. Owning even a minority of that new dominant Dehomag could be vastly more valuable than the Dehomag IBM owned today. Albert emphasized that in the very near future, "a minority of shares might be even materially of higher value than the present majority." He added that the notion of stockholder "control" was actually becoming a passé notion in Germany since the Reich now directly or indirectly controlled virtually all business. "A majority of shares," he wrote Watson, "does not mean as much as it used to . . . [since] a corporation, company, enterprise or plant manufacturing in Germany is so firmly, thoroughly and definitely subjected to the governmental rules and regulations."[46] Clearly, it was not possible to continue doing business as a German company without becoming a virtual extension of the Reich war economy. That had been the reality for years.

Whether IBM reduced its control to a minority or retained its majority, or appointed any number of influential Nazis to its board or management staff, was immaterial to Germany's perception of IBM's subsidiary. The truth was now known. Dehomag could no longer continue under its former Aryan guise. "Neither public opinion nor the authorities," assured Albert, "would recognize the German character of the company [any longer]."[47]

Watson tried a number of compromises to redeem himself in German eyes. None of them worked. He offered a sizable donation to the German Red Cross. Rottke immediately wrote a letter to Geneva stating that the gift would never be accepted. Watson's hope that the furor would die down was unrealistic. Although the decoration was returned on June 6, Nazis were still roiling months later. German radio in neutral Sweden in mid-September declared Watson persona non grata, assuring he would never again be permitted to set foot in any territory controlled by Germany.[48]

Watson understood that unless he came to an accommodation with Germany, Dehomag was only the beginning. IBM operated profitable Dehomag-dominated subsidiaries in Italy, Poland, Czechoslovakia, Holland, Belgium, Romania, France, Sweden, and indeed almost everywhere in Europe. All of them could be targeted.

At about 11 P.M. on September 30, 1940, Taylor in Geneva telephoned IBM's New York headquarters with continuing reports about pressure against IBM subsidiaries in the wake of Watson returning his medal. Should America enter the war, Taylor asserted, one of the first subsidiaries to be placed under a German trustee would be Watson Norsk, the IBM operation in occupied Norway. Earlier, Taylor's office had sent several letters explaining how the seizure would work under just-espoused German military law. To allow the subsidiary to continue even after America might declare war, Taylor now suggested creating the appearance that Watson Norsk had been sold to Norwegians even though IBM NY would still own and control all aspects of the firm. "We should consider whether now is not the time," Taylor said, "to take the necessary action to make the company free from American interests. We have come to the conclusion to suggest that the royalty set-up should be considered, that the shareholders would be changed to avoid American holders." As it stood, IBM's name was not now listed as controlling the Norwegian firm. Norwegian records reflected four individuals as owners: IBM managers Holt and Milner, as well as two token Norwegians. But the two Americans were clearly IBM Geneva employees known to Dehomag. So Taylor offered a new list of reliable Norwegians to use as additional front men. He emphasized, "The shares of these [new] people should be in their name actually, and cash consideration given. Understood," he added, "they would be held for the IBM—but no rights." The stock transfers could be just a pen stroke away, he pointed out, because "the shares are in New York now."[49]

What's more, Taylor recommended, Watson Norsk's 400,000 Krone debt to IBM NY should be reduced on paper to further distance the subsidiary from American control. If a series of paper transactions involving 250,000 Krone were arranged as Taylor outlined, then the "estimated loss for 1940 is 75,000 Krone, plus a cash remittance in New York of 100,000 Krone. After deducting all those from the IBM account, [it] leaves a balance of approximately 100,000 Krone, which we think would be in order."[50]

IBM's European empire, primarily vested in Dehomag, appeared to IBM managers to be careening toward demise. If the company did survive its challenges, German custodians would confiscate it as enemy property as soon as America joined the war. Unlike his managers, however, Watson did not fear seizure by a German-appointed trustee. He actually preferred it.

A peculiarity of German law demarcated a strong distinction between the assets of racial inferiors such as Jews, Poles, Czechs, and other vanquished groups, and the property of what in the bizarre Nazi mindset constituted a genuine war adversary, such as Britain and the United States. If the U.S. entered the war, Germany did not believe it would occupy American territory, only defeat the country. During any war, Germany expected its commercial enterprises in America to be safeguarded, managed properly by a trustee, and then returned intact when the conflict ended. In that same spirit, the Third Reich would in turn safeguard, manage diligently, and return American enterprises. Germany's well-developed alien custody laws were still in effect.[51] So while Nazi Germany was voraciously plundering and pillaging the width and breadth of Europe, a profoundly different set of rules would apply to IBM and other "enemy property" seized in any of those occupied countries.

Watson understood the ironic benefits of German enemy trusteeship. Just a few years earlier, he fondly remembered his own experiences in a letter to Hjalmar Schacht, president of the *Reichsbank.* "From the day I returned to Germany after the [first world] war" wrote Watson, "to find my company's affairs in the best safekeeping by your Alien Property Custodian, well administered and conscientiously managed . . . I have felt a deep personal concern over Germany's fate and a growing attachment to the many Germans with whom I gained contact at home and abroad."[52]

Taylor's memos, citing military decrees regarding the potential for seizure, explained that during the years any alien corporation was under Nazi receivership, all the profits would be safely blocked in an account. "We presume," wrote Taylor in a mid-September 1940 letter, "any resulting income is for the benefit of the owner in enemy territory and may be paid over at the end of the hostilities in accordance with the payment of enemy debts in general." Taylor sent exact translations of the law to New York for Watson's study.[53]

Watson queried attorney Albert. Albert confirmed that the rules of receivership had not changed. In a detailed memo, Albert unambiguously reported back: "A custodianship of the Alien Property Custodian would by itself mean no special danger, as the law concerning the administration of enemy property, and the practice based on this law, are very conservative, protect the property and keep it alive and in order."[54]

Because the potential for seizure as enemy property was so encouraging, Albert could not help but comment that Watson's decision on caving in to Heidinger's demands was actually "all, a matter of [Watson's] temperament, of taste, of general business policy, of the outlook into the future and so on." Watson could rely on Albert's assessments. Albert himself had functioned as a key custodian of enemy property during World War I. He had distinguished himself as a keen businessman and now represented those same companies as clients. Enemy receivers in Germany and other Axis countries understood the potential for a rewarding business relationship when hostilities ended. Ultimately, the Italian enemy property custodian, Giovanni Fagioli, actually sent personal written word to Watson that he was prepared to operate the Rome subsidiary profitably. Fagioli only hoped he could "cooperate with the owners after the war."[55]

For IBM, war would ironically be more advantageous than existing peace.

Under the current state of affairs, IBM's assets were blocked in Germany until the conflict was over. Under an enemy custodian, those same marks would still be blocked—again until any war was over. As it stood, Heidinger was threatening daily to destroy Dehomag unless IBM sold or reduced its ownership; and he was demanding to cash out his stock. But if war with the U.S. broke out, Heidinger and the other managers would be summarily relieved of their management authority since technically they represented IBM NY. A government custodian chosen on the basis of keen business skills—and Albert might have the connections to select a reliable one—would be appointed to replace Heidinger and manage Dehomag. In fact, the Nazi receiver would diligently manage all of IBM's European subsidiaries. The money would be waiting when the war was over.[56]

While the custodian would do all in his power to run the company profitably, he would also serve the interests of the Reich.[57] The custodian would make the hard decisions, probably in tandem with IBM Geneva because there were nexus subsidiaries in Sweden, Switzerland, and other real or nominal neutrals that were indispensable to Dehomag's supply lines. Other IBM subsidiaries in Latin America, Africa, and in the colonial lands of conquered European nations would also cooperate with Dehomag, but only through the most indirect and purely legal routes. Plausible deniability would be real. Questions—would not be asked by IBM NY. Answers— would not be given by IBMers in Europe or Reich officials.[58]

The revealing records would not be kept in New York but in Europe where they could never be uncovered and examined. They would be kept abroad in filing cabinets in subsidiary offices. Many of New York's records from the pre-war years would simply be destroyed. No one would ever be able to identify exactly what IBM NY did and did not know about the use of the Hitler Holleriths, or how many IBMers in Europe circuitously shared their information with New York. Indeed, a war-time Justice Department investigator examining IBM's collusion with Nazi Germany wrote: "IBM is in a class with the Nazis." But the investigator was forced to conclude: "This is a story told in circumstantial evidence."[59]

Watson would be satisfied with not knowing the specifics held by his European subsidiaries and managers—so long as those subsidiaries tenaciously pressed the Nazi regimes for proper rent payments on each and every machine, on every last one of billions of punch cards, on every spare cog and plate, and on all maintenance calls, all according to carefully worded contracts. Those demands for payment would start with the machines just removed from Paris by Reich officers in August 1940.[60]

Watson's micro-management of the most infinitesimal details would now end. That power would be delegated to trusted senior managers, managers who would be rewarded for their most loyal and most difficult service with generous salaries, and then anointed with great promotions in the powerful foreign divisions of the global IBM that they themselves built. Corporate security for these men would be seemingly endless. Even their children would find lucrative association with International Business Machines. In the company's literature, they would be remembered as "heroes."[61]

The corporate haze would last for decades. With all the European intermediaries, ownership nominees, corporate intrigues, belligerent German managers, and Nazi custodians, it would be impossible to reliably point a finger at the New York office. Hollerith machines could be placed in museums in exhibits tying their use to the most heinous aspects of the Third Reich, but the deniability would be unshakable. For, in truth, from 1933 until the summer of 1940, Watson personally micro-managed virtually every Dehomag decision. From August 1940, IBM NY made sure it did not know most of the gruesome details of Hollerith use. It was better not to know.

The company that lionized the word THINK now thought better of its guiding mandate. Incriminating dealings with Nazis did surface from time to time as frustrated war-besieged subsidiary managers would invariably become too specific in the cables to New York. These communications were discarded, however, and if necessary disowned by IBM NY.[62] By placing itself in the dark, IBM could forever truthfully declare it made millions during the war without knowing the specifics.

An emboldened Watson now decided more than ever to fight back. Immediately after Taylor's September 30 telephone call warning of German receivership, Watson elected to confront Heidinger head on. To do so, he would need the strongest ally. He knew who to call.

Watson contacted the U.S. State Department.

IBM HAD BEEN cultivating contacts at the State Department for years, starting at the top with Secretary of State Cordell Hull, and, of course, President Franklin D. Roosevelt. But entrenched influence was sought at all levels down to the lowliest clerks and bureaucrats in the Department's technical offices and overseas installations. Indeed, it was these people who rendered the most service.[63]

Commercial attachés and officers in the Foreign Service were supposed to assist U.S. business abroad. That has always been their charge. But with Watson's widely published letters of greetings, endorsements, and congratulations from Hull, the rank and file of the Foreign Service soon learned that Thomas J. Watson was more than just another citizen, and International Business Machines more than just another American company. Increasingly, diplomats and Foreign Service staffers became only too eager to please the firm and its stellar leader. Eventually, Watson assumed the status of unofficial ambassador-at-large, or perhaps something even larger. What was good for IBM became good for the United States. The protection and success of IBM was elevated to a defined "national interest." As such, IBM subsidiaries around the world learned to use American embassies and consulates as strategic partners in their routine business activities.[64]

The special relationship started in earnest in late 1936. Just after Watson was elected president of the International Chamber of Commerce, he managed to gain unprecedented levels of official recognition for the body and his assumption of its helm. Ambassadors, consuls general, and attachés were invited to attend, and IBM made special arrangements for their passage and hotels. Diplomats and other State Department bureaucrats were always welcome at the company's door or its lavish events. Watson traded on the perception throughout the Department that he was a personal and influential friend of Hull, and a major donor to Roosevelt. Designating who would represent the Department at a Watson event was frequently a process handled with great deliberation. A dozen or so memos might circulate back and forth to numerous offices and bureaus as the collective decision was carefully rendered.[65]

At first, rank and file State Department officers offered simple cooperation. For example, in fall 1936, the third secretary of the U.S. Embassy in Moscow conferred regularly with IBM's office there about Soviet government attempts to break IBM's monopoly. Cooperation was a two-way street. Watson would continuously check his busy travel and social schedule with State officials. In spring 1937, various letters were exchanged between the White House, the State Department, and Watson over whether he should extend official felicitations to the French government at a commemoration event.[66]

After Watson had received the medal from Hitler at the 1937 ICC Berlin Congress, junior officials at the State Department had begun advocating for IBM's unique business advantage. In particular, helping IBM avoid or reduce foreign taxes and tariffs was a continuing effort. For example, in August 1937, the U.S. Embassy in Paris helped IBM's French subsidiary gain a better tariff rate. Just days after the Paris Embassy helped with French customs, IBM sought similar assistance in Czechoslovakia. Tax authorities in Prague were raising IBM's tariffs. IBM's Foreign Division wrote to the Trade Agreement division in Washington, D.C., asking for help "to induce the [Czech] government to revert to the former classification."[67]

In some cases, the lower echelons of America's Foreign Service were eager to curry favor when they succeeded for IBM. In Bucharest, on September 28, 1938, Legation Secretary Frederick Hibbard sent report 543 entitled "Assistance Given International Business Machines Corporation," bragging, "Mr. Schotte of the Geneva office thanked a member of my staff for assistance given the company about a year ago. He stated that following the advice of the Legation, he [Schotte] had been able to prevent a tax suit against the Romanian subsidiary calling for the payment of 60 million lei in back taxes and fines. . . . This item should be added to the list of accomplishments of the Legation."[68]

Lavish letters of praise for individual ambassadors or their attachés were often sent by senior IBM executives to Hull to show gratitude and reward their effort.[69]

Watson's almost regal movements in Europe were regularly followed and reported with the utmost detail by American diplomats who were always on hand. Watson's visit to Oslo was typical. The U.S. Embassy there quickly reported "in quintuplicate" that "his train was met by a delegation representing the local membership of the International Chamber and by the Secretary of the Legation. Shortly after reaching the Legation, Mr. Watson received the press, responding to questions in a manner which evoked considerable favorable publicity in the newspapers."[70]

There seemed to be no limit to the service lower-echelon State Department staffers were willing to extend. Indeed, while World War II was raging, one Department administrator found time to write a letter to Frances Muños, an IBM employee in New York, passing along a message from a family member in Santiago, Chile, "stating that she desires to have you purchase shoes for her use."[71]

With as much service as State Department lower-echelon officers were enthusiastically providing, it is no wonder that Watson turned to America's commercial attaché in Berlin, Sam Woods, to use the weight of the United States government to help IBM confront Heidinger. Woods was enamored with Watson and only too glad to act as IBM's post-man, openly passing messages across the Atlantic through diplomatic pouch and coded cable, and providing clerical facilities within the embassy. More than that, Woods openly draped IBM's negotiation in the mantle of American officialdom that Watson hoped would make the difference.

On October 2, 1940, Watson sent a five-page letter to Heidinger's home passed through diplomatic pouch. Not only did Watson use the convenience of the diplomatic pouch, he took the unusual step of ostentatiously typing at the top: "Letter to be transmitted through the courtesy of the State Department to Mr. Willy Heidinger, Pöcking 56, am Starnberger See, Bavaria, Germany."[72]

Watson began with a cooperative tone. He confirmed, "On August 19 last, we telephoned our Geneva office to inform you that we would be glad to comply with your request for the election of Messrs. Schulte-Strathaus, Ziegler and Kiep as directors of Dehomag. We were later informed that they were duly elected . . . on August 31, 1940." He went on, "It has always been our desire to work in harmony with you for we realize how valuable your association with us has been . . . we maintain the highest respect for your judgment." He added, "We thought you were entirely right in the suggestions you made about enlarging the Board of Directors and placing thereon [three] men of affairs."[73]

At the same time, Watson stressed, questions of Dehomag being threatened unless IBM relinquished its majority was "a matter of such importance" that it needed to "be presented to our full Board of Directors [in New York] with all the facts obtainable for its careful consideration." He added, "You must realize that the economic conditions in the world, upset as they are, make it extremely difficult for us to decide promptly important matters such as you have suggested with respect to our interests in Germany without . . . all available facts and data."[74]

Specifically, IBM NY wanted to know whether there was genuinely an attempt to undermine Dehomag—privately or officially—in favor of a new company, unless it reduced its ownership and also repurchased Heidinger's shares. Ironically, as a savvy businessman, Watson understood the deeper fiscal meaning of Heidinger's actions against the subsidiary. Days earlier, IBM had confronted Heidinger with a completely unexpected scenario. If Dehomag was actually endangered because of Heidinger's disloyal actions, then the division's future was in fact worth far less. As such, Heidinger's shares were dramatically reduced in value as well. In other words, whatever Heidinger did to undermine Dehomag would impact the very Dehomag share value he was hoping to parlay. Heidinger angrily rejected this notion. But in his October 2 letter, Watson held fast: "We do not acquiesce in the statement that affairs of Dehomag following September 30th have no bearing on share purchases."[75]

Continuing with a hard line, Watson shocked Heidinger with another technicality. During the last round of corporate fisticuffs over bonuses, an automatic and generous buy-back was agreed upon. As was so often the case, when the negotiations were all written up, IBM preferred at the last minute that the final agreement should not be signed, but rather oral. At the time, Dehomag was reporting a continuous multimillion-mark income stream. Now Heidinger thought that when his shares would be repurchased, the per share price was a windfall guaranteed by the 1939 oral agreement. Watson's auditors had calculated these shares to be in excess of RM 2.7 million and Heidinger asserted they were valued at RM 3.8 million. If compelled to pay in dollars at an adverse exchange rate, as Heidinger expected, it would cost IBM millions.[76]

Not so, declared Watson in his letter. "You [Heidinger] say, 'Regarding the price basis, there is already an agreement between me and the IBM. . . . Your reference to an agreement . . . evidently refers to the then proposed agreement with Dehomag for the purchase of your shares, which we, as stockholders, were willing at that time to vote for. . . . You did not accept or execute these contracts, and, in view of the fact that the proposed contracts were not executed by you, of course none of their proposed provisions now apply."[77] In other words, a year after the contentious settlement was reached, IBM was now saying that without a signature, it would not honor the agreement.

"The only binding contract that exists between us," concluded Watson, "is one executed in New York City on the 8th day of May, 1936 . . . [and] executed in Berlin on the 10th day of June, 1936."[78]

Therefore, assured Watson, negotiation would be needed, maybe even a protracted arbitration process. "Our representative will meet you just as soon as he can secure the necessary documents to travel," he wrote.[79]

Mindful that his letter was being presented under the color of the State Department, Watson emphasized to Heidinger and to any colleagues in the Nazi Party he might share it with: "Our respective countries are at peace with each other, and we feel confident that there is no more desire on the part of the German authorities to interfere with United States business interests than there is a desire on the part of officials in the United States to interfere with business interests of Germany located in this country. . . . We believe that our two countries will continue to deal with each other fairly in all business matters."[80]

Watson's gambit worked. Heidinger became convinced he had to negotiate. At stake was the viability of the German automation program. Heidinger could not make the decisions alone. He had been in touch with a secret source in the Nazi Party who was familiar with Dehomag and its important uses for the Reich, and was willing to meet with Watson's negotiator in Berlin.[81]

On October 26, 1940, several cars motored to La Guardia Field. A delegation of senior IBM executives, led by Watson himself, accompanied the one man upon who rested the future of Dehomag and, in fact, IBM's entire European business. The vehicles pulled up to the Pan Am terminal. There a decorous IBM attorney named Harrison K. Chauncey alighted, ready to board Pan Am's *Dixie Clipper* to Portugal. A company notice for what was expected to be protracted travel appeared in the employee newsletter. The item was headlined: "Mr. Chauncey Leaves by *Clipper* on Trip to Europe for IBM." Nothing in the item mentioned visiting Germany. The subhead explained only, "Member of Legal Staff to Visit Switzerland, Portugal While Abroad."[82]

In truth, from neutral Lisbon, Chauncey would make his way to wartime Berlin for face-to-face negotiations with the still enraged Nazis. The newspapers that month were filled with terrifying reports that would have intimidated anyone traveling to the Third Reich. American corporate employees thought to be Jewish were tortured in Romania under Gestapo instruction.

British bombs hailed onto Berlin. Jews were entering the first phases of persecution in Nazi-dominated Vichy France and being tragically ghettoized and enslaved elsewhere. Moreover, if Roosevelt declared war, no one could even imagine the fate of Americans trapped in Nazi-controlled land.[83]

Although a loyal employee for thirteen years, beginning in the company controller's office, Chauncey understood little about the innermost affairs of Dehomag and its spreading influence with other IBM subsidiaries. He couldn't even spell newly elected board member Otto Kiep's name correctly. But Watson was counting on him. So Chauncey said goodbye to his wife and accepted Watson's assignment. Studious and reasoned in his approach, Chauncey's briefcase contained his own private plan of action, labeled "Program." The ten-page "Program" bookishly outlined his challenge in perfect classroom-style Roman numeral and A-B-C format, step-by-step: the questions he would ask in Berlin, the tactics he would employ with Heidinger along with their various financial implications, and how the U.S. Embassy would assist him. In the event IBM was forced to arbitrate Heidinger's demands, for instance, he planned to claim the business was over-valued because "the amount of business which may be attributable to the war [also means] the present profit rate is not a normal permanent profit rate."[84]

To some, Chauncey might have looked like a schoolboy in a dark suit and tie. He offered a polished, clean-shaven face with wide eyes, and ears that stuck out from behind nipped sideburns beneath a closely cropped haircut. But he was a sharp, fiercely tenacious attorney who would pursue his adversaries. He set aside qualms about flying into a dangerous Nazi setting and was completely focused on his historic corporate mission: save IBM Europe. For his efforts, Watson called him "the bravest man in IBM."[85]

CHAUNCEY'S PHYSICALLY tiring trip to Germany via Bermuda, Lisbon, and Geneva did not dampen his enthusiasm. His first stop was Munich where he spent several days in discussions with Heidinger. At first, Chauncey tried to reason with his sometimes emotional adversary. He told the embittered Dehomag founder that Watson wanted him to stay on, not force the repurchase of his shares. Mostly, he hoped Heidinger would help Watson comprehend the competitive forces that might be arraying against IBM. But Heidinger was not interested in compromise. Chauncey purchased a small vase for the Heidingers as a personal gift from Watson. Heidinger refused it. Most striking to Chauncey was Heidinger's contradictory arguments, and his elaborate, and occasionally bizarre, air of secrecy.[86]

The main Nazi objection, however, was made clear: IBM NY, now proven disloyal, would discover the secret planned uses of the Hollerith machines. Chauncey and his fellow Berlin-based attorneys did everything they could to constantly repeat the assurance that they would not ask questions or learn details. He told Heidinger he was willing "to go to any officials to show that IBM had not obtained any information of the confidential matters being done by Dehomag."[87] Again, IBM NY made a fine distinction between what its headquarters in New York would discover and the day-to-day knowledge its managers, engineers, and servicemen on site would be required to know to do their job.

A confusion of unwarranted alarms, false starts, and sudden rumors surrounded Chauncey as he tried, in his proper legalistic way, to make sense of it all. But after a few days of treadmill progress in Munich, Rottke telephoned from Berlin with something that appeared concrete. Rottke, too, was mysterious, but insisted it was imperative that Chauncey come to Berlin at once.[88]

When Chauncey arrived in Berlin, the sudden urgency of Rottke's telephone call dissipated as quickly as it appeared. As was so often the case in wartime Berlin, whispers and hazy conjecture ruled the day. Chauncey had hoped for a meeting with an influential Nazi. But as yet, that was not happening. So Chauncey immediately sought out board director Otto Kiep and attorney Albert in Berlin, each of whom offered a different suggestion for IBM's next move. Chauncey penciled voluminous notes and outlined various stratagems assessing the ifs and what-ifs of the predicament.[89]

As Chauncey waited to meet with the mysterious Nazi source, he lost no time scheduling a conference with Manager Karl Hummel. Hummel was generally perceived as more helpful in his views toward IBM because of his warm, personal relationship with Watson. This would be Chauncey's opportunity to learn firsthand the structure of Dehomag's business in war-ravaged Europe.

The conversation with Hummel was frank. Acting more like an attorney conducting a deposition, Chauncey first tried in his stiff way to understand the emotional Nazi mindset, why the medal's return was so threatening, and whether Dehomag could weather the rage.

> CHAUNCEY: When did you first observe difficulties . . . and what form did it take?
>
> HUMMEL: Sales resistance—before [the] war—because of [the] American ownership. Prior to that some government departments would not do

business with us even if they needed the machines, because they claimed [the] confidential nature of [the] department's activities prevented doing business with . . . [an] American-owned concern. War caused tremendous increase in those departments and they finally decided that they had to have the machines—but treated us very badly because of American ownership. About 35 percent of [our] business . . . is with government departments. [In the future,] even if [a] machine made in Germany is not as good at first as ours, the government will take the German machines and once that is done the private industries will follow. All of those industries are now under the government anyway, and only a suggestion is needed for them to change over.

CHAUNCEY: So . . . the form of any animosity was merely growling about having to do business with an . . . American-owned concern? Did any concerns actually refuse to do business with you because of American interest in Dehomag?

HUMMEL: There were no German machines. . . . The point . . . [will be] quite different when prospects have a choice between German machines and American machines . . . prospects kept saying that they would prefer to wait for the German machine.

CHAUNCEY: After the war commenced, did the difficulties increase?

HUMMEL: Sure! . . . [But] in my mind, [a] high percentage of difficulties were taken away because our people kept [the] friendship of the people! [A] number of companies took the machines but did not like it! "We don't want American machines," they said, but [the] Government ordered them.

CHAUNCEY: Notwithstanding that the animosity existed against Dehomag?

HUMMEL: In view of labor conditions, they could not do otherwise. This is when the Government realized the necessity of relying upon an American concern.

CHAUNCEY: What if anything did you report to IBM when this difficulty first arose and increased after the commencement of the war?

HUMMEL: When Schotte was here the difficulties had not increased so much and we did not think . . . it was so very much worse than it had always been . . . we always had been accustomed to the sales resistance because we were American owned! [90]

Chauncey turned to the issue of Hitler's medal. Hummel tried to be delicate but reflected the ire of many Germans. The photos of Hitler and Watson, and IBM's rejected letter offering a German Red Cross donation, were lying nearby.

CHAUNCEY: When did . . . the difficulty reach such a point that you thought . . . something [had] to be done?

HUMMEL: When Mr. Watson returned the medal. It came like a bomb. The man from the radio told us before anything [was] seen in the papers.

CHAUNCEY: Is it your feeling that this brought the thing to a climax, or was it really the reaction which you experienced with your customers and prospects?

HUMMEL: We excuse Mr. Watson because he looked at it from his own viewpoint—but it hurt us. In Italy it was as bad as in Germany . . .

CHAUNCEY: But let's have concrete examples. Was it merely talk, or did customers refuse to deal with you?

HUMMEL: You must remember that the Nazis, when they feel insulted, will make certain that they will pay back that injury. It shows [how] they feel when they refused the gift [of a Red Cross donation]!

CHAUNCEY: So they refer to the return of the decoration when they refused the gift?

HUMMEL: They expressed clearly "we do not want anything from that man." They said Watson and IBM's gift could not be accepted.

CHAUNCEY: Why was it presented as a gift of *Mr. Watson* and not of IBM [corporately]?

HUMMEL: They identify Watson and IBM as one person, just like you cannot divide Patterson and the National Cash Register Co.

CHAUNCEY: But Patterson owned the National Cash.

HUMMEL: But the letter was written in [such a] form that it was the instructions from Mr. Watson.

CHAUNCEY: Is there anything I could do to correct that misunderstanding, that it was IBM's gift and not Mr. Watson's?

HUMMEL: Don't try—they will treat you politely and let you go, because they will say or think that you cannot pay for an insult. Here is the letter from [IBM] Geneva, 24 July, saying that Mr. Watson had instructed that the money be given.

CHAUNCEY: Did you present it as a gift from Mr. Watson or as a gift from IBM?

HUMMEL: We had to show the letter. We could not risk saying it was a gift from IBM without having something to show. . . . It is personal danger to us . . . if we did not show the letter. If we failed to show the letter we would have been sent to the concentration camp. We had to take all of Mr. Watson's pictures down because of the visitors or officials who considered that when Mr. Watson insulted Hitler he also insulted them.

CHAUNCEY: Then when did you decide it was necessary to give up the [stockholder] majority—only after the return of the decoration?

HUMMEL: Oh, sure . . . when the medal was returned it showed that [the] . . . animosity against us was now proved. Do not worry but when things are settled they have their intentions to reply to Mr. Watson. The Americans refused to give Germany cotton, and Hitler said we will make cotton. Now we have cotton—and rubber and all the other things they wouldn't let us have without dollars.[91]

Chauncey turned to the economic outlook. Was Dehomag worth saving? Could it be saved? Hummel equivocated from moment to moment on the prospects. In truth, no one knew in this fluid wartime situation just what Germany's leaders would decide. Would they choose to angrily excise IBM and proceed with a dubious patchwork of punch card systems that would take months if not years to meet the Reich's escalating needs, or would some pragmatic modus vivendi be adopted?

CHAUNCEY: Then you are going to lose a lot of business after the war?

HUMMEL: I think . . . Hitler has so much in mind now, improvements, and you saw in the paper the housing plan! We feel that we will lose that business if German competition comes up. Otherwise not. Very few will discontinue machines after the war—except that they may and probably will change our machines for German machines. I think if we do not get German competition, our business will grow tremendously. . . .

CHAUNCEY: When did you first learn . . . that a new German company should be formed to compete with Dehomag?

HUMMEL: There are dozens of people who have discussed that and Heidinger believes he knows much more. People say, "We will build a factory—and we will get you." Take [the] case if Goering [Hitler's second-in-command] buys Bull patents and gets into the tabulating business. What do you think would happen then?

CHAUNCEY: What information have you obtained as to the purchase of Powers in Germany—I have heard now that it may not be Siemens?

HUMMEL: It may be Goering—whenever the Government feels that the industry should be started, it will put it in Hermann Goering Works. You may be sure that if that happens, Dehomag is no longer in business. Look at what Bull has been doing in France—they claimed that you tried to buy them out but that they would not sell out to Americans. Our security is—Rottke ['s] and mine—is continuing with IBM, because we would have great difficulty with [any new] German partners. We merely think in our hearts that we must show you the danger. If you don't act on it, all right! We were attacked and attacked, and when Mr. Watson got the decoration it helped us. We have a picture of it—here—and a picture of Mr. Watson and Hitler. It was advertising to us. When we wanted something we could show that and say: "You can't refuse." With officials and customers it was a good selling point, and when it was returned it had the opposite effect and worse.[92]

Chauncey now methodically reviewed for himself exactly what business arrangements Dehomag was engaged in throughout Europe, country by country. At the time, IBM had devised complicated and often circuitous methods of payment that generally but not always followed a 75–25 percent split of revenues between New York and Dehomag. IBM subsidiaries across Europe would generate orders for equipment, parts, and punch cards. Dehomag would supply these, either directly or through the subsidiaries it dominated in Nazi-conquered territory. IBM NY's 75 percent share of the money would sometimes be sent to Geneva, and sometimes to Berlin. Germany would often—but not always—receive its 25 percent share by crediting what it owed IBM for spare parts, the so-called "goods account." But all these payment procedures were frequently modified—or even set aside—as conflicting country-by-country wartime regulations emerged.[93]

IBM received its money either through Geneva, which openly transferred the sums to New York, or through Dehomag, which blocked the revenues until war's end, although they could be used to grow the subsidiary and purchase real estate.[94] Chauncey now wanted to make sure Dehomag was still abiding by the payment procedures as much as possible.

CHAUNCEY: Have you ever had any understanding with IBM in Geneva about the classification of machines for royalties?

HUMMEL: We feel obliged to pay on sorters and tabulators. The Devisenstelle [Foreign Exchange Office] will not permit us to pay royalties on other machines. Patents on the sorters will soon expire, and now there is a serious question whether they will say you can't pay royalties on expired patents. We have to get all the license statements verified by the Government.

CHAUNCEY: Well, I intend to reserve all our rights . . .

HUMMEL: Austria. IBM owes Dehomag nineteen thousand dollars. That was five or six years ago. . . . You agreed . . . to pay us nineteen thousand in cash. But you never paid it and every time we went to the Finance Department it made a serious problem for us.

CHAUNCEY: Go ahead and try to offset what you say is held in Austria for us against those items. Vienna Company?

HUMMEL: After incorporation of Austria in Germany, the tax people claimed that [with] the existence of that company there, that IBM had business in Germany and thereby [was] subject to the high tax. Every opportunity is taken by the tax authorities to fix liability on IBM for that higher tax. They have always contended that Dehomag is an "organ" of IBM and is subject to the tax. . . .

CHAUNCEY: Countries now incorporated into Germany?

HUMMEL: Austria, Sudetenland, German Poland, Alsace-Lorraine, Silesia.

CHAUNCEY: Bohemia Moravia?

HUMMEL: That is treated as a part of Germany.

CHAUNCEY: Poland?

HUMMEL: Very few customers left, the business is almost destroyed. Besides that they are using all the rentals to pay expenses and the Government will soon close the Company because they will not let it continue to lose money. Dehn [IBM's Polish subsidiary manager] says he can't continue to do business—all the industry [is] now in German hands and they won't do business with a Watson company.

CHAUNCEY: Can Dehne come to Berlin?

HUMMEL: Yes.

CHAUNCEY: Have him come here.

HUMMEL: Bohemia-Moravia—last month [the] frontier [was] given up, and since that time they have to buy machines. Geneva can no longer buy machines from us and they have to pay 100 percent for them. It is more or less included in the German territory. Not included *de jure,* but *de facto.*

CHAUNCEY: Are the employees there still the employees of the Prague Company?

HUMMEL: Yes.

CHAUNCEY: Silesia?

HUMMEL: We have taken over Silesia, which belongs to Germany. An arrangement was made with Schotte for that.

CHAUNCEY: What happened to our machines there?

HUMMEL: Some were sent to Romania and some to Hungary. Some are still there. Rental on IBM machines that are there still get 75 percent of the rentals—you have no expenses there and get 75 percent.

CHAUNCEY: Is the arrangement for Silesia in writing?

HUMMEL: Yes, a copy was sent to Geneva and agreed to by the Devisenstelle.

CHAUNCEY: Danzig?

HUMMEL: Only one customer. There was an agreement between Dehomag and Geneva. You had no customers there as that was always serviced by Dehomag. The people there refused to do business with Poland.

CHAUNCEY: Sweden? Are you furnishing machines, parts, or supplies to Sweden?

HUMMEL: Yes, if Geneva gives us orders. To every country, if Geneva gives us orders.

CHAUNCEY: How are you paid for them?

HUMMEL: 75 percent from the country [Sweden] and 25 percent from the goods account.

CHAUNCEY: Is there any dollar liability there?

HUMMEL: No.

CHAUNCEY: Suppose that Sweden should block its money, what would then be the position?

HUMMEL: Then you would not get permission to export the products to Sweden. But . . . there is a clearing agreement between Germany and Sweden and there is no possibility that that would happen.

CHAUNCEY: Norway?

HUMMEL: Just the same as Sweden.

CHAUNCEY: Denmark?

HUMMEL: Just the same.

CHAUNCEY: In those two countries, Norway and Denmark, are you in touch with the IBM people there?

HUMMEL: Certainly, we furnish parts and so on to them.

CHAUNCEY: Do you bill Geneva or the local company?

HUMMEL: We bill Geneva for the 75 percent. Sometimes . . . the authorities don't agree, then we have to bill 100 percent.

CHAUNCEY: Holland?

HUMMEL: Same condition in Holland.

CHAUNCEY: Belgium?

HUMMEL: Same condition.

CHAUNCEY: France?

HUMMEL: We have to bill direct to the French [IBM] company [in occupied France]. There is some exchange of goods. I don't think under present conditions we can bill Geneva. We sent them in exchange against parts for alphabetic machines. . . . eight kilos of paper. They . . . said they wanted to buy paper and we did not want to mix in that business. They buy direct from the German paper mill.

CHAUNCEY: Alsace-Lorraine. Have you taken over the territory?

HUMMEL: No, we have been called once for service.

CHAUNCEY: Who called you?

HUMMEL: The customers called on us only once.

CHAUNCEY: [Un]occupied France?

HUMMEL: We have no contact with that part of the country.

CHAUNCEY: You have not furnished anything for that part of the country?

HUMMEL: No. We helped [Roger] Virgile [director of CEC, the IBM subsidiary in France] get permission to go to both parts. This territory is taken care of by Virgile himself.

CHAUNCEY: Is the factory in operation?

HUMMEL: As far as I know, a little bit.

CHAUNCEY: Italy.

HUMMEL: We made an agreement with Geneva with consent of New York that in exchange for alphabetical tabulators which we received from IBM, we gave four used American multiplying punches . . . the first are delivered and the second will . . . be delivered in January. He [the Italian manager] is in great need for these machines. We pack the machines and send them back to Milan. . . . twelve multipliers equal to three alphabetic machines. He [is] still manufacturing but very limited.

CHAUNCEY: Romania?

HUMMEL: If Geneva gives us an order for Romania, we will fill it [under the] same conditions, 75 percent and 25 percent. We have not furnished any to Romania [directly]. Few machines sent from Silesia.

CHAUNCEY: Do you have to get a separate permission for each time you send a machine out?

HUMMEL: No, we have a general permission.

CHAUNCEY: Bulgaria?

HUMMEL: Same condition.

CHAUNCEY: Have you furnished any machines?

HUMMEL: No

CHAUNCEY: Yugoslavia?

HUMMEL: Nothing furnished.

CHAUNCEY: Would you be able to furnish machines?

HUMMEL: Yes, except for transportation.[95]

Chauncey continued pressing Hummel for payment details, country by country. Throughout, when referring to other subsidiaries in Nazi-dominated lands, he spoke as few words as possible—often speaking no more than the name of the invaded country. Not once in the long questioning of Hummel did Chauncey ever ask what the machines were being used for. Nor did Hummel offer any details. In dozens of pages of notes, reports, and messages sent from Chauncey to New York and back, the question never came up. No one wanted to discuss it.

———————————————

SECRECY, CONFUSION, and crisis continued to surround Chauncey's negotiations throughout November and December 1940 as he and IBM attorneys in Germany conferred with various influential personalities in the business community, German military, and Nazi Party. The tension was building as some, including Chauncey, began fearing for their safety.[96]

IBM attorney Albert had created a nine-page legal opinion with staunch recommendations. In his written opinion, Albert openly conceded that most German military agencies relied upon IBM machinery, and that the Reich was rightly worried that IBM knew the details of secret projects. The Reich's fear, Albert later wrote, "is not quite as unfounded as it might appear," based on the intimate knowledge Dehomag engineers required to create and service Hollerith punch card systems. He added, "It is no use to argue that this fear is absolutely theoretical." Nonetheless, Albert urged Watson to resist efforts to force IBM to relinquish its majority ownership.[97]

Chauncey was originally going to cable Albert's supportive opinion to New York, together with a six-page personal report. But at the last minute, he retreated to the Embassy, "for my own protection," where he typed his letter. "It is important," warned Chauncey, "that any reply you send me be sent in code and no reference made to this communication whatsoever." He added that he had shared its contents with no one except the Embassy staff. Embassy people in turn made copies for review by senior officials of the State Department in Washington, D.C., before they in turn delivered the correspondence to IBM.

Albert's nine-page opinion itself was undated. Chauncey was to destroy it after reading. But with the assistance of the Embassy, Chauncey elected to send it to Watson anyway, by diplomatic courier, writing, "Dr. Albert's [opinion] is contained in the enclosed memorandum, which I am sending to you, notwithstanding that I am supposed to return it to him for destruction." Before enclosing it, Chauncey, for extra measure, removed the first page of the opinion, which undoubtedly included identifying letterhead from Albert's law office. Chauncey shared his worry: "Our people must report their conversations with me, and in some respects they may be under the instruction of the military authorities."[98]

But writing from the security of the Embassy, Chauncey's own report freely outlined what was at stake for IBM NY in retaining its strategic alliance with Nazi Germany. He described the vast financial promise of the Third Reich where "plans are laid for the great economic future of Germany. One of the creeds here is 'Europe for Europeans,' and this probably means 'Europe for Germans.'"[99]

His report to IBM NY continued, "Naturally everyone here has no doubt about how the war will end, and they build on that. . . . consequently, they vision Dehomag doing business everywhere in Europe, and under the guidance of the new economic order in Europe, Dehomag would grow tremendously because all countries would use machines as Germany now does. . . . I suppose they [are] right." Chauncey added the converse: even "if Germany loses the war, [and] these things will not come into being . . . American-owned companies could probably resume business as theretofore."[100]

Clearly, Chauncey contended, the Nazis now understood that IBM's technology was vital to their war aims and too entrenched to be discarded. Replacing Holleriths, he argued, would be a long, difficult task in view of the military's "large use of Dehomag machines." Indeed, despite all "the animosity," Chauncey wrote, "the business has, however, gone forward . . . due to the need of the authorities."[101]

In fact, Germany had already thought better of its first hostile anti-Watson reaction and was trying now to find some rapprochement with the IBM Corporation. As for the machines snatched by the Nazis in France, noted Chauncey, "I understand . . . rental is being paid for them to our French company."[102]

IBM should rely on its decided technologic edge, suggested Chauncey, because of the profound difficulty in starting a punch card industry from scratch, especially if New York could block French Bull competition. In spite of the quality of its devices, French Bull was a very small company with very few machines. Bull's one small factory could never supply the Reich's continental needs. Ramping up for volume production—even if based within a Bull factory—would take months. Hitler didn't have months in his hour-to-hour struggle to dominate Europe. In a section entitled "Length of Time for Competition to Come in Actuality," Chauncey argued, "Unless the authorities, or the new company, operate in the meantime from the French Bull factory, it would appear that much time may elapse before such new company [could] . . . furnish machines in Germany."[103]

Watson, in fact, was ready to continue fighting to keep Bull out of the Nazi market. IBM had already preemptively acquired Swiss Bull's patent rights in Switzerland and was preparing to litigate to block the French sister corporation from functioning. IBM had concluded Bull infringed several IBM-owned patents, now that IBM NY had acquired Swiss Bull, which legally controlled French Bull's patents. Moreover, IBM believed that French Bull's use of an 80-column punch card violated IBM patents and could be swiftly enjoined by court action. So Chauncey added his prediction that even if French Bull did attempt to cooperate with the Nazis, there would be a great "length of time and difficulties for actual competition" to appear.[104]

It seemed that in spite of its autarkic impulses and collective rage against Watson, the cold fact remained: Nazi Germany needed punch cards. It needed them not next month or even next week. It needed them every hour of every day in every place. Only IBM could provide them.

"My inclination is to fight," Chauncey declared straight out. But the battle would be difficult. He knew that IBM was fighting a two-front psycho-economic war: Heidinger's demand to cash in his stock, and Nazi Party demands to take over the subsidiary. Clearly, the two were organically linked, but Chauncey could not be sure how.[105]

As they bickered, war and invasion proved it was still good business. By now, Dehomag's profits had mushroomed even more rapidly than expected, especially as a result of the Nazi takeovers of Belgium, Poland, and France. As the Reich expanded its voracious need for Holleriths in occupied lands, Dehomag's value was catapulting daily. The latest valuation of Heidinger's 10 percent stock, Chauncey advised, was now as much as RM 23 million—IBM accountants in Germany had already confirmed it. The new figure was as much as ten times higher than calculated just a few months earlier. It would be an enormous amount of money if payable in dollars— perhaps $5 or $6 million. Chauncey expected Heidinger to prevail in any court, should the Germans press his claim for repurchase. IBM's multi-million-mark blocked accounts in Berlin would be seized by the court to purchase those high-priced dollars, Chauncey warned. For this reason, Chauncey was continuously trying to finesse a settlement. "I am after him every day," he wrote.[106]

As for IBM's fight with the Nazi Party, Chauncey reiterated his willingness to "make any representations to the authorities that our managers need not reveal any information of the activities of Dehomag's customers. . . . but I cannot get the actual persons out in the open."[107] That chance would now come. After weeks of remaining in the background, Dr. Edmund Veesenmayer would finally come forward.

EVEN THOUGH Edmund Veesenmayer lived at August Strasse 12 in Lichter-felde, just around the corner from Dehomag's Berlin headquarters, he had declined to make his presence known to Chauncey until the first days of December 1940. Veesenmayer was one of Berlin's quiet but powerful Nazis, often feared, who helped to directly implement the most dramatic phases of Hitler's plans for Europe and the Jews. He was just a step or two removed from *der Führer*, and was from time to time summoned for consultations by Hitler personally—a claim few would dare make, but a claim that was nonetheless quite correct. Although Veesenmayer proudly wore the full uniform and regalia of his SS rank, he avoided noisy street riots and ghetto roundups in favor of boardrooms and embassies. Always lurking in the shadows as Eastern Europe's most heinous actions erupted, Veesenmayer was Hitler's most trenchant facilitator.[108]

Born Catholic in 1904 in the town of Bad Kissingen, amid the pastoral rolling hills and lush forests of Bavaria, Veesenmayer quickly took to political economics. He became a professor of economics and business administration at the Technical College in Munich. Veesenmayer joined the NSDAP early, in 1932, when he was only twenty-eight years old. When National Socialism came to power in 1933, he became the personal secretary and economic advisor to Wilhelm Keppler, Hitler's personal economic advisor. As such, Keppler functioned as Veesenmayer's direct connection to the *Führer* and the most powerful officials in Germany.[109]

Keppler was not only Hitler's personal economic advisor, he was also Germany's main nexus to American business. Dubbed "a Kodak Man" by U.S. military intelligence reports for his links to the Eastman Kodak film company, Keppler owed much to the Kodak Company. Before the rise of Hitler, Keppler enjoyed managerial positions with several firms that produced photographic gelatins, including one that exported heavily to Eastman Kodak in America and Kodak Limited in England. Kodak financed 50 percent of Keppler's Odin Company, which specialized in photo gels. Once Hitler came to power, Keppler advised a number of American companies on terminating their Jewish employees. He maintained good relations with executives connected to such companies as International Telephone and Telegraph and National Cash Register, and was Hitler's intermediary to such commercial giants as General Motors.[110]

Largely through his Keppler connections, Veesenmayer eventually joined the board of directors of the German subsidiaries of International Telephone and Telegraph and Standard Oil.[111] Veesenmayer traveled in executive circles and spoke the language of big business.

But Veesenmayer was more than just a corporate liaison. He was arguably considered Reich Foreign Minister von Ribbentrop's most important personal troubleshooter and advance man. A technical expert on the eradication of Jewish communities, Veesenmayer was invaluable as a behind-the-scenes organizer in Hitler's war against the Jews. As such, he had a keen appreciation for statistics and Hollerith capabilities. U.S. military intelligence described his meteoric ascent within the Reich's anti-Jewish destruction machine as "an amazing career which took him on missions to Southeastern Europe always, it would seem, at a moment of trouble."[112]

In the months leading up to the March 1938 *Anschluss* with Austria, Veesenmayer functioned as the Foreign Office's principal economic expert in Vienna. The day before Austria was taken over, March 12, Veesenmayer shuttled Himmler from a Vienna airfield to the German Embassy to help form a new Austrian Nazi regime. The next day, however, before the puppet Austrian government could be installed, Hitler annexed the country altogether.[113]

A year later, in early March 1939, Veesenmayer traveled to Bratislava to help engineer the destruction of Czechoslovakia and the declaration of a puppet state in Slovakia. On about March 11, he drove two handpicked Slovak leaders to Vienna where they met Keppler and then flew on to Berlin for a meeting with Hitler. On that same day, Veesenmayer wired the Foreign Office, *"alle Juden in der Hand,"* that is, "all Jews in hand." He remained in Bratislava on March 15 while Czechoslovakia was dismantled. Jews were quickly identified in the days to come.[114]

Veesenmayer was a frequent liaison to foreign militant movements. In early 1940, he was assigned to coordinate with two members of the Irish Republican Army visiting Berlin. Later, in Rome, he met with the virulent anti-Semites Amin Husseini, the Grand Mufti of Jerusalem, and Rashid Ali Gailani, former Iraqi premier. He escorted both men to Berlin for meetings with Hitler.[115]

It was Veesenmayer, who, in April 1941, brokered a written political agreement between Yugoslavian Fascists and a murderous Croatian militia known as the Ustashi, helping the Croats remain in power as Nazi surrogates with the support of the German Foreign Office. Indeed, the same day he brokered the Ustashi pact, Germany invaded Zagreb. Ustashi militias were allowed free rein under Veesenmayer's eye. It was Veesenmayer's job to liaison with Ustashi leader, Ante Pavelich. In the annals of wartime savagery against the Jews, there was no group as sadistic as the Croatian Ustashi. Using chainsaws, axes, knives, and rocks, frenzied Swastika-bedecked Ustashi brutally murdered thousands of Jews at a time. Ustashi leaders openly paraded about Zagreb with necklaces comprised of Jewish tongues and eyeballs cut and gouged from women and children, many of them raped and then dismembered or decapitated. Pavelich himself was fond of offering wicker baskets of Jewish eyeballs as gifts to his diplomatic visitors.[116]

In the first days of December 1940, just after completing his assignment with the Irish Republican Army and four months before leaving for his behind-the-scenes work with the Ustashi, Veesenmayer telephoned Heidinger and Albert to make the Reich's views on Dehomag known. Then he met with Chauncey.

MEMORANDUM OF CONVERSATION WITH DR. VEESENMAYER
Chauncey in Berlin to IBM New York

Dr. Veesenmayer is the right hand man of Dr. Keppler. Dr. Keppler, I am informed, is and has been Hitler's personal economic advisor. The organization of which Dr. Keppler is the head is a Nazi Party organization called . . . The Department for Policies and Economics. It's not formally a part of the government but has, of course, immense power . . . because it instructs . . . the government on what the Nazi party decides shall be economic policy.

I was present when Mr. Heidinger received a request or summons to visit Dr. Keppler and the morning afterwards when I saw Dr. Albert, he told me he had not slept all night. . . . Until this time, Dr. Albert had been ardently fighting Mr. Heidinger with respect to any reorganization of Dehomag. . . . The only question of competition was whether or not the managers were strong enough to fight, and whether our machines and prices could meet the competition.

Dr. Albert did not tell me what the conversation was between Mr. Heidinger, Dr. Keppler and himself, but did tell me of the conversation with Dr. Veesenmayer which conversation was after the talk with Dr. Keppler. Dr. Albert informed me that Dr. Veesenmayer had said that under no circumstances would any coercion be used to force the IBM to give up the majority but that it appeared advisable that the IBM should do so.

Dr. Veesenmayer had asked that Dr. Albert and Mr. Heidinger agree on a plan to effect the reorganization and that I should agree in writing to such a plan subject to the approval of the Board of Directors of the IBM. Dr. Albert attempted to get me to agree, which I refused on the ground that any such tentative agreement would lead to the belief officially that it would be carried out. . . . If the IBM did not desire to approve it . . . [then] IBM's position would [only] be more difficult with the officials. I told Dr. Albert that all I would authorize him to say to Dr. Veesenmayer was that there had been several plans submitted to me and these I would in turn submit to the IBM.

Dr. Albert told me that Dr. Veesenmayer had [then] expressed a desire to see me but not in his office, as he would like the conversation to be unofficial. Tentative arrangements were made for me to meet him at lunch. However, Dr. Albert called me one day and informed me that he was going to see Dr. Veesenmayer on the next day. . . . Dr. Albert called me later and said that I should go with him to Dr. Veesenmayer's office.

Dr. Veesenmayer stated [to me] that there were advantages to be gained by friendly agreements between industries in America and Germany and that it was not unusual to find a desire to have industries owned by the nationals of a country. I told him that I appreciated the advantages of a nationally-owned company whether in Germany or elsewhere. I pointed out to him that competition could be used [just as easily] against Dehomag [if it were] partly-owned by the IBM as it could be used when IBM practically owned the entire company . . . I asked him what guarantees IBM could have for the protection of its minority, assuming that it gave up its majority. He [Veesenmayer] suggested that no guarantees could be made in writing but that if the Government approved of the act of increasing the capital and the disposition of it to Germans, that should be all the security we need ask for. Dr. Veesenmayer did not speak English very well but I understood him to say that he had been instrumental in assisting in the re-organization of the International Telephone Company in Spain. Subsequently I attempted, through Dr. Albert, to have Dr. Veesenmayer give me the names of American companies which he had also assisted in re-organizing. The reply was that he could not give me the names but that he could tell me that he had just about closed the arrangements with two other American companies. In this connection I saw for a moment the names of three German companies which have been re-organized. I did not have the opportunity to get down these names, which were in German, nor could I identify them with any American company. . . .

Dr. Kiep seemed to be of the opinion that Dr. Keppler's introduction into the matter was occasioned by Mr. Heidinger. This may be so but I do not believe that Mr. Heidinger himself got in touch with Dr. Keppler or Dr. Veesenmayer because he appeared to be as much concerned about the call to Dr. Keppler's office as was Dr. Albert. It is possible, however, that through his other friends he [Heidinger] may have brought Dr. Keppler into the subject.[117]

Soon after Chauncey met with Veesenmayer, Albert delivered to Chauncey a short unsigned, unaddressed note, typed on plain paper. Chauncey forwarded that to New York as well through diplomatic pouch.

> The party with whom you have discussed the matter of IBM is Mr. Veesenmayer. He is the right hand of Dr. Keppler, Secretary of State in the Ministry of Foreign Affairs, but at the same time being entrusted, as an important member of the party with certain special duties and responsibilities, F.I. [for instance] concerning questions of political economic organizations. Mr. Veesenmayer confirmed the official attitude that no pressure should be brought on IBM to transfer its majority into German hands, but that he thought it advisable to do so. His recommendation to you was to lose no time in reporting to IBM and then to return as soon as possible to Berlin in order to carry the plan through.[118]

Things began happening rapid-fire. On December 5, Heidinger suddenly agreed to accept a vastly lower purchase price for his shares, just RM 3.9 million. What's more, he would accept payment in IBM's blocked marks and no longer insist upon dollars. A contract with IBM was quickly drawn up and signed on December 13, 1940.[119]

IBM felt Heidinger's war was on hold, at least for the moment. But the continuing pressure for IBM to relinquish its majority remained intense. Equally manifest was the air of tight-lipped mystery surrounding what the Nazis had in mind for the machines. Chauncey studiously avoided ever asking what additional tasks the machines were intended for. He nonetheless pressed ahead, demonstrating IBM NY's intention to remain a reliable vendor to the Reich. He began organizing new support for Germany's needs in occupied France, and declared his readiness to integrate IBM's Polish subsidiary into Dehomag proper. He even offered to extend Dehomag's territory into Russia, which many believed Germany was preparing to invade.[120]

Even still, a new plan was emerging. The Third Reich was now hoping to expand Dehomag and all its dominated European IBM subsidiaries into a huge all-inclusive Nazi cartel governed by the *Maschinelles Berichtwesen*, the Reich's agency for punch card technology. This cartel would be strengthened by the inclusion of the marginal European branches of Powers, as well as all local companies in invaded lands, such as Bull in France and Kamatec in Holland. Machines would be transported from country to country, like so many mortars, across war-ravaged Europe to the precise locales needed. Once their mission was accomplished, the devices would be shifted to the next hot spot. The pillars of the cartel would be the well-developed IBM subsidiaries in Italy, France, and Holland. In fact, a special Dehomag employee named Heinz Westerholt, the Nazi Party's direct agent within the subsidiary, had already traveled to France to initiate the arrangements in both Vichy and occupied territory. The Germans working through French authorities had already demanded a test integration of Bull systems with Hollerith tabulators and sorters.[121]

The planned punch card cartel would then be able to accomplish all the Reich's most important objectives without channeling requests through the IBM corporate bureaucracy or submitting to Watson micro-management. Germany's IBM-based cartel could function as a binary with Watson's non-European operation.

Ultimately, the attempted cartel would be bitterly fought by Watson, deploying every technologic, legal, financial, and political argument at IBM's disposal. Eventually, by mid-1941, the Nazis concluded that connecting Holleriths to other systems was mechanically impossible, and operationally naive. Unlikable as it was, Germany needed an agreement with Watson in which he agreed to supply all the Reich's needs, receive proper payment, but remain detached from the local details his managers and engineers would necessarily possess. Ironically, such a modus vivendi appealed greatly to Watson.

IBM as a company would know the innermost details of Hitler's Hollerith operations, designing the programs, printing the cards, and servicing the machines. But Watson and his New York directors could erect a wall of credible deniability at the doors of the executive suite. In theory, only those down the hall in the New York headquarters who communicated directly with IBM Geneva, such as IBM European General Manager Schotte, could provide a link to the reality in Europe. But in fact, any such wall contained so many cracks, gaps, and hatches as to render it imaginary. The free flow of information, instructions, requests, and approvals by Watson remained detailed and continuous for years to come—until well into 1944.

Subsidiary managers were authorized by New York to negotiate special equipment rental and service agreements from the *Maschinelles Berichtwesen* and other Reich officials. Projects in Europe were approved and customers prioritized with New York's permission. Machines were moved from place to place to meet the demand. IBM Europe's managers received special permission from the Nazi authorities to travel back and forth between neutral nations, Nazi-held territory, and Germany itself. They regularly sent IBM NY letters and reports. Some were simply handwritten notes. Others were dense sales and machine status reports, or meticulous monthly summaries, all sent from Axis-controlled subsidiaries to New York through neutral cities.[122]

When Geneva executives were pressed for time, they telephoned New York. Using codes and oblique references, they nonetheless all spoke the same language, even when the language was vague. As one previous European General Manager, John Holt, urged an IBM NY colleague early in the war: "wire Schotte for the information which you need, care being taken that your request is so worded that it can pass the censor. It goes without saying that any information covering military activity is apt to get the recipient, as well as the sender, into considerable 'hot water.'"[123]

Together the continuous reports, summaries, cables, and telephone calls offered minute-to-minute operational details of IBM's activities in France, Italy, and Sweden; the serial number and location of equipment; and precisely which machines were destined to be shipped to Dehomag or the German army. Devices and spare parts going into the Reich or elsewhere in Nazi-conquered Europe were tracked by New York—from the most complex collator to the simplest sorting brush. Despite the turmoil of Dehomag's revolt, throughout 1940 and 1941 the fluid decision to build new factories to supply Nazi Germany, the stocking of those factories, and the year-to-year ordering of expensive machine tools, these decisions were made by IBM NY based on the most current market information. Paper factory output and anticipated shortages throughout Europe were monitored to anticipate problems before they occurred.[124]

Millions of punch cards were routinely shipped from IBM in America directly to Nazi-controlled sources in Poland, France, Bulgaria, and Belgium, or routed circuitously through Sweden or colonies in Africa. When IBM's American presses did not fill orders, subsidiaries themselves would ship cards across frontiers from one IBM location to another.[125]

All money was accounted for and audited down to the franc and lira. All expenses were deferentially proposed to New York and carefully approved or rejected. Watson was even told that the French subsidiary had charged an extra 1.5 francs for wine with lunch in the company canteen.[126]

But in December 1940, things were different. The plan for an *MB* cartel was still very much alive in the Nazi game plan. Moreover, the constantly evolving special plans for Hitler's Holleriths were beginning to take shape. Periodically, when Chauncey inadvertently raised an issue that came close to the cartel question, the managers at Dehomag would mysteriously comment, "there were concentration camps," and then become completely silent. On December 13, 1940, Chauncey wrote to Watson, "I mentioned to Hummel that now might be a good opportunity to acquire our rights from Bull, he vaguely hinted that perhaps the Bull Company in France has already been acquired by others. When I pressed him for an explanation, he would say nothing more. When I reach a point with these fellows, they begin to talk of concentration camps, etc."[127]

A few days later, on December 17, Chauncey was discussing the issue of Heidinger defecting to a competitive company and destroying the subsidiary. Hummel first swore Chauncey to secrecy and then revealed, "Heidinger would never fight Dehomag." Chauncey then reported to IBM NY that he "went along with him [Hummel] in the hopes that he would not retire within a shell, or completely shut up with the explanation that 'there were concentration camps'!"[128]

About that time, Otto Kiep surprised Chauncey by mysteriously stating it was better for directors to decline any stock in Dehomag—even token stock. On December 13, Chauncey wrote to Watson without elaborating, "it is Mr. Kiep's opinion that no shares should be issued to the directors, because of something he has learned." Like the other messages, Chauncey channeled the message through the Embassy.[129]

Chauncey made clear to Watson in his various writings that Germany's use of machines throughout conquered Europe would be profoundly lucrative, and IBM could not give up the profits. Albert described an enticing Axis-wide punch card monopoly that would rule in "Germany's possible future economic space comprising not only the increased [Reich] territory [itself], but the sphere of . . . Central Europe to the Balkans, the African possessions, and the Near East."[130]

But to remain a viable member of the Nazi juggernaut, Albert explained, Watson would have to adopt a decision not to just do business with and extract profit from Nazi Germany, but to ensure that Dehomag become an organic facet of the Third Reich itself. In a twenty-one-page recommendation to Watson, Albert circumlocutiously described the cooperation Veesenmayer expected. "The structure of the German economic system," Albert wrote, "requires that every German undertaking is completely, loyally and without any reservation a member of that system, as formed by National Socialist leadership. What matters is . . . the spirit of German economic leadership—and not who is the owner of the shares. . . . the business policy of the German company . . . [must be] in complete harmony with the German national interests, and it is the business of the men at the head of the German undertaking to see to that. Of course, if the company's interests are not so defended, either because the parties concerned grow weary under the weight of those difficulties, . . . [or] perhaps because at heart they themselves share the adversarial point of view . . . the company will suffer."[131]

Watson was willing to cooperate—as he had done since the first days of the Third Reich. But why was it necessary to give up majority ownership? Majority ownership was something a man like Watson could not bear to relinquish. But everything seemed to rest on that very fulcrum: IBM becoming a minority owner of its own enterprise.

Only if IBM reduced its ownership to less than 50 percent would the contemplated competition be suppressed and Watson's profits be protected. Yet the guarantees, all oral, seemed too vague for IBM to trust. Chauncey wrote Watson, "Dr. Veesenmayer . . . stated that he was not in a position to give me any written statement," and added that "the transaction must be approved by the [German] government and that would be all the guarantee we needed." Chauncey also reported his conversation with a director of the Deutsche Bank, Dr. Kimlich, who concurred with Veesenmayer. "Dr. Kimlich stated that his organization [Deutsche Bank] would take care of any competition, . . . [a] statement he would not amplify, but only repeated."[132]

Reducing ownership to a minority bothered Chauncey's sense of profit as well. "IBM will have reduced its interest in the German company to less than 50 percent," he complained to New York, "and its share of the future profits proportionately."[133] IBM wanted both—to remain a commercial part of the Nazi domination in Europe and keep all the profits.

Only Watson could decide. Chauncey confirmed to Watson and the other senior executives in New York that he had promised Veesenmayer that he would fly back to America and brief company officials. Then he would immediately fly back to Berlin and personally deliver to Veesenmayer IBM's answer.[134]

Veesenmayer would now play a special role both with IBM and the Third Reich's war against the Jews. As statistics and human sorting continued in the drama of Jewish destruction, the two would intertwine. Chauncey's chaotic consultations with Veesenmayer and others about the future of IBM in Europe would keep the young attorney in Berlin and Geneva until late March 1941.[135]

Just days after Chauncey finally departed for New York, Veesenmayer would travel to Yugoslavia to oversee the Reich's affairs with the Ustashi. By early April, Veesenmayer was arranging with Croat leaders and the Ustashi "an exact plan for the assumption of power."[136]

But Veesenmayer ultimately emerged as much more than just Hitler's

envoy to communal destruction. He would soon become a technical sched-
uler of actual genocide.

One of the earliest episodes occurred in fall 1941. Germany's Minister
to Yugoslavia, Fritz Benzler, asked for an expert to handle difficulties with
the Jewish situation. The Foreign Office sent Veesenmayer. On September 8,
Veesenmayer and Benzler proposed that 8,000 Jews in Serbia be deported
down the Danube on barges into Romania for further action. Berlin did not
answer quickly enough, so forty-eight hours later Veesenmayer and his colleague sent a follow-up dispatch: "Quick and draconian settlement of the
Serbian Jewish question is most urgent. . . . Request authorization from the
Foreign Minister to place maximum pressure on the Serbian military commander. No opposition is to be expected from the Serb government."[137]

Soon, the question was routed to Adolf Eichmann, the Reich's expert
for Jewish affairs. The reply: "Eichmann proposes shooting." By September
28, the German general commander in the area wanted all 8,000 rounded up
for "immediate elimination." In early October 1941, German army commanders in conjunction with Serb mayors and police began picking up Jews
from cities and towns in a lightning *Aktion,* or Action. Victims were driven
and then marched to an open pit in a remote location, and there ordered to
kneel over the trench. German soldiers at ten paces would fire rifles at their
head and chest. Line by line, thousands of murdered Jews slumped into the
earth.[138]

Days later, the Foreign Office rebuked Benzler and Veesenmayer for
becoming too involved in the technical and military aspects. They were
reminded to confine themselves to such matters as simply arranging transportation.[139]

Later, in July 1943, Foreign Minister von Ribbentrop wanted President
Tiso of Slovakia to accelerate the "cleanup" of the Jewish question there. The
Slovakians were reluctant because the war was not going well for Germany
and Slovakian leaders could no longer plead ignorance of the genocide. In
December 1943, Veesenmayer was again sent to Bratislava. In one meeting
with Eichmann's expert Dieter Wisliceny, Veesenmayer angrily reviewed
Eichmann's detailed statistical reports of Slovakian Jews both by ancestry
and religious belief. Veesenmayer was impatient for action. He vowed to talk
"bluntly" with President Tiso. After their talks, Tiso agreed to transport the
remaining 16,000 to 18,000 unconverted Jews to concentration camps—no
exceptions permitted. Shortly thereafter, 10,000 baptized Jews were added
to the rolls.[140]

In spring 1944, after a stint at *der Führer*'s headquarters, Veesenmayer would be sent East again, this time as Minister to Hungary. His instructions were to form a new puppet government in Budapest and organize the Hungarian railroads.[141]

Veesenmayer was for the first time completely in charge of German operations in a puppet nation. In Budapest, he formed a close alliance with Eichmann and together they orchestrated the systematic destruction of Hungarian Jewry. According to Veesenmayer's 1941 census statistics, 724,307 Jews lived in Hungary. Another 62,000 were considered Jewish by blood. But Hungarian leaders, although rabidly anti-Semitic, were reluctant to continue their on-again off-again persecution of the Jews. The Allies had already announced that there would be war crime tribunals for genocide. Warnings conveyed by neutral leaders and the Vatican were coming in continuously. Russian troops were steadily advancing from the East. The Hungarians were openly worried.[142]

But Veesenmayer, with Eichmann at his side, hammered out a domestic power-sharing agreement with those Hungarian leaders that would ignore the Allies and cooperate with Hitler's mandate. To ensure close supervision, he installed his own expert in the Hungarian Office of Jewish Affairs to monitor a torrent of anti-Semitic decrees. Veesenmayer described the progress as one of "unusual rapidity under local conditions."[143]

A few weeks later, with confiscation and ghettoization nearly complete, the deportations began. Veesenmayer divided Hungary into five zones, plus Budapest. But Zone 1, the Carpathians, required a full seven weeks to empty because not enough trains were available. On April 20, 1944, Veesenmayer complained to the Foreign Office that he was unable to locate enough freight cars for his task. But by the end of April, two trains were arranged. Each carried 4,000 Jews from the Kistarcsa internment camp. Destination: Auschwitz.[144]

Veesenmayer would learn to locate freight cars and schedule them in and out of Hungary like clockwork. As efficiency increased, only ten days would be needed per zone. After the zones were emptied in late June, 437,402 Jews were gone. But then a struggle ensued as to whether Budapest's Jews would be deported to their death as well. Hungarian leaders hated Jews but feared war crimes trials more. Veesenmayer did not care how close the Russians were. A stalemate developed with Hungarian Chief of State Admiral Miklos Horthy. Eichmann sent one train filled with Budapest Jews to a death camp only to have Horthy order it stopped at the border and sent back.[145]

Horthy eventually dismissed the puppet leaders Veesenmayer had installed and ordered their arrest. Veesenmayer protested bitterly and complained to Berlin. Von Ribbentrop telegraphed a warning: "The *Führer* expects that the measures against the Budapest Jews will now be taken without any further delay by the Hungarian government . . . no delay of any kind in the execution of the general measures against Jews [will be permitted]."[146]

Veesenmayer then warned Horthy that two additional *Wehrmacht* armored units would soon be sent to Hungary. Horthy still refused to cooperate. Eventually, Veesenmayer ordered Horthy's son kidnapped. Bundled into a blanket, the son was driven to an airfield and flown to Mauthausen concentration camp in Austria. Veesenmayer threatened to have the younger Horthy shot if Hungary did not comply.[147]

Compromises, broken and amended, were made with Hungarian leaders. Eventually, Hungary agreed to deport 50,000 Jews to Austria and, the remainder of Budapest Jewry were sent to concentration camps. Beginning on October 20, 1944, thousands of terrified, weeping Jews were pulled from their apartments and homes in all-day operations. There weren't enough freight cars. So within days, the 27,000 assembled Jews were sent on a death march to the Austrian border. Lines of marching Jews stretched out from Budapest, miles and miles long, girded by a parallel of corpses heaped along the road. Veesenmayer reported that 2,000 to 4,000 were being added daily. Many thousands died en route from the exhaustion, exposure, and starvation. They were in fact marched to death.[148]

During the war years, IBM supplied elaborate Hollerith systems to nearly all the railways of Nazi-dominated Europe.[149] Knowing how many freight cars and locomotives to schedule on any given day in any given location, anywhere across the map of Europe, required the computational capabilities of Hollerith.[150] Punch card systems identified the exact location of each freight car, how much cargo it could accept, and what schedule it could adhere to for maximum efficiency.[151] In fact, the main method of tracking freight cars was a network of Hollerith systems installed at railroad junctions across Europe.[152] Using IBM equipment, freight car locations were updated every forty-eight hours. Without it, the location of rolling stock would generally be more than two weeks out of date and useless in a wartime setting.[153] In 1938 alone, more than 200 million punch cards were printed for European railroads.[154] In Nazi Poland, the railroads, which constituted some 95 percent of the IBM subsidiary's business, were accustomed to using more than 21 million cards annually.[155] In Nazi-allied Romania, the railroads used a large installation of machines in the Ministry of Communications.[156]

In Yugoslavia, where Veesenmayer worked with the Ustashi, the railroads used Ministry of Commerce machines in Belgrade.[157] In Hungary, where Veesenmayer and Eichmann coordinated continuously with the railroads, the machines were Holleriths.[158] Standardized forms on daily reports registered every detail of train operation from passenger load per car and fuel consumed per train, to locomotive efficiency and which government department would be billed for the freight.[159] Hollerith made the trains run on time in Nazi Europe. These were the trains Veesenmayer and his cohorts relied upon.

During all the genocide years, 1942–1945, the Dehomag that Watson fought to protect did remain intact. Ultimately, it was governed by a special Reich advisory committee representing the highest echelons of the Nazi hierarchy. The Dehomag advisory committee replaced the traditional corporate board of directors. As with any board, the committee's duty was to advise senior management, approve and veto special projects, and mandate priorities. The day-to-day decisions were left to managers to execute. When needed, it coordinated with IBM Geneva or its representatives in other subsidiaries. Four men sat on the advisory board. One was a trustee. Second was Passow, chief of the *Maschinelles Berichtwesen*. Third was Heidinger. Fourth was Adolf Hitler's personal representative.[160]

Hitler's representative on Dehomag's advisory committee was Dr. Edmund Veesenmayer.[161]

PART **THREE**

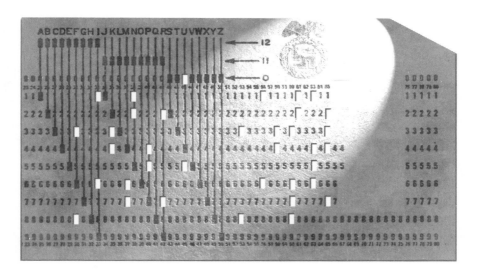

I
II
III
IV
V
VI
VII
VIII
IX
X
XI
XII
XIII
XIV
XV

THE STRUGGLE TO STAY IN THE AXIS

DURING THE WINTER OF 1940–1941, AS CHAUNCEY NEGOTIATED
with Nazis in Germany, war enveloped Europe. While Watson and
IBM executives were fighting daily to retain their commercial primacy in the Axis conquest machine, millions of Jews
were fighting to stay alive in a continent overrun with highly organized, intensely automated Nazi forces and their surrogates. Newspaper articles, dramatic photos, and newsreels continued to tell the
tragic, even if by now familiar, story of Jewish destruction.

November 9, 1940, *New York Times*, "Reich Jews Sent to South
France; 10,000 Reported Put Into Camps." *At Camp de Gurs, the refugees, it was said, were forced to live in small wooden barracks without
enough water and practically no food supply.*[1]

November 26, 1940, *New York Times*, "Walls Will Enclose Warsaw Jews Today; 500,000 Begin 'New Life' in Nazi-Built Ghetto." *By
German decree, all Jews in Warsaw have been required to take up residence in the ghetto . . . with as many as seven persons living in one room
in some buildings. The wall—unusual in modern times, surrounds 100
or more city blocks and closes off 200 streets and even street car lines.*[2]

December 5, 1940, *New York Times*, "Rumania Emerges From
'Revolution'; Death Toll Nearly 400, Wounded Exceed 300—Terror
Reign Lasted for Eight Days." *Moldavian Iron Guard "Purists" launched
a pogrom of large proportions. Jews were kidnapped, beaten and killed at*

Galati and Turnu Severinu, Giurgiu and Craieva. . . . In daytime raids, Iron Guards confiscated Jewish shops in Brasov, Timisoara and Ploesti.[3]

December 5, 1940, *New York Times,* "Cholera Killing Men in Concentration Camps in France." *Refugees transferred from one camp to another . . . were locked into cattle cars without food, water or sanitary equipment for as long as four days at a time . . . nearly all of the 15,000 inmates were stricken with cholera and approximately 500 died. "There were no shovels to dig graves with and no coffins to bury the bodies in," [an imprisoned doctor said]. "We dug shallow graves with our hands and cremated those we could."*[4]

December 17, 1940, *New York Times,* "Property of Jews in Alsace Is Confiscated." *The property of Jews is confiscated and will be distributed either gratis or at low prices. . . . The finer furnishings . . . have been sent to Germany by the trainload.*[5]

January 14, 1941, *New York Times,* "Netherland Jews Must Register." *All Jews must register within six weeks, under a decree issued today by the German Commissioner for the Netherlands.*[6]

January 25, 1941, *New York Times,* "300 Jews Reported Slain." *Some of the more extreme elements of the insurgent Iron Guard in Bucharest implemented the threat to oust the Jews . . . by killing an estimated 300 Jews [that] they had herded into cellars and then turned machine guns on.*[7]

January 26, 1941, *New York Times,* "Misery and Death in French Camps." *In some of the camps, . . . an "unbreathable atmosphere of human hopelessness" was reported, with "an intense desire to die" attributed to most of the older refugees. . . . [A Gurs camp source reported] "They will not fight any more; apathetic, they lie on their straw mattresses, often refusing food and waiting for the end."*[8]

Despite all the atrocity stories being broadcast, Watson was waging his own struggle. His was an undying determination to retain IBM's favored dominance in the Third Reich's commercial-industrial complex. The struggle was not going well.

In the first week of January 1941, German Finance Ministry officials ruled that IBM's settlement with Heidinger, worth almost $900,000, could not be transacted using the company's blocked Reichsmarks. In frustration, Chauncey sent word to New York that he would "have to begin all over again." One of the main government objections was the continuing existence of IBM's so-called royalty program, which was considered a sham to extract profits from Germany in the form of fake expenses. Why else, critics complained, did IBM's own subsidiary pay the parent company royalties?[9]

At the same time, Party circles continued to demand IBM shed its majority ownership. IBM executives began to wonder if they might sell some shares to the Hitler government itself, going into a direct partnership with the Reich, "provided, simultaneously, official formal recognition by the government . . . [of] the validity and binding nature of the royalty agreement." On January 24, 1941, a Nazi official at the Deutsche Bank met with Chauncey and repeated the assertion that if IBM ceded the majority, "we will take care of any new competition." New York did not mind making a token transfer to some German nationals, but Watson still hoped he would not be forced to reduce IBM's ownership to a minority.[10]

By the very end of January, a tired Chauncey was hoping to return to Manhattan to make his confidential report in the security of IBM headquarters. Once he obtained the board's decision, he would fly back to Berlin and again confer with Veesenmayer as promised. By now, Chauncey had learned when speaking over the phone to refer to Veesenmayer obliquely as "that official" or "an official." Chauncey went to Geneva and phoned New York for his next instructions. The conversation, as usual, was conducted in code and studded with cryptic allusions.[11]

JANUARY 31, 1941, 4:45 P.M.
Chauncey at IBM Geneva
John G. Phillips and Charles R. Ogsbury at IBM NY

PHILLIPS: Hello, Harry, this is Phillips. . . .

CHAUNCEY: Yes. There are two courses open to me at the moment. I shall send you a report of the big question [retaining the majority], which I cannot even here send to you completely in all respects, over the telephone or written. . . . Or I could come back to the United States and give you a written report. . . . [But] then I [must] return to Germany at the request of "an official."

PHILLIPS: You cannot define that any more?

CHAUNCEY: No, but you can understand. Because of the time that may be involved, I promised "that official" that I would go back to America with some degree of haste and return as soon as possible.

PHILLIPS: Does it need you, Harry, to complete it?

CHAUNCEY: He asked me to do that, notwithstanding the fact that I had left with our lawyer a power [of attorney] to complete whatever we may decide to do, because that man—our man [attorney Albert]—will have to go into discussions. . . . I am [now] going to read to you from a part of a letter from "our best friend," which has been mailed to Mr. Watson. Quote: "The introduction of influential industrial interests as new shareholders would inure to the benefit of both IBM and Dehomag. Dissatisfaction has evidently found expression in criticism of the price, and other policies—and in the demands for the creation of competition, if necessary, by Governmental initiative or at least with official support." End quote.[12]

Turning to the threat of a Reich cartel effort that might merge French Bull and Dehomag, Chauncey suggested he try to stem the plan at once.

CHAUNCEY: The transfer of the interest recently acquired in the French German Company [the planned German cartel] was offered for the majority holding in Dehomag . . . which, of course, would not be to our advantage. You see that? I am going to attempt to get in touch with our French people.

PHILLIPS: I have a question here on that. You are going to attempt to get in touch with our French People. Now Mr. Ogsbury has made some notes here with Mr. Schotte as to [three] things you might want to think about: The Bull suit. The general Bull situation. And any conversations between [IBM French subsidiary director Roger] Virgile and Germany in connection with a merger and buying.

OGSBURY: Harry, what will you do? Will you try to see Virgile in Paris or have him go over there?

CHAUNCEY: I know he will have to come into unoccupied parts [Vichy France]. They [Nazi authorities] would not let us go to Paris.

OGSBURY: There has apparently been some negotiations between Virgile and Dehomag with respect to the manufacture of parts and certain machines. I think you will find all that correspondence with Taylor. I think you ought to get acquainted with it and see who is sponsoring that. It looks as though the French Company [IBM's subsidiary in Paris] is sponsoring it, and it certainly is being done without the consent over here. See what I mean? That ought to be looked into. . . . None of these things do we concur in. . . . How long will you be there?

CHAUNCEY: I am perfectly willing to stay here. While I want to be in New York, I am perfectly willing to stay here. The thing is that you cannot understand what it is [like] here [in Europe].

OGSBURY: The thing is that if you should return [to New York], these other matters can all wait. You see what I mean? These things that I am talking to you about are only in the event that they are the practical thing for you to do, in view of how long you have to remain there.

CHAUNCEY: I will have to be here [in Geneva] two or three weeks before I can get through to Lisbon and get visas, etc. . . . I am going to write you a report as soon as I can. . . . I have sent word to Virgile. It may be necessary for us to go to Italy. I think I should make that connection down there. I think I better find out what it is all about.

OGSBURY: That will be all right, if it isn't going to interfere with the other things you ought to do.

PHILLIPS: Harry, the thing that worries me this afternoon is this. Both Mr. Watson and Mr. Nichol are home with colds. . . . One or the other or both will probably be back on Monday, and we cannot do anything over the weekend anyway. And we will cable you and talk with you again on Monday. How is that? . . .

CHAUNCEY: I am going over with Taylor everything that is open.

PHILLIPS: Harry, can you answer this question? Do you consider that you should return and then go back?

CHAUNCEY: I have given my promise that I shall return to "this official."[13]

DURING IBM'S day-to-day struggle to stay in the Axis during wartime, the firm relied on the cooperation of the State Department to act as postman. Every message relayed through an American Embassy or Legation was not just blindly passed on. Multiple copies were made for senior staff in Washington. Periodically, Watson sent letters of gratitude for the on-going help. For example, on January 8, 1941, Watson mailed Paul T. Culbertson, European Affairs division assistant chief: "I wish to thank you for the courtesy you extended our company in connection with the transfer of a letter to me from Mr. Harrison K. Chauncey, representative of our company, who is temporarily in Berlin. The promptness in which this matter was handled has been a real help to us and all of the officers of our company join me in expressing our appreciation to you."[14]

The Department's desire to secretly advance the commercial causes of IBM persevered in spite of the nation's officially stated opposition to the Hitler menace. For this reason, it was vital to Watson that nothing be done to embarrass or even annoy the Department publicly. This caution was only heightened by an on-going FBI investigation into IBM's operation as a potential hotbed of Nazi sympathizers. Avoiding embarrassing moments was difficult given the far-flung global empire of IBMers so deeply involved with Fascist and Axis countries, and accustomed to speaking supportively of their clients' military endeavors.

Walter G. Ross, affectionately known as "Capt. Ross," was one of IBM's most adventurous and freewheeling European agents stationed on the Continent, triumphantly concluding important deals for the company. He was once described by IBM as "one of the colorful ones," whose "zeal and dedication . . . [and] exploits" would be recounted for decades. Capt. Ross was primarily assigned to Fascist Spain, where he concentrated on the Spanish Railways. In 1940, the popular Ross was ready to retire. He would leave behind a newly organized IBM subsidiary in Spain and would continue on as a special advisor. When he came back to the United States in August 1940, the flamboyant salesman made some comments to a local newspaper, the *Brooklyn Eagle.*[15] Those comments caused a furor.

In his candid remarks, Ross predicted that England would be forced into an armistice within two weeks, thereby abandoning Europe. Moreover, he openly revealed his approval of and cooperation with the Hitler regime. "He [Ross] . . . has first-hand knowledge, having lived in the same building as the German Minister . . . On reaching these shores, the Captain was 'simply terrified and appalled' by the ultra-frank outbursts of American officials against Hitler and Mussolini, which, he opines, were in the manner of 'spindly boys tweaking the neighborhood bullies' noses.' . . . 'I am an American,' he sums up, 'but I say that before you start calling names be sure you're prepared: This country thinks it's going to spend a lot of money and make soldiers overnight. You can't do it. Germany worked at it for five years' . . . The Germans, he contends, had better trained soldiers, superior equipment and streamlined generals." Ross also declared he had conceived a plan in which Watson could use his channels to funnel money to destitute civilians in Europe.[16]

The seemingly inconsequential article did not escape the attention of those in Washington on the lookout for Nazi sympathizers. Assistant Secretary of State Adolf Berle sent a clipping to J. Edgar Hoover at the FBI declaring, "the remarks . . . follow the same pattern used in all German propaganda." Copies of the article made the rounds at the State Department and IBM. Quickly, Watson learned of the embarrassment. In an example of how Watson, if so moved, could act with swift corporate wrath to protect the company's interest, Watson immediately turned on Ross. In an instant, Ross' decades of colorful accomplishments for IBM were forgotten. He was summarily cut off.[17]

On September 6, 1940, Watson wrote Ross a humiliating termination letter. "I have before me a clipping from the *Brooklyn Eagle* of August 28, 1940, in which you pretend to speak as a representative of our Company," Watson began. "You were our agent working on a commission basis in Spain for several years, until we arranged with you in Paris, in August 1939, for your retirement. . . .

"You used my name in connection with a plan which you state you have of sending monetary aid to refugees and destitute civilians in France, in which you say I am willing to cooperate. I have never discussed any such matter with you, and I am not interested in any plan you have in mind. I am already extending my cooperation through other channels approved by our Government.

"You have no right to involve our Company, my name, or any of the Company representatives in any statements. Furthermore, you made statements in regard to the countries at war, and criticized our country's policies, for which you must accept sole responsibilities as an individual. I demand that you inform the *Brooklyn Eagle* that the statement attributed to you was an expression of your own opinion and not made as a representative of International Business Machines Corporation, any of its officers or members of the organization; and that your statement was made without the knowledge or consent of anyone connected with our Company. . . .

"This matter is so serious from the standpoint of our Company that it is necessary to advise you that effective immediately we must sever all relations between us. We had discussed the possibility of making use of you in some other capacity in our business, but the statement you made in the article referred to makes it impossible for us to do so. I am attaching to this letter the regular cancellation notice of your contract."[18]

On September 6, 1940, Ross indeed wrote the editor of the *Brooklyn Eagle* a stultifying retraction that sounded as though it had been typed in Watson's office. The typewriter seemed to be the same as the one used for Watson's letter, and the typist's identifying initials, "LH," were at the bottom of both letters. Moreover, Ross' retraction used the nearly identical first sentence as Watson's letter of the same day. "I have before me a clipping from the *Brooklyn Daily Eagle* of August 28, 1940," Ross' retraction stated, "which purports to be an interview with one of your reporters at your office. I wish to correct an erroneous impression which this article has given to the public. In the first place, I am not a representative of the International Business Machines Corporation . . . and was only acting in an advisory capacity in Spain. For this reason, the name of the International Business Machines Corporation, and that of Mr. Watson, should not have appeared in your article. What I said to your reporter was my own personal opinion, and I did not speak on behalf of the International Business Machines Corporation, or any of its officers. I wish you would do me the favor of publishing this letter in your paper at your earliest convenience."[19]

That same September 6, Watson personally dispatched copies of Ross' termination and his retraction to a number of senior State Department officials, including Secretary of State Cordell Hull.[20] When the dust had settled on the brief but turbulent Ross episode, Watson had proved once again that when he wanted to control the people in his organization, he could be mercilessly blunt and ruthless.

In other instances, some IBMers pushed the State Department's diplomatic pouch to the limits of propriety. It was one thing to help an American company protect its investment in Germany, but using diplomatic channels to deepen IBM's Nazi relationships in occupied countries sometimes made the Department recoil. On October 2, 1940, IBM's man in occupied Denmark, Max Bodenhoff, sent Watson a letter through the American Legation suggesting the company hire a personal friend of German Foreign Minister von Ribbentrop as a special business agent to further the subsidiary's work with the Nazis there. America's interim chargé in Copenhagen, Mahlon F. Perkins, was dubious about transmitting such a letter through official channels.[21]

"Max Bodenhoff . . . represents Mr. Watson's organization in Copenhagen," wrote the rankled chargé in a complaint sent in triplicate to Washington. "This letter is not transmitted in the manner prescribed by Diplomatic Serials 3267 and 3268 of August 9, 1940, since it is considered that the Department should decide upon the propriety of transmitting it. It will be noted that Mr. Bodenhoff suggests to Mr. Watson the employment of Dr. Orla Arntzen, who is a close friend of the German Foreign Minister, to act as a special representative of the International Business Machines Corporation. This procedure would appear to involve questions of policy and ethics which the Department may desire to consider."[22]

Perkins' objection was reviewed by no fewer than eight officials. All concurred that his judgment should be vindicated by sending Bodenhoff's letter back to Copenhagen with the declaration: "The Department does not believe it would be advisable to transmit the letter mentioned and it is accordingly returned to the Legation."[23]

At one point, a State Department officer notified IBM NY: "The Department understands that commercial telegraphic facilities are available between the United States and Germany. Should you experience difficulty in communicating . . . the Department will be pleased to consider the transmission . . . through official channels at your expense provided you supply the full names of the persons or firms abroad whose interests are affected thereby, and inform the Department as to the nature of those interests, and whether such persons or firms have American nationality. I believe you will readily appreciate that the Department, especially in these extraordinary times, must reserve its facilities for the service of legitimate American interests."[24]

Despite the occasional realization that the State Department was becoming an all too indispensable player in the proliferation and protection of

IBM's lucrative relations with the Nazis in Europe, its role would soon exceed the realm of postman. Soon, diplomats in Berlin would become IBM's special operatives in saving the company's niche in the Nazi Axis.

CHAUNCEY RETURNED to Berlin to renew his excruciating negotiations with Heidinger. Ironically, as the United States edged closer to entering the war, Heidinger believed his options were becoming more limited. In the strange praxis of German law, once Dehomag became enemy property, the subsidiary would be seized by a receiver and all ownership frozen. In such a case, Heidinger's hope to cash out would also be frozen. If competition supplanted IBM, his stock holdings could soon become worthless.

By early March 1941, Heidinger agreed to a new settlement—RM 2.2 million in exchange for giving up his preferential stockholder status. He would still own his shares, and those shares could still be sold only to IBM upon his departure from the company—but the price would be the book value.[25]

Reich economic bureaucrats approved because the transaction wasn't as much a sale as a reduction in status—and Heidinger was handsomely compensated for his various overdue bonuses.[26]

But Veesenmayer was still insistent that IBM relinquish its majority or face a newly created cartel. And now the cartel had a name: Wanderer-Werke. The old-line German motorcycle and toolmaker, Wanderer-Werke, was being primed by the Reich to host a merger of French Bull and Powers interests, allowing a new punch card enterprise to be forged. The Powers companies were now controlled by Hermann Goering Works under an overlapping board of directors. By now, Germany had realized that neither of the marginal firms, Bull or Powers, possessed the necessary production capacity. A completely new German-owned factory would be needed. Bull schematics and blueprints had already been brought to Berlin to launch a new machine series in case IBM would not yield. Germany could not afford an immediate separation from the IBM empire. But if Watson would not comply voluntarily, a steady combination of tactics from preferential business contracts for Wanderer-Werke to mandatory price reductions at Dehomag would compel an eventual sell-out. This approach is what Veesenmayer considered "no pressure."[27]

Opinions flagged from day to day on whether the Reich could proceed without IBM. Even with a crash program to build new machines, it would take months before the first machine would roll off assembly lines. Without a source for punch cards, it would be like producing guns without bullets. Understandably, Veesenmayer's pressure was carefully applied. If IBM withdrew and suddenly stopped servicing the Reich, Nazi automation would soon rattle to a halt.

"We are threatened with possible elimination of Dehomag through competition," Chauncey reported to New York on March 10, 1941, "which may be sponsored by the authorities. We are also threatened with attack on the royalty agreement; and further threatened with a substantial reduction in prices if we do not give up the majority."[28]

Chauncey could only repeat, "Dr. Veesenmayer . . . stated that no pressure [would] be brought to bear to surrender the majority but that it was advisable to do so. He told me all that was wanted was a friendly agreement. . . . I asked Dr. Veesenmayer for some assurance of protection for our minority in the event we relinquished the majority. He replied . . . there could not be any writing of assurance."[29]

There was no pretense that Dehomag's management was still a group of independent-minded employees or executives. They were openly pawns of the Nazi Party. "Mr. Heidinger and several other members of the board are Nazi members," stressed Chauncey. "As nearly as I can learn, they have to follow any order issued by the Nazi Party."[30]

But a rebellious Chauncey still clung to his revulsion over what he called "blackmail threats." Giving up the majority would not protect the company's investment, he argued. "Upon giving up the majority," he asserted, "we can obtain no assurance that the next attack would not be against the [remaining IBM] minority and even against the payment of royalties." Chauncey had termed the German unhappiness as mere "growling." It was easy to talk about starting a new cartel. The reality was unchanged: "The government at the present time needs our machines. The army is using them presently for every conceivable purpose."[31]

So while IBM came to believe they could not be dislodged from the Axis, they did fear the diminishment of profit that any attempted competition, howsoever tenuous or distant, might pose. The man who would not even tolerate competition from used cash registers would now only intensify his effort to block competition from diluting IBM profits. Ironically, the diligence of IBM auditors to certify and report that profit never paused during the entire Dehomag Revolt. Even as Watson expended maximum resources to protect his monopoly, the accountants were busy double-checking every penny.

Every Dehomag invoice to every client for every machine and punch card was reviewed by IBM Geneva for correctness and then verified by financial supervisors in New York. This fiscal procedure applied to both

Dehomag's billing within Germany and in the conquered nations and territories of Nazi Europe.[32]

For example, Dehomag generated four small invoices in spring 1940. Invoice #04/26469 billed March 13, 1940; invoices #04/28499 and #04/28500 both billed May 21; and invoice #04/28612 billed May 27, 1940. These invoices were missing from Dehomag's periodic submissions. To track them, New York accountants made a written request to Geneva on December 23, 1940. Taylor in Geneva issued a detailed two-page single-spaced item-by-item response on February 14, 1941, with a simultaneous written request to Dehomag in Berlin to resubmit the invoices in duplicate. On February 26, 1941, Dehomag accountants sent a letter in German to Geneva confirming that a new reconciliation statement would be sent out; a translation into English was forwarded to New York. The four invoices were ultimately tracked: one was for $525.60, a second was for $46.77, a third was for $23.44, and the fourth was for $1.52.[33] At IBM, every penny counted.

But on March 12, 1941, Germany's cracking wartime economy put an even greater strain on the flow of money from Dehomag. Reich Economics Minister Walther Funk warned at the annual *Reichsbank* stockholders luncheon that "drastic restrictions" on corporate profits would soon be announced. Dividends in excess of 6 percent would be subjected to "prohibitive taxation." The only way to correct reduced profits was a voluntary increase in capitalization permissible during a brief investment window; 6 percent of the higher capital investment would of course yield greater profit sums. In other words, only those who further invested in the German economy could continue to reap significant profits. Funk's words sent off alarm bells throughout IBM.[34]

More bells sounded when, in late May 1941, IBM realized that Dehomag was cutting prices to support the German war effort without IBM's permission.

MEMORANDUM TO THOMAS J. WATSON
From: J. C. Milner
Subject: German Rental Prices
May 23, 1941

We have heard from the Geneva office that the German Company have reduced their rental prices to customers by approximately ten percent. This will naturally mean that our royalties will be affected in the same proportion. Although we have no recent figures from Germany, we would estimate that the ten percent reduction would mean a reduction of approximately 1,500,000 Reichsmarks in the gross annual rentals of the German Company.[35]

On June 12, 1941, the Reich issued its profit-restricting regulations. Those profit limits affected not only IBM, but profit bonuses for Heidinger, Rottke, and Hummel as well. The German managers knew that if IBM did not increase its investment, bonuses would not be possible. A loophole in German law, however, allowed the board of directors—with or without majority approval—to reinvest its funds in the company. Dehomag had accrued millions of blocked Reichsmarks in undistributed profits waiting to be allocated. The Nazi board could vote to reinvest that money, thus increasing the stock of the company. More stock meant more shares. Under German law, when a company increased its shares with new investment, the new shares were allocated in the identical proportions as the existing ownership. In other words, the percentages would remain the same—just everyone would own more—as in any stock split. These new shares would be distributed without taxes.[36]

Heidinger and company decided they would rush a vote through to double the capital of the company, from about RM 7.7 million to about RM 15 million, using IBM's blocked profits. They would force a vote with or without IBM precisely because the law allowed directors to vote reinvestment without shareholder consent.[37]

Much more was at stake for IBM than just reinvesting its profits into the Dehomag. Up until now, although IBM retained about 85 percent of the shares, the 15 percent owned by Heidinger, Rottke, and Hummel were restricted shares. Unlike most stock holdings, Dehomag shares could not be routinely sold, collateralized, or transferred like ordinary shares in any company. The shares were owned only so long as the three managers remained with the company and could not be sold to anyone other than IBM. Moreover, each man had obtained the shares not by an ordinary purchase but through a large paper loan from IBM that was canceled when the loans were "given back." In essence, the three German managers owned captive stock that Watson controlled.[38]

If Dehomag's total stock doubled to RM 15 million, the new shares would be distributed 85 percent to IBM and 15 percent to the Germans—with one extraordinary difference. Fifteen percent of the new shares would proportionately flow to the three Germans automatically. Restrictive covenants would not apply to the new shares. Heidinger, Rottke, and Hummel could sell or trade their shares to anyone, including the new cartel. And the shares would be distributed free—no loans, no payments.[39]

Matters began coming to a head when the Dehomag requested that an additional profit should be declared so bonuses could be paid. IBM took a hard line. On August 27, 1941, Schotte, who was now permanently headquartered in New York, cabled Geneva: "Re: Dehomag. No dividends to be declared." IBM Europe Manager W. C. Lier was about to dictate a letter to Dehomag advising as much when distressing correspondence arrived from Albert in Berlin. Albert warned that the German board's true intentions were not just to declare profits, but to double the stock from blocked funds and distribute shares before any restrictive covenants could be imposed.[40]

Lier shelved his letter to Dehomag. Instead he cabled IBM NY: "Albert confidentially advises: Dehomag preparing another meeting which may decide without IBM represented. According Albert, Dehomag planning increase capital to such extent as to get [shares] out of IBM control. . . . Kiep not sufficient since can be outvoted."[41]

All understood that IBM would be compelled to vote in favor of—or more precisely, authorize—the stock split. There were so many reasons. First, it was the only way to extract a hefty 12 percent dividend from revenues and circumvent the Reich's new profit restriction. New York wanted that. Moreover, Albert knew IBM could not control the numerical vote of the board. The vote to split would prevail in any event. But New York could not allow a vote to be taken without IBM's consent or involvement—even if that consent was pressured or begrudged. Such a precedent would lead to unending business decisions without IBM's involvement. First it would be Dehomag. Then Dehomag would maneuver the other European subsidiaries. Watson would not permit it.[42]

Most of all, if IBM voted against reinvestment in Germany at this crucial stage in the negotiations with the Nazi Party it would only reinforce the perception that Watson was unfriendly to the Third Reich.

Albert urged IBM to be represented at the meeting, which seemed to be planned for mid-September, and unequivocally vote its majority in favor of the stock split. If nothing else, IBM could cooperate in the stock split on the condition that the new shares distributed to Germans were brought under the same restrictive agreements as the prior shares. However, to appear for IBM, Albert needed a proxy. Chauncey had foreseen such an emergency before he left Germany in the spring. He left a formal proxy in the custody of a third party, a secret source he could trust to follow his explicit instructions— a source in Berlin, one who was beyond the reach of the Nazis.[43]

Albert physically needed the sequestered proxy in hand so he could display it at the board meeting. August 29, late in the day, Lier cabled NY: "Albert stating third party holding IBM proxy for him. Desirable proxy handed to him. . . . Albert states imperative he obtain proxy in order [to] protect IBM interests. Suggests you cable third party hand him proxy. Also suggests we cable Dehomag Albert our attorney who should be invited all meetings and participate all Dehomag affairs. Albert urging speedy decision. Please advise."[44]

It was morning in New York when Chauncey received Lier's emergency dispatch from Geneva. He responded before the end of the day, Friday, August 29, instructing his secret source in Berlin. The source did not receive the cable until the next Wednesday, September 3.[45]

SEPTEMBER 3, 1941
Harrison Chauncey
International Business Machines Corporation
590 Madison Ave.
New York

Dear Chauncey:

Your cable of August 29 requesting me to turn over the power of attorney to Dr. Albert has been received and your instructions were carried out this morning when I personally handed him the document in question and gave him your message. He assured me that your instructions would be carried out to the letter. If developments do not move smoothly, there is a possibility that I shall call you on the telephone or write you in detail as Dr. Albert advises. Briefly he stated that Mr. Heidinger was attempting to take advantage of the dividend limitation decree, which was issued since you left Germany, to force the issuance of new stock.

When you left here I thought we would see each other in New York before this time, but as events are moving so slowly I have settled down for the winter. Paul Pearson, whom you will remember, is scheduled for home leave and may be passing through New York next month. There is a possibility that he will bring you a message if developments between now and then justify such action. Please remember me to Mr. Watson and Mr. Nichol, and with all good wishes to you.

Sincerely Yours,
Sam E. Woods
Commercial Attaché
United States Embassy
Berlin[46]

Although five Germans now sat on the Dehomag board, few of them could appear in Berlin for the rush meeting Heidinger planned for September 19—not even Heidinger himself. Heidinger lived in Munich. So did Schulte-Strathaus. Dr. Vogt, Heidinger's brother-in-law, lived in Berlin but was in poor health, and not available on such short notice. Arrangements were made for all three unavailable directors to sign proxies. Each signed on September 16 proxy forms prepared by Hans Mahr, a Dehomag attorney. These proxies empowered either Kiep or Ziegler to vote per specified instructions—to generate a stock split. Kiep was loyal to Watson, but the former German consul in New York was still an official of the German Foreign Ministry. The pressure on him was immense. He would have no choice but to vote as instructed on the proxy by Heidinger and his clique. There was no chance Kiep could cast his personal vote against reinvestment in Germany, so he would have to join with the majority.[47]

Albert was holding IBM's proxy, conveyed by Woods, but no instructions from Watson. The new German law did not *require* profit taking; it only offered corporations a window to double their dividends on the condition that more money was reinvested in the Reich. But IBM would have to vote for the stock split for a host of reasons—that seemed clear. Albert needed a decision—fast. If IBM was isolated by its own board, and voted against German economic support, it would only seal the view that IBM was an enemy of the Hitler regime.

Yet, at a time when America was closer than ever to entering the war, Watson was profoundly uncertain how doubling the investment would be perceived. If it could appear that the investment was somehow compulsory, then IBM could simply explain it was required to comply with the law. Woods could not provide such a statement, since the law was clearly optional. But he was willing to read such a statement from Albert to IBM NY, allowing IBM to transcribe the conversation and in so doing create a record of what appeared to be government coercion. A phone call was arranged.

SEPTEMBER 17, 1941, 10 A.M. NEW YORK TIME

WATSON: Hello, Mr. Woods.

WOODS: Hello, Mr. Watson. I am going to read a message to you from your attorney. This is the message:

"As you know, a special law, enacted June 12, 1941, provides that the dividends of any and all companies organized under German law are from now on restricted to six percent. . . . they can, according to certain detailed descriptions, increase their share capital out of their surplus. This is to be done by the board of directors, not by general [shareholder] meeting.

Dehomag intends to increase their share capital out of surplus by 100 percent—RM 15,400,000—and will then be entitled to declare six percent dividends on the 15,400,000 Marks, which is equivalent to 12 percent on the original 7,700,000. The obvious advantages of this are . . . transfer of surplus . . . without shareholders paying well-known high taxes. . . . This law can practically be considered compulsory. (In other words, it is compulsory that this be done). . . . I strongly recommend you send a cable of approval."

The message was transcribed as coming from Woods and therefore was enveloped in the authority of the commercial attaché.[48]

Joining Watson in the conference call were Nichol and Chauncey. Woods was actually excited to speak to Watson himself. Indeed, Woods immediately had Albert's message typed into a letter to IBM NY, adding, "It was good to hear your voices and I am looking forward eagerly to seeing you when I pass through New York the next time I am at home."[49]

In the conversation with Woods, Watson told the attaché he agreed in principle to the stock split, provided the Germans restricted their new stock as well. But IBM could not yet formally authorize it. Why? General Ruling 11 made it against the law.[50] Complying with General Ruling 11 would take time. Time was something Watson did not have.

As America advanced toward the moment it would enter the war, the Roosevelt Administration had recently espoused General Ruling 11, an emergency regulation forbidding any financial transactions with Nazi Germany without a special Treasury Department license involving written justifications. Even certain corporate instructions of a financial nature were subject to the rule. This was something completely new to contend with in IBM's Nazi alliance. IBM would now be required to seek a complicated, bureaucratic approval for each financial instruction it ordered for its overseas subsidiaries under Nazi control. General Ruling 11 would not affect subsidiaries in neutral countries, such as Sweden or Switzerland. Even still, it would severely hamper all communications with Dehomag itself, and open a government window into many of IBM's complex transactions.[51]

How much time did IBM have?

The board meeting was scheduled in Berlin for late the next day.

New York immediately cabled Woods that it approved Albert's recommendation to double the investment to RM 15.4 million—an increased reinvestment of about $2 million extra. But there was a condition. The new stock issued to the three Germans must be restricted under the existing captive share agreements. That was imperative.[52]

Quickly, IBM people had to complete the two-page sworn affidavit application to authorize the doubling of stock. It needed to be signed by the corporation's secretary-treasurer, John G. Phillips. But he was not available. No time to waste. Someone signed Phillips' name to both lines where it was required, and then dutifully placed their cursive lowercase initials—*aer*— under the signature to show it was affixed by a person designated to sign.[53]

But Phillips' signature had to be executed and certified in the presence of a notary. No problem. Someone found a notary in Queens. He verified the signatures as genuine, stamped his name and commission number just beneath the Phillips signature, and then pressed his embossing seal onto the application. A short transcript of Woods' telephone conversation with Watson was attached to prove the urgency of the transaction. The carefully quoted dialogue fragment included Albert's well-structured explanation that what was really an optional profit-taking regulation "can practically be considered compulsory."[54]

The application clearly stated that it could only be presented at the Federal Reserve Bank in Manhattan. But by the time the application was signed and sealed, it was just too late. The Federal Reserve was closed. Dealing with the phlegmatic Fed would be too slow anyway. Chauncey headed to Washington D.C. He would go over the head of the Fed, right to Treasury itself.[55]

The next morning, September 19, Chauncey appeared at the Treasury Department. The Dehomag board meeting would soon get under way—and IBM would not be there to vote for reinvestment unless the license was issued at once. Clearly agitated and pressured, Chauncey demanded the review officer issue the license to authorize the stock split.[56] When? Right now.

But Mr. Rueffer, the review officer at Treasury, was in no real hurry. He bureaucratically informed Chauncey that such an application would take some time and must first be submitted through proper channels—namely the Federal Reserve Bank in New York. An impatient Chauncey now became riled. This application was too important, it could not wait. He insisted that if the Treasury license was not rendered at once, IBM's German affiliate would take its own action in what was "probably a matter of compulsion."[57]

Rueffer was not fazed.[58] The matter just could not be done quickly. Take it to New York.

Meanwhile, in Berlin, a Dehomag attorney, Hans Mahr, had been called to certify the proper form of the board meeting. The session would be held not at Dehomag's headquarters, where a last-minute cable from New York could be received, but at the Hotel Adlon—Watson's favorite. Kiep and Ziegler would be there to vote their proxies as instructed by Heidinger. The meeting would convene soon—at 5 P.M.[59]

Back in Washington, Chauncey could not wait. He demanded to see Assistant Secretary J. W. Pehle for faster action. That was not possible.[60]

Then could he meet with a senior member of the staff?[61]

One of Mr. Rueffer's supervisors agreed to meet Chauncey. But the reality that the application would have to creep through the slow channels of the Federal Reserve Bank was sinking in. In frustration and futility, Chauncey laid out the financial transaction to the supervisor. Surplus money blocked in Germany, RM 7.7 million, would be reinvested in the company, doubling the capital of Dehomag. He stressed that even though IBM NY would be required to approve the recapitalization, no funds would be transferred from the U.S. In fact, the transaction would still leave an additional surplus of RM 10 million.[62]

Chauncey added that he had just been to Germany, and then his story began to wend into all sorts of permutations. The Treasury supervisor recalled that Chauncey "claims that unless the proposed change is made, the German authorities will make the change themselves . . . German interests will acquire control of the company."[63]

In truth, when the stock split was ratified, the proportion of ownership would remain identical. The three Germans would still own the same 15 percent. The government would not effectuate the split; that was strictly a business decision for Dehomag's board. The Treasury supervisor remained unconvinced. He noted, "His [Chauncey's] explanation of this was somewhat vague and had to do with present German laws about which he was very uncertain."[64]

Chauncey was again told by the supervisor that Rueffer was correct. Under the law, IBM needed to provide a proper detailed explanation of the stock split and file that with the license application at the Federal Reserve Bank. Knowing that time was running out for some sort of instruction to Berlin, Chauncey pressed the supervisor for at least an opinion. Might such a transaction be approved? It was all speculation. The supervisor just could not predict.[65]

But it was "extremely urgent," insisted Chauncey. It didn't matter. Nothing he said that day could make the license happen.[66]

Time was running out. The vote was about to proceed, and Albert needed to authorize the vote. But Watson could not authorize it. Chauncey could not authorize it. No one at IBM NY would authorize it without a Treasury license.

So Sam Woods authorized it. He called Albert and told him to proceed. [67]

Albert informed Dehomag officials that IBM NY was authorizing the stock split and would not challenge the reinvestment. In a brief corporate event, Kiep and Ziegler assembled at Berlin's Hotel Adlon at 5 P.M. Kiep officially opened the meeting and stated the sole agenda item. He and Ziegler verbally agreed in the presence of attorney Mahr, who certified every procedural step of the two men. The stock was split. [68]

Watson must have been furious. For decades, IBM had tiptoed through the serpentine regulations of seventy countries—whether at war, in peace, or anything in between. From Fascist states to revolutionary regimes, the company had always managed to avoid legal infractions of any kind. Now it appeared that General Ruling 11 had been violated. General Ruling 11 was essentially a precursor to Trading with the Enemy regulations. It was more than important. Moreover, Chauncey's name was on the proxy that effected the transaction. Everyone began explaining themselves in carefully worded memos and letters.

Albert wrote to Chauncey on October 9, "It is true that Mr. Watson stated he would send me a cable immediately authorizing such procedure and that I have not received such a cable; on the contrary, I have been informed that this cable . . . could not be sent due to the fact that IBM have not yet received license from Treasury Department. . . . I have not waited . . . but had informed the Dehomag . . . that they were authorized to go ahead." In so doing, Albert added, he was able to show IBM's willingness to cooperate in the German economy. In consequence, "everything had been amicably settled," he continued, which allowed more objectionable decisions by the board to be avoided. "I took the responsibility of approval upon myself." [69]

Understanding that Chauncey might have to answer to the Treasury Department, Albert's apologia went on, "I hope you do not get into difficulties with your [Treasury] Department. They will certainly understand. . . . For obvious reasons, I am not sending any more particulars than are already in IBM's hands." [70]

That same day, October 9, IBM's Werner Lier wrote a formal four-page letter to Watson explaining events. He had gone over the complete file in Albert's office. "I noted therefrom the decision taken by Dr. Albert, upon advice of Mr. Woods, to increase the capital by 100 percent. . . . [But] we wish to remind you in this connection of Mr. Woods' telephone call . . . and from which he deducted [*sic*] your agreement." Lier declared the urgent move was required "to avoid a precedent of Dehomag overstepping the prerogatives of the IBM."[71]

IBM couldn't be sure what to do. Its license application was slowly percolating through the Federal Reserve Bank and the Treasury Department. A series of formal letters and cables began papering the files reflecting official IBM non-authorization. On September 26, a week after the stock was split, IBM cabled Woods at the Embassy: "Regret we have not been able [to] cable you in response your telephone message due to [the] fact that we have not yet received license from Treasury."[72]

The Embassy was surely confused because shortly thereafter it sent back a message for clarification. A week later, Chauncey replied to the Embassy, "Re: your cable of September 29, representative may not act in absence of license . . . and permission requested therefore is denied."[73]

General Ruling 11 would make it impossible for IBM to continue doing business in the freewheeling cross-border fashion it was accustomed to. The company could not wait weeks for every instruction to be approved by the Treasury Department. Indeed, just after Dehomag doubled the capitalization, two of Watson's confidants were to meet with Lier from IBM Geneva, undoubtedly to discuss how to deploy the additional investment. That would only further the appearance of IBM ratification. On September 22, the Embassy cabled Chauncey one of many cryptic messages: "Your two friends wish Swiss representative to meet Dehomag people. Do you agree?"[74]

Chauncey tried to stop Lier from traveling from IBM Geneva to Germany. An immediate cable was sent to the Geneva office. But it was too late. The office replied, "Already en route. Left Saturday morning. Tried reach him border without success. . . . Only Bachofen [Lier's assistant] can reach him safe discreet way." Lier arrived in Berlin anyway and began working on vital Dehomag projects such as moving Dehomag machines from Poland into Romania where they were urgently needed for a census.[75]

On October 9, 1941, Milner in the New York office sent a memorandum to Chauncey regarding "Shipment of Dehomag Machines to Various Countries." Milner worried that it might have become too difficult to continue business as usual with the Hitler regime. "As you know, on June 15, 1941 we cabled the Geneva office regarding the President's [Franklin D. Roosevelt's] proclamation, and instructed them not to make any move involving IBM assets without securing advice from the American Consulate. This was to avoid their unintentionally violating any provision of the President's decree. I am wondering whether you would deem it advisable to definitely instruct

Geneva that none of the European countries which can be controlled should order any goods from Dehomag. This, of course, is a serious step, as some of the countries are using Dehomag machines and currently require repair parts. It might be well for us to discuss this subject at your convenience."[76]

IBM would not place a stop on any of its Dehomag business, or any subsidiary's interaction with it. IBM filed another request with the Treasury Department, this time to send an instruction to all of its European subsidiaries and agencies, as well as its divisions in Japan. The instruction: "In view of world conditions we cannot participate in the affairs of our companies in various countries as we did in normal times. Therefore you are advised that you will have to make your own decisions and not call on us for any advice or assistance until further notice." It was sent to the State Department on October 10, 1941, with a request for comment.[77]

A State Department official replied some two weeks later, "While this Department is glad to be informed of your intentions in this matter, it has no specific comment to make at this time." To this perfunctory response, Chauncey very cautiously answered, "Thank you very much for your letter of October 23, 1941."[78]

IBM's cable to all subsidiaries involved with Axis nations was approved. Watson's October 1941 instruction did not order his subsidiaries to stop producing punch cards for Nazi Germany. It did not order them to cease all operations. It did not set limits on which projects they could participate in. It did not require offices in neutral companies to stop supporting Hitler's program. It did not proscribe uses in census or registration operations. It did not even demand that spare parts no longer be sent to machines in concentration camps. All that business continued. The cable merely directed managers not to "call on us for any advice or assistance until further notice."

On October 21, 1941, the Treasury Department finally issued IBM a license to communicate the authorization to split the stock—more than a month after the fact.[79] A week later, long after IBM submitted its license to instruct all subsidiaries to stop communicating, Chauncey spoke again to Commercial Attaché Woods.

CHAUNCEY: We have received a license from the Treasury Department for the increase in the Dehomag stock and are sending out a cable to that effect.

WOODS: It has been done. Your attorney here had it done the next day after my telephone conversation with Mr. Watson because Mr. Watson had said that it would be all right.

CHAUNCEY: Was the stock issued proportionately?

WOODS: Yes, you have received your full share. . . .

CHAUNCEY: But the stock at present has been issued so that IBM is [the] owner of its proportionate amount of the increase?

WOODS: Yes.

CHAUNCEY: What I called you for was to explain that in authorizing this increase we wish to be sure that the additional shares to the other stockholders were included in their existing agreements and their agreements made to conform to the present circumstances.

WOODS: I do not know about that.

CHAUNCEY: Will you see Dr. Albert and have him arrange accordingly? Also, have Dr. Albert return to you the power of attorney which I gave him because of my personal liability for any act which I might commit under it. If, in the future, anything is required to be done we can release the power with specific instructions provided we have a license from the Treasury Department.

WOODS: I will see the attorney in a few minutes and tell him. Do you want me to destroy the power of attorney when it is returned?

CHAUNCEY: No, you keep it.

WOODS: Well, you know it is possible that we may leave here [in the event war is declared], and then do you want me to destroy it?

CHAUNCEY: Yes.

WOODS: Dr. Kiep and the others send their regards to all of you.

CHAUNCEY: We, in turn, send our regards to them.[80]

IBM faced countless additional emergencies throughout fall 1941, large and small, as it sought to protect its profits and control of its extended Dehomag subsidiary. In one such crisis, Heidinger was waging yet another voting *putsch*. On December 3, as America sensed it stood at the brink of war, a clearly nervous Chauncey again appeared at the State Department with yet another emergency message to be conveyed to Berlin. Mr. Luthringer was the officer on duty. Chauncey gave his IBM business card to the clerk. The card had no address, title, or phone number on it, just the imprint "Harrison K. Chauncey, International Business Machines Corp., New York."[81]

The clerk wrote on the card, "Do you want to see[?]" and drew an arrow to Chauncey's name. Luthringer agreed to see him.[82]

Chauncey was carrying a message, and again there was no time to secure a Treasury License. Would the State Department object to sending it? This way, the U.S. government would be sending the message, not IBM. IBM's message was intended for Dehomag through the Geneva office. It read: "Resolution of Executive and Finance Committee of Board of Directors that we will not consent to any change in authority to vote our stock in Dehomag. Dehomag is owned by IBM to the extent of approximately 84 percent and IBM cannot consent to any change in voting control or any other changes until emergency is over. Please inform Albert and Kiep."[83]

Luthringer kept notes on his conversation with Chauncey, whom he had met before. "During a previous visit," Luthringer wrote, "he had referred to the fact that the German army used quantities of his company's accounting machinery. Apparently, the Germans move such machinery along with the army in the field." Luthringer added, "I had a feeling from Mr. Chauncey's general remarks that he is somewhat perturbed for fear that his company may some day be blamed for cooperating with the Germans."[84]

Four days later, Pearl Harbor was bombed. The U.S. finally joined the war against Germany. Dehomag and all Watson subsidiaries under Reich control would now be managed by Nazi-appointed trustees. IBM Europe was saved.

I
II
III
IV
V
VI
VII
VIII
IX
X
XI
XII
XIII
XIV
XV

FRANCE AND HOLLAND

HOLLAND WAS INVADED IN MAY 1940. QUICKLY, THE COUNTRY was subjugated to a German civil administration. More than 140,000 Jews, as well as thousands of refugees from Nazism, lived in Holland on the day of invasion.[1]

France fell a month later. After the June 1940 armistice, France was divided into two zones. A so-called Occupied Zone in the north, which included Paris, was ruled by a German military governor backed up by the army and Himmler's Gestapo units. In the south, a collaborationist regime was popularly referred to as Vichy France, after the town of Vichy where the government was headquartered. Alsace-Lorraine was annexed. Approximately 300,000 Jews lived in all of France prior to occupation and dismemberment. About 200,000 of those lived in the Paris area.[2]

German intentions in both countries were nearly identical and unfolded in a similar sequence throughout the war years. But everything about the occupation of these lands and their involvement with Hitler's Holleriths was very different. For the Jews of these two nations, their destinies would also be quite different.

Germany frequently exploited ethnic antagonism between national groups in Eastern Europe and ignited long simmering anti-Semitism with Fascist surrogates in such lands as Yugoslavia, Slovakia, Romania, and Hungary. Jews in Eastern Europe often lived apart from the larger society and were subject to class resentment exacerbated by religious isolation. By clever manipulation, the Third Reich was able to divide and conquer democratic or monarchical sovereignties, and then enlist the aid of local Jew-haters to legislate and regiment the methodical destruction of the Jewish community.

But it was different in France and Holland.

In the Netherlands, the population was, with notable exceptions, fundamentally homogeneous. Certainly, traditional Portuguese, colonial, and recent refugee groups each occupied their own niche. Ethnic rivalries, however, were largely non-existent and could not be exploited. Dutch Jews maintained a closely knit community. Only some 12,400 (less than 10 percent) did not affiliate with either of the two leading Jewish ancestral groups. Less than an estimated 2,000 had drifted into Christianity. But Dutch Jews were nonetheless almost completely integrated. Jews could be found among the leaders of literature, jurisprudence, physics, medicine, and manufacturing. Jewish organizations were secularized. Intermarriage was common. By 1930, some 41 percent of the community was in a mixed marriage. Dutch Jewry lived in harmony and acceptance as productive citizens of Holland.[3]

France was ethnically diverse, weaving Jews, Christians, and Moslems from across Europe, Asia, and Africa into the fabric of French society. Certainly, strong racial and religious undercurrents continuously rippled, and sometimes exploded. Anti-Semitism had been a fact of life in France for generations—as it had been throughout Europe. The term *J'Accuse* was born amidst the outrage over the Dreyfus Affair. Yet the French had by and large learned to live with ethnic diversity as a strength of their national culture. French Jewry was as completely assimilated as many of their coreligionists in Germany. Jews in France achieved prominence in science, the arts, and politics. France cherished her Jewish painters Pissaro, Chagall, and Modigliani. Theatergoers loved Sarah Bernhardt. Men of letters such as Marcel Proust and Henri Bergson enjoyed wide followings. In 1936, Léon Blum became the first Jew elected premier. Yet Talmudic studies all but disappeared. Baptized or unaffiliated Jews were commonly found throughout a Jewish community that considered itself French first.[4]

In Holland, punch cards were a well-developed statistical tool. As early as 1916, the Central Statistical Bureau began tracking import and export data on Hollerith machines purchased from an agent for the German company. By 1923, Dutch industry was adopting the technology. The Amsterdam City Electricity Works became the first public utility in the world to use an actual punch card as a regular customer bill. After two Dutch statisticians visited

Berlin for demonstrations, the Netherlands chose Hollerith machines to tabulate its 1930 census. By 1937, a centralized "machine park" was developed to serve a multiplicity of government clients. To save money, the Dutch government integrated some locally produced punchers manufactured by Kamatec and Kamadex.[5]

Watson established a card printing plant in the Netherlands in 1936. In 1939, IBM located a training school in Amsterdam for its European sales force. By that time, the Netherlands was preparing for wartime disruptions by inventorying all sources and stores of the nation's food stocks. Ration cards were regularly issued to all civilians. All information was punched onto cards and sorted by IBM equipment.[6]

From the outbreak of World War II, Holland standardized on IBM devices. By 1941, the Ministry of Agriculture alone operated 40 machines, which used 1 million Hollerith cards monthly, continuously punched by a staff of 120 punching secretaries. The Statistical Bureau of the Ministry of Economics utilized 98 IBM machines. The Central Statistical Bureau's usage had employed 64 machines. All tolled, the Dutch federal government leased 326 machines from IBM, with an additional 176 Holleriths located in 21 provincial offices, municipal bureaus, and semi-official agencies. Fifteen key corporations used 169 machines. More than 320 machines were employed by nonessential private enterprises. Having surpassed its own card printing needs, by 1941, IBM NY was annually shipping Holland 132 million cards printed in America. Unquestionably, Holland automated its data with Holleriths.[7]

Ironically, IBM did not operate a subsidiary in Holland throughout the twenties and thirties. The company relied upon highly paid sales agents to close deals. Dehomag in conjunction with IBM Geneva supplied the equipment and expertise. Watson had opened new subsidiaries in Poland and other conquered territories just before or after the Germans invaded. It was no different in Holland. On March 20, 1940, just as Hitler was preparing to launch his spring invasions of the Low Countries and Western Europe, Watson rushed to incorporate Watson Bedrijfsmachine Maatschappij N.V.—the Dutch name for Watson Business Machines Corporation. Reich armies took Denmark on April 9, Norway on May 2, and Luxembourg on May 10. On May 10, Germany also launched its conquest of Holland—it only took five days.[8]

Throughout the spring invasions, the flow of punch cards to Holland was uninterrupted. Just before the war came to the Netherlands' border, IBM approved an agreement with the Central Statistical Bureau to supply enough cards to last a year. When the Germans entered Holland, they took possession of that supply.[9]

When originally incorporated in March 1940, two owners of Watson Bedrijfsmachine were listed. IBM NY was shown owning 90 percent of the Dutch company, with 10 percent held by J. W. Schotte, General Manager of IBM Europe. Although a mere nominee, Schotte's shares created the appearance of a Dutch national as principal. Even though Schotte lived in New York, IBM initially listed him as general manager of the Dutch subsidiary. Quickly, however, IBM NY decided to vest all real power in another manager named Pieter van Ommeren. Since by that time the Netherlands was occupied, IBM's secretary-treasurer, J. G. Phillips, on September 17, wrote to the Netherlands Consulate General in exile for permission to circumvent the rules of incorporation. Phillips' sworn letters to the Consulate never identified Schotte as IBM's European General Manager in New York, but merely as a Dutch "merchant" who was "sojourning in the United States."[10]

Some months later, on December 7, 1940, as part of Watson's move to create the appearance of non-communication and reassure Nazi occupiers of non-control, van Ommeren filed an unusual amendment to the articles of incorporation. This amendment deleted the standard clause of closely held corporations to facilitate communications. The words "by telegraph" were removed from the phrase "Shareholders can be consulted in lieu of meeting by writing or telegraph." From December 1940 to mid-June 1941, IBM executives undertook the protracted legal applications to ensure that the exiled Dutch consulate approved the power of attorney given to Ommeren.[11] IBM wanted to make sure that all of its corporate acts in Holland were recognized not only by the Nazi civil administration, but the exiled government as well.

IBM's operation in France was "promising"—but from the first years, a small and fragmented market. In 1919, CTR established its first European sales office in Paris, using Heidinger's original Dehomag as sales agent. With only a dozen French customers, IBM France, in 1925, opened a manufacturing factory and a branch in Lyon. As late as 1927, IBM was fighting a pitched battle with rival Powers Company for the small French market. Each firm had snared just 30 customers using approximately 50 sorters and tabulators fed by about 300 punching stations. Then in 1931, the Swiss company, Bull, appeared in France with a new low-cost integrated machine that seemed to outperform the Hollerith. Bull's first installation was at the French Ministry of Labor.[12]

Even though Bull enjoyed but a single client in 1931, Watson saw the new company as a significant threat. IBM ramped up its competitive machinery to neutralize the new firm. Watson personally inspected Bull machines at French government offices with an eye toward buying the company outright.

At about that time, IBM signed up the French Ministry of War, which would become a major client for complex Hollerith systems. By 1932, IBM France had expanded to more than sixty-five customers. Protracted discussions between Watson and French Bull owners broke down. So IBM purchased the original Bull rights in Switzerland, this to the shock of French Bull. Immediately after closing the deal, Watson went further, hiring Emile Genon, the very Bull manager who had sold IBM the Swiss rights. French Bull voted to dishonor the contract as anti-competitive and even moved to separate from its Swiss sister company. The serpentine Bull acquisition controversy led to years of lawsuits in Switzerland and France as IBM challenged Bull's right to sell its own designs, and Bull sued for unfair competition.[13]

Watson restructured his French organization in 1936, creating a new subsidiary named Compagnie Electro-Comptable de France, or CEC. By the outbreak of war, CEC had hundreds of machines installed, many of them concentrated in just three sectors: banking, railroad, and the military. IBM now dominated the French market with about 65 percent of usage in France proper, and virtually the entire market in France's colonies, especially North Africa and Indochina. Bull, beset by financial problems, undoubtedly linked to its endless litigation with IBM, secured only 25 percent of the French market share, mainly among governmental and banking clients. Powers clung to its marginal 10 percent segment.[14]

As France edged closer to war in the late thirties, French War Ministry orders greatly exceeded CEC's limited factory output. From 1937, excess French military orders were placed directly with IBM NY. In the approximately two years before war erupted in 1939, IBM NY shipped the French military alphabetizers yielding nearly a half million dollars in rentals, as well as $350,000 in spare parts. All of France utilized some 426 million punch cards in those two pre-war years; they were printed locally, ordered from other European subsidiaries, or imported from the U.S.[15]

But everything changed in French automation when the country was partitioned in June 1940. The Franco-German June armistice was signed less than three weeks after Watson returned Hitler's decoration. Dehomag's revolt was in its initial tempest state. Nazi forces immediately seized hundreds of CEC Holleriths. A special "requisitioning" platoon familiar with IBM tabulators was attached to the First Panzer Division to effect the confiscation. Machines were carted off from CEC's warehouse and workshops, and even removed from CEC's customers, such as the electric company in Strasbourg and a gamut of armament firms. The largest collection of Holleriths was swept from France's War Ministry, especially the Ministry's tabulator service.[16]

In all, 319 Holleriths were commandeered, spirited out of France, and dispersed to waiting Reich customers throughout Germany. Dozens of verifiers, sorters, and alphabetizers were placed at the *Maschinelles Berichtwesen* and its many punch card field offices throughout conquered Europe. Many of the devices were assigned to key German war industry companies. Some were deployed at Nazi occupation offices in Krakow and Prague. The largest group of Holleriths was transported to *Luftwaffe* bases and the German High Command.[17]

CEC officials logged each machine by original client location, serial number, and leasing valuation so CEC could make a claim in Berlin for payment. These logs were sent to IBM NY for review as soon as they became available. Likewise, German authorities kept meticulous records of each of the 319 requisitioned machines by original site, monthly leasing cost, and new location within Nazi Europe. Although the machines at first were forcibly removed, IBM actually found the action conducive to better relations with the Reich and quite profitable. CEC managers billed the Reich for each machine, and company representatives squabbled with the authorities over precisely how much would be paid for each device. In the fourth quarter of 1942 alone, the German Army paid CEC 9.4 million French francs—equal to about $100,000—for leasing, service, spare parts, and punch cards.[18]

Quickly, CEC's profits soared. Volume doubled from 1939 to 1942 to FF101 million for 1942. During that same period profits almost quadrupled to FF26.6 million in 1942, of which FF16.3 million was designated "royalties." Those monies were derived almost entirely from orders placed by Dehomag and German agencies. For example, the 250 sorters manufactured by CEC in 1942—double the 1938 output—were all ordered by Dehomag. What domestic activity CEC did undertake was generally some miscellaneous card printing and reconditioning of the oldest machines not yet requisitioned.[19]

Clearly, CEC had been converted into a captive supply source for Dehomag. This was done with IBM NY's full concurrence. In fact, to meet Dehomag's increasing demand, Watson in 1941 approved the construction of two new factory sites. One plant was added to the manufacturing complex at Vincennes, outside of Paris. A second factory compound was erected at Essonnes, twenty miles south of Paris, not far from rail facilities. A March 24, 1941, report from CEC management to IBM NY explained, "The equipment demanded by our customers . . . has caused that the capacity of our present factory at Vincennes was bound to be exceeded very rapidly." Until the new factory was completed, CEC would use outside "jobbers" to supply parts.[20]

IBM NY was continuously kept informed about CEC's progress by a variety of formal and informal means. Sometimes, it was just a handwritten letter, such as the one written in English to a manufacturing executive at Endicott by Dehomag engineer Oskar Hoermann. Hoermann was a principal IBM liaison between the German company, the *MB* in Berlin, and CEC.

LYON, FRANCE
April 30, 1942

Dear Jimmy,

I am on a business trip in the unoccupied France and take this opportunity of giving a sign of myself. I am not in the army yet, since we have become increasingly important. Even C.E.C. Paris works for us now. We opened up a small assembly plant in Kuchen, 50 miles from Sindelfingen, and will soon open up another little plant about 100 miles away. Not because we think it wise to decentralize, but because we have to move our work where we have workers available. Once in a while I go to Paris. They have purchased a second little plant at Essonnes, about 30 miles from P[aris]. The main office has moved to Place Vendome.

How are you people at Endicott? . . .

With my very best regards to you and your family,

I remain yours

Sincerely,

O.E. Hoermann[21]

IBM Endicott's executive offices received Hoermann's handwritten letter July 20, 1942, in the morning mail.[22]

But most reports to Watson were far more detailed. For example, in early 1943, more than a year after the U.S. entered World War II, IBM NY received CEC's regular quarterly financial report for the fourth quarter of 1942. The thirty-two-page, single-spaced report summarized in great detail, and illustrated with numerous tables, all the fiscal pluses and minuses of CEC's business with Germany. Income columns for each month, expressed in French francs, showed the increase over the previous year, with a 1942 total of FF16.311 million compared to 1941's FF11.377 million. January

1942 income was particularly impressive, showing revenue of FF1.2 million—double from a year earlier. Special notes attributed FF9.4 million, or about $100,000, "paid by the German Army for rental of requisitioned machines." CEC managers were careful to include detailed charts of how the subsidiary's performance measured up against its assigned profit quota—a point system—established by IBM NY.[23]

Sales and expenses were analyzed by financial quarter and product. Competitor activities at Bull and Powers were summarized for both the Occupied Zone and Vichy. Line items were entered for maintenance on the machines used by the German High Command, FF304,059, plus an extra adjustment of FF3.79 million for yet another category of machines and maintenance provided to the German High Command.[24]

CEC's report also emphasized France's dire paper shortages. The Nazis had temporarily authorized a Dehomag paper vendor to supply CEC, but that permission had ended because of Europe's general scarcity. "The outlook was very dark," CEC's report confessed, adding, "we tried to obtain paper by all available means." By scrounging from source to source, CEC hoped it could persevere a few weeks at a time. Among its precious remaining stock of 262 rolls was a cache of 93 rolls from IBM NY.[25]

Symptomatic of the paper scarcity, CEC reported, was the summer 1942 crisis at Mandeure, the French subsidiary's one remaining paper supplier. Mandeure warned CEC that it could not supply further paper for punch cards without additional shipments of the vital coal and cellulose it needed for pulping. Claiming an emergency, CEC was able to intervene with Nazi rationing authorities, "pressing them for an allotment of coal and cellulose to 'Mandeure'. . . . This allows us," reported CEC, "to live under the most drastic restrictions which we imposed on our customers." But by the end of 1942, even CEC's compromise alternative suppliers were being exhausted.[26]

Yet CEC could only hope profits would continue to rise based on increased machine orders for the Reich supplemented by ancillary punch card services. CEC's 1942 report itemized for IBM NY a wealth of Dehomag orders aggressively being filled despite wartime conditions. Order #52769 for 50 collators would commence shortly with five machines monthly. Order #55158 for an additional 100 collators would be scheduled as soon as raw materials permitted. Order #52768 for 50,000 sorting brushes would be satisfied with 5,000 per month.[27]

In addition, CEC's report listed its crucial training courses for punch card operators. Course #10B enrolled 45 keypunch students. Course 11B enrolled an additional 45 students. Course #12B taught 36 students. Schools for Hollerith operators were conducted night and day with course #131 training 94 evening students, course #133 training 16 day students, and courses #134 and #135 enrolling a total of 86 more.[28] Germany's voracious labor and military draft requirements had created a punch card emergency. CEC was not only churning out machines and punch cards, but also skilled operators to make them work for Germany.

To further expand its market, CEC was aggressively serving clients in France's colonial territories now controlled by Vichy. Of CEC's 848 employees, 5 worked at CEC offices in Algeria, 5 in Casablanca, and 3 in Indochina.[29]

CEC had become a veritable satellite of Dehomag. The subsidiary maintained a direct link to the Nazi Party. Although Watson's director general was Roger Virgile, the Nazis had appointed one of their own men, a Dehomag agent named Heinz Westerholt, to act as CEC's *Kommissar*. Westerholt was more than a Dehomag employee. He joined the NSDAP (Nazi Party) on May 1, 1933, shortly after Hitler assumed power; the Party issued him membership #2,781,981. Later that year, Westerholt was inducted into the SS, which issued him identification #272,239. In October 1934, Westerholt became a management employee of Dehomag.[30]

IBM NY was aware of Westerholt and his Party connections from the outset. Westerholt first became active in CEC's business when he visited Paris in summer 1940 during the Nazi effort to create a punch card cartel. Chauncey kept tabs on Westerholt by a combination of rumors and reports relayed through IBM Geneva, and remained in constant contact with CEC, as well as Otto Kiep and attorney Albert in Berlin. Chauncey clearly identified Westerholt to New York as the Dehomag agent with Nazi Party status who was deployed to undermine IBM's interest in Paris. For his part, Westerholt was among those incensed at Watson for slighting *der Führer*. At one point, Westerholt openly repeated Dehomag's prevailing view: Watson's opinions were "not of great importance" because he had returned Hitler's medal.[31]

But cooperation with the Third Reich was imperative for Watson. The recurring crisis of IBM retaining its dominance in Axis punch card operations was again peaking in fall 1941. The urge to create a German-controlled cartel was again confronting IBM NY. In that vein, the Reich began to view CEC as one of a geographical triad of IBM subsidiaries along with Belge Watson in Brussels and Watson Bedrijfsmachine Maatschappi in Amsterdam.

The director of Belge Watson was former Bull Director Emile Genon. The director of CEC was Roger Virgile. P. Taylor was Watson's trouble-

shooter in IBM Geneva. In September 1941, Genon wrote a confidential letter to Taylor at IBM Geneva discussing Watson's intentions for CEC. A copy
of Genon's letter ended up in the hands of Justice Department investigators
looking into IBM's many special Treasury licenses. The Justice Department
and State Department summarized the letter: "Political affairs in France.
Transmits copies of letter addressed to Mr. P. Taylor, International Business
Machines Corporation and written by E. Genon, which indicates that Mr.
T.H.J. Watson approved Mr. Virgile's policy of collaboration with Germany."[32]

In France, IBM's collaboration required working with the SS via Westerholt. Indeed, IBM NY suspected that when America entered the war, Westerholt might be designated custodian of CEC, since he had poignantly
discussed the issue of enemy receivership with Virgile. In the second week of
October 1941, Westerholt returned to Paris for further consultations with
Virgile. Westerholt met Virgile on October 13, when he warned that Dehomag was now prepared to break its contract with IBM NY on a legal "pretext." The German authorities understood that Bull lacked the manufacturing
muscle to supply the Reich, but Berlin still hoped it could use Bull designs
and patents to start its own factory. Toward that aim, license agreements had
already been signed. In view of the threat to IBM Europe if the company did
not cooperate, Westerholt wanted an immediate meeting at Lyon in Vichy. He
sent word to Werner C. Lier, Watson's most senior official at IBM Geneva.[33]

While Lier considered Westerholt's invitation, he filed a full report with
IBM NY. In his note, Lier warned that if the U.S. entered the war, as most
imminently expected, a custodian for CEC would "have the effect of reducing the amount of reports which we have been able to receive from CEC . . .
and create a situation somewhat similar to that of the Dehomag." That in
mind, Lier needed New York's permission to attend and bring CEC Sales
Manager William Borel as Virgile's representative.[34]

Three days later on October 16, an impatient Lier cabled IBM NY:
"Competition affair serious. Genon learned Vichy . . . definitely able destroy
our European business in cooperation with foreign group, previously mentioned. . . . Following telephone call Borel I received today written report
stating Westerholt confirmed Virgile reality our fears. . . . Also threatened
appointment foreign custodian Paris with program suppressing relations with
Geneva. Westerholt wants see me Lyon. . . . Will see him only with your approval. Please instruct all matters."[35]

The next day, Lier contacted Berlin to obtain the latest intelligence on
Dehomag's rebellious actions. He summarized the effort for New York. "Due
to the courtesy of the American Consulate in Geneva," Lier reported, "it was

possible for us to speak on the morning of October 17th to the United States Embassy in Berlin. Mr. Woods, the Commercial Attaché, being absent, we explained to his assistant our desire to find out something more definite concerning Dehomag's intention of breaking the contract with us. In the afternoon Mr. Woods called us in Geneva and told us that he had seen Dr. Albert who had admitted, though in a rather vague manner, that he had heard certain rumors about Dehomag's intention but . . . could not give a definite opinion as to the legal aspects of the matter."[36]

Thereafter, Lier concluded that a meeting with Westerholt could no longer be postponed. Lier cabled New York, "Recab [re: cable] competition. Intend go Vichy with Genon Wednesday trying prevent or slowing juridical materialization agreement between two groups." On October 20, IBM NY replied, "No objection your seeing Westerholt. Make no commitments and take no action." Lier confirmed that he would immediately leave for Lyon because it was "in the best interests of the IBM to delay as much as possible the official ratification of the agreement between the Bull and W [Wanderer-Werke] groups."[37]

The initial meeting between Lier and Westerholt was only the beginning. The Nazis wanted a second, much broader conference, this one in Berlin, and involving CEC's entire senior staff. Again, Lier would not proceed without Watson's specific permission. On November 17, 1941, CEC cabled IBM NY: "Meeting Berlin November 21 with Virgile Westerholt . . . Suggest you instruct Lier at once to attend that meeting even if you have not reached decision on Kiep's cable November 6 to Watson. Have met Westerholt with Lier. Impression good. Reports follow."[38]

The meetings with Westerholt in Berlin were part of the constellation of intrigues that compelled Chauncey to rush to the State Department in early December, just days before Pearl Harbor, to circumvent Treasury license requirements and issue financial instructions to Dehomag. Ultimately, after the U.S. joined the war against Germany, Westerholt was appointed the custodian of CEC.[39] The Nazis were able to do with CEC as they pleased so long as IBM was paid. The looming competition with Bull never came to fruition. It was more of a bargaining chip than a genuine threat. Unable to replace IBM, the Third Reich pressured the company into relinquishing Watson's troublesome micro-managing in favor of the faster and more coordinated action the Reich required.

But even though CEC and IBM were able to retain their dominance as a vital supplier of Reich automation, by the end of 1943, the bleak facts about the punch card business in France had become undeniable. CEC could no longer obtain reliable supplies of paper or raw materials. IBM's subsidiary no longer produced machines for the French market. Key workers with special Hollerith skills were being systematically drafted or transferred to punch card projects in the Greater Reich. The French company's entire manufacturing capacity—machines and parts—was being shipped out of the country to Germany and beyond. Despite its soaring revenues, the French subsidiary saw a moment of utter corporate collapse looming in the near future.[40] In the beginning of 1943, just as CEC was reporting doubled volumes and trebled profits, Virgile was compelled to warn IBM NY: "The situation of CEC at the end of 1942 is very precarious, both from the point of view of specialized personnel, which is subject to forced transfer to Germany at any moment, and from the point of view of card supply which is assured for only a few weeks. Manufacture is proceeding with enormous and ever increasing delays. Subcontractors have had to close down suddenly or decrease their activity sharply as a result of personnel requisitions. The greater part of our skilled labor is subject to immediate call. Under those conditions, it is impossible to venture as much as a guess as to the future."[41]

Powers had been all but marginalized in France. The Germans were required to transfer workshops from Germany to Paris just to keep its almost inactive operation functioning. Even though Bull had promising equipment with numerous installations in France, it was financially and operationally incapable of ramping up. Some Bull machines had also been removed by the Germans and were being serviced by IBM personnel in occupied territories. Bull was also desperate for raw materials to fabricate machines and paper to manufacture cards. Berlin's one and only order for leased Bull machines had to be canceled before any could be delivered.[42]

Germany wanted the Jews identified by bloodline not religion, pauperized, and then deported to camps, just as they were elsewhere in conquered Europe. The Jews of France stood vulnerable under the shadow of destruction. Hitler was ready.

In France, the Holleriths were not.

HOLLAND SURRENDERED to Germany on May 15, 1940, after just five days of fierce attack. The Reich immediately began planning the complete destruction of the Dutch Jewish community. Believing that the total of ancestral and practicing Jews in Holland to be about double their actual number, Nazi experts assumed the campaign against Dutch Jewry would be phased. More than that, they realized all too well that the local population did not welcome the arrival of Hitler's forces. Certainly, rabid Dutch Nazis were eager to cooperate with the occupation. But in significant measure, at times citizens of Holland demonstrated open solidarity with persecuted Jews and displayed an unwillingness to deliver their neighbors. Repressive measures against Jews provoked a strike by laborers, frequent demands by Christians to be included with the Jews in their misery, and even some violent riots.[43]

The Reich needed a very special expert to help to engineer the roundups. They needed a man who understood the administrative statistical landscape of Holland, one who was adept at Hollerith technology and willing to cooperate in the face of popular resistance. In an occupied nation beset by neighborhood ambushes against German soldiers, outrageous catcalls at the cinema when Nazi propaganda films flashed onto the screen, and coordinated sermons in churches everywhere to condemn anti-Semitism, Berlin needed someone uniquely qualified to step forward.[44]

They found their man in Jacobus Lambertus Lentz. He was not a Nazi. Those who have studied him have not proven his innate anti-Semitism. Instead, Lentz was a population expert, cocooned in his own stacked and tabulated world of ratios, registration programs, and rattling Hollerith machines. Perfection in human cataloging was for Lentz more than a matter of pride, it was a crusade.[45]

In 1936, as Inspector of Population Registries, Lentz standardized local population registers and their data collection methodology throughout the Netherlands—an administrative feat that earned him a royal decoration. That same year, he outlined his personal vision in *Allgemeines Statistisches Archiv*, the journal of the German Statistical Society: "Theoretically," predicted Lentz, "the collection of data for each person can be so abundant and complete, that we can finally speak of a *paper human* representing the natural human."[46]

One can only imagine the deep inner satisfaction Lentz derived from indexing one segment of the population after another with infallible precision. He bragged about his data, defensively stood by his summaries and always anticipated the next German request for Jewish names—if for no other reason than to self-validate his own "censual" foresight. When light streamed through the punch card, Lentz surely saw something no one else could. German occupiers were resented nearly everywhere in Holland. But for Lentz, his new Nazi masters had in fact liberated him from the dissatisfying ennui of peacetime social tracking. Now, under Nazism, he could unleash all his ideas of registration and powers of ratiocination restlessly waiting to be tested. He would declare war on population ambiguity. Lentz would be the man to deliver the Jews of Holland. His motto was "to record is to serve."[47]

Step one, on July 3, 1941, was the identification of Jewish refugees living in Amsterdam, a number the Germans erroneously believed was between 120,000 and 150,000. Using police stations normally charged with registering aliens, Lentz organized a systematic count. His numbers ultimately showed far fewer refugees than expected, about 20,000.[48]

Then, on August 17, Lentz devised a unique tamper-proof personal identification card that could not be forged. Translucent inks were employed to print key words that disappeared under a quartz lamp. The stamp franking was acetone-soluble. Photos of the individual were affixed front and back through a window transparently sealed and adhered with permanent glue. A fingerprint of the person's right index finger was then impressed upon the back of one of the photos so it always displayed through the small window. The individual's signature on watermarked paper completed the document, which included numerous personal details. Lentz' card was a masterpiece of human documentation.[49]

Lentz first conceived his complex card in 1939 when war in Europe broke out and the government considered foolproof food rationing cards. However, as recently as March 1940, a Dutch government commission thought that such a card would treat average people like criminals, and was inconsistent with the nation's democratic tradition. But with no one to hold him back, Lentz perfected his original card idea by adding the photograph and fingerprint features.[50]

When Lentz offered his specimen to the Criminal Technology Institute of the Reich Criminal Police Office, it was eagerly approved. His innovation outshone anything the German police had ever developed, and clearly could defeat the many local attempts to forge papers. Within weeks, German civil administrators began requiring all Dutch citizens over the age of fourteen to sign up. It took about a year before everyone was registered. But Lentz' personal card was more than just an advanced domestic identification. A second portion detached at issuance created a card-like receipt. Those card receipts were retained and organized into massive files cataloging the personal details of all who lived in the Netherlands.[51]

Every Dutch adult was required to carry Lentz' personal identification card. But a feature was added that only affected Jews. Eventually the letter *J* was stamped on every identification card carried by those defined as Jewish. The manual card file receipts became the first stepping-stone toward comprehensive automated Dutch Jewish registration.[52]

On October 22, all Jewish enterprises were compelled to register. Jews were defined, as in the Nuremberg Laws, according to their grandparents, not their current religious affiliation. Businesses were deemed Jewish if any member of the ownership or management was Jewish or had Jewish ancestors, again mimicking the decrees espoused earlier in the Reich. A Bureau of Economic Investigation was formed to decide whether suspect companies were actually Jewish under rigid ancestral definitions. As soon as German civil authorities in Holland announced the Jewish commercial registration, the nation erupted in protest. Virtually all Protestant churches, that next Sunday, condemned from the pulpit a Jewish registration they called "un-Christian."[53]

By early 1941, the Germans felt they were ready to begin the last phase before deportation. On January 10, 1941, Nazi State Secretary Friedrich Wimmer issued the all-important decree VO6/41 requiring all Jews—Dutch and foreign—to register at their local Census Office. Wimmer's deadline was four weeks for those residing outside of Amsterdam and ten weeks for Amsterdam residents. Since the 1930 census, Dutch Census Offices were completely automated with Hollerith systems. By comparing the Jewish registrations to the existing total population card index created by the Lentz card, the authorities could pinpoint any Jew who failed to sign up.[54]

Although nearly all of Holland angrily condemned the Nazi registration, the Jews did as instructed. With few exceptions, every Dutch Jewish family dutifully picked up its questionnaires, filled them out completely, and filed with the nearest registration office. The uncanny compliance was based on traditional Dutch respect for laws and regulations, as well as the stated penalty for not registering—five years in prison and the confiscation of property. Jews also understood that resistance was futile because their names had already long been innocently registered as "Jewish" in numerous statistical and registration bureaus throughout the Netherlands, and especially in the new card indices created by Lentz' personal identification program. Even though some Jews rioted in early February 1941, the entire community nonetheless filled out the forms as required. More than 157,000 questionnaires were ultimately returned in the first months—more than the entire Jewish community because many sympathetic Dutchmen actually volunteered to register alongside their Jewish countrymen. Lentz' punching cadres began converting the Jews to Hollerith records as quickly as possible.[55]

But none of it was fast enough for the Nazis. There were many delays. Although decree VO6/41 was espoused on January 10, 1941, German administrators did not release it to the media until January 14, when the news was published around the world, including in the *New York Times*. Because the registration ruling did not become effective until January 24, the official Dutch government gazette did not publish the details for census administrators until its February 3 issue. Hence local Census Offices across the country lost time in setting up registration facilities. Nonetheless, the offices remained open all day and night to speed the process. Each day, thousands of Dutch Jews marched into the local Census Office, paid a token guilder, and filled out the elaborate questionnaires providing the Germans with everything they needed to know about their possessions, families, and parentage.[56]

The German authorities at first praised the Census Office for "exemplary" service. But as Wimmer's early April deadline approached and the tallies were far from complete, Lentz' organization was challenged and rebuked for tardiness. The Germans even suggested some localities were sabotaging the program.[57]

Nazi administrators feared sabotage for good reason. Outraged Amsterdam workers had spontaneously called a strike, in large part over repressive measures. Nazi occupiers suppressed the defiance by throwing hand grenades and firing machine guns at crowds of protesters. Violent reprisals followed. The city of Amsterdam itself was fined 15 million guilders for the strike.[58]

But Lentz bristled at any suggestion his operation was doing less than its best. As Inspector of the Population Registries, he defended his national operation down to the local office. On March 25, he bluntly wrote Wimmer, "The government Inspectorate has thus far received approximately 30,000 registrations from the local registration posts. . . . the delay in registration is definitely not based on registration posts not willing to cooperate, or any sabotage, but on the circumstances, that the employees of the registration posts have been overburdened (specifically caused by the identification card decree); and on top of that, we just could not appoint key, reliable employees. The delay is also caused by the great number of dubious cases and interrogations." Acknowledging that more than a quarter million names were expected, Lentz assured, "I have ordered a circular letter by the Ministry of the Interior to the local registration posts, in which I have again asked for the greatest haste."[59]

Part of Wimmer's problem was that the Nazis simply could not take a Jewish census in Holland. A traditional census or population count required an army of enumerators visiting every citizen's home, diligently filling out forms. German administrators could not find reliable census takers to serve among the outraged masses. A registration, on the other hand, depended upon Jewish subjects voluntarily walking into the Census Office to fill out forms. That process was impeded by the general day-to-day reluctance that gripped Dutch Jewry, overcome only incrementally by each Jewish family. Moreover, a storm of venomous attacks in the popular underground media of Amsterdam made even the staffers of local Census Offices queasy.[60]

Two weeks later, on April 9, Lentz was still offering the Germans excuses for the slow progress, explaining that many local burgomasters had not yet read the government gazette, which came out in February.[61]

Of 1,050 municipalities outside Amsterdam, he reported, 1,019 had already completed their registration. As an example of local difficulties, he cited the town of Apeldoorn's "difficulty registering the inmates of the local Jewish insane asylum." The poor inmates could not provide cogent responses. But by May 5, most burgomasters had completed their registration. For many, the task was easy; some 483 localities had not a single Jew to report.[62]

By mid-May, Wimmer's office was beginning to understand that the constellation of overlapping local registrations in Holland fell short of what the Nazi program of destruction needed. Lentz' numerous Census Offices lacked the coordinated ability to identify, cross-index, and organize Jewish names nationally. Only a centralized Hollerith operation could do that. Moreover, Wimmer wanted the Jews alphabetized. Without alphabetizing, an organized step-by-step round-up and deportation to camps could not occur.

On May 19, 1941, Wimmer decided "that besides the registers that have been constructed so far, a special alphabetical register should be made, that [lists] all Jews and Jews of mixed blood, who are and have been reported after decree 6/41." This extra dimension would have tasked Lentz' overworked operation. To date, Lentz' bureaus had not even turned in reports on the first 78,119 questionnaires filed. While the Germans wanted to press Lentz to the maximum, they didn't want to pressure him too much.[63]

So some days later, Lentz was notified, quite carefully, by Hans Calmeyer, Wimmer's chief expert on Jewish affairs. "Dr. Wimmer would like to see constructed a register like the Hollerith punch card system," wrote Calmeyer. "The register must [contain] age, profession, and gender . . . [and] the category (Jew, Mixed I, Mixed II) to which the registered belongs. I don't deny that the compilation of such a register would form a serious burden for the Population Registries. However, without such an alphabetic register alongside the register on identity cards, and besides the already existing registers on municipalities, the [Jewish] registration just won't be sufficient.[64]

"You will soon have to be prepared for many . . . requests about information on individuals," Calmeyer continued. "These requests won't be able
to name the last residence of the requested person in every case. Such
requests will form an extraordinary workload for your office if the aforemen-
tioned alphabetical register is not compiled, because thus far, the requests
can only be answered after searching through all municipal registers. Of
course, the municipal registers should not be neglected. . . . Pray, also let me
know what kind of punch card system you think most efficient and most easily introduced." Calmeyer ended his note asking how long Lentz would need
to complete the alphabetical register.[65]

Lentz was ahead of Wimmer and Calmeyer. With barely suppressed
braggadocio, Lentz replied the next day, "With much interest I have taken
notice of your letter of 26th of May 1941, in which you informed me of the
wishes of Sir Secretary of State Dr. Wimmer concerning the making of
[another] punch card system. I am glad to inform you that the Inspectorate
has already been creating such a system according to the Hollerith method
for several weeks."[66]

Two months earlier, Lentz had requested permission from the Interior
Ministry to rent an extra Hollerith from the local IBM subsidiary. His
expense request was approved on April 23 and he was waiting for the equipment. But as soon as the approval was granted, he began to advance work. "I
immediately commenced the execution of the plan," Lentz informed Calmeyer. "We have already made much progress with the so-called 'coding' of
the data and the punching is almost ready too, thanks to the co-operation of
another government department. I add a model of the punch card for your
information. The machinery has not arrived yet, but measures have been
taken, so that this will soon become available."[67]

There was a major problem, though, confessed Lentz. His entire program was based on numerical identification of individuals, not alphabetical.
He emphasized to Calmeyer, "the [new] Hollerith punch card system is not
suited for functioning as an alphabetical register since the cards are not
punched by name, but by number. Punching alphabetically is possible, but
there are so many technical difficulties connected with it." As a result, Lentz
declared he would regretfully bypass all other projects and concentrate on
the alphabetizing. "I will now have an alphabetical register made that will
contain the names of all Jews and *Mischlinge* [people of mixed blood] who
have reported for registering."[68]

To further reduce delays, Lentz declared he would split the task into
two: those Jews in Amsterdam and those outside the city. Since the areas

outside Amsterdam were already complete, Lentz promised that list first. "This part will be ready about mid-June." If on the other hand, Wimmer and Calmeyer preferred Amsterdam first, Lentz could deliver that list just slightly later. "If you would like to have the names of the registered people in Amsterdam put into the alphabetical register as well," he stated, "then I would be able to have that completed by the end of June or in the beginning of July."[69]

On May 30, 1941, a German civil occupation official summarized the on-going overlapping Hollerith projects to Wimmer and the many technical obstacles. "Besides the already constructed and to be constructed registers," the report described "a special alphabetical register, possibly with the Hollerith punch card-system, for all people who have to report." But the punch cards for the new alphabetical file could not be printed without a careful design of data. So, the official added, his office would first have to determine exactly which punch card columns needed to be allocated to yield the desired data.[70] This was a question only Hollerith engineers could answer. Only IBM could print the cards.

"The Central Register has already requested the material and the machines for the construction of the Hollerith system," the official continued. Repeating Lentz' warning, he told Wimmer, "The Central Register, however, points out that the [existing] Hollerith punch card system, which currently assigns a number to every processed form and registered person, is not appropriate for the compilation of an alphabetic register. The alphabetic punching is connected to so many technical difficulties that a [quick] change of the system towards alphabetic processing seems just not possible in practice."[71]

"I don't deny," the report continued, "that this [additional] processing of persons who are obligated to report from Amsterdam (over 85,000 persons), will greatly increase the workload of the Central Office, and it will also delay the completion of the special registers."[72]

But for Wimmer, no time could be wasted. He ordered all alphabetizing projects to go forward at full speed, regardless of the difficulty. That was the priority. Lentz' devoted efforts prevailed. By June 14, 1941, Wimmer's office had received ten copies of a completed preliminary survey "of all persons of Jewish blood." The alphabetical index would be ready shortly. "Very soon," the report to Wimmer promised, "we shall be able to start categorizing certain groups through the Hollerith method." Now that the Jews were almost entirely alphabetized, demographic segments could be cross-indexed, sorted, and then called up by age, gender, and profession, all in alphabetical order.[73]

The system was soon ready. In early June 1941, anti-Nazi Dutch resistance groups detonated two bombs in Amsterdam. In reprisal, the Germans took action against 300 Dutch Jews, as well as a number of German refugees between the ages of 18 and 30. The Nazis relied upon Jewish organizational lists to round up Jewish youth workers. British intelligence reports asserted that when the number of Jews the Germans wanted fell short, additional hostages were taken. A British intelligence officer, citing a Dutch Jewish refugee, reported the additional action this way: "The Gestapo came with lists, from *Standesamt* [the Registry Office], carrying out searches in houses and looking for Jews in certain alphabetical groups. On one occasion, they took all the Jews whose names came within the alphabetical register S to V." The British report added that all seized Jews seized were eventually shipped to Mauthausen concentration camp, "and most of them also died" within several weeks."[74]

By June 16, 1941, Lentz reported that his office had almost completed the total registration of Jewish persons commanded by decree V06/41, except for a few "stragglers." He added that his Inspectorate "will now begin the registration of different groups via Hollerith method." Lentz wondered whether the Germans wanted any specific Jewish population segments sorted first. "I can process and pass on information," he wrote, "in case police services or German services urgently are looking for special groups, for example, artists or dentists."[75]

A few weeks later, on July 26, 1941, Lentz notified Calmeyer that the Inspectorate had established his own priorities. Processing by age was already underway. Next, he would tackle those of Jewish blood who had served in the Dutch military. "It is my intention," assured Lentz, "after these duties, to start with the control on the punching of Hollerith cards to improve the coding of professions." He would need a few weeks to finish these tasks if approved in that order. "I hope to hear from your side soon if you accept this proposal."[76]

Within a month, virtually all "stragglers" had been found out or had come forward. By September 5, Wimmer was about to review summaries that identified the exact number of Jews, broken down by specific categories. Lentz had registered, sorted, and tabulated 118,455 Dutch Jews; 14,495 German Jews; and 7,295 others, as well as 19,561 mixed breed *Mischlinge,* for a total of 159,806. This included 700 so-called racial Jews who were practicing Roman Catholicism; 1,245 belonging to Protestant churches; and 12,643 with no religious affiliation.[77]

Lentz reflected on his mammoth accomplishment while jotting notes in his personal handwritten journal, entitled *Memoires I, Registration of Jews (Source and Development)*: "I rented a Hollerith installation," he penned, "with which the professional statistical survey has been composed, which satisfied the Germans very much, and gave them the convictions that my opinions had been correct."[78]

He also thanked his Nazi overseers for their recognition for all his technical achievements. "I would like to express appreciation," Lentz wrote to Wimmer's office, "of the confidence you repose in myself and my staff. Thanks to this and to your cooperation, the Census Office was able to contrive ways and means of carrying out its often-difficult task. May I express the hope that we shall continue to enjoy your confidence." He also wrote, "This encourages us to strive with utter devotion to do justice to our slogan, 'to record is to serve.'"[79]

IBM's hastily established subsidiary in Holland, Watson Bedrijfsmachine Maatschappij, at 34 Frederiksplein in Amsterdam, listed impressive numbers for the first eight months of 1940.[80]

> Cash: $180,088.[81]
> Accounts receivable: $495,692.[82]
> Plant, office equipment, rental machines, and parts investment:
> $965,803.00.[83]

The subsidiary reported a gross profit of $116,651.90 for its eight months of operation in 1940.[84]

Ironically, by the time the subsidiary's profits were merged into charges added on the New York books, including $522,709.03 described only as "Other," as well as Eliminations and Adjustments, IBM reported a net loss for its Dutch subsidiary of $122,668.70.[85]

During 1941, IBM sent Holland 132 million punch cards from America; the subsidiary was by that time operating near its capacity of 150 million cards annually. Those cards were sold for $106,920.[86]

Ten days after the census ordered by decree VO6/41 was fully compiled, punched, and sorted, Nazi authorities demanded all Jews wear the Jewish star. Again a number of Dutch people reacted with outrage and protest. British diplomats reported that in one town, when the burgomaster ordered Jews to affix the star, many non-Jews wore one as well.[87]

But it was not the outward visage of six gold points worn on the chest for all to see on the street, it was the 80 columns punched and sorted in a Hollerith facility that marked the Jews of Holland for deportation to concentration camps. The Germans understood this all too well. On October 2,

1941, H. Böhmcker, a key Nazi official in Amsterdam, gleefully wrote to Arthur Seyss-Inquart, German *Kommissar* for Holland: "Thanks to decree 6/41, all Dutch Jews are now in the bag."[88]

FRANCE EXCELLED at many things. Punch card automation was not one of them. Although IBM had been able to install several hundred Hollerith devices, mainly for high-volume military, railway, and banking users, Reich forces had in large part confiscated those machines. The rest of France simply did not possess the punch card orientation of many other European countries, such as Holland and Germany. IBM learned early that its brand of technologic change came slowly to some markets. France was a prime example.

Holland's census and registration projects were masterminded by a fanatical population registrar commanding hundreds of advanced machines still intact in a well-entrenched Hollerith infrastructure supplied with decamillions of punch cards flowing from IBM NY and other European subsidiaries. Decades of Dutch registration that had innocently recorded religion and personal details could, under Lentz, be centralized into a clenching social dragnet.[89]

But France lacked a tradition of census taking that identified religion. Henri Bunle, chief of the General Statistics Office of France, explained to Vichy collaborators on March 4, 1941: "The General Statistics Office of France is not in a position to rectify published numbers as the last religious census in our country was undertaken in 1872. Since that date, the individual questionnaires used for counting have never touched upon questions of the religion of those counted." Later, on April 12, 1941, he informed the newly established General Commission for Jewish Questions (GCJQ): "France is actually the only country in Europe, or almost, where the number of Jews in its population is unknown, not to mention their age statistics, nationalities, professional affiliations, etc."[90] It was common to proclaim that no one really knew how many Jews lived in either France or even Paris.[91]

Inexorably complicating identification was a confusing patchwork of geopolitical social realities. Since the rise of Hitler in 1933, masses of refugees had been streaming in and out of France. In some cases, some members of refugee families remained while others in the group relocated. Most estimated that there were hundreds of thousands of undocumented refugees and other foreign-born Jews in France when Germany invaded in 1940. After France was bifurcated into an Occupied Zone in the north, including

Paris, and the Unoccupied Zone in the south, which became the Vichy col-laborationist regime, thousands of Jewish families in the north flocked to Vichy for safety. In some cases, German forces in the north actually expelled Jews to Vichy as a preliminary measure, much as Jews were expelled to Poland before the Reich invaded. During spring and summer 1940, when things settled down in the north, thousands of families cautiously ventured back to look after their businesses, possessions, or family members left behind. Jews routinely returned to Paris as late as November 1940. During May 1941, special trains transported 8,000 Jews from Vichy back to the north. Undeniably, Jews were constantly on the move between the two French zones. Addresses changed constantly. No one knew how many of the migrating Jews were foreign or native born.[92]

In either French territory, many of the Jews, whether stationary or migrating, did not identify with Judaism, or hid their religious background. Many genuinely doubted their lineage would qualify under the Reich's rule about Jewish grandparents. Who could even trace or identify one's ancestry, especially if earlier generations hailed from outside France? Ambiguities about the dimensions of Jewish existence in France persisted even as many Jews reacted to looming anti-Jewish measures by openly attending syna-gogues. There was no way to quantify the number of Jews in France or gen-eralize about their character.[93]

The problems of ancestral tracking, shifting addresses, and other popu-lation uncertainties were only multiplied by the twin French jurisdictions. Sometimes anti-Jewish measures were executed in one zone and not the other. Sometimes such measures were enacted months apart, or with vastly differing tenets. Aryanization of Jewish business, for example, was decreed on October 24, 1940, in Occupied France; the similar decree in Vichy France was not issued until ten months later, August 27, 1941. Adding in Jewish commercial and social existence in French colonies such as Morocco and Algeria, and making special provisions for the uniqueness of Paris itself, only further muddied the ability to promulgate and enforce actions.[94]

Berlin could overcome much of the geographical and ethnic confusion in France if it had enjoyed the regimented cooperation of its collaborators, whether reluctant or eager. However, for many leaders in Vichy France, will-ful collaboration with the Reich was strained through a French rightist mindset, which in many ways mimicked the early days of the Hitler move-ment. In the beginning phases of Nazism, foreign Jews in Germany, so-called Eastern Jews, were targeted first and foremost. In Nazi Germany,

German Jews who fought for the Reich in WWI were initially afforded special status. So too, the French right wing conceptualized foreign Jews, especially refugees, as France's scourge. By this ultra-patriotic French thinking, the Jews chiefly deserving of brutal persecution were not the established Jews of France, and especially not those who had distinguished themselves with great national service. War veterans and even those contributing to France's cultural and scientific realms were worthy of special consideration. To do otherwise could be seen by French rightists as an encroachment on certain French prerogatives.[95]

No less a Vichy commander than Admiral Francois Darlan, vice prime minister of Vichy with direct oversight of the anti-Jewish bureaus, was quoted as telling his Cabinet: "The stateless Jews who, for the past 15 years have invaded our country do not interest me. But the others, the good old French Jews, are entitled to all the protection that we can give them: I even have some of them in my family." Hence, a long list of special exemptions crept into the official French enforcement of anti-Semitic statutes, on either side of the Vichy line.[96]

Those in both zones quickly learned that their anti-Jewish collaboration would be dealt with when France was liberated. As early as November 11, 1940, the leader of Free French forces, Charles DeGaulle, issued Nazi surrogates in Vichy a warning: "Be assured . . . the cruel decrees directed against French Jews can and will have no validity in Free France. These blows are no less a blow against the honor of France than they are an injustice against her Jewish citizens. . . . the wrongs done in France itself [will] be righted." DeGaulle broadcast his remarks from recaptured French Equatorial Africa, and then asked that they be proclaimed to a meeting of the American Jewish Congress at Carnegie Hall.[97]

Oppressive Nazi rule could have dictated its iron will to all reluctant French authorities, and conquered the demographic uncertainties of a French Jewry in two zones if only the Holleriths could be deployed. That is precisely what Holleriths brought to any problem—organization where there was disorder and tabular certainty where there was confusion. The Nazis could have punch-carded the Jews of France into the same genocidal scenario in force elsewhere, including Holland. But in the aftermath of the *MB*'s technologic ravages, France's punch card infrastructure was simply incapable of supporting the massive series of programs Berlin required. Even if the machines could have been gathered, transferred, or built—CEC just didn't have the punch cards.

CEC had openly reported to IBM NY about its inability throughout 1941 and 1942 to locate a dependable paper supply. Even with its reduced customer load, CEC clients required 50 tons of paper monthly. But the French subsidiary's deliveries were generally rationed to as little as 15 tons per month—a mere ten-day supply. The Reich was diverting the bulk of the cellulose needed for pulping into nitro-cellulose at explosive plants throughout France. On January 1, 1942, CEC's punch card paper stocks totaled 318 tons. One year later, CEC informed IBM NY that the on-hand inventory had dwindled to just 222 tons, of which only 71 tons were from a paper mill that could reliably produce the high-tech stock tabulators required; the remaining 151 tons had come from a new and untested vendor. Bad paper only jammed Holleriths, worsening the situation.[98]

No wonder CEC bluntly informed IBM NY, "The outlook was very dark . . . we tried to obtain paper by all available means." Only by scraping the barrels of substitute suppliers could CEC "live under the most drastic [paper] restrictions, which we imposed on our customers."[99]

In September 1940, just after German forces transferred hundreds of French Holleriths to the Greater Reich, the first census was ordered in Occupied France.[100]

During the months and war years to come, exactly which censuses were taken, by whom, and by what method, would constitute a maze of mysteries, befuddling all in France and Germany. Registrations and census efforts would be announced and scheduled, and then delayed and rescheduled. They would take place over a period of months, but often the deadlines would be extended because the results were so incomplete. Some counting efforts were undertaken just in Vichy, some just in Occupied France, some in both. Many campaigns counted Jews; many counted the entire French population. Most were executed by a myriad of ad hoc census styles from the inept to the diligent. Incomplete, inaccurate, and inconsistent data ruled the entire enterprise. Heads of households were often counted instead of entire families. Children were often not included. Addresses were not infrequently omitted. Confused officials were on occasion forced to admit they simply had no idea where many of the Jews of France were.[101]

No wonder the Prefect of Tarn complained in a December 22, 1941, letter to the General Commission for Jewish Questions, or GCJQ, that the results of the census ordered just months earlier were already obsolete since the method did not systematically record changes of address.[102]

A later census inspector's report summarizing a major inquiry into the head-counts of eight provinces concluded: "If it was needed, this work is proof that the census of Jews prescribed by the June 2, 1941 law was poorly done . . . a new census is necessary."[103]

Germany's mushrooming labor needs only intensified the counting havoc. By 1942, Berlin had demanded as many as 600,000 French conscript laborers under a strict recruitment schedule as the requirements of the Reich's war work changed. In October 1942, the Reich demanded France deliver 35,000 of its railway workers for assignments in Germany. Earlier, France had suggested the release of 50,000 French prisoners of war in exchange for 150,000 skilled workers. Recruitment projects required waves of age-specific worker registrations. One labor census ordered all French men and women between the ages of 18 and 50, plus anyone working less than thirty hours per week, to register. A second survey sought unmarried women between the ages of 21 and 35 by professional category. Yet another sought to immediately register all young men in a major youth movement over the age of 21. All three census and registration programs were ordered within weeks during fall 1942.[104] Dozens more, equally disorganized, were undertaken during the occupation years.

A new census program would be launched before the previous one was completed. Germany was of course accustomed to multiple, overlapping census and registration programs, but only because it could organize them with battalions of card punchers and fleets of Holleriths fed by endless IBM cards. Those simply did not exist in France.

Cascading chaos as Germany sought to count Jews and others in France ensured that the multifarious census and registration efforts would not only be misreported, misunderstood, and mishandled throughout the war years, but would be misinterpreted for decades after liberation as well.[105]

A fundamental cause of France's profound counting disarray arose from its decentralized, almost anarchic, registration infrastructure. Registration was not implemented by professional statisticians or experienced census offices. With no one to do the job properly, Germany assigned it to the nation's police departments, the prefectures. That stood to reason, since police departments for years were accustomed to registering refugee Jews who entered their jurisdiction. Each prefecture executed its own count in its own way, employing its own interpretations, and not always using the same forms as the next prefecture. They did not use punch cards, but small colored pieces of paper and index cards. The machines they utilized were not IBM Holleriths whirring at great speed, but Remington typewriters with sticking keys that constantly broke down. Pen and pencil were readily used when typing ribbon was not available.[106]

The first real effort to systematically count French Jews had been rumored since the summer, but was finally announced in late September 1940. Jews in the Occupied Zone were ordered to register with information about their businesses at police stations on specified days, according to an alphabetical sequence. The entire process was to take eighteen days.[107]

The numerical tally for the Seine province, including Paris, was reported as 149,734; of these, 85,664 were categorized as French nationals and 64,070 foreign born. The northern Jewish group registered approximately 11,000 Jewish businesses as well. Outside the Paris area, an additional 20,000 Jews were counted. These numbers were for the Occupied Zone only.[108]

It was one thing to count the Jews numerically even if the count was approximate. It was quite another to track them month in and month out, and organize them centrally for either ghettoization or deportation. With a Hollerith, that diverse information would be sorted, tallied, and summarized to yield the desired results. But rather than compile information in succinct automated tabulated results, French information was segmented into a series of traditional paper forms: yellow, beige, white, and red—often as many as five forms to complete a single personal file. The forms, which came into use in January 1941, were known as Tulard files, named for the Vichy police bureaucrat André Tulard, stationed in Paris. Quickly, the Tulard file became famous within French authoritarian circles, which, under the circumstances, seemed the best means of tracking Jews. Soon, the Tulard system, which had first been implemented in the Occupied Zone, was adopted in Vichy as well.[109]

Unlike a Hollerith, which proofed and verified all its information to avoid errors, the Tulard system had no method of automatically deleting duplications. After the October 1940 counts for the Occupied Zone, some French newspapers began extrapolating the raw numbers for all of France. On March 4, 1941, Bunle, head of the General Statistics Office of France, advocated another national census. "Certain newspapers have recently published fanciful evaluations of the numbers of Jews in France," Bunle wrote. "These very exaggerated evaluations equal several times the actual number of Jews in the territory."[110]

So a second major census was launched on June 14, 1941. This one covered both zones, counting 287,962 Jews in 87 of France's 90 geographic "departments." German forces oversaw the count in Occupied France. Vichy performed the function in the south.[111]

The Jewish catalog that emerged required six pages of instructions sent to the police prefectures. Each multi-card file would be marked with various letters: J for Jewish; NJ for non-Jewish, or for someone cleared of Jewish ancestry; N for nationality; D for domicile information; and P for their professional details. Multiple manual catalogs were set up for foreign Jews and French-born Jews. One whole card was designated just to record a woman's maiden name.[112]

Confusion and lack of preparation were everywhere. A May 15 letter from the General Commission on Jewish Questions to the Attorney General tautologically clarified, "If a Jew has not declared equipment for use in the practice of his profession, this constitutes a non-declaration of goods." Another explanatory letter from the GCJQ, on June 24, 1941, confirmed to an inquiring government official that the census laws simply did not apply to certain colonial territories. On July 9, the GCJQ informed the President of the Council that it extended the June 14 census deadline "because the prefectures have not had time to prepare." Ads were placed in the newspapers publishing the new deadline. That same day, July 9, a census staffer jotted a notation that the census forms had been received, and they "will be done as soon as the Department of the Interior has the necessary personnel."[113]

A December 1, 1941, letter from a provincial administrator to the Prefect of Police explained that only Jews who had a residence in France were required to register. That left out the many dislocated Jews residing in hotels or living with another family, including many refugees. One survey of French provinces returning census reports itemized a long list of data missing from their forms: many left out gender, profession, nationality, and in many cases, all three. Many lists bore numerous typos and overtyped sections, so some names and addresses were illegible.[114]

When the Interior Ministry dispatched its long list of instructions to all prefects in France, it included a caution: "Since the number of these cards is limited due to their high price, please let me know, after creating the cards, the categories in which you have extra cards. This way I can distribute them to other Prefectures who have a shortage, as they will also be letting me know which cards they are short on."[115]

As France began its census activities, none of it was being recorded on punch card for automated retrieval. The operating budget reports for the GCJQ listed every expenditure for rentals, ribbons, and repairs on seven Remington and Underwood typewriters, but not a franc on punch card services.[116]

Even as French prefects and the GCJQ struggled to keep up with the waves of registrations, the Germans besieged their offices with unending requests for specific data that stretched their manual capabilities to the maximum. The experience of a single prefect was typical. On January 29, 1942, a German official asked the Prefect of Eure for the personal declarations made by district Jews, as well as inventories of their Jewish goods and enterprises. That same day, he also requested information from the provisional administrators of Jewish housing. On March 14 and again on April 2, the Prefect of Eure furnished the Police for Jewish Concerns with selected demographic information. On June 5, 1942, the Eure Prefect sent the Police for Jewish Concerns various tables listing Jews by age, gender, nationality, and profession—all in duplicate. On July 3, 1942, the Police for Jewish Concerns needed the number of Jews between ages 16 and 45 wearing the yellow star, all Jews between 16 and 45 required to wear the yellow star even though married to an Aryan, Jews older than 45 wearing the yellow star, and those Jews who because of their nationality did not wear the yellow star at all. All names were to be typed by gender listing all names and addresses where available.[117]

In a move to centralize all the information into a single, easily accessible catalog, 100,000 forms were sent to a special police unit headquartered in the Hôtel de Russie in Vichy. In December 1941, the Police for Jewish Concerns could finally visualize the massive quantity of census and registration forms to be sorted. The police bureau told CGJQ director Xavier Vallat that the task was impossible. On December 19, 1941, Vallat acknowledged the crisis. "The file would normally be established by your police service," asserted Vallat, "but it has become apparent from several conversations with your offices that it has neither the personnel required nor the equipment necessary for this operation. Due to this situation we have thought to ask [for] help."[118]

Vallat unexpectedly found the help he needed. René Carmille, comptroller general of the French Army, had for years been an ardent advocate of punch cards. More than that, he had machines in good working order at his government's Demographic Service. Carmille came forward and offered to end the census chaos. He promised that his tabulators could deliver the Jews of France.[119]

WHEN GERMAN requisition teams began pilfering Hollerith machines in August 1940, René Carmille, a mysterious French military technocrat, rescued his tabulators. Under cover of night, he moved the precious devices from his military finance office to a hiding place in a garage. In so doing, the French military's punch card capability was preserved. A few months later, on November 14, 1940, Carmille single-handedly created France's Demographic Service in Vichy. It was just a few weeks after the first Jewish census in the Occupied Zone, and from the Nazi viewpoint, the new agency was wholly compatible with Berlin's labor recruitment and racial agenda. The Vichy government entrusted his agency with the responsibility for all social statistics projects. It operated at least twenty offices on both sides of the zone boundary.[120]

Once established, Carmille carefully began strengthening his small arsenal of tabulators. Not only did he work with Holleriths, but he also had access to a Bull and even a Powers machine. In 1941, Carmille signed a 36-million-francs contract with Bull for new machines, even though the chance of delivery from their new plant in Lyon was in great doubt. He also signed a multi-million-franc contract with CEC calling for a series of powerful machines to be delivered on a strict schedule; millions of francs in fines and penalties were to be paid by CEC if they could not maintain the delivery regimen.[121]

When Carmille began the Demographic Service, he was not allied with the General Commission on Jewish Questions, the anti-Semitic Vichy agency coordinating Jewish registrations. But he was certainly hoping to attract the agency's attention. In March 1941, he made a point of informing GCJQ Director Vallat that his statistics for Jewish students were incorrect.[122]

Carmille had been working for months on a national Personal Identification Number, a number that would not only be sequential, but descriptive. The thirteen-digit PIN number would be a manual "bar code" of sorts describing an individual's complete personal profile as well as professional skills in great detail. For example, one number would be assigned for metal workers, with a second modifying number for brass, and then a third modifying number for curtain rods. Tabulators could then be set to whisk through millions of cards until it located French metal workers, specializing in brass with experience in curtain rods. Those metal workers could also be pinpointed in any district. The system mimicked a concurrent Reich codification system that assigned a descriptive bar code–like number to every product and component in Germany. Carmille's number would ultimately evolve into France's social security number.[123]

In spring 1941, Carmille was readying the professional July 1941 census of all French citizens aged 14 to 65. Question 11 asked Jews to identify themselves not only by their professed religion but also by their grandparents. The program was highly publicized. An article in the *New York Times* several weeks later reported, "Special registering machines are being used in this census. By a system of perforations—every citizen will receive a number composed of thirteen digits—information will be obtainable . . . county by county." An interesting emphasis in the questionnaire was on agricultural skills. A second *New York Times* article on the census actually identified the program as tied to an agricultural drive.[124] Any Vichy official or Nazi representative in France would surely approve of such a census. It would not only identify the workers, including farm laborers, but the Jews among them.

In mid-June 1941, Vichy launched the second major census of Jews, this one in both zones. The question was how would the questionnaires be processed, through manual methods with paper files, or with the dynamic capabilities of Holleriths?

LYON, JUNE 18, 1941
To Xavier Vallat
General Commissioner for Jewish Questions
Object: Census of the Jews

The June 2, 1941 law, published in the *Journal Officiel* on June 14, 1941, orders a census of all persons who are considered Jewish in the eyes of the law of that same date regarding the status of Jews.

   The inquiry that . . . your General Commissariat is going to undertake greatly interests the Demographics Department, which was given responsibility for all statistical operations regarding the population of France. . . .

   This Service just organized, in the unoccupied zone, the first census about professional activities of all persons 14 to 65 years old. The information gathered, as well as all information coming from further inquiries conducted in both the occupied and unoccupied zones, will be used to create and maintain an updated file on each individual summing up their activities. This will be used to produce, at any given moment, the general demographic profile of the nation.

   It seems to me that in these conditions, the special [June 14] census of the Jews could possibly bring complementary information that is even more interesting given that the inquiries cover not only people, but their belongings as well. These considerations lead me to ask you to please tell me right now how your inquiry will be conducted, details about the questions asked, and later on, the results you will have obtained.

In case the model of Jewish census forms is not definitively established, I am at your service to study . . . a form that should permit your General Commissariat, as well as the Demographics Department, to unify all useful information about the Jews. This will allow us to discover those [Jews] who have not yet made their declaration, so we can organize an inquiry as to the status of their belongings and their potential transfer . . . and definitively clarify the Jewish problem.

I am sending an Administrator of the Demographics Department to explain to you the organization of the Service, its work methods, and the results obtained by using tabulation processes to manage individual files. He will also examine with you the conditions in which collaboration between the Services concerned would be advantageous to you.

René Carmille [125]

Like many French bureaucrats, Vallat was resistant to Carmille's contraptions. He worried that commencing a punching operation from scratch would delay the reports. Vallat trusted the Tulard system, even though it was manual—and probably because it was manual. So on June 21, Vallat wrote back to Carmille, "I have thought about integrating this census with the operations your department handles, but it did not seem possible to me, first to prolong the process, given the economic urgency of the census of Jewish persons and belongings, and second, given the particular nature of the information that I need. And I decided to immediately order a [Tulard] file which has proved valuable in the occupied zone and which I will distribute to prefects and mayors in the coming week. I will always be happy to provide you with any information thus obtained." [126]

Only when Vallat's people were confronted with the mountains of forms to be assimilated did they realize that Carmille presented the only hope of efficiently identifying the Jews. Vallat transferred the processing assignment to him. On October 11, 1941, Carmille formed the National Statistical Service, which subsumed the General Statistics Office of France and merged it with the Demographic Service. Carmille stated, "The new statistical service would have a different point of departure, namely to establish files for individuals." He added, "We are no longer dealing with general censuses, but we are really following individuals." Carmille made clear, "the new organization must now be envisioned in such a way that the information be obtained continuously, which means that the updating of information must be carefully regulated."[127] Carmille was now France's great Hollerith hope.

On December 2, 1941, Vallat notified Carmille, "The Jewish census operations in the occupied zone, as ordered by the law of 2 June 1941, is finished; we collected approximately 140,000 declarations."[128] On December 19, a seemingly impatient Vallat complained to the Ministry of the Interior, "The file would normally be established by your Police service. But it has become apparent from several conversations with your offices that it has neither the personnel required nor the equipment necessary for this operation. Due to this situation we have thought to ask the help of the designated Demographic Service to ensure the completion of this task for which they are equitably suited. They have agreed and they have offered to forward this task to their tabulating workshops in Clermont-Ferrand and Limoges."[129]

Vallat later asked the Ministry to pay the considerable cost of the tabulation services, 400,000 francs, and to arrange for transportation of materials to Carmille offices. That was approved.[130] Now the Jewish forms were all in the possession of Carmille.

But the numbers were just not matching up. Vallat was to have sent 140,000 personal declarations. But on June 3, 1942, Carmille's office confirmed it had "received to date 109,066 declarations, of which 20% (exactly 17,980 declarations) were not received until 4 May 1942."[131] Things were going much slower than anyone expected.

To further delay the operation, CEC was now defaulting on its rigid delivery schedule. CEC just could not manufacture machines as required while Dehomag was usurping all its resources. In early 1943, the subsidiary in Paris informed IBM NY, "A certain number of transactions with the National Statistical Service have . . . caused the application of penalties. . . . The amount of these penalties might reach a figure of 4 million [francs] in view of the size and importance of the deals, and because of the company's inability to deliver machines according to contract schedules. . . . A one year delay and waving of penalties was requested."[132]

In the meantime, Berlin would not wait. Using the less efficient Tulard cards, it began organizing round-ups of Jews in Paris. In early May 1941, 6,494 summonses were left at presumed Jewish residences, mainly foreign Jews. They were instructed to report on May 14 to one of seven centers with their identification in hand. Nazi-allied officials could not be certain exactly which addresses were accurate and up-to-date. With Carmille's tabulations not yet ready, the Germans, in essence, relied on the Jews to turn themselves in. The results yielded only half what the Nazis had hoped for.

On the appointed day, May 14, 1941, an estimated 3,400 to 3,700 Jews, mainly of Polish origin, did report as requested. They were immediately sent to camps.[133]

A second raid was conducted on August 20, 1941. This time, French professionals in Paris' 11th Arrondissement were targeted. The Tulard files offered precise lists of names and addresses and even stairwells of many Jews. But the numbers again fell short. Police units cordoned off major intersections—and even blocked the subway exits, grabbing any Jewish man between the ages of 18 and 50. But only 3,022 Jews were arrested. For three more days, the authorities tried to locate more Jews. The inefficient operation only netted 609 on August 21. Then on August 22, they located 325 more. On August 23, as the word spread and Jews everywhere in the District tried to disappear, only 122 Jews were nabbed. The total for the four days was 4,078. The men were sent to the Drancy transit concentration camp. Paris was shocked and outraged because the raids seized both foreign and French-born Jews.[134] But for the Germans, it meant the updated data from Tulard was profoundly inefficient.

A third major raid on December 12, 1941, hoped to snare 1,000 Parisian professionals. The obsolete Tulard files only yielded 743 correct addresses. To round out the numbers, foreign Jews were picked up at random on Paris streets.[135]

Where was Carmille? Where were his Holleriths?

By the end of 1941, numerous Vichy officials had concluded the elaborate census of June 1941 conducted in both zones was completely nonfunctional. A new one was needed.[136]

On January 13, 1942, the Vichy Finance Minister, conscious of the extraordinary expense, bitterly objected to the Interior Ministry. "A general census of the Jews has already been done," the Finance Minister complained. "If all the desired information had been requested at the time, it would be superfluous to undertake a new census a few months later. I ask you please do not proceed with the projected census or with other measures of this nature without consulting the National Statistics Service. Their experience in this matter could be helpful in avoiding gaps or repeated information that could present serious problems from a technical as well as a financial point of view."[137]

Again, where was Carmille?

By February 1942, Eichmann's office in Paris reported that the prefecture lists were completely insufficient, asserting, "our offices are constantly demanding corrections."[138] Something needed to be done.

German officials began turning to the French Jewish Council for names. The Union Générale des Israélites en France, the so-called UGIF, became a prime source for the Gestapo. The UGIF was vested with the sole authority for all Jewish welfare and any other communication between the Jews in Occupied France and the German authorities. Therefore, Jews invariably came to the UGIF offices to sign up for welfare services and submit inquiries about interned loved ones. French Jews even paid special communal assessments to the UGIF. The Germans granted the UGIF unprecedented access to all Vichy census lists and allowed the organization to manually update them. These were then turned over to the Nazis by the UGIF. In fact, the UGIF maintained a whole department for providing lists to the authorities. They called it Service 14.[139]

When one list was not up-to-date, the Germans asked for a revision— again and again until perhaps on the fourth revision the names were complete.[140]

In many cases, Nazi agents merely waited to abduct those Jews who ventured to the constantly watched UGIF office.[141]

Although many Parisian Jews feared appealing to the UGIF for assistance, at some point of economic, emotional, or familial desperation, a number would risk the approach. All too often, that contact would presage their apprehension. The UGIF's efforts to comply with German demands for continually updated names could only be described as relentless.[142]

For example, in July 1942, the UGIF *Bulletin* published a notice regarding the children of incarcerated parents. These children, living in terror, were essentially being hidden by family friends and relatives. "We are composing a central listing," read the UGIF notice, "of all those Jewish children whose parents were arrested recently. If the children were taken in by a private organization or by individual families, and you have knowledge of this, we request you let us know immediately." The notice was published within the framework of UGIF welfare services that sought to render financial assistance to abandoned or orphaned Jewish children.[143]

However, in a telling rebuttal some weeks later, another quasi-sanctioned Jewish organization aligned with the resistance declared: if welfare assistance to the displaced children involved produced a list of the families who have taken them in, the UGIF should not bother.[144]

Later, when the UGIF tried to impose a special head tax to finance a new UGIF census, the underground press condemned it in no uncertain words.

NOTICE FROM THE JEWISH UNDERGROUND

In order to participate in the expenses of the Union Générale des Israélites en France, and to compensate for the insufficient voluntary contributions, all Jews . . . will be subject to a head-tax of 120 francs for the occupied zone, and 360 francs for the non-occupied zone. . . . The tattletaling . . . enterprise created by the Gestapo needs money and, filled with audacity, imposes a contribution upon its victims, "whose voluntary contributions" are insufficient— and with good reason. . . . Everyone knows how the UGIF helps the unfortunates. Like in Paris, where she turns over to the Gestapo the children entrusted to her care; like in Marseilles where the Jews who go to collect their dole are immediately attacked by the Gestapo, forewarned by this organization of traitors. . . . Solidarity is practiced by the Jews . . . [but not by] the traitors who want one more chance to earn the salary their masters in Vichy and Berlin allocate for them, by organizing a new census of the Jews. For this is also the meaning of the new contribution. . . .

Boycott this new census! Do not give a penny to the UGIF!
Not a penny to the Germans![145]

In July 1942, Eichmann arrived in Paris with direct orders from Himmler. All the Jews of France—foreign or native-born—were to be immediately sent to camps. Eichmann began personally supervising the systematic deportation of Jews. Berlin had assigned 37,000 freight cars, 800 passenger cars, and 1,000 locomotives to Occupied France. But local authorities were constantly falling short on the quotas.[146]

On July 15, one train could not leave on time. Eichmann was outraged, calling the missed departure "disgraceful" in view of how much effort had gone into the schedule. A Nazi official assigned to the Jewish solution recalled the moment: Eichmann threatened, the Nazi recalled, that perhaps he might "drop France entirely as a country to be evacuated." The beleaguered Nazi promised Eichmann no more trains would be late. Frantic local officials did everything they could to comply with Eichmann's obsessive demand for Jews. Hence all attempts to create a hierarchy of exemptions within the French ultra-conservative mindset, such as for women or children, or French nationals or war veterans—these all quickly eroded.[147]

Typical was the frenzy exhibited by one French policeman when he scribbled a note on September 12, 1942: "Under our current obligation to come up with one thousand deportees on Monday, we must include in these departures . . . the parents of sick [children] and advise them that they could be deported, with their child remaining in the infirmary."[148]

Throughout 1942, the Germans must have wondered what had happened to Carmille's operation. GCJQ Commissioner Vallat had assured the Ministry of the Interior that Carmille would provide "day-to-day maintenance of the file using perfected tabulation processes. . . . our Services will have permanent access to an updated database for its work." To this end, Carmille had been given a card file of 120,000. He had the only copy. There was no duplicate.[149]

But Carmille continued a mystery.

In October 1943, René Carmille traveled under an assumed name to the town of Annemasse, near the Swiss border, for a secret meeting with relatives of Emile Genon, director of IBM Belgium. Genon was now stationed in Geneva and had been assigned by IBM NY to maintain up-to-date information on all European subsidiaries being operated by German-appointed custodians. Genon wanted intelligence about Westerholt, the SS man appointed CEC trustee. What were his strengths and weaknesses? Carmille gladly provided it, as he needed the continued help of IBM for his punch card operation. Indeed, just after the War, Watson would dispatch a personal emissary and long-time aide, J. J. Kenney, to meet with Carmille's widow in Paris at the Hôtel Georges V. At that post-war meeting, Kenney extended Watson's personal thanks for Carmille's regular information.[150]

Clearly, Carmille was running an active tabulator operation. Why wasn't he producing the Jewish lists?

By November 8, 1942, the Americans, along with some British troops, had landed in Algeria. As many hoped, local French forces joined the Allied campaign against Hitler. On December 5, 1942, French forces seized the entire National Statistics Service branch office in Algiers. Using Carmille's system of tabulators and punch card files, DeGaulle's people were able to organize a seemingly miraculous rapid mobilization of thousands of Frenchmen and others into specific units. As soon as January 17, 1943, the loyal French elements in Algeria were ready to fight as a cohesive and efficient army.[151]

Instantly mobilized French forces in Algeria fiercely fought the German army along the Algerian-Tunisian border until the Reich was dislodged. It was the beginning of the end of Hitler's army in North Africa. Those French units proceeded to Italy and continued to fight throughout the war.[152]

The Germans could not understand how the French army in Algeria was assembled so quickly. Carmille's office there had only been tracking Jews, farm workers, and general laborers.

Just days after the French mobilized in Algeria the Nazis discovered that Carmille was a secret agent for the French resistance. He had no intention of delivering the Jews. It was all a cover for French mobilization.

SECTION III F
German Intelligence

The Section received from Paris a dossier in which there was found information about a special bureau in Lyon which, under the cover of a census of the population, was in fact a secret mobilization office. We had been informed that nearly all the directors of that office were General Officers or Superior Officers [of the resistance]. The Demographic Office could find, in a matter of moments, using special cards, all the specialists (Aviators, Tank Drivers, Mechanics, etc. . . . [both the] officers and enlisted personnel) needed to make up organized units. . . . This was not a census bureau but rather an office of mobilization.

Walter Wilde
special agent[153]

Carmille had deceived the Nazis. In fact, he had been working with French counter-intelligence since 1911. During the worst days of Vichy, Carmille was always considered one of the highest-placed operatives of the French resistance, a member of the so-called "Marco Polo Network" of saboteurs and spies. Carmille's operation had generated some 20,000 fake identity passes. And he had been laboring for months on a database of 800,000 former soldiers in France who could be instantly mobilized into well-planned units to fight for liberation. Under his plan, 300,000 men would be ready to go. He had their names, addresses, their military specialties, and all their occupational skills. He knew which ones were metal workers specializing in curtain rods, and which were combat-ready troops.[154]

As for column 11 asking for Jewish identity, the holes were never punched—the answers were never tabulated.[155] More than 100,000 cards of Jews sitting in his office—never handed over.[156] He foiled the entire enterprise.

Two punch cards were secretly obtained and sent to Gestapo headquarters at Hôtel Lutetia in Paris. Carmille was exposed. Some German officers demanded his immediate arrest along with the fourteen-member senior staff of the National Statistics Services. But German intelligence officer Wilde reasoned that someone needed to run the tabulators so that crucial work brigades could still be marshaled to Germany. After all, the strictly occupational information was indeed up-to-date. So Carmille was allowed to continue his operation. But automated Jewish information was now beyond Nazi reach.[157]

Suspecting he was under suspicion, Carmille nonetheless fearlessly addressed the 1943 graduating class of the Polytechnic School in Paris where his remarks could easily be overheard:

> *"No power in the world," he exhorted them, "can stop you from remembering that you are the heirs of those who defended the country of France, from those who stood on the bridge of Bouvines . . . to those who fought at the Marne. Remember that!*
>
> *"No power in the world can stop you from remembering that you are the heirs of Cartesian thought, of the mysticism and mathematics of Pascal, of the clarity of the writers of the 16th Century, and the perennial accomplishments of the 19th Century thinkers, all this—in France. Remember that!*
>
> *"No power in the world can stop you from realizing that your institution has furnished the world with [great] thinkers . . . that freedom of thought has always existed . . . with rigor and tenacity. Remember that!*
>
> *"No power in the world can stop you from knowing that the motto inscribed in gold letters on the pavilion: 'For Country, For Knowledge, and For Glory,' and the weighty heritage that constitutes the immense work of your ancestors, is for you a categorical imperative which must guide your path of conduct. Remember that!*
>
> *"All this is written in your soul, and no one can control your soul, because your soul only belongs to God."*[158]

In early 1944, SS security officers ordered Carmille arrested. He was apprehended in Lyon at noon on February 3, 1944. He was taken to the Hôtel Terminus where his interrogator was the infamous Butcher of Lyon, Klaus Barbie. Barbie was despised as a master of torture who had sadistically questioned many members of the resistance. Carmille went for two days straight under Barbie's hand. He never cracked.[159]

ON JUNE II, 1942, Germany had ordered 15,000 Jews immediately deported from Holland. Eichmann's people used the word "evacuated." The ultimate destination for Dutch Jewry would be the death camps of Auschwitz and Sobibor.[160]

France's quota was 100,000 drawn from both Zones. But Theodor Dannecker, Eichmann's assistant in Paris, realized he could never meet his quota. On June 22, 1942, the numbers suddenly changed.[161]

France's new quota was reduced to 40,000 Jews. Holland's was increased to 40,000.[162]

Holland's Hollerith program under Lentz was a model of efficiency. By March of 1944, *Waffen*-SS commanders in The Hague had ordered a new bombproof facility for Lentz' Population Registry. The new center was to be laced with bunkers to protect the Holleriths and their precious cards. Separate punching, tabulating, and alphabetizing rooms were arranged around a massive punching pool. One corner office was designated just for "lost cards." Administrative and control offices completed the complex.[163]

With Dutch Jewry handily identified, residentially confined under ghetto-like conditions, and constantly tracked, all that remained now was to organize their efficient deportation to concentration camps. Their names could be called up in an orderly fashion by demographic sector, age, or geographic locale, and of course always alphabetized.

It began in July 1941. Names were taken from the Central Office card indices. Special demographic maps at the Amsterdam Municipal Bureau of Statistics identified the Jewish population, district by district, using red numbers for Jews and blue numbers for non-Jews. In some maps, "dots" were marked onto city maps to more graphically identify Jewish population density by district—the more dots in a district, the more Jews. By July 1942, regular transports started running to a Dutch transit camp called Westerbork. The Dutch *Judenrat,* known as the *Joodsche Raad,* sent a contingent from its own staff to Westerbork to function as a registration department. Arrivals in Westerbork were directed into a large registration hall manned by about sixty registrars, who would take the prisoners' identity papers, ration cards, and other personal documents.[164]

One British intelligence report at the time declared, "The human being [now] becomes a number. . . . A duplicate of the new barracks number card goes into the card index. . . . a special card index [is maintained] in the camp. The identity papers of the deported Jews are then sent to the headquarters of the Population Register at the Hague which thus received the names of almost all the Jews who were deported from Westerbork to Poland." From Westerbork, they were transported to Auschwitz and other death camps. Twice weekly trains began July 15, 1942.[165]

Soon, the call up of names in Holland was so efficient, the Nazis regularly exceeded their quotas. For example, during one period, orders originally called for 3,000 Jews to be transported between January 11 and January 31, 1943. But 600 additional Dutch Jews were gathered, so a total of 3,600 occupied the five transports. The next four transports carried 4,300.[166]

By the close of 1942, virtually the entire 40,000 initial quota was met. Deportations continued. The 8,000 Jews residing in insane asylums and sanatariums were targeted next. The largest was the facility near Apeldoorn, the institution where inmates had such difficulty responding coherently to detailed census questions. January 21 and 22, 1943, SS detachments arrived at Apeldoorn hospital. In what was recorded as a particularly brutal episode, the SS men sadistically beat and herded the bewildered inmates, including many children, into cattle wagons—and from there to the train depot.[167]

It never stopped in Holland. The Population Registry continued to spew out tabulations of names. The trains continued to roll.

Meanwhile, in France, the Germans also deported Jews to death camps as often as possible. But in France, Nazi forces were compelled to continue their random and haphazard round-ups.[168]

Carmille was sent to Dachau, prisoner 76608, where he died of exhaustion on January 25, 1945. He was posthumously honored as a patriot although his role in dramatically reducing the number of Jewish deaths in France was never really known and in some cases doubted. How many lives he saved will never be tabulated. After the war, Lentz explained he was just a public servant. He was tried, but only on unrelated charges, for which he was sentenced to three years inprison.[169]

Holland had Lentz. France had Carmille. Holland had a well-entrenched Hollerith infrastructure. France's punch card infrastructure was in complete disarray.

The final numbers:

Of an estimated 140,000 Dutch Jews, more than 107,000 were deported, and of those 102,000 were murdered—a death ratio of approximately 73 percent.[170]

Of an estimated 300,000 to 350,000 Jews living in France, both zones, about 85,000 were deported—of these barely 3,000 survived. The death ratio in France was approximately 25 percent.[171]

I
II
III
IV
V
VI
VII
VIII
IX
X
XI
XII
XIII
XIV
XV

IBM AND THE WAR

THOMAS J. WATSON HAD CULTIVATED A LOYAL FOLLOWING OF employees throughout the IBM empire, as well as a nation of admiring executives, a fascinated American public, and enamored officials throughout the U.S. government. He enjoyed close social relations with President Franklin D. Roosevelt, the First Lady, and Secretary of State Cordell Hull. Chiefs of state and royal families on several continents welcomed his company. His veneration internationally, and his esteem in America, overcame any incongruities and embarrassing curiosities of his little-understood multinational technocracy. Even when some American diplomats and Washington financial bureaucrats balked at sanctioning what clearly seemed like IBM's marginal or improper actions against American interests, the reluctance was quiet and cautious. These were exceptions to the rule of deference and cooperation always afforded America's almost regal industrialist.

But as the stream of IBM's Treasury license requests to transact business with Nazi Germany or Fascist Italy multiplied—whether directly or circuitously through neutrals such as Spain, Sweden, or Switzerland—one man did take notice. He was not a politician, an executive, or a member of high society dazzled by Watson's gleam or IBM's corporate prestige. Rather, he was just a simple person waging a war at home while America's troops fought overseas. His name was Harold J. Carter.

Carter was a little-noticed investigator working in a little-noticed group that functioned under various names, and wended its bureaucratic way through a variety of federal organizational charts. But the unit was most frequently referred to as the "Economic Warfare Section" attached to the Department of Justice. Its mission was to acquire economic intelligence and confound enemy commerce. Carter was also looking into a category of crimes loosely styled "trading with the enemy." He understood that foiling the commercial and technologic infrastructure of the Axis powers was as important as deploying tanks and troops. Carter's combat was waged not with carbines and grenades, but with subpoenas and indictments. During 1942 and early 1943, he began looking at International Business Machines.

Working out of a fourteenth floor office at 30 Broad Street in lower Manhattan, Carter must have comprehended that he was but a very small person looking into a very big operation run by very powerful people. Watson could pick up the phone and call the White House, the Secretary of the Treasury, or the most senior Army officials. But Carter was unaffected by the Watson gravisphere. He saw something very different in the haze and maze of IBM's involvement with Nazis. Carter was determined to put the pieces together.[1]

After reviewing Treasury license requests, media reports, financial filings, intelligence intercepts from Switzerland, and other materials, Carter concluded that IBM had constructed a unique international cartel responsible for about 90 percent of the punch card technology in the world. This included Nazi Germany, which had developed an extraordinary punch card industry used extensively for all manner of commerce, aggression, and persecution. Carter concluded that IBM's cartel and its special leasing practices, as well as its complete control of the punch cards needed to operate Hollerith systems, meant that the company possessed a virtual monopoly on the technology. But far more than that, because of its grip on punch cards and spare parts, and its ownership of all machines, IBM exercised virtual dominion over any Hollerith's day-to-day ability to function. As a result, IBM wielded a crucial continuing impact on Nazi Germany's ability to plan and wage war.[2]

Carter saw IBM not as a great American company, but a global monster. In Carter's view, Watson was no capitalist luminary but an opportunist to be classed with the Nazis themselves. The only way to secure the evidence he needed to begin prosecution against IBM and its executives was to walk into their headquarters and seize the documents. He needed a subpoena.[3]

An eighteen-page draft preliminary report was prepared, complete with diplomatic intercepts, summaries of telephone conversations between CEC and IBM Geneva, translations of letters between IBM's Werner Lier in Geneva and attorney Heinrich Albert in Berlin, as well as corporate correspondence outlining IBM's tenacious fight against the Dehomag revolt. Carter was cautious in building his case. But he used plain words to portray the gravity of his investigation and explain the unique and less-than-apparent forces at work. He entitled his undated draft "Control in Business Machines."[4]

"CONTROL IN BUSINESS MACHINES"

This is a story of a peculiar type of cartel. Generally speaking, the cartel arrangements which have been heretofore considered deal with instances wherein the cartel control stems from Germany, or one of the other Axis countries, and into the United States for the purpose of curtailing production of critical materials following a deliberate plan of Nazi economic warfare. Previously a villain like I.G. Farben or Siemens Halske has reached its tentacles into American Industry and curtailed production through patents, licensing agreements, and other types of control. This story deals with an American firm which has deprived not only our own citizens by limiting supply but also the citizenry of the world. Americans and Germans alike have felt the pinching hand of Thomas J. Watson and International Business Machinery manifested through universal limited production and international high prices. In this case, the monopoly control originates in the United States and operates throughout the world. And what Hitler has done to us through his economic warfare, one of our own American corporations has also done. In this "arsenal of democracy," which supplies materiel for over half the warring world, limited production spells our worst enemy. Hence IBM is in a class with the Nazis.

Further, we have a peculiar clash of interests. This [World War] is a conflict of warlike nationalistic states, each having certain interests. Yet we frequently find these interests clashing diametrically with the opposing interests of international corporate structures, more huge and powerful than nations. These corporate entities are manned not by staffs of citizens of any nation, but by citizens of the world looking solely to the corporate interest and pledging loyalty thereto. We see revealed [in] this clash, this dichotomy of culture between our nation and an international corporation whose interests do not coincide. . . .

Dr. Hollerith was employed by the U.S. Bureau of Census in 1880 where it was necessary for him to spend much time in the routine of addition and subtraction. As a timesaving device, he invented these tabulating machines run by electric current for the use of the Census Bureau. He sold his patents to the predecessor of International Business Machines Company, who set up their legal monopoly based on these patents. The patents have since expired but so many additional patents were taken out by IBM on improvements and refinements of the original Hollerith machines that the field has been entirely weighted down and the legal monopoly extended. The monopoly still exists because of the many patents taken out by IBM on many small technical changes but all based upon the original Hollerith patents. A question might well be raised as to whether the patents belong to Dr. Hollerith or the U.S. Government in the first place. . . . Since Dr. Hollerith was an employee of a branch of our government and since there was a definite connection between his work of computing and his invention, the question might well be raised as to whether the patents belonged to Dr. Hollerith and were his to sell or to the U.S. Government at the time of their grant. . . .

As to the fact that these monopolies [IBM and the ones IBM imposed on Powers and Remington Rand in the U.S.] existed, there can be little doubt. These companies deliberately conspired to limit production, dictate price and restrain competition as much as possible. This fact has been declared by the United States Supreme Court. We see a monopoly inflicted on the people of the United States. We shall now attempt to show the effect of this monopoly on the outside world, the international cartel arrangement.

This is a story of circumstantial evidence. Practically no documentation or direct evidence can be produced proving the existence of the cartel. Yet one indirect source after the other points to that ultimate conclusion and the indirect evidence is so frequent as to be almost undeniable. . . .

These international corporations have grown so large that very often their interests and the national interests within which they are supposedly contained do not coincide. The personnel of IBM, though nominally citizens of the United States, is actually composed of citizens of the world. Their loyalties to their corporation know no national bounds. Mr. Thomas J. Watson, President of IBM, was one of the leading figures in the international peace movement—not for altruistic motives alone. IBM's far-flung empire was going much too smoothly to be interrupted by war and Mr. Watson's goal is profit. . . .

Certainly it can be said that his company is not an American company, but an international company. . . . The company has not only worked hardship on the people of the U.S. but also people in Germany. When the German section of the world monopoly grew too burdensome on the German people, the

Hitler Government apparently sought to interfere. . . . The entire world citizenry is hampered by an international monster and the indirect evidence herein presented seems to the writer conclusive enough to warrant an extensive search into files of the companies mentioned so that direct evidence may be obtained.[5]

THROUGHOUT 1942, a number of American companies were grandly exposed for extensive dealings with Nazi Germany. A so-called "Proclaimed List" of blacklisted companies had grown from 1,800 in the summer of 1941 to 5,000 European and Latin American companies by mid-January 1942. These prohibited firms were considered either Nazi-owned or Nazi-connected, whether located in Nazi Europe or in neutral countries such as Portugal, Spain, or Switzerland. Of course, all direct trading with Germany and Italy was prohibited. Some firms were included merely because they were considered Axis sympathizers.[6]

For example, on January 14, 1942, five controlling senior executives of General Aniline and Film Corporation, America's third-largest dyestuff manufacturer, were banned from the company by the Treasury Department. All were American citizens, but of German birth, and had for years been suspected of close ties to the German conglomerate I.G. Farbenindustrie. The suspicion was that I.G. Farben either secretly owned Aniline, or could dominate it through the five German-Americans.[7]

On March 26, 1942, a Congressional Committee castigated Standard Oil of New Jersey for turning over synthetic rubber processes to the German Navy while withholding the same technical information from the United States and British militaries. Investigators cited company correspondence and a secret pre–Pearl Harbor trade arrangement with I.G. Farbenindustrie to permit a "modus vivendi which would operate through the term of the war, whether or not the United States came in." Senator Harry Truman, who headed up a special defense investigating committee, publicly excoriated Standard Oil's arrangement as "treason" and "an outrage." An assistant U.S. attorney general described the pact as a "devise for the continuation of the conspiracy through the war." In reporting the scandal, the *New York Times* ran an adjacent article headlined "Standard Oil Men Silent on Charges."[8]

Further revelations documented that Standard Oil tried to do business with Nazi firms in Occupied France, including the construction of an aviation fuel refinery. In its allegations against Standard Oil, the Justice Department repeatedly emphasized that scores of American companies had been quietly capitalizing on relationships with Nazi Germany. In fact, said the Justice Department, Farben alone had consummated contracts with more than 100 hundred American firms, and that those efforts had retarded America's military preparedness by tying up patents and resources.[9]

Certainly scores of American firms used international connections to trade with the enemy. None of them needed more than their own profit motive to pursue such deals. Many of them were proud members of the International Chamber of Commerce, which, during Watson's tenure, espoused an official enthusiasm for trade with the Hitler regime.

Ironically, none of IBM's subsidiaries were on the Proclaimed List because they fell into a double-edged corporate identity as "American-owned property." The same applied to all American-owned subsidiaries in Axis-controlled lands. So even though corporate parents, such as IBM, were not permitted to communicate with their own subsidiaries because they were in Axis territory, these companies were deemed American property to be protected. In fact, since IBM only leased the machines, every Dehomag machine, whether deployed at the *Waffen*-SS office in Dachau or an insurance office in Rome, was considered American property to be protected.[10]

Hence, Dehomag could simultaneously exist as a U.S. interest and a tool of the Nazis doing business with the same Farben and Siemens entities that brought other American companies utter denunciation and often prosecution.

The confusion and inconsistency inherent in the classification of IBM subsidiaries as "friend or foe" was evident virtually every time the matter was raised. For example, on June 16, 1942, the American Consul in Bern asked that IBM's Swiss subsidiary, Watson A.G., not be blacklisted. "This is an American firm," wrote the Consul, "and American interests would probably suffer should it be listed. Axis firms would profit by the listing because it is believed that they have in stock a substantial number of office machines manufactured in Germany and exported to countries later occupied by Germany and Italy. . . . Such machines have already reached the Swiss markets carrying instructions for assembly, use, etc. in the Spanish, Yugoslav, Rumanian, etc., languages. . . . This Consulate General concurs . . . that Watson A.G. should not be listed."[11]

No wonder the British Foreign Office was increasingly disturbed at America's blacklisting inconsistencies. One confidential memo from the British Embassy regarding the blacklist evoked a handwritten marginal note: "It is only too clear that where U.S. trade interests are involved, these are being allowed to take precedence over 'hemispheric defense,' and . . . over cooperation with us."[12]

Because the legalities were so gray, and IBM so stellar an American concern, Carter was not permitted to work with much speed. Alleging treacherous business when the firm was as prominent as IBM, and its leader as well connected to the White House as Watson, was not to be undertaken lightly by any branch of the U.S. government.

So Carter was unable to obtain a subpoena. But he was allowed to visit IBM headquarters and conduct interviews in mid-July 1943. To prepare for his visit, Carter typed an outline with nine topics. His emphasis was how IBM could not just lease products but actually control its customers. Topic 1 on Carter's typed outline: "Importance of the [Dehomag] plant for the efficient management of the German war machine." Topic 2: "Cards imported from the United States per year." Topic 3, with a checkmark: "The source of raw materials with particular emphasis on the possible bottleneck in supplying paper pulp for the manufacture of cards." Topic 7: "Control exercised by IBM over their customers through the policy of renting equipment and the sale of cards." [13]

A second list of ten typed questions focused strictly on Dehomag factories in Sindelfingen and Lichterfelde. Carter wanted to know about "alphabetical printers . . . why the sudden interest now." He also wanted the "name of railroads" Dehomag worked with, and the volume of cards it produced and had imported from IBM NY over the years. [14]

Carter began June 14, 1943, by interviewing Jurriaan W. Schotte, IBM's New York–based General Manager for Europe, in the company's headquarters. Although Schotte, a Dutch national, was the firm's European General Manager, he was permanently stationed in New York. From his office at IBM NY headquarters, Schotte continued to regularly maintain communication with IBM subsidiaries in Nazi territory, such as his native Holland and Belgium. [15]

Carter found Schotte a font of information. The interview lasted three days. During that time, Carter scribbled copious notes about IBM customers, uses for Hollerith machines, paper suppliers, biographies of leading IBM and Dehomag personalities, and terms of use. Since Carter represented the Justice Department, his request to examine hundreds of pages of material was complied with. [16]

Carter perused collections of documents, allowing him to piece together an extraordinary global enterprise, one that in Europe centered on Nazi Germany. It was all micro-managed from IBM's world headquarters. He saw correspondence, typed and sometimes handwritten, detailing sales, installations, Dehomag's revolt, and IBM's struggle to retain its position in the Axis. Machine tool orders were itemized by factory, order date, and anticipated delivery date. Quarterly financial reports and monthly narratives from subsidiaries in enemy territory, received even after Pearl Harbor, relayed the latest business developments and the vicissitudes of competitor information. Up-to-date customer account information enumerated long lists of machines and rental prices, as well as specific war applications. Card consumption figures summarized the volume both by country of manufacture and country of import, all organized by year. Most of all, anyone could discern the ease and frequency of contact IBM maintained with foreign branches.[17]

Clearly, IBM NY possessed a wealth of detailed information about its overseas operations, from CEC to Dehomag to the units peppered throughout the Balkans. Carter was able to type twenty-five pages of notes based just on his three days of interviews with Schotte. A significant portion of those notes centered on two aspects: IBM's ability to manage all aspects of the railroads of Europe, from identification of freight to scheduling, and IBM's incontrovertible control of punch cards.

In the case of the railroads, Carter learned that the Nazis could not schedule cargo or locate a boxcar or locomotive without Hollerith cards. "The German government," Carter wrote, "is at present partly subsidizing freight shipments . . . dependent upon IBM machines in such a way that if the card system were not permitted to function, the railroads would be unable to ascertain that portion of the expense which the government had contracted to bear. . . . Statistics as to the expense to the railroad of freight running between certain points depends upon the card system. In allocating freight charges between railroad systems in different countries, the cards are invaluable."[18]

Carter continued, "the location of the number of trains available in a particular territory can be ascertained, which record would only be about two days late. The only other method would be a spot check which would be two weeks late and, of course, in any system such as a railroad with the tremendous flux of traffic, a two-week gap would be worthless."[19]

Regarding punch cards, Carter noted, "In the manufacture of cards, special machinery is needed. No one but an IBM affiliate can make IBM cards because in Germany the contracts contain a clause that the German customer cannot use cards except those of IBM manufacture. . . . At present, with paper shortages, stockpiles are probably not permitted for more than one month. The replacement requirements of cards are tremendous."[20]

Carter was even able to comprehend IBM's controversial "royalty" agreement. "A peculiar situation arises with regard to the Dehomag company," recorded Carter, "in that here is an almost completely owned subsidiary which, in addition to paying the usual stock dividend, is also required to pay royalties to the American company. . . . However, probably, the true explanation is that the legal limits of stock dividends prevented IBM from getting the return it wanted from the German company, and hence this is a method devised for additional returns."[21]

Clearly, if he could reconstruct as much as he did with a simple request, a full search was called for. Carter returned, this time for a systematic "file search." But he was still hobbled by the lack of a subpoena; his superiors would still not approve one. As such, he was dependent upon the voluntary cooperation of the very people he was investigating.[22]

In IBM's warehouse, at 75 Murray Street in Manhattan, Carter found ten file drawers. Files were arranged alphabetically by country covering the years 1934 to 1940. They contained correspondence relating to punch card production, machine and parts inventories, tariff files, repair records, customer complaints, lists of international fairs and visitors entertained.[23]

But where were the key European files listing "the customer, location, type of business, ownership . . . card consumption and name of salesman" for each machine? Most importantly, where were the "application studies," that is, the specific analysis of each machine's purpose, how well it performed its task, and how it could improve? Schotte's answer: all those records were located in the offices of IBM Geneva.[24]

Where were the records for 1933? Schotte's answer: destroyed.[25]

At IBM World Headquarters, 590 Madison Avenue, Carter first asked for Schotte's files. But now, cooperation had substantially narrowed. Carter was not permitted to examine the actual file drawers. Instead, Schotte brought the folders into his office for Carter's review. Again, all the files were arranged alphabetically by country. The covered years spanned 1940 to IBM's most recent correspondence, containing monthly narrative reports by subsidiary, the details of the IBM machine installations, and "in many instances, applications of the machines." But no "application studies" were found for Germany, France, or Japan.[26]

Where were the copies of Schotte's personal correspondence with the subsidiaries? Schotte's answer: none were in America—they were all kept in the files of the various subsidiaries.[27]

Hence, to examine Schotte's instructions, Carter would have to travel to all the capitals of Europe.

Second, Carter asked for the files of Fred Nichol, executive vice president and general manager of IBM. Nichol was second-in-command to Watson, continuously in touch with Harrison K. Chauncey, W. C. Lier, and others in Europe, and had for years maintained daily scrutiny over foreign operations. Nichol's files were arranged chronologically from 1936 to 1942, but again Carter could not review the entire file. Carter noted, "I was not permitted to take the material from the general file, but the material was chosen for me." Schotte explained that whatever was brought out "comprises the entire file on the foreign subsidiaries."[28]

Nichol's files contained analyses of sales performance and quotas, personnel problems, operating efficiencies at overseas branches, general records of business volume, and details of foreign visitors including "Good Will Ambassadors." Nothing was available on operations in Germany, France, or Italy that was not shown on Carter's previous visits.[29]

Third, Carter wanted to see Watson's files. Again, Carter was not permitted to examine the actual file location. Instead, twenty-six folders covering the years from 1938 to 1942 were brought into Schotte's office. Schotte presented the folders as "the complete file." They included details of Watson's tour as ICC president, lists of top sales achievers, copies of overseas information previously given, correspondence involving tax rates and subsidiary voting shares, letters from and about friends moving from Europe to the Americas, and exchanges of Season's Greetings.[30]

Where was all of Watson's business correspondence? Schotte's answer: Since Watson traveled in Europe extensively, "much of the business was transacted orally." If written materials did exist, then they would be in Geneva.[31]

Carter left IBM's offices with little. He typed a note to file:

> Because of the meager information contained in the files, especially on the European subsidiaries, it is reasonable to assume that either the important files are in the offices of the European headquarters in Geneva, Switzerland, or IBM has not made full disclosure.[32]

ALTHOUGH WATSON had been America's chief peace exponent during the Hitler years before Pearl Harbor, he had prepared for the day when the United States would enter the conflict. As early as August 1940, the War Department began speaking to Watson about converting IBM's manufacturing muscle to war use—but not for Holleriths. The War Department wanted IBM to make machine guns.[33]

On March 31, 1941, long before the U.S. was attacked, Watson had incorporated a new subsidiary, Munitions Manufacturing Corporation. The president of a long-time IBM supplier was designated president. Two small canning buildings were purchased for $201,546. Within sixty days of the December 1941 attack on Pearl Harbor, Watson unveiled a fully equipped 140,000-square-foot manufacturing facility, staffed by 250 employees. The first product was a 20mm anti-aircraft cannon. Eventually, Munitions Manufacturing Corporation produced approximately thirty-two different weapons and other military items, including Browning automatic rifles, gas masks, bombsights, 90mm anti-aircraft gun directors, and 345,500 units of the 30-caliber M1 carbine rifle. IBM logos were stamped on most of the products, including the carbine rifle butts. By 1943, eventually two-thirds of IBM's entire factory capacity had shifted from tabulators to munitions.[34]

More than just a manufacturer, IBM undertook sophisticated research on ninety-nine strategic military research projects, including ballistics trajectory studies, aircraft design, automated inventory control, transportation routing, aircraft fire control systems, and an advanced wireless, electronic messaging unit called Radiotype.[35]

One special defense project involved an experimental system requested by the Army Air Corps. It needed a device that could read holes in telegraphic paper and translate the results to punch cards. Watson was ready for such a request because he had already produced a preliminary design for a company identified as "National Analine." IBM did not complete the work for "National Analine" and instead transferred the project to the U.S. military.[36]

IBM also developed powerful mobile Hollerith units transported in thirty-foot rubber-padded trailers pulled by 2.5-ton tractors. The first sixteen mobile units were delivered by spring 1942 with more than 260 similar such units deployed throughout the war. In the Pacific, mobile Holleriths were hopscotched from one Pacific atoll to the next. In the European theatre, Hollerith vans were brought ashore in Tunisia and Sicily along with all other mobile equipment. Understanding their strategic value, the German High Command had issued priority orders to capture such a unit, with its crew, if possible. That never happened.[37]

Machine Record Units [MRUs] were nothing less than IBM-trained military units specializing in deploying IBM-made equipment. They were also designated to help capture any Holleriths discovered in Europe or the Pacific theatre. A typical MRU detachment was staffed by twenty-nine enlisted men and three officers proficient in punch card operations. To churn out the MRUs, IBM's school at Endicott was converted into a military academy where about 1,300 soldiers were trained to use Holleriths under war conditions. Many of these units were commanded and serviced by IBM employees on leave. They formed a cohesive group of troops, affectionately called "IBM Soldiers," with distinct loyalties to their company and Watson.[38] These IBM Soldiers would have special roles when they came upon IBM factories in Europe.

To coordinate IBM's dozens of war projects for the U.S., Watson created his own corporate "Department of Logistics." This company bureau helped IBM focus its resources on some of America's most sensitive military projects. Watson appointed IBM General Manager Nichol head of this department. Ironically, Nichol was at the same time overseeing IBM's foreign operations in Nazi Europe. Watson explained that Nichol "is eminently fitted for this important work by reason of his broad executive experience . . . combined with military knowledge." He added, "He has intimate knowledge of foreign industrial methods and resources."[39]

IBM and its technology were in fact involved in the Allies' most top-secret operations. The Enigma code crackers at Bletchley Park in England used Hollerith machines supplied by IBM's British licensee, the British Tabulating Machine Company. Hut 7 at Bletchley Park was known as the Tabulating Machine Section. As early as January 1941, the British Tabulating Machine Company was supplying machines and punch cards not only to Bletchley Park, but to British intelligence units in Singapore and Cairo as well.[40]

By May 1942, IBM employees had joined America's own cryptographic service. A key man was Steve Dunwell, who left Endicott's Commercial Research Department to join other code breakers in Washington, D.C. The group used a gamut of punch card machines made by IBM as well as Remington Rand to decipher intercepted Axis messages. Captured enemy code books were keyed into punch cards using overlapping strings of fifty digits. The punched cards were sorted. Each deciphered word was used to attack another word until a message's context and meaning could laboriously be established. At one point, Dunwell needed a special machine with electromechanical relays that could calculate at high speed the collective probability of words that might appear in a theoretical message bit. Dunwell sought permission from Watson to ask that the device be assembled at IBM. Watson granted it. Later, Watson rewarded Dunwell for his service to the nation by allowing him to spend his honeymoon in Watson's personal suite at the IBM Country Club.[41]

It was an irony of the war that IBM equipment was used to encode and decode for both sides of the conflict.[42]

IBM was there even when the Allies landed at Normandy on June 6, 1944. Hollerith machines were continuously used by the Weather Division of the Army Air Forces to monitor and predict the tempestuous storms afflicting the English Channel. When Allied troops finally landed at Normandy, MRUs went in soon after the beachhead was secured.[43]

War had always been good to IBM. In America, war income was without equal. Within ninety days of Pearl Harbor, Watson was able to inform the media that IBM had secured more than $150 million in munitions and other defense contracts. Total wartime sales and rentals tripled from approximately $46 million annually in 1940 to approximately $140 million annually by 1945.[44]

IBM machines were not just used to wage war. They were also used to track people. Holleriths organized millions for the draft. Allied soldiers missing in action, as well as captured Axis prisoners, were cataloged by IBM systems. The location of every serviceman anywhere in the world, from George S. Patton to the most anonymous buck private, could be determined by punching a request into a Hollerith. All military payments were automated and continuously distributed by IBM tabulators. A National Roster of Scientific and Specialized Personnel was assembled to aid in the war effort.[45]

A central reason IBM machines could yield such extraordinary people tracking capabilities in America arose from its extensive use in the 1940 census. This census asked a number of detailed, personal questions. A national campaign of gentle persuasion was launched to convince people to provide the answers. In one radio address, First Lady Eleanor Roosevelt promoted the 1940 census as "the greatest assemblage of facts ever collected by any people about the things that affect their welfare." She acknowledged, "Much doubt has been raised as to the propriety of some of the questions." But, she added, they were designed to yield "facts which will provide illuminating data on problems which have become particularly pressing."[46]

On Sunday, December 7, 1941, Japan attacked Pearl Harbor. Within forty-eight hours, the Bureau of the Census published its first report on Japanese Americans entitled *Japanese Population of the United States, Its Territories and Possessions*. The next day it published *Japanese Population by Nativity and Citizenship in Selected Cities of the United States*. On December 10, it released a third report, *Japanese Population in the Pacific Coast States by Sex, Nativity and Citizenship, by Counties*. Using IBM applications, the Census Bureau had tracked the racial ancestry of Japanese Americans based on their responses to the 1940 census.[47]

Census Director J. C. Capt confirmed, "we didn't wait for the [American] declaration of war [which was proclaimed Monday afternoon, December 8]. On Monday morning, we put our people to work on the Japanese thing." Since only 135,430 Japanese Americans lived in the United States, the results were tabulated quickly. A single sort was necessary: race.[48]

Divulging specific addresses was illegal. So the Census Bureau provided information that located Japanese-American concentration within specific census tracts. Census tracts were geographic areas generally yielding 4,000 to 8,000 citizens. When necessary, the Census Bureau could provide even finer detail: so-called "enumeration districts," and in some cities "census blocks." With this information, the American government could focus its search in select communities along the West Coast—even if it did not have the exact names and addresses.[49]

A Census Bureau official explained to a federal commission that he was happy to provide "a detailed cross-tabulation for even the most minute areas . . . for which data were collected. In other words, enumeration districts and in some instances cities by blocks. . . . Sheets of paper from the tabulation machines were sent out to WCCA [Wartime Civil Control Administration, which was responsible for the internment] . . . and became the basis for the WCCA statistical activities."[50]

The maps displaying Japanese population density were marked with dots, one for each ten persons. American and Dutch census bureaus simultaneously used Hollerith systems in 1943 to create racial "dot maps" as a means of organizing transfers to concentration camps. Hollerith experts dedicated to such projects seemed to work according to an established protocol on either side of the Atlantic, almost as though they had the same consultant. Lentz and his colleagues published highly detailed articles describing their registration programs. These articles appeared not only in Dutch statistical journals, but were translated into German for the journal of the German Statistical Society, and then translated into English for the journal of the American Statistical Association. The *Journal of the American Statistical Association* was regularly read by everyone in the American statistical community as well as the engineers and consultants at IBM.[51]

If locating the Japanese by census block was insufficient, the Census Bureau was willing to take the next step to deliver actual names and addresses. "We're by law required to keep confidential information by individuals," Census Director Capt declared at the time. He added, "But in the end, [i]f the defense authorities found 200 Japs missing and they wanted the names of the Japs in that area, I would give them further means of checking individuals."[52]

By February 19, 1942, President Roosevelt could confidently sign Executive Order 9066 authorizing the internment of Japanese Americans on the

West Coast. On March 22, 1942, the evacuations began in Los Angles. The U.S. Supreme Court later upheld the legality of such a measure based on ancestral grounds alone.[53]

Ironically, on April 29, 1945, an all-Japanese-American regiment helped free Dachau.[54]

Thomas Watson was more than the leader of one of America's most valued wartime corporations. He seized the opportunity to become the nation's chief industrial patriot. Just as he had sermonized for peace during the thirties and early years of war before America's entry, Watson now epitomized the loyal warrior capitalist. As early as January 1941, Watson had assured reporters, "The leaders of government, business and industry to whom the execution of our defense program has been entrusted will have the loyal cooperation of every businessman in the United States. We are willing to make sacrifices to achieve this, because we appreciate our privileges as American citizens and will always stand together in defense of our form of government and our American ideals, while also endeavoring to assist and cooperate with all right-thinking people throughout the world."[55]

On Independence Day, 1941, Watson reported that during the previous six weeks he had helped stage theatrical performances for more than 650,000 American soldiers and sailors stationed at sixty posts. As chairman of the Citizens Committee for the Army and Navy, Watson raised funds among major industrialists to entertain the troops. This included a substantial donation of his own.[56]

On July 15, 1941, Watson declared, "We are a peace-loving people and we love peace to such an extent that we are willing to fight for it. We cherish our civilization in this country above everything else and we are going to be adequately prepared to protect it and to continue to develop it."[57]

In October 1941, Watson's Citizens Committee helped Eleanor Roosevelt organize a "Knit for Defense" tea at the Waldorf-Astoria. At the event, he introduced the First Lady as "the first knitter."[58]

Throughout 1941, even as Watson was broadcasting jingoistic statements and organizing patriotic services, he was also waging his own private war against the Dehomag revolt. However, his struggle to remain in the Axis war machine did not deter him from continuing to mobilize America.

In 1942, Watson purchased full-page display ads in leading newspapers proclaiming his great "WE-ALL." The few lines of large type beneath the headline "WE-ALL" exhorted: "Our slogan now is WE-ALL, which means every loyal individual in the United States. We are facing a long, hard job, but when the United States decides to fight for a cause, it is in terms of WE-ALL, and nothing can or will stop us. President Roosevelt, our Commander-in-Chief, can be certain that WE-ALL are back of him, determined to protect our country, our form of government, and the freedoms which we cherish." The advertisements bore the thick, swashing signature of Thomas J. Watson as "President, International Business Machines Corporation."[59]

Watson's patriotic crusade never diminished in fervor. It wasn't just corporate. It was personal.

In 1943, as Harold J. Carter sat in IBM's offices at 590 Madison Avenue, he was investigating more than a powerful business. Carter never had a chance. He was going against a corporation that was intensely vital to almost every aspect of the U.S. war effort, including its most secret operations, and against executives who occupied the glittering apex of America's rally for defense. In fact, Watson had even declined a recent Democratic suggestion to run for Governor of New York.[60] No wonder Schotte could decide what documents Carter would and would not receive. IBM and Watson were untouchable. Carter learned the immutable truth in the very words he had written months earlier:

> This [World War] is a conflict of warlike nationalistic states, each having certain interests. Yet we frequently find these interests clashing diametrically with the opposing interests of international corporate structures, more huge and powerful than nations.

IBM was in some ways bigger than the war. Both sides could not afford to proceed without the company's all-important technology. Hitler needed IBM. So did the Allies.

By late 1943, Carter learned that whether he concurred or not, IBM was not to be treated as a suspect corporation trading with the enemy, but as a precious war asset in the Allied struggle for liberty. IBM now entered a wholly new phase. Since all of Nazi Europe administratively functioned with Holleriths, IBM's help would be crucial to the post-war control of Europe's administrative and economic infrastructure. Simply put: IBM had the keys to Europe—or rather the cards. Now, all its expertise in punch card technology would be utilized to create an orderly conquest and liberation of the Continent.

Carter's Economic Warfare Section now regularly turned to IBM to learn the many intricacies of German and Italian Hollerith use—not for the purposes of criminal prosecution or documenting culpability, but for the purposes of military intelligence and sustaining Allied victory.

In December 1943, Carter prepared a memo entitled "Use of Mechanized Accounting Systems in Axis and Axis Occupied Territory" based completely on information gleaned from Schotte and other IBM executives. Carter's focus had now shifted, recording the details of Hollerith deployment in Nazi Holland, Germany, and Italy, including the street addresses of major punch card processing agencies and repositories. For example, his memo pinpointed the Ministry of Corporations at Via Vittorio Veneto in Rome as maintaining "complete records in punch card form of all Italian industrial commercial, transportation, and agricultural enterprises, together with the employment and vocational records of all personnel engaged in these enterprises. By putting the punched cards and business machines at this location to use, it would be possible to secure quickly and accurately" a long list of operational information needed to control a post-war occupied Italy.[61]

The memo similarly listed key data bureaus in Holland and Germany. Carter stressed that IBM subsidiaries supplied and helped organize all the enemy installations. He closed with the observation: "In order to utilize the data located in the governmental agencies described above, it is suggested that special measures be instituted in conjunction with the military authorities to seize and safeguard the punch cards and business machines in these offices. These measures might include the constituting of a special unit with detailed knowledge of the applications of business machines and punch cards . . . and a prearranged plan of action."[62]

One of Carter's colleagues, Harold Ungar, prepared another confidential memo further outlining the new approach. "The German Government," wrote Ungar, "through the intensive use of standardized accounting practices and business machines, has achieved a highly centralized control of the financial and industrial activities of Germany and of the occupied countries. This control is so centralized that a sudden collapse of the German Government may produce such chaos in the functioning of the German economy as to make extremely difficult whatever administration the Allied authorities may seek to impose [after the war]. Whatever system the occupation authorities intend to adopt, therefore, one action with high priority is to prepare in advance to seize and utilize the existing German economic control apparatus."[63]

IBM had come full circle. The firm had now become a strategic partner in the war against the Third Reich—even as it continuously supplied the enemy, as before, through its overseas subsidiaries. Carter's investigation was finished. The crusade to save the machines was on.

Carter now produced memo after memo—hundreds of pages—detailing the inner workings of Dehomag, Watson Italiana, and the way the

Third Reich ran railroads and organized military operations across Europe using punch cards. The complete blueprint of Nazi Germany Holleriths was documented. His investigative reports were converted into operational manuals for both invasion forces and the civilian administrators who would follow. As late as June 1944, Carter's section was even able to learn from an IBM executive that critical economic policy files of the Nazi Party had been reduced to punch cards which could be reconstructed if recovered. IBM knew where they were: in Veesenmayer's office.[64]

For the Allies, IBM assistance came at a crucial point. But for the Jews of Europe it was too late. Hitler's Holleriths had been deployed against them for almost a decade and were continuing without abatement. Millions of Jews would now suffer the consequences of being identified and processed by IBM technologies.

After nearly a decade of incremental solutions the Third Reich was ready to launch the last stage. In January 1942, a conference was held in Wannsee outside Berlin. This conference, supported by Reich statisticians and Hollerith experts, would outline the Final Solution of the Jewish problem in Europe. Once more, Holleriths would be used, but this time the Jews would not be sent away from their offices or congregated into ghettos. Germany was now ready for mass shooting pits, gas chambers, crematoria, and an ambitious Hollerith-driven program known as "extermination by labor" where Jews were systematically worked to death like spent matches.

For the Jews of Europe, it was their final encounter with German automation.

EXTERMINATION

I
II
III
IV
V
VI
VII
VIII
IX
X
XI
XII
XIII
XIV
XV

NEARLY EVERY NAZI CONCENTRATION CAMP OPERATED A Hollerith Department known as the *Hollerith Abteilung*.

In some camps, such as Dachau and Storkow, as many as two dozen IBM sorters, tabulators, and printers were installed.[1] Other facilities operated punches only and submitted their cards to central locations such as Mauthausen or Berlin.[2] IBM's equipment was almost always located within the camp itself, consigned to a special bureau called the Labor Assignment Office, known in German as the *Arbeitseinsatz*.[3] The *Arbeitseinsatz* issued the all-important daily work assignments, and processed all inmate cards and labor transfer rosters. This necessitated a constant traffic of lists, punch cards, and encodeable documents as every step of the prisoner's existence was regimented and tracked.[4]

Hitler's Reich established camps all over Europe, but they were not all alike. Some, such as Buchenwald in Germany, were labor camps where inmates were worked to death. Several, such as Westerbork in Holland, were transit camps, that is, staging sites en route to other destinations. A number of camps, such as Treblinka in Poland, were operated for the sole purpose of immediate extermination by gas chamber. Some camps, such as Auschwitz, combined elements of all three.[5]

Without IBM's machinery, continuing upkeep and service, as well as the supply of punch cards, Hitler's camps could have never managed the numbers they did.

The major camps were assigned Hollerith code numbers for their paperwork: Auschwitz . . . 001; Buchenwald . . . 002; Dachau . . . 003; Flossenbürg . . . 004; Gross-Rosen . . . 005; Herzogenbusch . . . 006; Mauthausen . . . 007; Natzweiler . . . 008; Neuengamme . . . 009; Ravensbrück . . . 010; Sachsenhausen . . . 011; Stutthof . . . 012.[6]

Auschwitz, coded 001, was not a single camp, but a sprawling complex, comprised of transit facilities, slave factories and farms, gas chambers, and crematoria. The *Arbeitseinsatz* housed the Hollerith equipment. In most camps, the *Arbeitseinsatz* tabulated not only work assignments, but also the camp hospital index and the general death and inmate statistics for the Political Section.[7]

In August 1943, a timber merchant from Bendzin, Poland, arrived among a group of 400 inmates, mostly Jews. First, a Polish doctor examined him briefly to determine his fitness for work. His physical information was noted on a medical record for the "camp hospital index." Second, his full prisoner registration was completed with all personal details. Third, his name was checked against the indices of the Political Section to see if he would be subjected to special cruelty. Finally, he was registered on Hollerith equipment in the labor index of the *Arbeitseinsatz* and assigned a characteristic five-digit Hollerith number, 44673.[8] This five-digit number would follow the Polish merchant from labor assignment to assignment as Hollerith systems tracked him and his availability for work, and reported it to the central inmate file kept at Department DII. Department DII of the SS Economics Administration in Oranienburg oversaw all camp slave labor assignments.[9]

Later in the summer of 1943, the timber merchant's same five-digit Hollerith number, 44673, was tattooed on his forearm. Eventually, during the summer of 1943, all non-Germans at Auschwitz were similarly tattooed.[10]

Tattoos, however, quickly evolved at Auschwitz. Soon, they bore no further relation to Hollerith compatibility for one reason: the Hollerith number was designed to track a working inmate—not a dead one. Once the daily death rate at Auschwitz climbed, Hollerith-based numbering simply became outmoded. Clothes would be quickly removed from any cadaver, making identification for the Hollerith-maintained death lists difficult. So camp numbers were inked onto a prisoner's chest. But as the chest became obscured amidst growing mounds of dead bodies, the forearm was preferred as a more visible appendage. Soon, ad hoc numbering systems were inaugurated at Auschwitz.

Various number ranges, often with letters attached, were assigned to prisoners in ascending sequence. As people died, the numbers were reused, sometimes even stolen so people could "disappear" using the corpse's identity. Dr. Josef Mengele, who performed bizarre experiments, tattooed his own distinct number series on patients. Tattoo numbering ultimately took on a chaotic incongruity all its own as an internal Auschwitz-specific identification system.[11]

But Hollerith numbers remained the chief method of centrally identifying and tracking prisoners at Auschwitz, especially when responding to Berlin's orders. For example, in late 1943, some 6,500 healthy, working Jews were ordered to the gas chamber by the SS. But their murder was delayed for two days as the Political Section meticulously checked each of their numbers against the Section's own card index. The Section was under orders to temporarily reprieve any Jews with traces of Aryan parentage.[12]

Sigismund Gajda was processed by Hollerith. Born in Kielce, Poland, Gajda was about forty years of age when on May 18, 1943, he arrived at Auschwitz. A paper form, labeled "Personal Inmate Card," recorded all of Gajda's personal information. He professed Roman Catholicism, had two children, and his work skill was marked "mechanic." The reverse side of his Personal Inmate Card listed nine previous work assignments. At the bottom of the card's front panel was a column to list any physical punishments meted out, such as flogging, tree-binding, or beating. Once Gajda's card was processed by Auschwitz's Hollerith machines, a large indicia in typical Nazi Gothic script letters was rubber-stamped at the bottom: *Hollerith erfasst,* or "Hollerith registered." That designation was stamped in large letters on hundreds of thousands of processed Personal Inmate Cards at camps all across Europe.[13]

Auschwitz's print shops produced the empty Personal Inmate Cards for Hollerith operations at most other concentration camps. Sometimes the Auschwitz presses simply could not keep up with demand. In one instance, on October 14, 1944, the leader of Ravensbrück's Hollerith Department sent a letter to his counterpart at Flossenbürg's Hollerith Department confirming that a work gang of 200 females had been dispatched for slave labor at the Witt Company in Helmbrechts. "The inmates' personal cards as well as the Hollerith transfer lists are being submitted," the Ravensbrück officer leader wrote. But, he added, "Since at the moment, no [Inmate] Cards can be obtained from the Auschwitz printers, temporary cards had to be made for that part of the transport."[14]

All Auschwitz inmate information, including workers still alive, deaths, and transferees, was continuously punched into the camp's Hollerith system. Tabulated totals were wired each day to the SS Economics Administration and other offices in Berlin by the various camp Hollerith Departments. Hollerith tracking was the only system for monitoring the constantly shifting total population of all camps.[15]

The "Central Inmate File" at the SS Economics Administration was a mere paper file, but all its information was punched into the central Hollerith banks in Berlin and Oranienburg. Each prisoner was tracked with a single paper card boldly labeled at the top *Häftlingskarte,* that is, "Inmate Card." That paper card was filled with personal information handwritten in fields next to the corresponding Hollerith code numbers to be punched into IBM equipment. No names were used to identify prisoners in this file—only their assigned Hollerith numbers, generally five digits long, but often six digits when a zero was prefixed. Each five- or six-digit number was coupled with a concentration camp number. Hence, each camp could potentially register 999,999 inmates.[16]

For instance, one nameless inmate was assigned the six-digit number, 057949, which was to be punched into columns 22 and 27 of a Hollerith card. He was born on October 7, 1907, which was punched into section 5: The Security Police, which was coded 1 for column 2, took the man into custody in the town of Metz, which was punched into a different row. November 11, 1943, was the arrest date, which was punched into section 3. Prisoner 057949 was marked as a Communist Spaniard, coded 6 for column 4. As a male, box 1 for column 6 was checked; but since he was unmarried, box 1 for column 7 was also checked; his one child necessitated an additional mark for column 8. Prisoner 057949 was transferred to Dachau, coded "03" for columns 21 and 26.[17]

Along the bottom of Prisoner 057949's card was a series of lines for each concentration camp to which he was assigned. At the right of each camp entry line was a grid marked *Holl. Verm.* for "Hollerith Notation" above two separates boxes: one marked "In," and the next marked "Out."[18]

At the bottom right of every Inmate Card was a special processing section labeled *Kontrollvermerk*. Under *Kontrollvermerk* were three boxes:

> *ausgestellt* for "issued"
> *verschlüsselt* for "encoded"
> *Lochk. geprüft* for "punch card verified."[19]

The punch card operator's number was hand-stamped in the "punch card verified" box to maintain quality control.[20] Millions of identical Inmate Cards were run through the system, all featuring column-numbered data fields, the distinctive "Hollerith Notation" grid, and control boxes to certify the punch card processing details. When a number holder deceased, his number was simply re-issued. Of the millions produced, more than a hundred thousand such Inmate Cards survived the war.[21]

Hollerith tracking worked so well that the SS Economics Administration was able to authoritatively challenge the slave labor reports they were receiving on any given day. For instance, at one point in the latter part of 1943, the central office asked for the number of Auschwitz Jews fit for reassignment to an armaments plant. On August 29, Auschwitz replied that only 3,581 were available. Senior SS Economics Administration Officer Gerhard Maurer knew from DII's Hollerith sorts that fully 25,000 Jews were available for work transfers. Four days later, Maurer dispatched a brash rejoinder to Auschwitz Camp Commandant Rudolf Hoess himself. "What are the remaining 21,500 Jews doing?" Maurer demanded. "Something's amiss here! Please again scrutinize this process and give a report."[22]

Later, in January 1945, a number of Russian prisoners were delivered to Auschwitz. Each of them was classed *Nacht und Nebel,* which translated to "Night and Fog," essentially designating them as covert inmates. *Nacht und Nebel* Russians were coded 14 in Auschwitz records.[23]

Hollerith Departments at camps could not be operated by miscellaneous labor. They required so-called Hollerith experts trained by an IBM subsidiary, either Dehomag in Germany, or any of the others depending upon location. At Auschwitz, the key man running the card index systems was Eduard Müller. Müller was a fat, aging, ill-kempt man, with brown hair and brown eyes. Some said, "He stank like a polecat." A rabid Nazi, Müller took special delight in harming inmates from his all-important position in camp administration.[24]

Buchenwald, coded 002, was established in July 1937, long before the war started. From its inception, Buchenwald was a cruel destiny for Germany's social undesirables, including politicals, hardened criminals, so-called work-shy misfits, Jehovah's Witnesses, homosexuals, and Jews. Hollerith machines were needed from the outset to code and segregate each type of inmate, and then ensure the prisoner was subjected to a regimen of maltreatment and deprivation prescribed for his category.[25]

Ironically, when many Jews, homosexuals, and Jehovah's Witnesses registered at Buchenwald, they were required to write "career criminal" on the front of their Personal Inmate Card as a welcoming humiliation ritual. Their real occupation was noted on the back. Those who balked at listing themselves as criminals were severely beaten.[26]

So many hundreds of thousands of IBM cards, all with the characteristic red Dehomag logo printed along the edge, clicked through the Hollerith machines of Buchenwald, and its many sub-camps, that spent cards were typically cut in half so the backs could be used for note pads. For example, the flip side of a punch card recording production details at the Zwieberge sub-camp was re-used to request shift assignments. The commander scribbled on the back: please deploy Alfred and Schneider to *Kommando 1*. "They are to be transferred to a shift . . . in Block 12."[27]

Deaths were so numerous at Buchenwald that the hospital staff jotted individual details on the back of used IBM cards. Typically, the deceased inmate's five- or six-digit number, sometimes with barracks number appended, was scrawled next to the name and nationality, next to two dates: entry into the hospital and death. German Prisoner 52234 entered April 11 and died April 12. French prisoner 71985 entered on April 14 and exited on April 15. French Jewish prisoner 93190 entered April 14 and departed two days later. A tell-tale array of hole punches was always clearly visible on these square scraps.[28]

Dachau, coded 003, was the Reich's first organized concentration camp, established in March 1933 in the first weeks of the Hitler regime. Several detention camps had been erected early on. But Dachau, set up just ten kilometers from Munich, was the first Nazi camp created to inflict hellish cruelty on the Reich's undesirables, especially Communists and Jews. Offices of the merciless *Waffen*-SS and its predecessor organizations, located at Dachau, utilized at least four multi-machine sets of IBM machines, including Dehomag's most advanced. *Waffen*-SS units were militarized SS troops that actively participated in some of the bloodiest murders of the war.[29]

While Dachau was originally established for Germans, once the Reich conquered Europe, inmates from many countries were processed through its Hollerith machines. Middle-class Parisian prisoners were in abundance. Prisoner 072851, a French salesman, was taken by the Security Police in Paris; Hollerith operator number 8 processed his card. Prisoner 072850, a chef, was also taken by the Security Police in Paris; Hollerith operator number 8 also processed his card. Prisoner 072833 was a gardener, taken by Security Police in Paris; Hollerith operator 8 punched his information as well. The very next card in the sequence belonged to Prisoner 072834, a baker taken by Security Police in Paris; that card was punched by Hollerith operator 9.[30]

Dachau's equipment was managed by several Hollerith experts and non-technical supervisors. Albert Bartels, head of the SS machine record agency, with no particular expertise, functioned as the senior official. Herbert Blaettel possessed the technical knowledge since he was a former Dehomag dealer and later worked in Dehomag's training department. Blaettel was aided by Heiber, considered a virulent SS man. Busch, another technical expert, had been a Dehomag dealer since 1932 and finally joined the SS in 1943 to help the SS operate its machines. Because Dachau was just ten kilometers from Willy Heidinger's hometown near Munich, and the well-established Dehomag branch office there, Dachau was always close to the epicenter of Hollerith automation development. For example, Dachau received Dehomag's very first advanced alphabetizer, the DII-A.[31]

Flossenbürg, coded 004, was another camp built in Germany before the war. The giant facility, built near the town of Floss, continuously worked inmates to death at a nearby granite quarry and Messerschmitt aircraft factory. When enfeebled prisoners by the thousands dropped dead from malnutrition and exhaustion, their bodies were quickly cremated.[32]

Because Flossenbürg was primarily a slave labor camp, it relied heavily on Hollerith machines to coordinate the work battalions transferring in and out from other major camps or its own sub-camps. The camp's well-developed Hollerith Department tracked its slaves by name and number. During September 1944, thousands of prisoners were transferred to Flossenbürg proper from its smaller sub-camps. On September 1, 1944, for example, Flossenbürg's Hollerith Department received secret notice #1049/44, specifying that six of those sub-camps were transferring a total of 2,324 cards corresponding to the attached "Hollerith Transfer Lists." From Camp Neurohlau: 561; from Camp Zwodau: 887; from Camp Graslitz: 150; from Holleischen: 603; and from Camp Helmbrechts: 100. Seventeen women were also transferred to a special Flossenbürg detachment. The secret notice to Flossenbürg's Hollerith Department explained: "The inmates' files have been kept in the records of the local camps up until and including August 31, as was already reported by telegram. The transfer lists for the Hollerith card file are attached as well."[33]

Notice #1049/44 to Flossenbürg also stressed that although 2,324 cards were accompanying the Hollerith transfer printouts, six women had escaped during the past few months. "The inmates' files have been removed from the records of local camps, after their escape," the notice instructed, "and their records have to be reinserted into the files upon their capture." The six women were listed by name and Hollerith number:

#22941 Basargina, Elena	#23021 Edwokimenko, Diana
#30279 Baranecka, Lena	#28803 Krlanisch, Valentina
#29306 Saganjatsch, Nadia	#34434 Hildinberg, Gertrud[34]

Printouts from Flossenbürg's Hollerith Department were used to organize and accompany the transfer not only of large slave groups numbering more than 1,000, but small work gangs as well. On January 24, 1945, Flossenbürg's *Arbeitseinsatz* received notice from another camp's Hollerith Department: "We are submitting inmate personal cards for 200 inmates transferred to work camp Helmbrechts and 200 inmates transferred to work camp Dresden . . . Hollerith lists are included." Several months before, on September 1, 1944, Flossenbürg's *Arbeitseinsatz* received a similar order but for half as many inmates. "In the attachment," the September 4, 1944, notice informed, "find enclosed the inmate personal cards for 100 inmates transferred to work camp Witt in Helmbrechts on August 31, 1944. The Hollerith transfer list is included."[35]

Hollerith lists could be produced for as few persons as needed. On November 13, 1944, Flossenbürg's *Arbeitseinsatz* received orders involving just four women: "The inmate personal cards for 4 female inmates transferred to work camp Helmbrechts on November 9, 1944, as well as Hollerith transfer list Number 123 are submitted in the attachment. We are requesting the speediest delivery of personal file cards for the 4 transferred inmates."[36]

Among the many punch card operations in concentration camps, perhaps the most active was the massive Hollerith Department at Mauthausen. The giant Austrian camp was really an extensive complex of slave labor quarries and factories, operated with a brutal furor calculated to quickly work inmates to death. Sadistic labor conditions amid unspeakable daily atrocities killed thousands. Numerous Mauthausen sub-camps functioned as satellites in a similar vein. Moreover, as camps consolidated late in the war, captives were continuously shipped into the camp so Mauthausen received many transfers from other facilities. Hollerith operators located in the *Arbeitseinsatz,* across from the Political Section, could see the entire parade grounds, including the arrival of every prisoner transport.[37]

A low-level SS officer supervised Mauthausen's Hollerith Department. But day-to-day sorts and tabulations were undertaken by a Russian-born French army lieutenant POW named Jean-Frederic Veith. Veith arrived at Mauthausen on April 22, 1943, just days before his fortieth birthday. He was quickly assigned to the tabulators. Among Veith's duties was processing the many Hollerith lists from other camps, not only transferred prisoners for new assignment, but also those the sorts had determined were misrouted.[38]

Veith compiled both the voluminous death lists and new arrival rosters, and then dispatched the daily "strength numbers" to Berlin. His section stamped each document *Hollerith erfasst*—"Hollerith registered"—and then incorporated the figures into the camp's burgeoning database. Hence, the enormity of Mauthausen's carnage was ever-present in his mind as he ran the machines.[39]

Mauthausen "Departure Lists" were fundamentally roll calls of the dead. A typical handwritten "Departure List" ran on for many pages, thirty lines per page. No names were used, just the inmate's five- or six-digit Hollerith identity, listed on the left in numerical order for efficient punching into column 22 of the Dehomag cards printed for camp death tallying. The victim's birth date was penned into the next table for punching into section 5. Death dates were scrawled in the right field set aside for section 25.[40]

Cause of death was recorded for column 24. Generally, the murdered inmate itemized on the top line was coded C-3, the Hollerith designation for "natural causes." For convenience, ditto marks signifying "natural causes" would then be dashed next to every inmate number. But these death citations were faked. For amusement, Mauthausen guards might force an inmate to jump off the quarry cliff at a spot called "the Parachute Jump." Exhausted laborers might be crowded into the tiled gas chamber below the sick bay where carbon monoxide billows would suffocate their lives. Undesirables might be terminated in "Operation K" actions—a bullet administered at close range. Or special cases might be hoisted by their arms tied behind their backs until they died from the socket-wrenching excruciation. All these murders were almost always dittoed C-3, "natural causes."[41]

The Hollerith installations at Auschwitz, Buchenwald, Dachau, and Mauthausen were only part of an extensive network of camp punching and tabulating services that stretched across Europe. At Stutthof camp in Poland, coded 012, the Hollerith Department used six-digit registrations beginning with zero. At the nightmarish Gusen camps, the Hollerith cards were not only set up to record personal biographical and work assignments, they also recorded the gruesome details of painful punishments administered to prisoners, such as floggings and hanging from a tree with arms bound in back. At Westerbork transfer camp in Holland, Hitler's Holleriths were used to schedule efficient trainfuls of prisoners destined for Auschwitz gas chambers, and then report the numbers back to the registration office.[42]

At Bergen-Belsen, where surviving prisoners were described by liberators as "emaciated apathetic scarecrows huddled together in wooden huts," the Hollerith cards were maintained in a barracks dubbed "the lion's den," located in the *Arbeitseinsatz*. To obliterate all evidence of the mass murders documented by the Hollerith records, Himmler ordered all camp card indices to be destroyed before the Allies arrived.[43]

At Ravensbrück woman's camp, coded 010, the busy Hollerith Department used its own "Ravensbrück" rubber stamp to save time writing. Punch card operators at Ravensbrück often identified their work by letter, rather than number. A stream of Hollerith transfer lists always accompanied Ravensbrück slave women transported to various factory sites and camps. One could live as long as one could work. Ravensbrück women always knew fellow prisoners were about to be exterminated when a trusty abruptly retrieved their cards. One British inmate recalled in a secret letter written at the time, "The selected ones have to wait in front of the Block . . . while the [trusty] . . . who has noted their numbers goes to the *Arbeitseinsatz* and gets their cards (which are only removed if the prisoner is dead). An hour later she returns with the cards and a lorry and they go—never to return."[44]

The SS Economics Administration, under the leadership of *Gruppenführer* Oswald Pohl, utilized Hollerith systems for more than specific prisoner tracking. IBM machinery helped the SS manage the massive logistics of the entire camp system. Although millions, representing many nationalities and religions, were imprisoned at various times in hundreds of installations, the total camp capacity on any given day was between 500,000 and 700,000.[45] That required population management. Jews from across Europe were being continuously transported into the camps. At the same time, slaves within camp confines died or reached the limits of their utility to the Reich. The prodigious task of efficiently scheduling deportation from cities and ghettos in many countries, the daily work assignments, and outright extermination timetables would have been impossible without the daily strength reports. When the camps reached the maximum of even their inhumane overcrowded capacity, orders went out from Berlin to reduce the density. Those periodic orders issued by the SS Economics Administration were based on the well-honed statistics provided by the Holleriths both in the camps and at camp administration headquarters.[46]

In fact, a special statistical bureau was eventually established in January 1944 to coordinate and tabulate all new registrations, death lists, daily strength reports, and transfers from site to site. This virtually unknown secret punch card facility was simply called *Zentral Institut,* that is, the "Central Institute." Each day, camps would forward copies of their strength reports to *Zentral Institut,* located on a quiet, residential street in Block F at 129 Friedrichstrasse in Berlin.[47]

Although the location was tranquil, the traffic in and out was constant. Couriers delivered weekly "Departure Lists" from the various camps. For example, Mauthausen's list for week 37 of 1944 was six pages long—virtually all deceased. For week 40, the list was seven pages long. For week 41, it was six pages, recording 325 deaths. For week 44, seven pages listed 369 prisoners. An October 17, 1944, delivery of prisoner cards from Mauthausen's Hollerith Department included data on 6,969 males and 399 females.[48]

Zentral Institut, at Block F, 129 Friedrichstrasse, was able to render the big picture only because it processed the most individualized details. For instance, on January 2, 1944, the SS officer in charge of Mauthausen's Hollerith Department informed his counterparts at Flossenbürg's Hollerith Department about three named and numbered prisoners who had recently transferred in. One died in transport and two others were utilized in an unspecified secret project. Since they were never actually registered at Mauthausen, the Hollerith Department suggested their names just be sent to *Zentral Institut* as "departures."[49]

Zentral Institut's elaborate Hollerith banks at Block F, 129 Friedrichstrasse were expensive Dehomag systems. But the SS could more than justify the cost because slave labor was sold by the SS Economics Administration and managed as a profit center. Enterprises as large as the heavy industries of I.G. Farben, as delicate as Hotel Glasstuben, and as small as a local business, routinely contracted for slave labor with Department DII, which governed all slave labor assignments. For instance, in late July 1942, farmer Adam Bär of Würzelbrunn, short on farmhands for his beet fields, applied to DII for two farm slaves from Flossenbürg.[50]

The SS Economics Administration, which had total operational control of all camps, could supply exactly the skilled workers required and transfer people from camp to camp, and factory to factory, by setting the dials of their Hollerith systems that had stored the details of all inmate cards. Two important inmate cards were utilized. The Personal Inmate Card was used for on-site camp registration and stayed with the individual in the field. DII's centralized version was simply called "Inmate Card." Every Inmate Card held in DII's Central Inmate File listed the prisoner's profession in a field to be punched into column 10 of the IBM card. For example, Spanish inmate 30543 was listed as a lumberman. That qualified 30543 to be assigned by the Neuengamme concentration camp as a "helper" in any slave enterprise. Occupational details for column 10 were provided by the top line of the reverse side of the Personal Inmate Card.[51]

Maschinelles Berichtwesen, the Reich's central punch card agency, had helped develop the slave labor punch card in conjunction with Dehomag engineers. These cards listed inmates by nationality and trade. After matching any of the millions of slaves and conscripted workers, both in camps and incoming foreign labor battalions, to the numerous requests by both private companies and public works, DII could promptly deploy workers where they were needed, when they were needed.[52] In this sense, DII acted like any worker placement agency.

Charges for DII's workers could be easily tabulated on Dehomag's well-established hourly wage cards, thereby generating instant slave billings. A typical monthly charge to Messerschmitt airplane works for Flossenbürg slaves was the one itemized on DII's invoice #FLO 680, which was issued December 1, 1944:

- 50,778 full-time skilled slaves at RM 5 per day
- 5,157 part-time skilled slaves at RM 2.50 per day
- 53,071 full-time helpers at RM 3 daily
- 5,600 part-time helpers at just RM 1.50 daily

Messerschmitt's total invoice for the month of November 1944 was RM 434,395.50. Although Messerschmitt employed 114,606 Flossenbürg slaves in November 1942, once the month closed on November 30, DII was able to generate an itemized invoice within twenty-four hours. Prompt payment was requested.[53]

Slave revenues for all camps totaled RM 13.2 million for 1942. This program of working inmates to death had a name. The Reich called it "extermination by labor." Atop the ironwork entrances of many slave camps was an incomprehensible motto: *Arbeit Macht Frei*—"Work will set you free."[54]

EVERY HELL has its hierarchy. Each Hollerith code carried consequences. In the concentration camps, the levels of inhumanity, pain, and torture were not the happenstance of incarceration as much as a destiny assured by Hollerith coding. Many unfortunate groups were shipped to the camps. But the Jews, coded as they were, were singled out for special cruelties that forced them to either live a more tortured life or die a more heinous death.

It was impossible to shirk one's Hollerith code. Most camps classed prisoners into sixteen categories:

Political Prisoner 1	Asocial 9
Bible Researcher 2	Habitual Criminal 10
Homosexual 3	Major Felons 11
Dishonorable Military Discharge 4	Gypsy 12
Clergy 5	Prisoner of War 13
Communist Spaniard 6	Covert Prisoner 14
Foreign Civilian Worker 7	Hard Labor Detainee 15
Jew 8	Diplomatic Consul 16.[55]

On arrival, all prisoners would register and receive their five-digit inmate number, as well as a striped uniform sewn with a color-coded triangular chest patch. The patch identified the man at a distance to both guards and more privileged prisoners. Generally, but not always, political criminals wore red patches. Homosexuals wore pink. Serious criminals wore green. Jews, coded 8, were forced to wear two triangular patches forming the six-pointed Star of David. Various additional markings and colors on the yellow star connoted either "race polluter" or political Jew.[56]

As horrific as camps were for all, Jews coded by number experienced an additional nightmare of unspeakable dimension. Because Jews were instantly recognizable by their patches, they could be denounced at every turn as "Jewish swine," or "Jewish muck," with the attendant physical abuse.[57] One could never escape his code.

Coded maltreatment also meant segregated quarters and more severe work conditions for Jews. In Buchenwald, for example, Jews were almost always confined to the so-called Little Camp, where prisoners were housed sixteen to a 12' x 12' "shelf," triple-decked. Many new inmates were initiated by spending time in the Little Camp, where they were expected to quickly lose about 40 percent of their body weight, and then move on to other barracks. But Jews were not released. Emaciated Jewish prisoners who "had been around long enough" or who refused to be mentally broken, were arbitrarily condemned to death—generally an entire shelf at a time.[58]

Once the murder decision had been made, all sixteen Jews in the shelf were immediately marched to a small door adjacent to Buchenwald's incinerator building. The door opened inwards creating a short, three-foot-long corridor. Jews were pushed and herded until they reached the corridor end. There, a hole dropped thirteen feet down a concrete shaft and into the Strangling Room. A camp worker recalled, "As they hit the floor they were garroted . . . by big SS guards and hung on hooks along the side wall, about 6½ feet above the floor . . . any who were still struggling were stunned with a wooden mallet . . . An electric elevator . . . ran [the corpses] up to the incinerator room."[59]

In another camp, Jews were once singled out on Hanukkah, the Jewish festival of lights that features the lighting of small candles. Guards ordered Jews to gather round. Eight were selected and strung upside down. The Jews were then forced to douse the hanging men with oil, and ignite them one by one. As the immolating Jews shrieked in pain, the unfortunate audience was compelled to joyously sing the Christmas carol "Silent Night."[60]

For the smallest of infractions, including not standing completely erect or speaking out of line, Jews were regularly flogged in an official method prescribed by Berlin administrators. For example, Jews were tied to a board for twenty-five lashes on the buttocks delivered by exuberant guards who often jumped into the air to increase momentum. If the Jew screamed out, the beating was increased ten more strokes. Because they were Jews—and only because they were Jews—if the guard was in the mood he could increase the number to sixty lashes.[61]

Many random cruelties such as floggings, kicking, testicle beatings, and other sadistic acts were inflicted against Jews, especially by those of higher rank among the prisoners, such as Poles or German criminals. Other prisoners often attempted to curry favor with their guards by brutalizing Jews. Guards often demanded it as sport. Jews, no matter how broken or bloody, could not be admitted to the infirmary at some camps; one inmate recalls Jews were classed as "well or dead."[62]

Hollerith codes afflicted not just Jews, but others at the bottom of the hierarchy of camp victims. For example, Jehovah's Witnesses were coded 2. Known as "Bible Researchers," Jehovah's Witnesses were singled out for their abstinent refusal to register for the German draft and their Christian rejection of anti-Semitism. They were rewarded with a greater level of maltreatment than almost any prisoner other than a Jew coded 8. To relieve their daily agony of beatings and camp killings, Jehovah's Witnesses need only to sign a declaration denouncing their church and submit to the military draft. This they steadfastly declined to do. For their courage and conscience, Jehovah's Witnesses were tortured and slaughtered.[63]

Each special incarcerated group bore the horrors inflicted by their codes. Homosexuals coded 3 and assigned pink triangles were singled out for bestial treatment. Even traditional Germans who had been classed as "work-shy" or "asocial," that is, people who simply did not fit the Nazi mold, found themselves the targets of specially prescribed mistreatment in ways that other coded prisoners were not. The bottom of the Personal Inmate Card logged prescribed tortures in a section headed *Strafen im Lager,* "Punishment Administered in Camp." In addition to daily random brutalities, officially prescribed punishment was often meted out on specific orders issued by the SS Economics Administration in Berlin. The agency had instant access to an inmate's history of prior infractions and punishment. Typical was the Personal Inmate Card for Auschwitz III prisoner 11457; directly over the section entitled *Strafen im Lager* was the telltale stamp, *Hollerith erfasst.*[64]

When transferring to another camp, one's coded identity was never left behind. *Zentral Institut* Hollerith Transfer Lists always included it. Even in death, Nazi victims were coded. Four main death codes were punched into *Zentral Institut* Hollerith cards:

Death by natural causes	C-3
Execution	D-4
Suicide	E-5
SB Special Treatment	F-6[65]

Most death reports were coded C-3, even when people were openly murdered. But the fourth death code was in fact a secret one. F-6 stood for *SB, Sonderbehandlung* or "Special Treatment." Any punishment coded F-6 was in fact an order for extermination, either by gas chamber or bullet.[66]

The multitude of columns and codes punched into Hollerith and sorted for instant results was an expensive, never-ending enterprise designed to implement Hitler's evolving solutions to what was called the Jewish problem. From Germany's first identifying census in 1933, to its sweeping occupational and social expulsions, to a net of ancestral tracings, to the Nuremberg definitions of 1935, to the confiscations, and finally to the ghettoizations, it was the codes that branded the individual and sealed his destiny. Each code was a brick in an inescapable wall of data. Trapped by their code, Jews could only helplessly wait to be sorted for Germany's next persecution. The system Germany created in its own midst, it also exported by conquest or subversion. As the war enveloped all Europe, Jews across the Continent found themselves numbered and sorted to one degree or another.

By early 1942, a change had occurred. Nazi Germany no longer killed just Jewish people. It killed Jewish *populations*. This was the data-driven denouement of Hitler's war against the Jews.

Hollerith codes, compilations, and rapid sorts had enabled the Nazi Reich to make an unprecedented leap from individual destruction to something on a much larger scale. No longer were such vague notions as "destruction" and "elimination" bandied ambiguously in speeches and decrees. From early 1942, the prophetic new Nazi word openly pronounced in newspapers was *extermination*. The context, as spoken in Europe and widely reported in the media, always connoted but one objective: *mass killing*. Systematic coordinated extermination would yield an unimaginable new solution to the Jewish problem in Europe. This ultimate phase was known as *Endlösung*. In German, the term conveyed a singular meaning: "The Final Solution."[67]

SEVERAL FORCES were in play on January 1, 1942, as Hitler set the Final Solution in motion.

First, the Reich was well along in implementing its policy of pauperizing and enslaving European Jewry. In this campaign, the goal of emigration had become essentially curtailed or nonexistent, replaced by a program of "extermination by labor," organized ghetto starvation, and pit massacres. Still many Jews were hearty enough, or lucky enough, to survive the rigors of inhumane Nazi-style "forced labor," or escape into the forests.

Second, the long-standing goal of the Nazi movement, that is, the complete destruction of the Jewish people, was now crystallizing. For years, the debate within Nazi circles had taken many forms, including physical extermination. Hitler had publicly prophesied in 1939 that if the world again returned to war, he would utterly destroy the Jewish people. In Hitler's view, the conflict in Europe became a "World War" when America entered after Pearl Harbor was bombed in December 1941. *Der Führer* was now determined to unleash a long contemplated campaign of systematic, automated genocide, thus once and for all ridding the world of Jews.[68]

Just weeks after America entered the war with Germany, the two related campaigns accelerated: extermination by labor, and the new drive to exterminate all Jews by the most expedient method possible. On January 20, 1942, a top-secret conference of Hitler's key lieutenants was held in a Berlin suburb at the elegant terraced villa located at Am Grossen Wannsee 56–58. The purpose: coordinate the efficient murder of millions of Jews. The secret gathering was limited to senior Nazi leadership, including Reinhard Heydrich, the head of Security Police, and Gestapo Chief Heinrich Müller. Yet the conferees in many ways relied upon three key lower-level experts. One was Roderich Plate, a racial census expert. The second was Richard Korherr, Himmler's handpicked statistical overlord. The third was Adolf Eichmann. Plate was Korherr's assistant and both were established Hollerith experts.[69]

During the meeting, Heydrich presented a long list of Jewish populations, broken down by territory and country. Eichmann provided the list based on compilations by Korherr and Plate. Working with a coterie of current and former Dehomag experts, they developed the statistics. The conclave at Wannsee resulted in a Protocol, which outlined the massive demographic and geographic logistical challenge. The printed Protocol's centerpiece was, in fact, the statistical report on the mission ahead.[70]

Germany: 131,800; Ostmark region: 43,700; Eastern territories: 420,000; Occupied Poland: 2,284,000; Bialystok: 400,000; Bohemia and Moravia: 74,200; Latvia: 3,500; Lithuania: 34,000; Belgium: 43,000; Denmark: 5,600;

Occupied France: 165,000; Unoccupied France: 700,000; Greece: 69,600; Netherlands: 160,800; Norway: 1,300. . . . The long enumeration of population statistics went on, country after country, and even included England and Ireland.[71]

The Protocol's grand total was 11 million including the British Isles and a broad estimate of 5 million for Russia. The conference was told, "the number of Jews given here for foreign countries includes, however, only those Jews who still adhere to the Jewish faith, since some countries still do not have a definition of the term 'Jew' according to racial principles."[72]

Korherr's estimates for the conference were profoundly inflated. Certainly, Reich experts had been able to create precise population tables for Greater Germany and most of the occupied territories. But, at the time, the Nazis simply lacked accurate information about many other countries, especially Russia. Nonetheless, for the Nazi leadership assembled, the numbers, howsoever inaccurate, presented the outline of the genocidal task they faced. It was massive and unprecedented.

A two-tiered genocide was emphasized: extermination by labor and expedient mass murder. "In the course of the final solution the Jews are to be allocated for appropriate labor in the East," the Protocol recorded. "Able-bodied Jews, separated according to sex, will be taken in large work columns to these areas for work on roads, in the course of which action, doubtless, a large portion will be eliminated by natural causes. The possible final remnant will, since it will undoubtedly consist of the most resistant portion, have to be treated accordingly, because it is the product of natural selection and would, if released, act as the seed of a new Jewish revival.[73]

"In the course of the practical execution of the Final Solution, Europe will be combed through from west to east. . . . The evacuated Jews will first be sent, group by group, to so-called transit ghettos, from which they will be transported to the East." Jews in Poland were specified as "epidemic carriers" and "of approximately 2.5 million Jews, the majority is unfit for work."[74] In the parlance of Wannsee, those "unfit for work" were to be put to death as soon as possible.

As daunting as the deportation campaign would be, the Nazis insisted it be subordinated to their own Nuremberg racial theories. A complicated list of mandatory or potential exceptions was laid out. For example, "persons of mixed blood of the first degree married to persons of German blood" would be "treated essentially as Germans."[75]

The Wannsee Conference and its Protocol were considered by many to be the next major step in the Final Solution of the Jewish problem in

Europe. Although most of the bizarre formulaic exceptions would be eventually discarded, and although the true number of Jews existing in Europe was vastly overstated in the meeting, this much was apparent: the Final Solution would require an enormous amount of statistical information. Korherr, assisted by Plate, was ready to provide it.

Plate was an experienced Hollerith expert. After a stint as administrative assistant with the Reich Statistical Office, he joined the Race Political Office of the NSDAP in 1935. Soon thereafter, he assisted noted raceologist Friedrich Burgdörfer in compiling an estimate of all racial Jews in Germany. Later, he helped produce a second estimate, this one of World Jewry. In succeeding years, Plate functioned as the Reich Statistical Office's liaison to Eichmann's *Referat* II 112, also known as the Jewish Division. Plate was described by colleagues as an expert "in all important questions regarding the census, religious and race statistics, special counts of Jews, special counts of foreigners, and minority statistics." Plate, a civilian when Wannsee convened, was required to sign an oath of secrecy three days before the conference and was drafted into the military five days later.[76]

Korherr was the most important statistics man in the Nazi hierarchy. Irritable, defensive, and almost possessive about his Hollerith machines, Korherr had been developing race-oriented punch card programs for years. Always a rabid raceologist and statistical adventurer, his early writings denounced the "niggerization" of France and urged the defense of the "white race."[77]

His career included work with the Reich Statistical Office, and later, service as the Director of Population Politics and Statistics for Deputy Führer Hess. But Korherr did not become the undisputed syndic of all Nazi statistics until December 9, 1940. On that day, Himmler issued and personally signed two explicit orders. The first appointed Korherr Inspector of Statistics for the SS as well as for the Chief of the German Police. The second outlined Korherr's broad portfolio. By any reading, it was an extraordinary entitlement and cachet for one who might be viewed as a mere statistical technician. But Korherr was more than just a number cruncher.[78] He would become the keeper of the state's most incriminating genocidal secrets.

"The Inspector reports directly to me and receives his instructions from me personally," ordered SS Chief Himmler in Korherr's bona fides. "The Inspector is solely responsible for the totality of statistics of all units and offices in my area. The work of the Inspector is to be supported in every way possible in light of the necessity and significance [of] . . . practical statistics.

. . . The Inspector is the sole point of contact between the Reich and provincial and Party statistics."[79]

Korherr was more than willing to jealously guard his domain of Hollerith expertise, even if it meant tangling with Nazidom's top generals. For example, one general at the Wannsee Conference was *Gruppenführer* Otto Hofmann, the general in charge of the powerful SS Race and Settlement Department. *Gruppenführer* Hofmann was excited about his new Hollerith installation, and had already suggested expansive changes in statistical campaigns and the creation of new racial registration offices across Greater Germany. Korherr openly denigrated Hofmann's ideas as unnecessary and duplicative.[80]

Shortly after the Wannsee Conference, Korherr wrote to a colleague, "I would like to mention that the understandable lack of statistical expertise at the Race and Settlement Office, coupled with their urgent wish for a large statistics office with a Hollerith system and for an SS population card file, made [recent] negotiations extraordinarily difficult. For the statistician, the best proof of an amateur is when someone wants to begin—and end—his statistical work with a card file . . . Since *Reichsführer* [Himmler] appointed me the sole liaison for Reich statistics . . . I see *Gruppenführer* Hofmann's behavior as deliberately . . . undermining my position."[81]

Korherr snidely added, "The person in charge at the Reich Statistical Office was astonished at *Gruppenführer* Hofmann's plans and asked: then why did *Reichsführer* [Himmler] hire me and Dr. Plate. We were both amused at the idea of a Hollerith survey of the entire popular [German] movement . . . I suggested the numerical continuation of the [existing] inventory instead of a [new] Hollerith system . . . I should just float above it all."[82]

Korherr's expertise was so valued, Himmler sided with him even over a prominent SS general. Eventually, Himmler issued Korherr an additional directive: "in order to avoid jurisdictional conflicts and streamline work procedures, you are to be given responsibility for processing all statistical matters for [*Gruppenführer* Hofmann's] Race and Settlement Office."[83]

As Himmler's plenipotentiary for all statistical matters, Korherr was able to coordinate the data activities of numerous Reich agencies, and call upon many Hollerith experts who had been either trained by Dehomag, or were employees transferred or loaned to government offices for the war period. One example was Albert Bartels, head of the SS machine record agency and in charge of *Waffen*-SS Holleriths at Dachau. Bartels also worked at the complex at 129 Friedrichstrasse. In one typical packet, Bartels sent Korherr "work progress forms and punch cards used in my office. I ask you . . . for the necessary evaluations." Bartels' assistant was Busch, the former Hollerith dealer who ran the *Waffen*-SS machines at the Storkow camp. Herbert Blaettel, a veteran of Dehomag's training department, worked at Dachau's Hollerith Department. Dehomag's Munich dealer, Herr Asmis, sold the Nazi Party office its original leases; he only left the subsidiary in August 1944 to work with government projects. The *Maschinelles Berichtwesen* was the clearinghouse for all punch card technology, and their resources could be continuously tapped.[84]

In January 1943, Korherr was required to provide Himmler with a status report on the Final Solution. To do so, Korherr worked frantically to determine exactly how many Jews had been killed, country by country. He demanded a stream of data from all the ghettos and other territories where Eichmann had been working. Eichmann remembered that he provided Korherr "all our top-secret stuff. That was the order. All the shipments [of Jews] insofar as they had been reported to us." Eichmann added, "The statistician [Korherr] was with me, a week or maybe two, in my office, day after day, making his inquiries, he sent telegrams etc. all over the place."[85]

Korherr eventually produced a sixteen-page draft report, but was required to condense the tabulated data to just seven pages so Hitler could review it. When Korherr completed the summary, the perfectionist in him was still frustrated. "Despite the expended sweat, an accurate number for this time period cannot be given," he asserted, but he assured the report nonetheless did offer "useful clues." Korherr's progress report was submitted to Hitler on March 23, 1943.[86]

This time, the numbers were precise, enumerating Jewish communities throughout Europe, by ghetto and territory. The word "evacuation" was used to designate gassing in killing centers such as Treblinka and Sobibor. To eastern Russia: 1,449,692 Jews; to camps in occupied Poland: 1,274,166; through camps in the Warthe region: 145,301. Occupied France: 41,911; Netherlands: 38,571; Belgium: 16,886; Norway: 532; Slovakia: 56,691; Croatia: 4,927. Total evacuations including Special Treatment: 1,873,519. The total was written as more than 2.5 million to date.[87]

Himmler was so pleased with the report and Korherr's subsequent performance, he eventually appointed the statistician to a specially created agency known as the Statistical Scientific Institute of the *Reichsführer* SS. It, too, was located at Block F, 129 Friedrichstrasse. Korherr's new office now had the most up-to-the-minute access to all concentration camp information streaming into the *Zentral Institut*. By early 1944, Korherr was able to report to Eichmann a total of 5 million Jews eliminated by "natural decrease, concentration camp inmates, ghetto inmates, and those who were [simply] put to death."[88]

The offices at Block F, 129 Friedrichstrasse, undoubtedly processed more information than any other single office in Germany about the mass murder of Europe's Jews. More than a statistical bureau, by its very nature, the Hollerith complex at Friedrichstrasse helped Hitler, Himmler, Heydrich, and Eichmann prioritize, schedule, and manage the seemingly impossible logistics of genocide across dozens of cities in more than twenty countries and territories. It was not just people who were counted and marshaled for deportation. Boxcars, locomotives, and intricate train timetables were scheduled across battle-scarred borders—all while a war was being fought on two fronts. The technology had enabled Nazi Germany to orchestrate the death of millions without skipping a note.

Amidst the whirlwind of the Final Solution, the Third Reich's transition from the blind persecution of a general population to the destruction of individuals had come full circle. In genocide, the Jews lost their identity. They had been reduced to mere nameless data bits. Now each murdered Jew no longer even represented an individual death. Now every corpse comprised a mere component in a far larger statistical set adding up to total annihilation.

When Jews were worked to death, they were tracked with Inmate Cards, Hollerith Transfer Lists, punch cards, and endless sorters. It was expensive, but, in the Nazi view, a necessary cost allowing the Reich to track and regiment a Jew's every move. When enslaved Jews in work camps were about to be killed, their cards were taken—they no longer needed one.[89]

When ghettoized Jews were selected for deportation, and dispatched by Hollerith-scheduled trains to killing stations in Poland, they received no cards. Their names were not printed on any Hollerith Transfer List. When they arrived at the mass murder centers in Treblinka, Sobibor, Belzec, or any of the others sites reserved for eradication, a doctor briefly glanced at victims hurriedly filing past. A wave to the left meant reporting to the camp entrance for the prospect of laboring for a few days, perhaps a month. But most were never registered in any *Arbeitseinsatz*.[90] They had outlived the potential for usefulness. They were expeditiously directed to their final destiny: the showers.

The synchrony was exquisite. From the moment a Jew stepped onto the train platform in the ghetto, to the moment he was violently thrashed out of the boxcar at the final stop and led to his death, there were never any delays. Precision timing and scheduling was indispensable to the process. No longer worth the expense of a bullet, victims were gassed in large groups. At Auschwitz—2,000 at a time. Prussic acid pellets, *Zyklon B,* were dropped into water buckets to accomplish the mass asphyxiation. The screaming, clanging on the steel doors, and shrieks of ancient Jewish incantation, *Sh'ma Yisra'el,* stopped after fifteen minutes. Generally within an hour of stepping off the train, the Jews in a transport were successfully exterminated.[91]

Nor were any death records transmitted. It was enough to inform *Zentral Institut* that the people had boarded a train. Hence, the machines only tabulated the evacuations. No more was necessary. From these trains, there was no escape, no need for tracking, no further utility, and no further cost would be expended. At this point, the Jews were no longer worth a bullet, nor the price of a single punch card.[92]

Only at the moment of extermination did the Jews of Europe finally break free from Hitler's Holleriths.

GERMANY HAD forced Jews to help organize their own annihilation by establishing *Judenräte,* that is, Jewish councils. These councils were generally comprised not of communal leaders, but of arbitrarily selected Jewish personalities, frequently engineers. Engineers were chosen because they could relate to the mechanics of the numerical process underway. *Judenrat* leaders Ephraim Barash of Bialystok and Adam Czerniakow of Warsaw, for example, were both engineers. Eichmann considered himself an engineer by trade.[93]

Those council members who did not cooperate, or who even hesitated, were quickly murdered—often on the spot. Amid accusations of collaboration that would reverberate forever, the *Judenräte* were faced with the impossible choice of functioning—literally at gunpoint—as best they could, as long as they could. With their dismal ghetto communities starving, and rotting corpses piled high in the streets for lack of mortuary facilities, the councils hoped to somehow survive the brutalities of ghetto life, hour to hour.[94] Stories about gas chambers at the end of the railway track were circulating. So by their cooperation with constant census and registration projects, as well as organized evacuation, and, in many instances, the virtual self-selection of names to fill the trains, the enormity of Nazi intent took shape.

Quickly it became apparent to the men of the *Judenräte* that they were not conducting census and other statistical duties for the purposes of survival under a brutish occupation, or evacuation to less crowded settlements —but for organized extermination. In essence, these men were metering their own deaths in cadence to the overall Nazi timetable. Some were able to withstand the awesome personal nightmare, and functioned as demanded until the end. However, many reached a point of personal defiance. When that point came, their sole means of briefly slowing down the Nazi machine was suicide or suicidal refusal.

Arye Marder, head of Grodno ghetto's statistical department, submitted his resignation in November 1942, when German plans became inescapable. His name was placed on the next transport. He committed suicide. So his family was sent in his place.[95]

Moshe Kramarz refused to sign a document claiming the Minsk ghetto was "deporting" its Jews by choice. He tore the document into little pieces in front of people and loudly warned all within earshot that whether called "resettlement" or "evacuation," the process was really extermination. Gestapo officers immediately pummeled him and his colleagues, dragged the group away, and executed them all.[96]

In Lukow ghetto, *Judenrat* member David Liberman collected donations from residents thinking it was a ransom to save lives. When he learned the money would only be used to pay their own freight to the Treblinka death camp, he shouted at a German supervisor, "Here is your payment for our trip, you bloody tyrant!" He tore the bills into bits and slapped the German's face. Ukrainian guards killed Liberman where he stood.[97]

The Bereza Kartuska ghetto *Judenrat* was ordered to produce a list of Jews to assemble at the marketplace on October 15, 1942, "for work in Russia." The men of the council understood the people would be traveling to their doom. Unwilling to issue the lists, the council members assembled and collectively hanged themselves in the council offices. Two physicians and their families joined the protest by committing suicide as well.[98]

At Pruzana ghetto, forty-one members of the *Judenrat* staged a Masada action. Rather than submit to a Nazi-imposed death, they and their families gathered. Poison was distributed. The children swallowed first. Then the women. Finally the men. One man held back to make sure all had died. Then he gulped his. But the impoverished *Judenrat* simply did not have enough poison to formulate lethal doses. Some people emerged from mere drowsiness. So one man closed the chimney flu, sealed the windows, and turned on the oven. When the bodies were found the next morning, all but one was revived, and eventually deported to the camps.[99]

Adam Czerniakow, the head of Warsaw's ghetto *Judenrat*, the man who so tirelessly organized the census, began to see the process as wholesale murder. One day, when the Nazis demanded he increase the deportation lists from 6,000 to 10,000, he drew a line. Czerniakow also ended his duties by ending his life.[100]

Judenrat resistance never effectively delayed any German action in the ghettos. With scores of Jews dying of starvation or disease each week, a collection of suicides and executions simply became part of the hellscape. But their sacrifice made one thing clear. Even though they never comprehended the technologic intricacies of the process underway, and although most had never seen a punch card, they did sense that all the registrations and endless lists added up to a single odious destiny. They fought back with their only remaining weapon: the power to control their own extinction.

I
II
III
IV
V
VI
VII
VIII
IX
X
XI
XII
XIII
XIV
XV

THE SPOILS OF GENOCIDE, I

NO ONE WILL EVER KNOW EXACTLY HOW MANY IBM MACHINES clattered in which ghetto zone, train depot, or concentration camp. Nor will anyone prove exactly what IBM officials in Europe or New York understood about their location or use. Machines were often moved—with or without IBM's knowledge—from the officially listed commercial or governmental client to a deadly Nazi installation in another country, and then eventually transferred back again.[1]

Most importantly, it did not matter whether IBM did or did not know exactly which machine was used at which death camp. All that mattered was that the money would be waiting—once the smoke cleared.

In fact, a pattern emerged throughout war-ravaged Europe. Before America entered the war, IBM NY and its subsidiaries worked directly with Germany or Italy, or its occupying forces. As part of the strategic alliance, it also worked with German sympathizers and allies in countries such as Romania, Yugoslavia, and Hungary.[2] Watson would even order new subsidiaries established in conquered territories in cadence with Nazi invasions.[3] Even after America declared war, IBM offices worldwide would openly transact with these clients, or with other subsidiaries, until the moment General Ruling 11 was triggered for that particular territory. As the war in Europe expanded, General Ruling 11 jurisdiction was extended as well until all of

Nazi-dominated Europe was proscribed.[4] Once U.S. law prohibited transactions, IBM NY's apparent direct management of its European operations seemed to end. But, in truth, executives in New York could still monitor events and exercise authority in Europe through neutral country subsidiaries. These overseas units always remained under the parent company's control. Moreover, special bureaucratic exemptions were regularly sought by IBM NY, or its subsidiaries, to continue or expand business dealings throughout occupied Europe.[5] Official American demands that business be curtailed were often ignored.[6]

Once the United States entered the war, Axis custodians would be appointed as titular directors of subsidiaries in occupied territory. But these enemy custodians never looted the IBM divisions. Rather, they zealously protected the assets, extended productivity, and increased profits. Existing IBM executives were kept in place as day-to-day managers and, in some instances, even appointed deputy enemy custodians. In France, for example, although SS Officer Heinz Westerholt was appointed enemy custodian of CEC, he, in turn, appointed Dehomag's Oskar Hoermann as deputy custodian. CEC's Roger Virgile continued as managing director to keep the company profitable and productive. In Belgium, Nazi custodian H. Garbrecht remained aloof, allowing IBM managers Louis Bosman and G. Walter Galland to remain in place and virtually in command. In Germany, Dehomag's board of directors was superseded by custodian Hermann Fellinger. Fellinger replaced Heidinger, and then insisted that Rottke, Hummel, and all the other managers in Dehomag's twenty offices continue producing record profits.[7] Whether overseen by Nazi executives or Watson's own, IBM Europe thrived.

In the later war years, as the Allies moved across the western and eastern fronts, various liberated or about-to-be liberated territories emerged as exempt from prohibited trading under General Ruling 11. Sometimes the applicable regulations changed on an almost daily basis. IBM NY or IBM Geneva would tenaciously check with American authorities for permission to communicate or transact with previously proscribed subsidiaries. When direct contact was not possible, American legations passed the messages as a courtesy.[8]

During IBM's continuing wartime commerce, the world was always aware that the machinery of Nazi occupation was being wielded to exterminate as many Jews as possible as quickly as possible. After endless newspaper and newsreel reports, and once the Allies confirmed their own intelligence revelations in summer 1942, the conclusion became inescapable: Germany's goal was nothing short of complete physical extermination of all European Jewry. On December 17, 1942, the Allies finally declared there would be "war crime" trials and punishment. The Allies warned that all who cooperated with Hitler's genocide would be held responsible before the bar of international justice. In Parliament, members rose in awed silence as one MP rang out, "There are many today who . . . but for the grace of God . . . might have been in those ghettos, those concentration camps, those slaughter-houses." The Allies' joint declaration of war crimes for genocide was broadcast and published as the top news in more than twenty-three languages the world over.[9]

A *New York Times* article was headlined "Allies Describe Outrages on Jews," and sub-headlined "Extermination Is Feared." It led: "What is happening to the 5,000,000 Jews of German-held Europe, all of whom face extermination." The Allied report emphasized calculated starvation, group gassing, mass shooting, ghetto street scenes "beyond imagination," and intense deportation campaigns by railroad.[10]

IBM's business was never about Nazism. It was never about anti-Semitism. It was always about the money. Before even one Jew was encased in a hard-coded Hollerith identity, it was only the money that mattered. And the money did accrue.

Millions in blocked bank accounts scattered across Europe were waiting for IBM, as well as its newly acquired real estate, numerous Hitler-era factories and presses, and thousands of Hollerith machines. Much of the money and plant expansion was funded by a fundamentally bankrupt Third Reich, which financed its rapacious operations by slave labor, massive plunder, and cost-effective genocide. Where did Hitler's Germany get the money to pay for all the services, cards, and leases? Nazi gold and currency was fungible—whether carted away from banks in Prague or pried from the teeth of Jewish carcasses at Treblinka. The Reich could afford the best. And it purchased the best with the assets it stole.

Managing overseas branches and conducting commerce within the broken lines of changing wartime regulations was itself an intensive effort. Each IBM subsidiary in Europe spawned its own epic collection of bureaucratic correspondence, spanning months and even years. Life and death dramas became daily realities in Belgium, Czechoslovakia, Italy, and elsewhere as IBM employees and Hollerith technology intersected with the victors and vanquished of Nazi Europe.

World War II finally ended in Europe on May 8, 1945. Almost immediately, IBM rushed in to recover its machines and bank accounts from enemy territory. The wealth of stories could take many volumes to chronicle, but this much was clear: there was no realm where IBM would not trade, and none where they failed to collect—country by country.

ROMANIA'S ANTI-JEWISH campaign was in full force by fall 1940. Germany had already inspired a murderously anti-Semitic regime in Bucharest. Romanian strong man Marshal Ion Antonescu's Fascist regime had replicated Reich anti-Semitic laws of professional ousters and property confiscation. Rapidly in 1940, Romania pauperized thousands of Jews in a highly publicized campaign. Soon forced Jewish labor decrees and sporadic pogroms across Romania were breeding the usual headlines.[11]

For example, in January 1941, squads of vicious Iron Guard militants rampaged through Bucharest brutally massacring scores of Jewish residents. Some 120 Jews were beaten, mercilessly bullwhipped and bludgeoned with metal rods. Some were made to drink from bloody basins. At the local slaughterhouse, several Jews were fiendishly dismembered.[12]

Carnage in Bucharest and in other areas was followed by waves of official banishment for many to various regions and internment in camps. More than 100,000 Jews were thought to have been brutally murdered in the riparian provinces during summer 1941. Yet Eichmann and other Nazis at times tried to restrain their Romanian allies because the Reich believed the random acts of violence were "planless and premature."[13] The Germans favored a more orderly, comprehensive, and scientific approach that would systematically annihilate all of Romanian Jewry.

Population estimates in Romania were wildly exaggerated. The previous census, held in 1930, counted 756,930 individuals who routinely identified themselves as Jewish. The scheduled 1940 census lacked funding and was delayed. But by spring 1941, German experts estimated that as many as half of Romania's Jewish citizens had already been murdered, deported, or had fled as refugees.[14]

Nonetheless, hysterical speculation in the Romanian press suggested as many as 2 million Jews remained within the country. The speculation was based on a misreading of the prior census. The 1930 summaries reported that of the 756,930 practicing Jews, 728,000 considered themselves "ethnic Jews" even if not religious, and 519,000 primarily spoke Yiddish. Wrongly, those three numbers were *added* together by some Romanians to create a false total of 2 million. Only a proper, up-to-date census could answer what Nazi raceologists called "the Jewish question" in Romania.[15]

Eventually, the new census was scheduled for April 1941. This would be no ordinary household count, but rather a comprehensive inventory of every individual, enterprise, farmland, animal, building, profession, and asset in Romania. The counting itself would span ten days. German statisticians and IBM would assist in every way. Friedrich Burgdörfer, President of the Bavarian Statistical Office, was invited to attend as an official observer, accompanied by Dehomag expert Ludwig Hümmer.[16]

W. C. Lier confirmed in a letter to Chauncey in New York, "As regards the Census . . . neither we nor the Dehomag have been able to obtain any precise information as regards the specifications of the machines which are needed in Bucharest. I agreed, exceptionally, to Mr. Hümmer going to Bucharest together with a representative of the German Statistical Office in order to analyze the whole situation. The commercial side of these two subjects has been dealt with direct with Mr. Schotte and Mr. Milner."[17]

The Romanian business was not in Dehomag's portfolio. It was an enterprise of IBM NY. Watson had been preparing for the Romanian census for years. "During 1940," J. C. Milner wrote Headquarters in 1938, "the census will be taken in several countries, and we expect a number of orders." Milner hoped Endicott could develop a special IBM census tabulator in time.[18]

The population segment of Romania's sweeping ten-day count was scheduled for April 6, 1941. Article 2 of the census decree required a special Jewish census on April 11 and 12. The entire nation mobilized. Posters were prominently displayed in post offices, hotels, and public buildings. Radio programs, editorials, and presidential speeches encouraged everyone to cooperate. For accuracy's sake, volunteers were shunned in favor of 29,000 paid census takers, each responsible for about 120 households. The women hired to punch the Hollerith cards were mainly high school graduates, which in itself was thought to increase the processing accuracy. One thousand inspectors would oversee the overall endeavor. Even Burgdörfer admitted in a journal article that Romania's Central Statistical Institute was "unusually well-equipped."[19]

Questions designed to pinpoint so-called "race Jews" were included in both the Jewish and general census questionnaires. The religion question not only asked for an individual's current faith, but also his religion at birth; the same information was solicited about the person's father and mother. Under the ethnicity and mother tongue categories, similar questions were posed for both the individual and again for his parents. Ethnicity questions were also asked in the agricultural census and job census. Even the commercial ownership survey solicited responses from businessmen about their Jewish partners and employees. The mass of overlapping data would enable IBM tabulators to triangulate on the intended target: anyone of Jewish ancestry—even if the person were unaware of it.[20]

Specially trained enumerators worked one-on-one to evoke true ethnic responses from the population. One report indicated that when a Gypsy declined to admit his ethnicity, the suspicious census taker finally said, "Now, write: Gypsy."[21]

Romania's census was intended to identify all the nation's Jews, even if they were refugees or interned in concentration camps. So IBM's punch card was designed to record such designations as "temporarily absent" for refugees and "concentrated" (that is, located in a concentration camp). Summing up in a journal article, Burgdörfer praised the census as "an extraordinarily extensive (maybe too vast) program of registration . . . the Jewish question is treated in great detail."[22]

Because the Romanian census involved not just individuals, but livestock, property, professions, businesses, and virtually every other aspect of Romanian life, more IBM machines would be needed. In fall 1941, shortly after Chauncey left Germany at the height of Dehomag's revolt, Lier arrived in Berlin to represent IBM NY's interest. He wanted to make sure that Rottke and Hummel could be relied upon to carry out IBM projects elsewhere in Europe. Previously, when Chauncey had inquired whether tabulators had been dispatched to Romania, Hummel responded with what might seem a lack of initiative. "We have not furnished any to Romania," replied Hummel. He seemed to be waiting for direct orders, saying, "If Geneva gives us an order for Romania, we will fill it."[23]

For Lier, Romania was clearly a priority. "One of the first matters discussed with them," Lier reported to Chauncey on October 10, 1941, "was that of the Romanian census and the machines destined for this business, which are actually blocked in Poland." The day before, Lier had sent a more formal letter to Watson to allay any concerns: "On the occasion of my visit to Berlin," Lier wrote, "I also settled a few pending matters, such as the machines blocked in Poland [and] the Romanian census . . . I am addressing separate reports to the executives concerned in New York."[24]

Lier felt that if only he could contact the Romanian Embassy, diplomats could use their connection with Reich offices in occupied Poland to forward the machines through the war zone. He called IBM's best contact in Berlin, U.S. Commercial Attaché, Sam Woods. "Thanks to Mr. Woods," Lier reported to IBM NY, "I obtained an interview with the Romanian Commercial Attaché who immediately endeavored to obtain the freeing of approximately seventeen machines at present blocked in Poland from the *Devisenstelle* [Foreign Currency Office] and the German Authorities . . . I have been given every assurance as to the satisfactory outcome of this demand." Shortly thereafter, Lier did effect the transfer of Dehomag machines to IBM's Romanian subsidiary.[25]

A few days before Romania entered the war on June 22, 1941, Marshal Antonescu demanded lists of "all Jews, Communists and sympathizers in each region." In addition, all Jews aged sixteen to sixty in towns between the Siret and Prut rivers were to be rounded up and immediately shipped to a concentration camp on already scheduled trains. It was all to be done in forty-eight hours. Half the eastern city of Iaşi's 100,000 population was Jewish. Identifying the victims in a lightning operation could have been an impossibility. But Antonescu's Second Section intelligence unit, which monitored ethnic groups, relied on three statistical offices, including one in Iaşi. The Romanians generated the names and addresses. An intelligence officer recalled that the Second Section was crucial "in paving the groundwork for the Iaşi pogrom [in that] Junius Lecca, SSI station chief [of Iaşi] had played a major role by supplying intelligence concerning Jewish residences and centers."[26]

Thousands of Iaşi Jews were dragged from their homes, many still in their sleeping clothes. For several days, German and Romanian policemen and soldiers, as well as wild citizen mobs, perpetrated unspeakable violence on the identified. Corpses began piling onto the street as Jews were mercilessly clubbed to death with metal bars, rifles, and rocks, and then ceremoniously spat upon. Infants were not spared. Thousands more were loaded onto death trains where they would be viciously murdered in boxcars en route. As many as 13,000 painfully lost their lives.[27]

In late 1941, the statistics on Jews yielded a total of 375,422 Jews still surviving in Romania. In January 1942, the Wannsee Conference Protocol listed the number as 342,000 including Bessarabia, but not including certain other regions.[28]

A spring 1942 Jewish census showed that 300,000 Romanian Jews were still alive. On August 31, 1942, Antonescu reviewed not the spring data, but the late 1941 statistics. When he saw the number 375,422 Jews, he wrote, "a very large number." Next to Bessarabia's 6,900 Jews, he wrote, "Impossible! My order was to have all the Jews deported." Even though the Bukovina figure of 60,708 Jews was about a year old, he scribbled in a rage, "Impossible. Please verify. My order stated that only ten thousand Jews should remain in Bukovina. Please check. This is fantastic! Judaized cities, simply, purely Judaized."[29]

By September 1942, Eichmann had readied a schedule for Romanian Railroads to transport some 280,000 of those Jews to Belzec's gas chambers. But by now, Romania's Antonescu was reluctant to cooperate further. Like other Nazi surrogates in Eastern Europe, Antonescu feared the onslaught of the Russians, and rumors circulated of a forthcoming war crimes announcement. Jewish bribes—including 100 million lei to Antonescu's personal physician—also helped. The trains did not roll.[30]

On November 17, 1943, Antonescu again reviewed census data with his generals. "According to the latest statistics we have now in Transnistria a little over 50,000 Jews," said Antonescu. Adding 10,000 Jews from the Dorohoi area and others, Antonescu tallied "70,000 to 80,000." General Constantin Vasilu objected, "There was some mistake. We have talked with Colonel Radulescu, who has carried out a census. There are now exactly 61,000."[31]

By the end of the war, after a bloody series of Romanian-German executions and deprivations, more than 270,000 Jews had been brutally killed or starved. Hundreds of thousands more died in bordering regions under Romania's jurisdiction.[32]

IBM's subsidiary in Bucharest was incorporated on March 4, 1938, as Compania Electrocontabila Watson with approximately $240,000 in equipment, punch cards, and leaseable machines. Quickly, the unit became profitable. The subsidiary's main clients were the Communications Ministry, census bureaus, statistical offices, and railroads. Watson's decision to incorporate coincided with Romania embarking on an enhanced war footing. This martial program would include massive orders of Hollerith equipment and punch cards. IBM Europe was unable to fill all the leases requested by Bucharest, but it ramped up production to meet the need. IBM NY was kept apprised of the progress.[33]

Company executives had worked with Romanian military committees early in the war to scrutinize each commercial installation in the country, identifying which could be requisitioned by the Ministry of War. These machines were to be relocated to secure sites in the countryside when fighting broke out. Special arrangements with the Romanian Ministry of War exempted IBM supervisors and engineers from the draft to assure continuity of service.[34]

A few months after Lier arranged the shipment of seventeen additional machines from Poland to Bucharest, America declared war. Shortly thereafter, Romania was deemed enemy territory under General Ruling 11. But IBM needed to finalize commissions owed to the Italian bank in Bucharest that covered delivery guarantees. Writing on corporate letterhead co-equally displaying the name of IBM in New York and IBM Europe in Geneva, on June 18, 1942, Lier tried to secure from the American Commercial Attaché in Bern a special license to pay the bank commissions. Lier wrote, "In the middle of last year, our Romanian company contracted a large order with the Romanian census authorities for the execution of the census of the population of Romania. Prior to giving that order to our Romanian company, the Romanian Government required a bank guarantee to be filed with the Banque Commerciale Italienne et Roumaine in Bucharest to cover the delivery of the equipment foreseen by the order . . . May we therefore request you to issue a license which would authorize us to cover the amount of Lei 111,348 by remitting this amount in Swiss Francs to the Societe de Banque Suisse in Geneva."[35]

The American legation denied Lier's request and suggested he contact the Treasury Department in America. Lier asked IBM NY to handle the matter directly with Washington.[36]

As late as January 1944, Schotte in New York acknowledged to Department of Justice investigator Harold Carter that he knew that punch cards at the Central Institute of Statistics contained information on census, population trends, and "special studies of all minority groups in Romania." Schotte also confirmed that Romania's railroads maintained "a large installation of machines" located at the Ministry for Communications. The railroad's Statistical Department alone utilized as many as 1.7 million cards annually, and its Traction Department 3.34 million more. Those cards were printed on IBM's Swift Press in its busy Bucharest facility, which was functioning at its absolute capacity of 20 million cards per year.[37]

Romania was liberated from domination by Russian occupiers in late August 1944. On September 2, 1944, IBM Bucharest cabled a report to IBM Geneva: "Company in working order. Cable instructions for changed circumstances. Arrange urgently protection of property and personnel." A second brief report was cabled on October 5. General Ruling 11 had not yet been lifted, so IBM could not reply. Lier, on September 18, petitioned the American Legation in Geneva for permission to respond. IBM was in fact the first corporation to ask permission to resume normal business. America's Commercial Attaché ruled, "Romania is still enemy territory under General Ruling Number 11. . . . Until such time as General Ruling Number 11 is specifically revoked or amended for Romania, the International Business Machines Co. may not communicate with that country without license."[38]

Eventually, Lier's request was routed to the State Department through the American Embassy in London. When a response was finally permitted,

IBM, in its very first communication, answered, "Your telegram of the 12th October seems to indicate that your present situation is normal and that you are proceeding with your work as best you can."[39]

The company then asked for a comprehensive eleven-point report on all financial statements, including profit or loss, and rental revenues by customer, for the years 1942, 1943, and 1944. In addition, the company also wanted an immediate estimate of future prospects in war-ravaged Romania, broken down by machines that could be rented, personnel needed, and spare parts required. New York also wanted to know if Romania had made its quota: asking for "points installed and uninstalled to date." This way, the Romanian subsidiary could take its rightful place in IBM's Hundred Percent Club for outstanding performance.[40]

Romania was liable for war reparations, including $20 million to pay American claims, £10 million in Britain for its claims, and approximately $300 million for Russian claims.[41]

By late July 1945, IBM had lodged its own compensation claims for war damage. The total of $151,383.73 included $37,946.41 for damaged Hollerith machines. It also called on State Department intermediaries to secure its bank accounts in Romania.[42]

For IBM Romania, the war was over.

BULGARIA RELUCTANTLY joined the Axis bloc in March 1941. In exchange, it received German military support for its territorial ambitions in the Balkans. The Bulgarian military occupied Thrace and Macedonia in neighboring Greece. But Bulgarian society—from its churches to its government—overwhelmingly rejected German anti-Semitism for the nation's 48,000 well-integrated Jews. Under extreme pressure from Germany, the country half-heartedly issued anti-Jewish legislation, but deliberately laced the professional exclusions and property confiscations with many exceptions, including conversion.[43]

Bulgaria did everything it could to frustrate German plans for Bulgarian Jewry. At one point, when German-pressured regulations called for Jews to wear an identifying Star of David, senior Bulgarian church officials thwarted the move. Sermonizing that no man had the right to torture Jews, the Metropolitan of Sofia arranged for all so-called baptized Jews to be freed from the obligation. When that measure was not enough, the government cut off electricity to the factory producing the stars, claiming it was a power shortage.[44]

Eichmann's office wanted the Jews deported from the beginning. But the Bulgarian people were so opposed to the deportation plans that farmers had threatened to throw their bodies across the railroad tracks to stop any trains. Nonetheless, by late November 1941, German Foreign Minister von Ribbentrop, in a conference with Bulgarian Foreign Minister Popov, declared it the "unalterable decision of *der Führer*" that all Jews would be removed from Europe. As an "intermediate step," Bulgaria was instructed, the nation's 48,000 Jews would be concentrated in Poland. The method: deportation by train.[45]

IBM's subsidiary in Sofia, formed on March 17, 1938, was Watson Business Machines Corporation, Ltd. Its single most important customer was the Bulgarian Railroads. As with virtually all railroads since the turn of the century, punch cards made it possible to efficiently schedule trains, locate rolling stock, and deploy boxcars. Without Holleriths, it could take any European railway company up to two weeks to locate its boxcars in peacetime. In wartime, fast deployment was even more difficult. Using Holleriths at every major stop, train authorities could schedule within forty-eight hours. For this reason, whatever part of the war or the genocide that ran on track and rail was vitally dependent on IBM.[46]

Punch cards cost money. In spring 1942, just as the Bulgarian government had cut electricity off from the factory making Stars of David, the authorities also froze the railroad's payments to IBM, forcing the money into a blocked account. By spring, Watson Business Machines Corporation of Sofia was on the verge of bankruptcy. Unless that money was quickly released, the company would be compelled to close its doors. Bulgarian Railroads would then not receive its punch cards nor any further parts and service for its machines.[47]

On May 2, 1942, the IBM manager in Sofia, Pavel A. Datsoff, contacted Lier at IBM Geneva. "As you are informed," wrote Datsoff, "we have to receive from the railways the rent for the current 1942 year, but until now this amount is not paid due to the newly created conditions, and will be locked up in the National Bank. . . . As we have money which will be able to cover our expenses only for another four months, and if in the meantime we do not succeed to arrange . . . rent from the Railways, we shall be left with no money for our rent, salaries and other expenses. . . . I beg you . . . to open a current account through Bank Suisse for us in the Italian Bank, as it was in the past . . . to cover our expenses to the end of the current year. Otherwise, remaining with no money, it will be necessary to inform the personnel to look for other jobs and according [to] the law, we must notify them three months ahead."[48]

But IBM NY could not fund its Bulgarian operations without violating General Ruling 11. Lier sent Datsoff's letter to the American consulate: "From this letter," appealed Lier, "you will see that the situation of our Bulgarian company is jeopardized by the fact that the Bulgarian Government will not release any money paid by the Bulgarian Railroads which has been placed into a blocked account with the National Bank, and that this money served in the past for financing the operations of the Bulgarian company . . . Do you think that there is any chance of obtaining a special license to provide the Bulgarian company with funds . . . in order to avoid its complete bankruptcy?"[49]

The American legation rejected Lier's entreaty, explaining that monies could be funneled into "enemy territory through the Swiss Government only to cover the minimum subsistence requirements of American citizens who are entitled to receive such relief payments." Even still, the legation said it would transmit Lier's request on to the State Department, in case Washington wanted to forward the correspondence to IBM NY.[50]

However, on June 22, 1942, the Geneva legation went further, sending Lier's request to Washington, and actually suggesting that copies of both Lier's letter and Datsoff's financial distress call be passed to IBM NY.[51]

Unwilling to wait for a Treasury license, Lier in early July 1942 urgently asked the Geneva legation if somehow American diplomats might convince the Swiss government to appeal to Bulgarian officials to "deblock the account." Lier was again refused.[52]

The record is unclear exactly how funds were funneled to the Bulgarian company. But IBM Bulgaria was indeed funded and continued to supply punch card services to Bulgarian Railroads. In fact, more than a year later, Schotte told Carter that an extensively utilized range of IBM equipment was still in operation in Sofia, including a vital installation serving Bulgarian Railroads.[53]

On September 15, 1942, the Reich Foreign Office elected to delay the move to deport Bulgarian Jewry. Foreign Minister von Ribbentrop scribbled the words "wait some more" on a report summarizing the Bulgarian situation. By the end of September 1942, however, he suddenly told Eichmann's people to proceed.[54]

Bulgaria was unwilling to sacrifice its Jews. But in January 1943, Eichmann's representative arrived from France, demanding at least 20,000. So Bulgaria painfully agreed to a terrible choice. It consented to the deportation not of its own Jews, but the 14,000 Jews in the territories occupied by the

Bulgarian army—Thrace and Macedonia. Bulgarian Jewry was saved. Greek Jews would go to their death. Soon, the trains would roll.[55]

On March 2, 1943, the Bulgarian cabinet, still under intense pressure from Germany, ratified the number of trains to be allocated. A few days later, about 7,100 Macedonian Jews were pulled from their homes, congregated in tobacco warehouses, and later marched in long lines through the street. The women wore scarves and carried small bundles for the journey. The men carried larger objects on their backs. They walked passively with helpless expressions on their faces. At the end of the street was the railroad station, Bulgarian Railroads.[56]

In Thrace, the scenes were the same as more than 4,200 were marched to the boxcars. Standing before simple wooden tables, little children looked up with uncertainty as their parents gave their names to men in black uniforms jotting on note pads. Families crowded along the long ramp between the drab railroad building and the trains towering above them. Finally, they bustled into the cold boxcars for the long journey to a place they could not imagine.[57]

Pulling through the still snowy mountains, creating long curving lines of boxcars and cattle cars, Bulgarian Railroads delivered its freight to the Danube port of Lom. From there, the Jews were shipped by boat to Vienna. At Vienna, they were transferred to other trains en route to their final destination, Treblinka.[58]

With or without punch cards, efficiently or inefficiently, a determined Reich would have deported the doomed Greek Jews from Thrace and Macedonia. If locomotives and cattle cars were not available, Eichmann would have ordered a death march, as was done elsewhere in Eastern Europe. Even in the Bulgaria action, river barges were employed. But Berlin's most consistently used transport mode was rail. At the height of the deportations, Himmler beseeched his Minister of Transport, "If I am to wind things up quickly, I must have more trains. . . . Help me get more trains." Trains were Himmler's most valuable tool—and railroads were among IBM's most lucrative clients in Europe.[59]

February 14, 1945. With the war over in Bulgaria, IBM Geneva received permission from the American Consulate to re-establish relations with Watson Business Machines of Sofia. As they had in other countries, IBM NY asked for all financial records for the years 1942, 1943, and 1944. Datsoff, the manager, was asked to be sure to include a customer list reflecting "points installed and uninstalled to date" for review of Bulgaria's quota.[60]

On July 29, 1946, IBM NY filed a war compensation claim for losses sustained by its Bulgarian unit. The total was exactly $1,000 including $89 in damaged furniture and $836 for "time clock and typewriter supplies." The company also asked the State Department to help it regain control over its two bank accounts in Sofia.[61]

For IBM Bulgaria, the war was over.

IN THE NETWORK of European railroads that delivered Jews to the Germans, Bulgarian Railroads was but a minor player. The Polish railroads transported millions to their fate, either to ghettos, forced worked sites, or the gas chambers of Auschwitz and Treblinka. IBM's subsidiary in Poland, Watson Büromaschinen GmbH, serviced the railroads as its main account. Other IBM machines not used for the railways were moved into nearby *Maschinelles Berichtwesen* field offices or into Germany for service there.[62]

When the war was over, IBM NY made a priority of recovering the machines and assets of the machines used in Poland. In government filings, the company listed its prewar subsidiary, Watson Business Machines on Ossolinskich 6, not the one it incorporated during the German occupation under the name Watson Büromaschinen GmbH on Kreuzstrasse 23. Nor did IBM list its print shop across from the Warsaw ghetto at Rymarksa 6. But IBM NY did entreat the State Department and military liaisons to help recover its bank accounts, including two at Bank Handlowy and one at Bank Emosyjny, as well as deposits in a post office credit account. Even after Poland was liberated, when Polish machines transferred to Germany proper were used, the Berlin-based enemy property custodian made sure IBM's leasing fees were protected. He opened an additional account at Deutsche Bank to deposit those remittances.[63]

After more than two years of liaison through the State Department, IBM straightened out which of its machines in Poland belonged to Dehomag and which to the Polish unit. With the Holleriths back and its money recouped, the war was over for IBM Poland.

OPERATING IN Nazi Europe took fortitude by IBM. But the company was willing to provide service anywhere its Holleriths were needed. Frequently, this meant working with regimes that tolerated the most barbaric renegades, and doing business in areas subject to the most tempestuous military upheaval. Yugoslavia was an example. Germany and its Axis cohorts dismembered Yugoslavia into regions occupied by German, Italian, Hungarian, and Bulgarian forces. Hitler also supported the breakaway region of Croatia, which was the scene of Ustashi tortures.[64]

But local conditions, no matter how atrocious, were always put aside. On January 3, 1942, for instance, the *New York Times* prominently described the horrible bloodlust underway in Croatia. The article reported what it termed "'only a pale picture' of the ghastly reign of terror . . . [where] hundreds of persons were killed, but before they died many of them had their ears and noses cut off and then were compelled to graze on grass. The tortures most usually applied were beating, severing of limbs, gouging of eyes and breaking of bones. Cases are related of men being forced to hold red-hot bricks, dance on barbed wire with naked feet, and wear wreaths of thorns. Needles were stuck in fingers under the nails and lighted matches were held under noses."[65]

The area's most savage concentration camp was at Jasenovac where unspeakable crimes were committed by Ustashi guards. Jasenovac was situated on the Belgrade-Zagreb railroad line.[66]

Despite any horrors, IBM continued its thriving enterprise in Yugoslavia, known as Yugoslav Watson AG. Before America entered the war, IBM NY had been shipping Belgrade as many as 3 million punch cards annually. In 1942, the German enemy custodian appointed IBM's manager, Vilimir Bajkic, to remain in charge of the subsidiary. Bajkic was to coordinate with Germany's military commander in the area. Dr. Veesenmayer, Hitler's personal representative to the Dehomag advisory committee, was a close ally of the Ustashi during their reign of terror. Throughout the war, IBM cards and tabulators were used mainly by the Yugoslav army, the Ministry of Commerce, and Yugoslav railways. As in other Balkan states, IBM had made arrangements to service the military machines in remote locations after war broke out.[67]

Just before the Russians finally overran Yugoslavia in October 1944, many of the subsidiary's machines were hastily relocated to German territory, transferred to the nearest *MB* field office, or placed at the disposal of the German Navy. IBM's people in Belgrade forwarded the billing records to Germany before the Russians arrived. Hence, the Reich could continue lease payments into a special custodial account opened in Berlin at the Deutsche Bank. The Reich's last regular payment to Yugoslav Watson, issued April 3, 1945, remitted RM 3,114.15. On April 20, 1945, with the Red Army at the outskirts of Berlin, the enemy custodian submitted a special invoice of RM 51,970.24 for various services. Wehrmacht paymasters remitted the money just before the collapse of the Third Reich, but in the turmoil, the custodian could not deposit the check. Instead, he kept it safe, and later, on August 2, 1945, handed it to Capt. Arthur D. Reed, the U.S. Army's Property Control Officer, for transmission to IBM NY.[68]

But IBM NY needed all its Yugoslav assets restored. So it asked the U.S. military and State Department contacts to help it recover eighteen specified sorters, tabulators, and alphabetizers moved from its Yugoslavian unit to Germany; serial numbers were provided. The company also asked the State Department to reclaim its bank account at Jugobanka in Belgrade.[69]

For IBM Yugoslavia, the war was over.

IN THE EARLY morning hours of August 25, 1944, the bells of Notre Dame began to clang. Soon the other churches joined in welcoming the liberation of Paris. The next day, German POWs, their hands atop their heads, were led through the streets as Parisians celebrated their regained freedom.

On September 6, 1944, CEC Director Roger Virgile and Sales Manager Gabriel Lavoegie were arrested by French Forces of the Interior [FFI]. No charges were levied. Virgile had worked closely with Nazi agents and the Paris office of the *MB*, known as *MB West*. He also coordinated with Dehomag's custodian, working out lucrative leasing arrangements for IBM machines transported from France to Germany, occupied Czechoslovakia, and Poland. By mid-1943, CEC was holding Nazi orders totaling more than FF 38 million, or RM 760 million; of this amount FF 7.4 million had already been advanced.[70]

Virgile was released briefly, but then re-arrested on September 19 along with CEC Assistant Sales Manager Pierre Bastard. Other CEC officials feared they would be arrested as well. The American Embassy was notified and an urgent cable was sent to Watson. During the next few weeks, efforts to obtain the release of CEC staffers were unsuccessful. Watson was kept informed.[71]

By October 17, 1944, William Borel, who had been appointed interim manager, wired Watson through the Embassy that IBM staffers were still in jail. "With your intervention, we sincerely hope that the company will soon be operating normally. Two days later, Borel cabled Watson again that key people were "investigating situation which appears to have several angles. Everything is being done to clarify the whole matter."

Shortly thereafter, IBMers were suddenly released. Lavoegie resigned and Virgile took leave from the company. No charges were ever preferred. CEC resumed normal business by November 2, 1944. Even though General Ruling 11 was still in effect, the subsidiary began sending IBM NY copies of new orders through "various channels."[72]

About a year later, Captain Gamzon, a Jewish officer from the French resistance was speaking to the United Jewish Appeal charity in New York. The UJA was raising funds to assist decimated Jewish populations in Europe. The *New York Times* reported his remarks under the headline "Jews in France Saved by Others." The article reported, "Almost all surviving Jews in France owe their lives to non-Jews who risked everything to save them from the Nazis when they overran and occupied that country. . . . Captain Gamzon, a former leader of the Maquis of France . . . told the delegates that it can be said without exaggeration that any Jew now living in France has been saved at one time or another by a non-Jew—by the police, who made believe they did not see those wanted by the Nazis, and by others; many of them French officials who furnished false ration and identification cards to Jews who were successfully hidden in the various districts. The children specially have been saved, he said, by a people touched and saddened by the deportation of entire families."[73]

Captain Gamzon stressed that 25,000 families were lost. But so many more were saved due to the heroism and sacrifice of the resistance. He saluted the men and women of the underground, people who had been tortured and deported to concentration camps, but never cracked. René Carmille was not there to hear those words. Carmille was one of the valiant who died in Dachau rather than make the punch cards work.[74]

It took more than a year of petitions through the State Department, but IBM was able to recover all of its French machines from across Europe. Eventually, it secured all the money in its bank accounts at Credit Lyonnais. With the Holleriths back and the money recouped, the war was over for IBM France.[75]

SWITZERLAND WAS the commercial nexus of World War II. Its famous financial secrecy laws, neutrality, and willingness to trade with enemies made Switzerland the Reich's preferred repository for pilfered assets and a switchboard for Nazi-era commercial intrigue. In 1935, when talk of war in Europe became pervasive, Watson moved the company's European headquarters from Paris to Geneva. Doing business with Nazi Europe via Geneva involved a constant ebb and flow of incoherent blacklist enforcement and acquiescence by American commercial attachés. Deals and denials characterized virtually the length and breadth of IBM's presence in Geneva.[76]

Murky transactions were fundamentally untraceable since they could filter through a maze of banks or their branches, many of them newly created by Germany, scattered across occupied and neutral countries. New York branches of Swiss banks only complicated the trail, prompting Treasury officials in Washington to dispatch squads of investigators to Manhattan seeking evidence of trade with the enemy.[77]

Information even reached the Treasury that IBM might help establish its own international bank to link Nazi and American economic interests, thus only further obscuring Reich transactions and financing projects. In early 1942, the Treasury Department's Monetary Research Division moved quickly to block any such initiative. On July 13, 1942, Acting Treasury Secretary D. W. Bell took the unusual precaution of contacting Watson directly to stymie the possibility. Watson quickly declared neither he nor his company were involved in the enterprise, directly or through surrogates. For emphasis Acting Secretary Bell sent Watson an extraordinary, almost accusatory acknowledgment of his declaration: "Treasury takes note of your statement that the International Business Machines Corporation has no knowledge of any plan for the formation of an inter-continental credit bank financed jointly by American, French, and German capital. The Treasury also acknowledges your statement that the International Business Machines Corporation has not authorized and will not authorize anyone to act for it in the formation of such a bank."[78]

Bell added this clear warning to Watson: "You are, of course, aware that any action in connection with such a bank would be illegal unless done in conformity with the provisions of the Trading with the Enemy Act and Foreign Funds Control."[79]

Watson snapped back to Bell with a rare one-sentence letter: "Referring to the last paragraph of your letter of July 13, I was aware that the plans were illegal and that is why I wanted the Treasury Department to know that no one with our company had discussed or had anything to do with the proposition."[80]

Any illusion that IBM NY would not receive regular reports from its European agents about the most detailed operational vicissitudes was contradicted by the numerous Monthly Narratives, quarterly financial reports, and special punch card requests funneled through Sweden, Switzerland, Spain, and America's own diplomatic pouches.[81]

Certainly, the record was well-papered to protect IBM's legal position. From 1942 to 1945, IBM NY would wire uncharacteristically verbose and belabored instructions to its managers in neutral Europe to repossess machines, stop trading with subsidiaries in enemy countries, and terminate contracts with blacklisted firms.[82] Each such instruction stood out as a veritable disquisition of deniability laced with highly patriotic rationales for obeying the law against trading with the enemy. But when blacklists arrived, Watson's most trusted managers in Sweden and Switzerland would "get strangely busy," as one IBM internal probe termed it. Or managers would ignore New York's lengthy tractates to stop direct trading with Axis nations—sometimes delaying more than a year.[83] In many instances, elaborate document trails in Europe were fabricated to demonstrate compliance when the opposite was true.[84] Nonetheless, the true record would be permanently obscured.

During the war years, IBM's own internal reviews conceded that correspondence about its European business primarily through its Geneva office was often faked.[85] Dates were falsified.[86] Revised contract provisions were proffered to hide the true facts.[87] Misleading logs and chronologies were kept.[88]

During the protracted delays, millions of punch cards would be hurriedly shipped by IBM's neutral country subsidiaries to enemy countries or blacklisted customers.[89] At IBM, time was more than money. Time was punch cards. Once a million cards were punched, they could never be unpunched.

At the vortex of every economic masque in Switzerland was Werner Lier, IBM's European Manager in Geneva until Germany surrendered. As such, he was the company's top officer in Europe involved with virtually every transaction in every country throughout the war.[90] Yet even IBM's own review at the time concluded that Lier's dates, declarations, and documentation amounted to a prolonged and elaborate series of charades.

For instance, in late March 1942, Lier negotiated contracts with two blacklisted Swiss munitions companies. Yet on April 27, 1942, Lier sent a cable to IBM NY pretending that the two newly negotiated contracts were actually signed before the war, and then openly asking New York to petition the U.S. government for a special exemption: "U.S. Commercial Attaché Bern requests we cancel contracts," cabled Lier. "Can you intervene to maintain installations on basis contracts signed before war."[91] But IBM's own internal review later confirmed, "This is a definitely misleading statement because, apart from the two contracts here under consideration, three other contracts had been signed by the customer after the United States had entered into the war . . . the machines were supplied and billed by Geneva, and payment accepted. Mr. Lier made thereby a deliberately misleading statement. . . . This deception is the more serious since none of the contracts signed before the war existed any longer."[92]

IBM also found a pattern of falsified dates. For instance, Lier sent IBM NY a cable July 21, 1942, asserting that a Type 954 Hollerith was installed at a blacklisted customer site in Switzerland on December 31, 1941. However, IBM's own fraud review, citing its Installation Report No. 22, proved the machine was actually installed on March 31, 1942, with rent beginning in April 1942.[93]

Foot-dragging, false logs, and contrived chronologies were common-place at IBM Geneva. For example, Lier had created an extensive log to demonstrate how he regularly complied with American consular officials in Bern who demanded IBM cease business with blacklisted companies. Eventually, IBM had to admit in a letter: "Thus it has taken Mr. Lier thirteen days to inform Mr. Herzog [an IBM sales manager] that two of his customers appeared on the 'Black List,' when he [Lier] could have informed Mr. Herzog by telephone on the day he was in possession of this information—namely on March 25 [1942].[94] In consequence," the company letter continued, "[American Commercial Attaché Daniel] Reagan had pierced the mystery surrounding this case and [refused] . . . to accept Mr. Lier's . . . chronological report, inasmuch as he accuses him of having had these contracts five days after he [Lier] knew that these customers were on the Black List."[95]

On occasion, even IBM NY could no longer unravel the ruses its key managers were weaving. IBM's own internal review of one case confessed that after June 1942, "we lose track of the case as the correspondence relating thereto was withdrawn from the files."[96]

Despite IBM's own internal reviews summarizing a pattern of improprieties, Watson allowed Lier to continue at his pivotal post.

Watson himself set the stage for IBM Europe's wartime conduct. In October 1941, he circulated instructions to all subsidiaries: "In view of world conditions we cannot participate in the affairs of our companies in various countries as we did in normal times. Therefore you are advised that you will have to make your own decisions and not call on us for any advice or assistance until further notice."[97] That instruction never asked IBM executives to stop trading with the Hitler regime, or place a halt on sales to the camps, the war machine, or any German occupying authority. Watson only asked his companies to stop informing the New York office about their activities.

Despite the illusion of non-involvement, IBM NY continued to play a central role in the day-to-day operations of its subsidiaries. Company subsidiaries regularly traded with Axis-linked blacklisted companies in neutral countries, and even directly with Germany and Italy.[98] It was business as usual throughout the war.

As a Swiss national, Lier freely traveled to and from Germany, occupied territories, and neutral countries micro-managing company affairs for Watson.[99]

Six months after Watson declared IBM Headquarters to be cut off from its overseas units, Lier himself defined IBM Geneva's role not as an autonomous, detached office—but as a nexus, which simply implemented the business decisions made by IBM NY. On April 29, 1942, Lier outlined for the American Consul in Geneva exactly how IBM Geneva operated. "You will readily understand," explained Lier, "that this office is a clearing office between the local organizations in the various countries and the New York Headquarters." Lier added that IBM NY made all the decisions. His function was simply to monitor the business and keep the records. "The European Headquarters in Geneva," he explained, "are, in a way, a representative of the World Headquarters in New York, whose job it is to manage and control European affairs. . . . In short, the functions of the Geneva Office are purely administrative."[100]

Lier emphasized, "When the local offices require machines or material from our factories in the United States, they pass the order to the Geneva Office which, in turn, transmits it to the New York Headquarters for handling and supplying the machines direct to the local office."[101]

Perhaps IBM's business philosophy was best expressed by an executive of Belge Watson in an August 1939 letter to senior officers of IBM NY. The letter detailed the company's growing involvement in Japan's aircraft industry. The IBM Brussels executive declared: "It is none of our business to judge the reasons why an American corporation should or would help a foreign Government, and consequently Mr. Decker and myself have left these considerations entirely out of our line of thought. . . . we are, as IBM men, interested in the technical side of the application of our machines."[102]

But as European territory was liberated in late 1944 and early 1945, re-established national authorities began to hold commercial collaborators responsible. French arrests of IBM people in Paris—despite their ultimate release—were characteristic of the liberation fervor gripping Europe. Lier himself had been the center of many rumors. One story suggested that he had transported Dehomag money to Vichy in harrowing nighttime runs across occupied France.[103] Another story hinted that Lier was wanted by the post-War authorities even in Switzerland for bending the financial statutes.[104]

All the facts surrounding IBM's cloudy dealings in Geneva will probably never come to light, but this much became clear at the time: once the war ended, Lier needed to disappear from Geneva in a hurry. Lier had no choice. He could only escape by traveling through France. So at the end of 1944, just after French intelligence arrested CEC managers, Lier tried to arrange his immediate departure from Europe by applying for a French travel visa at the French Consulate in Geneva.[105] But on January 3, the French Foreign Ministry instructed the French Consulate to deny Lier's visa request, thus keeping him where he was. The French Consulate took its time informing Lier, and only confirmed the denial on January 12, 1945.[106]

Moreover, even if Lier could leave Switzerland, commercial officers at the American Legation in Bern were reluctant to grant him a temporary visa to enter the United States on the grounds his entry might be "detrimental to the public safety." They expressed themselves in an exchange of correspondence on January 16. But several days later, senior diplomats intervened. American Consul Paul Squire was told in a letter by legation officer J. Klahr Huddle. "Supplementing my letter," wrote Huddle, "I now have to inform you that the files in the case of Werner C. Lier have been carefully examined by the interested officers of this Legation. After careful consideration of the case, it is our considered opinion that Mr. Lier's entry into the United States on a temporary visitor's visa would not prove 'detrimental to the public safety,' and it is believed that in your discretion you may act accordingly with respect to Mr. Lier's application for a visa."[107]

However, even when U.S. officials agreed to issue a visa, Lier still could not enter French territory to effect his exit from Europe and travel to America. Yet sometime in the first two weeks of February 1945, Lier did indeed suddenly disappear.[108]

Camille Delcour, a longtime French IBM director, was astonished when he reported to the Paris subsidiary on February 12. He penned a message.

On coming to the IBM office on Monday morning, February 12, a notice was pinned on the notice board. This notice informed us that Mr. Lier was on his way to the States, "a rapid means of transportation necessitating a hurried departure having been placed at my disposal" and that he regretted not having the opportunity to take leave of the staff.

What is surprising to us is not only his strange way of eloping, but how he has found his ways and means to cross France since we know for a definite fact that the French transit visa for which he applied . . . was refused to him on January 12, 1945.

It seems that the invitation for him to go over to the States emanates from Mr. Schotte. Whether this invitation was extended without a direct provocation by Lier is uncertain. I am cabling Mr. Watson warning him not to be guided by anything Lier may say before a responsible N.Y. official has investigated the whole Geneva situation.

Camille Delcour
IBM[109]

No one could understand how Lier managed to escape. As late as summer 1945, Bern Commercial Attaché Reagan had written to the French Embassy reviewing the French Foreign Ministry's decision to deny Lier the right to enter their territory. "We have since learned," informed Reagan, "that Mr. Lier successfully reached the United States and we would like to know how he could have traveled through France without the necessary visa. If you have information about this subject, I would be grateful if you would inform me."[110]

But it should have been plain to consular officials in Bern. The man in Switzerland who intervened for Lier was America's Military Attaché, Brig. Gen. Barnwell Legge, an experienced hand at smuggling people into and out of Switzerland. Consular officials had already explained in a prior letter that General Legge was one of two senior foreign service officers who had proffered his written justification for allowing Lier into the United States. The other was the Consul General himself, a man who had transferred in from the German Embassy in Berlin. That new Consul General was Sam Woods—the same Sam Woods who helped IBM during Dehomag's revolt, and who later helped Lier move Holleriths from Poland to Romania.[111]

For Werner C. Lier and IBM Geneva, the war was over.

I
II
III
IV
V
VI
VII
VIII
IX
X
XI
XII
XIII
XIV
XV

THE SPOILS OF GENOCIDE, II

WHEN WORLD WAR II ENDED IN EUROPE, THE CONTINENT was shattered and in disarray. Millions of all faiths and nationalities were dead. For millions more—displaced persons, tattered victims, and fatigued combatants—it would be years before they could recover.

Yet, Dehomag emerged from the Hitler years with relatively little damage and virtually ready to resume business as usual. Its machines had been salvaged, its profits preserved, and its corporate value protected. Hence, when the war ended, IBM NY was able to recapture its problematic but valuable German subsidiary, recover its machines, and assimilate all the profits.

As early as December 1943, the United States government concluded that Hitler's Holleriths were strategic machines to save, not destroy. Dehomag's equipment held the keys to a smooth military occupation of Germany and the other Axis territories. By June 1944, Carter's investigative reports on IBM and Dehomag had been adapted into a confidential War Department Pamphlet, 31-123, entitled *Civil Affairs Guide: Preservation and Use of Key Records in Germany*. Over several dozen pages, key government and Party offices were listed by street address with a description of their punch card machines and data. On page 18, the Ministry of Labor entry declared, "Their records are of the utmost importance as they are the means by which the Germans controlled and shifted manpower, and should therefore be a valuable source of information for the occupying authorities. On pages 19–20, the Ministry of Transportation entry explained, "The up-to-date reports disclose the location and number of trains available in each territory, traffic density, tonnage over a particular line, type of cars used, type of materials shipped. . . . As the smooth running of the railroad system is of primary importance . . . in administering the occupied territory, all records should be placed under military custody."[1]

The War Department's *Civil Affairs Guide* citation on page 21 for Police Records specified, "records on aliens and Jews are kept by a special department of the police, the *Fremdenpolizei* (alien police). . . . By an elaborate technique, that is kept rigorously up to date, the police are enabled to trace the movements of practically everyone in the country." On page 58, in the "Gestapo Card Index," section subsection B was entitled "Register of Inmates of Concentration Camps." It confirmed: "The Gestapo Directorates and Offices keep the register of inmates of concentration camps in the areas under their jurisdiction. Copies are to be found in the concentration camps themselves."[2]

Appendix B of the *Civil Affairs Guide* identified the Dehomag factories and summarized the operational basics of Hollerith tabulators, sorters, verifiers, and multipliers.[3]

British intelligence was also keen to maintain German Holleriths intact to facilitate the occupation. A British paper reviewing the Reich Statistical Office asserted, "If the German statistical staffs at the Ministry of Economics and at subordinate levels continue to function, it will not require a great number of people to take charge. If, however, the German system . . . has been disrupted and the records sabotaged, it would be a long and arduous, though necessary, task to reconstitute it."[4]

German forces were just as eager to safeguard their IBM equipment, albeit for their own reasons. As the Allies liberated territories from the east and west, precious machines were moved behind defensible lines for the Reich's continued use. As late as 1945, *der Führer* himself had issued a decree placing a new emphasis on punch card technology for registering and tracking all Germans needed for the defense of the Reich. He appointed Karl-Hermann Frank, former military governor of occupied Czechoslovakia as a new plenipotentiary for punch card registration. Frank would be able to supercede the authority of the *Maschinelles Berichtwesen (MB)*, the *Zentral Institut*, and all other party and state offices. "In this capacity, he has to answer to me personally," declared Hitler. *Der Führer* added that the committee advising Frank would be chaired by Rudolf Schmeer, the official who spoke for the Party at the original 1934 opening of Dehomag's Lichterfelde factory. Schmeer still enjoyed a commanding role at the *MB*.[5]

More than just the strategic need to evacuate the equipment to safer ground, Hitler's Holleriths constituted damning evidence. Hence, when concentration camps were abandoned, the machines were moved and files destroyed to obliterate the record of war crimes. In many cases, Hollerith devices from various Reich sites were not redeployed, but simply hidden to keep them from Allied confiscation. However, as the Allies closed in on Berlin, military intelligence tracked many of the machines.[6]

A major *MB* punching operation of almost 100 Hollerith machines at its Wendisch-Reitz office was shifted in part to Otto's Hotel, while its tabulators were installed at a nearby castle, and the remaining devices were shipped by rail to Neudientendorf for reassembly in the basement of the Riesbeck brewery. Allied forces arrived at the brewery before the machines could be activated. Machines from Krakow and Posen were also moved to sites in Neudietendorf. Tabulators and sorters in Koenigsberg were thought to have been loaded onto a boat that escaped before Allied armies arrived. Holleriths at Hannover were moved to Elze. Nuremberg machines were relocated to Brauhaus Street in Ansbach. Tabulator experts at Kassel shipped their gear to Oberaula, but first removed several small components, rendering them inoperative if Allied forces discovered the systems.[7]

With both sides trying to protect the Holleriths, the evidence on exactly where and how thousands of machines were used was all but obscured. This was particularly the case in concentration camps where the Hollerith Departments were generally dismantled before liberators arrived, even if some of the cards, decoding keys, and telltale Hollerith transfer paper were left behind.[8]

Thus, almost as soon as Germany capitulated, IBM could begin the process of recovering its valuable equipment from frequently innocuous sites.

IBM's money was protected with equal fervor. During the war, the Reich needed IBM subsidiaries in Nazi Europe to continue operating in a reliable, profitable mode. At first, the Reich appointed a temporary enemy property custodian, Dr. Köttgen. He simply re-appointed IBM's most trusted managers in virtually all the territories.[9]

By 1943, however, the Reich Economics Ministry had designated Hermann B. Fellinger as custodian over Dehomag. Fellinger was one of Germany's most reliable and commercially adept *Kommissars*. In WWI, he had served as the chief *Kommissar* overseeing all other custodians of enemy property. In France, where Westerholt officiated as preliminary custodian at CEC,

Fellinger was empowered to supersede and ultimately replace him. Ultimately, Fellinger's authority extended not only to Dehomag, but also to IBM companies in Norway, Yugoslavia, Czechoslovakia, Poland, and France. Fellinger also coordinated closely with a second custodian, H. Garbrecht, who oversaw the IBM operating units in Belgium and Holland, and with Rome's appointed official at Watson Italiana. Real estate attorney Oskar Möhring was named custodian for IBM's property and other commercial interests in Nazi Europe.[10]

On assuming his position, Fellinger immediately re-designated IBM's best managers to keep the subsidiaries productive and profitable. He only excised one IBM personality: Dehomag Chairman Willy Heidinger. A four-man Advisory Committee, including Veesenmayer, quickly replaced Dehomag's Board of Directors. That outraged the combative Heidinger who saw his power suddenly neutralized. On June 18, 1943, Heidinger wrote a long, bitter defense of his involvement with the company, going back to its inception in 1910. His diatribe railed that Watson's interference had been the cause of all problems. Dehomag was German not American, he argued, and should not be administered for IBM's benefit, but instead completely Aryanized.[11]

"Contrary to what has on occasion been alleged," protested Heidinger, "it was, therefore, not a case of us Germans participating in an American enterprise, but rather of Americans participating in a German enterprise that I created . . . I have been blamed for many other things, in an unfounded and partly contradictory manner. Among other things, I was told I was merely a figurehead for the Americans; on the other hand, it was not very nice of me to act so aggressively towards the Americans now that I had waxed rich because of them. The opposite is true: It is not a case of my having become wealthy because of the Americans, but rather of the Americans having become wealthy because of me."[12]

Further undercutting him, Fellinger ruled that the company was no longer obligated to re-purchase Heidinger's stock. Heidinger would have undoubtedly pressed claims against Fellinger and done his utmost to regain control of Dehomag. But Heidinger's battle came to an end several months after his angry apologia to Fellinger. Deteriorating health eventually won out over the indomitable Dehomag founder. In 1944, Heidinger died of natural causes.[13]

With Heidinger out of the way, Fellinger was free to operate Dehomag and its sphere of influence as he saw fit. In that vein, he was far more than just an inert oversight officer. Fellinger functioned with as much commercial zeal and dedication to the IBM enterprise as any senior executive Watson could have personally selected. It was exactly as Watson had envisioned. Germany's custodian, Fellinger, was the perfect solution to the Dehomag revolt and the predicament of a business alliance with the Third Reich while America was fighting a war with Germany.

In Norway, Fellinger received regular progress reports from Watson Norsk's longtime manager, Jens Tellefson. Fellinger limited his involvement to "smoothing his [Tellefson's] path with [various Reich] departments, and especially the German occupation authorities." When machines and parts could no longer be imported directly from New York, Fellinger arranged for imports from Watson Italiana and Dehomag. Tellefson purchased the Italian and German machines not in the Norwegian subsidiary's name, but in the name of IBM NY to preserve the American parent company's claim to the property being used in occupied Norway. When the Norwegian company ran low on card stock, Fellinger also arranged for supplies through Dehomag's paper vendors.[14]

At one point, Norwegian saboteurs used explosives to destroy Watson Norsk's offices. They hoped to disrupt the company's in-house servicing of the Nazi labor office, which coordinated both conscripted and slave workers. Anticipating such an attack, Tellefson had arranged for Nazi records to be moved off-site daily. Nonetheless, most of the IBM machines serving the labor office were crippled in the bomb attack. So Fellinger approved relocating the IBM office to a more secure neighborhood with replacement machinery. This allowed IBM's lucrative service to continue. In Norway, annual revenues doubled from 161,000 crowns in 1940 to 334,000 crowns in 1943, and declined only slightly in 1944, the year Norway was liberated. Fellinger attributed Watson Norsk's excellent performance to "wartime conditions."[15]

In Czechoslovakia, Fellinger allowed Watson's handpicked director, Emil Kuczek, to remain in command. Fellinger was pleased that "Kuczek has conducted the business with great care and expert knowledge . . . acting conscientiously in the interest of that company." He remembered that Kuczek "always acted in complete harmony with myself." The Czech subsidiary's card printing capacity was doubled thanks to a transfer of printing presses and paper cutters from Dehomag. In turn, the Czech subsidiary filled Dehomag's punch card orders. A number of Czech machines were assigned to "German railways in the East." Kuczek accepted all machine rental payments, but did not provide any receipts. He deposited the money in IBM's account at Prague Kreditbank. IBM Geneva in turn notified Kreditbank that Kuczek was permitted to freely spend up to 20 percent of the deposits to pay for ordinary subsidiary operations, such as salaries and rent.[16] In this way, Czech operations were routinely funded without any written instructions from IBM NY, and service rendered with a minimal paper trail.

Fellinger worked hard to keep the Czech division's profits high. He insisted on eliminating discounts, limiting expenses, and even added a bonus to Kuczek's contract based on net profits. From 1941 to 1944, Czech punch card revenue alone doubled from 2.6 million crowns to nearly 5.3 million.[17]

Fellinger showed equal diligence in his administration of the other IBM subsidiaries under his control, such as Poland and Yugoslavia. The devoted receiver never failed to demand the best terms and formulate the most conservative business decisions to protect the companies he administered.[18]

Fellinger even put IBM's interest before that of the Third Reich, constantly badgering Berlin to pay more rent, and clear up its delinquencies. He even demanded that the *Wehrmacht* pay for CEC machines the German military seized from occupied France. It took months of burdensome legal wrangling, but Fellinger successfully argued that the German military had no right to remove CEC's machines without properly compensating IBM. His argument hammered away at the theme that because the plundered machines were leased items, they never belonged to the French government, but to IBM. As such, the transferred devices were not subject to traditional rules of "war booty." Only after reams of Fellinger's dense briefs, supported by attestations by CEC Managing Director Roger Virgile, did the *MB* finally consent to nearly a million Reichsmarks in back rent for machines transported out of France.[19]

Even when 308 leasing contracts—one for each requisitioned machine —were printed and submitted to CEC, at the last minute Fellinger asked Virgile to withhold signature. Fellinger learned that the *MB* had negotiated slightly better maintenance discounts with the custodian for IBM units in Belgium and Holland. Only after an adjustment guaranteeing parity did Fellinger finally agree. To replace the 308 now obsolete leasing contracts, Fellinger proposed reducing the entire agreement to a punch card but wondered about the validity of a "punch card signature." Ultimately, the parties relied on traditional written contracts.[20]

Dehomag engineer Oskar Hoermann, who doubled as CEC's deputy custodian, transmitted the basic format for the 308 leases to Paris. During the war years, Hoermann stayed in contact with IBM NY by various means, including posting ordinary letters—casual and formal—from Vichy France. For example, in April 1942, while transiting from Berlin through Vichy, Hoermann mailed a handwritten "Dear Jimmy" letter to manufacturing executives at Endicott, New York, routinely reporting factory developments at

Dehomag and CEC. From Vichy, Hoermann also was free to communicate with Lier in Geneva. The protracted negotiations with the *MB* specified the number of hours IBM machines could be used each month, thus limiting wear and tear, as well as monthly rental fees. CEC managers in combination with Fellinger stubbornly held out for the best terms, yielding the most money for IBM. Until the agreement was finalized, CEC was willing to just wait for its back rent.[21]

On June 16, 1944, an *MB* official finally noted for his file, "Fellinger has received the basic agreement signed by us and will give it today to his CEC representative, Mr. Hoermann, who is currently in Berlin. Mr. Hoermann will take it with him to Paris, where General Director Virgile will sign it. . . . The essential factor, however, is that after four years [of negotiation dating back to the invasion of France], a basic agreement is being signed."[22]

Fellinger's counterpart in Amsterdam, H. Garbrecht, who administered IBM companies in Holland and Belgium, exhibited similar assiduity in securing payment for machines removed from subsidiaries under his control. Working with IBM managers in Brussels and Amsterdam, Garbrecht finalized contracts that were typeset into a formal lease contract. Each contract declared at the top that the agreement was between the *Maschinelles Berichtwesen* in Berlin and "International Business Machines Corporation–New York" through the German administrator in Amsterdam or alternatively in Brussels. Details about the specific machine, its serial number, monthly rent, permissible hours of usage each month, and service terms were typed into the provided spaces. Although the numerous contracts were all executed on September 15, 1943, rental terms and fees were made retroactive to the summer of 1942, depending upon when the specific machines were transferred to Reich offices.[23]

For example, contract series #091/1/0094/43 for a model 034 duplicating alphabetizing puncher, serial number 10167, specified rent at RM 127.47 per month, retroactive to August 13, 1942; the device was deployed at the *MB* field office in Munich. A model 405 alphabetizing tabulator with an automatic cart, serial number 13430, cost RM 945.76 monthly, retroactive to August 26, 1942. Monthly billing tallies were generated until war's end, specifying combined rental fees at such departments as the Foreign Ministry, German Navy, *Luftwaffe*, or Inspectorate Seven. None of the contracts executed through custodian Garbrecht exploited IBM. In fact, German officials complained the hard bargain they agreed to was fundamentally unfair because the Reich was liable to pay for any damage caused by war action.[24]

With all the fervor of a Watson devotee, Fellinger also blocked any potential rivals. For example, in early August 1944, when the potential competition posed by the Wanderer-Werke alliance appeared, Fellinger challenged its patent rights in Germany. To avoid litigation, Wanderer-Werke was forced to accept Fellinger's stringent, almost dictatorial licensing agreement. Dehomag would receive a 4 percent royalty on every Bull machine imported into Germany. The 4 percent level was expressed as a temporary wartime royalty, to be increased after the conflict stopped. Fellinger's agreement demanded, "You will inform us about the type, the number, the date of import and the final purpose of every Bull machine imported." To further hush Wanderer-Werke's presence in the market, the license agreement stipulated, "You will not use these machines for advertising purposes." In the end, Fellinger's many procedural delays in Germany and the liberation of France in August 1944 combined to effectively stymie the delivery of any Bull machines into the Reich.[25] Thus, Dehomag's virtual monopoly was preserved.

Through the devoted administration of Fellinger and other Axis custodians, Dehomag and the other IBM subsidiaries in Europe thrived. Their custodial authority stopped when Germany surrendered. It would be a long bureaucratic and uncharted process for IBM to reclaim its property. Fortunately, Watson could rely upon another column of support: the IBM Soldiers.

AMERICAN SOLDIERS in Europe fought valiantly to defeat the Nazi nemesis. Part of their mission was to take control of German facilities and seize evidence of Nazi war crimes and collaboration. Whether the target was an industrial site, a bank, a military base, or a concentration camp, it was all enemy property to be referred to commanders, and possibly war crime prosecutors.

But among American forces, there existed a cohesive group of men with a common identification. As former employees of International Business Machines on leave from their company jobs, they affectionately referred to themselves as "IBM Soldiers."

The framework for IBM's continuing bond with its employees at war began long before America joined the conflict. At Christmas 1940, Watson informed all employees soon to be drafted into the military that they would be granted three months pay, up to $4,000, while absent. The money would be paid to inductees in twelve monthly installments, a comforting stipend for the family back home while the men were in uniform.[26]

Making it clear they were still part of the IBM Family with careers waiting after military service, Watson announced, "We shall miss you during the time you are away, but we feel that your year's training will be beneficial to you physically, mentally and morally. As a result of this training, we believe you will come back to our company better equipped for future service in the IBM. . . . If such is the case, you will be given an opportunity to earn increased compensation. We want you to know that your friends in the company are back of you in every way, and if at any time we can be of help to you please let us know."[27]

When the U.S. military formed its Machine Record Units (MRU), IBM employees, or those IBM had trained, became the backbone of the elite MRU forces. IBMers also commanded in other key areas, especially in administrative units, where their experience would be instrumental. In the minds of many of these men, unswerving loyalty to Thomas Watson and devotion to IBM was completely consistent with military discipline in the field and loyalty to the Allied cause. As a result, when IBM Soldiers happened upon Dehomag equipment and factories, they did not see evidence of a war crime to docket or a key Nazi industrial installation to capture. They saw something inspiring and beloved that needed protection and to be returned to its rightful owner. IBM's cause was their cause.

SOMEWHERE IN GERMANY
Thursday, April 26, 1945

Dear Mr. Watson:

Today I received your letter of congratulations upon my promotion to Corporal. It is impossible to state the wonderful effects your letter gives me especially as a morale builder. And in this respect I feel certain that I am speaking for each and every one of the fellow IBM Soldiers. Your letters and those of the executives received by us go a long way to make our lives over here in the ETC [European Theater Command] a much happier one.

It seems appropriate that today I should receive your letter; the day I returned from paying a visit to the "Deutsche Hollerith Maschinen Gesellschaft" in Sindelfingen. My Captain, a fellow [IBM] soldier, and myself were the first Americans to set foot in the plant since the war. [Dehomag employees] Mr. Otto Haug and Mr. Wiesinger were our personal guides and I can assure you, Mr. Watson that I felt a little thrilled seeing on a small scale what I witnessed in your factory at Endicott in the winter of 1940. The entire [Dehomag] factory is intact, spared for some unknown reason by our airmen.

At Sindelfingen, I found a sub-assembly plant with many parts on hand and in very good condition. Every tool, every machine is well-preserved ready to start work at a moment's notice. . . . a card stock of over a million cards [is] ready for shipment plus two hundred rolls of paper stock, stored away securely in a properly ventilated cellar.

At Holzgerlingen, six kilometers south of Sindelfingen there is a service bureau; two tabulators type 297, one multiplier—601, two sorters—080, 522 summary key punch and four key punches—016. Mr. Haug moved the service bureau here because it appeared safer from bombing attacks.

Time and duty did not permit me to investigate further but the following items Mr. Haug gave me: all spare parts and replacement parts were moved from Stuttgart to Kuchen. Here also you shall find the wiring department, plugboard and small assembly plants. Hechingen is the gathering point for all sub-assemblies. Here everything was assembled and Mr. Haug believes the plant is not bombed but in good condition. At Berlin, there is still a sub-unit assembly plant. Mr. Rottke, Mr. Hummel and Mr. Haug sometime in last autumn made all the above changes . . . as a safety measure. At Sindelfingen, Mr. Haug and Mr. Wiesinger have done a wonderful job in spite of very trying difficulties and the plant being 100 % intact could be very beneficial to the Allied Armies for spare parts, paper stock and such.

As you so well know Mr. Watson, fraternization is forbidden, but in this instance I was working under orders handed down in a directive to all MRUs from the Supreme Headquarters. All my dealings with Mr. Haug and Mr. Wiesinger were only of this nature but I know they would like to be remembered to you.

Sincerely yours,
James T. Senn
Fourth MRU[28]

Senn's letter was typical. Watson received reports from any number of sources, whether IBM Soldiers or Dehomag employees. Dehomag staffers were able to direct their messages through IBM Soldiers, who would pass them on through the ordinary mail. Whether an IBM Soldier or a Dehomag employee, most asked for instructions guiding their next effort on behalf of the corporation.

For example, on May 10, just two days after Berlin fell, Dehomag engineer Alfred Dicke, dutifully dispatched an emergency message to Watson in New York: "Hereby I wish to inform you," reported Dicke, "of the transfer of the Patent Department . . . from the plant in Berlin to Hechingen/Hohen-zollern, a town . . . which you know from your visit in former days. On account of the frequent air attacks on Berlin and the approach of the Allied Armies it became impossible to remain in Berlin any longer, and it was necessary to bring the valuable patent files, of which many documents cannot be reproduced, to safer places.[29]

"The plant in Berlin," Dicke continued, "has been gradually destroyed by incendiary bombs since 1943. Most of the departments have been transferred to different places in southern Germany, so that one cannot speak any more of a main office in Berlin. . . . Would you find it advisable to move the complete files to the 'Compagnie Electro-Comptable' . . . [in] Paris or to the 'International Business Machines Corporation' in Geneva?"[30]

On August 22, 1945, Capt. Leonard V. Salisbury, A Company, 750 Tank Battalion, sent a short note to IBM advising that a letter from IBM's Berlin tax attorney had been sent via the Rochester, New York, factory. Salisbury also dispatched a report of his own personal inspection of the Lichterfelde factory and office. "The outstanding observation I noticed," reported Salisbury, "was the optimism of [Dehomag managers] Mr. Cimbal, Mr. Kölm and Mr. Brockman for the future business of IBM in this, a shattered city. With such a spirit, the future is very bright. If I can be of any aid as liaison or otherwise will be only be too glad to do so . . . I hope to see all my IBM friends by Christmas."[31]

The same steady flow of information reached IBM NY from American forces elsewhere in liberated Europe. In one instance, IBM became impatient for reports on the Dehomag facility in Austria when it had heard no news for three weeks. William W. Bass of IBM NY's Foreign Trade Department communicated with his son, an army lieutenant stationed in Vienna. Lieutenant Bass in turn provided a report which was passed from the military headquarters in Vienna to the State Department in Washington, and from there to IBM NY.[32]

In the chaotic first months of the Allied occupation of Germany, a faithful, if officious, network of IBM Soldiers tried to outdo each other in advancing the cause of Dehomag. Perhaps none caused the waves that Lt. Col. Lawrence G. Flick did. The Russians arrested Rottke on May 11 for his Nazi connections. Allied forces arrested Hummel shortly thereafter. Lieutenant Colonel Flick, an MRU officer, tried his best to help IBM by restoring Dehomag's prior management.[33]

On September 2, 1945, Flick wrote a long letter to Watson. "I am leaving Berlin tomorrow for Frankfurt," he advised. "There I shall endeavor to locate Karl Hummel and do what I can to expedite his return to Berlin. As you will see later, there is a considerable difference of opinion amongst those involved in handling the affairs of Dehomag. But on two things all seem to be agreed. One is the return of Dr. Rottke. This I am afraid is highly problematical. Although some have returned after arrest by the Russians, they are few and usually not in the best physical condition. Second is the return of Hummel. This can be accomplished if his health permits his travelling under the existing very trying conditions.[34]

"Last evening," continued Flick, "I spent with Captain Arthur D. Reed, Property Control Officer of the Military Government. He is the custodian of all businesses, a highly intelligent and earnest man of about forty. . . . Captain Reed is in accord with any personal efforts I have and can make on behalf of my company. He is sold on . . . Fellinger, and has given him a position of trust with his section, that of trustee of former Nazi businesses. He also uses Fellinger as counsillor on IBM policy.[35]

"After my conversation with Captain Reed," Flick went on, "it was agreed that I might communicate with Fellinger through him, and, if you so desire, I will forward any directions in this manner until more normal communications are restored. Also through Reed, I was able to locate Major Andrew Haensel from whom you may have heard through [Watson aide] Jack Kenney. I spent the morning with Haensel and am forwarding some reports on this meeting as enclosures hereto. . . . Haensel has done an outstanding job of cooperation insofar as he can do so within existing regulations. The same is true of Captain Reed. I made arrangements with Haensel, to forward any communications to the present executives of the company here in Berlin, with a copy to Reed and vice versa. Thus, any correspondence will be entirely on the up and up, and will by the same token be subject to military screening. The three of us will keep in touch with one another as stated."[36]

Flick also addressed the difficulty of significant cash accounts in Germany that were blocked and therefore unavailable to defray the day-to-day needs of Dehomag.

"The company [Dehomag] needs cash," wrote Flick. "Reed, Haensel, and Fellinger have all indicated that a matter of one hundred fifty thousand marks will keep the breath of life in the organization for a period of three months when it might be possible to operate more normally once again. If I get to Hamburg I will endeavor to do something about this if it can be done within existing regulations. Haensel, who is quite thoroughly informed, holds out little hope that any capital in Berlin will be available for a long time."[37]

Flick concluded his long report to Watson, "In the meanwhile I would appreciate hearing from you on the matter of how much interest any of the

IBMers should continue to take in European business, etc. Until I hear further, I shall endeavor to pick up any and all data that may be of interest to you. It is of course obvious that much of the data may already be available to you or may duplicate information, which you have had for some time. There is no way of avoiding this, and it is only with the hope that what is gathered may be of help to the home office, that we in the field, are gathering with considerable difficulty, the material which is being sent in."[38]

Watson did not appreciate the help. In IBM's view, the IBM Soldiers rendered invaluable service to the company. But he saw Flick's helpfulness trying to restore Hummel as unwanted interference. Watson had no intention of re-empowering the leaders of the Dehomag revolt, and any manager with a claim to a percentage on profits. Watson possessed the ability to send a single letter from his office that would reach directly into the bombed-out sectors of Berlin. He wanted Flick silenced and removed. He ordered Chauncey to Washington with a letter.

SEPTEMBER 20, 1945
The Honorable William L. Clayton
Assistant Secretary of State
Washington D.C.

Dear Mr. Secretary,

I have just received a letter from Lt. Col. Lawrence G. Flick, who is on leave of absence from the International Business Machines Corporation, in the Military Service, a photostatic copy of which I enclose. In the first and fourth paragraphs he refers to restoring Mr. Karl Hummel to the Management. We do not want any of our IBM people in the Military Service discussing anything of this kind with any of our German representatives because we do not know how many of the German employees we will take back into the organization, when our business is re-instated in Germany.

We would like to have Colonel Flick notified of this, and I am asking you to advise Mr. H. K. Chauncey, who presents this letter, as to how the matter can be handled, consistent, of course, with the policies and wishes of the Military authorities in charge.

Sincerely,
Thomas J. Watson
President[39]

The response was swift. Several days later, Assistant Secretary of State Clayton wrote to his counterpart at the Pentagon.

Dear General Hilldring:

On 21 September 1945 Mr. H. K. Chauncey, of the International Business Machines Corporation, delivered two letters to the Department, copies of which are attached for your information, which indicate that Lt. Colonel Lawrence G. Flick, now on leave from the International Business Machines Corporation and currently assigned to G5 Industry Branch in Berlin, is actively interfering in the management of the German subsidiary of the International Business Machines Corporation. You will note that Mr. Thomas J. Watson, President of the International Business Machines Corporation, requests in his letter to me that Lt. Colonel Flick and any other personnel now on leave from the International Business Machines Corporation while in the military service, be restrained from discussing policy with respect to the affairs of the German subsidiary. I assume that you will request the proper authorities to notify Colonel Flick to this effect. . . .

Sincerely yours,
William Clayton
Assistant Secretary [40]

Clayton reported back to Watson the same day.

My Dear Mr. Watson:

Pursuant to the suggestion advanced in your letter of September 20, delivered by Mr. Chauncey to officers of this Department, I have addressed a communication to General Hilldring of the War Department General Staff, Civil Affairs Division, notifying him that it is your desire that former employees of the International Business Machines Corporation, now in the military service, shall not perform any actions relating to the management or operation of your German subsidiary. I have advised General Hilldring that the Department at this time does not favor the restoration of private business connections or relations with German firms by persons who are or claim to be acting for the benefit of principals located in the United States.

Sincerely yours,
William Clayton
Assistant Secretary [41]

In mid-November, Major General Hilldring at the Pentagon forwarded a copy of Watson's letter directly to Gen. Lucius Clay, Deputy Military Governor in Berlin. This prompted a full army brass investigation of Flick's well-intentioned actions. By November 19, General Clay had completed the investigation. On November 27, 1945, Hilldring reported back to the State Department, "Lt. Colonel Flick is being returned to the United States for retirement from the Army. Therefore, General Clay has recommended that no further action is necessary."[42]

Dehomag, the Berlin company so integral to the Hitler war machine, was never treated as an enemy entity. It was welcomed back as a precious American interest and still under the control of Thomas J. Watson.

RECAPTURING DEHOMAG was a long, involved process that began within days of Germany's surrender. On May 18, 1945, IBM NY sent three letters to the State Department's War Problems Division. The first explained that IBM owned a company called Dehomag that installed equipment around Germany. Certainly, much of that machinery had been moved in the last days of the Third Reich. IBM wanted State Department help in locating every one of those devices. "From January 1937," IBM's letter claimed, "Dehomag has failed to give us detailed information of installations in Germany. . . . Consequently, we do not know the exact location of the machines. We attach a list of the places in which at one time we knew machines were located." A two-column list itemized eighty-eight German cities and towns where Holleriths had been installed. The statement about not knowing addresses since 1937 was made in spite of IBM's assistance in preparing the *Civil Guide,* which included up-to-date addresses as of 1944 on numerous key Hollerith installations.[43]

The company's second letter to the War Problems Division included the addresses of two residential properties that had been managed by IBM's tax attorney. IBM wanted the rents. "He has, no doubt, accumulated a substantial amount of money for the rentals of the buildings."[44]

A third letter just reminded the State Department that by immediately establishing communications with Dehomag, a list of the precise locations of shifted equipment could be obtained.[45]

Shortly thereafter, the State Department sent instructions to American foreign service officers in Germany and Austria to "extend such protection as may be possible to the property."[46]

On October 24, 1945, Chauncey returned triumphantly to Germany to reclaim Dehomag. The setting was quite different from his last visit. Then, in 1941, he never knew from moment to moment whether he would run afoul of the Nazi Party. Now he was in the company of victors.[47]

Chauncey's journey began in liberated France, where the U.S. Army assigned Capt. Philip Kober as his escort. The two men traveled to Frankfurt where another escort, Capt. Philip Hayter, joined them. Their first stop was IBM's Frankfurt office. As he entered the property, Chauncey was abundantly cautious in his demeanor. General Eisenhower had decreed strict "non-fraternization," forbidding such common courtesies as shaking hands with Germans, engaging in friendly conversation, or visiting in German homes. IBM could adapt to any geo-political setting. When the rule was banquets and social graces, the company could summon up corporate celebrations and partake of festive extravangazas at a moment's notice. Now under strictures of cold communication, IBM could exhibit regulation chilliness. In that vein, Chauncey visibly asked his military escorts' permission before conversing with anyone, spoke only in the presence of officers, and even declined to look at papers unless cleared in advance. After first obtaining permission to speak to IBM's Frankfurt manager, Chauncey, in a dispassionate, formal tone, requested a complete list of financial data on the office. Little more was discussed with the Dehomag manager.[48]

From Frankfurt, the trio traveled the next day to Stuttgart, hoping to inspect the vital Dehomag factory in nearby Sindelfingen. In Stuttgart, Chauncey first met with Maj. J. M. Teasdale, the U.S. officer in charge of Dehomag and other commercial property in the area. When Chauncey asked if there was any existing procedure for an American company to regain control of its property, Teasdale replied that none yet existed. But if it would help, Teasdale offered to make Chauncey the custodian. He explained that if Chauncey accepted the custodianship, he would be functioning not in IBM's interest as much as in the army's interest. Chauncey was not receptive, feeling, "I think it unwise for any IBM man to be in charge." In any event, Teasdale declared he would not permit any German to continue working for an American firm against the American company's wishes. That included Dehomag.[49]

What's more, there was business to be done. The U.S. military needed more Hollerith alphabetizers in France and Germany. The army was prepared to sign leases for equipment. Teasdale declared he was more than willing to permit Dehomag to fill those orders. He then assigned a field investigator, Private Schufert, to accompany Chauncey and his escorts to Sindelfingen.[50]

Dehomag's Sindelfingen plant was undamaged. No bombs had struck. Chauncey and the three military men were met by Oskar Hoermann. Taut and unfriendly, Chauncey informed Hoermann he would not converse with him except with the permission and within earshot of "the Army people . . . accompanying me." Having been authorized to speak, Chauncey stated that the army wished IBM to recover the Holleriths the German Army had removed from France. Hoermann replied, as Chauncey noted in his report, that "Dehomag had little information, since the taking of the machines was done by the German Army and not with the cooperation of Dehomag." Ironically, few knew more about those transferred machines than Hoermann. Hoermann, of course, was deputy Nazi custodian of CEC, the key Dehomag engineering manager in charge of French equipment, and aware of page after page of CEC billing demands on the Reich. What's more, Hoermann functioned as the intermediary between CEC and the *MB* as Fellinger negotiated and finalized all 308 machine-specific lease contracts. Chauncey did not correct Hoermann.[51]

Instead, Chauncey merely went on to the next order of business. The U.S. Army, said Chauncey, was anxious to obtain German-made alphabetizers, especially the advanced D11-A. Hoermann replied that although five such machines were placed into production, only one was fully assembled and in operation—the machine used at Dachau. Then in the presence of two special military escorts and an army field investigator, Chauncey inspected the Dachau machine. It was partially dismantled. He noticed that the device, which featured a rotary printing mechanism, seemed larger than the Model 405 American alphabetizer. Hoermann asserted that the Dachau machine never worked as well as it should. Captains Kober and Hayter also examined the device. In reporting back to IBM NY about the D11-A, Chauncey wrote, "This machine was used at Dachau, but was sent to the Dehomag at Sindelfingen through the cooperation of Mr. Hendricks." Sergeant Hendricks was a U.S. Army industry liaison that headed up "a special installation" at Bad Nauheim.[52]

As Chauncey turned to leave, the gregarious Hoermann tried to ask several questions about his IBM friends. He had openly corresponded with them during the war years. But Chauncey stiffly cut him off, asserting that no personal conversation or other pleasantries could be exchanged. Hoermann demurred.[53]

That day, the group returned to Frankfurt where they met with Hendricks, who had just returned from Berlin. Hendricks had inspected the damaged Lichterfelde facility, and was carrying an envelope for IBM containing a full report from the German staff there. Lieutenant Colonel Flick had conveyed the report to Hendricks. In the awkward moment that followed, Hendricks pulled the envelope out of his pocket, but Chauncey declined to actually accept it. Instead, Chauncey immediately handed the envelope—

without looking inside, to Captain Kober standing next to him. Kober, who read German, skimmed the reports and then granted permission for Chauncey to review it as well. Chauncey did so, but quickly realized the reports "convey no information not previously known."[54]

Hendricks told Chauncey some additional information about Dehomag managers. Rottke's imprisonment by the Russians for Nazi connections was considered a lost cause because Mrs. Rottke was known for pronounced Nazi views. But Hummel was back. After Hummel was released from the Allied prison at Bad Kreuznach, Hendricks saw no harm in transporting him to Stuttgart in a truck.[55] Even though Watson had wanted Hummel excised, he had already been restored to the company.

On October 30, 1945, Chauncey returned under escort to Paris to continue the methodical process of reclaiming the German subsidiary. He continued to petition various offices of the occupying authorities in Europe and the State Department in Washington. Even though a complete policy on resumption of corporate control had not yet been defined, as soon as any ad hoc element of the policy was espoused, IBM was ready to swiftly act on it. During late summer and fall 1945, the bureaucratic barriers gradually began to crumble.[56]

The Berlin and Sindelfingen operations were administered as two distinct entities. During the summer, the military had initially appointed Dehomag Manager H. Beckmann as custodian of the Berlin operation. But he was extremely inefficient and depressed over Germany's fortunes. His son had been killed in the war. His wife had her teeth knocked out during an altercation with Russian soldiers. Chauncey called Beckmann "a broken man." What's more, he was on bad terms with Fellinger. Beckmann ordered guards to stop Fellinger at the gate. Fellinger complained. So the military replaced Beckmann with another Dehomag manager, W. Cimbal, who was more to Fellinger's liking. Whoever was appointed to run Dehomag was dependent upon Fellinger for transitional help. After all, Fellinger had been effectively running the subsidiaries since 1943. Nonetheless, occupation authorities, overlooking Fellinger's Nazi Party connections, designated him a special advisor to Cimbal.[57]

Although IBM had not regained control of Dehomag, the company was now allowed to resume its normal operations as quickly as possible. Considerable monies were still frozen in bank accounts. An August 1945 review reported that salaries had not been paid since the fall of Berlin. So Cimbal rallied Lichterfelde's resources, cut expenses and salaries, and re-established monthly leasing patterns. To earn extra cash, toys were produced from scrap metal. Soon Lichterfelde's tabulators were rattling again. Punch cards were rolling off the presses. By September 1945, more than 320 prior German installations were in operation, including Holleriths at public utilities, insurance companies, and railroads. One plant filling card orders for the French and U.S. armies was already at 75 percent capacity; it had produced 58 million cards from September to November. A military order for 17 million was waiting to be produced. Cimbal was compelled to seek IBM NY permission to order $12,000 in additional machine tools to restart the manufacturing program.[58]

Before the end of the year, Chauncey would be able to report in a letter to Watson, "Cimbal has done a good job. The territory under him is operating on a cash basis profit. You know already of their manufacture of toys from scrap and novelties from American Army discarded tin cans. The rentals, however, remain the backbone of the revenue."[59]

In August 1945, the military instructed Fellinger to prepare comprehensive reports on his command of IBM subsidiaries in Germany, Norway, France, Yugoslavia, Czechoslovakia, and Poland, as well as his knowledge in other territories. In addition to a resumé of activities, Fellinger was required to forecast the prospects for each division. Fellinger addressed some reports directly to Watson. But most of the surveys were formally submitted to American military government for IBM's review.[60] These extensive country-by-country summaries, backed up by financial data, contained most of the information IBM NY needed to resume control.

Shortly after the submission, an unidentified branch of the military arrested Fellinger.[61] That was end of his involvement with IBM.

On December 3, 1945, the American military government in Stuttgart passed a message for Chauncey through an army office in Paris. Firm policies were still unresolved on restoring American property. But Chauncey could again travel to Germany to resume discussions.[62]

The next day, December 4, Chauncey and another IBM officer, Mr. Warrin, flew from Paris to an airport near Frankfurt. The late connecting flight to Berlin was canceled due to poor weather. They tried again in the morning, but the weather was unimproved. While waiting in Frankfurt, they again called on Captain Hayter, who asked IBM to prepare whatever contract it deemed appropriate to allow the military to begin the widespread leasing of needed Dehomag machines and secure repair services for mobile U.S. machines in the area.[63] Chauncey was happy to comply.

With the weather still difficult, Chauncey and Warrin resorted to an overnight train. Purchasing tickets at the last minute, they were required to travel all the way to Berlin in regular seats instead of first-class berths. Once in Berlin, they sought out Major Curry at the local Property Control Office. He authorized Chauncey to finally inspect the Lichterfelde facility. No escort would be necessary and any useful discussion could take place.[64]

When Chauncey and Warrin arrived at Lichterfelde, December 6, 1945, an American flag was flying atop the Dehomag factory roof. They were met by Cimbal and a delegation of Dehomag employees. From the outset, Chauncey announced, as before, no "friendly discussion" could take place, but only an exchange of business information required by IBM NY.[65]

The next day, Chauncey received a message to come to Cimbal's home to speak to Major Curry. That evening, Chauncey and Warrin arrived at Cimbal's home as requested, and met Curry. But when they walked in a bit further, they saw a beautifully set dinner table. It was nothing like the grandiose banquets IBM had staged during the war, but Mrs. Cimbal had spent some time trying to be hospitable with the little they had. Abruptly, Chauncey stopped and harshly demanded that no party-like atmosphere could ensue. Adhering to a strict non-fraternization ethic, he insisted only business in a business-like setting could be discussed.[66]

Just then, Lieutenant Colonel Flick entered the dining room. In a few days, Flick was due to return home. But for now he was still in authority. He berated both Chauncey and Warrin for their unfriendly attitude toward the Cimbals. At that, Chauncey retorted: had he known he was being invited to a party, he would have refused. The two IBM men turned around and abruptly left.[67]

After first checking with several ranking occupation officers, Chauncey softened his manner with Cimbal. In subsequent contacts, he was able to extract the key information about Dehomag's Berlin operation, including its customer list, financial condition, a review of blocked bank accounts, and the prospects for profitable continuation. Eventually, he learned that the Sindelfingen plant alone had produced some $3.07 million in cards and equipment during the war years. One site alone, Plant II, averaged 39 million cards per month. At the cessation of hostilities, the Berlin factory controlled about 1,000 total installations, representing as many as 6,000 machines, worth $2.34 million. Some 1,314 punches, verifiers, sorters, and tabulators were damaged at user sites, representing an approximate loss to IBM of $1.61 million.[68]

Dehomag machines were located throughout what had been known as the Greater Reich and adjacent occupied territories. In Poland: 444 punches and verifiers, 144 sorters, 124 tabulators, and 74 auxiliary machines. In Austria: 447 punches and verifiers, 117 sorters, 91 tabulators, and 53 auxiliary machines. In Czechoslovakia: 108 punches and verifiers, 37 sorters, 26 tabulators, and 17 auxiliary machines. All tolled, some 2,348 Holleriths were identified for recovery.[69]

Chauncey sought out IBM attorney Heinrich Albert. Albert was now functioning as custodian for Ford Motor Company's operation in Berlin. Although many of the records relating to Dehomag were lost, Albert was able to sign enough affidavits and certificates to document that IBM NY was in fact the lawful owner of Dehomag and all its Holleriths.[70]

Machine by machine, office by office, IBM NY began recouping the proceeds of Dehomag's service to the Third Reich. In doing so, the utmost care was taken to walk the thin green line between conquest and commerce. Chauncey summarized his own conduct in a report to New York. Uppermost in his mind, was the "desire that neither I nor IBM should be in any way criticized."[71]

Chauncey was completely successful. Endless additional meetings ensued with the many transient bureaucratic faces of what was known as OMGUS (Office of the Military Governor–U.S.), as well as its counterparts in the Russian occupying administration. IBM was cautious, persistent, and consistently above reproach. This perception was indispensable because with the horror of 6 million murdered Jews, and perhaps an equal number of other Europeans, as well as billions of dollars, francs, and crowns in plunder and devastation, war crime trials were being organized. Reparations from the German commercial sector were being readied. IBM very much wanted to be excluded.

MILITARY LAW NO. 52 was a problem.

Article I stated: "All property in occupied territory is subject to seizure of possession or title of management, supervision or otherwise, which is owned or controlled in any way by: (a) The German Reich or any sub division or agency thereof; (b) any Governments or nationals at war with the United Nations at anytime since September 1, 1939; (c) the outlawed NSDAP . . . or its agencies; (d) persons held by Military Government under detention." Dehomag qualified on all accounts. It was controlled by known Nazis, Heidinger and Rottke, who also owned 10 percent of the shares. Rottke and Hummel had been arrested for their Nazi affiliations. The company's Board of Directors since 1941 was completely Nazified. As part of the war machinery, Dehomag was under the jurisdiction of the *Maschinelles Berichtwesen,* a wartime agency.[72]

Chauncey had reviewed a summary of Military Law No. 52 and other Allied decrees as early as May 21, 1945.[73] IBM sought to be carved out of the sphere of culpability and absorbed into the apparatus of victory. It wanted restitution for its war-damaged property, not to become a candidate for reparations. IBM did not want to join the roster of all those deemed part of what was termed "Nazi conspiracy and aggression." Fortunately for IBM, there seemed to be a concerted effort to keep Watson and the company out of the reparations discourse.

On October 16, when Assistant Secretary of State Clayton first wrote to the Pentagon about the troublesome Lieutenant Colonel Flick and Dehomag, the third paragraph originally referred to the issue of potential reparations. "As you know," Clayton initially asserted, "this Government's policy towards German reparations, external assets, and combines is not fully implemented and it is my belief that for these and other reasons it is undesirable at this time to foster or support the restoration of private business relationships." But a State Department policy review of the proposed draft objected to the paragraph. "Attached is a redraft version of the Clayton-Hilldring letter concerning the activities of Lt. Colonel Flick," wrote Walt Rostow. "As you will note, I have simply removed the offending paragraph." A large X was drawn across the draft, and a shorter version mailed.[74]

On Chauncey's first post-war visit to occupied Stuttgart, in October 1945, Major Teasdale indicated that all the corporate enterprises in the heavily industrial Sindelfingen area were slated to be liquidated for reparations. Chauncey's report back to New York confirmed, "He [Major Teasdale] stated that all of the property in the American zone belongs to the American government for reparations, and that if and when property owned by an American was turned over to him, it would reduce the reparation claim of the United States and consequently the reparation claim of the American owner."[75]

On his second trip, Chauncey arranged for a personal visit to Deputy Military Governor Clay's office where he was introduced to General Clay's assistant, Gen. William Draper. Draper, a friend of Watson's, headed up OMGUS' Economic Branch. Draper, in turn, introduced Chauncey to Col. John A. Allen, the man in charge of the Restitution Branch. Chauncey argued IBM's case "that the American viewpoint would be the restoration of American-owned concerns to their owners, and that it would not be . . . that such companies would be used for general reparations, as has been proposed." Chauncey was told that no decision had yet been formulated.[76]

IBM's view held that even if their machinery and corporate acumen had helped organize and optimize the Third Reich's aggression, they should be held exempt—ipso facto—by virtue of its American ownership. The company contended that its Nazi payments were protected revenues.

However, the prevailing thought among the Allies and those who demanded justice was that all in government and the private sector who helped Hitler destroy Europe and commit genocide should be held accountable in war crimes. Their war gains and economic wherewithal were not sacrosanct. Rather, they should be sacrificed as reparations to the victims—nations and individuals both. Whether dressed in jackboots and swastikas, or suit and tie, accountability was demanded. Indeed, the world understood that corporate collusion was the keystone to Hitler's terror. Businessmen who cooperated with Hitler were considered to be war criminals or "accessories to war crimes."[77]

OMGUS established a Division of Investigation of Cartels and External Assets to identify those responsible for the financing and corporate support of Nazi Germany. By November 1, 1945, twenty-one major bankers were arrested for their role in helping German rearmament and the plunder of occupied nations. Twenty more bankers were targeted. The financial institutions identified included Germany's most respected: Deutsche Bank, Dresdner Bank, and Commerzbank.[78]

German magnates from the steel, finance, automotive, and chemical industries were also arrested and sent to the Nuremberg dock. Names such as Krupp, Thyssen, and Flick became synonymous with corporate war criminality. Even companies with American ownership or affiliation were spotlighted. For example Roehm & Haas of Darmstadt was investigated. The firm, which manufactured Plexiglas bulletproof materials in Germany, was affiliated with its American-owned counterpart in Philadelphia. Each of the corporate twins was half-owned by German and American citizens. The *New York Times* reported, "Files located in Darmstadt reveal the history of the joint efforts of the German Roehm & Haas and the American Roehm & Haas to nullify the action of the Alien Property Custodian and restore the German interest in the American firm."[79]

By January 5, 1946, hundreds of German factories were slated to be sold to Americans to effect reparations. These factories covered a range of industry from entrenched armament firms, such as the Borgward torpedo plant at Bremen, to Norddeutsche Dernierwerke's factory number 4 at Rothebeck, which manufactured simple household utensils and beds.[80] They were sold both because they represented economic assets of the German people to be liquidated in war culpability, and because they were war vendors.

Within another week, OMGUS had destroyed or liquidated half of I.G. Farben's forty-two German plants. Two dozen of its directors and corporate managers were indicted on five war crimes. One count specified "the planning, preparation, initiation and waging of wars and invasions of other countries." A second identified "crimes against humanity through participating in the enslavement and deportation for slave labor of civilians." A third count accused the executives of "participation in a common plan or conspiracy to commit crimes against peace." Ten of the defendants were acquitted. The remainder were found guilty and sentenced to varying terms in prison.[81]

By fall 1946, the Allies had selected 658 German plants to be liquidated for reparations: 157 in the American zone, 444 in the British zone, and 57 in the French zone. Only half of the firms were from the war industry. Russia had already received 15,500 tons of commercial deliveries as part of its reparations levy.[82]

In Belgium, prosecutors tried industrialists for commercial cooperation with the Reich. Defendants included a textile company executive, as well as financiers. All revenues received from Nazi Germany were confiscated; prison sentences ranged from four to eight years. Newspapers reported the Belgian court's declaration that the executives had embarked upon a "two-way gamble designed to pay rich dividends either way—if Hitler won the war or lost it."[83]

Justice Robert H. Jackson, chief Nuremberg prosecutor, told Armed Forces Radio that he feared that while German industrialists were "one of the chief causes of the war," most would never be brought to justice. Jackson's fellow prosecutors felt the number of defendants would simply be too large to pragmatically try in the first wave of Nuremberg Trials. The other Allied prosecutors suggested that perhaps businessmen could be indicted later. "I feared failure to include them," said Jackson, "would mean they never would be tried. Time only will tell which was right."[84]

Indeed, the trial process was slowed by the necessity of translating all documents, exhibits, and testimony into several languages of the war crime tribunal: French, Russian, German, and English. Justice Jackson turned to a newly invented process called "simultaneous translation." One company reviewed all the evidence and translated it not only for real time usage at the trial proceedings, but for posterity. That company was International Business Machines. It made the final translated record of all evidence back and forth from French, Russian, German, Polish, and English. Watson offered to undertake the massive evidence handling free of charge.[85]

Many wealthy men stood in the dock at Nuremberg. Publishers, financiers, bankers, and industrialists were summoned to account for their commerce. Hjalmar Schacht himself, former president of the *Reichsbank* and out of power for years, although ultimately acquitted, was forced to explain his involvement at the bar of justice.[86]

But it was a far different story for IBM. It seemed to be immune from the debate itself. Every bloodstain and barracks blueprint in the camps was examined, catalogued, and probed. Machines such as Dachau's D11-A, inspected by Chauncey, and those at Auschwitz, Buchenwald, Westerbork, and at the Warsaw Ghetto, were simply recovered and resorbed into the IBM asset list. They would be deployed another day, another way, for another client. No answers or explanations would be provided. Questions about Hitler's Holleriths were never even raised.

IBM WAS MORE than important to the Allies. It was vital.

The Supreme Headquarters Allied Expeditionary Force (SHAEF) was the Allied high command in Europe under General Eisenhower. SHAEF had established a classified statistical analysis office in Bad Nauheim, which in summer 1945 was serving the United States Strategic Bombing Survey (USSBS). Roosevelt had established the Bombing Survey in November 1944 to evaluate the devastating effects of Allied bombing on Germany. This was to include the effects of civilian morale and whether bombs hardened the national will to fight, or collapsed it.[87]

The Bad Nauheim site was completely dependent upon Hollerith machines and Dehomag operators for its numerous calculations of bomb destruction and predictions of the resulting social disruption. The so-called Morale Division, staffed with a platoon of social scientists, psychologists, and economists relied upon the machines to quantify public reaction to severe bombing. Regular debriefing of civilians and experienced Gestapo agents regarding the dimensions of political dissension, as well as survey questionnaires, were all reduced to researchable punch card data.[88]

The USSBS was denied nothing. When its officers asked for one Hollerith, eight sets were flown overnight from the United States to London, along with the staff needed to operate them; from London, the units were rushed to Bad Nauheim. When another USSBS statistical office at Jena needed to be evacuated before being absorbed into the Russian zone, a convoy of trucks was immediately provided to transfer all the punch cards, machines, and German technicians in a single move.[89]

The man who made the Holleriths run at Bad Nauheim was Sergeant Hendricks. Hendricks was the same man who transferred the D-11A from Dachau to Dehomag's Sindelfingen plant. He was also the man who drove

Hummel from his prison release to Stuttgart. In Bad Nauheim, Hendricks had the knowledge and expertise to convert the prior Hollerith installation of a former Reich industry association into a pure USSBS operation. Hendricks made sure a continuous stream of army questionnaires on economic capacity were methodically processed by a range of industries in occupied Germany. In this way, the Allies could assess the ability of German industry to recover from the massive bombing it had endured. The system was identical to that employed by the *MB* when it monitored industrial output during the Nazi era. Hendricks even used the same forms.[90]

On July 30, 1945, a group from the Planning and Intelligence Branch of SHAEF's Economic Division, led by a Brigadier General, visited the Bad Nauheim facility. Three days later, the Brigadier General reported on his visit and Hendricks' indispensable value. "[T]he party was shown round by Sgt. Hendricks," the General wrote, "in civilian life an employee of the International Business Machines Company, who are the patentees of the Hollerith system. Sgt. Hendricks has supervised a number of installations on behalf of his firm, and is obviously a competent technician in this particular field." At Bad Nauheim, the General wrote, Sergeant Hendricks was supervising about sixty "carefully screened German personnel" operating fourteen sorters, two tabulators, and a host of punchers and verifiers. Hendricks told the tour group, the report noted, "There was practically no limit to the information obtainable through the Hollerith system, *provided the right questions were asked at the outset.*" In the General's original report, the words were underlined.[91]

The August 2, 1945, tour report noted that Hendricks was scheduled to complete the USSBS's last economic surveys on August 4. Then the unit's job in Germany would be finished. The USSBS was scheduled to leave the facility on August 15, the note explained.[92]

From its inception, a stated mission of the USSBS was to apply all bombing impact information compiled in Germany to America's air war against Japan. On August 6, a U.S. bomber dropped an atomic bomb on Hiroshima. Three days later, Nagasaki was bombed. USSBS statistical analyses and predictions of economic and social ruination had been part of the decision-making process. On August 15, President Harry Truman instructed the USSBS to begin evaluating the effects of America's atomic bombing of Japan. Anticipating the order, the statistic team had already departed Bad Nauheim. They left all their Hollerith equipment behind.[93]

As the best-equipped punch card center in occupied Germany, Sergeant Hendricks assured that with the USSBS gone, the Bad Nauheim location could serve all industrial data needs in the American zone. Sergeant Hendricks added that a similar data facility could be erected for the British zone. For their part, the Russians in their zone were already utilizing the experienced staff and IBM machinery of the Reich Statistical Office in Berlin.[94] There was no need for the American and British to have anything less.

But industrial statistics were only the beginning. When occupying authorities needed a census of all Germans in the territories, they knew whom to call. Dehomag stepped forward. The company's census experts simply took its existing census tabulation regimens and made certain adjustments for Allied requirements. Some of the column headings were adjusted slightly, but little else. Columns 1–6: unchanged. Column 7: Family Status. Column 8: Religion. Column 9: Mother Tongue. Column 10: National Descent (or Ethnicity). Column 11: Nationality. At one point in the preparations an American officer complained that some of the German column headings requesting ethnicity were "of Nazi memory and implying a racial idea which was most undesirable." Eventually, however, American objections subsided.[95]

The Russians permitted the Reich Statistical Office, controlled in their zone, to help Dehomag implement the project. The four powers agreed that completed census forms would be destroyed after two years—but only after the individual information was transferred to punch cards. For Dehomag, the 1946 census of occupation was a project organized quickly and economically. People counting was what they did best. The questions remained the same. Only the client name changed.

By 1947, it was time to change the subsidiary's name as well. On July 4, 1947, IBM's Foreign Trade Vice President J. T. Wilson wrote to Watson, "Apparently now is a good time to change the name of the company and to discontinue the name 'Hollerith.' I have, therefore, given instructions to start the necessary proceedings to call it 'IBM Germany.'"[96]

As Germany was emerging from its occupation, Dehomag was edging back to IBM NY's dominion. The company had received permission to undertake various contractual agreements with Dehomag. But only upon formal decontrol would IBM NY regain genuine custody of its German operation. In the meantime, Dehomag's financial success was impressive. By the end of 1946, it had emerged from a bombed and dissected Germany with a valuation of more than RM 56.6 million and a gross profit of RM 7.5 million.[97]

A key toward regaining total control was fortifying the argument that Dehomag was not a German company, but an American-owned enterprise. On November 14, 1947, custodian Karl Hummel filed papers with OMGUS and German financial authorities averring that the token German shares in Dehomag that he, Rottke and Heidinger owned were not genuine stock ownership. "We cannot understand how our relationship with our parent can be subject to Law No. 56. . . . While a minority interest exists in Germany, such minority interest was granted as an inducement to the managers of the company; but they are not shareholders in the general sense of the term, because they are not free to sell their shares, but can sell them only to the company and only for their book value. They were retaining the share only during their holding a leading position in the company. Only one remains today. Mr. Heidinger died in 1944 and Mr. Rottke is reported to have died in a Russian camp."[98] Ironically, the one remaining shareholder was Hummel himself.

Before the end of 1947, IBM would finally receive a Treasury License to repurchase the stock of Rottke, Heidinger, and Hummel, thus regaining 100 percent ownership of its German unit. Ownership still did not convey control. It took two years of additional bureaucratic wrangling before IBM could legally change Dehomag's name to IBM Deutschland. That happened in April 1949.[99]

In the years that followed, IBM's worldwide stature became even more of a beacon to the cause of progress. It adopted a corporate motto: "The Solutions Company." Whatever the impossible task, IBM technology could find a solution. The men who headed up the IBM enterprise in Nazi Europe and America became revered giants within the corporation's global community. Chauncey became chairman of the IBM World Trade Corporation, and the European subsidiary managers were rewarded for their loyalty with top jobs. Their exploits during the Nazi era were lionized with amazing specificity in a promotional book entitled *The History of Computing in Europe,* published in 1967 by IBM itself. However, an internal IBM review decided to immediately withdraw the book from the market. It is no longer available in any publicly accessible library anywhere in the world.

Eventually, after ceaseless efforts, IBM NY regained control of its German subsidiary. The name had been changed, the money regained, the machines recovered, the record clear. For IBM the war was over.

But for the descendants of 6 million Jews and millions of other Europeans, the war would never be over. It would haunt them and people of conscience forever. After decades of documentation by the best minds, the most studied among them would confess that they never really understood the Holocaust process. Why did it happen? How could it happen? How were they selected? How did the Nazis get the names? They always had the names.

What seemingly magical scheduling process could have allowed millions of Nazi victims to step onto train platforms in Germany or nineteen other Nazi-occupied countries, travel for two and three days by rail, and then step onto a ramp at Auschwitz or Treblinka—and within an hour be marched into gas chambers. Hour after hour. Day after day. Timetable after timetable. Like clockwork, and always with *blitzkrieg* efficiency.

The survivors would never know. The liberators who fought would never know. The politicians who made speeches would never know. The prosecutors who prosecuted would never know. The debaters who debated would never know.

The question was barely even raised.

I: NUMBERED PEOPLE

1. "Recollection of Hanna Levy-Hass" in Eberhard Kolb, *Bergen-Belsen: From "Detention Camp" to Concentration Camp, 1943–45*, trans. Gregory Claeys and Christine Lattke (Göttingen: Vandenhoeck & Ruprecht, 1985), p. 66; see *Encyclopaedia Judaica*, s.v. "Bergen-Belsen," p. 611; Kolb, pp. 29, 41, 94, 98, as well as the photos; General Glyn-Hughes, Cité in Le grand livre des témoins, FNDIRP, Ramsey, 1995, p. 291; also see photos, The Nizkor Project, www.nizkor.org; Judith Jaegermann, "Memories of My Childhood," Oral History in *A History of Jews in Hamburg*, Hamburg University, www.rrz.uni-hamburg.

2. Hadassah Rosensaft Collection, United States Holocaust Memorial Museum (USHMM) Photo Archives; *Encyclopaedia Judaica*, s.v. "Bergen-Belsen," p. 611; Kolb, p. 29.

3. Hadassah Rosensaft crematorium photo, April 28, 1945, USHMM.

4. *Encyclopaedia Judaica*, s.v. "Bergen-Belsen," p. 612; Brigadier Hugh Llewelyn Glyn-Hughes in "Excerpts from *The Belsen Trial, Pt. 2 of 5: Testimony Concerning Water and Food*," The Nizkor Project, www.nizkor.org; see Raymond Philips, ed., *The Trial of Josef Kramer and 44 Others: The Belsen Trial* (London: William Hodge and Co., 1949); Kolb, p. 40.

5. Papers of Rudolf Martin Cheim, Joodsche Raad Voor Amsterdam, p. 26, YIVO RG804; Kolb, p. 29; see *Encyclopaedia Judaica*, s.v. "Bergen-Belsen," p. 611.

6. Papers of Rudolf Martin Cheim, Joodsche Raad Voor Amsterdam, p. 26, YIVO RG804.

7. Papers of Rudolf Martin Cheim, Joodsche Raad Voor Amsterdam, p. 26, YIVO RG804.

8. Papers of Rudolf Martin Cheim, Joodsche Raad Voor Amsterdam, p. 26, YIVO RG804; see NA RG242/338, T1021, Roll 5, Frame 126.

9. Papers of Rudolf Martin Cheim, Joodsche Raad Voor Amsterdam, pp. 26–27, YIVO RG804; see NA RG242/338, T1021, Roll 5, Frame 126; Testimony of and Concerning Irma Grese in "Excerpts from *The Belsen Trial, Pt. 5 of 5: The Trial of Adolf Eichmann, Session 101 (Pt. 3 of 4)*, The Nizkor Project, www.nizkor.org"; Jamie McCarthy and Ken McVay, "The Meaning of Special Treatment, Pt. 1 of 3," *Deceit and Misrepresentation: The Techniques of Holocaust Denial*, The Nizkor Project, www.nizkor.org; Raul Hilberg, *Documents of Destruction: Germany and Jewry 1933–1945* (Chicago: Quadrangle Books, 1971), pp. 219–223.

10. Papers of Rudolf Martin Cheim, Joodsche Raad Voor Amsterdam, p. 28, YIVO RG804.

11. Papers of Rudolf Martin Cheim, Joodsche Raad Voor Amsterdam, pp. 27–28, YIVO RG804; Memo and Transfer List, Ravensbrück Concentration Camp Labor Deployment

Office to Flossenbürg Concentration Camp Labor Deployment Office, September 1, 1944, D II NA RG242/338, T1021 Reel 17.

12. Operation of D II, *IMT*, 5:980–992; sound recording, Heinrich Himmler's Speech at Posen, October 4, 1943, NA RG238, PS 1919.

13. Papers of Rudolf Martin Cheim, Joodsche Raad Voor Amsterdam, p. 27, YIVO RG804.

14. Papers of Rudolf Martin Cheim, Joodsche Raad Voor Amsterdam, pp. 27–28, YIVO RG804.

15. Papers of Rudolf Martin Cheim, Joodsche Raad Voor Amsterdam, p. 26, YIVO RG804.

16. Thomas J. Watson, Jr., and Peter Petre, *Father, Son & Co.: My Life at IBM and Beyond* (New York: Bantam Books, 1990), pp. 29–30; CSDIC, "Secret Report: PW Intelligence Bulletin No. 2/57," April 25, 1945, p. 4, NA RG226; "Deutsche Hollerith Maschinen: Confidential Report 242," p. 8, submitted by Harold J. Carter, December 8, 1943, Department of Justice, War Division, Economic Warfare Section, NA RG60.

II: THE IBM-HITLER INTERSECTION

1. Edwin Black, *The Transfer Agreement: The Dramatic Story of the Pact Between the Third Reich & Jewish Palestine* (New York: Macmillan, 1984; Washington, DC: Dialog Press, 1999), pp. 3–7, 26; Letter, Thomas J. Watson to Dr. Hjalmar Schacht, August 18, 1937, IBM Files.

2. Peter N. Stearns and John H. Hinshaw, eds., *The ABC-CLIO World History Companion to the Industrial Revolution* (Santa Barbara, Calif.: ABC-CLIO, 1996), p. 223.

3. From V. Hollerith, "Biographical Sketch," interviews with Madeline and George Hollerith, January 19, 1972, and May 18, 1970, cited in Geoffrey D. Austrian, *Herman Hollerith: Forgotten Giant of Information Processing* (New York: Columbia University Press, 1982), p. 350.

4. Emerson W. Pugh, *Building IBM: Shaping an Industry and Its Technology* (Cambridge: The MIT Press, 1995), pp. 2–3; Robert Sobel, *IBM: Colossus in Transition* (New York: Truman Talley Books, 1981), p. 14; Austrian, p. 4; Saul Engelbourg, *International Business Machines: A Business History* (Arno Press, 1976), pp. 2–3, and author's typescript.

5. Sobel, p. 14.

6. Sobel, p. 14.

7. Sobel, p. 14; see Austrian, p. 15.

8. Austrian, pp. 6, 22, 40–42; see Pugh, p. 11.

9. Sobel, pp. 13–14; Pugh, pp. 1–3; 17; Austrian, pp. 82–83, 124–141.

10. Pugh, pp. 12–13.

11. Austrian, pp. 58, 69.

12. Austrian, pp. 88, 170–171, 221; Sobel, pp. 17, 20; Pugh, pp. 16, 17; see Austrian, pp. 120–121.

13. Austrian, pp. 206–207.

14. Austrian, pp. 207–208, 236–237.

15. Austrian, pp. 80, 103, 122.

16. Austrian, p. 78.

17. Austrian, pp. 146–149; *Encyclopaedia Judaica*, s.v. "Russian brutal regime," pp. 444–450.

18. Austrian, p. 97.

19. Austrian, p. 225.

20. Austrian, p. 225.

21. Austrian, p. 225.

22. Austrian, pp. 234–237, 260–261, 277, 279.

23. Austrian, pp. 274–275.

24. Austrian, pp. 199–202, 273–274, 288–305.

25. Austrian, pp. 306–307.

26. Austrian, pp. 327–328; W. Heidinger, "Declaration to the IBM Advisory Panel," June 18, 1943, IBM Files.

27. Sobel, pp. 4–5, 11–12; see Charles R. Flint, *Memories of an Active Life* (New York: G.P. Putnam's Sons, 1923).

28. Sobel, pp. 4–5; Flint, 85–88, 180–184, 196–225, 247–249; see Thomas Graham Belden

and Marva Robins Belden, *The Lengthening Shadow: The Life of Thomas J. Watson* (Boston: Little, Brown and Company, 1962), p. 90; also see Robert Wistrich, *Who's Who in Nazi Germany* (New York: Macmillan, 1982).

29. Sobel, p. 5.
30. Austrian, p. 308; see Sobel, p. 5.
31. Sobel, pp. 10–12; see Pugh, p. 24; also see Austrian, p. 312.
32. Sobel, pp. 10–12; see Pugh, pp. 24–26.
33. Pugh, p. 27; Sobel, pp. 10–12; Austrian, pp. 312–313.
34. Austrian, p. 323.
35. Austrian, pp. 323–324.
36. Belden and Belden, pp. 6–7.
37. Belden and Belden, p. 4.
38. Belden and Belden, p. 5.
39. Belden and Belden, pp. 6–11.
40. William Rodgers, *Think: A Biography of the Watsons and IBM* (New York: Stein and Day, 1969), p. 27.
41. Rodgers, pp. 16, 29–34.
42. Rodgers, pp. 31–33; Belden and Belden, p. 22.
43. Rodgers, pp. 33–35.
44. Rodgers, pp. 33–35; Belden and Belden, p. 27.
45. Rodgers, p. 40; see Thomas J. Watson, Jr., and Peter Petre, *Father, Son & Co.: My Life at IBM and Beyond* (New York: Bantam Books, 1990), p. 141.
46. Rodgers, pp. 40–41.
47. Rodgers, pp. 40–41.
48. Rodgers, pp. 41–43.
49. Rodgers, p. 42.
50. Rodgers, p. 42.
51. Rodgers, pp. 42–43.
52. Rodgers, pp. 48, 57.
53. Rodgers, pp. 48, 52.
54. Rodgers, pp. 53–55.
55. Rodgers, p. 60.
56. Rodgers, pp. 62–63; see Sobel, p. 42; also see Belden and Belden, pp. 76–80.
57. Rodgers, pp. 63–65; Belden and Belden, pp. 76–80; Sobel, p. 42.
58. Rodgers, pp. 63–64; Sobel, pp. 42–43; Watson, Jr., and Petre, pp. 141–142.
59. Rodgers, pp. 64–65; Belden and Belden, pp. 86–87.
60. Rodgers, pp. 64–65; Belden and Belden, pp. 86–87; Watson, Jr., and Petre, p. 13; Belden and Belden, p. 87.
61. Belden and Belden, pp. 90–91; also see Flint.
62. Belden and Belden, pp. 91–94; see Rodgers, pp. 68–71.
63. Belden and Belden, p. 93; see Rodgers, p. 69.
64. Belden and Belden, pp. 93–94; see Watson, Jr., and Petre, p. 15.
65. Belden and Belden, pp. 93–94.
66. Pugh, pp. 29–30; Watson, Jr. and Petre, p. 74; Rodgers, pp. 48, 79; Engelbourg, p. 83.
67. Engelbourg, pp. 195–200; Rodgers, pp. 75, 76.
68. Pugh, p. 30; Austrian, pp. 333–335; Rodgers, pp. 79–80.
69. Rodgers, pp. 77, 79, 81; James Connally, *History of Computing in Europe* (IBM World Trade Corporation, circa 1967), p. 15; Carl H. Dassbach, *Global Enterprises and the World Economy: Ford, General Motors and IBM, the Emergence of the Transnational Enterprise* (New York: Garland Publishing, 1989), p. 166.
70. Rodgers, p. 76.
71. Rodgers, p. 76; Watson, Jr., and Petre, pp. 69, 82.
72. Rodgers, pp. 82–83.
73. Belden and Belden, p. 125.
74. Engelbourg, p. 183.
75. Engelbourg, p. 196.

76. Engelbourg, pp. 196, 199–202.
77. Rodgers, p. 91; Watson, Jr., and Petre, p. 30.
78. Watson, Jr., and Petre, pp. 69, 82.
79. Watson, Jr. and Petre, p. 82.
80. Engelbourg, p. 93; Watson, Jr., and Petre, pp. 29–30.
81. Engelbourg, p. 94.
82. Engelbourg, p. 189.
83. Belden and Belden, pp. 126–136; Pugh, p. 337.
84. Watson, Jr., and Petre, pp. 69, 82; "International Business Machines," *Fortune*, January 1940, p. 37.
85. Letter, Thomas J. Watson to Dr. Hjalmar Schacht, circa 1937, IBM Files.
86. Letter, Thomas J. Watson to Dr. Hjalmar Schacht, circa 1937, IBM Files.
87. Letter, Thomas J. Watson to Dr. Hjalmar Schacht, circa 1937, IBM Files.
88. W. Heidinger, "Declaration to the IBM Advisory Committee," June 18, 1943, p. 5, IBM Files.
89. W. Heidinger, "Declaration to the IBM Advisory Committee," June 18, 1943, pp. 5, 9, IBM Files.
90. W. Heidinger, "Declaration to the IBM Advisory Committee," June 18, 1943, p. 9, IBM Files.
91. "Watson Belge, S.A. Balance Sheet December 31, 1940," "Societa Internazionale Macchine Commerciali and Watson Italiana S/A Balance Sheet April 30, 1940," "A.B. Svenka Watson Sweden Balance Sheet December 31, 1942," NA RG131.
92. IBM Correspondence, January 17, 1934, IBM Files.
93. Black, p. 217.
94. Black, 217; Saul Friedländer, *Nazi Germany and the Jews, Vol. 1: The Years of Persecution, 1933–1939* (New York: HarperCollins, 1997), p. 17.
95. Black, pp. 71, 93.
96. Black, pp. 177–185, 217.
97. Black, pp. 41–42.
98. Black, pp. 104–105.
99. Black, pp. 104–105.
100. Black, p. 119; also see photo pp. 208–209.
101. See: Files of Non-Sectarian Anti-Nazi League, Columbia University Lehman Suite; phone number cards of Joint Boycott Council, New York Public Library Manuscript Division; Records of Jewish War Veterans, American Jewish Historical Society.
102. Watson, Jr., and Petre, p. 33.
103. Letter, H.K. Chauncey to IBM, November 29, 1940, NA RG59 662 1111/28.
104. Dr. Friedrich Zahn, "Die Statistik im nationalsozialistischen Großdeutschland," *Allgemeines Statistisches Archiv (ASA)* 29 (1939/40): 370.
105. Götz Aly and Karl Heinz Roth, *Die restlose Erfassung: Volkszählen, Identifizieren, Aussondern im Nationalsozialismus* (Berlin: Rotbuch Verlag, 1984), pp. 28–29.
106. Biehler, "Lochkartenmaschinen im Dienste der Reichsstatistik," *ASA* 28 (1938/39): 90–100.
107. Dr. Johannes Müller, "Die Stellung der Statistik im neuen Reich," *ASA* 24 (1934/35): 244.
108. Dr. Karl Keller, "Zur Frage der Rassenstatistik," *ASA* 24 (1934/35): 134, 136, 138.
109. Keller, p. 139.
110. Keller, pp. 140–142.
111. Dr. Friedrich Zahn, "Fortbildung der Deutschen Bevölkerungsstatistik," *ASA* 27 (1937/38): 181.
112. Zahn, "Die Statistik im nationalsozialistischen Großdeutschland," *ASA* 29 (1939/40): 369.
113. Zahn, "Die Statistik im nationalsozialistischen Großdeutschland," *ASA* 29 (1939/40): 370.
114. Aly and Roth, 29–35; see Raul Hilberg, *The Destruction of the European Jews* (New York: Quadrangle Books, 1961; Harper Colophon, 1979), pp. 31–32.
115. CSDIC, "Secret Report: PW Intelligence Bulletin No. 2/57," April 25, 1945, pp. 4–17, NA

RG226; "Deutsche Hollerith Maschinen GmbH: Confidential Report 242," pp. 1–7, submitted by Harold J. Carter, December 8, 1943, Department of Justice, War Division, Economic Warfare Section, NA RG60.

116. CSDIC, "Secret Report: PW Intelligence Bulletin No. 2/57," April 25, 1945, pp. 4–17, NA RG226; "Deutsche Hollerith Maschinen GmbH: Confidential Report 242," pp. 1–7, submitted by Harold J. Carter, December 8, 1943, Department of Justice, War Division, Economic Warfare Section, NA RG60.

117. Letter, W. Heidinger to O.E. Braitmayer, November 14, 1935, IBM Files.

118. *Denkschrift zur Einweihung der neuen Arbeitsstätte der Deutschen Hollerith Maschinen Gesellschaft m.b.H. in Berlin-Lichterfelde*, January 8, 1934, p. 23, USHMM Library.

119. *Denkschrift zur Einweihung der neuen Arbeitsstätte der Deutschen Hollerith Maschinen Gesellschaft m.b.H. in Berlin-Lichterfelde*, January 8, 1934, pp. 39–40, USHMM Library.

120. *Denkschrift zur Einweihung der neuen Arbeitsstätte der Deutschen Hollerith Maschinen Gesellschaft m.b.H. in Berlin-Lichterfelde*, January 8, 1934, pp. 39–40, USHMM Library.

121. Memorial Program, Opening of the Dehomag Plant in Lichterfelde, January 8, 1934, and IBM's translated version, IBM Files.

122. Belden and Belden, photo 144–145; see Rodgers, 48.

III: IDENTIFYING THE JEWS

1. Raul Hilberg, *The Destruction of the European Jews* (New York: Quadrangle Books, 1961; Harper Colophon, 1979), p. 54.

2. Edwin Black, *The Transfer Agreement: The Dramatic Story of the Pact Between the Third Reich & Jewish Palestine* (New York: Macmillan, 1984; Washington, D.C.: Dialog Press, 1999), pp. 166–167.

3. Black, pp. 166–167.

4. Black, pp. 166–167.

5. Black, pp. 166–167.

6. Black, pp.166–167.

7. Black, pp. 166–176.

8. F. Burgdörfer, "Die Volks-, Berufs- und Betriebszählung 1933," *Allgemeines Statistisches Archiv (ASA)* 23 (1933/34): 146; also see Götz Aly and Karl Heinz Roth, *Die restlose Erfassung: Volkszählen, Identifizieren, Aussondern im Nationalsozialismus* (Berlin: Rotbuch Verlag, 1984), pp. 29–33.

9. Ludwig Hümmer, "Die Aufbereitung der Volks- und Berufszählung 1933 im Hollerith-Lochkartenverfahren," *Hollerith Nachrichten (HN)* 28 (August 1933): 343; Dr. Richard Couvé, "Der Mensch im Lochkartenverfahren," *HN* 36 (April 1934): 445.

10. Letter, Dr. Karl Koch to Thomas J. Watson, May 26, 1933, IBM Files.

11. Letter, Dr. Karl Koch to Thomas J. Watson, May 26, 1933, IBM Files.

12. Letter, Dr. Karl Koch to Thomas J. Watson, May 26, 1933, IBM Files.

13. Letter, Thomas J. Watson to Dr. Karl Koch, June 20, 1933, IBM Files.

14. Hümmer, pp. 343–355; see Letter, W.D. Jones to Thomas J. Watson, January 10, 1934, IBM Files.

15. Hümmer, p. 346.

16. Aly and Roth, p. 21.

17. Hümmer, p. 346.

18. "Inventur eines Volkes," *Berliner Tageblatt* 13 (January 9, 1934); see Hümmer, pp. 343–346, 347; *Illustrierter Beobachter*, January 6, 1934, p. 5.

19. Hümmer, pp. 345–347.

20. Hümmer, pp. 345–347.

21. Hümmer, pp. 345–346, 447.

22. Aly and Roth, p. 145.

23. "Inventur eines Volkes," *Berliner Tageblatt* 13 (January 9, 1934).

24. Aly and Roth, p. 56.

25. "Inventur eines Volkes," *Berliner Tageblatt* 13 (January 9, 1934).

26. "Die Glaubensjuden im Dritten Reich," *Statistik des Deutschen Reichs* 415/5 (1936): 5 cited in Aly and Roth, p. 55.

27. Hümmer, pp. 343, 348, 351–355.

28. "Die Glaubensjuden im Dritten Reich," *Statistik des Deutschen Reichs* 415/5 (1936): 5 cited in Aly and Roth, pp. 57–59.

29. "Die Glaubensjuden im Dritten Reich," *Statistik des Deutschen Reichs* 415/5 (1936): 5 cited in Aly and Roth, pp. 57, 59; exhibit photo of Census Poster, USHMM.

30. Dr. Friedrich Zahn, "Die Statistik im nationalsozialistischen Großdeutschland," *ASA* 29 (1939/40): 370.

31. Cablegram, Thomas J. Watson to W. Heidinger, May 19, 1933, IBM Files; also see Memorandum, W. Heidinger to W.F. Battin, July 14, 1933, IBM Files; Letter, M.G. Connally to W.F. Battin September 6, 1934, p. 3, IBM Files; Letter, F.C. Elstob to J.F. Gormley, January 19, 1934, IBM Files; Confirmation of Cable, January 20, 1934, IBM Files, Letter, J.F. Gormley to H. Karst, January 22, 1934, IBM Files.

32. Memorandum, W. Heidinger to W.F. Battin, July 14, 1933, IBM Files.

33. Letter, H.K. Chauncey to J.C. Milner, November 19, 1935, IBM Files; see Letter, O.E. Braitmayer to J.E. Holt, March 7, 1936, IBM Files; Letter, W. Heidinger to R. Kugler, December 18, 1933, IBM Files.

34. "Sails for Paris Meeting," *NYT,* October 5, 1933; Letter, W. Heidinger to Thomas J. Watson, January 2, 1934, IBM Files; also see "Sees Business Gain Generally," *NYT,* October 25, 1934.

35. Letter, W. Heidinger to Thomas J. Watson, October 31, 1933, IBM Files.

36. Letter, W. Heidinger to Thomas J. Watson, January 2, 1934; Letter, W.D. Jones to Thomas J. Watson, January 10, 1934, IBM Files.

37. Letter, Dehomag to J.T. Wilson, November 16, 1935, IBM Files; also see, "Davis Named IBM Secretary," *NYT,* February 22, 1940.

38. Cablegram, W. Heidinger to Thomas J. Watson, August 27, 1934, IBM Files; Radiogram, Thomas J. Watson to W. Heidinger, August 23, 1934, IBM Files; also see Letter and handwritten cover note on carbons, Thomas J. Watson to W. Heidinger, September 11, 1934, IBM Files.

39. Radiogram, K. Hummel and Managers to Thomas J. Watson, November 8, 1933, IBM Files.

40. William Rodgers, *Think: A Biography of the Watsons and IBM* (New York: Stein and Day, 1969), p. 57; "Cummings to Push Anti-Trust Suits," *NYT,* March 31, 1934.

41. Letter, M.G. Connally to W. Heidinger, November 18, 1933, IBM Files.

42. Cablegram, W. Heidinger to Thomas J. Watson, August 27, 1934.

43. Radiogram, Thomas J. Watson to W. Heidinger, August 28, 1934, IBM Files.

44. Letter and handwritten cover note on carbons, Thomas J. Watson to W. Heidinger, September 11, 1934; Memorandum, W. Heidinger to H.B. Fellinger, June 18, 1943, p. 9, IBM Files.

45. Radiogram, Thomas J. Watson to W. Heidinger, August 28, 1934; Letter and handwritten cover note on carbons, Thomas J. Watson to W. Heidinger, September 11, 1934.

46. "German Socialists Reported Tortured," *NYT,* March 18, 1933.

47. "German Fugitives Tell of Atrocities at Hands of Nazis," *NYT,* March 20, 1933.

48. "Nazis to Put Bavarian Foes in Concentration Camp," *NYT,* March 21, 1933.

49. "3 More Americans Attacked in Berlin As Raiding Goes On," *NYT,* March 10, 1933; "German Socialists Reported Tortured," *NYT,* March 18, 1933; "Terror in Germany Amazes Novelist," *NYT,* March 21, 1933; "Nazis Hunt Arms in Einstein Home," *NYT,* March 21, 1933; "German Jailings Spreading Terror," *NYT,* March 27, 1933; "Hitlerites Order Boycott Against Jews in Business, Professions and Schools," *NYT,* March 29, 1933; "Boycott Spreads in Reich but Hitler Bans Violent Acts," *NYT,* March 30, 1933; "Nazis Cut Boycott Today with Threat of Renewal if World Does Not Recant," "Nazis Oust Jews From Law Courts," *NYT,* April 1, 1933; "Boycott at End, Germany Believes," "Germans Fearful Under Nazi Regime," *NYT,* April 3, 1933; "Nazis to Control Lutheran Church," *NYT,* April 6, 1933; "Nazis Seize Power to Rule Business," "Nazis Demand Ban on Old Testament," *NYT,* April 7, 1933; "Nazis Herd Enemies Behind Barbed Wire in Big Prison Camps," "Nazis Hold Foes in Prison Camp," "Reich Authors Oust Non-Nationalists," "Nazis Demand Divorce of Jewish Wives by Officials if They Are to Retain Jobs," *NYT,* April 8, 1933; "Schwarz Ousted As Reich Counsel," *NYT,* April 12, 1933; "10,000 Jews

Flee Nazi Persecution," *NYT,* April 15, 1933; "Nazi Book-Burning Fails to Stir Berlin," *NYT,* May 11, 1993; "League Will Hear Jews on Oppression by Nazis; Drummond Forces Issue," *NYT,* May 21, 1933.

50. "Reich Post Ministry Is Sifting Out Jews," "Nazi Jewish Policy Assailed in Senate As Peril to Peace," *NYT,* June 11, 1933.

51. "Nazis Hold 80,000, Camp Study Shows," *NYT,* August 29, 1933.

52. Black, p. 188.

53. Black, pp. 41–42.

54. Black, p. 42.

55. Black, p. 42.

56. Black, p. 45.

57. Letter, Dehomag Senior Management to Thomas J. Watson, March 31, 1933, IBM Files.

58. Dehomag Board of Directors Minutes, April 1, 1933, IBM Files.

59. Account Receipt, Deutsche Bank und Disconto-Gesellschaft, August 7, 1933, IBM Files.

60. William L. Shirer, *The Rise and Fall of the Third Reich: A History of Nazi Germany.* (New York: Simon and Schuster, 1960), pp. 196–204; "Nazis Seize Power to Rule Business; Our Firms Alarmed," *NYT,* April 7, 1933.

61. "Nazis Seize Power to Rule Business," *NYT,* April 7, 1933.

62. "Germany Cautions Foreign Business," *NYT,* April 28, 1933.

63. "Reich Issues Orders for New Labor Units," *NYT,* May 21, 1933.

64. See: Files of Non-Sectarian Anti-Nazi League, Joint Boycott Council, Jewish War Veterans, American Jewish Congress, and World Jewish Congress.

65. Rodgers, p. 107; Thomas Graham Belden and Marva Robins Belden, *The Lengthening Shadow: The Life of Thomas J. Watson* (Boston: Little, Brown and Company, 1962), p. 196.

66. Rodgers, p. 107; Belden and Belden, p. 196.

67. Thomas J. Watson, Jr., and Peter Petre, *Father, Son & Co.: My Life at IBM and Beyond* (New York: Bantam Books, 1990), p. 43.

68. Belden and Belden, p. 197.

69. Draft Letter, Thomas J. Watson to Dr. Hjalmar Schacht, circa August 1937, IBM Files.

70. "G.W. Davidson, T.J. Watson Named to Succeed Wiggin and Woodin on Reserve Bank Board," *NYT,* April 18, 1933; also see "Directors Elected by Reserve Bank," *NYT,* May 4, 1933; "Columbia Trustees," *NYT,* June 16, 1933; Rodgers, pp. 109, 122, 140.

71. Watson, Jr., and Petre, pp. 43–45.

72. Watson, Jr., and Petre, p. 44.

73. Watson, Jr., and Petre, pp. 44–45.

74. Watson, Jr., and Petre, p. 45.

75. Letter, W. Heidinger to Dehomag Management, October 27, 1933, IBM Files.

76. Letter, Dr. Otto Kiep to Thomas J. Watson, August 8, 1933; Letter, Thomas J. Watson to Dr. Otto Kiep, June 15, 1933; Letter, Thomas J. Watson to Dr. Otto Kiep, August 21, 1933, IBM Files.

IV: THE IBM-NAZI ALLIANCE

1. Affidavit, W. Heidinger to H.B. Fellinger, June 18, 1943, IBM Files.

2. Affidavit, W. Heidinger to H.B. Fellinger, June 18, 1943, pp. 5, 9, IBM Files.

3. Affidavit, W. Heidinger to H.B. Fellinger, June 18, 1943, p. 7, IBM Files.

4. James Connally, *History of Computing in Europe* (IBM World Trade Corporation, circa 1967), pp. 24, 29.

5. Letter, J.F. Gormley to F.C. Elstob, January 22, 1934, IBM Files; Letter, M.G. Connally to W.F. Battin, April 14, 1934, p. 2, IBM Files; Letter, J.F. Gormley to W.F. Battin, April 3, 1934, p. 1, IBM Files.

6. Connally, p. 18.

7. Letter, W.D. Jones to O.E. Braitmayer, July 5, 1934, IBM Files.

8. Letter, W. Heidinger to Political and Economics Division NSDAP, December 18, 1933, IBM Files.

9. Letter, W. Heidinger to Political and Economics Division NSDAP, Question 2, December 18, 1933, IBM Files.

10. Letter, W. Heidinger to Political and Economics Division NSDAP, Question 5, December 18, 1933, IBM Files.
11. Letter, W. Heidinger to Political and Economics Division NSDAP, Question 6, December 18, 1933, IBM Files.
12. Letter, W. Heidinger to Political and Economics Division NSDAP, December 18, 1933, IBM Files; also see German version, IBM Files.
13. Memorandum, Foreign Division to W.M. Wilson, January 7, 1934, IBM Files; Letter, M.G. Connally to F.C. Elstob, October 31, 1934, IBM Files.
14. Dehomag By-laws, June 23, 1934, pp. 11–13, IBM Files.
15. Dehomag By-laws, June 23, 1934, pp. 11, 12, IBM Files.
16. "Aus der Geschichte der Hollerith Maschinen Gesellschaft," *Hollerith Nachrichten (HN)* 55 (November 1935): 9; Dehomag Board Meeting Minutes, November 14, 1934, IBM Files.
17. Letter, K. Hummel to Thomas J. Watson, April 26, 1934, p. 2, IBM Files; Radiogram, Thomas J. Watson to H. Rottke, December 14 and December 15, 1933, IBM Files.
18. Radiograms, Thomas J. Watson to H. Rottke, December 14 and December 15, 1933, IBM Files; Cablegram, H. Rottke to Thomas J. Watson, December 18, 1933, IBM Files; Letter, W. Heidinger to Thomas J. Watson, December 20, 1933, IBM Files.
19. Letter, W. Heidinger to Thomas J. Watson, December 20, 1933, IBM Files.
20. Letter, W. Heidinger to Thomas J. Watson, December 20, 1933, IBM Files.
21. Cablegram, Thomas J. Watson to H. Rottke, December 20, 1933, IBM Files.
22. Letter, Thomas J. Watson to W. Heidinger, January 10, 1934, IBM Files.
23. Letter, W. Heidinger to Thomas J. Watson, January 23, 1934, IBM Files.
24. Letter, W. Heidinger to Thomas J. Watson, January 23, 1934; Radiogram, Thomas J. Watson to H. Rottke, December 14, 1933, IBM Files.
25. See photo in *Denkschrift zur Einweihung der neuen Arbeitsstätte der Deutschen Hollerith Maschinen Gesellschaft m.b.H. in Berlin-Lichterfelde,* January 8, 1934, p. 13, USHMM Library; "Die erste Fabrikeinweihung im Jahre 1934," *Der Deutsche,* January 9, 1934.
26. *Denkschrift zur Einweihung der neuen Arbeitsstätte der Deutschen Hollerith Maschinen Gesellschaft m.b.H. in Berlin-Lichterfelde,* January 8, 1934, pp. 31–33, USHMM Library; also see Letter, W.D. Jones to Thomas J. Watson, pp. 1–2, January 10, 1934, IBM Files.
27. *Denkschrift zur Einweihung der neuen Arbeitsstätte der Deutschen Hollerith Maschinen Gesellschaft m.b.H. in Berlin-Lichterfelde,* January 8, 1934, pp. 39–40, USHMM Library.
28. *Denkschrift zur Einweihung der neuen Arbeitsstätte der Deutschen Hollerith Maschinen Gesellschaft m.b.H. in Berlin-Lichterfelde,* January 8, 1934, pp. 39–40, USHMM Library.
29. "Die erste Fabrikeinweihung im Jahre 1934," *Der Deutsche,* January 9, 1934; photo in *Denkschrift zur Einweihung der neuen Arbeitsstätte der Deutschen Hollerith Maschinen Gesellschaft m.b.H. in Berlin-Lichterfelde,* January 8, 1934, p. 14, USHMM Library; Letter, W. D. Jones to Thomas J. Watson, p. 2, January 10, 1934, IBM Files.
30. "Die erste Fabrikeinweihung im Jahre 1934," *Der Deutsche,* January 9, 1934; *Denkschrift zur Einweihung der neuen Arbeitsstätte der Deutschen Hollerith Maschinen Gesellschaft m.b.H. in Berlin-Lichterfelde,* January 8, 1934, p. 14, USHMM Library.
31. "Die erste Fabrikeinweihung im Jahre 1934," *Der Deutsche,* January 9, 1934; *Denkschrift zur Einweihung der neuen Arbeitsstätte der Deutschen Hollerith Maschinen Gesellschaft m.b.H. in Berlin-Lichterfelde,* January 8, 1934, pp. 14, 39–40, USHMM Library.
32. *Denkschrift zur Einweihung der neuen Arbeitsstätte der Deutschen Hollerith Maschinen Gesellschaft m.b.H. in Berlin-Lichterfelde,* January 8, 1934, pp. 13–14, USHMM Library; Letter, W.D. Jones to Thomas J. Watson, Jan 10, 1934, IBM Files.
33. *Denkschrift zur Einweihung der neuen Arbeitsstätte der Deutschen Hollerith Maschinen Gesellschaft m.b.H. in Berlin-Lichterfelde,* January 8, 1934, p. 13, USHMM Library.
34. *Denkschrift zur Einweihung der neuen Arbeitsstätte der Deutschen Hollerith Maschinen Gesellschaft m.b.H. in Berlin-Lichterfelde,* January 8, 1934, p. 17, USHMM Library; "Die erste Fabrikeinweihung im Jahre 1934," *Der Deutsche,* January 9, 1934.
35. Letter, W.D. Jones to Thomas J. Watson, January 10, 1934, attachment 1, IBM Files.
36. Letter, W.D. Jones to Thomas J. Watson, January 10, 1934, IBM Files; Connally, p. 28.

37. Letter, W.D. Jones to Thomas J. Watson, January 10, 1934, IBM Files.

38. Letter, W.D. Jones to Thomas J. Watson, January 10, 1934, IBM Files.

39. Letter, W.D. Jones to Thomas J. Watson, January 10, 1934, IBM Files; also see photo in *Denkschrift zur Einweihung der neuen Arbeitsstätte der Deutschen Hollerith Maschinen Gesellschaft m.b.H. in Berlin-Lichterfelde,* January 8, 1934, p. 16, USHMM Library.

40. Letter, W.D. Jones to Thomas J. Watson, January 10, 1934, IBM Files.

41. Letter, W.D. Jones to Thomas J. Watson, January 10, 1934, IBM Files; also see Edwin Black, *The Transfer Agreement: The Dramatic Story of the Pact Between the Third Reich & Jewish Palestine* (New York: Macmillan, 1984; Washington, D.C.: Dialog Press, 1999), pp. 368–369.

42. Letter, W.D. Jones to Thomas J. Watson, January 10, 1934, IBM Files.

43. *Denkschrift zur Einweihung der neuen Arbeitsstätte der Deutschen Hollerith Maschinen Gesellschaft m.b.H. in Berlin-Lichterfelde,* January 8, 1934, p. 27, USHMM Library.

44. *Denkschrift zur Einweihung der neuen Arbeitsstätte der Deutschen Hollerith Maschinen Gesellschaft m.b.H. in Berlin-Lichterfelde,* January 8, 1934, p. 17, USHMM Library.

45. "Die erste Fabrikeinweihung im Jahre 1934," *Der Deutsche,* January 9, 1934.

46. Letter, W.D. Jones to Thomas J. Watson, January 10, 1934, IBM Files.

47. Letter, Thomas J. Watson to W. Heidinger, February 26, 1934, IBM Files; also see *Denkschrift zur Einweihung der neuen Arbeitsstätte der Deutschen Hollerith Maschinen Gesellschaft m.b.H. in Berlin-Lichterfelde,* January 8, 1934, USHMM Library.

48. "Die erste Fabrikeinweihung im Jahre 1934," *Der Deutsche,* January 9, 1934.

49. Connally, pp. 20, 35.

50. Letter, W.D. Jones to Thomas J. Watson, January 10, 1934.

51. "Deutsche Hollerith Maschinen GmbH: Confidential Report 242," submitted by Harold J. Carter, December 8, 1943, Department of Justice, War Division, Economic Warfare Section, NA RG60.

52. "EAM Accounts and Revenue by Industry Class," January 1, 1937, pp. 1, 2, Department of Justice, War Division, Economic Warfare Section, NA RG60.

53. "EAM Accounts and Revenue by Industry Class," January 1, 1937, pp. 1, 2, Department of Justice, War Division, Economic Warfare Section, NA RG60; "Deutsche Hollerith Maschinen GmbH: Confidential Report 242," submitted by Harold J. Carter, December 8, 1943, Department of Justice, War Division, Economic Warfare Section, NA RG60.

54. "Deutsche Hollerith Maschinen GmbH: Confidential Report 242," submitted by Harold J. Carter, December 8, 1943, Department of Justice, War Division, Economic Warfare Section, NA RG60.

55. "Deutsche Hollerith Maschinen GmbH: Confidential Report 242," pp. 2–4, submitted by Harold J. Carter, December 8, 1943, Department of Justice, War Division, Economic Warfare Section, NA RG60.

56. CSDIC, "Secret Report: PW Intelligence Bulletin No. 2/57," April 25, 1945, pp. 4–17, NA RG226.

57. Götz Aly and Karl Heinz Roth, *Die restlose Erfassung: Volkszählen, Identifizieren, Aussondern im Nationalsozialismus* (Berlin: Rotbuch Verlag, 1984), p. 23; also see *Handbuch für das Deutsche Reich 1936,* NA RG242, A3345-B Roll 172, Frames 7–253.

58. "Deutsche Hollerith Maschinen GmbH: Confidential Report 242," pp. 2–4, submitted by Harold J. Carter, December 8, 1943, Department of Justice, War Division, Economic Warfare Section, NA RG60; IBM Corporation, *Kleine Chronik der IBM Deutschland,* 1993.

59. "Deutsche Hollerith Maschinen GmbH: Confidential Report 242," pp. 2–4, submitted by Harold J. Carter, December 8, 1943, Department of Justice, War Division, Economic Warfare Section, NA RG60.

60. "Deutsche Hollerith Maschinen GmbH: Confidential Report 242," pp. 8, 15–18, submitted by Harold J. Carter, December 8, 1943, Department of Justice, War Division, Economic Warfare Section, NA RG60.

61. "Report to Associates of Dehomag," October 6, 1936, IBM Files.

62. "Die Glaubensjuden im Dritten Reich," *Statistik des Deutschen Reichs* 415/5 (1936): 8 cited in Aly and Roth, p. 57.

63. "Letter of Resignation of James G. McDonald to Secretary General of the League of Nations," December 27, 1935, FO 371/19918; "Reich Adopts Swastika As Nation's Official Flag; Hitler's Reply to 'Insult,'" *NYT,* September 16, 1935.

64. "Die Glaubensjuden im Dritten Reich," *Statistik des Deutschen Reichs* 415/5 (1936): 8 cited in Aly and Roth, p. 57.

65. "Letter of Resignation of James G. McDonald to Secretary General of the League of Nations," December 27, 1935, FO 371/19918; "Reich Adopts Swastika As Nation's Official Flag; Hitler's Reply to 'Insult,'" *NYT,* September 16, 1935; "Die Glaubensjuden im Dritten Reich," *Statistik des Deutschen Reichs* 415/5 (1936) cited in Aly and Roth, pp. 56, 57.

66. *Handbuch für das Deutsche Reich 1936,* NA RG242, A3345-B Roll 172, Frames 7–253.

67. *Handbuch für das Deutsche Reich 1936,* NA RG242, A3345-B Roll 172, Frames 7–253.

68. *Handbuch für das Deutsche Reich 1936,* NA RG242, A3345-B Roll 172, Frames 7–253.

69. *Handbuch für das Deutsche Reich 1936,* NA RG242, A3345-B Roll 172, Frames 7–253.

70. *Handbuch für das Deutsche Reich 1936.* NA RG242, A3345-B Roll 172, Frames 7–253.

71. RMBliV (1940): 2121; also see A. Schultze-Naumburg, "Die Tätigkeit der Reichsstelle für Sippenforschung," *Zeitschrift für Standesamtwesen* 17 (1937): 283 cited in Aly and Roth, p. 70 and n35.

72. ZSTAP/M, Rep.77, 343, 1:107 cited in Aly and Roth, p. 37.

73. Hannah Arendt, *A Report on the Banality of Evil: Eichmann in Jerusalem* (New York: Viking Penguin, Inc., 1963; Penguin Books, 1965), p. 42; Aly and Roth, p. 71.

74. Edgar Schultze, "Die verfeinerte Auswertung statistischer Zusammenhänge mit Hilfe des Hollerith-Lochkartenverfahrens," *HN* 40 (August 1934): 505–517.

75. Aly and Roth, p. 100; *HN* 45 (January 1935): 586–7; CSDIC, "Secret Report: PW Intelligence Bulletin No. 2/57," April 25, 1945, p. 17, NA RG226.

76. Aly and Roth, 98; also see Henry Friedlander, *The Origins of Nazi Genocide: From Euthanasia to the Final Solution* (Chapel Hill: The University of North Carolina Press, 1995), p. 27.

77. F. Zahn, "Vom Wirtschaftswert des Menschen als Gegenstand der Statistik," *ASA* 24 (1934/35): 461–464 cited in Aly and Roth, p. 99.

78. F. Zahn, "Vom Wirtschaftswert des Menschen als Gegenstand der Statistik," *ASA* 24 (1934/35) cited in Aly and Roth, p. 99.

79. Siegfried Koller, "Die Auslesevorgänge im Kampf gegen die Erbkrankheiten," *Zeitschrift für menschliche Vererbungs- und Konstitutionslehre* 19 (1935/1936): 257ff cited in Aly and Roth, pp. 99–100, n86.

80. Aly and Roth, p. 107; also see H. Friedlander, p. 17.

81. Hermann Krüger, "Das Hollerith-Lochkarten-Verfahren im Führsorgewesen," *HN* 47 (March 1935): 614; CSDIC, "Secret Report: PW Intelligence Bulletin No. 2/57," April 25, 1945, p. 17, NA RG226.

82. *HN* 47 (March 1935): 615, 618.

83. *HN* 47 (March 1935): 615; see illustration *HN* 47:2 ub.

84. *HN* 47 (March 1935): 615.

85. *HN* 45 (January 1935): 588.

86. *HN* 45 (January 1935): 588.

87. *HN* 45 (January 1935): 586.

88. *HN* 45 (January 1935): 620.

89. Kurt Holm, "Vereinfachung des ärztlichen Untersuchungsverfahren und Sammlung der Ergebnisse," *Deutsches Ärzteblatt* 65 (1935): 113 cited in Aly and Roth, pp. 103–104.

90. Friedrich Zahn, "Fortbildung der deutschen Bevölkerungsstatistik durch erbbiologische Bestandsaufnahmen," *ASA* 27 (1937/38), 194–195.

91. Ludwig Hümmer, "Die Aufbereitung der Volks- und Berufszählung 1933 im Hollerith-Lochkartenverfahren," *HN* 28 (August 1933): 345; see Schultz, p. 507; see Rudolf Gunzert, "Die Erfassung der persönlichen Verhältnisse und des Berufsschicksals der Arbeitslosen," *HN* 42 (October 1934); 555; see "Die Bearbeitung der Arbeitsunfähigkeit einzelner Krankenkassen im Hollerith-Lochkartenverfahren," *HN* 45 (January 1935): 588, see Krüger, pp. 614, 616; "Deutsche Hollerith Maschinen GmbH: Confidential Report 242," submitted by Harold J. Carter, December 8, 1943, Department of Justice, War Division,

Economic Warfare Section, NA RG60; see Aly and Roth, pp. 23–24, 26, 27, 107–108, 118–119; also see H. Friedlander, pp. 25–27.

92. H. Friedlander, p. 35; also see BA R22/1933 cited in Aly and Roth, pp. 100–101 and n21.

93. Zahn, "Fortbildung der deutschen Bevölkerungsstatistik durch erbbiologische Bestandsaufnahmen," *ASA* 27 (1937/38): 181.

94. Connally, p. 7.

95. "Deutsche Hollerith Maschinen GmbH: Confidential Report 242," p. 4, item 7 fn, submitted by Harold J. Carter, December 8, 1943, Department of Justice, War Division, Economic Warfare Section, NA RG60.

96. "Deutsche Hollerith Maschinen GmbH: Confidential Report 242," p. 3, item 6, Appendix A, submitted by Harold J. Carter, December 8, 1943, Department of Justice, War Division, Economic Warfare Section, NA RG60.

97. "Deutsche Hollerith Maschinen GmbH: Confidential Report 242," p. 3, item 6, Appendix A, submitted by Harold J. Carter, December 8, 1943, Department of Justice, War Division, Economic Warfare Section, NA RG60.

98. "Deutsche Hollerith Maschinen GmbH: Confidential Report 242," pp. 3, 4, item 6, Appendix A, submitted by Harold J. Carter, December 8, 1943, Department of Justice, War Division, Economic Warfare Section, NA RG60.

99. Saul Engelbourg, *International Business Machines: A Business History* (Arno Press, 1976), p. 127, plus author's typescript.

100. "Deutsche Hollerith Maschinen GmbH: Confidential Report 242," p. 10, submitted by Harold J. Carter, December 8, 1943, Department of Justice, War Division, Economic Warfare Section, NA RG60; also see Letter, W. Heidinger to Associates of Dehomag, October 6, 1936, p. 3, IBM Files.

101. Dispatch from British Embassy Berlin to Sir John Simon, May 17, 1934, PRO 581; see also Attachment, *Deutscher Reichsanzeiger und Preussischer Staatsanzeiger* No. 111, May 15, 1934, PRO FO371/17753.

102. Letter, M.G. Connally to W.F. Battin, September 6, 1934, IBM Files; Black, pp. 104–5; Letter and Cablegram, Thomas J. Watson to H. Rottke, January 16, 1934, IBM Files; Letter, M.G. Connally to W.F. Battin, April 14, 1934, IBM Files.

103. Letter, M.G. Connally to W.F. Battin, September 6, 1934; see handwritten notation at top of Letter, M.G. Connally to W.F. Battin, April 14, 1935, IBM Files; also see Memorandum, J.C. Milner to W.F. Battin, August 30, 1934, IBM Files; Letter, J.C. Milner to H.K. Chauncey, December 13, 1935, IBM Files.

104. Letter, W.D. Jones to Thomas J. Watson, September 25, 1933, IBM Files; Letter, F.C. Elstob to W.D. Jones, October 10, 1933, IBM Files.

105. Letter, F.C. Elstob to W.D. Jones, October 10, 1933, IBM Files.

106. Letter, W. Heidinger to M.G. Connally, November 14, 1933, IBM Files.

107. Letter, M.G. Connally to W.F. Battin, May 7, 1934, IBM Files.

108. Letter, J.T. Wilson to J.E. Holt, November 21, 1934, IBM Files.

109. Board Meeting Deleted Minutes, June 10, 1934, IBM Files.

110. Memorandum, W. Heidinger to Associates, October 6, 1936, IBM Files.

111. Letter, Thomas J. Watson to Dr. Otto Kiep, April 24, 1934, IBM Files; Letter, Thomas J. Watson to K. Hummel, December 7, 1934, IBM Files; Letter, K. Hummel to Thomas J. Watson, December 14, 1934, IBM Files; Notarized Contract, IBM and W. Heidinger, June 23, 1934, IBM Files.

112. Emerson W. Pugh, *Building IBM: Shaping an Industry and Its Technology* (Cambridge: The MIT Press, 1995), pp. 249–250.

113. Connally, pp. 30–32.

114. Abstract from Final Decision and Injunction 9th Chamber for Commercial Affairs, Provincial Court, Ref No. 409.0.18.34, April 18, 1934, IBM Files.

115. Abstract from Final Decision and Injunction 9th Chamber for Commercial Affairs, Provincial Court, Ref No. 409.0.18.34, April 18, 1934, IBM Files.

116. Reports, Dehomag to IBM, November 16, 1934, IBM Files.

117. BA R43II/720a cited in Aly and Roth, p. 101; Aly and Roth, pp. 10, 98.

118. FAAK materials, circa 1936–37, Rheinisch-Westfälisches Wirtschaftsinstitut, RWWA, 130–4001483/0.

119. *ASA* 24 (1934/35): 138 cited in Aly and Roth, p. 70.

120. "Deutsche Hollerith Maschinen GmbH: Confidential Report 242," submitted by Harold J. Carter, December 8, 1943, Department of Justice, War Division, Economic Warfare Section, NA RG60; also see Aly and Roth, p. 70.

121. See covers of *HN* 42 (October 1935).

V: A NAZI MEDAL FOR WATSON

1. "The Party: Marching Through Nuremberg During the Great Review," *NYT*, September 15, 1935; see photos, NA RG242, Items 242-HB-15046, 242-HB-15039a36, 242-HB-15039a56, 242-HB-15039a77; also see photo, RG242, Item 242-HB-15039a65, 242-HB-15026a11, 242-HB-15046, 242-HB-15037; "Hitler Hails the Spade," *NYT*, September 13, 1935.

2. Photo, NA RG242, Item 242-HB-15014M; Item 242-HB-15046; Item 242-HB-15012; "The Party: Marching Through Nuremberg During the Great Review," *NYT*, September 15, 1935.

3. "Reich's New Army Shows Its Power to Nazi Leaders," *NYT*, September 17, 1935; "Text of Hitler's Speech to Reichstag at Nuremberg," *NYT*, September 16, 1935.

4. Raul Hilberg, *The Destruction of the European Jews* (New York: Quadrangle Books; Harper Colophon, 1979), p. 58.

5. BA R22/1933 cited in Götz Aly and Karl Heinz Roth, *Die restlose Erfassung: Volkszählen, Identifizieren, Aussondern im Nationalsozialismus* (Berlin: Rotbuch Verlag, 1984), p. 153.

6. Hilberg, *Destruction of the European Jews*, p. 20; "Hope of Reich Jews Is Dimmed by Events," *NYT*, September 22, 1935; "New Drive Aimed at Jews in Reich," *NYT*, March 21, 1934.

7. "Hope of Reich Jews Is Dimmed by Events," *NYT*, September 22, 1935; also see Hilberg, *Destruction of the European Jews*, pp. 12, 21; "New Drive Aimed at Jews," *NYT*, March 21, 1934; "Large Jewish Store in Berlin Liquidated," *NYT*, August 20, 1937.

8. Hilberg, *Destruction of the European Jews*, pp. 46–47.

9. Burgdörfer, "Die Juden in Deutschland und in der Welt, Ein Statistischer Beitrag zur biologischen, beruflichen und sozialen Struktur des Judentums in Deutschland," *Forschungen zur Judenfrage*, Volume 3, Hamburg 1938, cited in Aly and Roth, p. 60, n32; Hilberg, *Destruction of the European Jews*, pp. 34, 37; also see Dispatch, British Embassy to Foreign Dept., June 14, 1935, FO 371/18861; "Text of Hitler's Speech to Reichstag at Nuremberg," *NYT*, September 16, 1935.

10. "Big Nazi Conclave Will Start Today," *NYT*, September 10, 1935.

11. "Hitler Gets Sword As Congress Opens," *NYT*, September 11, 1935; photo, NA RG242 Item 242-HB-15014M.

12. "Reich Adopts Swastika As Nation's Official Flag," *NYT*, September 16, 1934; Hilberg, *Destruction of the European Jews*, pp. 21–22.

13. Hilberg, *Destruction of the European Jews*, pp. 43–53.

14. Dispatch No. 135, British Consulate General, Munich to Eric Phipps, British Embassy ,Berlin, September 27, 1934, PRO FO 371/18881; "Bautzen County Summary for June 1, 1935 to December 31, 1937," Race Political Office, Main Office III to Reich Family Research Office, August 9, 1938, BA R1509/812.

15. Letter, Chief of the Security Police to the Chief of the Order Police, October 12, 1936, ZSTAP/M, Rep 77, Tit. 343 cited in Aly and Roth, p. 69.

16. Dispatch, British Embassy to Foreign Dept., June 14, 1935, FO C 4760; Hilberg, *Destruction of the European Jews*, pp. 34, 37, 43.

17. Burgdörfer, "Die Juden in Deutschland und in der Welt, Ein Statistischer Beitrag zur biologischen, beruflichen und sozialen Struktur des Judentums in Deutschland," *Forschungen zur Judenfrage*, Volume 3, Hamburg 1938, cited in Aly and Roth, p. 60; Hilberg, *Destruction of the European Jews*, p. 46.

18. "Text of Hitler's Speech to Reichstag at Nuremberg," *NYT*, September 16, 1935; photos, NA RG242 Items 242-HB-15014a, 242-HB-15012, and 242-HB-15022a45.

19. "Text of Hitler's Speech at Nuremberg," *NYT*, September 16, 1935; "Reich Adopts Swastika As National Flag," *NYT*, September 16, 1934.
20. "Text of Hitler's Speech at Nuremberg," *NYT*, September 16, 1935.
21. "Text of Hitler's Speech at Nuremberg," *NYT*, September 16, 1935.
22. "Text of Hitler's Speech at Nuremberg," *NYT*, September 16, 1935.
23. "Reich Adopts Swastika As National Flag," *NYT*, September 16, 1934.
24. "Text of Hitler's Speech at Nuremberg," *NYT*, September 16, 1935.
25. Letter of Resignation of James G. McDonald to Secretary General of the League of Nations, Annex, p. 1, December 27, 1935, FO 371/19918.
26. Hilberg, *Destruction of the European Jews*, p. 60.
27. Letter of Resignation of James G. McDonald to Secretary General of the League of - Nations, December 27, 1935, FO 371/19918.
28. "All Jews Quit Hersbruck," *NYT*, May 28, 1935; "German Town to Bar Jews," *NYT*, July 17, 1934.
29. Thomas J. Watson, Jr., and Peter Petre, *Father, Son & Co.: My Life at IBM and Beyond* (New York: Bantam Books, 1990), p. 54.
30. "Nazi Plan to Buy Out All Jewish Firms; Stress Bargains Resulting from the Boycott," *NYT*, September 24, 1935.
31. "Munich Seizes Passports to Curb Flight of Jews," *NYT*, January 20, 1936; Letter of Resignation of James G. McDonald to Secretary General of the League of Nations, 34, December 27, 1935, FO 371/19918.
32. Westphalen, "Die Hollerith Maschinen Gesellschaft im Dienste der Sparkassen-Statistik," *Hollerith Nachrichten (HN)* 54 (October 1935): 726.
33. James Connally, *History of Computing in Europe* (IBM World Trade Corporation, circa 1967), p. E-9; *HN* 55 (November 35); also see "EAM Accounts and Revenue by Industry Class," January 1, 1937, pp. 1, 2, Department of Justice, War Division, Economic Warfare Section, NA RG60; CSDIC, "Secret Report: PW Intelligence Bulletin No. 2/57," April 25, 1945, p. 9, NA RG226; *HN* 54 (October 1935).
34. CSDIC, "Secret Report: PW Intelligence Bulletin No. 2/57," April 25, 1945, p. 9, NA RG226.
35. Aly and Roth, p. 68.
36. Hilberg, *Destruction of the European Jews*, p. 82; N. Henderson, "Registration of Jewish Businesses in Germany," PRO FO 371/21635.
37. "Deutsche Hollerith Maschinen GmbH: Confidential Report 242," Appendix A, p. 4, submitted by Harold J. Carter, December 8, 1943, Department of Justice, War Division, Economic Warfare Section, NA RG60; CSDIC, "Secret Report: PW Intelligence Bulletin No. 2/57," April 25, 1945, p. 9, NA RG226.; Dispatch, British Embassy, Berlin to Foreign Office, No. 236E, February 24, 1936, PRO FO 871/19941; Walther Lauersen, "Organisation und Aufgaben des Maschinellen Berichtwesens des Reichsministers für Rüstung und Kriegsproduktion," December 5, 1945, pp. 3–4, BA R3/17a.
38. CSDIC, "Secret Report: PW Intelligence Bulletin No. 2/57," April 25, 1945, p. 9, NA RG226; Dispatch, British Embassy, Berlin to Foreign Office, No. 236E, February 24, 1936, PRO FO 871/19941; NA RG242, T-73, Reel 12, RMfRuK/320.
39. Connally, p. E-10, also see p. E-7; Banquet Guests List, November 26, 1935, IBM Files.
40. "Goebbels Utters Threats to Jews," *NYT*, May 12, 1934; "Nazis Warn Jews to Stay at Home," *NYT*, June 2, 1934.
41. Joint Boycott Council Box 22-E, NYPL; Connally, p. E-10; Dehomag Stationery, IBM Files.
42. Letter, Dehomag to J.T. Wilson, November 16, 1935, IBM Files; see Letter, Dr. Edgar Schulz to Thomas J. Watson, November 27, 1935, IBM Files; Letter, Thomas J. Watson to Dr. B. Fels, December 23, 1935, IBM Files; Letter, Dr. B. Fels to Thomas J. Watson, February 4, 1936, IBM Files; Letter, Thomas J. Watson to Dr. Edgar Schulz, December 19, 1935, IBM Files.
43. Connally, pp. E-11, 36; "Sales School Is Opened," *NYT*, July 15, 1936; Letter, H. Rottke to O. Gubelman, October 2, 1935, IBM Files.
44. Connally E-11; see Patent Agreement Between IBM and Gustav Tauschek, September 1, 1930, Department of Justice, War Division, Economic Warfare Section, NA RG60.

45. Connally, pp. 33, E-11.
46. Connally, p. E-11.
47. "Deutsche Hollerith Maschinen GmbH: Confidential Report 242," p. 10, submitted by Harold J. Carter, December 8, 1943, Department of Justice, War Division, Economic Warfare Section, NA RG60.
48. Connally, pp. E-11, E-12; CSDIC, "Secret Report: PW Intelligence Bulletin No. 2/57," April 25, 1945, p 4, NA RG226; "Deutsche Hollerith Maschinen GmbH: Confidential Report 242," p. 8, submitted by Harold J. Carter, December 8, 1943, Department of Justice, War Division, Economic Warfare Section, NA RG60.
49. "Workers, Wages, Sales Increased," *NYT*, March 17, 1934; "Business Machines Corporation Reports Steady Rise in Sales," *NYT*, April 4, 1934; "Business Machines Gains," *NYT*, April 11, 1934.
50. "Earnings Reports by Corporation," *NYT*, July 31, 1934; "Large Industrial Increases Income," *NYT*, October 27, 1934; "Dividend News," *NYT*, November 28, 1934.
51. "Business Leaders See Gain Continue," *NYT*, January 2, 1935; "Business Machines Increases Income," *NYT*, March 7, 1936.
52. Connally, p. 37.
53. "International Business Machines Corporation to Expand Near 32nd St.," *NYT*, February 20, 1934; "Insures 6,900 Employees," *NYT*, September 25, 1934; "Thousands Get Pay Raises and Bonuses As Industries' Gift at Yule Season," *NYT*, December 22, 1934; Watson, Jr., and Petre, p. 46, and also see "T.J. Watson an Optimist on $1,000-a-day-Income," *NYT*, April 30, 1934; "Watson Defends 6-Figure Income," *NYT*, April 8, 1936; "Business Unit Seeks Madison Ave. Site," *NYT*, June 28, 1936.
54. "Story of IBM: The Early Years 1890–1938," www.ibm.com/history; Oral History, Jack S. Futterman, January 23, 1974, www.ssa.gov/.
55. Oral History, Jack S. Futterman, January 23, 1974, www.ssa.gov/.
56. Oral History, Jack S. Futterman, January 23, 1974, www.ssa.gov/.
57. Oral History, Jack S. Futterman, January 23, 1974, www.ssa.gov/.
58. Thomas Graham Belden and Marva Robins Belden, *The Lengthening Shadow: The Life of Thomas J. Watson* (Boston: Little, Brown and Company, 1962), p. 163; Connally, p. E-13, and see Oral History, Jack S. Futterman, January 23, 1974, www.ssa.gov/; "Deutsche Hollerith Maschinen GmbH: Confidential Report 242," fn pp. 1–3, submitted by Harold J. Carter, December 8, 1943, Department of Justice, War Division, Economic Warfare Section, NA RG60.
59. Saul Engelbourg, *International Business Machines: A Business History* (Arno Press, 1976), p. 372.
60. Letter, Dehomag to F.C. Elstob, March 8, 1935, IBM Files; Letter, M.G. Connally to F.C. Elstob, February 21, 1935, IBM Files; Application for Relief, Konrad Matzdorf to The Central Revenue Board, February 27, 1935, IBM Files.
61. Letter, O.E. Braitmayer to J.E. Holt, February 21, 1935, IBM Files; Letter, O.E. Braitmayer to W. Heidinger, February 21, 1935, IBM Files; Letter, W. Heidinger to O.E. Braitmayer, March 8, 1935, IBM Files; Letter, W. Heidinger to J.E. Holt, January 20, 1938, IBM Files; Letter, F.C. Elstob to F.W. Nichol, March 20, 1935, IBM Files.
62. Letter, F.C. Elstob to F.W. Nichol, March 20, 1935, IBM Files; see Letter, W. Heidinger to J.E. Holt, January 20, 1938.
63. Letter, W. Heidinger to O.E. Braitmayer, March 3, 1935, IBM Files.
64. Letter, F.C. Elstob to F.W. Nichol, March 20, 1935, IBM Files.
65. Letter, J.C. Milner to H.K. Chauncey, December 13, 1935, IBM Files.
66. H.K. Chauncey, Draft IBM Memorandum, March 27, 1935, IBM Files.
67. Resolutions, Dehomag Board of Directors, April 20, 1936, IBM Files.
68. Report to Dehomag Board of Directors, July 25, 1935, IBM Files.
69. Report to Dehomag Board of Directors, July 25, 1935, IBM Files; Letter, H. Rottke to O.L. Gubelman, October 2, 1935, IBM Files.
70. Letter, H. Rottke to O.L. Gubelman, October 2, 1935, IBM Files.
71. Letter, J.C. Milner to Thomas J. Watson, March 23, 1937, IBM Files.

72. Letter, J.C. Milner to Thomas J. Watson, March 23, 1937, IBM Files.
73. Letter, J.T. Wilson to Dept. of State, May 18, 1945, NA RG59 362.115/5–1845.
74. Private and Confidential Report, Price Waterhouse to IBM Geneva, April 24, 1937, IBM Files; Connally, p. E-10.
75. Memorandum, Proposal for Change of the Contract, J.C. Milner to H.K. Chauncey, December 13, 1935, IBM Files.
76. Memorandum, Heidinger-Watson Agreement, circa May 1936, IBM Files; see also Radiogram, J.E. Holt to Thomas J. Watson, March 20, 1936, IBM Files.
77. Letter, O.E. Braitmayer to J.E. Holt, May 12, 1935, IBM Files.
78. Notarized Agreement, circa 1938, and attached Affidavit of J.G. Phillips, January 26, 1937, IBM Files; Letter, W.A. Pithie to W.F. Battin, September 4, 1936, IBM Files.
79. "Reich Seizing 25% of Fortunes of Jews; Ruin of Many More Businesses Forecast," *NYT,* September 8, 1936.
80. "Nazi Penalties Heavier," *NYT,* September 17, 1936.
81. "Streicher Advises Foreigners on Jews," *NYT,* September 16, 1936.
82. "McDonald in Poland on Refugee Problem," *NYT,* April 19, 1934; Letter of Resignation of James G. McDonald to Secretary General of the League of Nations, December 27, 1935, p. 34, FO 371/19918; "German Refugees Placed at 125,000,"*NYT,* September 5, 1937.
83. Letter of Resignation of James G. McDonald to Secretary General of the League of Nations, December 27, 1935, p. 34, FO 371/19918.
84. American Section Meeting of the International Chamber of Commerce, May 1, 1934, Hagley ACCT1960, Box 7.
85. White House Telegram, Franklin D. Roosevelt to Thomas J. Watson, February 14, 1935, NA RG59 600.0031/1377; see also Letter, Chauncey Snow to Cordell Hull, May 15, 1933, NA RG59 600.001171/337, Letter, Cordell Hull to Chauncey D. Snow, June 1, 1935, NA RG59 600.001171/337; see also Letter from Assistant Secretary to Carr, May 24, 1935, NA RG59 600.00171/337; see also Letters to J.T. Wilson, May 27, 1935, and Carr, May 25, 1935, NA RG59 600.00171/337.
86. Telegram, Cordell Hull to Thomas J. Watson, November 6, 1935, NA RG59 600.001171/361A.
87. Program, Eighth General Congress of the International Chamber of Commerce, Paris, June 24–29, 1935, NA RG59 600.00171/337.
88. Program, Eighth General Congress of the International Chamber of Congress, Paris, June 24–29, 1935, NA RG59 600.00171/337; "Business Is Divided on 2-Nation Pacts," *NYT,* June 28, 1935; "World Chamber Lays Trade Ills to Government Rule of Industry," *NYT,* June 30, 1935.
89. ICC Meeting transcripts, American Section Meeting of the International Chamber of Commerce, April 26, 1936, American Chamber of Commerce, Hagley ACCT 1960 Box 8.
90. "NRA Called a Help to Business Ethics," *NYT,* June 9, 1935; "Watson Appeals for World Trade," *NYT,* January 27, 1935; "Business Is Divided on 2-Nation Pacts," *NYT,* June 28, 1935; "France Is Cautious in New Tariff Policy," *NYT,* November 17, 1935; "World Now Seeks New Trade System," *NYT,* May 22, 1936; "T.J. Watson Returns," *NYT,* August 11, 1936.
91. ICC Meeting transcripts, American Section Meeting of the International Chamber of Commerce, April 26, 1937, p. 500, American Chamber of Commerce, Hagley ACCT1960 Box 8.
92. ICC Meeting transcripts, American Section Meeting of the International Chamber of Commerce, April 26, 1937, p. 501, American Chamber of Commerce, Hagley ACCT1960 Box 8.
93. ICC Meeting transcripts, American Section Meeting of the International Chamber of Commerce, April 26, 1937, p. 505, American Chamber of Commerce, Hagley ACCT1960 Box 8.
94. ICC Meeting transcripts, American Section Meeting of the International Chamber of Commerce, April 26, 1937, p. 505, American Chamber of Commerce, Hagley ACCT1960 Box 8.

95. ICC Meeting transcripts, American Section Meeting of the International Chamber of Commerce, April 26, 1937, p. 500, American Chamber of Commerce, Hagley ACCT1960 Box 8.

96. "Watson for Freer Trade," *NYT,* April 25, 1937.

97. "Watson Defends 6-Figure Income," *NYT,* April 8, 1936; Watson, Jr., and Petre, p. 55; Belden and Belden, pp. 192, 195; William Rodgers, *Think: A Biography of the Watsons and IBM* (New York: Stein and Day, 1969), p. 121.

98. Draft Letter, Thomas J. Watson to Dr. Hjalmar Schacht, circa November 1937, IBM Files.

99. "Report to the Associates of the Dehomag Company," October 6, 1936, pp. 4–5, 9, IBM Files.

100. "Report to the Associates of the Dehomag Company," October 6, 1936, pp. 4–5, 9, IBM Files; Letter, J.E. Holt to J.G. Johnston, June 2, 1938, NA RG60.

101. "Thomas J. Watson Is Decorated by Hitler for Work in Bettering Economic Relations," *NYT,* July 2, 1937.

102. Letter, Thomas J. Watson to Cordell Hull, February 12, 1937, NA RG59 600.00171/369; Louis P. Lochner, ed. and transl., *The Goebbels Diaries 1942–1943* (New York: Doubleday & Co., Inc, 1948); also see "Salute for Hitler at Trade Union Congress," *NYT,* June 29, 1937; "Hitler Meets International Chamber Delegates," *NYT,* July 13, 1937.

103. Press Release, ICC, October 22, 1937, NA RG59; Letter, Decker to Taylor, May 26, 1939, Department of Justice, War Division, Economic Warfare Section, NA RG60; see Letter, Chevalerie to J.T. Wilson, August 4, 1939, Department of Justice, War Division, Economic Warfare Section, NA RG60.

104. Telegram, White House to Thomas J. Watson, June 27, 1937, NA RG59.

105. *Internationale Wirtschaft* 7/8 (July-August 1937): 6; *Völkischer Beobachter,* June 28, 1937.

106. "Salute for Hitler at Trade Union Congress," *NYT,* June 29, 1937.

107. "Salute for Hitler at Trade Union Congress," *NYT,* June 29, 1937.

108. "Salute for Hitler at Trade Union Congress," *NYT,* June 29, 1937.

109. "Germans Plead for Colonies at World C. of C.," *New York Herald Tribune,* June 29, 1937.

110. "Salute for Hitler at Trade Union Congress," *NYT,* June 29, 1937.

111. "Germans Plead For Colonies at World C. of C.," *New York Herald Tribune,* June 29, 1937; "Salute for Hitler at Trade Union Congress," *NYT,* June 29, 1937.

112. "Salute for Hitler at Trade Union Congress," *NYT,* June 29, 1937.

113. *Internationale Wirtschaft* 7/8 (July-August 1937): 6–8.

114. *The Goebbels Diaries 1942–1943,* pp. 20–21; Belden and Belden, p. 196.

115. *The Goebbels Diaries 1942–1943,* pp. 20–21.

116. "Thomas J. Watson Is Decorated by Hitler for Work in Bettering Economic Relations," *NYT,* July 2, 1937; "Watson Sends Hitler Notes of Gratitude," *NYT,* July 6, 1937; see also Watson, Jr., and Petre, p. 55; *Internationale Wirtschaft* 7/8 (July-August 1937): 7.

117. Rodgers, p. 114.

VI: WAR CARDS

1. "Watson Sends Hitler Notes of Gratitude," *NYT,* July 6, 1937.

2. Letter, Ilse Meyer to Thomas J. Watson, July 4, 1938, IBM Files.

3. "Reich Orders Jews to Hold No Meetings," *NYT,* April 14, 1937; "Jewish Cafes Closed in Reich," *NYT,* August 27, 1937; "Ghetto Zones for Jews Decreed in Berlin Parks," *NYT,* August 18, 1937; "Special Seats for Jews," *NYT,* September 16, 1937; "Germans to Raze Synagogue," *NYT,* September 28, 1938; "Munich's Main Synagogue Being Wrecked by Nazis," *NYT,* June 13, 1938.

4. "Jewish Clothiers Gain," *NYT,* October 9, 1937; "Warns Jews Owning Boarding Houses," *NYT,* September 2, 1938; "Jews to Lose Permits," *NYT,* September 21, 1938; "'Business Ghetto' Is Berlin's Aim," *NYT,* June 27, 1938; "Anti-Jewish Drive Covers All Reich; Arrests Mounting," *NYT,* June 19, 1938; "Anti-Jewish Raids Continue in Berlin," *NYT,* June 18, 1938.

5. James Connally, *History of Computing in Europe* (IBM World Trade Corporation, circa 1967), p. E-12.

6. Götz Aly and Karl Heinz Roth, *Die restlose Erfassung: Volkszählen, Identifizieren, Aussondern im Nationalsozialismus* (Berlin: Rotbuch Verlag, 1984), p. 25.

7. Connally, p. E-12; Memorandum, J.G. Johnston to J.E. Holt, March 25, 1938, Department of Justice, War Division, Economic Warfare Section, NA RG60; Letter, J.E. Holt to J.G. Johnston, June 2, 1938, Department of Justice, War Division, Economic Warfare Section, NA RG60.

8. *Völkischer Beobachter,* Ausg. Köln, 30 (December 1937) cited in Aly and Roth, p. 24.

9. ZSTAP/M, Rep.77, Title 343, Volume 1, No.107 cited in Aly and Roth, p. 76.

10. "Austria Absorbed in German Reich: The Austrian Situation," "Vienna Jews Beaten; Stores Plundered," "Nazi Purge in Linz Now in Full Swing," *NYT,* March 14, 1938; "Austrian Shake-Up Is Pressed by Nazis," "Schuschnigg Under Arrest," "Hitler Enters a Cheering Vienna," *NYT,* March 15, 1938; "Jews Humiliated by Vienna Crowds," *NYT,* March 16, 1938; "Jews Scrub Streets in Vienna Inner City," *NYT,* March 24, 1938.

11. "Vienna Nazis Widen Drive on Jews; Every Family Reported Suffering," *NYT,* June 20, 1938.

12. "Vienna Prisoners Sent to Camp or to Hard Labor on Projects," *NYT,* June 3, 1938; "Arrests Continue," *NYT,* June 9, 1938; "Non-Jews Hard Hit by Drive in Berlin," *NYT,* June 23, 1938.

13. "Austrian Province Ousts 3,000 Jews," *NYT,* April 24, 1938.

14. "Employer in Vienna Dismisses 30,000 Jews," *NYT,* July 1, 1938.

15. "Freud Leaves Vienna for London Refuge, Declaring He Plans to Come Here Later," *NYT,* June 5, 1938.

16. "Jews Scrub Streets in Vienna Inner City," *NYT,* March 24, 1938, "New Suicide Wave Breaks Out in Vienna," *NYT,* May 7, 1938; "Wave of Suicides Renewed in Vienna," *NYT,* June 28, 1938.

17. "Hitler Enters a Cheering Vienna," *NYT,* March 15, 1938.

18. Connally, pp. E-9, E-10, E-12,19, 24; "German Nazis Point for Austrian Jews," *NYT,* March 13, 1938; Handwritten Notes, circa 1945, IBM Files; see H.B. Fellinger, Enclosure 6, July 19, 1945, p. 15, IBM Files.

19. Jochen von Lang, ed., *Eichmann Interrogated: Transcripts from the Archives of the Israeli Police,* transl. Ralph Manheim (New York: Farrar, Strauss & Giroux, 1983), pp. 46–47.

20. von Lang, pp. 46–47.

21. Letter J.G. Johnston to J.E. Holt, June 14, 1938, p. 2, Department of Justice, War Division, Economic Warfare Section, NA RG60; Bruno Blau, "The Jewish Population of Germany 1939–1945," *Jewish Social Studies,* p. 162.

22. "Goering Starts Final Liquidation of Jewish Property in Germany," *NYT,* April 28, 1938.

23. "Youth Beheaded by Reich," *NYT,* December 22, 1938; "Treatment of Prisoners in Concentration Camp at Buchenwald," B.L. Bracey to Lord Halifax, December 28, 1938, PRO FO 371/21757; "Nazi Tortures Detailed by Britain; Concentration Camp Horrors Told," *NYT,* October 31, 1939; "Anti-Jewish Drive Covers All Reich; Arrests Mounting," *NYT,* June 19, 1938; "Memorandum of the Concentration Camp at Sachsenhausen," PRO FO 371/230006; "1,410,000 Nazis' Captives," *NYT,* October 31, 1939.

24. "25 More Lose Citizenship," *NYT,* March 4, 1936; "Reich Bars Jews in Trade, Fines Them Billion Marks; Cardinal's Palace Stoned," *NYT,* November 13, 1938; "Half of the Persecuted in Reich Are Christians," *NYT,* November 18, 1938; "Viennese Unhappy Under Nazi Rule," *NYT,* December 28, 1938.

25. "Berlin Raids Reply to Death of Envoy," *NYT,* November 10, 1938; "Anti-Jewish Measures and Treatment of Jews in Germany," Dr. Bruno Stern, Beresford to Sir S. Gaselee, January 13, 1939, p. 4, PRO FO 371–19918; "Nazis Smash, Loot and Burn Jewish Shops and Temples Until Goebbels Calls Halt," *NYT,* November 11, 1938.

26. "Nazis Smash, Loot and Burn Jewish Shops and Temples Until Goebbels Calls Halt," *NYT,* November 11, 1938; "Anti-Jewish Measures and Treatment of Jews in Germany," Dr. Bruno Stern, Beresford to Sir S. Gaselee, January 13, 1939, PRO FO 371–19918.

27. "Nazis Smash, Loot and Burn Jewish Shops and Temples Until Goebbels Calls Halt," *NYT,* November 11, 1938; "Anti-Jewish Measures and Treatment of Jews in Germany," Dr. Bruno Stern, Beresford to Sir S. Gaselee, January 13, 1939, PRO FO 371–19918.

28. "Nazis Smash, Loot and Burn Jewish Shops and Temples Until Goebbels Calls Halt," *NYT,* November 11, 1938.

29. "Nazis Smash, Loot and Burn Jewish Shops and Temples Until Goebbels Calls Halt," *NYT,* November 11, 1938.

30. "Washington Calls Envoy from Berlin," *NYT,* November 15, 1938; Haskel Lookstein, *Were We Our Brothers' Keepers? The Public Response of American Jews to the Holocaust, 1938–1944* (Toronto: Hartmore House, 1985; New York: Vintage Books, 1988), p. 42; "U.S. and British Voters Found Skeptical on Hitler Pledge to End Demands in Europe," *NYT,* November 11, 1938; "Hungary Curbing Nazis," *NYT,* July 13, 1938; American History in the 20th Century, "The House on Un-American Activities Committee's Hearings and the People It Affected," dorit.ihi.ku.dk/.

31. "Jews Are Ordered to Leave Munich," *NYT,* November 11, 1938; "Reich Jews' Flats Causing Scramble," *NYT,* November 28, 1938; see "Reich Orders Ouster of Stateless Jews," *NYT,* May 19, 1939.

32. "Extremists Sway Nazis and Jews Are Menaced with More Drastic Rule," *NYT,* November 14, 1938; "Jews in Germany Get Extermination Threat," *NYT,* November 30, 1938.

33. Letter, J.E. Holt to J.G. Johnston, June 2, 1938, Department of Justice, War Division, Economic Warfare Section, NA RG60; Letter, Thomas J. Watson to Cordell Hull, September 23, 1939, NA RG59 600.00171/386.

34. "Reich in Great Need of Raw Materials," *NYT,* November 17, 1936; "Germans Are Asked to Economize on Fats," *NYT,* January 26, 1936; "Plane Designers Win Nazi Awards," *NYT,* September 7, 1938; "Germans Anxious Over 1937 Events," *NYT,* January 1, 1937; "Germany Puts Planes in Terrible War Role," *NYT,* March 19, 1936; "Reich Restricting Passenger Trains," *NYT,* February 4, 1939; "Reports Nazi Mobilization Plan," *NYT,* January 16, 1937.

35. "U.S. Trade Efforts Lauded by Watson," *NYT,* January 25, 1938; also see "Hull Sees Danger in Autarky's Rise," *NYT,* May 26, 1938; "Watson Back from Tour: Manufacturer Finds 'Best Ever' Business in Europe," *NYT,* November 18, 1938; see "World Team Work Asked by Watson," *NYT,* November 23, 1938; "Approves Trade Treaties: Thomas J. Watson at Vassar Hails Pacts As Peace Aid," *NYT,* April 14, 1938; "Watson for Freer Trade," *NYT,* April 24, 1937; "Reich in Great Need of Raw Materials," *NYT,* November 17, 1936; "Germans Are Asked to Economize on Fats," *NYT,* January 26, 1936.

36. "Nazi Prosecution Bars Trade Pacts," *NYT,* April 24, 1937; Transcript, Seventeenth Annual Dinner, American Section, International Chamber of Commerce, May 2, 1938, Hagley Accession 1960, Box 8.

37. Thomas J. Watson, *Men, Minutes, Money: A Collection of Excerpts From Talks and Messages Delivered and Written at Various Times* (New York: International Business Machines, 1934), pp. 781, 885.

38. Draft Letter, Thomas J. Watson to Dr. Hjalmar Schacht, November 25, 1938, IBM Files.

39. Draft Letter, Thomas J. Watson to Dr. Hjalmar Schacht, November 25, 1938, IBM Files.

40. Letter, Thomas J. Watson to Adolph Hitler, November 25, 1938, IBM Files.

41. Letter, Thomas J. Watson to Adolph Hitler, November 25, 1938, IBM Files; Secretary's Follow-Up, March 7, 1939, IBM Files; Thomas J. Watson, Jr., and Peter Petre, *Father, Son & Co.: My Life at IBM and Beyond* (New York: Bantam Books, 1990), p. 44.

42. "Watson Back from Tour," *NYT,* November 18, 1938; compare to Letter, Thomas J. Watson to Cordell Hull, September 5, 1938, NA RG59 600.00171/386; "Foreigners Studying in Company School," *NYT,* May 9, 1939.

43. "Foreigners Studying in Company School," *NYT,* May 9, 1939; Transcript, 18th Annual Dinner, ICC American Section, May 1, 1939, Hagley Accession 1960; William Rodgers, *Think: A Biography of the Watsons and IBM* (New York: Stein and Day, 1969), p. 74.

44. "World Team Work Asked by Watson," *NYT,* November 23, 1938; "T.J. Watson Asks Resources Parley," *NYT,* June 27, 1939; Transcript, 18th Annual Dinner, ICC American Section, May 1, 1939, Hagley Accession 1960.

45. Letter, J.E. Holt to J.G. Johnston, June 2, 1938, Department of Justice, War Division, Economic Warfare Section, NA RG60; Protocol, Decisions Taken During Shareholders Meeting, June 24, 1938, IBM Files.

46. Shareholders' Meeting Minutes, June 24, 1938, p. 1, IBM Files; Protocol, Decisions Taken During Shareholders Meeting, June 24, 1938, pt. 6, IBM Files.

47. Joint Letter, H. Rottke and K. Hummel to O.L. Gubelman, July 6, 1938, p. 2, IBM Files.
48. Joint Letter, H. Rottke and K. Hummel to O.L. Gubelman, July 6, 1938, p. 2, IBM Files.
49. Joint Letter, H. Rottke and K. Hummel to O.L. Gubelman, July 6, 1938, p. 2, IBM Files.
50. Joint Letter, H. Rottke and K. Hummel to O.L. Gubelman, July 6, 1938, p. 2, IBM Files.
51. Joint Letter, H. Rottke and K. Hummel to O.L. Gubelman, July 6, 1938, p. 2, IBM Files.
52. Letters, Thomas J. Watson to J.E. Holt, August 2, 1938, IBM Files.
53. Letter, J.C. Milner to J.T. Wilson, August 4, 1938, IBM Files.
54. Letter, J.C. Milner to J.T. Wilson, August 4, 1938, IBM Files.
55. Letter, J.C. Milner to J.T. Wilson, August 4, 1938, IBM Files.
56. Letter, J.T. Wilson to J.E. Holt, August 25, 1938, IBM Files; Memo, J.T. Wilson to H.K. Chauncey, August 25, 1938, IBM Files; Letter, J.E. Holt to J.T. Wilson, September 14, 1938, IBM Files.
57. Letter, J.E. Holt to J.T. Wilson, September 14, 1938, IBM Files.
58. Letter, J.E. Holt to J.T. Wilson, September 14, 1938, p. 2, IBM Files.
59. Draft Letter, Thomas J. Watson to Dr. Hjalmar Schacht, August 18, 1937, IBM Files; Edwin Black, *The Transfer Agreement: The Dramatic Story of the Pact Between the Third Reich & Jewish Palestine* (New York: Macmillan, 1984; Washington, D.C.: Dialog Press, 1999), pp. 185, 186, 264.
60. Letter, J.C. Milner to J.T. Wilson, August 4, 1938, IBM Files; Memorandum, J.T. Wilson to H.K. Chauncey, August 25, 1938, IBM Files.
61. Letter, J.C. Milner to J.T. Wilson, August 4, 1938, IBM Files; Memorandum, J.T. Wilson to H.K. Chauncey, August 25, 1938, IBM Files.
62. State Department Document, American Section of ICC to Secretary of State, January 19, 1934, NA RG G551.2A3A/73; "Double Taxation Convention, United States and France, 1932," March 24, 1938, NA RG 59 512351.
63. Memorandum, J.T. Wilson to H.K. Chauncey, August 25, 1938, IBM Files.
64. Walther Lauersen, "Organisation und Aufgaben des Maschinellen Berichtwesens des Reichministers für Rüstung und Kriegsproduktion," December 5, 1945, pp. 3–4, BA R3/17a; H.B. Fellinger, Enclosure 4, July 19, 1945, p. 15, IBM Files.
65. MB Report, February 23, 1938, NA RG242 T-73 Reel 11.
66. Draft Letter to Armaments Inspectorate re: Fink Memorandum to Reich Defense Committee, March 31, 1939, NA RG242 T-73 Reel 11.
67. "Many Jews Quit Berlin," *NYT,* July 4, 1937; "Christian Churches Hold 92% of Reich Population," *NYT,* December 25, 1937; "Demands Jewish Names," *NYT,* August 20, 1938; "Reich Limits Goods for Jewish Concerns," *NYT,* December 30, 1937. "August 17, 1938," www.ushmm.org/outreach/locatchr.htm.
68. "10 Big Reich Cities Lose 40% of Jews," *NYT,* May 15, 1938.
69. "Migration Register Is Started in Germany; Plan to Recapture All Emigrants for Race," *NYT,* June 22, 1938; "Nazis Hunting 333,000 Wives for Farmers," *NYT,* May 6, 1935; "Political Divorces Proposed in Reich," *NYT,* January 23, 1936.
70. Letter, Pastor Stich to *Reichssippenamt,* November 12, 1935, BA R1509/576; see Letter, *Reichssippenamt,* to Pastor Stich, November 25, 1935, BA R1509/576; also see Memorandum to Düsseldorf NSDAP, March 19, 1937, BA R1509/812 and Anweisung für Sonderfälle, April 1936, BA R1509/576.
71. Letter, Pastor Stich to *Reichssippenamt,* November 12, 1935, BA R1509/576.
72. Letter, *Reichssippenamt* to Pastor Stich, November 25, 1935, BA R1509/576.
73. Memorandum to Düsseldorf NSDAP, March19, 1937, BA R1509/812.
74. Anweisung für Sonderfälle, April 1936, BA R1509/576.
75. Memorandum to Düsseldorf NSDAP, March 19, 1937, BA R1509/812.
76. Working Report, Race Political Office, County Bautzen, June 1–December 31, 1937, BA R1509/812.
77. Working Report, Race Political Office, County Bautzen, July 5, 1938, BA R1509/812; "Census of Persons Who Must Possess a 'Labour' Book," Sir N. Henderson to Foreign Office, No. 934E, September 4, 1938, PRO FO C9467/138/18; Letter to Reichsführer-SS, BA R1509/555.
78. Letter, J.E. Holt to J.G. Johnston, June 2, 1938, Department of Justice, War Division,

Economic Warfare Section, NA RG60; Report, H. Rottke to J.G. Johnston, December 18, 1937, Department of Justice, War Division, Economic Warfare Section, NA RG60.

79. "Deutsche Hollerith Maschinen GmbH: Confidential Report 242," submitted by Harold J. Carter, December 8, 1943, Department of Justice, War Division, Economic Warfare Section, NA RG60; IBM List, December 1, 1937, Department of Justice, War Division, Economic Warfare Section, NA RG60.

80. Memorandum, J.G. Johnston to J.E. Holt, March 23, 1938, pp. 1, 4, Department of Justice, War Division, Economic Warfare Section, NA RG60; Letter, J.E. Holt to J.G. Johnston, June 6, 1938, Department of Justice, War Division, Economic Warfare Section, NA RG60.

81. Memorandum, J.G. Johnston to J.E. Holt, June 14, 1938, pp. 1, 3, Department of Justice, War Division, Economic Warfare Section, NA RG60.

82. William L. Shirer, *The Rise and Fall of the Third Reich: A History of Nazi Germany.* (New York: Simon and Schuster, 1960), p. 41.

83. Shirer, p. 417.

84. "Czechs Yield Area to Poles, Disorder Marks Sudeten Entry," *NYT,* October 2, 1938; "German Oppression Charged," *NYT,* June 5, 1938; "Sudetens Halt Firemen As Jews House Burns," September 9, 1938.

85. "Refugees Pour Into Prague," *NYT,* October 3, 1938.

86. "Terror Reported in Sudenten Areas," *NYT,* November 12, 1938; "Czechs Let Refugees in for 48-Hour Stay," *NYT,* November 14, 1938; "Ousted Jews Live in Sudeten Fields," *NYT,* October 20, 1938; "Jews Left to Starve Near Czech Frontier," *NYT,* October 21, 1938; "Czechs Order Relief for Trapped Jews," *NYT,* October 22, 1938; "Sokols Ask Prague to Expel Many Jews," *NYT,* October 24, 1938; "Nazis Bar Violence on the Czech Jews," *NYT,* March 19, 1938.

87. "Ousted Jews Live in Sudeten Fields," *NYT,* October 20, 1938; "Czechs Order Relief for Trapped Jews," *NYT,* October 22, 1938.

88. "Jews Left to Starve Near Czech Frontier," *NYT,* October 21, 1938.

89. "Czechs Will Expel Majority of Jews," *NYT,* February 2, 1939; Shirer, p. 448.

90. "Nazis Bar Violence on the Czech Jews," *NYT,* March 19, 1938.

91. "Suicide Club," *NYT,* August 5, 1939; "Nazis Bar Violence on the Czech Jews," *NYT,* March 19, 1938.

92. "Reich Curbs Jews in the Czech Area on Trade Dealings," *NYT,* June 22, 1939.

93. H.B. Fellinger, Enclosures 3 and 5, July 19, 1945, IBM Files; Connally, pp. E-9, E-11; Letter, Dr. J. Polak to IBM, September 16, 1937, NA RG59 611.60F31/311; also see Letter, IBM to Harry C. Hawkins, September 20, 1937, NA RG59 611.60F31/311.

94. Letter, Dr. G. Schneider to Thomas J. Watson, 1, July 4, 1945, IBM Files; H.B. Fellinger, Enclosure 3, July 19, 1945, IBM Files; Tabular graph, circa 1938, NA; Aly and Roth, p. 10.

95. Draft Letter, H.K. Chauncey to J.E. Holt, January 11, 1939, IBM Files.

96. Draft Letter, H.K. Chauncey to J.E. Holt, January 11, 1939, IBM Files.

97. Draft Letter, H.K. Chauncey to J.E. Holt, January 11, 1939, IBM Files.

98. Draft Letter, H.K. Chauncey to J.E. Holt, January 11, 1939, IBM Files.

99. Revised Letter, H.K. Chauncey to J.E. Holt, January 17, 1939, IBM Files.

100. Revised Letter, H.K. Chauncey to J.E. Holt, January 17, 1939, IBM Files.

101. Letter, W. Heidinger to J.E. Holt, January 20, 1938, IBM Files; "Tabulation of Profits 1938–39," IBM Files; Letter, H.K. Chauncey to O.E. Braitmayer, April 25, 1938, IBM Files.

102. Letter, W. Heidinger to J.E. Holt, January 20, 1938, IBM Files.

103. Letter, H. Rottke to J.C. Milner, April 11, 1938, IBM Files; also see Letter, H. Rottke to Thomas J. Watson, May 20, 1938, IBM Files.

104. Letter, J.C. Milner to H. Rottke, March 24, 1938, IBM Files; Letter, J. C. Milner to H. Rottke, April 6, 1938, IBM Files; see Letter, H. Rottke to J.C. Milner, April 11, 1938, IBM Files.

105. Letter, H. Rottke to J.C. Milner, April 11, 1938, IBM Files.

106. Letter, Thomas J. Watson to J.E. Holt, August 2, 1938, IBM Files; Letter, W. Heidinger to

H. Albert, November 29, 1938, IBM Files; "Report on Dehomag," Price Waterhouse, December 30, 1938, IBM Files; Letter, Thomas J. Watson to J.E. Holt, August 2, 1938, IBM Files; Draft Letter, H.K. Chauncey to J.E. Holt, January 11, 1939, IBM Files.

107. Protocol of the Special Meeting of the Shareholders of June 24, 1938, IBM Files.
108. "Tabulation of Profits 1938–39," IBM Files.
109. Letter, W. Heidinger to H. Albert, November 29, 1939, p. 4, IBM Files.
110. Letter, W. Heidinger to H. Albert, November 29, 1939, pp. 2, 4, IBM Files.
111. "Report on Dehomag," Price Waterhouse, December 30, 1938, pp. 8, 9, IBM Files.
112. "Report on Dehomag," Price Waterhouse, December 30, 1938, pp. 7, 9, IBM Files.
113. Memorandum, A.R. Van Doren to F.W. Nichol, January 3, 1939, IBM Files.
114. Letter, J.C. Milner to Thomas J. Watson, January 6, 1939, IBM Files.
115. Letter, J.C. Milner to Thomas J. Watson, January 6, 1939, IBM Files.
116. Letter, J.C. Milner to Thomas J. Watson, January 6, 1939, IBM Files.
117. Letter, J.C. Milner to N.F. Lenssen, December 5, 1938, p. 1, IBM Files.
118. Letter, H. Rottke to J.C. Milner, March 13, 1939, p. 1, IBM Files.
119. Letter, H. Rottke to J.C. Milner, March 13, 1939, p. 1, IBM Files.
120. Letter, J.C. Milner to H. Rottke, March 15, 1939, p. 1, IBM Files.
121. J.C. Milner to J.G. Phillips, March 15, 1939, IBM Files.
122. Letter, H.K. Chauncey to J.G. Phillips, March 21, 1939, IBM Files.
123. Radiogram, J.E. Holt to Thomas J. Watson, March 31, 1939, IBM Files; see Letter, W. Heidinger to Thomas J. Watson, April 26, 1939, p. 1, IBM Files.
124. Cablegram, Thomas J. Watson to J.E. Holt, March 31, 1939, IBM Files; Letter, J.C. Milner to J.G. Phillips, March 15, 1939, IBM Files; Letter, H. Albert to N.F. Lenssen, April 24, 1939, IBM Files; Letter, W. Heidinger to Thomas J. Watson, April 26, 1939, IBM Files.
125. Letter, W. Heidinger to Thomas J. Watson, April 26, 1939, IBM Files.
126. Letter, H. Rottke to Thomas J. Watson, May 20, 1939, IBM Files.
127. Letter, H. Rottke to Thomas J. Watson, September 9, 1939, IBM Files; see Letter, Thomas J. Watson to H. Rottke, September 13, 1939, IBM Files; Letter, H. Rottke to Thomas J. Watson, September 9, 1939, IBM Files; see Telephone Notes of Thomas J. Watson and H. Rottke's Conversation with J.W. Schotte, September 29, 1939, IBM Files.

VII: DEADLY COUNT

1. "Reich Census on May 17," *NYT,* April 4, 1939; also see "Reich to Take Census of Her 80 Millions," *NYT,* May 17, 1939; "National Registry in Germany," Sir. N. Henderson to Foreign Office, February 14, 1939, PRO FO 371/23006.
2. "Reich to Take Census of Her 80 Millions," *NYT,* May 17, 1939.
3. "Reich Housing Laws Segregate Jews," *NYT,* May 4, 1939.
4. RMBliV (1938), pp. 369f cited in Götz Aly and Karl Heinz Roth, *Die restlose Erfassung: Volkszählen, Identifizieren, Aussondern im Nationalsozialismus* (Berlin: Rotbuch Verlag, 1984), p. 24, fn16.
5. "Aus dem Volkszählungshaus in Berlin," *Der Stromkreis* (Werkzeitschrift DEHOMAG), Berlin, 66 (February 1940): 1–8, cited in Friedrich W. Kistermann, "Locating the Victims: The Nonrole of Punched Card Technology and Census Work," *IEEE Annals of the History of Computing,* 19:2 (April–June 1997); Hollerith-Tabelliermaschine D-11 mit Zähleinrichtung (D 11 VZ), (Berlin: Dehomag, 1939) cited in Kistermann, "Locating the Victims: The Nonrole of Punched Card Technology and Census Work"; Letter, J.G. Johnston to J.E. Holt, June 14, 1938, Department of Justice, War Division, Economic Warfare Section, NA RG60; also see Biehler, "Lochkartenmaschinen im Dienste der Reichsstatistik," *Allgemeines Statistisches Archiv (ASA)* 28 (1938/39): 90ff, 93.
6. RMBliV (1938), p. 369f cited in Aly and Roth, p. 24, fn16.
7. "National Registry in Germany," Sir. N. Henderson to Foreign Office, February 14, 1939, PRO FO 371/23006; ZSTAP/M, Rep. 77, Tit. 343, Volume 1, No. 107 cited in Aly and Roth, p. 23, fn17.
8. Kistermann, "Locating the Victims: The Nonrole of Punched Card Technology and Census Work"; Klaus Drobisch, "Die Judenreferate des geheimen Staatspolizeiamtes und des

Sicherheitsdientes der SS 1933 bis 1939," *Jahrbuch für Antisemitismusforschung,* 1993, p. 2 cited in Saul Friedländer, *Nazi Germany and the Jews: Vol. 1: The Years of Persecution, 1933–1939,* (New York: HarperCollins, 1997), p. 199 fn77.

9. Kistermann, "Locating the Victims: The Nonrole of Punched Card Technology and Census Work."

10. Aly and Roth, 20; Kistermann, "Locating the Victims: The Nonrole of Punched Card Technology and Census Work."

11. Kistermann, "Locating the Victims: The Nonrole of Punched Card Technology and Census Work"; Klaus Drobisch, "Die Judenreferate des Geheimen Staatspolizeiamtes und des Sicherheitsdientes der SS 1933 bis 1939," *Jahrbuch für Antisemitismusforschung,* 1993, p. 2, cited in S. Friedländer, *Nazi Germany and the Jews,* p. 199 fn77.

12. Letter, Statistical Office for Reich Gau Ostmark to Reich Kommisar for Reunion, December 15, 1939, in "Translation of Document 1948-PS," *Nazi Conspiracy and Aggression, Vol. IV: Office of United States Chief of Counsel for Prosecution of Axis Criminality* (Washington, D.C.: U.S. Government Printing Office, 1946), pp. 566–590, NA RG 238.

13. Bruno Blau, "The Jewish Population of Germany 1939–1945," *Jewish Social Studies,* pp. 11–172; Letter, Statistical Office for Reich Gau Ostmark to Reich Kommisar for Reunion, December 15, 1939, in "Translation of Document 1948-PS," *Nazi Conspiracy and Aggression, Vol. IV: Office of United States Chief of Counsel for Prosecution of Axis Criminality* (Washington, D.C.: U.S. Government Printing Office, 1946), p. 588, NA RG 238.

14. Edwin Black, *The Transfer Agreement: The Dramatic Story of the Pact Between the Third Reich & Jewish Palestine* (New York: Macmillan, 1984; Washington, D.C.: Dialog Press, 1999), pp. 260–262; Frank Stoakes, "The Supervigilantes: The Lebanese Kataeb Party As Builder, Surrogate, and Defender of the State," *Middle Eastern Studies* 11:3 (October 1975), pp. 215–236, cited in Rex Brynen, *Sanctuary and Survival: The PLO in Lebanon* (Boulder: Westview Press, 1990).

15. Helmut Krausnick et al., *Anatomy of the SS State,* transl. Richard Barry et al. (New York: Walker and Company, 1968), p. 541; "Nazis Urged to Maintain Race Purity," *NYT,* September 3, 1940; "Goering Threatens Jews on Boycott," *NYT,* September 3, 1937.

16. "Migration Register Is Started in Germany," *NYT,* June 22, 1939; "Goering Threatens Jews on Boycott," *NYT,* September 3, 1937.

17. "Czechs Still Wait for Guarantees," *NYT,* February 21, 1939.

18. "Sofia Decree Limits Civil Rights of Jews," *NYT,* October 9, 1940; "Rumanian Premier Acts Against Jews," *NYT,* July 31, 1937; "Wider Threats Reported," *NYT,* March 25, 1939; "Polish Jews Fear Fate for Germany," *NYT,* January 26, 1937; "Czechs Still Wait for Guarantees," *NYT,* February 21, 1939; "Hungary Planning to Take Jews Lands," *NYT,* January 13, 1939; also see "Jewish Influence Scored," *NYT,* December 31, 1937; "For Strict Ban on Jews," *NYT,* April 22, 1939; "Modifies Anti-Jewish Act," *NYT,* April 3, 1939; "Curb on Jews Held Official in Poland," *NYT,* April 22, 1937; "Polish Jews Fear Fate of Germany's," *NYT,* January 26, 1937; "Polish Jews Held in Immediate Need," *NYT,* February 26, 1937; "Warsaw Students Bar Gate to Jews," *NYT,* January 29, 1937; "Poland Presses Jewish Migration," *NYT,* February 9, 1937; "Polish Jews Offer Solution of Plight," *NYT,* February 10, 1937; "More Riots at Universities," *NYT,* February 12, 1937.

19. Letter, C. Fust to *Reichssippenamt,* June 29, 1936, BA R1509/555.

20. Meeting Minutes of Breslau Party Comrades, July 2, 1936, NA RG242, T-175, Reel 410, Frames 2934957–58; Aly and Roth, 74.

21. "Sales School Is Opened," *NYT,* July 15, 1936; "Confidential Report on Our Dealings with War Ministries in Europe," J.W. Schotte to L.H. La Motte, p. 1, circa spring 1940, Department of Justice, War Division, Economic Warfare Section, NA RG60; see Letter, H. Rottke to Thomas J. Watson, September 9, 1939, IBM Files.

22. "Monthly Average Card Cost and Selling Price Per Country, Three Months Ended March 31, 1939," Department of Justice, War Division, Economic Warfare Section, NA RG60.

23. "Aryan to Be Dropped by Reich Law Texts," *NYT,* February 17, 1939.

24. "Japan Withdraws Parley Bid," *NYT,* January 27, 1938; Letter, Thomas J. Watson to Franklin D. Roosevelt, June 9, 1939, NA RG59 600.00171/399.

25. Memorandum, William D. Hassett to Cordell Hull, June 13, 1939, NA RG59 600.00171/ 399.
26. Letter, Thomas J. Watson to Franklin D. Roosevelt, July 5, 1939, p. 1, NA RG59 600.00171/ 402.
27. Letter, Thomas J. Watson to Franklin D. Roosevelt, July 5, 1939, p. 1, NA RG59 600.00171/ 402.
28. "Terrors of Nazis Related by Benes," *NYT,* June 3, 1939. Shirer, p. 448.
29. "Terrors of Nazis Related by Benes," *NYT,* June 3, 1939.
30. "Terrors of Nazis Related by Benes," *NYT,* June 3, 1939.
31. Broadcast Transcript, Station WJZ, June 29, 1939, p. 8, NA RG59 600.00171/402; Transcript, Closing Address, Thomas J. Watson to ICC Congress, July 1, 1939, p. 3, NA RG59 600.00171/402.
32. Letter, Thomas J. Watson to Franklin D. Roosevelt, July 5, 1939, NA RG59 600.00171/402.
33. See Franklin D. Roosevelt's "Memorandum for the State Department for Preparation of Reply for My Signature," July 15, 1939, from State Department's Adviser on Political Relations, Division of International Conferences, and Division of European Affairs; also see Note, Division of Protocol to Fenstermacher, Department of State, July 16, 1939, NA RG59 600.00171/402; also see Note, Adviser on International Economic Affairs, Department of State, July 21, 1939, NA RG59 600.00171/402.
34. Draft Letter, Franklin D. Roosevelt to Thomas J. Watson, circa July 22, 1939, and see accompanying memos July 19–22, 1939, NA RG59 600.00171/402.
35. Review Memo, J. Hickerson to Reviewers, Department of State, Division of European Affairs, July 19, 1939, NA RG59 600.00171/402, 600.00171/405.2
36. Memorandum, Stinebower, Department of State, Advisor on International Economic Affairs, July 20, 1939, NA RG59 600.00171/402.
37. Memo, Department of State, Assistant Secretary, October 6, 1939, NA RG59 600.00171/402.
38. William L. Shirer, *The Rise and Fall of the Third Reich: A History of Nazi Germany.* (New York: Simon and Schuster, 1960), pp. 594–595, 597.
39. "Hitler in Warsaw, Cites It As Warning," *NYT,* October 6, 1939; see Shirer, p. 597.
40. "250,000 Jews Listed As Dead in Poland," *NYT,* January 23, 1940; "Sikorski Calls Nazis Barbarians in Poland," NYT, November 30, 1939; also see "Polish Atrocities Charged by Nazis," *NYT,* September 9, 1939.
41. Raul Hilberg, *The Destruction of the European Jews* (New York: Quadrangle Books, 1961, Harper Colophon Books, 1979), p. 126; Notes for an Oral Report, prepared by Blaskowitz, February 6, 1940, NO-3011 cited in Hilberg, *The Destruction of the European Jews,* p. 127; see "Nazis Hint Purge of Jews in Poland," *NYT,* September 13, 1939.
42. "Nazis Hint Purge of Jews in Poland," *NYT,* September 13, 1939.
43. Letter, H. Rottke to Thomas J. Watson, September 9, 1939, IBM Files.
44. Robert Sobel, *IBM: Colossus in Transition* (New York: Truman Talley Books, 1981), pp. 80, 86; James W. Cortada, *Before the Computer: IBM, NCR, Burroughs, and Remington Rand and the Industry They Created, 1865–1956* (Princeton, NJ: Princeton University Press, 1993), p. 134; James Connally, *History of Computing in Europe* (IBM World Trade Corporation, circa 1967), pp. E-11, E-13; see Emerson W. Pugh, *Building IBM: Shaping an Industry and Its Technology* (Cambridge: The MIT Press, 1995), p. 53, plus attached photo; Letter, H. Rottke to Thomas J. Watson, September 9, 1939, IBM Files.
45. Cortada, 134.
46. Sobel, 80; Dehomag Notes on Telephonic Discussions with Geneva, September 29, 1939, IBM Files; Letter, H. Rottke to Thomas J. Watson, September 9, 1939, plus attached statement, IBM Files.
47. Letter, Thomas J. Watson to H. Rottke, date-stamped September 13, 1939, IBM Files.
48. Letter, Thomas J. Watson to H. Rottke, date-stamped September 13, 1939, IBM Files; Letter, Watson's Secretary to J.C. Milner, September 13, 1939, IBM Files; Letter, J.C. Milner to J.G. Phillips, Geneva, March 15, 1939, IBM Files; Letter, J.C. Milner to H.K. Chauncey, April 6, 1938, IBM Files; Letter, H. Rottke to J.C. Milner, April 11, 1938, IBM Files.

49. Letter, H. Rottke to Thomas J. Watson, November 17, 1939, IBM Files; Dehomag Notes on Telephonic Discussions with Geneva, September 29, 1939, p. 1, IBM Files; Connally, pp. 43, E-15.

50. Dehomag Notes on Telephonic Discussions with Geneva, September 29, 1939, IBM Files.

51. Dehomag Notes on Telephonic Discussions with Geneva, September 29, 1939, IBM Files.

52. Dehomag Notes on Telephonic Discussions with Geneva, p. 2, September 29, 1939, IBM Files.

53. Letter and Attached Statement, H. Rottke to Thomas J. Watson, September 9, 1939, IBM Files.

54. Express Letter, Heydrich to *Einsatzgruppen*, September 21, 1939, USHMM Folder B; Reinhard Heydrich, Implementation Order No.1 for the Regulation of October 26, 1939 for the Introduction of Forced Labor for the Jewish Population in the Government-General, December 11, 1939, VBIGG, 1939, pp. 231–232 cited in Arad et al., eds., *Documents on the Holocaust*, trans. Lea Ben Dor (Lincoln: University of Nebraska Press, 1981; Bison Books, 1999), pp. 179–180.

55. Express Letter, Heydrich to *Einsatzgruppen*, September 21, 1939, USHMM Folder B; Heydrich, Implementation Order No.1 for the Regulation of October 26, 1939, for the Introduction of Forced Labor for the Jewish Population in the Government-General, December 11, 1939, VBIGG, 1939, pp. 231–232 cited in Arad et al., pp. 179–180.

56. Express Letter, Heydrich to *Einsatzgruppen*, September 21, 1939, USHMM Folder B; Heydrich, Implementation Order No.1 for the Regulation of October 26, 1939, for the Introduction of Forced Labor for the Jewish Population in the Government-General, December 11, 1939, VBIGG, 1939, pp. 231–232 cited in Arad et al., pp. 179–180.

57. Express Letter, Heydrich to *Einsatzgruppen*, September 21, 1939, p. 2, USHMM Folder B; Heydrich, Implementation Order No.1 for the Regulation of October 26, 1939 for the Introduction of Forced Labor for the Jewish Population in the Government-General, December 11, 1939, VBIGG, 1939, pp. 231–232 cited in Arad et al., pp. 179–180.

58. Express Letter, Heydrich to *Einsatzgruppen*, September 21, 1939, pp. 2–3, USHMM Folder B; Heydrich, Implementation Order No.1 for the Regulation of October 26, 1939, for the Introduction of Forced Labor for the Jewish Population in the Government-General, December 11, 1939, VBIGG, 1939, pp. 231–232 cited in Arad et al., pp. 179–180.

59. Express Letter, Heydrich to *Einsatzgruppen*, September 21, 1939, pp. 3–4, USHMM Folder B; Heydrich, Implementation Order No.1 for the Regulation of October 26, 1939, for the Introduction of Forced Labor for the Jewish Population in the Government-General, December 11, 1939, VBIGG, 1939, pp. 231–232 cited in Arad et al., pp. 179–180.

60. Express Letter, Heydrich to *Einsatzgruppen*, September 21, 1939, pp. 3–4, USHMM Folder B; Heydrich, Implementation Order No.1 for the Regulation of October 26, 1939, for the Introduction of Forced Labor for the Jewish Population in the Government-General, December 11, 1939, VBIGG, 1939, pp. 231–232 cited in Arad et al., pp. 179–180.

61. Express Letter, Heydrich to *Einsatzgruppen*, September 21, 1939, pp. 3–4, USHMM Folder B; Heydrich, Implementation Order No.1 for the Regulation of October 26, 1939, for the Introduction of Forced Labor for the Jewish Population in the Government-General, December 11, 1939, VBIGG, 1939, pp. 231–232 cited in Arad et al., pp. 179–180.

62. Aly and Roth, pp. 83, 85.

63. Raul Hilberg et al., eds., *The Warsaw Diary of Adam Czerniakow*, transl. Stanislaw Staron (New York: Stein and Day, 1979), p. 76; Isaiah Trunk, *Judenrat: The Jewish Councils in Eastern Europe Under Nazi Occupation* (New York: Macmillan, 1972; Lincoln: University of Nebraska Press, 1972), p. 1; Yisrael Gutman, *Resistance: The Warsaw Ghetto Uprising* (New York: Houghton Mifflin Co., 1994), opposite p. 107.

64. Hilberg et al., pp. 78, 79, 80, 81.

65. Abraham I. Katsh, ed. and transl., *The Warsaw Diary of Chaim A. Kaplan* (New York: Collier Books, 1965), p. 52.

66. Hilberg et al., pp. 81–86.
67. Turkin, "Polish Territory Occupied by Union of Soviet Socialist Republics in September 1939," PRO FO 371/24470/C1523/116/55; Hilberg et al., p. 28.
68. Hilberg et al., pp. 54, 84; see photo, "SS Man Publicly Humiliating a Religious Jew in Warsaw," Bildarchiv Preussischer Kulturbesitz (Berlin, Germany, 1939); see Katsh, p. 54.
69. Hilberg et al., p. 84.
70. Hilberg et al., p. 84.
71. Hilberg et al., pp. 85, 90.
72. Hilberg et al., pp. 85, 87, 90.
73. Hilberg et al., pp. 85, 86.
74. Katsh, p. 55.
75. Katsh, p. 57.
76. Katsh, p. 59.
77. Katsh, p. 86.
78. Kenneth Barker, ed., *The NIV Study Bible* (Grand Rapids, MI: Zondervan Publishing House, 1995), p. 604.
79. Hilberg et al., p. 86.
80. Hilberg et al., p. 86; Joseph Kermish, ed., *To Live with Honor and Die with Honor: Selected Documents from the Warsaw Ghetto Underground Archives*, "O.S." [Oneg Shabbath], (Jerusalem: Yad Vashem, 1986), p. 137.
81. Hilberg et al., pp. 86–87.
82. Hilberg et al., pp. 90–91; "Jews' Plight Held Critical in Poland," *NYT*, December 10, 1939; Kermish, p. 138.
83. *Encyclopaedia Judaica*, s.v. "Warsaw," p. 342; Hilberg et al., pp. 59–60, 88; "Jews' Plight Held Critical in Poland," *NYT*, December 10, 1939; www2.dsu.nodak.edu/users/dmeier/Holocaust/deportations.html. Trunk, pp. 356, 382.
84. Connally, p. E-10.
85. Connally, p. E-10.
86. J.W. Schotte, Curriculum Vitae, circa 1940, Department of Justice, War Division, Economic Warfare Section, NA RG60; see Connally, p. 30.
87. J.W. Schotte, Curriculum Vitae, circa 1940, Department of Justice, War Division, Economic Warfare Section, NA RG60; see Connally, p. 30.
88. Connally, p. 30.
89. Connally, p. 30.
90. Connally, p. 30.
91. Connally, p. E-12, 31; H.B. Fellinger, Enclosure 4, p. 5, July 19, 1945, IBM Files; www.ibm.com website.
92. H.B. Fellinger, Enclosure 4, July 19, 1945, pp. 1, 5, 7, 11, IBM Files; Connally, p. E-12.
93. H.B. Fellinger, Enclosure 4, July 19, 1945, pp. 1, 6–7, IBM Files; Connally, p. E-12; CSDIC, "Secret Report: PW Intelligence Bulletin No. 2/57," April 25, 1945, section II, p. 4, NA RG226; "Confidential Report on Our Dealings with War Ministries in Europe," J.W. Schotte to L.H. La Motte, Appendix Item 2, circa spring 1940, Department of Justice, War Division, Economic Warfare Section, NA RG60.
94. H.B. Fellinger, Enclosure 4, July 19, 1945, p. 3, IBM Files; Connally, p. E-12.
95. H.B. Fellinger, Enclosure 4, July 19, 1945, pp. 4, 11, IBM Files; Connally, p. E-12; *Encyclopaedia Judaica*, s.v. "Warsaw," p. 342.
96. H.B. Fellinger, Enclosure 4, July 19, 1945, pp. 2 (subsection 1), 88–9, 15, IBM Files; Connally, p. E-12.
97. H.B. Fellinger, Enclosure 4, July 19, 1945, p. 9, IBM Files.
98. H.B. Fellinger, Enclosure 4, July 19, 1945, pp. 12–13, IBM Files.
99. H.B. Fellinger, Enclosure 4, July 19, 1945, pp. 12–13, IBM Files.
100. H.B. Fellinger, Enclosure 4, July 19, 1945, p. 9, IBM Files.
101. Correspondence to Author, July 14, 2000; H.B. Fellinger, Enclosure 4, July 19, 1945, p. 9, IBM Files; also see Letter and attached photo, *Zydowski Instytut Historyczny* (Jewish Historical Institute), July 14, 2000, and map #4 in Abraham Lewin, *A Cup of Tears: A Diary of the Warsaw Ghetto*, transl. Christopher Hutton (Oxford: Basil Blackwell), p. 4.

102. Trunk, pp. 172–175.
103. Aly and Roth, p. 10; see Trunk, pp. 259, 286; Aly and Roth, p. 11.
104. Aly and Roth, pp. 10–11.
105. Aly and Roth, pp. 10–11.
106. Aly and Roth, p. 11.
107. Aly and Roth, p. 11.
108. Aly and Roth, p. 80.
109. Letter, H. Rottke to Thomas J. Watson, December 6, 1939, IBM Files.
110. Dehomag Profit Statement, circa spring 1940, IBM Files.

VIII: WITH BLITZKRIEG EFFICIENCY

1. "How Hitler Has Changed the Map of Europe," *NYT,* June 2, 1940.
2. "Center of Rotterdam Devastated After Its Commander Surrendered," *NYT,* May 21, 1940; "Nazi Newsreel Shows Rotterdam in Flames," *NYT,* May 23, 1940; "Brussels Is Raided," *NYT,* May 10, 1940.
3. "Terrors' of Nazis Related by Benes," *NYT,* June 3, 1939; "Big Haul for Nazis in Dutch Invasion," *NYT,* May 16, 1940; "Transport of Jews in Stettin Reported," *NYT,* February 14, 1940; "Jewish Camp Set Up," *NYT,* September 30, 1939; "New Deportations of Jews," *NYT,* January 21, 1940; "Conscript Labor Put at 2,500,000 in Reich," *NYT,* February 2, 1940; "Big Haul for Nazis in Dutch Invasion," *NYT,* February 22, 1940; "Nazis Said to Remove Lublin Ghetto Plan," *NYT,* February 27, 1940; "Poles Charge Nazis Aim to End Nation," *NYT,* April 3, 1940.
4. "Poland Protests German 'Horrors,'" *NYT,* December 3, 1939; "Refugees Are Pouring Into England and France with Harrowing Tales," *NYT,* May 13, 1940; "Big Haul for Nazis in Dutch Invasion," *NYT,* May 16, 1940.
5. "Jews Said to Face Famine in Poland," *NYT,* November 6, 1939; "Fears for Polish Jews," *NYT,* January 22, 1940.
6. "Jews in Cracow Move to Ghettos," *NYT,* March 16, 1940.
7. H.B. Fellinger, Enclosure 3, July 14, 1945, IBM Files; Letter, Thomas J. Watson to H. Rottke, September 13, 1939, IBM Files; Letter, Dutch Consulate to Commission of Mobility of Law in War Time, December 4, 1940, DNA RG2.06.09 Box 7; see Letter, J.G. Phillips to Dutch Consulate U.S., September 17, 1940, and Letter, Dutch Consulate U.S. to Commission of Law in War Time, June 20, 1941, DNA RG2.06.09 Box 7; Letter, Commission of Mobility of Law in War Time to Dutch Consulate U.S., July 12, 1941, DNA RG2.06.09 Box 7; Letter, J.G. Phillips to Dutch Consulate, June 10, 1941, and see Letter, Commission of Mobility of Law in War Time to Dutch Consulate, April 16, 1941, DNA RG2.06.09 Box 7; also see Memorandum to Files Re: Application NY-203330, Department of Justice, War Division, Economic Warfare Section, NA RG60.
8. "Butler Sees Navy as Force for Peace," *NYT,* May 5, 1940.
9. "Foreigners Study in Company School," *NYT,* May 9, 1940.
10. "IBM Group Holds Busman's Holiday," "They Are All Coming on 12 Special Trains," *NYT,* May 13, 1940; Thomas J. Watson, Jr., and Peter Petre, *Father, Son & Co.: My Life at IBM and Beyond* (New York: Bantam Books, 1990), p. 84; "IBM Employees Dine," *NYT,* May 14, 1940; "Program for Today at World's Fair," *NYT,* June 23, 1940; see Letter, F.W. Nichol to Cordell Hull, April 15, 1939, NA RG59 811.607.
11. "They Are All Coming on 12 Special Trains," "IBM Group Holds Busman's Holiday," *NYT,* May 13, 1940.
12. "Confidential Report on Our Dealings with War Ministries of Europe," J.W. Schotte to L.H. La Motte, circa spring 1940, p. 1, Department of Justice, War Division, Economic Warfare Section, NA RG60.
13. "Confidential Report on Our Dealings with War Ministries of Europe," J.W. Schotte to L.H. La Motte, circa spring 1940, p. 1, Department of Justice, War Division, Economic Warfare Section, NA RG60.
14. "Confidential Report on Our Dealings with War Ministries of Europe," J.W. Schotte to L.H. La Motte, circa spring 1940, p. 1, Department of Justice, War Division, Economic Warfare Section, NA RG60.

15. "Confidential Report on Our Dealings with War Ministries of Europe," J.W. Schotte to L.H. La Motte, circa spring 1940, p. 1, Department of Justice, War Division, Economic Warfare Section, NA RG60.

16. "Confidential Report on Our Dealings with War Ministries of Europe," J.W. Schotte to L.H. La Motte, circa spring 1940, p. 1, Department of Justice, War Division, Economic Warfare Section, NA RG60.

17. "Confidential Report on Our Dealings with War Ministries of Europe," J.W. Schotte to L.H. La Motte, circa spring 1940, p. 2, Department of Justice, War Division, Economic Warfare Section, NA RG60.

18. "Confidential Report on Our Dealings with War Ministries of Europe," J.W. Schotte to L.H. La Motte, circa spring 1940, p. 2, Department of Justice, War Division, Economic Warfare Section, NA RG60.

19. "Confidential Report on Our Dealings with War Ministries of Europe," J.W. Schotte to L.H. La Motte, circa spring 1940, pp. 2, 4, Department of Justice, War Division, Economic Warfare Section, NA RG60.

20. "Confidential Report on Our Dealings with War Ministries of Europe," J.W. Schotte to L.H. La Motte, circa spring 1940, p. 2, Department of Justice, War Division, Economic Warfare Section, NA RG60.

21. "Confidential Report on Our Dealings with War Ministries of Europe," J.W. Schotte to L.H. La Motte, circa spring 1940, pp. 2–3, Department of Justice, War Division, Economic Warfare Section, NA RG60.

22. "Confidential Report on Our Dealings with War Ministries of Europe," J.W. Schotte to L.H. La Motte, circa spring 1940, p. 3, Department of Justice, War Division, Economic Warfare Section, NA RG60.

23. "Confidential Report on Our Dealings with War Ministries of Europe," J.W. Schotte to L.H. La Motte, circa spring 1940, p. 3, Department of Justice, War Division, Economic Warfare Section, NA RG60.

24. "Confidential Report on Our Dealings with War Ministries of Europe," J.W. Schotte to L.H. La Motte, Attachment, circa spring 1940, p. 5, Department of Justice, War Division, Economic Warfare Section, NA RG60.

25. "Confidential Report on Our Dealings with War Ministries of Europe," J.W. Schotte to L.H. La Motte, circa spring 1940, p. 6, Attachment, Department of Justice, War Division, Economic Warfare Section, NA RG60; see "Deutsche Hollerith Maschinen GmbH: Confidential Report 242," p. 2, IIA, submitted by Harold J. Carter, December 8, 1943, Department of Justice, War Division, Economic Warfare Section, NA RG60.

26. "Confidential Report on Our Dealings with War Ministries of Europe," J.W. Schotte to L.H. La Motte, circa spring 1940, p. 5, Attachment, Department of Justice, War Division, Economic Warfare Section, NA RG60.

27. "Confidential Report on Our Dealings with War Ministries of Europe," J.W. Schotte to L.H. La Motte, circa spring 1940, p. 5, Attachment, Department of Justice, War Division, Economic Warfare Section, NA RG60; Walther Lauersen, "Organisation und Aufgaben des Maschinellen Berichtwesens des Reichministers für Rüstung und Kriegsproduktion," December 5, 1945, pp. 3–4, BA R3/17a "Conscript Labor at 2,500,000 in Reich," *NYT,* February 2, 1941.

28. "Deutsche Hollerith Maschinen GmbH: Confidential Report 242," p. 2, IIA, submitted by Harold J. Carter, December 8, 1943, Department of Justice, War Division, Economic Warfare Section, NA RG60.

29. "Confidential Report on Our Dealings with War Ministries of Europe," J.W. Schotte to L.H. La Motte, circa spring 1940, p. 5, Attachment, Department of Justice, War Division, Economic Warfare Section, NA RG60.

30. "Confidential Report on Our Dealings with War Ministries of Europe," J.W. Schotte to L.H. La Motte, circa spring 1940, p. 5, Attachment, Department of Justice, War Division, Economic Warfare Section, NA RG60; Secret German Police Activities, Summary 4, p. 7, April 1940, PRO HW16/3.

31. Summary of Enemy Economic Developments #90, Ministry of Economic Warfare, June 4, 1940, p. 12, Item 61, PRO FO 337/440.

32. "Confidential Report on Our Dealings with War Ministries of Europe," J.W. Schotte to L.H. La Motte, circa spring 1940, p. 5, Attachment, Department of Justice, War Division, Economic Warfare Section, NA RG60.

33. Summary of Economic Developments #90, Ministry of Economic Warfare, June 4, 1940, p. 12, Item 65, PRO FO 337/440; H.J. Carter, Draft Interview Notes with J.W. Schotte, June 14–16, 1943, Department of Justice, War Division, Economic Warfare Section, NA RG60; see Lauersen, p. 15, BA R3/17a fol.1.

34. "Confidential Report on Our Dealings with War Ministries of Europe," J.W. Schotte to L.H. La Motte, circa spring 1940, p. 5, Attachment, Department of Justice, War Division, Economic Warfare Section, NA RG60; see CSDIC, "Secret Report: PW Intelligence Bulletin No. 2/57," April 25, 1945, section III, p. 13, NA RG226.

35. "Confidential Report on Our Dealings with War Ministries of Europe," J.W. Schotte to L.H. La Motte, circa spring 1940, p. 5, Attachment, Department of Justice, War Division, Economic Warfare Section, NA RG60; see CSDIC, "Secret Report: PW Intelligence Bulletin No. 2/57," April 25, 1945, section III, pp. 12–13, NA RG226; "Deutsche Hollerith Maschinen GmbH: Confidential Report 242," IIA, submitted by Harold J. Carter, December 8, 1943, Department of Justice, War Division, Economic Warfare Section, NA RG60.

36. "Confidential Report on Our Dealings with War Ministries of Europe," J.W. Schotte to L.H. La Motte, circa spring 1940, p. 5, Attachment, Department of Justice, War Division, Economic Warfare Section, NA RG60.

37. Lauersen, p. 15, BA R3/17a fol.1.

38. "Machines as of September 30, 1940," IBM Files.

39. "Machines as of September 30, 1940," IBM Files.

40. "Confidential Report on Our Dealings with War Ministries of Europe," J.W. Schotte to L.H. La Motte, circa spring 1940, p. 2, Department of Justice, War Division, Economic Warfare Section, NA RG60; H.B. Fellinger, General Report, August 8, 1945, p. 2, IBM Files.

41. Letter, IBM to H.K. Chauncey, October 20, 1941, RG60; see CSDIC, "Secret Report: PW Intelligence Bulletin No. 2/57," April 25, 1945, section III, pp. 12–13, NA RG226.

42. "Deutsche Hollerith Maschinen GmbH: Confidential Report 242," submitted by Harold J. Carter, December 8, 1943, Department of Justice, War Division, Economic Warfare Section, NA RG60; Pugh, p. 48: H.J. Carter, Draft Interview Notes with J.W. Schotte, June 14–16, 1943, Department of Justice, War Division, Economic Warfare Section, NA RG60.

43. Connally, pp. E-9–E-15; "Monthly Average Card Cost and Selling Price Per Country, Three Months Ended March 31, 1939," Department of Justice, War Division, Economic Warfare Section, NA RG60. Letter, J.G. Phillips to Netherlands Consulate General, September 17, 1940, DNA RG2.06.09 Box 7; H.J. Carter, Draft Interview Notes with J.W. Schotte, June 14–16, 1943, Department of Justice, War Division, Economic Warfare Section, NA RG 60.

44. J.W. Schotte, War Memorandum, April 1940, pp. 2–4, Department of Justice, War Division, Economic Warfare Section, NA RG60; NA RG242, T-73 Reel 8; Summary of Enemy Economic Developments #90, Ministry of Economic Warfare, June 4, 1940, p. 12, PRO FO 337/440.

45. NA RG242, T-73 Roll 8.

46. NA RG 242 T-73 Roll 8; Hümmer, "Die Aufbereitung der Volks- und Berufszählung 1933 im Hollerith-Lochkartenverfahren," Hollerith Nachrichten (HN) 28 (August 1933): 343; Böhlerwerk Card is author's copy; also see BA NS 48/6.

47. Böhlerwerk Card is author's copy.

48. BA NS 48/6.

49. Hümmer, p. 345; Lauersen, p. 15, BA R3/17a fol.1; "Deutsche Hollerith Maschinen GmbH: Confidential Report 242," pp. 3–4, submitted by Harold J. Carter, December 8, 1943, Department of Justice, War Division, Economic Warfare Section, NA RG60; Rudolf Lawin, "Die Auszählung einer Wohnungsbestandsaufnahme im Hollerith-Verfahren," HN 58 (February 1936): 773; "Reich Housing Law segregates Jews," NYT, May 5, 1939.

50. Rassenamt and Heiratsamt Cards, BA NS 48/6; Hümmer, p. 345; Böhlerwerk Card is author's copy; "Report on Deutsche Hollerith Maschinen GmbH: Confidential Report

242," p. 9, submitted by Harold J. Carter, Department of Justice, War Division, Economic Warfare Section, December 8, 1943, NA RG60.

51. "Card featuring POWs," NA RG 242, T-73, Reel 8.
52. "Card featuring POWs," NA RG 242, T-73, Reel 8.
53. "Card featuring POWs," NA RG 242, T-73, Reel 8.
54. CSDIC, "Secret Report: PW Intelligence Bulletin No. 2/57," section III, p. 13, NA RG226; "Oral Testimony of Jean-Frederic Veith," *The Avalon Project: Nuremberg Trial Proceedings, Vol. 6,* January 28, 1946, www.yale.edu/lawweb/avalon; schematic drawings, NA RG 242, T-73, Reel 8, Frames 1053289 and 1053381.
55. Dehomag Calculation of Bonus on Profits, February 16, 1940, IBM Files.
56. Letter, W.A. Pithie to F.C. Elstob, April 22, 1940, IBM Files.
57. "$5,996,482 Earned on Office Machines," *NYT,* July 26, 1940.
58. Transcript, American Committee of the International Chamber of Commerce, April 29, 1940, Hagley Accession 1960, U.S. Chamber of Commerce, Box 9, pp. 405, 410–412; "Van Zeeland Tells Business Key Role," *NYT,* April 30, 1940; "They Are All Coming on 12 Special Trains," *NYT,* May 13, 1940.
59. Transcript, American Committee of the International Chamber of Commerce, April 29, 1940, p. 405, Hagley Accession 1960.
60. Gallup Question, circa spring 1940, USGALLUP.051940.RK02B.
61. Letter, Cordell Hull to Thomas J. Watson, May 20, 1940, IBM Files; FBI, File No. 65–205, January 13, 1941, NA RG59 862.20211.
62. Letter, Cordell Hull to Thomas J. Watson, May 20, 1940, IBM Files.
63. "$3 Million for Dutch Relief," *NYT,* May 24, 1940.
64. "Sales School Is Opened," *NYT,* July 15, 1936; Connally, p. E-9; FBI, File No. 65–205, June 6, 1940, January 13, 1941, and attached material, Department of Justice, War Division, Economic Warfare Section, NA RG60 862.20211; "Leaders of Bund Indicted in New Jersey," *NYT,* October 12, 1940; "Nazis Aid Protesters," *NYT,* October 11, 1940; "Says Bund Mapped Wall St. Hangings," *NYT,* October 5, 1940.
65. FBI, File No. 862.20211, June 6, 1940, pp. 1–4, NA RG59 862.20211; FBI, Case Report, File No. 65–290, Karl Georg Ruthe, January 18, 1940, October 11, 1940, NA RG59 800.20211; FBI, Case Report, File No. 65–721, Karl Georg Ruthe, October 2, 1940, NA RG59 800.20211; FBI, Case Report, File No. 65–6344, Karl Georg Ruthe, February 13, 1941, NA RG59 800.20211.
66. FBI, Case Report, File No. 65–290, Georg Ruthe, October 11, 1940, April 8, 1941, NA RG59 800.20211; FBI, Case Report File No. 65–205, NA RG59 862.20211.
67. Letter, F.W. Nichol to Sumner Welles, June 10, 1940 NA RG 59 800.20211.
68. FBI, Case Report, File 65–290, Georg Ruthe, April 8, 1941, p. 2, NA RG 59 800.20211.
69. FBI, Case Report, File 65–290, Georg Ruthe, October 11, 1940, pp. 1, 2, April 8, 1941, NA RG59 800.20211.
70. FBI, Case Report, File 65–290, Karl Georg Ruthe, October 2, 1940, p. 1, October 11, 1940, p. 1, NA RG59 800.20211.
71. Letter, F.W. Nichol to Sumner Welles, June 10, 1940, NA RG59 800.20211.
72. Letter, F.W. Nichol to Sumner Welles, June 10, 1940, NA RG59 800.20211.
73. FBI, Case Report, File 65–721, Karl Georg Ruthe, October 2, 1940, NA RG 59 800.20211.
74. "200 Planes Drop 1,100 Bombs on Paris," *NYT,* June 4, 1940.
75. "'Better Learn German,' Nazi Says to a Brazilian," *NYT,* June 4, 1940.
76. "Refugee Describes Netherland Dread," *NYT,* June 7, 1940; "French Admit Loss," *NYT,* June 7, 1940; "From the European Cauldron," *American Hebrew,* June 7, 1940.
77. "1937 Hitler Decoration Is Returned by Watson," *NYT,* June 7, 1940; William Rodgers, *Think: A Biography of the Watsons and IBM* (New York: Stein and Day, 1969), p. 127.

IX: THE DEHOMAG REVOLT

1. Letter, H. Rottke to W. Heidinger, June 10, 1940, IBM Files.
2. Transcript, H.K. Chauncey Interview with K. Hummel, circa November 1940, IBM Files; Telephone Message, P. Taylor, August 19, 1940, IBM Files; *Völkischer Beobachter,* June 9, 1940, cited in Letter, H. Rottke to W. Heidinger, June 10, 1940, IBM Files.

3. Transcript, H.K. Chauncey Interview with K. Hummel, circa November 1940, p. 2, IBM Files; Letter, H. Rottke to Thomas J. Watson, June 10, 1940, pp. 1, 2, IBM Files; Telephone Message, P. Taylor, August 19, 1940, IBM Files.

4. Transcript, H.K. Chauncey Interview with K. Hummel, circa November 1940, p. 2, IBM Files; Memorandum, H.K. Chauncey to Thomas J. Watson, March 2, 1941, IBM Files.

5. Protocol, Dehomag Board Meeting, July 15, 1940, p. 2, IBM Files; Letter, Dehomag to P. Taylor, July 15, 1940, IBM Files.

6. Protocol, Dehomag Board Meeting, July 15, 1940, p. 2, IBM Files.

7. Protocol, Dehomag Board Meeting, July 15, 1940, p. 1, IBM Files.

8. Protocol, Dehomag Board Meeting, July 15, 1940, p. 2, IBM Files; Letter, Dehomag to P. Taylor, July 15, 1940, IBM Files.

9. Letter, Dehomag to P. Taylor, July 15, 1940, IBM Files.

10. Letter, Dehomag to P. Taylor, July 15, 1940, IBM Files.

11. Letter, Dehomag to P. Taylor, July 15, 1940, IBM Files.

12. Minutes, Dehomag Shareholder Meeting, July 29, 1940, pp. 2, 3, IBM Files.

13. Minutes, Dehomag Shareholder Meeting, July 29, 1940, p. 2, IBM Files.

14. H.J. Carter, Draft Interview Notes with J.W. Schotte, June 14–16, 1943, p. 20, Department of Justice, War Division, Economic Warfare Section, NA RG60; "Aus der Geschichte der Deutschen Hollerith Maschinen Gesellschaft," *Hollerith Nachrichten (HN)* 55 (November 1935): 730; also see Bradley E. Schaefer, "Conjunctions That Changed the World," *Sky & Telescope Magazine*, 1998, p. 33.

15. Memorandum, H.K. Chauncey, December 17, 1940, IBM Files; Transcript of August 19, 1940, Radiogram, P. Taylor to Thomas J. Watson, circa November 21, 1940, p. 3, IBM Files.

16. Minutes, Dehomag Shareholder Meeting, July 29, 1940, pp. 2, 3, IBM Files.

17. Summary of Enemy Economic Developments, #110, Ministry of Economic Warfare, p. 9, October 22, 1941, PRO FO/837/441; H.J. Carter, Draft Interview Notes with J.W. Schotte, June 14–16, 1943, p. 9, Department of Justice, War Division, Economic Warfare Section, NA RG60; "Deutsche Hollerith Maschinen GmbH: Confidential Report 242," pp. 1, 4, 6, 9, submitted by Harold J. Carter, December 8, 1943, Department of Justice, War Division, Economic Warfare Section, NA RG60; "Inventory of Card Printing Machinery in Foreign Countries of December 1941," circa 1942, p. 37, Department of Justice, War Division, Economic Warfare Section, NA RG60; "CEC Quarterly Report, Fourth Quarter 1942," Department of Justice, War Division, Economic Warfare Section, NA RG60.

18. Cablegram, W.C. Lier to H.K. Chauncey, July 14, 1941, IBM Files; "Deutsche Hollerith Maschinen GmbH: Confidential Report 242," pp. 6, 8, 10, submitted by Harold J. Carter, December 8, 1943, Department of Justice, War Division, Economic Warfare Section, NA RG60; H.J. Carter, Draft Interview Notes with J.W. Schotte, June 14–16, 1943, p. 9, Department of Justice, War Division, Economic Warfare Section, NA RG60.

19. Letter, SS-Major Dreher to Inspector for Statistics, November 30, 1942, BA NS 48/6; "Deutsche Hollerith Maschinen GmbH: Confidential Report 242," p. 4, submitted by Harold J. Carter, December 8, 1943, Department of Justice, War Division, Economic Warfare Section, NA RG60; Cablegram, W.C. Lier to H.K. Chauncey, July 14, 1941, IBM Files; "Tool-machines Already Ordered for the Sindelfingen Factory," December 1, 1937, pp. 1–3, Department of Justice, War Division, Economic Warfare Section, NA RG60; "Proposal Regarding a Survey of Materials Stored in the RuS Main Office on Genetics and Population Policy," November 11, 1942, p.2, BA NS 48/6.

20. "Proposal Regarding a Survey of Materials Stored in the RuS Main Office on Genetics and Population Policy," November 11, 1942, p. 2, BA NS 48/6.

21. "Proposal Regarding a Survey of Materials Stored in the RuS Main Office on Genetics and Population Policy," November 11, 1942, p. 2, BA NS 48/6.

22. "Proposal Regarding a Survey of Materials Stored in the RuS Main Office on Genetics and Population Policy," November 11, 1942, pp. 1, 3, 4, BA NS 48/6.

23. Letter, SS-Major Dreher to Inspector for Statistics, November 30, 1942, BA NS 48/6.

24. NA RG242, T-73 Reel 11 RmfRvK/297; "Demands of CEC," circa June 1944, pp. 1, 4, 5, NA RG242 T73, Reel 8, RmfRuK/173, Frames 1057532, 1057535, 1057536; Letter,

Maschinelles Berichtwesen to Herbst, August 3, 1944, NA RG242, T-73 Reel 8, RmfRvK/173; List of Machines in Contract of German Military High Command, September 5, 1941, NA RG242, T73 Reel 11, Frames 1057616–1057617; also see Letter, P. Taylor to F.W. Nichol, August 20, 1940, p. 2, IBM Files.

25. Letter, P. Taylor to F.W. Nichol, August 20, 1940, p. 2, IBM Files; James Connally, *History of Computing in Europe* (IBM World Trade Corporation, circa 1967), pp. 33, 34; see Letter, W.C. Lier to H.K. Chauncey, October 10, 1941, pp. 6, 7, IBM Files; "CEC I.B.M. Subsidiary in France: Confidential Report 332," p. 2, submitted by Harold J. Carter, April 10, 1944, Department of Justice, War Division, Economic Warfare Section, NA RG60; Groupe Bull Chronology perso.club-internet.fr/febcm/english/chronoa3.htm, pp. 1–2.

26. Memorandum, H. Albert to H.K. Chauncey, circa Fall 1940, pp. 3–4, IBM Files.

27. Memorandum, H. Albert to H.K. Chauncey, circa Fall 1940, p. 4, IBM Files.

28. Memorandum, H. Albert to H.K. Chauncey, circa Fall 1940, pp. 3–4, IBM Files.

29. Letter, P. Taylor to F.W. Nichol, August 20, 1940, p. 2, IBM Files.

30. Transcript of August 19, 1940 Radiogram, P. Taylor to Thomas J. Watson, circa November 21, 1940, p. 1, IBM Files.

31. Transcript of August 19, 1940 Radiogram, P. Taylor to Thomas J. Watson, circa November 21, 1940, p. 1, IBM Files.

32. Transcript of August 19, 1940 Radiogram, P. Taylor to Thomas J. Watson, circa November 21, 1940, p. 1, IBM Files.

33. Transcript of August 19, 1940 Radiogram, P. Taylor to Thomas J. Watson, circa November 21, 1940, p. 1, IBM Files.

34. Transcript of August 19, 1940 Radiogram, P. Taylor to Thomas J. Watson, circa November 21, 1940, pp. 1–2, IBM Files.

35. Transcript of August 19, 1940 Radiogram, P. Taylor to Thomas J. Watson, circa November 21, 1940, p. 2, IBM Files.

36. Transcript of August 19, 1940 Radiogram, P. Taylor to Thomas J. Watson, circa November 21, 1940, pp. 2–3, IBM Files.

37. Transcript of August 19, 1940 Radiogram, P. Taylor to Thomas J. Watson, circa November 21, 1940, p. 5, IBM Files.

38. Transcript of August 19, 1940 Radiogram, P. Taylor to Thomas J. Watson, circa November 21, 1940, p. 5, IBM Files.

39. Memorandum, H.K. Chauncey to IBM NY, March 10, 1941, pp. 1, 4, 5, IBM Files; Letter, W.C. Lier to Harrison K. Chauncey, October 10, 1941, pp. 8–9, IBM Files.

40. Letter, P. Taylor to F.W. Nichol, August 20, 1940, p. 2, IBM Files; Bruce Clements, *From Ice Set Free: The Story of Otto Kiep* (New York: Farrar, Straus, Giroux, 1972), p. 162; Dehomag Meeting Minutes, August 31, 1940, p. 1, IBM Files.

41. Letter and Attachment, P. Taylor to F.W. Nichol, August 20, 1940, IBM Files.

42. Typescript Notes, H.K. Chauncey, December 19, 1940, IBM Files; H.K. Chauncey, "Program," October 20, 1940, p. 2, IBM Files.

43. Letter Attachment, P. Taylor to F.W. Nichol, August 20, 1940, IBM Files; Letter, Thomas J. Watson to W. Heidinger, October 2, 1940, p. 2, IBM Files.

44. Radiogram, P. Taylor to Thomas J. Watson, August 19, 1940, IBM Files; Letter, J.C. Milner to P. Taylor, July 15, 1940, IBM Files; Letter, P. Taylor to F.W. Nichol, September 12, 1940, IBM Files; Telephone Message Transcript, H.K. Chauncey to P. Taylor, September 30, 1940, IBM Files.

45. Memorandum, H. Albert to IBM NY, circa Fall 1940, p. 7, IBM Files.

46. Memorandum, H. Albert to IBM NY, circa Fall 1940, p. 8, IBM Files.

47. Memorandum, H. Albert to IBM NY, circa Fall 1940, p. 9, IBM Files.

48. Telephone Message, P. Taylor to IBM NY, September 30, 1940, p. 1, IBM Files; Transcript of Conversation between H.K. Chauncey and K. Hummel, circa 1940, p. 3, IBM Files; Letter, P. Taylor to F.W. Nichol, August 20, 1940, p. 1, IBM Files.

49. Telephone Message, P. Taylor to IBM NY, September 30, 1940, p. 1, IBM Files; Letter, P. Taylor to F.W. Nichol, September 12, 1940, IBM Files.

50. Transcript, Telephone Message, P. Taylor to IBM NY, September 30, 1940, p. 2, IBM Files.

51. Letter, P. Taylor to F.W. Nichol, September 12, 1940, pp. 1–2, IBM Files; Memorandum, H. Albert to IBM NY, circa Fall 1940, IBM Files.
52. Draft Letter, Thomas J. Watson to Dr. Hjalmar Schacht, circa 1937, p. 2, IBM Files.
53. Letter, P. Taylor to F.W. Nichol, September 12, 1940, p. 2, IBM Files.
54. Memorandum, H. Albert to IBM NY, circa Fall 1940, p. 7, IBM Files.
55. Memorandum, H. Albert to IBM NY, circa Fall 1940, p. 8, IBM Files; Confidential Memorandum, H. Albert to H.K. Chauncey, circa December 1940, p. 8, IBM Files; Letter, G.H. Hackworth to IBM NY, June 8, 1943, cited in "S.A. Watson Italiana: Confidential Report 287," Appendix A, p. 2, submitted by Harold J. Carter, February 21, 1944, Department of Justice, War Division, Economic Warfare Section, NA RG60.
56. H.B. Fellinger, Enclosure 1, July 10, 1945, IBM Files; H.B. Fellinger, Enclosure 2, July 14, 1945, IBM Files; Memorandum, H. Albert to IBM NY, circa Fall 1940, pp. 11–14, IBM Files.
57. H.B. Fellinger, General Report, August 8, 1945, pp. 1, 5, 6, IBM Files.
58. Transcript of Conversation between H.K. Chauncey and K. Hummel, circa 1940, IBM Files.
59. H.J. Carter, "Memorandum for the Files," May 16, 1944, pp. 2–3, Department of Justice War Division Economic Warfare Section NA RG 60; H.J. Carter, "Control in Business Machines," circa Spring 1943, p. 8, Department of Justice War Division Economic Warfare Section NA RG60.
60. Affidavit, R.A. Virgile, August 8, 1944, NA RG242 Frame 1053876; see H.B. Fellinger, Enclosure 7, August 4, 1945, pp. 1–3, IBM Files; Draft of contract between MB and CEC, circa 1940, NA RG242, T-73 Reel 11 RmfRuK/297.
61. Connally, pp. 31, 42, 44.
62. "Justice in 2 Weeks Seen by Boro Expert," *Brooklyn Eagle*, August 28, 1940, NA RG59, 740.00119 European War 1939/497; Letter, W.G. Wilson to City Editor, September 6, 1940, NA RG59, 740.00119 European War 1939/497; Letter, T.J. Watson to W. Ross, September 6, 1940, NA RG59, 740.00119 European War 1939/497; Letter, T.J. Watson to Cordell Hull, September 6, 1940, NA RG59, 740.00119 European War 1939/497; Letter, P.T. Culbertson to T.J. Watson, September 16, 1940, NA RG59, 740.00119 European War 1939/497; Letter, Adolf A. Berle, Jr., to J.E. Hoover, September 18, 1940, NA RG59, 740.00119 European War 1939/497. See Letter, M.F. Perkins to Cordell Hull, October 5, 1940, NA RG59, 164.12/2778; also see Letter, Cordell Hull to Stockholm, September 11, 1942, Department of Justice, War Division, Economic Warfare Section, NA RG60.
63. Letter, Thomas J. Watson to Franklin D. Roosevelt, April 27, 1937, NA RG59, 711.0012 AntiWar/1521; Letter, Cordell Hull to Thomas J. Watson, May 3, 1937, NA RG59, 711.0012 AntiWar/1521; see Letter, F.W. Nichol to Cordell Hull, October 21, 1938, NA RG59, 123C11/574; Letter, H.M. Cochran to Cordell Hull, August 26, 1937, p. 2, NA RG59, 651.003/715.
64. Letter, M. Cochran to Cordell Hull, August 26, 1937, p. 2, NA RG59, 651.003/715; Letter and Reply Letters, W.A. Burton to Harry C. Hawkins, September 20, 1937, NA RG59, 611.60F31/311; see Letter, U.S. Embassy Moscow to Cordell Hull, September 21, 1936, NA RG59, 661.1115 Amtorg Trading Corp./175; also see Letter, Frederick P. Hibbard to Cordell Hull, September 28, 1938, pp. 1–2, NA RG59, 160/1400.
65. Letter, Thomas J. Watson to Cordell Hull, February 12, 1937, NA RG59, 600.00171/369.
66. Letter, Loy W. Henderson to Cordell Hull, September 21, 1936, State Department No. 1906, NA RG59 661.1115 Amtorg Trading Corp./175 and Attachments; Letter and Attachments, Thomas J. Watson to Franklin D. Roosevelt, April 27, 1937, NA RG59, 711.0012 Anti-War/1521.
67. H.M. Cochran to Cordell Hull, August 26, 1937, NA RG59, 651.003/715; Report, W.A. Burton to Harry C. Hawkins, September 20, 1937, NA RG59 611.60F31/311.
68. Report No. 543, Frederick P. Hibbard to Cordell Hull, September 28, 1938, pp. 1–2, NA RG59.160/1400; Report No. 494 and Attached Enclosure, Francisco Ugarte to Cordell Hull, September 30, 1938, NA RG59.352.115/365.
69. Letter, F.W. Nichol to Cordell Hull, October 21, 1938, NA RG59.123C11/574.
70. Report No. 35, Florence J. Harriman to Cordell Hull, September 23, 1937, p. 2, NA RG59

032/1065; Report, Fletcher Warren to Cordell Hull, June 14, 1938, pp. 2–3, NA RG59, 660N.00171/1.

71. Letter, Harry A. Havens to Frances Muños, May 3, 1943, NA RG59 125.840H3/ 5–345.
72. Letter, Thomas J. Watson to W. Heidinger, October 2, 1940, IBM Files.
73. Letter, Thomas J. Watson to W. Heidinger, October 2, 1940, pp. 1, 2, 4, IBM Files.
74. Letter, Thomas J. Watson to W. Heidinger, October 2, 1940, pp. 1, 2, IBM Files.
75. Letter, Thomas J. Watson to W. Heidinger, October 2, 1940, p. 3, IBM Files.
76. Letter, Thomas J. Watson to W. Heidinger, October 2, 1940, pp. 2–3, IBM Files; H.K. Chauncey, "Program," October 20, 1940, pp. 5–6, IBM Files; "Memorandum Regarding Conversations Relating to the Interest of IBM in Dehomag," circa Winter 1941, pp. 1, 2, IBM Files; "Memorandum on Dehomag," circa 1940, pp. 1–2, IBM Files; H.K. Chauncey, Memorandum on Heidinger, circa 1940, IBM Files.
77. Letter, Thomas J. Watson to W. Heidinger, October 2, 1940, pp. 2–3, IBM Files.
78. Letter, Thomas J. Watson to W. Heidinger, October 2, 1940, p. 3, IBM Files.
79. Letter, Thomas J. Watson to W. Heidinger, October 2, 1940, p. 3, IBM Files.
80. Letter, Thomas J. Watson to W. Heidinger, October 2, 1940, pp. 3–4, IBM Files.
81. H.K. Chauncey, "Program," October 20, 1940, p. 2, IBM Files.
82. "Chauncey Departs from La Guardia," *Business Machines,* October 31, 1940, IBM Files.
83. "Chauncey Departs from La Guardia," *Business Machines,* October 31, 1940, IBM Files; "Hadassah Backs Fight of Britain," *NYT,* October 31, 1940; "50,000 French Jews Hit by New Decree," *NYT,* October 8, 1940; "Vichy Drafts Plan to Deal with Jews," *NYT,* October 2, 1940; "Beating of Aliens Laid to Iron Guard," *NYT,* October 22, 1940; "The International Situation," *NYT,* October 28, 1940.
84. "Chauncey Departs from La Guardia," *Business Machines,* October 31, 1940, IBM Files; H.K. Chauncey, "Program," October 20, 1940, p. 10, IBM Files; Transcript, Telephone Conversation between H.K. Chauncey and J.G. Phillips, January 31, 1940, p. 4, IBM Files.
85. "Chauncey Departs from La Guardia," *Business Machines,* October 31, 1940, IBM Files; Connally, p. 44.
86. H.K. Chauncey, Potential Memorandum for Dr. Albert and Dr. Kiep, January 1, 1941, IBM Files; Letter, H.K. Chauncey to Thomas J. Watson, December 13, 1940, pp. 1, 2, IBM Files.
87. H.K. Chauncey, Potential Memorandum for Dr. Albert and Dr. Kiep, January 1, 1941, IBM Files.
88. H.K. Chauncey, Typed Running Notes, January 1, 1941, IBM Files.
89. H.K. Chauncey, Typed Running Notes, circa November 1, 1941, IBM Files.
90. Transcript, H.K. Chauncey Interview with K. Hummel, circa November 1940, pp. 1, 2, IBM Files.
91. Transcript, H.K. Chauncey Interview with K. Hummel, circa November 1940, pp. 2, 3, IBM Files.
92. Transcript, H.K. Chauncey Interview with K. Hummel, circa November 1940, pp. 2, 3–4, IBM Files.
93. Transcript, H.K. Chauncey Interview with K. Hummel, circa November 1940, pp. 4, 6, IBM Files.
94. Cablegram, Thomas J. Watson to J.E. Holt, March 31, 1939, IBM Files; H.K. Chauncey, "Program," October 20, 1940, pp. 3, 4, 6–7, IBM Files.
95. Transcript, H.K. Chauncey Interview with K. Hummel, circa November 1940, pp. 4–8, IBM Files.
96. H.K. Chauncey, Typed Running Notes, December 17, 1940, p. 4, IBM Files; Memorandum, H. Albert to H.K. Chauncey, circa 1941, p. 2, IBM Files; William L. Shirer, *The Rise and Fall of the Third Reich: A History of Nazi Germany* (New York: Simon and Schuster, 1960), p. 259; Notes, H.K. Chauncey to W. Heidinger, p. 1, IBM Files; H.K. Chauncey, Notes on Conversation with Dr. Kimlich, January 30, 1941, IBM Files; Cablegram, H.K. Chauncey to IBM NY, November 29, 1940, pp. 1–2, IBM Files.
97. H. Albert, Memorandum and Handwritten Notes, circa December 1941, pp. 4–5, IBM Files; H.K. Chauncey, "Memorandum of Conversation with Dr. Veesenmayer," circa December 1940, IBM Files.

98. Letter, H.K. Chauncey to IBM NY, November 29, 1940, pp. 4–5, IBM Files.
99. Letter, H.K. Chauncey to IBM NY, November 29, 1940, p. 1, IBM Files.
100. Letter, H.K. Chauncey to IBM NY, November 29, 1940, p. 3, IBM Files.
101. Letter, H.K. Chauncey to IBM NY, November 29, 1940, pp. 1–2, IBM Files.
102. Letter, H.K. Chauncey to IBM NY, November 29, 1940, p. 2, IBM Files.
103. Letter, H.K. Chauncey to IBM NY, November 29, 1940, p. 3, IBM Files.
104. Letter, H.K. Chauncey to IBM NY, November 29, 1940, p. 3, IBM Files; H.K. Chauncey, Typed Running Notes, December 17, 1940, p. 6, IBM Files.
105. Letter, H.K. Chauncey to IBM NY, November 29, 1940, p. 4, IBM Files.
106. Letter, H.K. Chauncey to IBM NY, November 29, 1940, p. 5, IBM Files.
107. Letter, H.K. Chauncey to IBM NY, November 29, 1940, p. 5, IBM Files.
108. SS Personnel Identity Card of E. Veesenmayer, NA RG242 A3343-SSO; Lichterfelde Map, NA RG169, entry 128; H.K. Chauncey, "Memorandum of Conversation with Dr. Veesenmayer," circa 1940, IBM Files; Letter, H.K. Chauncey to IBM NY, November 29, 1940, pp. 4–5, IBM Files; State Department Special Interrogation Mission, Interrogation of Dr. E. Veesenmayer, October 5, 1945, p. 16, NA RG165, 390/35/15/07, entry 179; also see Gerald Reitlinger, *The Final Solution: The Attempt to Exterminate the Jews of Europe, 1939–1945* (Beechhurst Press, Inc., 1953; New York: Perpetua, 1961), pp. 417, 419; Raul Hilberg, *The Destruction of the European Jews* (New York: Quadrangle Books, Inc., 1961; Harper Colophon Books, 1979), pp. 436–437, 453, 458, 471, 513, 526–528, 530–533, 541, 543, 547–554; Memorandum, H. Albert to H.K. Chauncey, circa December 1940, p. 18, IBM Files; Letter, E. Veesenmayer to Chief of SS-Personnel Main Office, December 18, 1944, NA RG242 A3343-SSO; see Letter, E. Veesenmayer to Reichsführer SS, November 1, 1940, NA RG242 A3343-SSO; also see Letter, E. Veesenmayer to Reichsführer SS, July 1935, NA RG242 A3343-SSO; also see Letter, SS-Obersturmführer to E. Veesenmayer, May 13, 1942, NA RG242 A3343-SSO.
109. Handwritten Biography from E. Veesenmayer's SS Personnel file, NA RG242 A3343-SSO; State Department Special Interrogation Mission, Interrogation of Dr. E. Veesenmayer, October 5, 1945, pp. 1, 2, 16, NA RG165 Entry 179.
110. State Department Special Interrogation Mission, Interrogation of Wilhelm Keppler, October 23, 1944, pp. 5–6, 7, 8, 10, NA RG165 Entry 179.
111. State Department Special Interrogation Mission, Interrogation of Dr. E. Veesenmayer, October 5, 1945, p. 3, NA RG165 Entry 179.
112. State Department Special Interrogation Mission, Interrogation of Dr. E. Veesenmayer, October 5, 1945, p. 2, NA RG165 Entry 179; also see Hilberg, *Destruction of the European Jews*, p. 436 and Reitlinger, p. 417.
113. State Department Special Interrogation Mission, Interrogation of Dr. E. Veesenmayer, October 5, 1945, pp. 2, 4, NA RG165 Entry 179.
114. State Department Special Interrogation Mission, Interrogation of Dr. E. Veesenmayer, October 5, 1945, pp. 5–6, NA RG165 Entry 179; Telegram, Seyss-Inquart to Minister Schmidt, March 11, 1939, p. 2, NA NG 5135, p. 2; Hilberg, *Destruction of the European Jews*, p. 458.
115. State Department Special Interrogation Mission, Interrogation of Dr. E. Veesenmayer, October 5, 1945, pp. 8, 11, NA RG165, 390/35/15/07, Entry 179.
116. State Department Special Interrogation Mission, Interrogation of Dr. E. Veesenmayer, October 5, 1945, p. 9, NA RG165, 390/35/15/07, Entry 179; also see SM, Library, Facts, srpska-mreza.com/library/facts; Ruth Mitchell, *The Serbs Choose War* (New York: Doubleday, Doran & Co., Inc., 1943), pp. 254, 255; also see "The Ustashi in Croatia Support Hitler," North Park University, Department of History WebChron, East Europe, campus.northpark.edu/history/WebChron//EastEurope/Ustashe.html; also see "Serbian Prelate Charges Killing of 180,000 in Nazi Invaded Croatia," *NYT*, January 3, 1942.
117. H.K. Chauncey, "Memorandum of Conversation with Dr. Veesenmayer," circa 1940, IBM Files.
118. H. Albert, Unmarked Typed Note, circa 1940, IBM Files.
119. Memorandum to H.K. Chauncey, January 16, 1941, IBM Files; Letter, H.K. Chauncey to Thomas J. Watson, p. 1, December 13, 1940, IBM Files.

120. Letter, H.K. Chauncey to Thomas J. Watson, p. 3, December 13, 1940, IBM Files; Memorandum, H.K. Chauncey to H. Albert, p. 2, December 23, 1940, IBM Files.
121. Connally, p. 44; Jan Van den Ende, *Knopen, kaarten en chips. De geschiedenis van der automatisering bij het Centraal Bureau voon de Statistiek* (Amsterdam: CBS, 1991), p. 53; H.B. Fellinger, General Report, August 8, 1945, p. 3, IBM Files; Letter, H. Albert to H.K. Chauncey, circa December 1940, pp. 7, 14, IBM Files; H.B. Fellinger, Enclosure 6, Supplement I, July 25, 1945, p. 4, IBM Files; H.B. Fellinger, Enclosure 5, July 30, 1945, p. 1, IBM Files; Transcript, "Resume of Telephone Conversation between W.C. Lier and W. Borel of the CEC on October 14, 1941, at 10 A.M. and 4 P.M.," pp. 1–2, IBM Files; H.K. Chauncey, Typed Running Notes, December 17, 1940, p. 2, IBM Files; Transcript, H.K. Chauncey Interview with K. Hummel, circa November 1940, p. 7, IBM Files; "Deutsche Hollerith Maschinen GmbH: Confidential Report 242," p. 1, submitted by Harold J. Carter, December 8, 1943, Department of Justice, War Division, Economic Warfare Section, NA RG60; Paraphrase of Telegram Received, American Legation Stockholm to Secretary of State, April 30, 1943, Department of Justice, War Division, Economic Warfare Section, NA RG60.
122. "List of Papers, Political Affairs-France," p. 236, 1941, Department of Justice, War Division, Economic Warfare Section, NA RG60; Letter, O.E. Hoermann to James Johnson, April 30, 1942, Department of Justice, War Division, Economic Warfare Section, NA RG60; Letters, Sidney Homer, Jr. to C.C. McIvor, pp. 2, 3, Department of Justice, War Division, Economic Warfare Section, NA RG60; "CEC I.B.M. Subsidiary in France: Confidential Report 332," pp. 2, 12, submitted by Harold J. Carter, April 10, 1944, Department of Justice, War Division, Economic Warfare Section, NA RG60; "S.A. Watson Italiana: Confidential Report 287," p. 7, submitted by Harold J. Carter, February 21, 1944, Department of Justice, War Division, Economic Warfare Section, NA RG60.
123. Letter, J.E. Holt to F.H. Cowles, November 3, 1939, Department of Justice, War Division, Economic Warfare Section, NA RG60; Transcript, Telephone Conversation between H.K. Chauncey and J.G. Phillips, January 31, 1941, p. 4, IBM Files.
124. Letter, O.E. Hoermann to IBM Endicott, April 30, 1942, Department of Justice, War Division, Economic Warfare Section, NA RG60; "CEC Quarterly Report, Fourth Quarter 1942," Department of Justice, War Division, Economic Warfare Section, NA RG60; "CEC I.B.M. Subsidiary in France: Confidential Report 332," pp. 2, 3–5, 8, 9, submitted by Harold J. Carter, April 10, 1944, Department of Justice, War Division, Economic Warfare Section, NA RG60; "Card Exports from U.S.A.," circa 1942, Department of Justice, War Division, Economic Warfare Section, NA RG60.
125. "Card Exports from U.S.A.," circa 1942, Department of Justice, War Division, Economic Warfare Section, NA RG60; "S.A. Watson Italiana: Confidential Report 287," pp. 2, 6, submitted by Harold J. Carter, February 21, 1944, Department of Justice, War Division, Economic Warfare Section, NA RG60.
126. "CEC Quarterly Report, Fourth Quarter 1942," p. 17, Department of Justice, War Division, Economic Warfare Section, NA RG60.
127. Letter, H.K. Chauncey to Thomas J. Watson, December 13, 1940, p. 3, IBM Files.
128. H.K. Chauncey, Typed Running Notes, December 17, 1940 and December 8, 1940, p. 3, IBM Files.
129. Letter, H.K. Chauncey to Thomas J. Watson, pp. 2, 4, December 13, 1940, IBM Files.
130. Letter, H.K. Chauncey to Thomas J. Watson, pp. 2, 4, December 13, 1940, IBM Files; Confidential Memorandum, H. Albert to H.K. Chauncey, circa December 1940, p. 4, IBM Files.
131. Letter, H.K. Chauncey to Thomas J. Watson, pp. 2, 4, December 13, 1940, IBM Files; Confidential Memorandum, H. Albert to H.K. Chauncey, circa December 1940, p. 11, IBM Files.
132. H.K. Chauncey, "Outline Submitted for the Reorganization of Dehomag," circa 1940, p. 10, IBM Files.
133. H.K. Chauncey, "Outline Submitted for the Reorganization of Dehomag," circa 1940, p. 3, IBM Files.
134. Confidential Memorandum, H. Albert to H.K. Chauncey, circa December 1940, p. 11,

IBM Files; Transcript, Telephone Conversation between H.K. Chauncey and J.G. Phillips, January 31, 1940, p. 4, IBM Files.

135. W. Heidinger, "Memorandum to Advisory Committee," January 18, 1943, p. 10, IBM Files.
136. Telegram, E. Veesenmayer to Ribbentrop, April 11, 1941, NA NG 5875; also see Hilberg, *Destruction of the European Jews,* p. 453.
137. Letter, E. Veesenmayer and Benzler to Foreign Office, September 10, 1941, NA NG 3354; see Hilberg, *Destruction of the European Jews,* p. 437; also see State Department Special Interrogation Mission, Interrogation of Dr. E. Veesenmayer, October 5, 1945, pp. 8–9, NA RG165, 390/35/15/07, Entry 179.
138. Hilberg, *Destruction of the European Jews,* pp. 437–438, 440.
139. Hilberg, *Destruction of the European Jews,* p. 440; State Department Special Interrogation Mission, Interrogation of Dr. E. Veesenmayer, October 5, 1945, p. 10, NA RG165, 390/35/15/07, Entry 179.
140. Letter, Wagner to von Sonnleithner, July 21, 1943, NA NG 4749; Hilberg, *Destruction of the European Jews,* p. 471; Affidavit, Dieter Wisliceny, June 11, 1947, pp. 1–2, NA NG 1823; Memorandum, E. Veesenmayer, December 22, 1943, pp. 1–2, NA NG 4651.
141. State Department Special Interrogation Mission, Interrogation of Dr. E. Veesenmayer, October 5, 1945, p. 10, NA RG165, 390/35/15/07, Entry 179; Hilberg, *Destruction of the European Jews,* pp. 472, 530.
142. Telegram, E. Veesenmayer to Ambassador Ritter, June 8, 1944, p. 2, NA NG 5620; Hilberg, *Destruction of the European Jews,* p. 513; State Department Special Interrogation Mission, Interrogation of Dr. E. Veesenmayer, October 5, 1945, pp. 16–18, NA RG165, 390/35/15/07, Entry 179.
143. Hilberg, *Destruction of the European Jews,* p. 531; also see State Department Special Interrogation Mission, Interrogation of Dr. E. Veesenmayer, October 5, 1945, pp. 16–18, NA RG165, 390/35/15/07, Entry 179.
144. Hilberg, *Destruction of the European Jews,* pp. 535, 538.
145. Hilberg, *Destruction of the European Jews,* pp. 547, 548–553.
146. Hilberg, *Destruction of the European Jews,* p. 550.
147. Hilberg, *Destruction of the European Jews,* p. 552.
148. Hilberg, *Destruction of the European Jews,* pp. 552–3.
149. Handwritten List, "1938 Card Consumption of European Countries," Department of Justice, War Division, Economic Warfare Section, NA RG60; see "Confidential Memorandum NY 249-C (Supplemental): Location, Number and Use of All Business Machines in the City of Rome," Appendix A, pp. vii, viii, submitted by H.J. Carter, January 14, 1944, Department of Justice, War Division, Economic Warfare Section, NA RG60; also see "Confidential Memorandum NY 249-D: Use of Business Machines by the Italian State Railways," pp. 1–3, submitted by H.J. Carter, March 8, 1944, Department of Justice, War Division, Economic Warfare Section, NA RG60; also see H.J. Carter, "Miscellaneous Remarks Pertaining to the Installation of Business Machines and Applications of Punched Cards in the Balkan States," January 14, 1944, pp. 2, 3, 5, Department of Justice, War Division, Economic Warfare Section, NA RG60.
150. Handwritten List, "1938 Card Consumption of European Countries," Department of Justice, War Division, Economic Warfare Section, NA RG60; "Deutsche Hollerith Maschinen GmbH: Confidential Report 242," pp. 1, 3, submitted by Harold J. Carter, December 8, 1943, Department of Justice, War Division, Economic Warfare Section, NA RG60.
151. "Deutsche Hollerith Maschinen GmbH: Confidential Report 242," pp. 1, 3, submitted by Harold J. Carter, December 8, 1943, Department of Justice, War Division, Economic Warfare Section, NA RG60; "Confidential Memorandum NY 249-D: Use of Business Machines by the Italian State Railways," pp. 1–2, 4, 6, 8–9, submitted by H.J. Carter, March 8, 1944, Department of Justice, War Division, Economic Warfare Section, NA RG60; see H.J. Carter, "Miscellaneous Remarks Pertaining to the Installation of Business Machines and Applications of Punched Cards in the Balkan States," January 14, 1944, pp. 2, 3, 5, Department of Justice, War Division, Economic Warfare Section, NA RG60; Handwritten List, "1938 Card Consumption of European Countries," Department of Justice, War Division, Economic Warfare Section, NA RG60.

152. Handwritten List, "1938 Card Consumption of European Countries," Department of Justice, War Division, Economic Warfare Section, NA RG60; "Deutsche Hollerith Maschinen GmbH: Confidential Report 242," pp. 1, 3, submitted by Harold J. Carter, December 8, 1943, Department of Justice, War Division, Economic Warfare Section, NA RG60.

153. "Confidential Memorandum NY 249-D: Use of Business Machines by the Italian State Railways," p. 8, submitted by H.J. Carter, March 8, 1944, Department of Justice, War Division, Economic Warfare Section, NA RG60; "Deutsche Hollerith Maschinen GmbH: Confidential Report 242," p. 3, submitted by Harold J. Carter, December 8, 1943, Department of Justice, War Division, Economic Warfare Section, NA RG60; H.J. Carter, Interview with J.W. Schotte, June 14–16, 1943, p. 13, Department of Justice, War Division, Economic Warfare Section, NA RG60.

154. Handwritten List, "1938 Card Consumption of European Countries," Department of Justice, War Division, Economic Warfare Section, NA RG60.

155. H.B. Fellinger, Enclosure 4, July 19, 1945, p. 9, IBM Files; Handwritten List, "1938 Card Consumption of European Countries," Department of Justice, War Division, Economic Warfare Section, NA RG60.

156. H.J. Carter, "Miscellaneous Remarks Pertaining to the Installation of Business Machines," January 14, 1944, pp. 3–4, Department of Justice, War Division, Economic Warfare Section, NA RG60.

157. H.J. Carter, "Miscellaneous Remarks Pertaining to the Installation of Business Machines," January 14, 1944, p. 5, Department of Justice, War Division, Economic Warfare Section, NA RG60.

158. H.J. Carter, "Miscellaneous Remarks Pertaining to the Installation of Business Machines," January 14, 1944, p. 5, Department of Justice, War Division, Economic Warfare Section, NA RG60.

159. "Confidential Memorandum NY 249-D: Use of Business Machines by the Italian State Railways," p. 4, submitted by H.J. Carter, March 8, 1944, Department of Justice, War Division, Economic Warfare Section, NA RG60.

160. H.B. Fellinger, Enclosure 6, July 19, 1945, pp. 2–3, IBM Files.

161. H.B. Fellinger, Enclosure 6, July 19, 1945, pp. 2–3, IBM Files.

X: THE STRUGGLE TO STAY IN THE AXIS

1. "Reich Jews Sent to South France; 10,000 Reported Put Into Camp," *NYT,* November 9, 1940.

2. "Walls Will Enclose Warsaw Jews Today; 500,000 Begin 'New Life' in Nazi-Built Ghetto," *NYT,* November 26, 1940.

3. "Rumania Emerges From 'Revolution'; Death Toll Nearly 400, Wounded Exceed 300— Terror Reign Lasted for Eight Days," *NYT,* December 5, 1940.

4. "One Arrival on Liner Nyassar Tells of Cholera Killing Men in Concentration Camps in France," *NYT,* December 5, 1940.

5. "Property of Jews in Alsace Is Confiscated; Finer Furnishings Sent to Reich by Trainload," *NYT,* December 17, 1940

6. "Netherland Jews Must Register," *NYT,* January 14, 1941.

7. "300 Jews Reported Slain," *NYT,* January 25, 1941.

8. "Misery and Death in French Camps," *NYT,* January 26, 1941.

9. Memorandum, W.C. Lier, January 16, 1941, IBM Files; Draft Letter, K. Horak to White, December 3, 1941, Department of Justice, War Division, Economic Warfare Section, NA RG60.

10. Letter, W.C. Lier to C.R. Ogsbury, January 16, 1941, p. 2, IBM Files; H.K. Chauncey, Notes of Conversation with Dr. Kimlich, January 30, 1941, IBM Files.

11. Letter, H. Albert to N.F. Lenssen, January 27, 1941, IBM Files; Transcript, Telephone Conversation between H.K. Chauncey, C.R. Ogsbury, and J.G. Phillips, January 31, 1941, IBM Files.

12. Transcript, Telephone Conversation between H.K. Chauncey, C.R. Ogsbury, and J.G. Phillips, January 31, 1941, pp. 1–2, IBM Files.

13. Transcript, Telephone Conversation between H.K. Chauncey, C.R. Ogsbury, and J.G. Phillips, January 31, 1941, IBM Files.

14. Letter, J.H. Keeley, Jr., to H.K. Chauncey, September 29, 1941, IBM Files; see Transcript, Telephone Conversation between Thomas J Watson and S.E. Woods, September 17, 1941, IBM Files; Letter, S.E. Woods to H.K. Chauncey, September 3, 1941, IBM Files; Letter, Thomas J. Watson to P.T. Culbertson, January 8, 1941, NA RG59 662.1111/29.

15. James Connally, *History of Computing in Europe* (IBM World Trade Corporation, circa 1967), p. 25; *The Brooklyn Eagle*, August 28, 1940, cited in NA RG59 740.00119.

16. *The Brooklyn Eagle*, August 28, 1940, cited in NA RG59 740.00119.

17. Letter, Adolf A. Berle to J. Edgar Hoover, September 18, 1940, IBM Files; Letter, Thomas J. Watson to W.G. Ross, September 6, 1940, p. 2, NA RG59 740.00119.

18. Letter, Thomas J. Watson to W.G. Ross, September 6, 1940, pp. 1–2, NA RG59 740.00119.

19. Letter, W.G. Ross to City Editor of the *Brooklyn Eagle*, September 6, 1940, NA RG59 740.00119.

20. Letter, Thomas J. Watson to Cordell Hull, Sumner Welles, P.T. Culbertson, and W.G. Ross, September 6, 1940, NA RG59 740.00119.

21. Letter, M.F. Perkins to Cordell Hull, October 5, 1940, NA RG59 164.12/2778.

22. Letter, M.F. Perkins to Cordell Hull, October 5, 1940, NA RG59 164.12/2778.

23. Letter, M.F. Perkins to Cordell Hull, October 5, 1940, NA RG59 164.12/2778.

24. Letter, J.H. Keeley to H.K. Chauncey, September 29, 1941, IBM Files.

25. Memorandum, H.K. Chauncey to IBM NY, March 10, 1941, IBM Files; Statement of Fact by Dehomag, circa 1941, p. 2, IBM Files.

26. Memorandum, H.K. Chauncey to IBM NY, March 10, 1941, p. 1, IBM Files.

27. Memorandum, H.K. Chauncey to IBM NY, March 10, 1941, pp. 1, 3–4, IBM Files; Letter, W.C. Lier to H.K. Chauncey, October 10, 1941, p. 5, IBM Files.

28. Memorandum, H.K. Chauncey to IBM NY, March 10, 1941, p. 1, IBM Files.

29. Memorandum, H.K. Chauncey to IBM NY, March 10, 1941, p. 3, IBM Files.

30. Memorandum, H.K. Chauncey to IBM NY, March 10, 1941, pp. 4–5, IBM Files.

31. Memorandum, H.K. Chauncey to IBM NY, March 10, 1941, pp. 4–5, IBM Files; Transcript, H.K. Chauncey Interview with K. Hummel, circa November 1940, p. 1, IBM Files.

32. Letter, P. Taylor to B.J. Wallace, February 14, 1941, IBM Files; see Translation, Dehomag Letter to IBM NY, February 26, 1941, IBM Files; also see, Memorandum, J.C. Milner to Thomas J. Watson, May 23, 1941, IBM Files.

33. Letter, P. Taylor to B.J. Wallace, February 14, 1941, IBM Files; Letter, B.J. Wallace to K. Zimmermann, February 14, 1941, IBM Files; see Translation, Dehomag Letter to IBM NY, February 26, 1941, IBM Files; also see Letter, P. Taylor to F.C. Elstob, March 10, 1941, IBM Files.

34. *Foreign Commerce Weekly*, June 21, 1941, p. 499, cited in Letter, W.C. Lier to H.K. Chauncey, September 12, 1941, IBM Files.

35. Memorandum, W.C. Lier to Thomas J. Watson, May 23, 1941, IBM Files.

36. Transcript, Resume of Telephone Conversation between H.K. Chauncey and S.E. Woods, September 17, 1941, IBM Files; Letter, S.E. Woods to H.K. Chauncey, September 17, 1941, IBM Files; also see "Statement with Respect to Agreement with Stockholders of Deutsche Hollerith Maschinen, Gesellschaft, m.b.H," attached to Department of Treasury License Request, License No. NY-253046, circa 1941, IBM Files; Transcript, Resume of Telephone Conversation between S.E. Woods and H.K. Chauncey, October 27, 1941, and attached Treasury Department License No. NY-253046, October 21, 1941, IBM Files.

37. Treasury Department License No. NY-253046, September 18, 1941, IBM Files.

38. Letter, S.E. Woods to H.K. Chauncey, September 17, 1941, IBM Files; also see "Statement with Respect to Agreement with Stockholders of Deutsche Hollerith Maschinen, Gesellschaft, m.b.H," attached to Department of Treasury License Request, License No. NY-253046, circa 1941, IBM Files; Transcript, Resume of Telephone Conversation between S.E. Woods and H.K. Chauncey, October 27, 1941, IBM Files; see Letter, S.E. Woods to H.K. Chauncey, October 29, 1941, and attached Cablegram, October 28, 1941, IBM Files.

39. Letter, S.E. Woods to H.K. Chauncey, September 17, 1941, IBM Files; Telegram, IBM NY to S.E. Woods, September 18, 1941, IBM Files; "Statement with Respect to Agreement with Stockholders of Deutsche Hollerith Maschinen, Gesellschaft, m.b.H," attached to

Department of Treasury License Request, License No. NY-253046, circa 1941, IBM Files; IBM Application to Secretary of Treasury, License No. 223994, September 18, 1941, IBM Files; Transcript, Telephone Conversation between Thomas J. Watson and S.E. Woods, September 17, 1941, IBM Files; see Letter, W.C. Lier to J.C. Milner, August 29, 1941, IBM Files; Transcript, Telephone Conversation between H.K. Chauncey and S.E. Woods, October 27, 1941, IBM Files.

40. Letter, W.C. Lier to J.C. Milner, August 29, 1941, IBM Files.
41. Letter, W.C. Lier to J.C. Milner, August 29, 1941, IBM Files.
42. Cablegram of August 27, 1941, cited in Letter, W.C. Lier to J.C. Milner, August 29, 1941, IBM Files.
43. Cablegram of August 27, 1941, cited in Letter, W.C. Lier to J.C. Milner, August 29, 1941, IBM Files.
44. Letter, W.C. Lier to J.C. Milner, August 29, 1941, IBM Files.
45. Letter, S.E. Woods to H.K. Chauncey, September 3, 1941, IBM Files.
46. Letter, S.E. Woods to H.K. Chauncey, September 3, 1941, IBM Files.
47. Proxy Documents, September 16, 1941, IBM Files; Letter, W.C. Lier to H.K. Chauncey, October 10, 1941, p. 2, IBM Files.
48. Transcript, Telephone Conversation between Thomas J. Watson and S.E. Woods, September 17, 1941, IBM Files.
49. Letter, S.E. Woods to H.K. Chauncey, September 17, 1941, IBM Files; see Telegram, IBM NY to S.E. Woods, September 18, 1941, IBM Files.
50. Letter, S.E. Woods to H.K. Chauncey, September 17, 1941, IBM Files; see Telegram, IBM NY to S.E. Woods, September 18, 1941, IBM Files.
51. Letter, S.E. Woods to H.K. Chauncey, September 17, 1941, IBM Files; see IBM Application to Secretary of Treasury, License No. 223994, September 18, 1941, IBM Files.
52. Cablegram, IBM to S.E. Woods, September 18, 1941, IBM Files; IBM Application to Secretary of Treasury, License No. 223994, September 18, 1941, IBM Files.
53. IBM Application to Secretary of Treasury, License No. 223994, September 18, 1941, IBM Files.
54. Transcript, Telephone Conversation between Thomas J. Watson and S.E. Woods, September 17, 1941, p. 2, IBM Files; IBM Application to Secretary of Treasury, License No. 223994, September 18, 1941, IBM Files.
55. Memorandums to Files, September 19, 1941, as Attachments to IBM Application to Secretary of Treasury, License No. 223994, September 18, 1941, IBM Files.
56. Memorandums to Files, September 19, 1941, as Attachments to IBM Application to Secretary of Treasury, License No. 223994, September 18, 1941, IBM Files.
57. Memorandums to Files, September 19, 1941, as Attachments to IBM Application to Secretary of Treasury, License No. 223994, September 18, 1941, IBM Files.
58. Memorandum to File, September 19, 1941, IBM Files.
59. 1941 Document Register, September 19, 1941, IBM Files.
60. Memorandum to File, September 19, 1941, IBM Files.
61. Memorandum to File, September 19, 1941, IBM Files.
62. Memorandum to File, September 19, 1941, IBM Files.
63. Memorandum to File, September 19, 1941, IBM Files.
64. Memorandum to File, September 19, 1941, IBM Files.
65. Memorandum to File, September 19, 1941, IBM Files.
66. Memorandum to File, September 19, 1941, IBM Files.
67. W.C. Lier to Thomas J. Watson, October 9, 1941, p. 1, IBM Files.
68. Document Register, Item No. 66, September 19, 1941, IBM Files; Letter, H.F. Albert to H.K. Chauncey, October 8, 1941, IBM Files.
69. Letter, H.F. Albert to H.K. Chauncey, October 8, 1941, pp.1–2, IBM Files.
70. Letter, H.F. Albert to H.K. Chauncey, October 8, 1941, p. 2, IBM Files.
71. W.C. Lier to Thomas J. Watson, October 9, 1941, pp. 1–2, IBM Files.
72. Cablegram, IBM NY to S.E. Woods, September 26, 1941, IBM Files.
73. Cablegram, IBM NY to Morris, October 7, 1941, IBM Files.
74. Telegram, Morris to H.K. Chauncey, September 22, 1941, IBM Files.

75. Cablegram, September 22, 1941, IBM Files; Letter, W.C. Lier to H.K. Chauncey, October 20, 1941, p. 1, IBM Files; Letter, H.F. Albert to H.K. Chauncey, October 8, 1941, IBM Files; Letter, W.C. Lier to H.K. Chauncey, October 10, 1941, p. 6, IBM Files; see Letter, W.C. Lier to Thomas J. Watson, October 9, 1941, p. 2, IBM Files.

76. Letter, J.C. Milner to H.K. Chauncey, October 9, 1941, IBM Files.

77. IBM Application to Secretary of Treasury, License No. 223994, September 18, 1941, IBM Files; Letter, J.G. Phillips to Cordell Hull, October 10, 1941, IBM Files.

78. Letter, H. Feis to IBM NY, NA RG59 840.51 4064; Letter, H.K. Chauncey to Cordell Hull, October 29, 1941, NA RG59 840.51 4064.

79. License Executive Order No. 8389, Federal Reserve Bank of New York, October 12, 1941, IBM Files.

80. Transcript, Telephone Conversation between H.K. Chauncey and S.E. Woods, October 27, 1941, pp. 1–2, IBM Files.

81. "International Business Machine Corp./2," December 3, 1941, NA RG59 362.115.

82. "International Business Machine Corp./2," December 3, 1941, NA RG59 362.115.

83. "International Business Machine Corp./2," December 3, 1941, NA RG59 362.115.

84. "International Business Machine Corp./2," December 3, 1941, NA RG59 362.115.

XI: FRANCE AND HOLLAND

1. "Ribbentrop Charges Allies Plotted with the Lowlands," *NYT*, May 10, 1940; see Jacob Presser, *The Destruction of the Dutch Jews,* transl. Arnold Pomerans (New York: E.P. Dutton & Co. Inc., 1969), p. 221.

2. William L. Shirer, *The Rise and Fall of the Third Reich: A History of Nazi Germany.* (New York: Simon and Schuster, 1960), pp. 738, 746; Saul Friedländer, *Nazi Germany and the Jews: Vol. 1: The Years of Persecution, 1933–1939* (New York: HarperCollins, 1997), p. 220; see *Encyclopaedia Judaica,* s.v. "France," pp. 32–33.

3. Bob Moore, *Victims and Survivors: The Nazi Persecution of the Jews in the Netherlands 1940–1945* (New York: Arnold, 1997), pp. 25, 37; *Encyclopaedia Judaica,* s.v. "Holland," pp. 983–984.

4. *Encyclopaedia Judaica,* s.v. "France," p. 32.

5. B. Erwich and J.G.S.J. van Maarseveen, eds., *Een eeuw statistieken. Historisch-methodologische schetsen van de Nederlandse officielle statistieken in de twintigste eeuw* (Amsterdam, 1999), pp. 71, 74, 357; James Connally, *History of Computing in Europe* (IBM World Trade Corporation, circa 1967), p. 20; Jan Van den Ende, *Knopen, kaarten en chips. De geschiedenis van de automatisering bij het Central Bureau voor de Statistiek,* (Amsterdam: CBS, 1991), pp. 53–54.

6. Connally, pp. E-12, 14; H.J. Carter, "Confidential Memorandum NY-256," December 20, 1943, pp. 2–3, Department of Justice, War Division, Economic Warfare Section, NA RG60.

7. Van den Ende, p. 58; Harold Ungar, "Confidential Memorandum NY-356: The Use of Standardized Accounting and Business Machines in the German Economy," June 28, 1944, p. 4, Department of Justice, War Division, Economic Warfare Section, NA RG60; H.J. Carter, "Card Production and Sales Statistics," 1943, Department of Justice, War Division, Economic Warfare Section, NA RG60.

8. Connally, p. E-14; Letter, J.G. Phillips to The Netherlands Consulate General, June 10, 1941, DNA, Archive of the Ministry of Justice in London 1940–1945, number 2.09.06, Box 7, Letter 4; see "Appendix to Nederlandsche Staatscourant of February 6, 1941, cited in Document of Amsterdam Chamber of Commerce, DNA 33054214/Commercial Register.

9. Van den Ende, p. 58.

10. Letter, J.G. Phillips to The Netherlands Consulate General, June 10, 1941, DNA, Archive of the Ministry of Justice in London 1940–1945, number 2.09.06, Box 7, Letter 4; Letter, J.G. Phillips to the Netherlands Consulate General, September 17, 1940, DNA, Archive of the Ministry of Justice in London 1940–1945, number 2.09.06, Box 7, Letter 1.

11. "Appendix to Nederlandsche Staatscourant of February 6, 1941, cited in Document of Amsterdam Chamber of Commerce, DNA 33054214/Commercial Register; Letter, General Consulate of the Netherlands, New York, NY, to U.S. Commission of Mobility of Law,

December 4, 1940, DNA, Archive of the Ministry of Justice in London 1940–1945, number 2.09.06, Box 7, Letter 2.

12. Connally, pp. E-3, E-5, E-6; Groupe Bull chronology, perso.club-internet.fr/febcm/english/chronoa2.htm.

13. Connally, pp. 34, E-9, E-10, E-11, E-14; Groupe Bull chronology, perso.club-internet.fr/febcm/english/chronoa3.htm.

14. Connally, pp. E-12, E-13; "CEC I.B.M. Subsidiary in France: Confidential Report 332," pp. 2, 12, submitted by Harold J. Carter, April 10, 1944, Department of Justice, War Division, Economic Warfare Section, NA RG60; Note, Fellinger, circa 1944, T-73 Reel 11 RmfRuK/297 Frame 1057532.

15. "CEC I.B.M. Subsidiary in France: Confidential Report 332," pp. 2–3, submitted by Harold J. Carter, April 10, 1944, Department of Justice, War Division, Economic Warfare Section, NA RG60; H.J. Carter, "Card Production and Sales Statistics," 1943, Department of Justice, War Division, Economic Warfare Section, NA RG60.

16. H.B. Fellinger, Enclosure 5, July 30, 1945, IBM Files; Lieutenant Colonel Schultz, "Demands of CEC," circa June 1944, NA RG242 T73, Reel 8, RmfRuK/173, Frames 1057532, 1057535, 1057536; "Inventory of Machines Taken Over by German Authorities as of December 31, 1940," Department of Justice, War Division, Economic Warfare Section, NA RG60; also see Letter, Dr. Springer to Captain Luedtke, February 19, 1944, NA RG242 T-73 Reel 8, RmfRuk/173, Frames 1053860–1053861; NA RG242 T-73 Reel 8, RmfRuk/173, Frames 1053881–92; "Confidential Report: War Economics and the Armament Office of the German High Command," December 1942, p. 29, PRO FO 371/35431.

17. "Leased machines of CEC," January 7, 1944, NA RG242, T-73 reel 8, RmfRuk/173 Frame 1057440; "List of Inventory at MB-Headquarters and Field Offices," NA RG242, T-73 Reel 8, RmfRuk/173 Frames 1053927–1053932; H.B. Fellinger, Enclosure 3, July 14, 1945, IBM Files.

18. "List of Requisitioned Machines," NA RG242 T-73 Reel 8, RmfRuk/173, Frames 1053881–92; Lieutenant Colonel Schultz, "Demands of CEC," circa June 1944, NA RG242 T73, Reel 8, RmfRuK/173, Frames 1057532–1057539; "CEC Quarterly Report, Fourth Quarter 1942," p. 2, Department of Justice, War Division, Economic Warfare Section, NA RG60.

19. "CEC I.B.M. Subsidiary in France: Confidential Report 332," pp. 1, 2, submitted by Harold J. Carter, April 10, 1944, Department of Justice, War Division, Economic Warfare Section, NA RG60.

20. "CEC I.B.M. Subsidiary in France: Confidential Report 332," p. 3, submitted by Harold J. Carter, April 10, 1944, Department of Justice, War Division, Economic Warfare Section, NA RG60; "Report on the Factory at Essones," March 24, 1941, p. 1, Department of Justice, War Division, Economic Warfare Section, NA RG60.

21. Letter, O.E. Hoermann to IBM Endicott, April 30, 1942, Department of Justice, War Division, Economic Warfare Section, NA RG60.

22. Letter, O.E. Hoermann to IBM Endicott, April 30, 1942, p. 2, Department of Justice, War Division, Economic Warfare Section, NA RG60.

23. "CEC Quarterly Report, Fourth Quarter 1942," pp. 1, 2, 3, Department of Justice, War Division, Economic Warfare Section, NA RG60.

24. "CEC Quarterly Report, Fourth Quarter 1942," pp. 3, 7, Department of Justice, War Division, Economic Warfare Section, NA RG60.

25. "CEC Quarterly Report, Fourth Quarter 1942," Department of Justice, War Division, Economic Warfare Section, NA RG60.

26. "CEC Quarterly Report, Fourth Quarter 1942," pp. 6, 6–2, Department of Justice, War Division, Economic Warfare Section, NA RG60.

27. "CEC Quarterly Report, Fourth Quarter 1942," p. 23, Department of Justice, War Division, Economic Warfare Section, NA RG60.

28. "CEC Quarterly Report, Fourth Quarter 1942," p. 16, Department of Justice, War Division, Economic Warfare Section, NA RG60.

29. "CEC Quarterly Report, Fourth Quarter 1942," p. 11, Department of Justice, War Division, Economic Warfare Section, NA RG60.

30. Westerholt Biography, May 1, 1933, NA RG242 A3340-MFOK-Y078, Frame 1532; see NA RG242 A3343-RS-G 5166, Westerholt, Heinz 25.07.1907 Rasse- und Siedlungshauptamt, Frame 370.

31. Transcript, Telephone Conversation between W.C. Lier and W. Borel, October 14, 1941, p. 2, IBM Files; Typed Running Notes, H.K. Chauncey, December 17, 1940, p. 2, IBM Files.

32. Purport List, List of Papers, Political Affairs–France, September 23, 1941, p. 236, Entry 2409, NA RG59 851.00.

33. Transcript, Telephone Conversation between W.C. Lier and W. Borel, October 14, 1941, p. 2, IBM Files.

34. Transcript, Telephone Conversation between W.C. Lier and W. Borel, October 14, 1941, p. 2, IBM Files; Letter, W.C. Lier to F.W. Nichol, October 21, 1941, IBM Files.

35. Letter, W.C. Lier to F.W. Nichol, October 21, 1941, IBM Files.

36. Letter, W.C. Lier to F.W. Nichol, October 21, 1941, IBM Files.

37. Letter, W.C. Lier to F.W. Nichol, October 21, 1941, IBM Files.

38. Radiogram, C. Delcour to IBM NY, November 17, 1941, IBM Files.

39. H.B. Fellinger, Enclosure 5, July 30, 1945, p. 6, IBM Files.

40. "CEC I.B.M. Subsidiary in France: Confidential Report 332," p. 25, submitted by Harold J. Carter, April 10, 1944, Department of Justice, War Division, Economic Warfare Section, NA RG60.

41. "CEC I.B.M. Subsidiary in France: Confidential Report 332," p. 25, submitted by Harold J. Carter, April 10, 1944, Department of Justice, War Division, Economic Warfare Section, NA RG60.

42. Connally, p. E-14; Transcript, H.K. Chauncey Interview with K. Hummel, circa November 1940, p. 9, IBM Files; "CEC I.B.M. Subsidiary in France: Confidential Report 332," p. 12, submitted by Harold J. Carter, April 10, 1944, Department of Justice, War Division, Economic Warfare Section, NA RG60; Memorandum, H.B. Fellinger to W. Beck, June 21, 1945, Item 9, IBM Files.

43. Moore, pp. 30, 66–67; "Netherlands Churches Assail Ban on Jews in Government Service," NYT, October 28, 1940; "Conditions in Holland," p. 1, Items 2, 8, PRO FO 371/26683.

44. Moore, pp. 63–64; "Germans' Reprisals Open in Netherlands," NYT, January 15, 1941; see "Netherlands Churches Assail Ban on Jews in Government Service," NYT, October 28, 1940.

45. Letter J.L. Lentz to Dr. Calmeyer, May 27, 1941, NIOD; see Moore, p. 124; also see Götz Aly and Karl Heinz Roth, Die restlose Erfassung: Volkszählen, Identifizieren, Aussondern im Nationalsozialismus (Berlin: Rotbuch Verlag, 1984), p. 66; see Presser, pp. 38, 301.

46. Moore, p. 196; H.W. Methorst and J.L. Lentz, "Die Volksregistrierung und das neve in den Niederlanden eingeführte System," Allgemeines Statistisches Archiv (ASA) 26 (1936/37): 65.

47. Presser, pp. 38, 301; see Moore, pp. 124, 138, 66; also see Aly and Roth, p. 66 and Letter, J.L. Lentz to Dr. Calmeyer, May 27, 1941, NIOD, DOC I-1045, J.L. Lentz, map B.

48. "To Register Refugee Jews," NYT, July 4, 1940; see Letter, J.L. Lentz to Interior Ministry, March 25, 1941, NIOD, Letter, J.L. Lentz to Interior Ministry, March 25, 1941, NIOD, Generalkommissar fur Verwaltung und Justiz GK VuJ, Hauptabteilung Inneres, 25–122b; Moore, p. 65.

49. Aly and Roth, p. 66; see Moore, p. 197.

50. Moore, p. 196.

51. Aly and Roth, p. 66; Moore p.197.

52. Presser, pp. 39–40.

53. Moore, p. 58; also see Presser, pp. 33–34 and "Netherlands Churches Assail Ban on Jews in Government Service," NYT, October 28, 1940.

54. "Netherland Jews Must Register," NYT, January 14, 1941; see Presser, pp. 35–37; B. Erwich and J.G.S.J. van Maarseveen, pp. 76–78; also see Van den Ende, pp. 52–59.

55. Moore, pp. 61–65; "Jews Fight Nazis in Amsterdam Riot," NYT, February 14, 1941; Presser, p. 36; also see "Amsterdam Fined for Nazi Clashes," NYT, March 2, 1941; Letter, National Inspection for Population Registration to Dr. Calmeyer, June 14, 1941, NIOD, GK VuJ, Hauptabt. Inneres, 25–122b; see Letter, Dr. Stüler to Dr. Wimmer, June 16,

1941, NIOD, GK VuJ, Hauptabt. Inneres, 25–122b; also see Letters, J.L. Lentz to Dr. Calmeyer, May 27, 1941, NIOD, DOC I-1045, J.L. Lentz, map B, and Letter, J.L. Lentz to Dr. Calmeyer, July 26, 1941, NIOD, DK VuJ Hauptabt. Inneres, 25–122b; also see Memorandum, Ministry of Interior Administration, March 25, 1941, NIOD, *Ministerialreferat Innere Verwalung,* GK VuJ, Hauptabt. Inneres, 25–122b.

56. "Netherland Jews Must Register," *NYT,* January 14, 1941; Presser, pp. 35, 36, 37; Diplomatic Dispatch, p. 3, January 29, 1941, PRO FO 371/26534.

57. Letter, J.L. Lentz to Interior Ministry, March 25, 1941 NIOD, GK VuJ Hauptabt. Inneres, 25–122b.

58. "Conditions in Holland," p. 1, Item 2, December 16, 1941, PRO FO371/26683. B.A. Sijes, De Februari-staking, 25–26 Februari 1941, H.J.W. Becht, Amsterdam 1954, pp. 153–155, 160–167, 176

59. Letter, J.L. Lentz to Dr. Wimmer, March 25, 1941, NIOD, GK VuJ Hauptabt. Inneres, 25–122b.

60. Letter, Dr. Stüler to Dr. Wimmer June 16, 1941, NIOD, GK VuJ Hauptabt. Inneres, 25–122b.

61. Presser, p. 37.

62. Presser, p. 37.

63. Letter, Dr. Wimmer's office to J.L. Lentz, May 26, 1941, NIOD, GK VuJ Hauptabt. Inneres, 25–122b.

64. Letter, Dr. Wimmer's office to J.L. Lentz, May 26, 1941, NIOD, GK VuJ Hauptabt. Inneres, 25–122b.

65. Letter, Dr. Wimmer's office to J.L. Lentz, May 26, 1941, NIOD, GK VuJ Hauptabt. Inneres, 25–122b.

66. Letter, J.L. Lentz to Dr. Calmeyer, May 27, 1941, NIOD, GK VuJ Hauptabt. Inneres, 25–122b.

67. Letter, J.L. Lentz to Dr. Calmeyer, May 27, 1941, NIOD, GK VuJ Hauptabt. Inneres, 25–122b.

68. Letter, J.L. Lentz to Dr. Calmeyer, May 27, 1941, NIOD, GK VuJ Hauptabt. Inneres, 25–122b.

69. Letter, J.L. Lentz to Dr. Calmeyer, May 27, 1941, NIOD, GK VuJ Hauptabt. Inneres, 25–122b.

70. Dr. Stüler, Report to Dr. Wimmer, p. 1, May 30, 1941, NIOD, GK VuJ Hauptabt. Inneres, 25–122b.

71. Dr. Stüler, Report to Dr. Wimmer, p. 2, May 30, 1941, NIOD, GK VuJ Hauptabt. Inneres, 25–122b.

72. Dr. Stüler, Report to Dr. Wimmer, p. 3, May 30, 1941, NIOD, GK VuJ Hauptabt. Inneres, 25–122b.

73. Report, Inspectorate to Dr. Calmeyer, June 14, 1941, NIOD, GK VuJ Hauptabt. Inneres, 25–122b.

74. "Conditions in Holland," Attachment 18, Items 4 and 5, December 16, 1941, PRO FO 371/26683. Jacob Presser, p. 69–70; and H.B.J. Stegeman and J.P. Vorsteveld, Het Joodse Werkdorp in de Wieringermeer 1934–1941, Zutphen 1983, pp. 122–127.

75. Letter, J.L. Lentz to Dr. Stüler, June 16, 1941, NIOD, GK VuJ Hauptabt. Inneres, 25–122b.

76. Letter, J.L. Lentz to Dr. Calmeyer, July 26, 1941, NIOD, GK VuJ Hauptabt. Inneres, 25–122b.

77. Moore, p. 65; Presser, pp. 37–38.

78. J.L. Lentz, *Memoires I, Registratie van Joden (oorsprong en ontwikkeling),* p. 10, unpublished journal, circa October 1944, NIOD, Dossier I-1045; also see J.L. Lentz, Ambtelijke Herinneringen, unpublished journal, circa October 1944, p. 25, NIOD, Doc. Dossier I-1045

79. Presser, p. 38.

80. "Report No. 38: Netherlands, Census of Property in Foreign Countries, Series C: Report of Interests in Primary Allied Organizations," Form TFR 500, Department of Treasury/Foreign Funds, NA RG131.

81. "Report No. 38: Netherlands, Census of Property in Foreign Countries, Series C: Report of Interests in Primary Allied Organizations," Section 6, Form TFR 500, Department of Treasury/ Foreign Funds, NA RG131.

82. "Report No. 38: Netherlands, Census of Property in Foreign Countries, Series C: Report of Interests in Primary Allied Organizations," Section 6, Form TFR 500, Department of Treasury/ Foreign Funds, NA RG131.

83. "Report No. 38: Netherlands, Census of Property in Foreign Countries, Series C: Report of Interests in Primary Allied Organizations," Section 6, Form TFR 500, Department of Treasury/Foreign Funds, NA RG131.

84. Statement of Income and Profit and Loss for the 8 Months Ended December 31, 1940, Attachment to "Report No. 38: Netherlands, Census of Property in Foreign Countries, Series C: Report of Interests in Primary Allied Organizations," Form TFR 500, Department of Treasury/Foreign Funds, NA RG131.

85. Statement of Income and Profit and Loss for the 8 Months Ended December 31, 1940, Attachment to "Report No. 38: Netherlands, Census of Property in Foreign Countries, Series C: Report of Interests in Primary Allied Organizations," Form TFR 500, Department of Treasury/Foreign Funds, NA RG131.

86. H.J. Carter, "Card Production and Sales Statistics," 1943, Department of Justice, War Division, Economic Warfare Section, NA RG60; "Report No. 38: Netherlands, Census of Property in Foreign Countries, Series C: Report of Interests in Primary Allied Organizations," Section 7, Form TFR 500, Department of Treasury/Foreign Funds, NA RG131.

87. "Netherland Jews to Wear Star," *NYT*, September 16, 1941; also see Letter, R. Boyard to Prefect of Beaune-Montbard, June 9, 1942, and four pages of attached lists, AJ 38/1142; "Conditions in Holland," Attachment Holland #18, Item 8, PRO FO 371/26683.

88. Presser, p. 35.

89. H.B. Fellinger, Enclosure 7, May 1, 1944, IBM Files; Moore, p. 64; also see Presser, p. 37; "Card Exports from USA," 1943, Department of Justice, War Division, Economic Warfare Section, NA RG60; "CEC I.B.M. Subsidiary in France: Confidential Report 332," fn p. 12, submitted by Harold J. Carter, April 10, 1944, Department of Justice, War Division, Economic Warfare Section, NA RG60; Connally, pp. E-10, E-13.

90. *Le "Fichier Juif:" Rapport de la Commission présidée par René Rémond au Premier Ministre* (France: Plon, 1996).

91. Jacques Adler, *The Jews of Paris and the Final Solution: Communal Response and Internal Conflicts, 1940–1944* (New York: Oxford University Press, 1987), p. 3.

92. Adler, pp. 5–6, 34; see "8,000 Parisians Sent Home," *NYT*, May 27, 1941; Michael R. Marrus and Robert O. Paxton, *Vichy France and the Jews* (New York: Schocken Books, 1983), pp. 65, 80.

93. Adler, pp.3, 8–9, 35.

94. Madrid Chancery, "Treatment of Jews in Unoccupied France," February 20, 1942, PRO FO 371/32056; Letter, Madrid Chancery to Refugee Department, Foreign Office, February 20, 1942; Foreign Research and Press Service, "Position of Jews in France," July 15, 1942, PRO FO 371/32056; Confidential Minute, "Jews in France: August 1941-June 1942," July 6, 1942, PRO FO 371/32056.

95. Marrus and Paxton, pp. 75–76, 86–87.

96. Adler, p. 87; also see Marrus and Paxton, pp. 84–85, 87, "Jew Exempted by Vichy," *NYT*, April 20, 1941, and "Vichy Keeps Jew in Office," *NYT*, January 25, 1941.

97. "DeGaulle Assails Anti-Jewish Laws," *NYT*, November 14, 1940.

98. *M.E.W.* [Ministry of Economic Warfare] *Intelligence Weekly* 44 (December 19, 1942): 1, PRO FO 837/15; "CEC Quarterly Report, Fourth Quarter 1942," pp. 6, 6–2, Department of Justice, War Division, Economic Warfare Section, NA RG60.

99. "CEC Quarterly Report, Fourth Quarter 1942," pp. 6, 6–2, Department of Justice, War Division, Economic Warfare Section, NA RG60.

100. Marrus and Paxton, pp. 100, 243.

101. "Censuses: A Critique of the Sources," *Analytical Franco-Jewish Gazeteer, 1939–45*, p. 87; "Vichy Warns All Jews to Obey New Decree," *NYT*, June 22, 1941; Typed Summary of Files, X. Vallat to Vice President Baur, March 2, 1943, YIVO Frame 416 #000002; Letter,

Head of Department of Provisional Administrators to Prefect of Police, December 1, 1941, AJ 38/118; Letter, General Commission on Jewish Questions to X. Vallat, October 6, 1941, AJ 38/1142; also see Handwritten Letters, circa July 1941, June 16, 1941, July 9, 1941, July 10, 1941, AJ 74 JA; also see Letter, X. Vallat to C. Platon, June 24, 1941, AJ 38/1142; Letter, Secretary of State of Interior to Prefects in Unoccupied Zone, July 29, 1941, AJ 38/118; also see Note, General Commission on Jewish Questions, January 26, 1943, AJ 38/118; Henri Phillipe Petain, "Loi: portent prolongation du delai prevu par la loi du 2 juin 1941 prescrivent le reconsement des juifs," AJ 38/ 1142; "Vichy Easing Jewish Law," *NYT,* July 13, 1941; also see Note, X. Vallat to Vice President of Council, July 9, 1941, AJ 38/1142; Letter, X. Vallat to Minister of Interior, January 23, 1942, AJ 38/61 M70; also see *Le "Fichier Juif,"* p. 65; "Census of All Jews Is Planned in France" *NYT,* April 22, 1941; Letter, X. Vallat to Secretary of State for National Economy and Finance, June 21, 1941, AJ 38/61M49; Letter, X. Vallat to Ministry of Interior, circa June 1941, AJ 38/69 M20.

102. *Le "Fichier Juif,"* p. 77; also see *Analytical Franco-Jewish Gazeteer 1939–1945,* p. 87.
103. *Le "Fichier Juif,"* p. 77.
104. *M.E.W. Intelligence Weekly* 44 (December 19, 1942): 2, PRO FO 837/15; *M.E.W. Intelligence Weekly* 37 (October 31, 1942): 1, PRO FO 837/15; *M.E.W. Intelligence Weekly* 34 (October 31, 1942): 3, PRO FO 837/15; *M.E.W. Intelligence Weekly* 84 (October 31, 1942): 5, PRO FO 837/15.
105. Typed Summary of Files, X. Vallat to Vice President Baur, March 2, 1943, YIVO Frame 416 #000002; "Censuses: A Critique of the Sources," *Analytical Franco-Jewish Gazeteer, 1939–45,* p. 87; "Vichy Warns All Jews to Obey New Decree," *NYT,* June 22, 1941; Letter, Head of Department of Provisional Administrators to Prefect of Police, December 1, 1941, AJ 38/118; Letter, General Commission on Jewish Questions to X. Vallat, October 6, 1941, AJ 38/1142; also see Handwritten Letters, circa July 1941, June 16, 1941, July 9, 1941, July 10, 1941, AJ 74 JA; also see Letter, X. Vallat to C. Platon, June 24, 1941, AJ 38/1142; Letter, Secretary of State of Interior to Prefects in Unoccupied Zone, July 29, 1941, AJ 38/118; also see Note, General Commission on Jewish Questions, January 26, 1943, AJ 38/118; Henri Phillipe Petain, "Loi: portent prolongation du delai prevu par la loi du 2 juin 1941 prescrivent le reconsement des juifs," AJ 38/ 1142; "Vichy Easing Jewish Law," *NYT,* July 13, 1941; also see Note, X. Vallat to Vice President of Council, July 9, 1941, AJ 38/1142; Letter, X. Vallat to Minister of Interior, January 23, 1942, AJ 38/61 M70; also see *Le "Fichier Juif,"* p. 65; "Census of All Jews Is Planned in France," *NYT,* April 22, 1941; Letter, X. Vallat to Secretary of State for National Economy and Finance, June 21, 1941, AJ 38/61M49; Letter, X. Vallat to Ministry of Interior, July 1941, AJ 38/69 M20.
106. *Le "Fichier Juif,"* p. 65; also see Letter, X. Vallat to Jean François, August 18, 1941, AJ 38/69 M70; Marrus and Paxton, pp. 54–56; see "50,000 French Jews Hit by New Decree," *NYT,* October 8, 1940; Handwritten Note, Chief of Statistical Service, April 19, 1943, YIVO Frame 466; Letter, F.O. Ambert to Paris Prefecture of Police, April 15, 1943, AJ 38/69; see Expense Reports for the Months of July and September, 1941, AJ 38/3800; see *Le "Fichier Juif,"* p. 81.
107. "50,000 French Jews Hit by New Decree," *NYT,* October 8, 1940; Adler, p. 28; also see "Paris Jews Forced to Sell Properties," *NYT,* January 15, 1941.
108. *Le "Fichier Juif,"* p. 64; Adler, p. 28.
109. *Le "Fichier Juif,"* p. 82; also see Marrus and Paxton, p. 243.
110. *Le "Fichier Juif,"* p. 69.
111. *Analytical Franco-Jewish Gazeteer 1939–1945,* p. 85; also see "Vichy Orders Census," *NYT,* June 1, 1941; Also see Marshal Petain Law, June 2, 1941, AJ38/1142.
112. *Le "Fichier Juif,"* p. 81; Letter, Secretary of the Interior to Police Prefectures, July 29, 1941, AJ 38/118; "Individual Declaration," AJ 38/1142.
113. Letter, General Commissioner on Jewish Questions to Admiral Platon, June 24, 1941, AJ 38/118; Note, X. Vallat to Vice President of Council, July 9, 1941, AJ 38/1142; Letter, X. Vallat to Platon, June 24, 1941, AJ38/1142; Note, Secretary of State of the Interior to Prefects of Occupied Zone, July 29, 1941, p. 5, AJ 38/118; Letter, Vichy to Director of

Agence HAVAS, July 15, 1941. Handwritten Note by Census Staffer, July 9, 1941, AJ38/74 JA.

114. Letter, Head of the Department of Provisional Administrator to Prefect of Police, December 1, 1941, AJ38/118; Typed Summary of Files, X. Vallat to Vice President Baur, March 2, 1943, YIVO Frame 416 #000002; Handwritten Note, April 19, 1943, YIVO Frame 466; Typed Lists with Handwritten Totals, Head Commissioner of Police of Eur-et-Loire to Police Chief of Orleans, June 6, 1942, AJ 38/1142.

115. Letter, Secretary of State of Interior to all Prefects, July 29, 1941, p. 5, AJ38/118.

116. Expense Report for September 1941, AJ 38/3800; also see Bill for Cleaning and Maintenance of Typewriters, March 24, 1943, AJ 38/3800.

117. Le *"Fichier Juif,"* pp. 72–73.

118. Le *"Fichier Juif,"* p. 85.

119. Letter, R. Carmille to X. Vallat, June 18, 1941, p. 2, AJ38/61 M49.

120. Robert Carmille, *Des Apparences A La Réalité: Mise Au Point, Le "Fichier Juif": Rapport de la Commission présidée par René Rémond au Premier Ministre* (1996). pp. 3, 69, 141; Letter, R. Carmille to X. Vallat, June 18, 1941, pp. 1–2, AJ 38/61/M49; *Geheim-Akten über Fremde Staaten (Frankreich)*, Oberkommando der Wehrmacht, Abteilung für Wehrmacht-Propaganda, OKW /1605, NA RG242, T-77 Reel 1027, Secret File on Foreign States, Item d.

121. Bull Computers Chronological History, perso.club-internet.fr.febcm/english/chronoa3.htm, p. 3; "CEC Quarterly Report, Fourth Quarter 1942," p. 25, Department of Justice, Department of War, Economic Warfare Section, NA RG60; Connally, p. E-14.

122. Le *"Fichier Juif,"* p. 143.

123. "Vichy Maps Plan of Identity Cards," *NYT*, October 22, 1941; also see Le *"Fichier Juif,"* p. 76; also see *Des Apparences A La Réalité*, p. 8; "Von der Ware zur Nummer," *Wirtschafts-blatt der Deutschen Allgemeinen Zeitung*, October 10, 1942.

124. "Vichy Maps Plan of Identity Cards," *NYT*, October 22, 1941; "Vichy Orders Census," *NYT*, June 1, 1941; Le *"Fichier Juif,"* p. 75; Letter, R. Carmille to X. Vallat, June 18, 1941, AJ 38 61 M49; René Carmille, *La Mécanographie dans les Administration*, 2nd edition, circa Fall 1941.

125. Letter, R. Carmille to X. Vallat, June 18, 1941, AJ 38/61/M49.

126. Letter, X. Vallat to R. Carmille, June 21, 1941, AJ 38/61/M49.

127. Le *"Fichier Juif,"* pp. 67, 68–69, 85.

128. Le *"Fichier Juif,"* p. 67.

129. Le *"Fichier Juif,"* pp. 84–85.

130. Le *"Fichier Juif,"* pp. 68, 85; Letter, X. Vallat to Puecheu, January 23, 1942, AJ38 61 M70.

131. Le *"Fichier Juif,"* p. 68.

132. "CEC Quarterly Report, Fourth Quarter 1942," p. 25, Department of Justice, War Division, Economic Warfare Section, NA RG60.

133. Annette Kahn, *Le Fichier* (Paris: Robert Laffont, 1993), p. 41; Adler, p. 76; Kahn, p. 41; also see Marrus and Paxton, p. 243 and "French War Camps Now Confine Jews," *NYT*, May 19, 1941.

134. Adler, pp. 75, 76; Kahn, pp. 61, 62–63.

135. Marrus and Paxton, pp. 225–226; also see Kahn, pp. 99, 102.

136. Le *"Fichier Juif,"* pp. 77–78, 80.

137. Le *"Fichier Juif,"* p. 78.

138. Cynthia J. Haft, *The Bargain and the Bridle: The General Union of the Israelites of France, 1941–1944* (Chicago: Dialog Press, 1983), p. 2.

139. Haft, pp. 22, 23; Letter, Georges Edinger to X. Vallat, April 8, 1943, YIVO Frame 450 #000032; Handwritten List, Chief of Service, April 19, 1943, YIVO Frame 466; also see six forms, n.d., UGIF, YIVO Folder 107 / 96 MK 490.86 UGIF records, 1940–1944, Frames 2, 5, 7–9 #000001, 000005–000007; also see note, UGIF to X. Vallat, April 1, 1943, YIVO Frame 447 #00029; also see Letter, A. Baur to X. Vallat, April 1, 1943, YIVO Frame 444 #000026; also see Letter, UGIF to X. Vallat, March 19, 1943, YIVO Frame 436 #000019.

140. Haft, p. 23.

141. Haft, pp. 22, 62.

142. Haft, pp. 62, 104.

143. *Bulletin* (col. I, no. 27), July 24, 1942, cited in Haft, p. 68.

144. Haft, p. 77.

145. Haft, p. 112.

146. Marrus and Paxton, pp. 246–247.

147. Marrus and Paxton, p. 246.

148. Marrus and Paxton, p. 255.

149. Letter, X.Vallat to Ministry of the Interior, January 23, 1941, AJ38/61 M70; *Des Apparences A La Réalité*, p. 10.

150. *Des Apparences A La Réalité*, p. 23.

151. *Des Apparences A La Réalité*, p. 6.

152. *Des Apparences A La Réalité*, p. 6.

153. *Des Apparences A La Réalité*, p. 33.

154. Le *"Fichier Juif,"* p. 145; *Des Apparences A La Réalité*, pp. 8, 13, 15, 22; "Vichy Maps Plan of Identity Cards," *NYT,* October 22, 1941.

155. *Des Apparences A La Réalité*, p. 10.

156. *Des Apparences A La Réalité*, p. 10.

157. *Des Apparences A La Réalité*, p. 19.

158. *Des Apparences A La Réalité*, p. 17b.

159. *Des Apparences A La Réalité*, pp. 19–20.

160. Moore, p. 91.

161. Moore, p. 91.

162. Moore, p. 91.

163. Floor Plan and Attached Memo, Central Administration for Building Construction, May 18, 1944, BA R83 Niederlande/54.

164. Moore, pp. 92–93, 218; Confidential Memorandum, circa 1946, p. 20, PRO FO 371/46796; Hilberg, *Destruction of the European Jews,* p. 372; Presser, 216; William Seltzer, "Population Statistics, The Holocaust, and the Nuremberg Trials," *Population and Development Review* 24(3): 525.

165. Confidential Memorandum, circa 1946, p. 20, PRO FO 371/46796; Presser, p. 482.

166. Presser, p. 483.

167. Moore, p. 100.

168. Marrus and Paxton, p. 226; Handwritten Note, X. Vallat, April 19, 1943, YIVO Frame 466; Typed Summary, X. Vallat to Baur, circa 1943, YIVO Frame 416#000002; also see Adler, p. 48.

169. Moore, pp. 198, 199; *Des Apparences A La Réalité*, pp. 2, 13; William Seltzer, "Population Statistics," pp. 525, 546.

170. Presser, p. 539; also see Moore, p. 2 and *Encyclopaedia Judaica,* s.v. "Netherlands," p. 989.

171. *Encyclopaedia Judaica,* s.v. "France," pp. 32–33; also see Adler, pp. xi, 3, 5; also see Marrus and Paxton, p. 343 and Moore, p. 2.

XII: IBM AND THE WAR

1. H.J. Carter, Memorandum for the Files, May 16, 1944, p. 1, Department of Justice, War Division, Economic Warfare Section, NA RG60; H.J. Carter, H.J. Carter, "Control in Business Machines," circa 1944, pp. 1, 18, Department of Justice, War Division, Economic Warfare Section, NA RG60.

2. H.J. Carter, Memorandum for the Files, May 16, 1944, pp. 1, 8, 14, Department of Justice, War Division, Economic Warfare Section, NA RG60; H.J. Carter, "Control in Business Machines," circa 1944, pp. 1, 18, Department of Justice, War Division, Economic Warfare Section, NA RG60.

3. H.J. Carter, "Control in Business Machines," circa 1944, pp. 1, 18, Department of Justice, War Division, Economic Warfare Section, NA RG60.

4. Typed Notes, IBM Geneva to H.K. Chauncey, October 20, 1941, p. 19, Department of Justice, War Division, Economic Warfare Section, NA RG60.

5. H.J. Carter, "Control in Business Machines," circa 1944, pp. 1–3, 8–9, 13, 7–18, Department of Justice, War Division, Economic Warfare Section, NA RG60.

6. "1,800 in Europe on New Blacklist; Windsor's Swedish Friend On It," *NYT*, January 15, 1942.

7. "U.S. Ousts Five Aniline Executives As 'Personifying' Nazi Domination," *NYT*, January 14, 1942.

8. "Arnold Says Standard Oil Gave Nazis Rubber Process," *NYT*, March 27, 1942; also see "Standard Oil's German Patents Demanded by Government Agency," *NYT*, May 25, 1944.

9. "Standard Oil Tried to Deal in France in '41, Says Arnold," *NYT*, March 28, 1942.

10. Maurice W. Altaffer, "Report on Watson A.G.," June 16, 1942, NA RG84, Foreign Service Posts of the Department of State, Bern 711.2 Watson.

11. "Report in Connection with the Proclaimed List of Certain Block Nationals," June 16, 1942, NA RG84, Foreign Service Posts of the Department of State, Bern 711.2 Watson.

12. *FO Minute*, PRO FO 837/311.

13. H.J. Carter, Attachment, Draft Notes of Interview with J.W. Schotte, circa June 1943, Department of Justice, War Division, Economic Warfare Section, NA RG60.

14. H.J. Carter, Attachment, Draft Notes of Interview with J.W. Schotte, circa June 1943, p. 2, Department of Justice, War Division, Economic Warfare Section, NA RG60.

15. H.J. Carter, Interview with J.W. Schotte, September 15, 1944, pp. 2–3, Department of Justice, War Division, Economic Warfare Section, NA RG60.

16. H.J. Carter, Draft Notes of Interview with J.W. Schotte, June 14–16, 1943, pp. 1, 3–4, 17–18, 20, Department of Justice, War Division, Economic Warfare Section, NA RG60; H.J. Carter, Memorandum for the Files, May 16, 1944, pp. 2–4, Department of Justice, War Division, Economic Warfare Section, NA RG60 ; H.J. Carter, "Use of IBM Machines," circa 1943, Department of Justice, War Division, Economic Warfare Section, NA RG60.

17. H.J. Carter, Memorandum for the Files, May 16, 1944, p. 3, Department of Justice, War Division, Economic Warfare Section, NA RG60; "CEC I.B.M. Subsidiary in France: Confidential Report 332," pp. 4–5, 6–7, 9, 13–14, submitted by Harold J. Carter, April 10, 1944, Department of Justice, War Division, Economic Warfare Section, NA RG60; H.J. Carter, Draft Notes of Interview with J.W. Schotte, June 14–16, 1943, Department of Justice, War Division, Economic Warfare Section, NA RG60.

18. H.J. Carter, Draft Notes of Interview with J.W. Schotte, June 14–16, 1943, p. 12, Department of Justice, War Division, Economic Warfare Section, NA RG60.

19. H.J. Carter, Draft Notes of Interview with J.W. Schotte, June 14–16, 1943, p. 13, Department of Justice, War Division, Economic Warfare Section, NA RG60.

20. H.J. Carter, Draft Notes of Interview with J.W. Schotte, June 14–16, 1943, pp. 4, 9, Department of Justice, War Division, Economic Warfare Section, NA RG60.

21. H.J. Carter, Draft Notes of Interview with J.W. Schotte, June 14–16, 1943, p. 23, Department of Justice, War Division, Economic Warfare Section, NA RG60.

22. H.J. Carter, "International Business Machines Corporation, File Search of the Foreign Division," May 16, 1944, pp. 2–4, Department of Justice, War Division, Economic Warfare Section, NA RG60.

23. H.J. Carter, "International Business Machines Corporation, File Search of the Foreign Division," May 16, 1944, pp. 1–2, Department of Justice, War Division, Economic Warfare Section, NA RG60.

24. H.J. Carter, "International Business Machines Corporation, File Search of the Foreign Division," May 16, 1944, p. 1, Department of Justice, War Division, Economic Warfare Section, NA RG60.

25. H.J. Carter, "International Business Machines Corporation, File Search of the Foreign Division," May 16, 1944, p. 2, Department of Justice, War Division, Economic Warfare Section, NA RG60.

26. H.J. Carter, "International Business Machines Corporation, File Search of the Foreign Division," May 16, 1944, pp. 1–2, Department of Justice, War Division, Economic Warfare Section, NA RG60.

27. H.J. Carter, "International Business Machines Corporation, File Search of the Foreign Division," May 16, 1944, p. 3, Department of Justice, War Division, Economic Warfare Section, NA RG60.

28. H.J. Carter, "International Business Machines Corporation, File Search of the Foreign

Division," May 16, 1944, p. 3, Department of Justice, War Division, Economic Warfare Section, NA RG60.

29. H.J. Carter, "International Business Machines Corporation, File Search of the Foreign Division," May 16, 1944, p. 3, Department of Justice, War Division, Economic Warfare Section, NA RG60.

30. H.J. Carter, "International Business Machines Corporation, File Search of the Foreign Division," May 16, 1944, pp. 3, 4, Department of Justice, War Division, Economic Warfare Section, NA RG60.

31. H.J. Carter, "International Business Machines Corporation, File Search of the Foreign Division," May 16, 1944, p. 4, Department of Justice, War Division, Economic Warfare Section, NA RG60.

32. H.J. Carter, "International Business Machines Corporation, File Search of the Foreign Division," May 16, 1944, p. 4, Department of Justice, War Division, Economic Warfare Section, NA RG60.

33. Thomas J. Watson, Jr., and Peter Petre, *Father, Son & Co.: My Life at IBM and Beyond.* (New York: Bantam Books, 1990), p. 87.

34. Emerson W. Pugh, *Building IBM: Shaping an Industry and Its Technology* (Cambridge: The MIT Press, 1995), pp. 90, 345; Watson, Jr., and Petre, p. 87; see James W. Cortada, *Before the Computer: IBM, NCR, Burroughs, and Remington Rand and the Industry They Created, 1865–1965* (Princeton: Princeton University Press, 1993), p. 201.

35. Pugh, pp. 95, 347–348; Cortada, p. 201.

36. Pugh, p. 94; also see "U.S. Ousts Five Aniline Executives," *NYT,* January 14, 1942.

37. Pugh, pp. 91–92; Watson Jr., p. 112.

38. Pugh, pp. 91–92, 347 fn13; Charles M.Province, "IBM Punch Card Systems in the U.S. Army," www.members.aol.com/PattonsGHQ; Letter, J.T. Senn to Thomas J. Watson, April 26, 1945, IBM Files.

39. "Heads Unit of Logistics of Business Machines," *NYT,* May 7, 1942; also see Pugh, pp. 91, 346.

40. Letter and Attachments, A. Cranfield to Travis, January 31, 1941, PRO HW 14/11 Government and Cipher School: Directorate, WWII Policy Papers.

41. Watson, Jr., and Petre, p. 112; Pugh, pp. 98–101, 348–349fn.

42. Cortada, pp. 201–202, 320; "Deutsche Hollerith Maschinen GmbH: Confidential Report 242," submitted by Harold J. Carter, December 8, 1943, Department of Justice, War Division, Economic Warfare Section, NA RG60; also see Letter and Attachments, A. Cranfield to Travis, January 31, 1941, PRO HW 14/11 Government and Cipher School: Directorate, WWII Policy Papers; also see List of Documents on Use of Machines for Crypto Purposes, Politisches Archiv, N Series to Cryptographic Office, pp. 14, 29, 50.

43. Pugh, pp. 93, 347fn; also see Thomas G. Belden and Marva R. Belden, *The Lengthening Shadow. The Life of Thomas J.Watson* (Boston: Little, Brown and Company, 1962), p. 209.

44. "Watson Tells of War Orders," *NYT,* March 15, 1942; Watson, Jr., and Petre, p. 113.

45. "IBM Punch Card Systems in the U.S. Army," p. 5; Cortada, p. 201.

46. "Census Plan Hailed by Mrs. Roosevelt," *NYT,* March 27, 1940.

47. William Seltzer and Margo Anderson, *After Pearl Harbor: The Proper Role of Population Data Systems in Time of War,* draft unpublished, March 28, 2000, p. 5.

48. Seltzer and Anderson, p. 5; "New Policy on Interned Japanese Urged by Senate Military Affairs Committee," *NYT,* May 8, 1943.

49. Seltzer and Anderson, pp. 6–7.

50. Seltzer and Anderson, p. 7.

51. Seltzer and Anderson, pp. 7, 24; also see William Seltzer, "Population Statistics, the Holocaust, and the Nuremberg Trials," *Population and Development Review* 24 (September 1998): 511–522, 525; also see H.W. Methorst, "The New System of Population Accounting in the Netherlands," *Journal of the American Statistical Association* (1936): 719–722, (1938): 713–714.

52. Seltzer and Anderson, p. 10.

53. "Chronology of the Japanese American Internment"; www.clpef.net/9066.html; 1944, Entries, pp. 2, 4, www.clpef.net/chrono.html.

54. "Chronology of the Japanese American Internment,"1945, Entry, p 4.
55. "Watson Says Defense Is First Consideration," *NYT,* January 2, 1941; "Advertising News," *NYT,* November 17, 1942.
56. "Mobile Shows on Tour," *NYT,* July 4, 1941.
57. "Foresees Success in Preparedness," *NYT,* July 15, 1941.
58. "Mrs. Roosevelt Urges All Women to Knit," *NYT,* October 1, 1941.
59. Full Page IBM Advertisement, *NYT,* January 5, 1942.
60. "Young Won't Run for Governorship," *NYT,* June 22, 1942.
61. H.J. Carter, "Confidential Memorandum NY-256," December 20, 1943, p. 1, Department of Justice, War Division, Economic Warfare Section, NA RG60.
62. H.J. Carter, "Confidential Memorandum NY-256," December 20, 1943, p. 4, Department of Justice, War Division, Economic Warfare Section, NA RG60.
63. Harold Ungar, "Confidential Memorandum NY-356: The Use of Standardized Accounting and Business Machines in the German Economy," June 28, 1944, p. 1, Department of Justice, War Division, Economic Warfare Section, NA RG60.
64. H.J. Carter, "Control in Business Machines," circa 1944, Department of Justice, War Division, Economic Warfare Section, NA RG60; also see H.J. Carter, Interview of J.W. Schotte, September 15, 1944, Department of Justice, War Division, Economic Warfare Section, NA RG60; also see H.J. Carter, "Confidential Memorandum NY-256," December 20, 1943, Department of Justice, War Division, Economic Warfare Section, NA RG60; also see H.J. Carter, "Confidential Memorandum NY-287 to Brigadier General Betts," December 14, 1943, Department of Justice, War Division, Economic Warfare Section; NA RG60; also see *Civil Affairs Guide, Preservation and Use of Key Records in Germany,* No.13–123, Department of Justice, War Division, Economic Warfare Section, NA RG60; H.J. Carter, Draft Notes of Interview with J.W. Schotte, June 14–16, 1943, Department of Justice, War Division, Economic Warfare Section, NA RG60; also see H.J. Carter, "Confidential Memo 249-D re: Use of Business Machines by the Italian State Railways," March 8, 1944, Department of Justice, War Division, Economic Warfare Section, NA RG60; also see "CEC I.B.M. Subsidiary in France: Confidential Report 332," submitted by Harold J. Carter, April 10, 1944, Department of Justice, War Division, Economic Warfare Section, NA RG60; also see "Deutsche Hollerith Maschinen GmbH: Confidential Report 242," submitted by Harold J. Carter, December 8, 1943, Department of Justice, War Division, Economic Warfare Section, NA RG60; Harold Ungar, "Confidential Memorandum NY-356: The Use of Standardized Accounting and Business Machines in the German Economy," June 28, 1944, p. 4, Department of Justice, War Division, Economic Warfare Section, NA RG60.

XIII: EXTERMINATION

1. CSDIC, "Secret Report: PW Intelligence Bulletin No. 2/57," April 25, 1945, NA RG226; "Oral Testimony of Jean Frederic Veith," *The Avalon Project: Nuremberg Trial Proceedings, Vol. 6,* January 28, 1946, cited in www.yale.edu/lawweb/avalon.
2. Letter and Attachment, Arbeitseinsatz Mauthausen to Arbeitseinsatz Ravensbrück, November 27, 1944, CAEN; Georgia Peet-Taneva, Telephone Interview by Author, November 29, 1999; also see "Oral Testimony of J.F. Veith," pp. 202, 203, 204.
3. Johannes Tuchel, *Die Inspektion der Konzentrationslager 1938–1945* (Berlin: Hentrich, 1994), p. 124; Oral Testimony of J.F. Veith, p. 202; also see Josef Kramer Statement, May 22, 1945, p. 3, PRO TS 26/903.
4. Letter, Arbeitseinsatz Ravensbrück to Kommandantur Concentration Camp Flossenbürg, October 14, 1944, NA RG242/338, T-1021/ Roll 17 JAG; see Letter, Arbeitseinsatz K.L. Ravensbrück to Arbeitseinsatz K.L. Flossenbürg, September 1, 1944, NA RG242/338, T-1021/Roll 17 JAG Frame 030201; see Tuchel, p. 124; also see Letter, G. Maurer to R. Hoess, September 4, 1943, cited in Tuchel, p. 128.
5. "Secret Report: Poland Birkenau (Auschwitz II) Concentration Camp," May 31, 1945, PRO WO 208/4296; see Benjamin B. Ferencz, *Less Than Slaves: Jewish Forced Labor and the Quest for Compensation* (Cambridge: Harvard University Press, 1979), p. 118; Affidavit of Rudolf Hoess, p. 2, U.S. Army Interrogation Division, NA RG238; Letter, G. Maurer to R. Hoess, September 4, 1943; cited in Tuchel, p. 128; "Inspection of German Concentra-

tion Camp for Political Prisoners Located at Buchenwald," April 16, 1945, Appendix A, p. 2, PRO FO 371/51185; Josef Kramer, "Confidential Report," circa 1945, p. 20, PRO FO 371/46796; see Bob Moore, *Victims and Survivors: The Nazi Persecution of the Jews in the Netherlands 1940–1945* (New York: Arnold, 1997), p. 102.

6. *Ziffernschlüssel für KL-Häftlingskartei,* NA RG242/338, T-21, Roll 5, JAG.
7. "Secret Report: Poland Birkenau (Auschwitz II) Concentration Camp," May 31, 1945, PRO WO 208/4296.
8. "Secret Report: Poland Birkenau (Auschwitz II) Concentration Camp," May 31, 1945, pp. 1–2, PRO WO 208/4296.
9. Tuchel, p. 124.
10. "Secret Report: Poland Birkenau (Auschwitz II) Concentration Camp," May 31, 1945, p. 2, PRO WO 208/4296.
11. Yisrael Gutman and Michael Berenbaum, eds., *Anatomy of the Auschwitz Death Camp,* (Indianapolis: Indiana University Press, 1994), pp. 7, 312; Piper Franciszek and Teresa Swiebocka, eds., *Auschwitz: Nazi Death Camp. Oswiecim: the Auschwitz-Birkenau State Museum, 1996,* pp. 60–61 cited in library.ushmm.org/faqs; Ferencz, p. 53.
12. "Secret Report: Poland Birkenau (Auschwitz II) Concentration Camp," May 31, 1945, p. 3, PRO WO 208/4296.
13. Auschwitz Museum, Item 51593; Mauthausen Card APMO, n.d., Syg. D-Mau/6.
14. Letter, K.L. Ravensbrück Arbeitsdienst to K.L. Flossenbürg, October 14, 1944, NA RG242/338, T-21 Roll 5 JAG.
15. Josef Kramer, "Confidential Report," circa 1945, Section II, p. 14, PRO FO 371/46796; Josef Kramer Statement, May 22, 1945, p. 2, PRO TS 26/903.
16. *Häftlingskartei,* BA NS3.
17. *Häftlingskartei,* BA NS3.
18. *Häftlingskartei,* BA NS3.
19. *Häftlingskartei,* BA NS3.
20. *Häftlingskartei,* BA NS3.
21. *Häftlingskartei,* BA NS3.
22. Letter, G. Maurer to R. Hoess, September 4, 1943, cited in Tuchel, p.128.
23. "Administration of German Concentration Camps," July 9, 1945, PRO FO 371/46979 July 9, 1945; "Decoding Key for Concentration Camp Card Index Files," n.d., NARG242/338, T-1021 Roll 5, JAG.
24. "Secret Report: Poland Birkenau (Auschwitz II) Concentration Camp," May 31, 1945, p. 4, PRO WO 208/4296.
25. "Treatment of Prisoners in Concentration Camp at Buchenwald," B.L. Bracey to Lord Halifax, December 28, 1938, p. 5, PRO FO 371/21757.
26. "Treatment of Prisoners in Concentration Camp at Buchenwald," B.L. Bracey to Lord Halifax, December 28, 1938, p. 5, PRO FO 371/21757.
27. "Daily Reports of Transfer of Inmates within Work Camp Zwieberge of Buchenwald Concentration Camp," January 7–February 21, 1945," NA RG242/338 T-1021 Roll 5, Frame 149.
28. "Hospital Cards of Sick Inmates at Work Camp Zwieberge of Buchenwald Concentration Camp," December 29, 1944–April 18, 1945, NA 242/338 T-1021 Roll 6, Frame 445.
29. Robert Jay Lifton, *The Nazi Doctors: Medical Killing and the Psychology of Genocide,* (Basic Books, 1986), p. 152; CSDIC, "Secret Report: PW Intelligence Bulletin No. 2/57," April 25, 1945, p. 16, NA RG226; Helmut Krausnick et al., *Anatomy of the SS State,* transl. Richard Barry et al. (New York: Walker and Company, 1965), p. 572.
30. *Häftlingskartei,* BA NS3.
31. CSDIC, "Secret Report: PW Intelligence Bulletin No. 2/57," April 25, 1945, p. 20, NA RG226; H.K. Chauncey, Memorandum, October 30, 1945, IBM Files.
32. Tuchel, pp. 136, 137, 143–145.
33. Letter, Arbeitseinsatz K.L. Ravensbrück to Arbeitseinsatz K.L. Flossenbürg, September 1, 1944, NA RG242/338, T-1021/Roll 17 JAG Frame 030201.
34. Letter, Arbeitseinsatz K.L. Ravensbrück to Arbeitseinsatz K.L. Flossenbürg, September 1, 1944, NA RG242/338, T-1021/Roll 17 JAG Frame 030201.

35. Letter, K.L. Ravensbrück Arbeitseinsatz to K.L. Flossenbürg Kommandantur, January 24, 1945, NA RG242/338 JAG T-1021 Roll 17; Letter, Arbeitseinsatz K.L. Ravensbrück to Arbeitseinsatz K.L. Flossenbürg, September 1, 1944, NA RG242/338, T-1021/Roll 17 JAG Frame 030201.

36. Letter, K.L. Ravensbrück to Kommandantur Flossenbürg, November 13, 1944, NA RG242/338 JAG T-1021 Roll 17.

37. "Captive in Germany Recalls Cannibalism," *NYT,* March 31, 1946; "Oral Testimony of J.F. Veith," p. 202; "Written Testimony of Gerhard Kanthack," Mauthausen Concentration Camp Memorial Archive (V/3/20), cited in www.mauthausen-memorial.gv.at/engl/Geschichte/10.07.Kanthack.html.

38. "Oral Testimony of J.F. Veith," pp. 201, 203; Letter, K.L. Mauthausen to Zentral Institut, October 17, 1944, USHMM RG-04.006M Reel 14, File 38.

39. "Oral Testimony of J.F. Veith," p. 204; "Report on Changes from Prison Camp," October 8, 1944, USHMM RG-04.006 M Reel 14, File 38.

40. "Abgangsliste No. 1," USHMM RG-04.006M Reel 14, File 38.

41. "Abgangsliste No. 1," USHMM RG-04.006M Reel 14, File 38; "Oral Testimony of J.F. Veith," p. 203; Tuchel, p. 100.

42. *Häftlingskartei,* BA NS3; Josef Kramer, "Confidential Report," circa 1945, p. 20, PRO FO371/46796; also see Moore, p. 94.

43. "Deposition of Lt. Col. James Johnson," pp. 1, 2, 3, PRO TS26/903; "Notes on Oswald Pohl," PRO WO311/435 p3.

44. Josef Kramer Statement, May 22, 1945, p. 3, PRO TS 26/903.

45. Gutman and Berenbaum, p. 47; also see Krausnick et al., p. 504.

46. Josef Kramer, "Confidential Report," Appendix, pp. 14–15, circa 1945, PRO FO371/46796.

47. Note, K.L. Mauthausen to Zentral Institut, September 14, 1944, USHMM RG-04.006 M Reel 14, File 38; Josef Kramer, "Confidential Report," Appendix, pp. 14–15, circa 1945, PRO FO371/46796.

48. Note, K.L. Mauthausen Arbeitseinsatz to Zentral Institut, September 12, 1944, USHMM RG-04–006 M Reel 14, file 38; Note, K.L. Mauthausen Arbeitseinsatz to Zentral Institut, October 3, 1944, USHMM RG-04–006 M Reel 14, File 38; Note, K.L. Mauthausen Arbeitseinsatz to Zentral Institut, October 17, 1944, USHMM RG-04–006 M Reel 14, File 38; Note, K.L. Mauthausen Arbeitseinsatz to Zentral Institut, November 13, 1944, USHMM RG-04–006 M Reel 14, File 38.

49. Letter, K.L. Mauthausen Arbeitseinsatz to Zentral Institut, January 2, 1944, USHMM RG-04–006 M Reel 14, File 38.

50. Tuchel, pp. 137, 143, 144–145, 149.

51. *Häftlingskartei,* BA NS3.

52. Punch Cards, NA RG242, Reel 8, T-73, Frames 1053480, 1053481.

53. Tuchel, p. 143.

54. Tuchel, p. 149; "Key to Sketches of Oswiecik Concentration Camp," n.d., p. 2, PRO WO 208/4296.

55. "Decoding Key for Concentration Camp Card Index File," NA RG242/338 JAG T-1021/Roll 5, Frame 99.

56. "Confidential Memo," circa 1945, p. 43, PRO FO 1038/35; also see Gutman and Berenbaum, p. 364.

57. "Treatment of Prisoners in Concentration Camp at Buchenwald," B.L. Bracey to Lord Halifax, December 28, 1938, p. 5, PRO FO 371/21757; Gutman and Berenbaum, p. 364.

58. "Inspection of German Concentration Camp for Political Prisoners Located at Buchenwald," April 16, 1945, pp. 1–2, PRO FO371/51185.

59. "Inspection of German Concentration Camp for Political Prisoners Located at Buchenwald," April 16, 1945, p. 3, PRO FO371/51185.

60. Video, "Testimony," Permanent Exhibit, USHMM.

61. "Treatment of Prisoners in Concentration Camp at Buchenwald," B.L. Bracey to Lord Halifax, December 28, 1938, Register, p. 414, PRO FO 371/21757; "Memorandum of

Concentration Camp at Sachsenhausen," circa February 1939, PRO FO 371/23006; Josef Kramer, "Confidential Report," p. 5, circa 1945, PRO FO371/46796.

62. "Treatment of Prisoners in Concentration Camp at Buchenwald," B.L. Bracey to Lord Halifax, December 28, 1938, pp. 3, 4, 7, 12, PRO FO 371/21757; "Statement by Jewish Ex-prisoner, August 1938," PRO FO 371/21757; Report on Buchenwald, circa February 1939, p. 7, PRO FO 371/23006.

63. "Translated Declaration," www.library.ushmm.org/jhvhwtns/declare2.htm; also see "Jehovah's Witnesses: Courageous in the Face of Nazi Peril," www.watchtower.org/library/9/1998/7/8/article_01.htm.

64. "Decoding Key for Concentration Camp Card Index Files," NA RG242/338, T-1021, Reel 5 JAG; Josef Kramer Statement, May 22, 1945, p. 7, PRO TS 26/903; also see "Memorandum of the Concentration Camp at Sachsenhausen," p. 6, circa February 1939, PRO FO 371/23006; Prisoner card, Auschwitz Museum.

65. "Decoding Key for Concentration Camp Card Index Files," NA RG242/338, T-1021, Reel 5 JAG.

66. "Decoding Key for Concentration Camp Card Index Files," NA RG242/338, T-1021, Reel 5 JAG.

67. Yitzhak Arad et al., eds., *Documents on the Holocaust: Selected Sources on the Destruction of the Jews of Germany and Austria, Poland, and the Soviet Union*, transl. Lea Ben Dor (Lincoln: University of Nebraska Press, 1981; Bison Books, 1999), pp. 342, 344; also see Letter, Anthony Eden to Polish Embassy, December 9, 1942, p. 2, PRO FO 371/30924; also see "1,000,000 Jews Slain by Nazis, Report Says," *NYT* June 30, 1942; also see "Two-thirds of Jews in Poland Held Slain," *NYT*, December 4, 1942.

68. Arad et al., p. 134.

69. Götz Aly and Karl Heinz Roth, *Die restlose Erfassung: Volkszählen, Identifizieren, Aussondern im Nationalsozialismus* (Berlin: Rotbuch Verlag, 1984), pp. 32–34, 60; "Questionnaire of Richard Korherr," n.d., BA NS 48/15; also see "Certificate of Character" of Korherr by Gauleitung Mainfranken, September 22, 1939, BA NS 48/15.

70. Jochen von Lang, ed., *Eichmann Interrogated: Transcripts for the Archives of the Israeli Police*, transl. Ralph Manheim (New York: Farrar, Straus & Giroux, 1983), pp. 88–89.

71. Wannsee Protocol, January 20, 1942, cited in Arad et al., p. 255.

72. Wannsee Protocol, January 20, 1942, cited in Arad et al., pp. 254–255; also see www.us-israel.org.

73. www.us-israel.org; also see Arad et al., p. 256.

74. www.us-israel.org; also see Arad et al., pp. 256, 260–261.

75. www.us-israel.org; also see Arad et al., p. 258.

76. Aly and Roth, pp. 60–61.

77. Aly and Roth, pp. 32–34.

78. H. Himmler, Decrees, December 9, 1940, BA NS 48/15.

79. H. Himmler, Decree, December 9, 1940 BA NS 48/15.

80. Letter, R. Korherr to R. Brandt, June 8, 1942, BA NS 48/6.

81. Letter, R. Korherr to R. Brandt, June 8, 1942, p. 2, BA NS 48/6.

82. Letter, R. Korherr to R. Brandt, June 8, 1942, pp. 2–3, BA NS 48/6.

83. Letter, Personal Staff Himmler to Korherr, August 10, 1943, BA NS 48/15.

84. CSDIC, "Secret Report: PW Intelligence Bulletin No. 2/57," April 25, 1945, p. 20, NA RG226; Letter, A. Bartels to R. Korherr, May 26, 1944, NA RG242 A 3343–550–201A, Frames 1018–1029; Walther Lauersen, "Organisation und Aufgaben des Maschinellen Berichtwesens des Reichministers für Rüstung und Kriegsproduktion," December 5, 1945, pp. 3–4, BA R3/17a.

85. von Lang, pp. 112, 115.

86. Manuscript Department, University Library, Göttingen No. 5193, cited in Aly and Roth, p. 87.

87. Manuscript Department, University Library, Göttingen No. 5194, cited in Aly and Roth, p. 87.

88. H. Himmler Personnel Order, December 31, 1943, BA NS 48/5; www.nizkor.org/people/

e/eichmann.adolf; von Lang, p.112; also see Raul Hilberg, *The Destruction of the European Jews* (New York: Quadrangle Books, Inc., 1961; Harper Colophon Books, 1979), p. 631.

89. Josef Kramer Statement, May 22, 1945 p. 3, PRO TS 26/903, PRO TS 26/903.

90. von Lang, pp. 111, 113, 115; also see Aly and Roth, pp. 86, 87; Arad et al., pp. 358–361.

91. Gutman and Berenbaum, p. 163; Affidavit of Rudolf Hoess, circa April 1946, p. 2, NA RG238.

92. von Lang, pp. 111, 113, 115; Arad et al., pp. 359, 360, 361; also see Aly and Roth, p. 87.

93. Arad et al., p. 262; Raul Hilberg et al., eds., *The Warsaw Diary of Adam Czerniakow: Prelude to Doom*, transl. Stanislaw Staron and the staff of Yad Vashem (New York: Stein and Day, 1979), p.1; Hannah Arendt, *Eichmann in Jerusalem: A Report on the Banality of Evil* (New York: Viking Penguin, Inc., 1963; Penguin Books, 1965), p. 28.

94. "Polish Jews in Tribute," *NYT*, April 20, 1946; also see Letter, Polish Embassy to A. Eden, December 9, 1942, PRO FO 371/30924.

95. Isaiah Trunk, *Judenrat: The Jewish Councils in Eastern Europe under Nazi Occupation* (New York: Macmillan, 1972; Lincoln: University of Nebraska Press, 1972) p. 444.

96. Trunk, p. 441.

97. Trunk, p. 443.

98. Trunk, p. 445.

99. Trunk, p. 446.

100. Raul Hilberg et al., pp. 384–385, 443; also see Letter, Polish Embassy to A. Eden, December 9, 1942, p. 6, PRO FO 371/30924; Confidential Report from Agent to Polish government on "Liquidation of the Warsaw Ghetto," n.d., p. 2, PRO FO 371/31097.

XIV: THE SPOILS OF GENOCIDE, I

1. H.K. Chauncey, Memorandum, October 30, 1945, IBM Files; Harold Ungar, "Confidential Memorandum NY-356: The Use of Standardized Accounting and Business Machines in the German Economy," June 28, 1944, p. 4, Department of Justice, War Division, Economic Warfare Section, NA RG60; Letter, H.K. Chauncey to the British Admiralty, April 6, 1948, PRO ADM 1/21025; also see James Connally, *History of Computing in Europe* (IBM World Trade Corporation, circa 1967), p. 42; also see Letter, H.B. Fellinger to William Esch, June 21, 1945, pp. 2, 3, IBM Files; also see Confidential Report, J.W. Schotte to L.H. La Motte, circa 1941, Department of Justice, War Division, Economic Warfare Section, NA RG60.

2. "Report on Card Exports from U.S.A., circa 1939–1940," Department of Justice, War Division, Economic Warfare Section, NA RG60; also see "Report on Card Production and Sales Statistics," circa 1943, Department of Justice, War Division, Economic Warfare Section, NA RG60; Confidential Report, J.W. Schotte to L.H. La Motte, circa 1941, p. 4, Department of Justice, War Division, Economic Warfare Section, NA RG60.

3. Letter, Commission of Mobility of Law to Dutch Consulate U.S., July 12, 1941, DNA Box 7; also see Connally, p. E-14.

4. Internal IBM Memorandum, circa May 1945, pp. 1, 2, 3, 5, NA RG84; Paraphrase of Telegram, McIvor to Cordell Hull, May 8, 1943, NA RG84.

5. "S.A.Watson Italiana: Confidential Report 287," pp. 3, 4, submitted by Harold J. Carter, February 21, 1944, Department of Justice, War Division, Economic Warfare Section, NA RG60; Paraphrase of Telegram, American Legation to Cordell Hull, June 27, 1943, NA RG84; Internal IBM Memorandum, circa May 1945, pp. 1–5, NA RG84.

6. "S.A. Watson Italiana: Confidential Report 287," p. 7, submitted by Harold J. Carter, February 21, 1944, Department of Justice, War Division, Economic Warfare Section, NA RG60; also see Letter, W.C. Lier to D. Reagan, May 8, 1942, p. 2, NA RG84.

7. Connally, pp. 41, 42; H.B. Fellinger, Enclosure 5, pp. 1–2, IBM Files; H.B. Fellinger, Enclosure 6, pp. 1–2, IBM Files.

8. Letter, P.A. Datsoff to W.C. Lier, May 2, 1942, NA RG84; also see Letter, L.J. Clairis to American Legation Bern, April 20, 1945, NA RG84; also see Letter, R.G. Martens to American Legation Bern, May 4, 1945, NA RG84; also see Letter, W.C. Lier to D. Reagan, June 9, 1942, NA RG84; also see Memorandum, J.H. Tait to D. Reagan, June 19, 1942, NA RG84; also see Letter, J.K. Huddle to W.C. Lier, June 22, 1942, NA RG84; also see

J.K. Huddle to Cordell Hull, June 22, 1942, NA RG84; also see Letter, W.C. Lier to J.K. Huddle, July 3, 1942, NA RG84; also see Memorandum, J.H. Tait to D. Reagan, July 8, 1942, NA RG84; Note, D. Reagan to IBM Geneva, April 30, 1945, NA RG84; also see Letter, W.C. Lier to Commercial Attaché, November 24, 1944, NA RG84.

9. "Nazi Retribution Widened by Eden," *NYT,* December 18, 1942.

10. "Allies Describe Outrages on Jews," *NYT,* December 20, 1942.

11. "Jewish Risings Reported," *NYT,* July 1, 1940; "Rumania Freezes Wealth," *NYT,* October 21, 1940; "Bucharest Seizes Farms," *NYT,* October 6, 1940; "Rumania Seizes Farms," *NYT,* September 28, 1940; "Rumania Decrees Anti-Jewish Laws," *NYT,* September 10, 1940; also see "Memorandum on Anti-Jewish Measures in Roumania Since the End of September, 1940," pp. 1, 2, 11, 13, 15, PRO FO 371/30002; Report, "The German Minority in Roumania," PRO FO 371/33266.

12. *Encyclopaedia Judaica,* s.v. "Rumania," p. 400; Radu Ioanid, *The Holocaust in Romania: The Destruction of Jews and Gypsies Under the Antonescu Regime, 1940–1944* (Chicago: Ivan R. Dee, 2000), pp. 57, 58.

13. Ioanid, pp. 57, 58, 111, 170, 196; "Jews Moved From Pruth Area," *NYT,* July 6, 1941.

14. Ioanid, p. xxi; Friedrich Burgdörfer, "Die rumänische Volkszählung 1941: Ein Reisebericht," *Allgemeines Statistisches Archiv* 30 (1941/42): 302, 303, 310.

15. Burgdörfer, p. 318.

16. Burgdörfer, pp. 302, 304–306, 307–311; also see Letter, Ludwig Hümmer to H.K. Chauncey, October 10, 1941, p. 3, IBM Files.

17. Letter, W.C. Lier to H.K. Chauncey, October 10, 1941, p. 3, IBM Files.

18. Letter, J.C. Milner to J.T. Wilson, August 4, 1938, IBM Files.

19. Burgdörfer, pp. 305, 306, 307, 310, 312, 320.

20. Burgdörfer, pp. 307, 309–310.

21. Burgdörfer, p. 315.

22. Burgdörfer, pp. 307, 310.

23. Transcript, H.K. Chauncey Interview with K. Hummel, circa 1940, IBM Files.

24. Letter, W.C. Lier to H.K. Chauncey, October 10, 1941, IBM Files; Letter, W.C. Lier to Thomas J. Watson, October 9, 1941, p. 4, IBM Files.

25. Letter, W.C. Lier to H.K. Chauncey, October 10, 1941, IBM Files; Letter, W.C. Lier to D. Reagan, June 16, 1942, NA RG84.

26. Ioanid, pp. 63–64, 64–65.

27. Ioanid, pp. 71–74, 80–90.

28. Ioanid, p. 276; Yitzhak Arad et al., eds., *Documents on the Holocaust: Selected Sources on the Destruction of the Jews of Germany and Austria, Poland, and the Soviet Union,* transl. Lea Ben Dor (Lincoln: University of Nebraska Press, 1981; Bison Books, 1999), p. 254.

29. Ioanid, p. 242, 276.

30. Ioanid, pp. 242–243, 245.

31. Arad et al., p. 506.

32. Ioanid, p. xxi.

33. "Report of Interests in Primary Allied Organizations, Roumania," November 23, 1943, NA RG131; Confidential Report, J.W. Schotte to L.H. La Motte, circa Spring 1940, pp. 1, 2, 3, 4, Department of Justice, War Division, Economic Warfare Section, NA RG60; H.J. Carter, "Miscellaneous Remarks Pertaining to the Installation of Business Machines and Application of Punched Cards in the Balkan States," January 14, 1944, p. 3, Department of Justice, War Division, Economic Warfare Section, NA RG60.

34. Confidential Report, J.W. Schotte to L.H. La Motte, circa Spring 1940, pp. 1, 2, 3, 4, Department of Justice, War Division, Economic Warfare Section, NA RG60.

35. Letter, W.C. Lier to D.J. Reagan, June 18, 1942, NA RG84.

36. Letter, J.K. Huddle to W.C. Lier, June 23, 1942, NA RG84; also see Letter, W.C. Lier to J.K. Huddle, June 30, 1942, NA RG84.

37. H.J. Carter, "Miscellaneous Remarks Pertaining to the Installation of Business Machines and Application of Punched Cards in the Balkan States," January 14, 1944, p. 3, Department of Justice, War Division, Economic Warfare Section, NA RG60; "Card Production and Sales Statistics," circa 1943, p. 2, Department of Justice, War Division, Economic War-

fare Section, NA RG60; H.J. Carter, "Inventory of Card Printing Machinery in Foreign Countries as of December 1, 1941," Department of Justice, War Division, Economic Warfare Section, NA RG60; H.J. Carter, "List of Card Consumption, 1938," Department of Justice, War Division, Economic Warfare Section, NA RG60.

38. Letter, W.C. Lier to P.C. Squire, September 18, 1944, NA RG84; Telegram, Harrison to American Embassy London, October 5, 1944, NA RG84; Letter, D.J. Reagan to P.C. Squire, September 22, 1944, NA RG84; Telegram, Secretary of State to Monetary Research Department, October 20, 1944, NA RG84. William L. Shirer, *The Rise and Fall of the Third Reich* (New York: Simon and Schuster, 1960), p. 1085.

39. Letter, R. Bachofen to I. Berindei, February 15, 1945, NA RG84.

40. Letter, R. Bachofen to I. Berindei, February 15, 1945, pp. 1–2, NA RG84.

41. "Rumania Pleased by Treaty Terms," *NYT*, August 3, 1946; "Rumania Asks Relief," *NYT*, November 16, 1946.

42. "Statement of War Losses and Damages in Roumania," Attachment to Letter, William R. Vallance to A.L. Williams, August 29, 1945, NA RG59 State Department 465.11 EW International Business Machines Corp./7–2946 CS/JEO; Letter, J.T. Wilson to A.E. Clattenburg, August 10, 1944, NA RG59 340.115/8–1045 XR.

43. Martin Gilbert, *The Holocaust: A History of the Jews of Europe During the Second World War* (New York: Holt, Rinehart and Winston, 1985), pp. 547–548; Raul Hilberg, *The Destruction of the European Jews* (New York: Quadrangle Books, 1961; Harper Colophon, 1979) p. 478.

44. Hilberg, *The Destruction of the European Jews*, p. 481; also see Gilbert, pp. 547–548.

45. Gilbert, p. 547; Hilberg, *The Destruction of the European Jews*, pp. 474, 475, 478, 479; Memorandum of Meeting between von Ribbentrop and Popov, November 26, 1941, p. 1, NA RG238, T-1139, Reel 38, Frames 298–314.

46. "Report of Interests in Primary Allied Organization, Bulgaria," November 23, 1943, NA RG131; Letter, W.C. Lier to D. Reagan, June 9, 1942, NA RG84; also see Letter, P.A. Datsoff to W.C. Lier, May 2, 1942, NA RG84.

47. Letter, P.A. Datsoff to W.C. Lier, May 2, 1942, NA RG84; Letter, W.C. Lier to D. Reagan, June 9, 1942, NA RG84.

48. Letter, P.A. Datsoff to W.C. Lier, May 2, 1942, NA RG84.

49. Letter, W.C. Lier to D. Reagan, June 9, 1942, NA RG84.

50. Letter, J.K. Huddle to W.C. Lier, June 22, 1942, NA RG84.

51. Letter, J.K. Huddle to Cordell Hull, June 22, 1942, pp. 1–2, NA RG84.

52. Letter, W.C. Lier to J.K. Huddle, July 3, 1942, NA RG84; also see Letter, D.J. Reagan to W.C. Lier, July 9, 1942, NA RG84; also see Memorandum, G. Tait to D.J. Reagan, July 8, 1942, NA RG84.

53. H.J. Carter, "Miscellaneous Remarks Pertaining to the Installation of Business Machines and Application of Punched Cards in the Balkan States," January 14, 1944, p. 2, Department of Justice, War Division, Economic Warfare Section, NA RG60; "Statement of War Losses and Damages in Roumania," Attachment to Letter, W.R. Vallance to A.L. Williams, August 29, 1945, NA RG59 State Department 465.11 EW International Business Machines Corp./7–2946 CS/JEO; Note, P.C. Squire to J.K. Huddle, January 20, 1945, NA RG84; also see Letter, L.J. Clairis to American Legation, Bern, April 20, 1945, NA RG84.

54. Note, Luther via Weizsäcker to von Ribbentrop, September 11, 1942, NA NG 2582 cited in Hilberg, *The Destruction of the European Jews*, pp. 480–481; Letter, Luther to Weizsäcker, September 24, 1942, NA NG 1517 Legal and Trade Political divisions, cited in Hilberg, *The Destruction of the European Jews*, p. 481.

55. Hilberg, *The Destruction of the European Jews*, p. 482.

56. Hilberg, *The Destruction of the European Jews*, p. 482; see two photos cited in www.motlc.wiesenthal.com/gallery/pg17/pg0/pg17054.html and 17052.

57. Hilberg, *The Destruction of the European Jews*, p. 482; Gilbert, p. 655.

58. Hilberg, *The Destruction of the European Jews*, p. 482; train photo cited in http://motlc. wiesenthal.com/gallery/pg17/pg0/pg17052.html; see *Encyclopaedia Judaica*, s.v. "Bulgaria," pp. 1486–1487.

59. Gilbert, p. 526.

60. Letter, R. Bachhofen to P. Datsoff, February 14, 1945, pp. 1, 2, NA RG84.

61. "Statement of War Losses and Damages in Roumania," Attachment to Letter, William R. Vallance to A.L. Williams, August 29, 1945, NA RG59 State Department 465.11 EW International Business Machines Corp./7-2946 CS/JEO.

62. H.B. Fellinger, Enclosure 4, July 19, 1945, pp. 14–15, IBM Files.

63. H.B. Fellinger, Enclosure 4, July 19, 1945, pp. 1, 13, IBM Files; Letter and Attachment, J.T. Wilson to A.E. Clattenburg, August 10, 1944, NA RG59 340.115/8–1045 XR; "Report of Interests in Primary Allied Organizations, Poland," November 23, 1943, NA RG131.

64. *Encyclopaedia Judaica,* s.v. "Yugoslavia," p. 874; Hilberg, *The Destruction of the European Jews,* p. 453.

65. "Serbian Prelate Charges Killing Of 180,000 in Nazi-Invaded Croatia," *NYT,* January 3, 1942.

66. *Encyclopaedia Judaica,* s.v. "Yugoslavia," p. 877.

67. H.J. Carter, "Report on Card Production and Sales Statistics," circa 1943, Department of Justice, War Division, Economic Warfare Section, NA RG60; H.B. Fellinger, Enclosure 4, July 19, 1945, p. 1, IBM Files; Hilberg, *The Destruction of the European Jews,* p. 453; H.J. Carter, "Miscellaneous Remarks Pertaining to the Installation of Business Machines and Application of Punched Cards in the Balkan States," January 14, 1944, p. 5, Department of Justice, War Division, Economic Warfare Section, NA RG60.

68. H.B. Fellinger, Enclosure 2, July 14, 1945, pp. 3–4, IBM Files; William L. Shirer, *The Rise and Fall of the Third Reich: A History of Nazi Germany* (New York: Simon and Schuster, 1960), p. 1112; Letter, Lawrence G. Flick to Thomas J. Watson, September 2, 1945, NA RG59 LM197, Reel 19, Frame 372.

69. H.B. Fellinger, Enclosure 2, July 14, 1945, IBM Files; Letter, J.T. Wilson to A.E. Clattenburg, August 10, 1944, NA RG59 340.115/8–1045 XR.

70. Telegram, Chapin to Cordell Hull, September 30, 1944, NA RG59 FW351.1121 Virgile, Roger/9–2344 CS/D; also see Letter, EC to IBM, November 2, 1944, NA RG84; H.B. Fellinger, Enclosure 5, IBM Files, pp. 4, 9, 11.

71. Telegram, Chapin to Cordell Hull, September 30, 1944, NA RG59 FW351.1121 Virgile, Roger/9–2344 CS/D; Letter, Kenneth C. Krentz to Thomas J. Watson, October 9, 1944, NA RG59 State Department FW351.1121 Virgile, Roger/9–2344 CS/D; Letter, Kenneth C. Krentz to Thomas J. Watson, October 9, 1944, NA RG59 State Department FW351.1121 Virgile, Roger/9–2344 CS/D; also see Telegram, E. Caffery to Cordell Hull, October 27, 1944, NA RG59 State Department FW351.1121 Virgile, Roger/9–2344 CS/D; Letter, Kenneth C. Krentz to Thomas J. Watson, October 9, 1944, NA RG59 State Department FW351.1121 Virgile, Roger/9–2344 CS/D.

72. Letter, Kenneth C. Krentz to Thomas J. Watson, October 17, 1944, NA RG59 State Department FW351.1121 Virgile, Roger/9–2344 CS/D; Letter, K.C. Krentz to Thomas J. Watson, October 31, 1944, NA RG59 State Department FW351.1121 Virgile, Roger/9–2344 CS/D; Letter, CEC to IBM, November 2, 1944, NA RG84.

73. "Jews in France Saved by Others," *NYT,* December 18, 1945.

74. "Jews in France Saved by Others," *NYT,* December 18, 1945; Robert Carmille, *Des Apparences a la Réalité: Mise Au Point, Le "Fichier Juif": Rapport de la Commission présidée par René Rémond au Premier Ministre* (1996), p. 13.

75. Memorandum No.3833, Colette Meyer to NA RG59 351.115 International Business Machine Corp./11-2645; also see Letter, J.T. Wilson to A.E. Clattenburg, August 10, 1944, NA RG59 340.115/8–1045 XR.

76. Connally, p. E-10; "Allies Offer Swiss Nazi Asset Share," *NYT,* April 4, 1946; also see "Swiss Stand Firm on German Assets," *NYT,* April 8, 1946; also see "Coercion on Funds Futile, Swiss Hold," *NYT,* April 13, 1946; also see "Swiss Concede Point on German Assets," *NYT,* April 19, 1946; also see "Swiss to Yield 50% of German Assets," *NYT,* May 22, 1946; also see "Accord on Assets Faces Swiss Fire," *NYT,* May 27, 1946; also see "Swiss To Debate Liquidation Pact," *NYT,* June 24, 1946.

77. "Investigation in the New York Agencies of Swiss Banks by the Treasury Department, Washington, June 2, 1942, cited in www.ourworld.compuserve.com/homepages/potomac/doc13.html, pp. 1–2.

78. Letter, D.W. Bell to Thomas J. Watson, July 13, 1942, Department of Justice, War Division, Economic Warfare Section, NA RG60.
79. Letter, D.W. Bell to Thomas J. Watson, July 13, 1942, Department of Justice, War Division, Economic Warfare Section, NA RG60.
80. Letter, Thomas J. Watson to D.W. Bell, July 20, 1942, Letter, D.W. Bell to Thomas J. Watson, July 13, 1942, Department of Justice, War Division, Economic Warfare Section, NA RG60.
81. Confidential Report, IBM Suisse to J.T. Wilson, October 4, 1943, NA RG84; H.J. Carter, "Memorandum for the Files," May 16, 1944, Department of Justice, War Division, Economic Warfare Section, NA RG60.
82. "S.A.Watson Italiana: Confidential Report 287," pp. 6, 7, submitted by Harold J. Carter, February 21, 1944, Department of Justice, War Division, Economic Warfare Section, NA RG60; also see Letter, W.C. Lier to D. Reagan, May 8, 1942, NA RG84.
83. Internal IBM Memorandum, circa May 1945, pp. 1–2, NA RG84; "S.A.Watson Italiana: Confidential Report 287," p. 7, submitted by Harold J. Carter, February 21, 1944, Department of Justice, War Division, Economic Warfare Section, NA RG60.
84. Internal IBM Memorandum, circa May 1945, pp. 1–4, NA RG84.
85. Internal IBM Memorandum, circa May 1945, pp. 1–4, NA RG84; also see Transcript, Telephone Conversation between J.W. Schotte and W.C. Lier, Department of Justice, War Division, Economic Warfare Section, NA RG60.
86. Internal IBM Memorandum, circa May 1945, pp. 1, 2, 3–4, 5, NA RG84.
87. Internal IBM Memorandum, circa May 1945, p. 5, NA RG84.
88. Internal IBM Memorandum, circa May 1945, pp. 1–2, NA RG84; also see W.C. Lier, "Chronological Record of Events in Connection with the Proclaimed Lists of Switzerland-IBM Geneva Office," circa 1945, NA RG84.
89. Letter, F. De Asua to F.W. Nichol, March 10, 1943, NA RG84; also see Letter, J.J. Reinstein to F.W. Nichol, August 14, 1943, NA RG84; also see "Card Production and Sales Statistics," circa 1943, Department of Justice, War Division, Economic Warfare Section, NA RG60; also see "S.A.Watson Italiana: Confidential Report 287," p. 6, submitted by Harold J. Carter, February 21, 1944, Department of Justice, War Division, Economic Warfare Section, NA RG60.
90. Letter, W.C. Lier to P.C. Squire, April 29, 1942, pp. 1–2, NA RG84.
91. Letter, W.C. Lier to D. Reagan, May 8, 1942, NA RG84.
92. Internal IBM Memorandum, circa May 1945, pp. 3, 4, NA RG84.
93. Cablegram, W.C. Lier to IBM New York, July 21, 1942, NA RG84; Internal IBM Memorandum, circa May 1945, p. 5, NA RG84.
94. Internal IBM Memorandum, circa May 1945, p. 2, NA RG84.
95. Internal IBM Memorandum, circa May 1945, p. 5, NA RG84.
96. Internal IBM Memorandum, circa May 1945, p. 5, NA RG84.
97. IBM Application for License to Secretary of Treasury, License No. 223994, September 18, 1941, p. 1, NA RG59 State Department 840.51 Frozen Credits/4064; Letter, J.G. Phillips to Cordell Hull, October 10, 1941, NA RG59 State Department 840.51 Frozen Credits/4064.
98. "S.A. Watson Italiana: Confidential Report 287," p. 6, submitted by Harold J. Carter, February 21, 1944, Department of Justice, War Division, Economic Warfare Section, NA RG60; "CEC I.B.M. Subsidiary in France: Confidential Report 332," pp. 1–2, submitted by Harold J. Carter, April 10, 1944, Department of Justice, War Division, Economic Warfare Section, NA RG60; Letter, D. Reagan to W.C. Lier, June 11, 1942, NA RG84.
99. Cablegram, C. Delcour to F.W. Nichol, November 17, 1941, IBM Files; also see Letter, W.C. Lier to H.K. Chauncey, October 10, 1941, IBM Files; also see Letter, W.C. Lier to Thomas J. Watson, October 9, 1941, IBM Files; also see Nancy Foy, *The Sun Never Sets on IBM* (New York: William Morrow & Company, Inc., 1975), pp. 30, 31; Letter, W.C. Lier to P.C. Squire, April 29, 1942, pp. 1, 2, NA RG84; also see Internal IBM Memorandum, circa May 1945, pp. 1, 2, 3, 5, NA RG84.
100. Letter, W.C. Lier to P.C. Squire, April 29, 1942, pp. 1–2, NA RG84.
101. Letter, W.C. Lier to P.C. Squire, April 29, 1942, pp. 1–2, NA RG84.

102. Letter, G. Daufresne de la Chevalerie to J.T. Wilson, August 4, 1939, Department of Justice, War Division, Economic Warfare Section, NA RG60.

103. Foy, p. 31.

104. Foy, p. 35.

105. Letter, P.C. Squire to D.J. Reagan, May 22, 1945, NA RG84.

106. Letter, P.C. Squire to D.J. Reagan, May 22, 1945, NA RG84.

107. Letter, J.K. Huddle to P.C. Squire, January 22, 1945, NA RG84.

108. Note, C. Delcour, February 13, 1945, NA RG84.

109. Note, C. Delcour, February 13, 1945, NA RG84.

110. Letter, D.J. Reagan to Marcel Vaidie, July 5, 1945, NA RG84.

111. Letter, J.K. Huddle to P.C. Squire, January 22, 1945, NA RG84; also see Foy, p. 35; *Diary of Charles Cassidy*, 303rd Bomb Group (Hells Angels) 360th Bmb. Sqdn cited at www.west.net/~macpuzl/internee.html, p4.

XV: THE SPOILS OF GENOCIDE, II

1. "Civil Affairs Guide: Preservation and Use of Key Records in Germany," June 6, 1944, OMGUS D802-83, U59 War Department Pamphlet No. 31-123, pp. 18, 20, Department of Justice, War Division, Economic Warfare Section, NA RG60.

2. "Civil Affairs Guide: Preservation and Use of Key Records in Germany," June 6, 1944, OMGUS D802-83, U59 War Department Pamphlet No. 31-123, pp. 21, 58, Department of Justice, War Division, Economic Warfare Section, NA RG60.

3. "Civil Affairs Guide: Preservation and Use of Key Records in Germany," June 6, 1944, OMGUS D802-83, U59 War Department Pamphlet No. 31-123, p. 47, Department of Justice, War Division, Economic Warfare Section, NA RG60.

4. British Intelligence Note, January 12, 1945, PRO FO 1032/1583; also see *FIAT Weekly Target Digest* 21 (February 10, 1946), PRO FO935/53.

5. Hitler Decree, circa 1945, NA RG242, T-73 Reel 10 Frames 1055461-1055462.

6. CSDIC, "Secret Report: PW Intelligence Bulletin No. 2/57," April 25, 1945, pp. 6-7, NA RG226; Notes, H.K. Chauncey, October 30, 1945, p. 3, IBM Files.

7. CSDIC, "Secret Report: PW Intelligence Bulletin No. 2/57," April 25, 1945, Item II, pp. 5, 6, NA RG226.

8. "Hospital Cards of Sick Inmates," circa April 1945, NA RG 242/338, T-1021, Roll 6, Frame 445; "Decoding Key for Concentration Camps," p. 126, NA RG242/338 T-1021/ Roll 6, Frame.

9. H.B. Fellinger, Enclosure 3, July 14, 1945, IBM Files.

10. H.B. Fellinger, Enclosure 5, July 30, 1945, p. 1, IBM Files; H.B. Fellinger, Enclosure 7, August 4, 1945, IBM Files; H.B. Fellinger, General Report, August 8, 1945, pp. 1-2, IBM Files.

11. W. Heidinger, Memorandum to Advisory Committee, June 18, 1943, p. 9, IBM Files.

12. W. Heidinger, Memorandum to Advisory Committee, June 18, 1943, pp. 6-7, IBM Files.

13. James Connally, *History of Computing in Europe* (IBM World Trade Corporation, circa 1967), p. E-15; Letter, H.K. Chauncey to Thomas J. Watson, December 23, 1945, p. 4, IBM Files.

14. H.B. Fellinger, Enclosure 1, July 10, 1945, pp. 2, 4, 9, IBM Files.

15. H.B. Fellinger, Enclosure 1, July 10, 1945, pp. 3, 8, IBM Files.

16. H.B. Fellinger, Enclosure 3, July 14, 1945, pp. 1, 2, 4, 6, IBM Files.

17. H.B. Fellinger, Enclosure 3, July 14, 1945, p. 10, IBM Files.

18. H.B. Fellinger, Enclosure 4, July 19, 1945, IBM Files; H.B. Fellinger, Enclosure 2, July 14, 1945, IBM Files.

19. Letter, H.B. Fellinger to MB, circa 1944, NA RG 242, T-73 Reel 11, RmfRuK/292, Frames 1057520-1057526; also see Note, Kurt Passow to H.B. Fellinger, January 5, 1945, NA RG242, T-73 Reel 8, Frame 1053840 RmfRuK/173; Dr. Springer, Memorandum for Files, June 16, 1944, NA RG242, T-73 Reel 8, Frame 1053858 RmfRuK/173; Memorandum, H.B. Fellinger to MB, circa July-August 1944, NA RG 242, T-73 Reel 11/292 RmfRuK.

20. Memorandum, H.B. Fellinger to MB, circa July-August 1944, pp. 3-5, NA RG 242, T-73 Reel 11/292, RmfRuK Frames 1057522-1057524.

21. Dr. Springer, Memorandum for Files, June 16, 1944, NA RG242, T-73 Reel 8, Frame 1053858 RmfRuK/173; also see Memorandum, H.B. Fellinger to MB, circa July–August 1944, pp. 3–6, NA RG242, T-73, reel 11/292 RmfRuK, Frames 1057522–1057525; Letter, O.E. Hoermann to Endicott Employee, April 10, 1942, Department of Justice, War Division, Economic Warfare Section, NA RG60.

22. Memorandum, H.B. Fellinger to MB, circa July-August 1944, pp. 3–5, NA RG 242, T-73 Reel 11/292, RmfRuK Frames 1057522–1057524.

23. "Lease Contract," September 15, 1943, NA RG 242, T-73, Reel 8/IBM contracts.

24. "Lease Contracts," September 15, October 6, 1943, NA RG 242, T-73 Reel 8/IBM contracts.

25. "Memorandum of Licensing Agreement between Wanderer-Werke and Dehomag," August 7, 1944, IBM Files.

26. "Holiday Bonuses Paid to Employees," *NYT,* December 24, 1940.

27. "Holiday Bonuses Paid to Employees," *NYT,* December 24, 1940.

28. Letter, James T. Senn to Thomas J. Watson, April 26, 1945, IBM Files.

29. Letter, Alfred Dicke to Thomas J. Watson, May 10, 1945, IBM Files; also see Cablegram, Alfred Dicke to Thomas J. Watson, May 10, 1945, IBM Files.

30. Letter, Alfred Dicke to Thomas J. Watson, May 10, 1945, IBM Files; also see Cablegram, Alfred Dicke to Thomas J. Watson, May 10, 1945, IBM Files.

31. Letter, Leonard V. Salisbury to IBM NY, August 22, 1945, IBM Files.

32. Letter, Lawrence C. Frank to Secretary of State, January 5, 1946, NA RG 363.115 International Business Machines Corp./1–546 OS.

33. Letter, Lawrence G. Flick to Thomas J. Watson, September 2, 1945, NA RG59 862.5034/9–2045 CS/LE; also see H.B. Fellinger, Enclosure 6, August 10, 1945, p. 5, IBM Files.

34. Letter, Lawrence G. Flick to Thomas J. Watson, September 2, 1945, NA RG59 862.5034/9–2045 CS/LE.

35. Letter, Lawrence G. Flick to Thomas J. Watson, September 2, 1945, NA RG59 862.5034/9–2045 CS/LE.

36. Letter, Lawrence G. Flick to Thomas J. Watson, September 2, 1945, pp. 1–2, NA RG59 862.5034/9–2045 CS/LE.

37. Letter, Lawrence G. Flick to Thomas J. Watson, September 2, 1945, p. 2, NA RG59 862.5034/9–2045 CS/LE.

38. Letter, Lawrence G. Flick to Thomas J. Watson, September 2, 1945, p. 2, NA RG59 862.5034/9–2045 CS/LE.

39. Letter, Thomas J. Watson to William L. Clayton, September 20, 1945, NA RG59 862.5034/9–2045 CS/D.

40. Letter, W.L. Clayton to J.H. Hilldring, circa October 1945, NA RG59 862.5034/9–2045 CS.

41. Letter, W.L. Clayton to Thomas J. Watson, circa October 1945, NA RG59 862.5034/9–2045 CS/LE.

42. Letter, J.H. Hilldring to W.L. Clayton, November 27, 1945, NA RG59 862.5034/11–2745 CS/D; Lucius D. Clay, 1897–1978, www.dhm.de/lemo/html/biografien/ClayLuciusD/.

43. Letter, J.T. Wilson to State Department, May 18, 1945, NA RG59 362.115 International Business Machines Corp./5–1845 CS/D.

44. Letter, J.T. Wilson to State Department, May 18, 1945, NA RG59 362.115 International Business Machines Corp./5–1845 CS/D.

45. Letter, J.T. Wilson to State Department, May 18, 1945, NA RG59 362.115 International Business Machines Corp./5–1845 CS/D.

46. Letter, State Department to U.S. Political Advisor, July 13, 1945, NA RG59 362.115 International Business Machines Corp./5–1845 CS/D.

47. Report, H.K. Chauncey, October 30, 1945, p. 1, IBM Files.

48. Report, H.K. Chauncey, October 30, 1945, pp. 1, 2, 3, 4, IBM Files.

49. Report, H.K. Chauncey, October 30, 1945, pp. 1, 2, IBM Files; H.K. Chauncey, "Report: Trip to Germany, October 24–30, 1945," H.K. Chauncey, "Trip Summary, November 16, 1945," IBM Files; H.K. Chauncey, Note, "Germany," November 16, 1945, IBM Files.

50. Report, H.K. Chauncey, October 30, 1945, pp. 2, 3, IBM Files.

51. Report, H.K. Chauncey, October 30, 1945, pp. 2, 3, IBM Files.

52. Report, H.K. Chauncey, October 30, 1945, pp. 2, 3, IBM Files.

53. Report, H.K. Chauncey, October 30, 1945, p. 3, IBM Files.

54. Report, H.K. Chauncey, October 30, 1945, p. 4, IBM Files.

55. Report, H.K. Chauncey, October 30, 1945, p. 4, IBM Files; also see "Report: Trip to Germany, October 24–30, 1945," p. 2, circa November 16, 1945; H.B. Fellinger, Enclosure 6, August 10, 1945, IBM Files.

56. Collect Telegram, Norman D. Cann to IBM NY, November 1, 1945, IBM Files; also see Memorandum #1339 to U.S. Political Advisor, "Property in Germany of the International Business Machines Corporation," November 19, 1945, NA RG59 462.11 EW International Business Machines Corp./11–1945 CS/D.

57. Confidential Report, H.K. Chauncey to Thomas J. Watson, December 23, 1945, IBM Files; also see H.B. Fellinger, Enclosure 6, August 10, 1945, IBM Files.

58. "Report on Conditions of IBM Affairs in Germany Sept–Nov 1945," circa December 1945, pp. 4, 5, IBM Files; H.B. Fellinger, Enclosure 6, August 10, 1945, IBM Files.

59. Letter, H.K. Chauncey to Thomas J. Watson, December 23, 1945, p. 2, IBM Files.

60. H.B. Fellinger, General Report, August 8, 1945, IBM Files; also see H.B. Fellinger, Enclosure 1, July 10, 1945, IBM Files; also see H.B. Fellinger, Enclosure 2, July 14, 1945, IBM Files; also see H.B. Fellinger, Enclosure 3, July 19, 1945, IBM Files; also see H.B. Fellinger, Enclosure 4, July 19, 1945, IBM Files; also see H.B. Fellinger, Enclosure 5, July 30, 1945, IBM Files; also see H.B. Fellinger, Enclosure 6, August 10, 1945, IBM Files; also see H.B. Fellinger Enclosure 7, August 4, 1945, IBM Files; Letter and Attachment, James W. Gantenbein to J.T. Wilson, November 5, 1946, IBM Files.

61. Letter, H.K. Chauncey to T.J. Watson, December 23, 1945, p. 2, IBM Files.

62. Letter, H.K. Chauncey to T.J. Watson, December 3, 1945, IBM Files.

63. H.K. Chauncey, "Report on German Trip," circa December 1945, pp. 1–2, IBM Files.

64. H.K. Chauncey, "Report on German Trip," circa December 1945, pp. 1–2, IBM Files.

65. H.K. Chauncey, "Report on German Trip," circa December 1945, p. 2, IBM Files.

66. H.K. Chauncey, "Report on German Trip," circa December 1945, pp. 2–3, IBM Files.

67. H.K. Chauncey, "Report on German Trip," circa December 1945, p. 3, IBM Files.

68. H.K. Chauncey, "Report on German Trip," circa December 1945, p. 6, IBM Files; "Report on Conditions of IBM Affairs in Germany Sept–Nov 1945," circa December 1945, pp. 1, 3, 4, IBM Files.

69. "Report on Conditions of IBM Affairs in Germany Sept–Nov 1945," circa December 1945, pp. 1–4, IBM Files.

70. Confidential Report, H.K. Chauncey to Thomas J. Watson, December 23, 1945, p. 4, IBM Files.

71. H.K. Chauncey, "Report on German Trip," circa December 1945, p. 6, IBM Files.

72. Memorandum for H.K. Chauncey, "American Military Laws–Germany," May 21, 1945, IBM Files.

73. Memorandum for H.K. Chauncey, "American Military Laws–Germany," May 21, 1945, IBM Files.

74. Letter, William L. Clayton to J.H. Hilldring, NA RG59 862.5034/9–2045 LM 197, Reel 19, Frames 379–380; Memorandum, W.W. Rostow to Thorp, November 1, 1945, NA RG59 862.5034/9–2045 LM 197, Reel 19, Frame 377.

75. Report, H.K. Chauncey, October 30, 1945, p. 1, IBM Files.

76. H.K. Chauncey, "Report on German Trip," circa December 1945, p. 4, IBM Files.

77. "15 Major Bankers Seized in Germany," *NYT*, November 2, 1945; also see "Allies Investigate German Magnates," *NYT*, February 17, 1946.

78. "15 Major Bankers Seized in Germany," *NYT*, November 2, 1945.

79. "German Magnate Tied to War Plan," *NYT*, January 2, 1946.

80. "Factories on Sale in Germany Listed," *NYT*, January 6, 1946.

81. "21 Farben Plants Wiped Out by U.S.," *NYT*, January 17, 1946; see caption on Photo 43042, I.G. Farben Trial, USHMM August 27, 1947, www.ushmm.org/uia-bin/.

82. "658 German Plants Listed for Payment," *NYT*, October 20, 1946.

83. "Industrial Quislings Convicted in Belgium," *NYT,* September 6, 1946.
84. "Fears Industrialists May Escape Trials," *NYT,* February 1, 1946.
85. Joseph E. Persico, *Nuremberg on Trial* (New York: Viking Penguin, 1994; Penguin Books, 1995) pp. 53, 54, 111; also see Ann Tusa and John Tusa, *The Nuremberg Trial* (New York: Atheneum, 1984), pp. 110, 218, 219.
86. "Schacht Insists He Opposed War," *NYT,* May 2, 1946; also see "Tribunal Dooms Keitel, Ribbentrop, Streicher, Rosenberg, Jodl," *NYT,* October 2, 1946.
87. "United States Strategic Bombing [USSB] Survey Summary Report (Pacific War)," July 1, 1946, www.anesi.com/ussbs; also see "Report on Visit to Statistical Office, Bad Nauheim," August 2, 1945, PRO FO 1046/61; also see Excerpts from *A Memoir, Part 2, "Tibor Scitovsky: A Proud Hungarian,"* 1999, www.hungary.com/hunq/; also see Gabriel Almond, "Size and Composition of the Anti-Nazi Opposition," *APSA Association News* (September 1999), www.apsanet.org; also see "The United States Strategic Bombing Survey," Statistical Appendix to Overall Report (European War), NA RG243, M1013 Final Report of the United States Strategic Bombing Survey, 1945–1947, Reel 1, Office of the Chairman.
88. Almond, "Size and Composition of the Anti-Nazi Opposition," *APSA Association News* (September 1999), www.apsanet.org.
89. Almond, "Size and Composition of the Anti-Nazi Opposition," *APSA Association News* (September 1999), www.apsanet.org.
90. Report, H.K. Chauncey, October 30, 1945, p. 1, IBM Files; also see "Report on Visit to Statistical Office, Bad Nauheim," August 2, 1945, PRO FO 1046/61.
91. "Report on Visit to Statistical Office, Bad Nauheim," August 2, 1945, pp. 1, 2, PRO FO 1046/61.
92. "Report on Visit to Statistical Office, Bad Nauheim," August 2, 1945, pp. 1, 2, PRO FO 1046/61.
93. "USSB Survey Summary Report (Pacific War)," July 1, 1946, www.anesi.com/ussbs.
94. "Report on Visit to Statistical Office, Bad Nauheim," August 2, 1945, pp. 1, 2, PRO FO 1046/61; Report, Sir Brian H. Robertson to Lucius D.Clay, September 17, 1945, PRO FO 1046/61.
95. "Minutes of the Fifth Meeting of the Technical Experts, Allied Control Authority, Directorate of Internal Affairs and Communications: Civil Administration Committee, Census/Registration Working Party," April 18, 1946, p. 4, PRO FO 1005/654; Minutes, "Fifth Meeting of Allied Control Authority," June 27, 1946, PRO FO 1005/656.
96. Letter, J.T. Wilson to Thomas J. Watson, July 4, 1947, IBM Files.
97. "Dehomag Balance Sheet as of December 31, 1946," NA RG260 IBM Dehomag.
98. Letter, K. Hummel to Decartelization Branch, November 14, 1947, NA RG260 IBM Dehomag.
99. Letter, H.K. Chauncey to State Department, September 27, 1949, NA RG59 363.115 International Business Machines Corporation/9–2749 CS/M.

MAJOR SOURCES

ARCHIVES AND REPOSITORIES

The following archives were accessed. If significant research was conducted within a record group, it was cited.

AJA	American Jewish Archives	Cincinnati
AJCm	American Jewish Committee Archives	New York
AJCo	American Jewish Congress Archives	New York
AJHS	American Jewish Historical Society	New York
AJPA	American Jewish Press Archives	Cincinnati
ACC	Amsterdam Chamber of Commerce Archives	Amsterdam
ANF	Archives Nationales	Paris
AJ 38	Commissariat Général aux Questions Juives	
AM	Auschwitz Museum	Oswiecim
BDBJ	Board of Deputies British Jews	London
BA	Bundesarchiv	Berlin
NS 3	SS-Wirtschafts- und Verwaltungshauptamt	
NS 19	Persönlicher Stab Reichsführer SS	
NS 48	Sonstige zentrale Dienststellen und Einrichtungen der SS	
R 2	Reichsfinanzministerium	
R 3	Reichsministerium für Rüstung und Kriegsproduktion	
R 7	Reichswirtschaftsministerium	
R 83 Niederl.	Reichskommissar für die besetzten niederländischen Gebiete	
R 87	Reichskommissar für die Behandlung feindlichen Vermögens	
R 1501	Reichsministerium des Innern	
R 1509	Reichssippenamt	
BAK	Bundesarchiv	Koblenz
BEA	Business Economics Archives	Rotterdam
CBS	Central Office for Statistics	Voorburg
CZA	Central Zionist Archives	Jerusalem
CDJC	Centre de Documentation Juive Contemporaine	Paris
CUL	Columbia University Library Lehman Suite	New York
CMA	Computer Museum of America	San Diego

DHM	Deutsches Historisches Museum	Munich
DOK	Dokumentationszentrum Oberer Kuhberg e.V.	Ulm
DNA	Dutch National Archives	The Hague

| FME | French Ministry of Economics Archives | Savigny Le Temple |

GO	Gallup Organization	Princeton
GDW	Gedenkstätte Deutscher Widerstand	Berlin
GKM	Gedenkstätte Konzentrationslager Mauthausen Archiv	Wien
GMS	Gedenkstätte und Museum Sachsenhausen Archiv	Oranienburg
GSPK	Geheimes Staatsarchiv Preussischer Kulturbesitz	Berlin
GFH	Ghetto Fighters House	Western Galilee

HAG	Hagley Museum	Wilmington
Accession 473	John J. Raskob Papers	
Accession 1057	National Industrial Conference Board	
Accession 1960	Chamber of Commerce, United States	

IBM	IBM Files, Courtesy New York University	New York
IWM	Imperial War Museum	London
IfZ	Institut für Zeitgeschichte—Archiv	Munich
YIVO	Institute for Jewish Research	New York
ISA	Israel State Archives	Tel Aviv

JHI	Jewish Historical Institute	Warsaw
JLC	Jewish Labor Committee Archives	New York
JWV	Jewish War Veterans Archives	New York
JBC	Joint Boycott Committee Archives	Cincinnati

| LBI | Leo Baeck Institute | New York |

| MGR | Mahn- und Gedenkstätte Ravensbrück | Fürstenberg |
| MWV | Ministry of War Veterans and War Victims Archives | Caen |

NA	National Archives	College Park
RG 59	General Records of the Department of State: Central Files of the Department of State	
RG 60	General Records of the Department of Justice: Records of the Antitrust Division: Records of the Economic Warfare Section: Subject File	
RG 84	Records of the Foreign Service Posts of the Department of State: American Legation Bern: Economic Section: Safehaven Name Files, 1942–49	
RG 131	Records of the Office of Alien Property: Foreign Funds Control Subject Files, 1942–60	
RG 165	Records of the War Department General and Special Staffs: Records of the Captured Personnel and Material Branch: Entry 179	
RG 169	Records of the Foreign Economic Administration: General Records: Entry 140; Entry 141A	
RG 226	Records of the Office of Strategic Services: Intelligence Reports 1941–45: Entry 16; Entry 19, XL8486, XL10762	
RG 238	Records of U.S. Military Tribunals at Nuremberg M 890 Records of the United States Nuremberg War Crimes Trials: United States of America v. Oswald Pohl et al. (Case IV) T 1139 Records of the U.S. Nuremberg War Crimes Trials, NG Series #:1543, 1628, 1823, 2192, 2770, 3004, 3354, 4651, 4749, 5135, 5725, 5875 PS-1919, Himmler Speech at Posen	
RG 242	National Archives Collection of Foreign Records Seized	

A 3340-MFOK Berlin Document Center, NSDAP Ortsgruppenkartei
A 3343-SSO Berlin Document Center, SS Officer Personnel Files
A 3343-RS Berlin Document Center, Rasse und Siedlungshauptamt
A 3345-DS Berlin Document Center, Miscellaneous Collections
A 3345-B Berlin Document Center, Library
A 3355 Miscellaneous Lists and Registers of German
    Concentration Camp Inmates
T 73 Records of the Reich Ministry for Armaments and War Production
T 77 Records of Headquarters, German Armed Forces High Command
242-HB photographs NSDAP Party Convention 1935, Nuremberg
    (Still Picture Research Room)

RG 242/338	Records of U.S. Army War Crimes Trials in Europe
	T 1021 German Documents Among the War Crimes Records of the Judge Advocate Division, Headquarters, United States Army, Europe
RG 243	M 1013 Final Reports of the United States Strategic Bombing Survey
RG 260	Records of U.S. Occupation Headquarters, World War II: Records of the Field Information Agency, Technical: IBM Bad Nauheim, IBM Equipment, IBM Dehomag
RG 306	Records of the United States Information Agency: Sound Recordings

NIOD	Netherlands Institute for War Documentation	Amsterdam
NYPL-J	New York Public Library Jewish Division	New York
NYPL-M	New York Public Library Manuscript Room	New York
NLPB	Niedersächsische Landeszentrale für Politische Bildung—Gedenkstätte Bergen Belsen	Loheide
NSANL	Non-Sectarian Anti-Nazi League Archives	New York

PA	Politisches Archiv des Auswärtigen Amts	Bonn
R 106 059	Vereinigte Staaten von Nord-Amerika, Jul.–Nov.1940	
R 114 751	Ausstellungswesen	
R 114 755	Ausstellungswesen	
R 114 911	Handelskongresse 1937-41	

PRO	Public Record Office	London
ADM 1	Admiralty, and Ministry of Defense, Navy Department	
ADM 116	Admiralty, Record Office	
FO 371	Foreign Office: Political Departments: General Correspondence	
FO 372	Foreign Office: Treaty Departments: General Correspondence	
FO 837	Ministry of Economic Warfare	
FO 935	Ministry of Economic Warfare, and Foreign Office Economic Warfare Department: Intelligence Objectives Sub-committee	
FO 1005	Foreign Office: Control Commission for Germany	
FO 1014	Control Commission for Germany and Austria and Foreign Office: Control Commission for Germany, Hamburg	
FO 1030	Control Commission for Germany: Various Private Office Papers and Administration and Local Government Branch Files	
FO 1031	Foreign Office: Control Commission for Germany, T Force and Field Information Agency Technical	
FO 1032	Economic and Industrial Planning Staff and Control Office for Germany and Austria: Control Commission for Germany, Military Sections at Headquarters Secretariat	
FO 1038	Control Office for Germany and Austria and Foreign Office: Control Commission for Germany, Military Divisions	
FO 1046	Control Office for Germany and Austria and Foreign Office: Control Commission for Germany, Finance Division	
FO 1050	Control Office for Germany and Austria and Foreign Office: Control Commission for Germany, Internal Affairs and Communications Division	

HW 3	Government Code and Cypher School: Personal Papers, Unofficial Histories, Foreign Office X Files and Miscellaneous Records
HW 5	Government Code and Cypher School: German Section: Reports of German Army and Air Force High Grade Machine Decrypts
HW 14	Government Code and Cypher School: Directorate: Second World War Policy
HW 16	Government Code and Cypher School: German Police Section: Decrypts of German Police Communications during Second World War
PREM 4	Prime Minister's Office: Confidential Correspondence and Papers
TS 26	Treasury Solicitor and HM Procurator General: War Crimes Papers
WO 204	War Office: Armed Forces, Mediterranean Theatre: Military Headquarters Papers, Second World War
WO 208	War Office: Directorate of Military Operations and Intelligence and Directorate of Military Intelligence
WO 209	Judge Advocate General's Office: Original Submissions
WO 309	War Office: Judge Advocate General's Office, British Army of the Rhine War Crimes Group (North West Europe)
WO 311	Judge Advocate General's Office, Military Deputy's Department, and War Office, Directorate of Army Legal Services and Personal Services: War Crimes

RWWA	Rheinisch-Westfälisches Wirtschaftsarchiv	Cologne
SF	Shoah Foundation	Los Angeles
SAJ	Special Administration for Justice Archives	The Hague
SH	Staatsarchiv Hamburg	Hamburg

TLA	Tamiment Institute Labor Archive	New York
USBC	United States Bureau of the Census Archive	Washington
USHMM	United States Holocaust Memorial Museum Archives and Collections	Washington
RG 02.148	Concentration camp	
RG 04.005	Correspondence, various concentration camps	
RG 04.008	Auschwitz inmate list (partial)	
RG 04.013	Camp log books and administrative records from the Auschwitz Memorial Museum	
RG 04.015	Official SHAEF report on Buchenwald	
RG 04.017	Selected records, Nationale Mahn- und Gedenkstätte, Ravensbrück and Sachsenhausen	
RG 04.031M	Häftlingspersonalbogen, Auschwitz	
RG 04.058M	Stutthof	
RG 04.063M	Auschwitz: Abteilung I—Kommandantur	
RG 04.064M	Auschwitz: Abteilung II—Politische Abteilung	
RG 04.077M	Fichier de Drancy	
RG 04.006M	Nazi concentration camp	
RG 11.001M.01	Reichssicherheitshauptamt, Berlin SD office	
RG 11.001M.02	Berlin Gestapo	
RG 11.001M.20	Concentration and POW camps, Germany	
RG 14.013M	Reichssippenamt Volkszählung, German minority census, 1938–1939	
RG 15.061M	Czestochowa Judenrat	
RG 41.001	Amsterdam City Archives	
RG 43.002.*01	"An Unpublished Chapter in the History of the Deportation of Foreign Jews from France in 1942" by Roswell McClelland	
RG 43.005M	Union Generale des Israelites de France	
RG 49.003	Crimes Against Serbs, Jews, Other Yugoslavs, World War II, Uncataloged Collections	
1996.A.0434	Commissariat General aux Questions Juives	
1997.A.0132	Auschwitz, Birkenau: from Auschwitz-Birkenau Museum	

1998.A.0020	Branch Office of the Ustasha's Intelligence Service, Jewish Section	
1998.A.0045	Camp de concentrations	
1998.A.0099	Gestapo France	
1999.A.0102	Auschwitz-Birkenau: Abteilung IV, Verwaltung	
Folder B	Heydrich Order 1939	
YV	Yad Vashem	Jerusalem
ZfA	Zentrum für Antisemitismusforschung, Technische Universität	Berlin

MAJOR LIBRARIES

Most major libraries carry distinct manuscript, monograph, pamphlet, and serial collections. The following libraries were accessed.

ASAL	American Statistical Association Library	Washington
AUL	American University Library	Washington
BFE	Bibliothek der Friedrich-Ebert-Stiftung	Bonn
BFN	Bibliothek der Friedrich-Naumann-Stiftung	Königswinter
BF	Bibliotheque Francais	Paris
BL	British Library	London
CU	Columbia University Library	New York
CUM	Columbia University Rare Book & Manuscript Library	New York
CZAL	Central Zionist Archives Library	Jerusalem
HBU	Hebrew University Library	Jerusalem
LC	Library of Congress	Washington
LCH	Library of Contemporary History	Stuttgart
NPL	Nashville Public Library	Nashville
NAL	National Archives Library	College Park
NYPL	New York Public Library	New York
NYPL-SIBL	New York Public Library-Scientific, Industry and Business Library	New York
NYUL	New York University Library	New York
TAU	Tel Aviv University Library	Tel Aviv
WL	Wiener Library	London
USHMM Library	United States Holocaust Memorial Museum Library	Washington
UBB	Universitätsbibliothek	Bonn
UNL	Universiteitsbibliotheek	Leiden
UL	University of Louisville Library	Louisville
UM	University of Maryland Library	College Park
UMBC	University of Maryland-Baltimore County Library	Baltimore
UT	University of Texas Library	Austin
YL	Yale University Library	New Haven

PERIODICALS

A number of publications were surveyed for the period 1933–1945. Modern period publications were also consulted.

ASA	*Allgemeines Statistisches Archiv*
AH	*American Hebrew*
AFG	*Analytical Franco-Jewish Gazeteer*
IEEE	*Annals of the History of Computing*
BT	*Berliner Tageblatt*
BM	*Business Machines*
DD	*Der Deutsche*

DWZ	*Deutsche Wirtschafts–Zeitung*
DZN	*Deutsche Zeitung in den Niederlanden*
FM	*Fortune Magazine*
HND	*Het Nationaal Dagblad*
HN	*Hollerith Nachrichten*
IB	*Illustrierter Beobachter*
IW	*Internationale Wirtschaft–Zeitschrift der Internationalen Handelskammer*
JSS	*Jewish Social Studies*
JASA	*Journal of the American Statistical Association*
MES	*Middle Eastern Studies*
NYHT	*New York Herald Tribune*
NYT	*New York Times*
NRC	*Nieuwe Rotterdamse Courant*
PDR	*Population and Development Review*
STM	*Sky & Telescope Magazine*
VV	*Volk en Vaderland*
VB	*Völkischer Beobachter*
WWZ	*Westdeutsche Wirtschaftszeitung*
WDAZ	*Wirtschaftsblatt der Deutschen Allgemeinen Zeitung*

INTERNET SITES

Reliable and established informational Internet sites were accessed continuously during research.

American Political Science Association Online	www.apsanet.org
Bull Computers Chronological History	perso.clubinternet.fr/febcm/ english/chronoa2.htm
Bundesarchiv	www.bundesarchiv.de
Anesi's Web Site	www.anesi.com
Civil Liberties Public Education Fund	www.clpef.net
Gedenkstätte Konzentrationslager Mauthausen	www.mauthausen-memorial.gv.at
German Historical Museum, Berlin	www.dhm.de
Humanities Faculty Copenhagen University	dorit.ihi.ku.dk
Hungary Network	www.hungary.com
IBM Punch Card Systems in the U.S. Army	members.aol.com/PattonsGHQ
International Business Machines	www.ibm.com
Jehovah's Witnesses	www.watchtower.org
National Archives	www.nara.gov
Public Record Office	www.pro.gov.uk
Regionales Rechenzentrum Universität Hamburg	www.rrz.uni-hamburg.de
United States Holocaust Memorial Museum	www.ushmm.org
United States Social Security Administration	www.ssa.gov
West.Net Communications	www.west.net
World Web News	ourworld.compuserve.com/ homepages/potomac

SEARCH ENGINES

Several general Holocaust search engines and other document databases were used and are recommended. In some cases, to facilitate reader access to documentation, we have listed those site addresses in the footnotes.

Nizkor Project	www.nizkor.org
Avalon Project	www.yale.edu/lawweb/avalon
Jewish Student Online Research Center	www.us-israel.org

American Book Exchange www.abe.com
Google www.google.com

BIBLIOGRAPHY

The Holocaust literature is virtually devoid of references to Hollerith technology with several notable exceptions. Although many of these works could only raise questions about the larger picture, most of them represented early attempts to learn the truth. During my research, I benefited from all these preliminary efforts.

The first of these is *Die restlose Erfassung: Volkszählen, Identifizieren, Aussondern im Nationalsozialismus,* by Götz Aly and Karl Heinz Roth, published in 1984 as a well-researched study arguing against registration policies in modern Germany. In the process, Aly and Roth traced numerous forms of Nazi registration and statistical abuses, including those undertaken with Hollerith machines.

In the 1990s, there were four more references. When the United States Holocaust Memorial Museum acquired its Hollerith machine, its census uses were mentioned in the museum's 1993 illustrated catalog, *The World Must Know.* Thereafter, three articles appeared in scholarly journals far from the Holocaust mainstream. The first was the excellent article "Locating the Victim: An Overview of Census-Taking, Tabulation Technology, and Persecution in Nazi Germany," by David Martin Luebke and Sybil Milton, which appeared in the *Annals of the History of Computing,* published by the Institute of Electrical and Electronics Engineers. Three years later, an attempt at rebuttal appeared in the *Annals of the History of Computing,* authored by Friedrich Kistermann, a retired IBM engineer and tabulator enthusiast; his work was entitled "Locating the Victims: The Nonrole of Punched Card Technology and Census Work."

The third article was William Seltzer's landmark work of scholarship entitled "Population Statistics, the Holocaust, and the Nuremberg Trials" in the September 1998 edition of *Population Development and Review.* Seltzer, a former United Nations statistical and census expert, assembled an impressive list of secondary references to census and registration during the Holocaust.

In 1997, Andreas Baumgartner offered a fleeting reference to Hollerith in a little known Austrian volume entitled *Die vergessenen Frauen von Mauthausen: Die weiblichen Häftlinge des Konzentrationslagers Mauthausen und ihre Geschichte.*

During my research, I consulted hundreds of books, articles, monographs, pamphlets, jubilee editions and other secondary materials, both in paper form and electronically. I cannot list them all, but the following identifies some of the more salient items.

Adler, Jacques. *The Jews of Paris and the Final Solution: Communal Response and Internal Conflicts, 1940–1944.* New York: Oxford University Press, 1987.

Aly, Götz and Karl Heinz Roth. *Die restlose Erfassung: Volkszählen, Identifizieren, Aussondern im Nationalsozialismus.* Berlin: Rotbuch Verlag, 1984.

Aly, Götz, Peter Chroust, and Christian Pross. *Cleansing the Fatherland.* Translated by Belinda Cooper. Baltimore: The Johns Hopkins University Press, 1994.

Arad, Yitzhak, Israel Gutman, and Abraham Margaliot, eds. *Documents on the Holocaust: Selected Sources on the Destruction of the Jews of Germany, and Austria, Poland, and the Soviet Union.* Translated by Lea Ben Dor. Lincoln: University of Nebraska Press, 1981; Bison Books, 1999.

Arendt, Hannah. *Eichmann in Jerusalem: A Report on the Banality of Evil*. New York: Viking Penguin, Inc., 1963; Penguin Books, 1965.

Armanski, Gerhard. *Maschinen des Terrors: Das Lager (KZ und GULAG) in der Moderne*. Münster: Verlag Westfälisches Dampfboot, 1993.

Austrian, Geoffrey D. *Herman Hollerith: Forgotten Giant of Information Processing*. New York: Columbia University Press, 1982.

Baumgartner, Andreas. *Die vergessenen Frauen von Mauthausen: Die weiblichen Häftlinge des Konzentrationslagers Mauthausen und ihre Geschichte*. Wien: Verlag Österreich, 1997.

Barker, Kenneth, ed. *The NIV Study Bible*. Grand Rapids: Zondervan Publishing House, 1995.

Belden, Thomas Graham and Marva Robins Belden. *The Lengthening Shadow: The Life of Thomas J. Watson*. Boston: Little, Brown and Company, 1962.

Berenbaum, Michael. *The World Must Know*. Boston: Little, Brown and Company, 1993.

Black, Edwin. The Transfer Agreement: *The Dramatic Story of the Pact Between the Third Reich and Jewish Palestine*. New York: Macmillan, 1984; Chicago: Dialog Press, 1999.

Borkin, Joseph. *The Crime and Punishment of I.G. Farben*. New York: The Free Press, 1978.

Bradsher, Greg, comp. *Holocaust-Era Assets: A Finding Aid to Records at the National Archives at College Park, Maryland*. National Archives and Records Administration, 1999.

Breitman, Richard. *Official Secrets: What the Nazis Planned, What the British and Americans Knew*. New York: Hill and Wang, 1998.

Browning, Christopher R. *The Path to Genocide: Essays on Launching the Final Solution*. New York: Cambridge University Press, 1992.

Brynen, Rex. *Sanctuary and Survival: The PLO in Lebanon*. Boulder: Westview Press, 1990.

Burleigh, Michael. *Death and Deliverance: 'Euthanasia' in Germany,' 1900–1945*. New York: Cambridge University Press, 1994.

Centre Historique des Archives Nationales. *Inventaire des Archives du Commissariat Général aux Questions Juives et du Service de Restitution des Biens des Victimes des Lois et Mesures de Spoliation*. Paris: Centre Historique des Archives Nationales, 1998.

Choldin, Harvey M. *Looking for the Last Percent: The Controversy Over Census Undercounts*. New Brunswick: Rutgers University Press, 1994.

Clements, Bruce. *From Ice Set Free: The Story of Otto Kiep*. New York: Farrar, Straus and Giroux, 1972.

Connolly, James. *History of Computing in Europe*. IBM World Trade Corporation, circa 1967.

Cortada, James W. *Before the Computer: IBM, NCR, Burroughs, and Remington Rand and the Industry They Created, 1865–1956*. Princeton: Princeton University Press, 1993.

Dassbach, Carl H. A. *Global Enterprises and the World Economy: Ford, General Motors, and IBM, the Emergence of the Transnational Enterprise*. New York: Garland Publishing, Inc., 1989.

De Jong, L. *Holland Fights the Nazis*. London: Lindsay Drummon.

Encyclopaedia Judaica. Jerusalem: Keter Publishing House, 1972.

van den Ende, Jan, *Knopen, kaarten en chips: De geschiedenis van de automatesiering bij het Centraal Bureau voor de Statistiek*, Amsterdam, 1991.

Engelbourg, Saul. *International Business Machines: A Business History*. Arno Press, 1976.

Erwich, B. and J.G.S.J. van Maarseveen, eds., *Een eeuw statistieken: Historisch-Methodologische schetsen van de Nederlandse officiële statistieken in de Twentigste eeuw*, Amsterdam, 1999.

Fein, Helen. *Accounting for Genocide: National Responses and Jewish Victimization During the Holocaust*. New York: The Free Press, 1979.

Ferencz, Benjamin B. *Less Than Slaves: Jewish Forced Labor and the Quest for Compensation*. Cambridge: Harvard University Press, 1979.

Foy, Nancy. *The Sun Never Sets on IBM*. New York: William Morrow & Company, Inc., 1975.

Flint, Charles R. *Memories of an Active Life: Men, and Ships, and Sealing Wax*. New York: G.P. Putnam's Sons, 1923.

Friedlander, Henry. *The Origins of Nazi Genocide: From Euthanasia to the Final Solution.* Chapel Hill: The University of North Carolina Press, 1995.

Friedländer, Saul. *Nazi Germany and the Jews. Volume 1: The Years of Persecution.* New York: HarperCollins, 1997.

Garr, Doug. *Lou Gerstner and the Business Turnaround of the Decade.* New York: HarperCollins, 1999.

Gilbert, Martin. *The Holocaust: A History of the Jews of Europe During the Second World War.* New York: Holt, Rinehart and Winston, 1985.

Goldhagen, Daniel Jonah. *Hitler's Willing Executioners: Ordinary Germans and the Holocaust.* New York: Alfred A. Knopf, 1996; Vintage Books, 1997.

Gutman, Israel. *Resistance: The Warsaw Ghetto Uprising.* New York: Houghton Mifflin Company, 1994.

Gutman, Yisrael and Michael Berenbaum, eds. *Anatomy of the Auschwitz Death Camp.* Indianapolis: Indiana University Press, 1994; published in association with the United States Holocaust Memorial Museum, Washington, D.C.

Haft, Cynthia J. *The Bargain and the Bridle: The General Union of the Israelites of France, 1941–1944.* Chicago: Dialog Press, 1983.

Herzberg, Abel J. *Between Two Streams: A Diary from Bergen-Belsen.* Translated by Jack Santcross. New York: I.B. Tauris,

Hilberg, Raul, ed. *Documents of Destruction: Germany and Jewry 1933–1945.* Chicago: Quadrangle Books, Inc., 1971.

Hilberg, Raul. *The Destruction of the European Jews.* New York: Quadrangle Books, Inc., 1961; Harper Colophon Books, 1979;

Hilberg, Raul, Stanislaw Staron, and Josef Kermisz, eds. *The Warsaw Diary of Adam Czerniakow: Prelude to Doom.* Translated by Stanislaw Staron and the staff of Yad Vashem. New York: Stein and Day, 1979.

Hirschfeld, Gerhard. *Nazi Rule and Dutch Collaboration: The Netherlands Under German Occupation, 1940–1945.* Translated by Louise Willmot. New York: Berg, 1988.

Hoess, Rudolf. *Commandant of Auschwitz: The Autobiography of Rudolf Hoess.* Translated by Constantine FitzGibbon. New York: Popular Library, 1959.

Ioanid, Radu. *The Holocaust in Romania: The Destruction of Jews and Gypsies Under the Antonescu Regime, 1940–1944.* Chicago: Ivan R. Dee, 2000.

Jagendorf, Siegried. *Jagendorf's Foundry: A Memoir of the Romanian Holocaust, 1941–1944.* New York: HarperCollins, 1991.

Kahn, Annette. *Le Fichier.* Paris: Robert Laffont, S.A., 1993.

Katsh, Abraham I., ed. and translator. *Scroll of Agony: The Warsaw Diary of Chaim A. Kaplan.* New York: The Macmillan Company, 1965.

Katsh, Abraham I., ed. and translator. *The Warsaw Diary of Chaim A. Kaplan.* New York: Collier Books, 1973.

Kermish, Joseph, ed. *To Live With Honor and Die With Honor: Selected Documents from the Warsaw Ghetto Underground Archives "O.S." ["Oneg Shabbath"].* Jerusalem: Yad Vashem, 1986.

Klee, Ernst. *"Euthanasie" im NS-Staat: Die "Vernichtung lebensunwerten Lebens."* Frankfurt am Main: S. Fischer Verlag GmbH, 1999.

Kleine Chronik der IBM Deutschland, IBM Corporation, 1993.

Kolb, Eberhard. *Bergen-Belsen: From "Detention Camp" to Concentration Camp, 1943–1945.* Translated by Gregory Claeys and Christine Lattek. Göttingen: Vandenhoeck & Ruprecht, 1985, 1986.

Krausnick, Helmut, Hans Buchheim, Martin Broszat, and Hans-Adolf Jacobsen. *Anatomy of the SS State.* Translated by Richard Barry, Marian Jackson, and Dorothy Long. New York: Walker and Company, 1968.

von Lang, Jochen, ed. *Eichmann Interrogated: Transcripts from the Archives of the Israeli Police.* Translated by Ralph Manheim. New York: Farrar, Straus and Giroux, 1983.

Lewin, Abraham. *A Cup of Tears: A Diary of the Warsaw Ghetto.* Antony Polonsky, ed. Translated by Christopher Hutton. New York: Basil Blackwell, 1989.

Lifton, Robert Jay. *The Nazi Doctors: Medical Killing and the Psychology of Genocide.* New York: Basic Books, 1986.

Lochner, Louis P., ed. and translator. *The Goebbels Diaries: 1942–1943.* New York: Doubleday & Company, Inc., 1948.

Lookstein, Haskel. *Were We Our Brothers' Keepers? The Public Response of American Jews to the Holocaust, 1938–1944.* Toronto: Hartmore House, 1985; Vintage Books, 1988.

Marrus, Michael and Robert O. Paxton. *Vichy France and the Jews.* New York: Schocken Books, 1983.

Marsalek, Hans. *Mauthausen.* Wien: Steindl-druck, n.d.

Maser, Werner. *Nuremberg: A Nation on Trial.* Translated by Richard Barry. New York: Charles Scribner's Sons, 1979.

Meacham, Alan D., ed. *The Punched Card Data Processing Annual: Applications and Reference Guide 2.* Detroit: Gille Associates, Inc., 1960.

Mitchell, Ruth. *The Serbs Choose War.* New York: Doubleday, Doran & Company, Inc., 1943.

Moore, Bob. *Victims and Survivors: The Nazi Persecution of the Jews in the Netherlands 1940–1945.* New York: Arnold, 1997.

Paxton, Robert O. *Parades and Politics at Vichy: The French Officer Corps Under Marshal Pétain.* Princeton: Princeton University Press, 1966.

Persico, Joseph E. Nuremberg: *Infamy on Trial.* New York: Viking Penguin, 1994; Penguin Books, 1995.

Presser, Jacob. *Ondergang: De vervolging en verdelging van het Nederlandse Jodentom.* 's-Graven-hage, 1965.

Presser, Jacob. *The Destruction of the Dutch Jews.* Translated by Arnold Pomerans. New York: E.P. Dutton & Co., Inc., 1969.

Proebster, W.E., ed. *Datentechnik im Wandel: 75 Jahre IBM Deutschland.* Berlin: Springer-Verlag, 1986

Pugh, Emerson W. *Building IBM: Shaping an Industry and Its Technology.* Cambridge: The MIT Press, 1995.

Rapport de la commission présidée par René Rémond au Premier ministre, *Le "Fichier Juif,"* Plon, 1996.

Reitlinger, Gerald. *The Final Solution: The Attempt to Exterminate the Jews of Europe, 1939–1945.* Beechhurst Press Inc., 1953; New York: Perpetua, 1961.

Remond, Rene. *Des Apparences a la Réalité: Le "Fichier Juif."* Paris, 1996.

Rodgers, William. *Think: A Biography of the Watsons and IBM.* New York: Stein and Day, 1969.

Shelley, Lore, ed. and translator. *Secretaries of Death.* New York: Shengold Publishers, Inc.,

Shirer, William L. *The Rise and Fall of the Third Reich: A History of Nazi Germany,* New York: Simon and Schuster, 1960.

Sijes, B.A., *De Februari-staking, 25–26 Februari 1941,* H.J.W. Becht, Amsterdam 1954.

Sloan, Jacob, ed. and translator. *The Journal of Emmanuel Ringelblum.* New York: McGraw-Hill Book Company, Inc., 1958.

Sobel, Robert. *IBM: Colossus in Transition.* New York: Truman Talley Books, 1981.

Somers, Erik and Mark Pier. *Archievengids van de Tweede Wereldoorlog: Nederland en Nederlands-Indië.* Zutphen: Walburg Druk.

Stearns, Peter N. and John H. Hinshaw, eds. *The ABC-CLIO World History Companion to the Industrial Revolution,* Santa Barbara, CA: ABC-CLIO, 1996.

Stegeman, H.B.J. and J.P. Vorsteveld, *Het Joodse Werkdorp in de Wieringermeer 1934–1941,* Zutphen, 1983.

Trunk, Isaiah. Judenrat: *The Jewish Councils in Eastern Europe under Nazi Occupation*. New York: Macmillan, 1972; Lincoln: University of Nebraska Press, 1996.

Tuchel, Johannes. *Die Inspektion der Konzentrations-Lager: Das System des Terrors 1938–1945*. Berlin: Edition Hentrich, 1994.

Tusa, Ann and John Tusa. *The Nuremberg Trial*. New York: Atheneum, 1984.

Watson, Thomas J. *Men—Minutes—Money: A Collection of Excerpts from Talks and Messages Delivered and Written at Various Times*. New York: International Business Machines, 1934.

Watson, Jr., Thomas J. and Peter Petre. *Father, Son & Co.: My Life at IBM and Beyond*. New York: Bantam Books, 1990.

Wistrich, Robert. *Who's Who in Nazi Germany*. New York: MacMillan, 1982.

PERIODICALS

"Aus der Geschichte der Deutschen Hollerith Maschinen Gesellschaft," *Hollerith Nachrichten*, 55 (Nov.1935): 729–738.

Biehler, "Lochkartenmaschinen im Dienste der Reichsstatistik," *Allgemeines Statistisches Archiv*, 28 (1938): 90–100.

Blau, Bruno, "The Jewish Population of Germany 1939–1945," *Jewish Social Studies*, 161–172.

Burgdörfer, Friedrich, "Die Volks- Berufs- und Betriebszählung 1933," *Allgemeines Statistisches Archiv*, 23 (1933/34): 143–171.

Burgdörfer, Friedrich, "Die Rumänische Volkszählung 1940–41: Ein Reisebericht," *Allgemeines Statistisches Archiv*, 30 (1941): 302–322.

"Censuses" in *Analytical Franco-Jewish Gazeteer 1939–45*: 85–88.

Couvé, Richard, "Der Mensch im Lochkartenverfahren," *Hollerith Nachrichten*, 36 (Apr.1934): 443–455.

"Das deutsche Volk wird gezählt," *Illustrierter Beobachter*, 9 (1), 6 Jan. 1934: 5–6, 20.

"Die erste Fabrikeinweihung im Jahre 1934," *Der Deutsche*, 9 Jan. 1934.

"Der Berliner Kongreß," *Internationale Wirtschaft*, Jul.–Aug.1937: 6–8.

"From the European Cauldron," *American Hebrew*, 7 Jun. 1940: 7.

Hümmer, Ludwig, "Die Aufbereitung der Volks- und Berfuszählung 1933 im Hollerith-Lochkartenverfahren," *Hollerith Nachrichten*, 28 (Aug.1933): 343–355.

"International Business Machines," *Fortune* (Jan.1940): 36–37.

"Inventur eines Volkes," *Berliner Tageblatt*, 9 Jan. 1934.

Keller, Karl, "Zur Frage der Rassenstatistik," *Allgemeines Statistisches Archiv*, 24 (1934/35): 129–142.

Kistermann, Friedrich W., "Locating the Victims: The Nonrole of Punched Card Technology and Census Work," *IEEE Annals of the History of Computing*, 19 (2) (Apr.–Jun. 1997): 31–45.

Krüger, Hermann, "Das Hollerith-Lochkartenverfahren im Fürsorgewesen," *Hollerith Nachrichten*, 47 (Mar.1935): 614–632.

Lawin, Rudolf, "Die Auszählung einer Wohnungsbestandsaufnahme im Hollerith-Verfahren," *Hollerith Nachrichten*, 58 (Feb.1936): 773–777.

Luebke, David Martin and Sybil Milton, "Locating the Victim: An Overview of Census-Taking, Tabulation Technology, and Persecution in Nazi Germany," *IEEE Annals of the History of Computing*, 16:3, (1994): 25–39.

Methorst, H.W., "The New System of Population Accounting in the Netherlands," *Journal of the American Statistical Association* (1936): 713-714, 719–722.

Methorst, H.W. and J.L. Lentz, "Die Volksregistrierung und das neue in den Niederlanden eingeführte einheitliche System," *Allgemeines Statistisches Archiv*, 26 (1936): 59–84 .

Müller, Johannes, "Die Stellung der Statistik in neuen Reich," *Allgemeines Statistisches Archiv*, 24 (1934): 241–250.

Schaefer, Bradley E., "Conjunctions that Changed the World," *Sky & Telescope* (May 2000).

Schultze, Edgar, "Die verfeinerte Auswertung statistischer Zusammenhänge mit Hilfe des Hollerith-Lochkartenverfahrens," *Hollerith Nachrichten,* 40 (Aug.1934): 507–517.

Seltzer, William, "Population Statistics, the Holocaust, and the Nuremberg Trials," *Population and Development Review,* 24 (3): 511–552.

"Watson neuer Präsident der Internationalen Handelskammer," in *Völkischer Beobachter,* 28 June, 1937.

Westphalen, "Die Hollerith Maschinen Gesellschaft im Dienste der Sparkassen-Statistik," *Hollerith Nachrichten,* 54 (Oct.1935): 721–726.

Zahn, Friedrich, "Vom Wirtschaftswert des Menschen als Gegenstand der Statistik," *Allgemeines Statistisches Archiv,* 24 (1934/35): 461–464.

Zahn, Friedrich, "Fortbildung der deutschen Bevölkerungsstatistik durch erbbiologische Bestandsaufnahmen," *Allgemeines Statistisches Archiv,* 27 (1937/38): 180–195.

Zahn, Friedrich, "Die Statistik im nationalsozialistischen Großdeutschland," *Allgemeines Statistisches Archiv,* 29 (1939): 369–392.

TYPESCRIPTS AND UNPUBLISHED MANUSCRIPTS

Engelbourg, Saul. *International Business Machines: A Business History,* typescript, 1954.

Kistermann, Friedrich, *The Way to the First Automatic Sequence-Controlled Calculator: The 1935 DEHOMAG D 11 Tabulator Title,* typescript, 1995.

Kistermann, Friedrich, *Locating the Victims: The Nonrole of Punched Card Technology,* typescript, 1997.

J.L. Lentz, *Memoires I, Registratie van Joden (oorsprong en ontwikkeling),* unpublished journal, circa October 1944.

J.L. Lentz, *Ambtelijke Herinneringen,* unpublished journal, circa October 1944.

Presser, Jacob. *Ondergang: De vervolging en verdelging van het Nederlandse Jodentom,* typescript.

Seltzer, William and Margo Anderson, *After Pearl Harbor: The Proper Role of Population Data Systems in Time of War,* an unpublished paper.

ABOUT THE AUTHOR

The son of Polish survivors, Washington-based writer EDWIN BLACK is the author of the award-winning Holocaust finance investigation, *The Transfer Agreement,* and is an expert on commercial relations with the Third Reich.